THE RELIGIOUS CENSUS OF 1851

A CALENDAR OF THE RETURNS RELATING TO WALES

THE RELIGIOUS CENSUS OF 1851
A CALENDAR OF THE RETURNS RELATING TO WALES

VOLUME I
SOUTH WALES

Edited by

IEUAN GWYNEDD JONES

and

DAVID WILLIAMS

With an introduction by Ieuan Gwynedd Jones

Published on behalf of the Board of Celtic Studies
History and Law Series No. 30

CARDIFF
UNIVERSITY OF WALES PRESS
1976

Printed in Wales by
D. Brown & Sons Ltd.,
Cowbridge and Bridgend

CONTENTS

PREFACE

It was Professor Emeritus David Williams, at the time Sir John Williams Professor of Welsh History at the University College of Wales, Aberystwyth, who first proposed to the History and Law Committee of the Board of Celtic Studies that a calendar of the returns made in Wales to the Religious Census of 1851 should be prepared and published under their auspices. He himself, with the assistance of Mr. Emlyn Sherrington, undertook the labour of transcribing the original entries, and by 1966 this first stage of the work had been completed. Professor Williams had also begun to prepare the standardized entries for the press and had completed some of the Monmouthshire Districts when his deteriorating health compelled him reluctantly to abandon the project. Subsequently, I accepted the invitation of the History and Law Committee to bring it to completion. The calendar for the south Wales entries which is now presented follows substantially the arrangement proposed by Professor Williams, but, as I explain in the introduction, additional material has been added from other contemporary sources which, it is hoped, will enhance its value as a major source for the study of the history of religion in Wales.

In addition to Mr. Sherrington, valuable assistance was given at an early stage by Dr. G. M. Bayliss, of the Department of History, University College of Swansea. Mrs. Eira Lewis, of the Department of Welsh History at this College, valiantly relieved me of the enormous burden of typing. Professor Glanmor Williams, the chairman of the Board of Celtic Studies, has given unstintingly of his advice and encouragement in a task which has been both arduous and time-consuming. To all these I desire to express my sincerest thanks. I am grateful also to the officers of the Public Record Office who, through the kind offices of its past Keeper, Sir David Evans, gave me unusual facilities for checking and re-checking the typescript. I wish particularly to thank Mr. W. A. Carter, Secretary to the Incorporated Church Building Society, for making their records available to me. Dr. R. Brinley Jones, Director of the University of Wales Press, has given unsparingly of his time in the preparation of the book for the press, and its appearance owes much to his expert and friendly advice. Above all, I wish to thank my wife for her cheerful readiness to relieve me of some of the labour involved in reading the proofs and preparing the index.

Finally, I must express my warmest gratitude to the Leverhulme Trust for making it possible, through a Fellowship, for this work to be completed.

I. G. J.

THE ARRANGEMENT OF THE CALENDAR

The system of reference is that adopted in the original returns (PRO. HO. 129/26-28) and in the Population Tables of the Census of 1851. The first figure gives the number of the district, the second the subdistrict, the third the parish or other division, and the final figure (in round brackets) the number of the individual place of worship as bound into the Enumeration Books. Thus, 579. 1.1(1) gives PONTYPOOL (District), Pontypool (Sub district), Llanhilleth (Parish), Crumlin Church of England Licensed School-room. The spelling of place-names under districts, subdistricts, parishes and other divisions is strictly as in the Population Tables, and any variations in the manuscript returns have been scrupulously preserved. The corrected forms are given in the index, the authority for these being Melville Richards, *Welsh Administrative and Territorial Units* (Cardiff, 1969).

Under each county, district, subdistrict and parish (or other division) is given its area and population, this information being given for all divisions irrespective of whether they contained places of worship. In the case of divided parishes, the area and population of the whole parish is given first. English parishes or townships included in Welsh districts or sub-districts have been excluded, and the necessary adjustments made to the population figures. Likewise, Welsh parishes in English districts have been added at the end of the relevant Welsh districts.

The information abstracted from the returns has been standardized so as to preserve all the details recorded in the returns. Wherever necessary, due to any obscurity, misunderstanding, or other idiosyncracy in the original, this information has been given *verbatim*. In all cases, the remarks made in the returns have been carefully transcribed so as to preserve the original spellings and punctuation, since these give some indication of the levels of literacy among clergymen, ministers, and chapel officials. Where accommodation figures for parish churches are not returned this information is supplied at the end of the entry from the *Report of the Commissioners of Inquiry into the Ecclesiastical Revenues of England and Wales*, 1835 (P.P. 1835, XXII), under the heading *ERCR*. Where the manuscript return is illegible, torn, or otherwise unreadable, the omissions are indicated between square brackets. Official endorsements are given at the end of the entry within square brackets. Contemporary errors in the numbering of individual returns are indicated at the end of the relevant parishes or divisions, and wherever possible the returns transferred to their correct locations and the cross-references supplied.

Below the entry for each parish church or chapelry, or, in those cases where there is no return for a parish church, immediately following the name and population details of the parish or chapelry, an entry from the 1848 edition of Samuel Lewis *A Topographical Dictionary of Wales* [headed *Lewis*] is appended. These entries are confined to details regarding the benefice, its description, income, and patronage. This is followed by an entry from a parliamentary return of 1850 entitled 'Numbers of Services performed in each Church and Chapel in Wales' (P.P. 1850, XLII (4)) [headed *C & C*], and, below this, an entry from a return of the same year entitled 'Returns of the names and residences of Curates and the stipends of each' (P.P. 1850, XLII (226)), [headed *I & C*]. Finally, there follows an entry of all grants made to Welsh parishes between 1818 and 1851 by the Incorporated Church Building Society [headed *ICBS*].

INTRODUCTION

Only once in modern times has there been an official and comprehensive count of the accommodation available for, and the actual attendance at, religious worship in Great Britain. Initiated by government, planned and supervised by the office of the Registrar-General, carried out by means of the sophisticated machinery available to him, and published by authority, the Census of Religious Worship of 1851 is a unique document providing a mass of statistical material which cannot be found elsewhere.[1] But it is also a highly perplexing document, and for all its appearance of objectivity and reliability its accuracy has always been suspect.[2] Partly this is due to the circumstances of its origin, which were shrouded in mystery; it was a purely administrative and bureaucratic act acquiesced in by the Liberal government of Russell without any overt political intentions. Partly the misgivings arose from the nature of the resulting Report itself, for this contained a great deal of highly speculative statistical analysis which, by drawing attention to the arithmetic involved, cast grave doubts on its main conclusions. What came to be called 'the arithmetic war'[3] had already begun even before the census was taken, the opening salvo being fired in the House of Commons on 18 March 1851 by Henry Goulburn, the ex-chancellor of the exchequer, to be followed a few days later by a broadside delivered by the Bishop of Oxford in the Lords.[4] Goulburn, while recognizing that the Act authorizing the decennial census empowered the Secretary of State to issue queries in addition to those actually mentioned in the Act, and thus to take the Religious and the Education Censuses, complained that the inquiries as framed were vague and imprecise in that they asked for information which ministers of religion could not possibly supply accurately, and also unwarranted in that

[1] P[arliamentary] P[apers] 1852-3, LXXXIX (1690). An octavo edition was also published with the title *Census of Great Britain, 1851. Religious Worship in England and Wales. Report and Tables* (London, 1853). The pagination of both editions is the same.

[2] The most important recent studies are the following: K. S. Inglis, 'Patterns of Religious Worship in 1851', *Journal of Ecclesiastical History*, II, i (April 1960), pp. 74-86; David Williams, 'The Census of Religious Worship of 1851 in Cardiganshire', *Ceredigion*, IV, ii (1961), pp. 113-128; Owen Chadwick, *The Victorian Church*, Part I (1966), p. 368 et. seq.; W. S.F.Pickering, 'The 1851 religious census—a useless experiment?', *British Journal of Sociology*, XVIII, iv (December 1967), pp. 382-407; Ieuan Gwynedd Jones, 'Denominationalism in Swansea and District; A Study of the Ecclesiastical Census of 1851', *Morgannwg*, XII (1968), pp. 67-96; David M. Thompson, 'The 1851 Religious Census: problems and possibilities', *Victorian Studies*, XI, i (September 1967), pp. 87-97; R. M. Goodridge, 'The Religious Condition of the West Country', *Social Compass*, XIV, iv (1967), pp. 285-296; Robert Currie, 'A Micro-theory of Methodist Growth', *Proceedings of the Wesley Historical Society*, XXVI (October 1967), pp. 65-73; Ieuan Gwynedd Jones, 'Denominationalism in Caernarvonshire in the Mid-nineteenth century as shown in the Religious Census of 1851', *Transactions of the Caernarvonshire Historical Society* (1970), pp. 3-40; John D. Gay, *The Geography of Religion in England* (1971), pp. 45-63; Ieuan Gwynedd Jones, 'The Religious Condition of the Counties of Brecon and Radnor, . .' in Owain W. Jones and David Walker (eds.) *Links with the Past* (1974), pp.185-214.

[3] Owen Chadwick, *op. cit.*, p. 368.

[4] *Hansard*, 3rd series, CXV, 18 March and 27 March 1851, cc. 112-113 and 629-31.

they sought information regarding the incomes of livings. Sir George Grey's answer was designed to allay such suspicions but was scarcely such as to increase confidence in the accuracy of the information which would be collected. He explained that the information asked for, though desirable, was not legally enforceable, and that the queries regarding incomes were of very little importance and could be withheld altogether. In the Lords, the criticisms were much more specific. There the prelates were unanimously of the opinion expressed in a petition of the clergy of the deanery of Newbury presented by the Bishop of Oxford, to the effect that the returns would inevitably be incomplete and imperfect, and that therefore, the general result 'might be conducive to the propagation of error rather than truth', and that, as the Bishop of Salisbury put it, 'from its imperfections inferences would be drawn, unjust, mischievous, and dangerous'.

These exchanges in Parliament, which seemed to have as their object the placing on record of the attitudes of the bench of bishops to the Census, do not appear to have received much publicity. None of the Welsh-language newspapers and magazines—not even *Y Cymro* and *Yr Haul*, the leading Anglican organs in Wales—made any reference to them, and, as we shall see, the few clergymen who refused to co-operate seem to have done so of their own volition rather than as part of a co-ordinated campaign. In any case, such difficulties and objections had been foreseen by the authorities, in particular, the opinion of the Law Officers that the religion returns would not be enforceable by law. A circular addressed to the clergy of the Established Church on 13 March 1851 by the Registrar-General makes this clear.[5] It was an appeal, couched in suitably deferential language, to the clergy to co-operate in the making of full and correct returns themselves and to exert their 'beneficial influence on the minds of their less educated neighbours' to do the same even though there was no legal obligation upon them to do so. It is worth bearing in mind also the fact that the bishops were not necessarily expressing the views of the Church as a whole. The purpose of the Census, as defined by the Registrar-General, was to ascertain 'how far the means of Religious Instruction provided in Great Britain during the last fifty years have kept pace with the population during the same period, and to what extent those means are adequate to meet the spiritual wants of the increased population of 1851'. 'Spiritual destitution' was a major preoccupation of the Church at the time, and although fairly detailed studies of the religious and moral condition of particular places had been made—more particularly, of the great cities and some of the manufacturing and mining regions—there existed no overall picture based on system-atically collected statistics covering the whole country. Most of the societies and voluntary bodies created by churchmen, even those which were required to co-operate closely with the Ecclesiastical Commissioners, felt that they were operating largely in the dark or in a twilight broken intermittently by flashes of revealing light. The Church Building Society, for example, whose

[5] Census of Great Britain 1851. PP 1851, XLIII (1339), p. 41, 'Instructions to Enumerators'.

annual and quarterly reports were circulated to all beneficed clergy, had no doubt whatsoever that the coming census would furnish information of considerable importance to the Church, particularly in 'determining how far the present provision meets the wants of the population'.[6] It pointed out that the only comprehensive survey available was that published in 1835 by the Ecclesiastical Commissioners,[7] and that this was highly defective, especially with regard to the numbers of sittings, 'there [being] no certainty as to the numbers actually furnished being taken by admeasurement, or only by guess'. The Society knew from its own experience how difficult it was to obtain this necessary information, and it welcomed the census as an authoritative way of obtaining it, in effect calling upon the clergy to make certain that the results obtained would be something more than a mere approximation to the truth 'and that the numbers of persons accommodated in each Church . . . be obtained by actual inspection and measurement'.[8] One can only speculate as to what effect the Registrar-General's appeal as reinforced by the Incorporated Church Building Society may have had upon their recipients: it is reasonable to suppose that numbers of them would have been sympathetic to the avowed aims and purpose of the census, and what evidence there is, as revealed in the enumeration schedules, would suggest that the vast majority acted in the spirit not of the petitioners to Parliament and the bench of bishops but in that of the Registrar-General and the Incorporated Society.

Accuracy—the first essential of a census—would obviously depend upon the quality and the co-operation of the persons taking it. Lacking legal sanctions and dependent ultimately upon the goodwill and integrity of individuals, the officials responsible for the taking of the census had to rely on the effectiveness of the machinery devised for the purpose. It is therefore important to understand the detail of this in order to assess the degree of accuracy attained. The Religious Census was taken as an essential part of the decennial Census of Population, and was thus the responsibility of the Registrar-General, by whom it was delegated to Horace Mann, one of the two senior officials at the Census Office. Mann was a barrister-at-law, for whom the notoriety subsequent upon the publication of his massive Report late in 1853 seems to have been as unexpected and as unwelcome as the almost total obscurity of his life up to that point seems to have been congenial. He was deeply resentful of the charges of partiality later brought against him, and one suspects that he would also have been mortified had he known that Gladstone, the chancellor of the exchequer at the time, regarded the inclusion in the introduction to the Report of a historical survey of religion in England and Wales as the equivalent of pre-facing the Army estimates with a treatise on the art of war.[9] He warmly

<hr>

[6] Incorporated Church Building Society, *Supplementary Report to the Quarterly Report*, No. 8 (1850).
[7] PP 1835, XXII, Table IV, Revenues.
[8] Church Building Society, *op. cit.*, p. 5.
[9] PRO, HO 45/5779, Gladstone to Palmerston, 31 January 1854.

refuted those charges of partiality to dissenters, and there is no reason to
question his claim that he and his subordinates, like the Registrar-General,
had been 'free even from the shadow of bias or sinister intention'. 'It was
next to impossible for him to be actuated by any hostile spirit towards the
Church of England, although he did not think that a sincere desire to
promote the best interests of the Church, was at all inconsistent with an
impartiality towards Dissenting bodies'. He added the not-altogether-
surprising information that only two of the twenty or thirty clerks who had
dealt with the returns were dissenters, 'and they were only occupied for a
portion of the time'.[10] In fact, we must conclude that what offended some
contemporary churchmen—though not dissenters—was the general 'tone'
of the Report, its readiness, that is, to accept and to treat all religious
denominations as having equal validity and to avoid using the patronizing
language so common in the religious literature of the time. The local
machinery was the responsibility of the Superintendent Registrars of the
Registration Districts.[11] In Wales there were 48 of these Registrars, their
Districts being more or less co-terminous with the Poor Law Unions. These
Districts were divided into 181 Subdistricts, each having a local registrar of
births and deaths. The subdistricts in turn were agglomerations of parishes,
townships, hamlets, chapelries and other lesser divisions, of which there
were 1,261 in Wales itself.[12] For the purpose of taking the census the subdistricts were divided by the local registrars into Enumeration Districts. So
far as possible these were based on existing parishes or other recognized
divisions and were such as could be enumerated by one person in the course
of a single day. Where parishes were too large to permit a perambulation in
one day they were divided, as were very populous parishes where, generally
speaking, a norm of about a hundred or so households was aimed at. It was
the duty of each of the enumerators to obtain a thorough and minute knowledge of his individual district, its boundaries, number of houses, etc., and
specifically 'with all Churches, Chapels, and other Places of Public Religious
Worship . . .; also with the residence of the minister, warden, or other
manager of every place of worship . . .'.[13] During the week ending 29 March
the enumerator was required, in the course of delivering the enumeration
schedules, to leave the Religious Worship forms either at the residence of
the officiating minister or at that of the warden or other official, and should
any such residences be outside his enumeration district he was to inform the
registrar of this fact. There were two forms—copies of which are given in

[10] Horace Mann, 'On the statistical position of religious bodies in England and Wales',
Journal of the Royal Statistical Society, XVIII, (1855) pp. 141-2.

[11] The Census machinery is described in PP 1851 XLIII (1339), 'Instructions to
Enumerators'. There is a convenient summary in Edward Cheshire, *The Results of the Census
of Great Britain in 1851; with the description of the machinery and processes employed to obtain
the returns* (1853). See also 'The Census, 1801-1891', by Michael Drake, in E. A. Wrigley
(ed.), *Nineteenth-century Society* (1972), pp. 7-46.

[12] These totals are exclusive of subdistricts and parishes wholly or partly in England
Thus the subdistricts of Lydney (in the Registration District of Chepstow) and Coleford (in
the Registration District of Monmouth), which were wholly in English counties, are excluded. To the total of *divisions* should be added those which were included in English
Registration Districts, namely, the parishes of Grosmont and Llangua (Monmouthshire).

[13] 'Instructions to Enumerators', *op. cit.*, p. 33.

the Appendix, pp. 675-8. Form A was for Anglican places of worship, and Form B for Nonconformist places. To avoid confusion the latter was printed in red ink. Having delivered the schedules, the enumerator was then required to make out a list of every place of worship within his district, its denomination, and the name and address of its minister or other responsible official, and send it to the registrar. There were printed forms for this purpose none of which, however, appears to have survived. The completed schedules were to be collected on the following Monday (the 31st), and it was the enumerator's task to see to the best of his knowledge that they had been properly filled up, 'and if any of the required particulars be omitted, he should ask the necessary questions, and himself enter the answers'. Finally, before 8 April, he was to deliver the schedules, as checked and, if necessary, corrected, to his registrar. There remained one supervisory check to be carried out by the registrar before sending them to Horace Mann at the Census Office in London by 22 April. He was to compare the completed returns with the lists previously supplied by his enumerators in order to ensure that a return had been received from all the places notified. In the event of non-returns the registrar, or his agent, was to obtain the necessary information and enter it upon a special form called an 'Informant's Form'. (See Appendix, p. 000.) He was likewise required to scrutinize all the returns and to check their accuracy 'in all particulars which might be known to him'.[14] The final check took place at the Census Office where twenty or thirty clerks were employed on the task.[15] In cases where further information was required or a return missing they corresponded directly with the ministers concerned or, if that brought no result, with the registrar.

How efficiently did this system work? Obviously, it is impossible to tell with any degree of certainty, but at least the present-day historian is in a better position to judge than were the critics of the Report when it was published. Since the published statistics were of aggregations in the Registration Districts only—the so-called 'Detailed Tables' of the Report which we reproduce in the Appendix (pages 681 to 687)—a pledge having been given that only general results would be made public in order to avoid 'facilities . . . for making invidious comparisons between particular individual parishes,'[16] the defenders of the accuracy of the Report—notably Mann himself—could do no more than appeal to the systematic checks and safeguards which we have described. Such appeals invited a sceptical response and very often got it. The individual returns now published enable us to reach at least general conclusions regarding its effectiveness. One indication might be the number of 'Informant's forms' to be found among the schedules. There are about 123 of these out of a total of 2,270 returns for the whole of south Wales, or a proportion of a little over five per cent. The great majority of these are in respect of deficiencies discovered by the registrars, but some are in reply to inquiries made subsequently by the

---

[14] 1851 Census Report. PP 1852-3, LXXXV (1631), p. xvi.
[15] Horace Mann, *art. cit.*, p. 142.
[16] Report, *op. cit.*, p. clxxi.

officials in London.[17] At least one instance can be discovered of a schedule not having been delivered on time to the minister of an Independent Chapel in Pembrokeshire, so that, as the minister explained, it 'could not be filled up' on the appointed day 'although all preparations thereto were made March 30'.[18] One assumes that he had made a note of the details. Even so, it is surprising that a number of places of worship are missing altogether. The weakness of the system lay in its first stage—the preliminary listing of places of worship. If this were defective there were no means available for correcting it. Mann took infinite care to account for and to supply any deficiencies in *the returns* as made and as checked against the preliminary list. But it is a serious criticism of the Census that so many places of worship were not listed in the first place and that Mann's officials in London did not, so far as Church of England places are concerned, efficiently check those lists against the *Clergy Lists* as they were required to do. Nor is it likely that these omissions were due to the intransigence of incumbents, for very few appear to have refused to co-operate. The vicar of Bron-gwyn and the vicar of Brynmawr were two such.[19] Others objected to giving specific details, such as the vicar of Whitchurch who regarded the queries on endowments as impertinent, though he gave them in detail, or the vicar of Manordeivy who, while himself giving information of questionable accuracy concerning his endowments, drew attention to the fallacy of imagining that accurate information would be forthcoming.[20] But the system should have taken care of such exceptions, so that some of the omissions are quite inexplicable. A number of adjacent parish churches in the western part of the Vale of Glamorgan are missing, as is the parish church of Laleston, and, most baffling of all, the ancient collegiate church of Llanddewibrefi in north Cardiganshire.[21] In this edition of the Census such omissions as have appeared by checking in Lewis's *Topographical Dictionary of Wales* (1848 edn.) and the *Clergy List for 1851* are indicated. Local historians will no doubt check the accuracy of the returns for their completeness respecting chapels. Evidently some are missing: for instance, possibly two in the parish of Betws Bledrws[22] and, most surprisingly, Ebenezer, the mother-church of the Independent cause in Aberdare. It should be noted, in this connection, that places of worship in workhouses and gaols were not required to be returned. In fact, there was no consistency in this matter. The gaols at Monmouth and Carmarthen were recorded, and the chapels in the workhouses at Monmouth, Llandovery and Llangadog (Carms.), but none of the others. These inconsistencies may have been due as much to the sectarian zeal of some

[17] H.O. 129 : 580. 1. 11(16) dated 12 January 1852, 580. 1. 11(19) dated 9 September 1852 and 580. 1. 11(24) dated 12 January 1852. All those returns are in respect of parish churches in the subdistrict of Caerleon.

[18] 593. 2. 6(15).

[19] 594. 2. 3(3), 601. 4. 6 (Brynmawr, Church of England).

[20] 593. 3. 6(13).

[21] Examples of missing parish churches are 583. 2. 6(31) and (34), 583. 3. 1(1), 583. 3. 11-12, 583. 3. 14-15, 598. 2. 14-15, 592. 4. 17 (34).

[22] 595. 3. 1. There were two nonconformist chapels in this parish according to Lewis, *Topographical Dictionary*.

ministers as to the incompetence of the enumerators.[23] Such deficiencies as
these, though obviously of vital importance to the local historian (who, however, will be able to detect them easily) are of minor importance in relation
to the whole, and we can probably conclude that, with some slight reservations, the machinery devised by the Census Office worked in a reasonably
efficient manner and that the list of places of worship is virtually
complete and certainly far more complete than any other list known to
exist.

A criticism often made of the Report at the time of its publication and
subsequently was that it did not define 'place of worship' with sufficient
clarity and exactness. Query V and VI of Form B asked whether the place
was 'a separate and entire building' and 'whether used exclusively as a Place
of Worship (except for a Sunday School)', and on the evidence of the replies
to these queries and his study of denominational statistics, Mann pointed
out that there was a striking difference between the kind of accommodation
provided by the Established Church and that provided by many dissenting
bodies, 'the former always consisting of substantial fabrics and commodious
pews or seats, while much of the latter [were] composed of rooms in dwelling-
houses with temporary seats or benches'.[24] According to his calculations
only about 1.5 per cent of church buildings in England and Wales were not
permanent and separate buildings wholly devoted to ecclesiastical objects,
but 16.0 per cent of all chapels were in this category. In his valuable and
pioneering analysis of the Report in 1860, the Rev. Abraham Hume took
this analysis a stage further by pointing out that virtually all of the churches
were permanently served by beneficed clergymen or curates, but that only
between one half and a third of the chapels were served by professional
ministers. And he concluded that a very large proportion of the chapels,
therefore, were no more than preaching stations 'served by pious and worthy
laymen . . . engaged in secular occupations during the week'.[25] The position
in Wales in both these respects can be ascertained with a fair degree of
accuracy from the returns, but caution must be exercised in making any
calculations because there is no means of knowing to what extent chapel
officials (and enumerators) understood the requirements of the forms. The
instructions defined 'separate' as denoting a building 'separated or set apart'
for religious workship, but one suspects that some officials returned their
buildings as 'not separate' on the grounds that they were physically attached
to other buildings, or being used for other non- or semi-religious purposes.
On the other hand, some buildings were returned as 'separate' which we
know to have been farm- or dwelling-houses. Mann himself attached less
importance to this criticism than did some of his critics on the sociologically
sound grounds that the type of building did not diminish 'the value of such
provision as affording opportunities of spiritual instruction: rather, perhaps,
the character of the accommodation has a special fitness for the classes who

[23] 587. 5. 1(2) and 601. 3. 1(4).
[24] Report, p. cxxxvi, cxliii.
[25] Abraham Hume, *Remarks on the Census of Religious Worship* (1860), pp. 6-7.

avail themselves of it'.[26] This remark applies with particular force to the pattern of organization in Wales, while Hume's judgment on the extent and importance of a professional ministry likewise loses some of its force when applied to Welsh Nonconformity if, while admitting the force of his observation, we add that many fully ordained ministers remained in full- or part-time occupation as craftsmen or tradesmen or farmers.

It was a relatively elementary and straightforward matter to devise ways and means of ensuring a complete list of *places* of worship. More problematical was the recording of exact information regarding the provision made by them—their seating capacity. Here Horace Mann and his assistants were very much at the mercy of individuals over whom they had virtually no control. As we have seen, the enumerators, immediately after collecting the completed forms, and the local registrars, before despatching them to London, were required to examine them carefully and to correct all erroneous entries which came to their notice. There is plenty of evidence that this was done. The registrar of Llanelli Subdistrict (Breconshire), for instance, added a remark to the effect that he did not think that Rehoboth Independent Chapel at Brynmawr provided sittings for 1,500: 'I do not think it will hold more than a thousand'.[27] But such a remark was the exception and there is no means of knowing whether the clerks in London took any notice of such comments. As a rule the enumerators and registrars confined their attention to information which was wrongly or insufficiently presented. Large numbers of forms, as can be seen, were defective due to the failure of the officials making the returns to understand exactly what was required. One reason for this may have been a certain imprecision in the wording of the relevant questions, particularly those on Form B. Form A, for Anglican places of worship, merely asked for the number of seats, distinguishing 'free' from 'other', or appropriated seats. It was assumed that this information would be readily at hand or easily obtainable by both incumbents and enumerators. This was not necessarily so. For example, the local registrar, 'by the representation of . . . the Rector', in answer to the query regarding sittings in Llanglydwen Parish Church, stated baldly, 'all in the Church'.[28] What could they have been thinking of? Form B, for non-Anglican places, in addition to asking for the 'space available for public worship', distinguishing 'free' from 'other', also asked for an estimate of the 'Free Space or Standing Room' available. This latter query was intended for Roman Catholic churches where it was customary, at least in some places, for standing room to be occupied by the poor. In an extraordinary number of cases, 'space' was taken to mean literally the area enclosed by the four walls, the internal measurements of the buildings being given. This is a bonus for the local historian, but it is not what Mann asked for. 'Standing room' baffled many ministers and deacons and, one suspects, enumerators as well. Many

---

[26] Mann, *op. cit.*, cxxxvi.
[27] 601. 4. 1(23).
[28] 590. 1. 3(82). Cf. also 590. 1. 1(2) where an obviously incorrect entry by the curate has been corrected.

chapel officials carefully measured every part of their buildings not actually occupied by seats—the aisles, passage-ways in galleries, porches and such like—while the more arithmetically inclined tried to work out how many individuals could stand in the space thus indicated.[29] Some contented themselves with wildly optimistic guesses. Others clearly took sittings to mean pews, in which cases the enumerators or registrars used multipliers of 6 or 7 to obtain total numbers. But this was not invariably done, and it is this inconsistency in the checking process, the failure on the part of the census officials to realize the nature of the mistake, which in a number of cases accounts for the gross disparity between sittings and attendants which sometimes occurs. Some of these returns are endorsed 'See Letter', and these must refer to communications from registrars drawing attention to such irregularities. But as these latter have not survived one can only surmise that this was their purpose. Nevertheless, despite the number of irregularly completed forms, one cannot but be impressed by the care with which this information was given in the vast majority of cases. At least a rough check of the accuracy of the returns from ancient parish churches can be made by comparing them with the information given in the Ecclesiastical Revenues Commission Report of 1835.[30] In this edition I have appended this information in all cases where it is lacking in the original parish returns.

It is not clear to what extent the query regarding 'free' and 'other' sittings was understood. The object of the distinction was to discover what proportion of the 'present provision [was] at the service of the poorer classes, without price'.[31] As we have seen, the instructions on Form A (Anglican) made no reference to it, presumably because it was assumed that incumbents would have precise information regarding the number of sittings appropriated by purchase, rental, or by custom to individual parishioners. Evidently Mann believed—on what evidence is not clear—that large numbers of incumbents took 'other' to mean sittings for which a rental was received and that other forms of appropriation of seats to the exclusive use of individuals had been ignored. It is quite impossible to tell from the returns themselves the extent to which this may have been true of the Welsh Anglican returns. There are exceptions. For example, the vicar of Swansea gave a detailed statement of the 953 'other' sittings in St. Mary's in order to show that 424 of them were not under the control of the church authorities.[32] The reader may find further examples of this kind of scrupulousness and understanding, but there is no way, except by the investigation of local records, of ascertaining whether this was typical of the majority. However, with this important caveat, the figures published in the Report, and with greater precision in the returns themselves, do give useful clues as to the extent to which the provision of church sittings was available freely and without distinction to all people. The uncorrected statistics show that about 45 per cent of its

---

[29] e.g. 592. 1. 6(20), 586. 1. 4(2), 588. 2. 2(4).
[30] PP 1835, XXII, Table IV.
[31] Report, *op. cit.*, p. cxxxiv pp. cxxxiv-v, clxx
[32] 585. 3. 1(1).

provision in south Wales was free compared with an estimated 37 per cent for England and Wales. It may also be suggested that it is the variations in these proportions as between Districts which are interesting and worthy of study. These range between 7.8 per cent in Tregaron District to 48.9 per cent in Abergavenny District.[33] Even allowing for a wide margin of error these figures point unmistakably to the fact that the provision of free accommodation by the Church tended to be least, not in the urban districts where Church extension was beginning to make a substantial impression, but in the rural areas where, as was suspected, some of the churches were 'little more than chapels of the privileged few, in which the people at large [had] no more concern than . . . in the Chapel Royal, or any nobleman's private chapel'.[34]

The distinction between 'free' and 'other' for nonconformist places of worship was more straightforward and designed to discover simply the proportion of seats which were let for a rental. The underlying concern was the same as in the Established Church, for though different in origin the system of pew rents, well nigh universal in all denominations, was held by its critics to have commercialised and degraded the old voluntary system to such an extent as to have made the chapels the preserve of those who could afford to worship but at the cost of excluding the poor.[35] That the system of pew-rents was common, if not universal, in Wales can be seen from the returns, though it does not follow from this that it necessarily had the same social consequences. 'Voluntary appropriation by payment', as described by the minister of a Baptist chapel in the town of Abergavenny,[36] certainly did not have such effects there, nor even in the iron districts where it appears that, on average, almost one half of the available seats were rented. In rural areas the proportion could be higher, for the reason, no doubt, that country chapels could not depend on, or even hope to attract, significant numbers of worshippers over and above their own members. Membership involved payment universally and pew rents was the usual form it took, but only rarely was there a fixed rate, and the system was such, according to Dr. Thomas Rees and other observers, as to bring membership obligations within the range of all people excepting paupers.[37] From this it might follow that the numbers of rented seats in chapels would give the approximate numbers of members as distinct from 'hearers'. But since we cannot be certain how the individual returns were made up such a conclusion would be somewhat hazardous.[38]

[33] Report, *op. cit.*, pp. cxxxiv-cxxxv, clxx; Table A, p. clxxviii, and pp. 120-126 [Districts 576 to 605 inclusive].

[34] PP 1857-8, IX (387), 'Select Committee on the means of divine service in populous district', p. 645. On church pews in general, see John Fowler, *Church Pews, their origin and legal incidents, with some observations on the propriety of abolishing them* (London) 1844. J. C. Fowler became stipendiary magistrate for Merthyr Tydfil and was very active in the Llandaff Church Extension Society.

[35] See, in general, W. R. Ward, *Religion and Society in England 1790-1850* (1973) *passim.*, and *The Congregational Economist* (1859), pp. 86 *et seq.* for an article on 'The Failure of Financial Plans', by the Rev. John Ross.

[36] 578. 3. 3(10).

[37] T. Rees, *Miscellaneous Papers on subjects relating to Wales* (1867), p. 29. See also Iorwerth Jones, *David Rees y Cynhyrfwr* (1971).

[38] e.g. 581. 2 5(23), 592. 1. 14(35), 592. 2. 2(7).

The returns enable us to study the denominational pattern in mid-century with a greater degree of exactitude than is possible from the detailed tables in the Report. As Mann himself recognized—though his brief prevented him from pursuing it in anything but elementary terms—this was one of the most interesting and baffling by-products of the census.[39] But as has been pointed out, the Report did not, despite the promise of Mann's elaborate introductory essay on the various denominations, distinguish between them with sufficient precision.[40] It is complained, for instance, that he lumped the Baptists together in the detailed tables of places, sittings, and attendants arranged in Registration Districts[41]—though, in fairness to Mann, in his summary tables he was careful enough to make the appropriate distinctions.[42] This is a less serious deficiency so far as Wales is concerned than for certain parts of England where there was greater denominational and sectarian variety. In the returns here published Independent chapels quite often describe themselves as 'Independent or Congregationalist', and many of them, no doubt, would have commended the precision of the minister of Bwlchygroes who noted that 'We are generally called Independents, but with more propriety we are called Congregationalists'.[43] Few sought to achieve the definitiveness of 'Independent Society Dissenting party' of Siloam, Llanegwad.[44] This latter was included in the Report as Independent, though it is doubtful whether it should have been.[45] On the other hand, the famous chapel of Ynys-gau, the mother church of orthodox independency in Merthyr Tydfil, was described as 'Protestant Dissenter', the person responsible for filling the form explaining that he thought it best to enter it thus as this is what he found in the chapel deed. Despite this legalistic precision—perhaps because of it—and this echo of old controversies, it was included in the category 'undefined', and the Independents thus failed to be credited with one of their oldest and largest chapels.[46]

A careful perusal of the returns might reveal further inconsistencies, but it is worth stressing that the basic simplicity of the denominational pattern in south Wales ensured that, by and large, the information given under this head is reliable, and the fact that deviant sectarian off-shoots were so few and so isolated makes it virtually certain that they would not escape the enumerators. As the summary tables in the Report made clear, and as the returns themselves confirm, the Baptist chapels recorded, whether they called themselves Strict, Calvinistic, or simply Baptist were in fact Particular Baptists. The General or Free Baptists—a distinction which was of considerable importance—were so very few as to make virtually no differences

---

[39] Report, p. cxi and *passim. ibid., art. cit.*; A. Hume, *op. cit.* See also Gray, *op. cit., passim.*

[40] Cf. D. M. Thompson, *art. cit.*, p. 89.

[41] Report, pp. 1-129.

[42] e.g. Tables, B, C, D, F, L. M.

[43] 594. 3. 1(1).

[44] 588. 3. 1(5).

[45] Report, p. 123, under Table 588, Llandilo Fawr. No mention of this chapel is made in *Hanes Eglwysi Annibynol Cymru*, gan T. Rees a J. Thomas, Cyf. III (1872).

[46] Report, p. 121, under Table 582, Merthyr Tydfil, below p. 682.

to the overall pattern, though the historian will note carefully their location.[47] Presbyterian, or Arminian Presbyterian, were correctly understood to mean Unitarian.[48] The Report, it should be noted, classified a total of 16 places as 'undefined'. The local historian will be able to identify them. One— Pwlldu in Abergavenny District—was almost certainly founded by and for Independents even though used by other denominations as well.[49] The congregations in Cardiff, Haverfordwest, and Crickhowell Districts described as 'Dissenters' were almost certainly Independent,[50] another three were inter-denominational mariners' chapels,[51] and another was genuinely 'mixed'. Three places in Swansea District was categorized as 'undefined' because they called themselves 'Independent Baptist'. Research into their histories might reveal special characteristics belonging to them at that time, but evidently they should be included as Baptist chapels for there is no evidence that they were outside the County Association.[52] Interdenominational co-operation was by no means rare. At Dale, in Pembrokeshire, for example, Anglicans, Independents, and Wesleyan Methodists worshipped together using their own chapels in rotation,[53] and Capel-y-Drindod, Llandysul, had been endowed by the local squire as an interdenominational place of worship.[54] Examples of genuinely 'undefined' congregations, in the sense that their declared denomination would not fit into Mann' schemes, or simply because they had omitted to state their allegiance, are very rare. The Tenby congregation of 'Brethren in Christ' might be one such example.[55]

It is reasonable to conclude, therefore, that the system devised by Mann, though far from perfect, achieved a fair degree of accuracy so far as the actual counting and recording of places of worship were concerned, their denominational allegiances, and the sitting accommodation they provided. There were anomalies certainly, and some of these can be corrected. Missing places of worship can sometimes be traced in topographical dictionaries, parish churches by reference to clergy lists and various parliamentary papers, and nonconformist chapels and congregations (though with greater difficulty and less certainty) in denominational publications and histories. Accommodation is more open to doubt, particularly with reference to chapels and meeting-houses—indeed, it is virtually impossible to check the figures given. Even so, one is impressed by the evident desire of most of the persons responsible to be accurate, and errors should be attributed in the first place not to a desire to deceive but rather to a failure to understand. Mann argued that the fact that the average number of sittings for chapels came out at less than that for churches (377 as against 240) was tolerable evidence of the

---

[47] There was a congregation of Unitarian or Free Baptists in Cilrhedyn—an area where Unitarianism was strong. See 594. 1. 4(11).
[48] e.g. 594. 3. 7(14), and 594. 3. 2(4).
[49] 578. 4. 2(6). See Rees and Thomas, Cyf. 1, t. 148.
[50] 581. 1. 1(34), 592. 2. 1(20), 601. 1. 1(2). See Rees and Thomas, *passim*.
[51] 580. 2. 2(15) and 585. 3. 1(28) and 591. 1. 3(6).
[52] 585. 1. 1(10), 585. 1. 2(12-13).
[53] 592. 1. 5(16).
[54] 594. 3. 1(4).
[55] 591. 1. 3(5).

reliability of the returns.[56] In south Wales the average for chapels was greater than that for churches (249 as against 210), and it seems improbable that this can have been far from the actual situation, bearing in mind, of course, the caveat already made, that we are not necessarily comparing similar things. It is also justifiable to point out as evidence for their basic reliability that the proportions as between church and chapel accommodation in different areas varied enormously. Some errors, such as duplicate returns, are not difficult to detect, and these are noted in the text. Likewise, the even more numerous errors due to the mis-binding of returns can fairly easily be rectified. Some registrars seem to have been extremely careless: the Aberystwyth District returns, for example, were very haphazardly put together. More often there was confusion over place-names. Llanelli in Carmarthenshire is sometimes confused with the place of the same name in Breconshire. Aberystruth appears as Aberystwyth and places properly located in the former bound in with returns from the latter by the London clerks. Not all of these are easy to detect, but most are indicated in the edition which follows by means of a note to that effect appended to both of the parishes or districts involved in such errors.

The accuracy of the attendance figures is also open to serious doubt, possibly more so than the accommodation figures, and it was these which gave rise to the most heated discussion when they were published in summary form in the Report. Underlying the references to the Census in Parliament to which we have already referred was the suspicion that the statistics would be used for partisan purposes. There was a presumption that Nonconformist figures would be exaggerated either consciously or unconsciously, and that, in any case, as Abraham Hume so justly remarked at a later date, 'Each religious body looks at facts through a medium of its own interposing; and each is anxious to show its importance through its numbers'.[57] The vicar of Abergwili, the Revd. Enoch Pugh, was convinced that this would be the case, and in his view, accuracy would be assured only by entrusting the enumeration to disinterested parties. 'This', he wrote, 'would prevent wilful exaggeration of which I could give shameful specimens in dissenting localities, as published in Welsh periodicals'.[58] The vicar must have had in mind the statistics of membership which were published from time to time in the denominational magazines and occasionally in English magazines as well.[59] But contemporaries were well aware of the difficulty of compiling such statistics and of the unreliability of such as were published, and probably most Welshmen would have agreed that James Bennett's conclusion concerning dissenters applied with even greater force in Wales, namely, 'that nothing has been more difficult than to obtain an

[56] *The Times*, 22 July 1870.
[57] A. Hume, *op. cit.*, p. 3.
[58] 589. 2. 4(21).
[59] See, for example, *Congregational Magazine*, New Series, 10 (1834), pp. 436, 711, 791 and 11, (1835), p. 199. Cf. also 'On the statistics of places of worship in England and Wales, founded on a table compiled by the Rev. T. Blisse', *J. R. Stat. S.*, xiv, (1851), p. 343.

accurate estimate of their churches, and members, and congregations, and ministers'.[60] Enoch Pugh was undoubtedly right to be sceptical as to the reliance to be placed on the returns, but wrong in his assumption that inaccuracy would be the product of a conscious desire to deceive. Moreover, he could not have been fully aware of the many safeguards built into the system to ensure a relatively high degree of objectivity in the country, and the tone of his remark more than suggests that he was typically the kind of person whom Mann had in mind as being ready to believe 'that ministers in humble life were less disposed than their superiors to adhere to the truth'.[61]

It is significant that the vicar of Abergwili was virtually alone in thus dismissing the Census as worthless. Neither before, during, nor immediately after the event were there serious attempts made by critics to sustain his point of view. One signing himself 'Mihangel', and claiming to have been employed as an enumerator in north Cardiganshire, complained, in a letter to *Yr Haul* in June 1851, that a Calvinistic Methodist chapel, one of six nonconformist chapels and three churches in a parish of 1,300 people, had returned an attendance figure of 1,400. Even this one instance, however, cannot be taken as anything but a mischievous attempt to stir up trouble, for none of the north Cardiganshire returns from Calvinistic Methodist chapels have been altered or amended or, indeed, return such a figure, which should have been the case if the facts alleged had been true. Nor were there any such allegations made in 1854 on the publication of the Report: in fact, very little notice of the Report was taken in Wales at the time. It became the centre of controversy only much later, in the 1860s, when the disestablishment campaign began in earnest.[62] There is no direct evidence, either, in the magazines and newspapers of the time that special preparations had been made by Nonconformists to achieve a good turn-out. The incumbent of Haverfordwest remarked that he had not given previous notice of the count to his congregation, and this, one supposes, can be taken as a kind of negative evidence that some ministers may have been less scrupulous than he.[63] But there is no evidence that this was so, and it is worth pointing out that if this had been the case then the advantage tactically would have lain with the Anglican ministers for they had all received specimen copies of the form they would be required to complete, whereas Nonconformists received theirs only a few days before the count. The lack of any evidence suggests that the practice alluded to could not have been general.

---

[60] James Bennett, *History of Dissenters*, Vol. 1 (1839), pp. 260-1, Vol. 2 (1839) p. 271 note.

[61] Horace Mann, *art. cit.*, p. 143.

[62] Most of the Welsh magazines of radical tendencies seem to have contented themselves in 1854 with references to, or summaries of, articles on the Report by Liberationists: e.g. *Y Cronicl* (1854), t. 57 summarizes Miall's article in *The Nonconformist* of January 1854, and *Y Dysgedydd* (1854), t. 199 Liberationist pamphlets. *Y. Methodist* (1854), t. 61 is mainly interested in Methodist numbers. An article in *Yr Eglwysydd*, Chwefror, 1854, t. 13, refers to the Church of England *Church and State Gazette* and *Y Cymro*, 6 Ionawr 1854.

[63] 592. 2. 4(10).

More serious is the criticism made by the same person that there was a conspiracy on the part of Dissenters to inflate numbers of attendants artificially by encouraging individuals to attend additional services in chapels other than their own.[64] This was a criticism widely made on the publication of the Report. Mann attempted to dismiss it by arguing that 'Double attendances would not benefit the conspirators, for they could not be in two places at the same time: they could only swell parish B at the expense of parish A'.[65] But, as has been pointed out, this would be the case only if both chapels were open at the same time.[66] This might or might not be the case. In towns and industrial areas, as the returns amply demonstrate, the pattern of services was universally to have preaching services, or possibly a preaching service and a prayer meeting, morning and evening, with a Sunday School in the afternoon. When it was known before-hand that there would be only one preaching service no doubt many worshippers might visit another chapel where there was preaching. But this was customary and to be expected. In rural areas the pattern varied considerably from place to place, with one service and one Sunday School being common for the simple reason that in such regions ministers often had the care of more than one chapel and served scattered congregations. Even so, for Enoch Pugh's observation to be valid it would be necessary to show that the preaching services had been so arranged, the ministers' rosters so contrived, as to permit such journeyings as he alleged were taking place. This does not appear to have been the case in his own parish, as can be seen from the returns, and it will also be noted that the attendance figures for the various chapels do not suggest that such interchanges of congregation were taking place. This does not exclude the possibility of worshippers moving from one parish to another: indeed, it would be strange if this did not take place, for the presence of a popular preacher would draw hearers from very wide areas. The pattern of services in the rural areas facilitated this kind of movement—may, indeed, have been designed to permit such movement. But this is a very different matter from the conscious deceit adumbrated by Enoch Hughes of Abergwili.

Conscious exaggeration of the number of attendants is another aspect of the same problem. In the nature of the evidence it is impossible to judge the truth of the allegations made, or the extent to which it was indulged. The local registrar, J. D. Palmour of the Begelly (Pembrokeshire) Subdistrict alleged that most of the returns from dissenting congregations were very far from the truth, and instanced the attendance figures of the Primitive Methodist chapel at Jeffreston.[67] But since the registrar appears to have been the curate of the parish his testimony is far from unimpeachable. His reference to the high average attendances given for that chapel does, nevertheless, draw attention to the fact that some of the persons making the returns were not

<hr>

[64] 589. 2. 4(21).
[65] Mann, *art. cit.*; p. 146.
[66] Thompson, *art. cit.*, p. 93
[67] 590. 6. 4(6).

certain of the meaning of the term.[68] On the other hand, most ministers and officials understood exactly what was involved and made returns as directed in the instructions. Many went to the trouble to explain any disparities between actual and average attendances. Some noted that the current depression in the iron-trade had had a disastrous effect on chapels in industrial and mining areas, and it was the consequent migration of families away from those neighbourhoods which, reasonably enough, accounted for the disparities.[69] Indeed, it would be difficult in the face of the evidence to sustain the argument that the value of the attendance statistics are vitiated by a conscious desire to exaggerate. No doubt, not all ministers, church-wardens and deacons actually counted the heads of their congregations: some are declared to be estimates only.[70] But some ministers obviously did make careful counts—like the minister of Carmel, Pontypridd, who arranged for his congregation to be counted as it assembled, children under nine years being excluded,[71] and clearly, some chapel officials were accustomed to making regular counts, like the Cardiganshire minister who explained that it would have taken too much time to have counted male and females separately as was their normal practice.

Evidence of an indirect kind will be found in the 'remarks' which were often added to the returns. Many of the ministers were preoccupied with this problem of having to record a smaller, or sometimes larger, attendance than average. In Monmouthshire and East Glamorgan, and in one place in south Radnorshire, it was pointed out that 30 March was Mothering Sunday —or Mid-lend Sunday—a day for family reunions.[72] Apologists for the Church of England argued that this must have reduced considerably the total of their attendance in such places, but the returns make it clear that Nonconformist chapels were likewise affected. Mothering Sunday, where it was observed, was a social rather than a religious custom.[73] The weather also affected many congregations, so far as one can tell, pretty generally throughout the whole country though most evidently in rural areas where worshippers had to travel considerable distances to worship. But again, as Mann rather bitterly remarked, 'the rain, at all events, cannot be accused of partiality'.[74] More specifically, attendances were affected adversely by the presence of an unpopular preacher,[75] or of a popular preacher in another chapel.[76] There was fever at Bassaleg and sickness at other places.[77] The vicar of Vaynor remarked that at that time of year the farmers were usually busy with their cattle, and the forms from fishing villages and coastal towns in Pembrokeshire and Cardiganshire drew attention to the fact that many of

[68] 583. 2. 7(15), 591. 3. 1(7), 592. 3. 16(35).
[69] 579. 1. 2(6), (14), (41), 580. 3. 7(14).
[70] 589. 3. 1(1), 590. 3. 2(3), 602. 2. 2(4).
[71] 582. 1. 1(7), 594. 3. 6(22). See also, 585. 3. 1(15), 593. 1. 4(14), 591. 2. 4(6).
[72] e.g. 577. 2. 7(12), 578. 1. 3(3), 579. 1. 2(6).
[73] e.g. 577. 4. 5(14), 579. 1. 2(26), 580. 2. 1(10).
[74] Mann, *op. cit.*, p. 145.
[75] 586. 2. 1(9).
[76] 603. 2. 1(15).
[77] 580. 3. 7(13), and, e.g. 591. 1. 14(25), 591. 2. 1(5), 592. 3. 7(30), 597. 1. 1(3).

their members were sailors and away at sea, or at home preparing for the
fishing season to open.[78] Others again emphasized that their attendance
figures gave no proper indication of the size of their membership. The shift
system kept the coppermen of Swansea and Llanelli away from chapel at
regular intervals, for example.[79] The Rev. William Roberts (Nefydd)
estimated that a fifth or a sixth part of the congregations of the districts where
he resided would be unable to attend regularly for domestic or employment
reasons.[80]

The distinction between 'general congregation' and Sunday scholars
presents some difficulties. When he drew up his Report Mann had the
English system of Sunday Schools in mind, that is to say, schools providing
secular education on Sundays, and where attendants at Sunday School were
shown separately, as being attended only by scholars, he disregarded them
in his calculations but included them where they were given as being present
at normal services.[81] But as is well known, Sunday Schools in Wales had a
different origin and philosophy and were organized on a different system,
operated in accordance with quite different principles. The Sunday School
in Wales was a characteristic mode of religious experience, an essential
characteristic of community belonging, and as a function of the chapel and
congregation it is not at all clear on what grounds the distinction between
general congregation and Sunday scholars was made. A majority of chapels
returned scholars as being present at all services indifferently, and one can
only assume in such cases that the distinction was simply as between adults
and children: the exclusion of children under nine years from the totals of
the congregations at the Rhondda chapel already referred to is interesting in
this respect.[82] Similarly, Sunday Schools were not necessarily made up of
young people and children. More than half of the Sunday School at Llangeler consisted of adults, and this was undoubtedly the case throughout the
whole country as had been often observed earlier, as was confirmed in the contemporary Education Census, and would again be stressed in future surveys
of educational provision.[83] It is a matter of the greatest regret that the
original returns of the Education Census are not preserved, for this would
have enabled historians to study in the greatest detail the age structure of the
Sunday Schools in Wales and have provided a means of checking the information given in the Religious Census. And it may be observed that the fact
that the same officials were responsible for making both returns must have
encouraged a greater degree of accuracy in both. Several of the returns

[78] 582. 3. 2(26), 593. 1. 3(12), 596. 2. 5(13).
[79] 584. 6. 1(7), 586. 2. 1(5).
[80] 578. 5. 1(18).
[81] Report, p. clxxi.
[82] Above, p. xxvii Cf. 597. 2. 1(9) where it is explicitly stated that no distinction is made
between general congregation and Sunday scholars.
[83] *Reports of the Commisioners of Inquiry into the state of Education in Wales* (1847), *passim.*
Census of 1851. Education, pp. lxxvi et seq. *Report of the Commisioners on popular
education in England*, PP 1861, xxi-xxvi (2794): Report of Assistant Commissioner John
Jenkins.

here reproduced refer to the Education Census,[84] but without the original returns it is impossible to assess clearly the exact significance of the entries here printed, though the general conclusion as to the overwhelming reliance of the Welsh people on the Sunday School is unmistakably borne out.

Both in his Report and in his subsequent writings, Horace Mann was careful to point out that the Census had counted not individuals, but visits.[85] It is impossible to distinguish between attendants and attendances. Given the declared purpose of the Census, which was to ascertain 'how far the means of Religious Instruction . . . have kept pace with the population, and to what extent these means are adequate to meet the spiritual wants of the increased population of 1851' this was a less serious deficiency for Mann than his critics, then and subsequently, have made out.[86] Mann was concerned with fairly large aggregations and approximations, and his very elaborate calculations, designed to distil actual numbers of individual worshippers from the numbers of attendants, were intended merely to provide a more or less comparative base in order to identify the relative spiritual destitution or deprivation of the various regions of the country. His method of adding together the whole of those who had attended in the morning, one half of those who attended in the afternoon, and one third of those who attended in the evening had no objective validity.[87] It was a device, based on guesswork, on impressions as to general religious practice, and Mann himself was not disposed to defend it in detail. He admitted that his method favoured the Church, and that this was so in Wales is obvious from the returns. Almost universally the best attended service with the Nonconformists was in the evening—or at the one preaching service in rural chapels. Only in urban and industrialized districts where 'spiritual destitution' was highest and the challenge of Nonconformity most acute would Mann's formula be more or less statistically fair, for in such areas the Church adapted itself to the worshipping habits of the majority. There are equally cogent objections to all the other methods of establishing the size of the worshipping population which have been suggested, and the conclusion must be that it is impossible to make accurate estimates.[88] Nevertheless, the attendance figures as given can be used for comparing the relative religiosity of one region with another without first having to establish numbers of individual attendants. This is the method adopted by Inglis and adapted by Gay, namely, establishing an Index of Attendance by adding together the morning, afternoon and evening attendances and expressing the resultant total as a percentage of the total population.[89] In the edition which follows the population of each Registration County, District, Subdistrict, and parish (or other division) is given to enable this to be done.

[84] e.g. 591. 2. 1(9), 594. 3. 5(17), 601. 4. 1(7) and (18).
[85] Report, *passim.*, *art. cit.*, p. 146.
[86] Census of Great Britain 1851, vol. 1, p. 41, 'Circular to the Clergy'.
[87] Report, pp. cli, et seq.
[88] These are discussed in Pickering, *art. cit.*, and John D. Gay, *op. cit.*, pp. 52ff.
[89] This was the method adopted by the present author in his studies of religious observance in Swansea, Caernarvonshire, and Brecon and Radnor.

This method can also be used to establish the relative strength of the various denominations, on the basis either of accommodation or attendance, within specific regions from the parish upwards. It is necessary to emphasize that this was not a primary object of the Census, still less, as Gay mistakingly believes, 'to discover how many people were outside the institutional church; and to show that the Church of England was still the church of the majority'.[90] The object of the Census was as stated in the official papers, or, as Mann explained in his paper to the Statistical Society and in his letters to *The Times*, "The inquiry undertaken in 1851 related to the provision for religious worship and the extent to which the means provided were made use of. It was not an enumeration of professed adherents to different sects'.[91] To have asked every individual to state his religious belief would have been 'far too inquisitorial to be ever adopted in England', and anyway would have produced utterly untrustworthy results, inevitably favouring the Church. In the circumstances Mann was probably right in preferring some kind of controlled observation, and on the basis of the information yielded by the returns it is possible to establish, subject to the reservations we have made, the pattern of provision and of attendance throughout south Wales with a fair degree of certitude by using the above method.

Since the primary purpose of the Census was to discover the extent to which the means of religious worship had kept pace with the increase in population since the beginning of the century, both Anglican and Nonconformist ministers were asked to give the date of erection or opening of their places of worship. Nonconformists were asked simply for the date if after 1800. In the vast majority of cases this was given accurately. Though not required specifically to say so chapels which had been rebuilt stated the fact (often with pride), sometimes adding interesting details, such as the decision to rebuild on a new site, difficulties in obtaining land, the additional sittings thus made available, the provision of vestries, school-rooms, and so on. On the basis of these returns it is possible to study the growth of Nonconformity regionally and by denomination in considerable detail, but caution is required in preparing any such statistics because one cannot always be certain that the buildings referred to were 'separate and entire buildings' and 'used exclusively as places of worship'. In a large number of cases this information has been corrected by the enumerator, the return being endorsed 'dwelling house', or, in one case, 'no place at all'.[92] Sometimes the date given refers obviously to the date of erection of the building, whether dwelling, hall, or some other, in which the service was held. In others it is taken to mean the date when the congregation first met for worship. Nevertheless, with those qualifications, it is possible to trace the growth of the denominations over the half century with a fair degree of certainty.

[90] Gay, *op. cit.*, p. 45.
[91] Mann, *art. cit.*, p. 142, *The Times*, 22 July 1860, p. 4, and 22 July 1870.
[92] 582. 2. 1(7).

Anglican ministers were asked for much more detailed information, including the date of consecration or licensing, and, in the case of additional churches, by whom they had been erected, and how the cost had been defrayed. This was the age of church extension, and though most, if not all, of the information asked for would have been available from other sources—returns to Parliament from the Church Commissioners and the reports of the Incorporated Church Building Society, for instance—the Census gives a complete picture of the results at a particular point in time of the efforts of the church, both at the official, statutory level and by means of private enterprise, to adapt itself in a changing society. In most cases the information given by the church authorities is full and correct. Church extension came relatively late in Wales and in most cases details would be fresh in the memories of the incumbents, and they would be in a position to supply details of local benevolence not otherwise available. Sometimes, however, the returns were made by curates who might not necessarily have the desired information, and it is for this reason that entries from the 1848 edition of Samuel Lewis's *Topographical Dictionary* have been appended to the returns from the parish churches. Likewise, many incumbents omitted to state whether grants from the Incorporated Society had been received, and an entry has therefore been made of all grants made by that Society from its foundation in 1818 until 1851.[93] Most of the Society's grants were for relatively small amounts and intended to assist in repairs and extensions rather than for the building of new churches or for rebuilding old ones, and although not required in the returns, this additional information is of importance in any assessment of the adjustment of the Church to the changing conditions of the time.

The most controversial class of information asked for concerned the endowments attached to benefices. Despite strong objections to the inclusion of this query and the Registrar-General's circular stating that there was no legal compulsion to supply the information, very few incumbents refused to comply. The incumbent of Whitchurch (Pem.) was unique in objecting that the query was impertinent: but he none the less gave the information accurately.[94] Stipendiary curates, of course, could not be expected to have the necessary facts. The entry from *Lewis* given under each parish church supplies the information as to endowments and income from tithe, etc., but we must rely on the returns for details of income from pew rents and Easter offerings. The entries from *Lewis* also give details—not asked for on the forms—of appropriations, and these can be checked against the official returns of the Church Commissioners.[95] In most cases, *Lewis* gives the name of the tithe-owner, and also the name of the patron. The relevance of

[93] Incorporated Church Building Society Annual Reports. The individual files to which reference is made are deposited in the Library of Lambeth Palace.
[94] 592. 3. 8(15).
[95] Returns of all tithes commuted and apportioned, PP 1847/8, XLIX (298), pp. 396-399, 324-392.

this information scarcely needs to be pointed out, and the frequency with which it is given by incumbents in their remarks is eloquent testimony to its great importance in the eyes of churchmen at that time. It was not unusual for incumbents, particularly in the diocese of St. David's, to allude to the fact that they received only a fraction of the tithe income of their parishes. The counties of Pembroke, Carmarthen, and Cardigan were the worst off in this respect, the incumbents of benefices in those countries receiving on average only 13, 16 and 33 per cent respectively of tithe rents.[96] The superbly detailed remarks of the vicar of Nevern illustrate perfectly the situation in large numbers of parishes in the western counties, and probably also the attitudes of frustrated incumbents who suffered in consequence.[97] Pluralities, likewise, were most endemic in those regions, and clearly they were a function of poor endowments caused primarily by appropriations.

Although the information returned regarding incomes from livings is generally full and accurate, not much can be gleaned from the returns regarding that numerous class of clergymen, the unbeneficed or stipendiary curate. Except incidentally—as, for example, when an incumbent states that he has deducted his curate's stipend from the gross income—the returns are silent regarding their duties, residences, and stipends. To supply this deficiency entries from a Parliamentary Return of 1850 entitled 'Incumbents and Curates' have been added to the parish church entries.[98] This particular return gives the name of the incumbent, states whether he was resident or not (and if the latter, whether legally non-resident), the name, residence and stipend of the curate. From this it will be seen that more than one half of the curates in the two south Wales dioceses (124 out of 194) served non-resident incumbents.[99] Some of these curates served more than one benefice, and it is interesting to note that while the proportion of curates serving non-resident incumbents had fallen dramatically since the late 1830s, the number serving resident incumbents had grown almost proportionately.[100] From this it is clear that while the Pluralities Act of 1838, which regulated the stipends of curates only in the case of non-resident incumbents, was having its desired effect, the creation of new districts, the consolidation of parishes, and the instilling of higher notions of parochial responsibilities were having a quite contrary effect.[101] This was particularly the case in the diocese of Llandaff and in the industrial regions of St. David's. Church extension in

[96] These calculations are based on returns of tithes commuted and apportioned up to 1848.

[97] 593. 1. 4(14).

[98] 'Return of the names and residences of incumbents and curates', PP 1850, XLII (226).

[99] A return of the same year gives the total of curates as 205, of whom 111 served non-resident incumbents. PP 1850, XLII (364), p. 136.

[100] In 1838 there were 175 curates in non-resident benefices and 15 in resident benefices in St. David's, and 70 and 27 respectively in Llandaff. Ten years later the numbers of curates on non-resident benefices had fallen to 67 in St. Davids and 44 in Llandaff, while the other class had risen to 49 in St. Davids and 45 in Llandaff. *Ibid.*, p. 130. In 1835 there had been a total of 273 curates serving non-resident benefices in the two diocese. Ecclesiastical Revenues Report, *op. cit.*

[101] 1 and 2 Vict. c. 106. For detailed studies see Walter T. Morgan, 'The Diocese of St. David's in the nineteenth century', *Journal of the History Society of the Church in Wales* No. 26 (1971).

south Wales often amounted to the creation of additional pauper benefices and a clerical proletariat.[102]

For the historian of religion in Wales one serious deficiency in the drafting of the queries for both Anglican and Nonconformist places of worship was the omission of any questions relating to the language in which services were conducted. This is highly regrettable, and also very strange, for the question of the use of the Welsh language in the services of the Church in Wales was invariably an issue at both the diocesan and the parliamentary levels whenever church extension was under discussion. Protagonists of a 'Welsh Church'—the advocates of the need to appoint Welsh-speaking Welshmen to the heriarchy, and for the conscientious enforcement of the law regarding appointment to Welsh benefices, such as Sir Benjamin Hall, were extremely active at this time, but the nearest they ever got to a comprehensive survey of the language pattern in the parishes was the return called for by John Williams, Member of Parliament for Macclesfield, entitled 'Number of Services performed in each Church and Chapel [in Wales]' which was published late in 1849.[103] In addition to the information set out in its short-title, the return also stated for each place of worship whether any such services were performed in English or Welsh, and in the case of the latter language, by whom, the incumbent or the curates. This return therefore gives a very considerable amount of important information not easily obtainable from other sources, and in this edition of the returns the relevant entry for each Anglican place of worship has been added to the parish details. Inevitably, it has largely to be taken on trust and local historians, no doubt, will be able to establish its accuracy and reliability. At the time of its publication it aroused considerable interest, being extensively reported and discussed in the newspapers of south Wales, but its basic accuracy was never seriously called in question by churchmen.[104] Indeed, judging by Bishop Copelston's prefatory letter to the Llandaff section, the bishops went to considerable trouble to make accurate returns, a task of some difficulty in those parts of the diocese where the two languages were intermixed 'and that in every conceivable proportion . . . [and] this proportion . . . continually fluctuating'.[105] Contemporaries were convinced that the alienation of the Church was largely due to its neglect of the language. A comparison of the attendance figures for church and chapel in the industrialized parts of the south Wales dioceses would seem to indicate not

---

[102] See, in general, Ward, *op. cit.*, E. T. Davies, *Religion in the Industrial Revolution in South Wales* (1965), and Wilton D. Wills, 'Ecclesiastical Reorganization and Church Extension in the Diocese of Llandaff, 1830-1870', unpublished M.A. thesis (Swansea), 1965. The Select Committee Report on the deficiency of the means of worship, PP 1857-8, IX (378), marshalled considerable evidence in support of this view.

[103] PP 1850, XLII (4).

[104] One Wm. Jones of Tredegar, wrote a letter to the *Cardiff and Merthyr Guardian*, 29 December 1849, drawing attention to the fact that at Tredegar there were two Welsh services on a Sunday and one weekdays, and not one as was stated in the Return.

[105] PP 1850, XLII (4), p. 91.   See also his successor's letter on the same subject in the *Cardiff and Merthyr Guardian* 2 March, 1850.

only that the Church was providing insufficient services but also failing to act upon the knowledge now abundantly available that, as Bishop Ollivant put it, 'The Welsh attach themselves to that place of worship, whether Church or Sectarian, in which their language is alone used',[106] or, as Bishop Burgess of St. David's had observed earlier, 'the Welsh language is with sectaries a powerful means of seduction from the Church'.[107] More succinctly, the vicar of Llandyfaelog, in whose church the last service in the month happened to be an English one, remarked, 'the Welsh who do not understand the language do not attend'.[108]

That some chapel officials may have had difficulty in understanding the instructions for filling in the forms might have been due to their infamiliarity with the English language. No Welsh versions of the forms had been prepared—a strange omission when we realize that Welsh versions of the population schedules had been made available in certain parts of the country.[109] No one in south Wales commented upon this: it was a north Walian who resented the failure to provide translations as an insult to the language.[110] A number of the returns seem barely literate, but it is remarkable that so few signed with a mark—less than a half of one per cent of the total signatures[111]—and it may be significant also that most of these were from urban areas. Many of the forms were completed by men in very humble circumstances. Unfortunately, the forms did not ask the signatories to state their occupations, and where these are given one assumes that it was for purposes of identification in areas of relatively recent settlement in order to supplement addresses which might otherwise be very vague. Addresses are given in all cases in this edition not merely by reason of its obvious utility to local historians but also as providing some indication of the pattern of ministerial services being provided for what were so often rural and scattered congregations.

The remarks columns often provide important and interesting information regarding the religious customs of particular congregations and regions, and these are copied out in full, the original spelling and punctuation being carefully preserved. As we have already observed, some of them are very long, detailed statements ranging far beyond the requirements of the

---

[106] *Ibid.*, cf. also Sir Benjamin Hall, *A letter to the Archbishop of Canterbury on the State of the Church* (1851), *Speech in the House of Commons, 1 July 1851* (1851), his letter to the *Cardiff and Merthyr Guardian*, 5 January 1850, explaining why he would not contribute to a memorial to the late Bishop Copleston, Bishop Ollivant's letter in *ibid.*, 2 March 1850 on the 'Churches and Chapels' Return', Archdeacon Thomas Williams's Open Letter to the Bishop of Llandaff, *ibid.*, 14 September 1850. For a Nonconformist view—not necessarily typical—see a review of the Return in *The Principality*, 15 March 1850, p. 4, which concludes, 'There is no Welsh Church. There was; but there is not'.

[107] Quoted in W. Morgan, *J.H.S.C. in W.*, 28 (1973), p. 26.

[108] 589. 1. 5(23).

[109] Census Report, PP 1852-3, LXXXV (1631), Population Report, Vol. 1, p. xiii, and E. Cheshire, *op. cit.*, p. 12.

[110] 'What was the care that you sent us these papers in English instead of Welsh. We believe that our Language ought to be loved by any heart that can talk it. We think it the best Language now in the whole earth and if you cant talk Welsh there we can talk English here. We love our dear language and we like to have every paper belonging to us in Welsh.' HO 129/621. 2. 2(25).

[111] Examples are 581. 4. 5(11), 584. 2. 1(3), 588. 1. 1(11), 589. 6. 2(5), 599. 3. 1(2).

forms.[112] This is where their value to the historian lies. The vicar of Kidwelly, for instance, is eloquently bitter on the immorality of his parish,[113] while the vicar of Angle and Warren in South Pembrokeshire gives some indication of the depressing effects of excessive poverty on the religious life of his neighbourhood—an impression confirmed by the remarks of the Baptist Home Missionary at work in the parish,[114] and by a Baptist deacon in near-by Camrose. Many incumbents take the opportunity to complain about dilapidations and the general state of the fabric, and an even greater number draw attention to the inconvenient situation of their parish churches. From such remarks we gather an impression of the efforts being made to find and adapt suitable additional premises, and we realize forcefully, what is so often ignored, that the spiritual struggle in the new heavily populated industrial regions was not so much between rival denominations but rather between organized Christianity as a whole and the constant spectre of a fundamentally irreligious society. If the Baptists of Llangynwyd were glad to make use of an old storehouse belonging to the Llynfi Iron Company, so too the Anglicans were not slow to adapt an old engine-house.[115] Indeed, this is the prevailing impression with which we are left. Polemical, partisan statements of belief are rare. The Baptists of Trevethin proclaim their belief in the need for disestablishment, the Anglicans of Rumney have a high turn-out for anti-papist reasons, and the Baptists of Llanelli (Breconshire), while emphasizing their voluntaryist attitudes, proclaim their attachment to the constitution and the queen.[116] At this particular point in time, perhaps it is the attitude of the vicar of Nevern which was most typical. His remarks vividly illustrate the decline in the influence of the Church, its age-old neglect of the outlying parts of the parish, and its inability, by reason of the in-difference and greed of a non-resident lay impropriator, to adopt more aggressive attitudes. The distant inhabitants of the parish 'would be living the lives of heathens had not the Dissenters built Chapels in different parts of the Parish, of which there are *six*'.[117] The key to the relative success of the Nonconformists is likewise to be inferred from the returns. Old-established chapels, serving scattered communities of farmers and labourers, suffered from their remoteness from large centres of population just as much as the parish churches,[118] but they accepted as normal and necessary the dispersed congregation, and their preachers were as ready to serve the faithful in farm-houses and dwelling-houses as the founding-fathers had been. White-cross Independent chapel in the industrial parish of Eglwysilan held their evening services in four different places.[119] This was the adaptation of an

[112] Excellent examples are the returns made by the vicars of Llangynwyd, 583. 1. 1(1), Nevern, 593. 1. 3(12), Llanddeti, 600. 4. 4(9), Llanvillo, 600. 4. 7(11), and the minister of the Independent Chapel at Llywel, 600. 2. 2(8).
[113] 586. 3. 2(12).
[114] 591. 2. 9(25-27).
[115] 584. 1. 2(8-9).
[116] 579. 1. 2(31), 581. 2. 2(5), 601. 4. 1(22).
[117] 593. 1. 4(14).
[118] e.g. Pont Estyll, 600. 3. 3(2).
[119] 581. 1. 1(15).

old rural pattern of religious organization to the new conditions of the coal-field.[120] Where the Church was resurgent this was also the pattern of its worship, a pattern it was increasingly prepared to adopt. But the Census, if it has any significance at all, is eloquent of the fact that by the 1850s the pattern of religious adherance in south Wales which was to survive in its main characteristics until our own times, had by then been established. It is hoped that the edition of the Census here presented will enable historians to study that pattern in greater detail and to greater effect than has heretofore been the case.

IEUAN GWYNEDD JONES

---

[120] Cf., e.g. almost any area in north Pembrokeshire, Carmarthenshire or Cardiganshire.

MONMOUTHSHIRE

Area of the Registration County within Wales: 457,922 acres.
Popn. 81,705 males, 74,479 females: total 156,184.

Area of the District within Wales: 49,393 acres. *Popn.* 5,879 males, 5,677 females: total 11,556.

1 SHIRE-NEWTON (Subdistrict)
Area: 37,623 acres. *Popn.* 2,683 males, 2,429 females: total 5,112.

1   Portscuett, or Portskewett Parish.
Area: 1,779 acres. *Popn.* 100 males, 87 females: total 187.

(1)   Portskewett with Southbrook Parish Church.
Endowed: tithe and glebe about £250.
Space: 144 total sittings.
Present: morn. 70 + 26 scholars.
Remarks: general congregation from 80 to 90; Sunday Scholars from 30 to 35.

E. J. Lewis.   Rector.

Lewis: discharged rectory, valued at £7. 2. 1; patron Thomas Lewis, Esq.; tithes commuted for £224. 16. 9; glebe of 52 acres and glebe-house.

C & C: 1 service in English.

I & C: resident.

2   Caldicott Parish.
Area: 3,158 acres. *Popn.* 338 males, 323 females: total 661.

(2)   Caldicott Parish Church.
Endowed: net income £180; fees applied to Parish Charities.
Space: None are Faculty seats; about 200 (inclusive of children's seats) with room for many more.
Present: morn. 90 + 45 scholars; aft. 80 + 20 scholars.
Average (6 months): morn. 100 + 50 scholars; aft. 60 + 30 scholars.
Remarks: About ⅓ of the Parish live at some distance from the Church.

E. T. Williams, M.A.   Vicar.

Lewis: discharged vicarage; valued at £6. 0. 7½; patron, Sir E. Keynton Williams; impropriator, T. Rowland, Esq.; great tithes commuted for £240, and the vicarial tithes for £188: glebe of 15 acres.

C & C: 2 services in English.

I & C: incumbent resident.

(3) Caldicott Weslean Chapel.   Wesleyan Methodist.
Erected: 1810.
Space: free 110, other 70.
Present: morn. 150.
Average: morn. 160.

Henry James.   Steward.

3   Ifton Parish
Area: 2,155 acres. *Popn.* 22 males, 12 females: total 34.

[(4) This return is misplaced through confusion with Itton, for which see 576. 1. 13 below.]

Lewis: the living of Ifton, a rectory not in charge united with that of Roggiet [576. 1. 4(5)]: church demolished.

4   Roggiet Parish.
Area: 2,905 acres. *Popn.* 38 males, 22 females: total 60.

(5) Rogiett cum Ifton Parish Church.
Endowed: By land, tithe, glebe.
Space: Free sittings for 45 and a gallery that will hold between 20 and 30 people, chiefly occupied by the school children, School mistress.
Present: morn. 45 + 20 scholars.
Average: morn. from 30 to 40 + 20 scholars.
Remarks: The Service is alternatively morning and afternoon during the summer months. There is generally a larger congregation.

Richard Williams.   Rector.

Lewis: discharged rectory with that of Ifton [576. 1. 3] united; valued at £12. 6. 0½. patron, Sir Charles Morgan, Bart.: tithes commuted for £65. 17: glebe, small cottage and 4 acres of land in Llanvihangel parish [576. 1. 5].

C & C: 1 service in English.

I & C: incumbent resident.

5   Llanvihangel near Roggiett Parish.
Area: 557 acres. *Popn.* 21 males, 21 females: total 42.

(6) Llanvihangel juxta Roggiett Parish Church.
Endowed: By land, tithe, glebe.
Space: free 30; other 20.
Present: morn. 12.
Average: morn. 12.

Stephen Williams.   Rector.

Lewis: discharged rectory; valued at £6. 9. 4½; patron, Sir C. Morgan, Bart.; tithes commuted for £123; glebe of 9 acres.

C & C: 1 service in English.

I & C: incumbent not resident.

6   Undy Parish.

Area: 3,717 acres. *Popn.* 192 males, 181 females: total 373.

(7)   UNDY PARISH CHURCH.
Endowed: land £40; tithe £140; glebe house £15; fees £2: gross annual value £197.
Space: about 100.
Present: morn. 25 scholars; aft. 76.
Average: morn. 60 + 20 scholars; aft. 70; even. 35.
Remarks: Average in the morning about 60; average in the afternoon about 70; average in the evening about 35.

William Jones.   Vicar.

Lewis: discharged vicarage, valued at £4. 10. 7½; patrons and appropriators, Dean and Chapter of Llandaff: great tithes commuted for £150, the vicarial for £140; appropriate glebe of 52 acres, and vicarial glebe of 4 acres with a glebe-house.

C & C: 1 service in English.

I & C: incumbent resident.

7   St. Bride Netherwent Parish, excluding the hamlet of Llandevenny
[580. 1. 7]
Area: 780 acres. *Popn.* 79 males, 52 females: total 131.

(8)   ST. BRIDES NETHERWENT PARISH CHURCH.
Endowed: land £58; tithe £133; permanent endowment £6; fees £1: gross annual value £198.
Space: free 70.
Present: morn. 20.
Average: morn. 20; aft. 30.
Remarks: It was consecrated in 1848, having been rebuilt from the foundation. Erected by the Patron chiefly. Cost defrayed by Parochial Rate £60; subscription £440; total cost £500.

William Jones.   Vicar of Undy.

Lewis: discharged rectory; valued at £6. 16. 3; patrons, family of Perry; tithes commuted for £148; glebe of 52 acres. Includes the hamlet of Llandevenny.

C & C: 1 service in English.

I & C: incumbent not resident: curate, who resides at Undy, 2 miles distant, has stipend of £70.

8-9   Caerwent Parish, consisting of [8] Caerwent and [9] the Hamlet of Dinham.
Area of the whole: 1,962 acres. *Popn.* 205 males, 215 females: total 420.

(9)   THE BAPTIST CHAPEL, CAERWENT
Erected 1815.
Space: free 120; other 30; standing 50.
Present: morn. 42 + 20 scholars; aft. 27 scholars; even. 74.
Average (12 *months*): morn. 50 + 30 scholars; aft. 35 scholars; even. 100.
Remarks: A day school is kept in it.
John Walter Morgan.   Minister.

(10)   ST. JOHN'S CAERWENT PARISH CHURCH.
Space: free 80; appropriated 120.
Usual number of attendants: morn. 70 + 30 scholars; aft. 80; even. no service.
Informant: James White.   Registrar.

[Informant's form.]

Lewis: discharged vicarage: endowed with the rectorial tithes and with the perpetual curacy of Llanvair Discoed [576. 1. 10(11)]: valued at £7. 11. 8: patrons, Dean and Chapter of Llandaff: tithes commuted for £249. 2.

C & C: 2 services in English.

I & C: incumbent not resident.

ICBS: grant of £25 in 1829.

[10-11]   Llanvair Discoed Parish, consisting of [10] Llanvair Discoed and [11] the Hamlet of Dinham.
Area of the whole: 1,986 acres. *Popn.* 103 males, 88 females: total 191.

10   Llanvair Discoed Parish.
Area: 1,316 acres. *Popn.* 85 males, 76 females: total 161.

(11)   LLANVAIR DISCOED PARISH CHURCH.
Space: 80.
Present: morn. 32.
Average (6 *months*): morn. 25; aft. 35.
Remarks: The service is performed once a day morning and afternoon alternately.
Edward Griffiths.   Licensed curate.

Lewis: perpetual curacy, united to the vicarage of Caerwent [576. 1. 8(10)]: appropriators, Dean and Chapter of Llandaff.

C & C: 1 service in English.

C & C: incumbent not resident.

11   Dinham Hamlet.
Area: 670 acres. *Popn.* 18 males, 12 females: total 30.
[No returns]
Lewis: ancient parish now considered only a hamlet: lay rectory belonging to the
Bp., Archdeacon and Chapter of Llandaff; tithes commuted for £83. There is no
trace of the church.

12   Shire-Newton Parish.
Area: 3,544 acres. *Popn.* 508 males, 425 females: total 933.

(12)   SHIRENEWTON PARISH CHURCH.
Endowed: tithe £310; fees £2.
Sittings: fee 99; other 58.
Present: morn. 78 + 37 scholars; aft. 92 + 24 scholars.
Remarks: The figures (those present) do not represent the average number
of attendants either of the general congregation or of Sunday Scholars, but
as no accurate account had been kept it is thought better not to make any
return in the following columns.

Edward Inwood Jones.   Rector.

Lewis: discharged rectory; valued at £9. 8. 1½; patron, the Crown in right of the
Prince of Wales; tithes commuted for £375. 5. 6, with glebe of 2 acres.

C & C: 2 services in English.

I & C: incumbent not resident.

ICBS: grant of £100 in 1852.

(13)   WESLEYAN CHAPEL.
Erected about 1825.
Sittings: free 80.
Present: even. 70.

Zechariah Jones.   Steward.

(14)   BIBLE CHRISTIANS, MYNYDD BACH.
Erected 1850.
Space: free 40.
Present: morn. 8; aft. 18; even. 11.
Average (12 *months*): 26.

James Penny.   Steward.

(15)   EARLSWOOD WESLEYAN METHODIST.
Erected 1799.
Space: free 150; standing 250.
Present: aft. 80.
Average (12 *months*): morn. 30 scholars; aft. 100.
John James.   Steward.

[Endorsed: See letter.]

(16)   MOUNT ZION, GAERLWYD.   WELSH CALVINISTIC METHODIST.
Erected 1842.
Space: free 100.
Present: morn. 37 scholars; aft. 69.
Average (12 *months*): morn. 35 scholars; aft. 60.
Remarks: A day school held within the chapel commencing March 31, 1851.

>   Edward Jones.   Member.
>   Caerlwyd

(17)   FISHERS PLACE.   BIBLE CHRISTIANS.
Present: even. 30.
Average (12 *months*): even. 30.
Remarks: This is a cottage in which there has been Religious Service for the last 10 or 12 years.

>   William Powell.   Steward.

[13-14]   Itton Parish, consisting of [13] Itton and [14] Howick Hamlet.
Area of the whole: 1,738 acres. *Popn.* 108 males, 92 females: total 200.

13   Itton Parish
Area: 1,103 acres. *Popn.* 84 males, 67 females: total 151.

(18)   ITTON PARISH CHURCH.
Space: free 100; other 48.
Number of attendants including Sunday Scholars: morn. 40; aft. 60; even. no service.

>   *Signed.* James White. Registrar.
>   *Dated.*   18 Sept. 1852.

The official return for Itton Parish Church is listed under 576. 1. 3(4) as follows:

ITTON PARISH CHURCH.
Sittings: free 80; other 20.
Present: aft. 42.
Average (12 *months*): morn. 40; aft. 60.
Remarks: The 5th question (how endowed) I consider an intrusive one and therefore decline answering it.

>   Joseph Camplin Prosser.   Rector.

Lewis: discharged rectory; valued at £4. 10. 10; patron, Mr. Curre: tithes commuted for £130, and £70 annual rental from a farm in St. Arvans Parish [576. 2.5]; glebe of 8 acres.

C & C: 1 service in English.

I & C: incumbent not resident.

14   Howick Hamlet.
Area: 635 acres. *Popn.* 24 males, 25 females: total 49.
[No returns]

[15-16]   Newchurch Parish, consisting of [15] East Division and [16] West Division.
Area of the whole: 5,434 acres. *Popn.* 382 males, 365 females: total 747.

15   East Division
Popn. 296 males, 290 females: total 586.

(19)   DEVANDEN CHAPEL.   CHURCH OF ENGLAND.
Consecrated 18 September 1837 as an additional chapel to the Mother Church.
Space: free 140; other 16.
Present: morn. 39 scholars; aft. 70 + 39 scholars; even. 59.
Average (12 *months*): morn. 46 + 20 scholars; aft. 80 + 20 scholars; even. 100.
Remarks: If any further information is required it shall be given if requested, *privately.*

David Jones. Off. Ministr.

Lewis: district chapel: perpetual curacy with a small endowment in the patronage of the vicar.

C & C: *sub* Newchurch [1.1.16.(21a)] : 2 services in the chapel in English.

(20)   GLYNN CHAPEL.   WESLEYAN.
Erected 1824.
Space: free 102; standing 15 or 20.
Present: aft. 35.
Remarks: One service at ½ 2 every Sabath and once in 3 weeks on Wednesday at 7 in the evening.

James White.   Steward.
Glen Vale

[Endorsed: See letter.]

(21)   MOUNT EPHRAIM.   WESLEYAN.
Erected 1841.
Space: free 75; standing 10.
Present: morn. 23.
Average (12 *months*): morn. 20; aft. 20.
Remarks: One service a day i.e., each Sabbath alternately Morning and afternoon.

Thomas Thomas.   Local Preacher.
Middle Street

16   West Division of Newchurch Parish.
Popn. 86 males, 75 females: total 161.

(21a) [The form is stamped 22]
NEWCHURCH PARISH CHURCH.
Space: free 74; other 48.
Present: morn. 15.
Average (12 *months*): morn. 30; aft. 50.
Remarks: The Congregation on 30th small because it was what is called Midlent or Mothering Sunday. The 5th question (i.e. how endowed) is an intrusive one and therefore I decline answering it.

Joseph Camplin Prosser.   Vicar.

Lewis: vicarage, in the patronage of the Duke of Beaufort; net income £176: impropriate tithes commuted for £172, and the vicarial for £65; glebe of 52½ acres, with a glebe-house built in 1832.

C & C: 1 service in English.

I & C: incumbent resident.

17   Kilgwrrwg Parish.
Area: 659 acres. *Popn.* 86 males, 68 females: total 154.

(23)   KILLGWRROGG PARISH CHURCH.
Erected: about 180 years 1671.
Space: free 30; other 20.
Usual number of attendants: morn. 25; aft. 35; even. no service. No Sunday Scholars.

Informant: James White. Registrar.

[Informant's form.]

Lewis: perpetual curacy; valued at £2. 4. 9½; net income £57; patron, Archdeacon of Llandaff.

C & C: 1 service in English.

I & C: incumbent resident.

(24)   ZION.   BIBLE CHRISTIANS.
Erected 1842.
Space: free 100; standing 20.
Present: morn. 40; even. 60.
Average (12 *months*): morn. 40; even. 60.

George M[?]   Local Preacher and Steward.
Micham, Killgwrrne Hill

18   Wolves-Newton Parish.
Area: 2,649 acres. *Popn.* 111 males, 108 females: total 219.

(25) WOLVESNEWTON PARISH CHURCH.
Endowed: land, tithe, glebe, total £198; fees about 10*s.*
Space: free sittings about 18; other about 60.
Present: morn. 18 + 9 scholars; even. 34 + 9 scholars.
Remarks: The number of attendants on March 30th 1851 in the morning under the head of General Congregation does not truly represent the average number throughout the year. It happened that 8 or 10 of the most regular attendants were absent.

David Jones. Rector.

Lewis: rectory; rated at £8. 2. 8½; patron, the Crown; tithes commuted for £244; glebe of 23 acres: accomodation for about 110 persons.

C & C: 1 service in English.

I & C: incumbent resident.

(26) NEBO. INDEPENDANT.
Erected 1818.
Space: free 120.
Present: morn. 30; aft. 32 (no scholars morn. or aft.).
Average (12 *months*): morn. 40; aft. 30.
Remarks: A Day School had been conducted in connexion with the Society meeting at the Chapel for the space of about ten years. It averaged about 25 scholars, but owing to the want of pecuniary support it ceased last week.

James Jones. Deacon.

19 Llangwm Parish, consisting of Icha Division and Ucha Division.
Area of the whole: 3,159 acres. *Popn.* 184 males, 180 females: total 364.

(26) LLANGWM PARISH CHURCH.
Space: free 40; other 84. The Sunday children have benches in the Church.
Present: aft. 36 + 35 scholars.
Average: 9 March: morn. 40 + 31 scholars.
            16 March: aft. 70 + 30 scholars.
Remarks: A very correct account cannot be sent in this schedule of this Parish, but I will (should it be wished) by letter give further information.

John Fleming. Vicar.

Lewis: sub Llangwym: discharged vicarage: valued at £4. 16. 8; net income £83; patron, prebendary of Llangwym in the cathedral of Llandaff.

C & C: 1 service in English.

I & C: incumbent resident.

(27)   LANGWM.   BAPTIST.
Erected 1840.
Space: all free except 11 pews.
Present: even. 66.
Average: general congregation from 80 to 100.

John Michael.   Minister.

(28)   LANGWM.   PENUEL.   BAPTIST.
Erected 1802.
Present: morn. 50.
Average: from 50 to 100.

John Michael.   Minister.

20   Llansoy Parish.

Area: 1,410 acres. *Popn.* 86 males, 80 females: total 166.

(29)   LLANSOY PARISH CHURCH.
Endowed: tithe £190; glebe £8; fees 10*s*.
Space: free 70; other 30.
Present: morn. 26 + 11 scholars; aft. 58 + 13 scholars.
Average: morn. 38 + 14 scholars; aft. 70 + 14 scholars.
Remarks: There is no other place of worship in the Parish.

Richard Macdonnell Evanson.   Rector.

Lewis: discharged rectory; valued at £6. 10. 10; net income £170; patron, Duke of Beaufort; glebe of 14 acres.

C & C: 1 service in English.

I & C: incumbent resident.

21   Llanvihangel-Tor-y-Mynydd Parish.

Area: 1,031 acres. *Popn.* 120 males, 110 females: total 230.

(30)   LLANVIHANGEL TORYMYNYDD PARISH CHURCH.
Present: morn. 45.
Remarks: No objection by a Private Communication to answer the Registrar General how endowed and other queries.

John Price.   Rector.

Lewis: discharged rectory; patron, Archdeacon of Llandaff: tithes commuted for £108. 10; glebe of 11½ acres.

C & C: 1 service in English.

I & C: incumbent resident.

(31) Cross Hands. Bible Christians.
Erected 1826.
Space: free 120; standing 15.
Present: aft. 55; even. 125.
Average: aft. 50; even. 100.

Cornelius Dening.   Minister.
Tintern Abbey.

[End of Shire-Newton Subdistrict]

2 CHEPSTOW (Subdistrict)
Area (excluding the parish of Tidenham in co. Gloucester): 11,770
acres. *Popn.* 3,196 males, 3,248 females: total 6,444.

1 Trelleck Grange Chapelry (Part of Trelleck Parish [577. 4. 5]).
Area: 1,774 acres. *Popn.* 85 males, 63 females: total 148.

(1) Trelleck Grange Church.
Endowed: land £70; glebe £6; permanent endowment £5; fees 15s.
Space: free 25; other 37.
Average attendance (12 *months*): morn. 20-30; aft. 20-30.
Remarks: a small neat building but very damp. March 30 1851 was Mid
Lent Sunday and most of the people of this parish visit their friends that
day. The few cottagers of Trelleck Grange may send their children to
Tintern National School consequently they are expected to attend there on
Sundays.

Henry Warrilow.   Incumbent Minister.

Lewis: chapelry in the parish of Trelleck: perpetual curacy: net income £74;
patron and impropriator, Duke of Beaufort: glebe of 85 acres.

C & C: 1 service in English.

I & C: incumbent resident.

2 Little Tintern Parish.
Area: 827 acres. *Popn.* 190 males, 180 females: total 370.

(2) Tintern Parva, St. Mary's Church.
Endowed: land, tithe, glebe, total £160. 5s.
Space: free 200.
Present: morn. 89 - 90 + 49 scholars; aft. 43 scholars, even. 125-130.

Remarks: Consecrated November 3rd 1845 after being rebuilt and considerably enlarged. Erected partially by the parish rate and public subscription. Parochial rate £33. 6. 1½*d.*, subscriptions £582. 14. 2½*d.*
> R. W. Ferguson, B.A.   Curate.

Lewis: discharged rectory; valued at £2. 1. 5½; net income £162: patron, W. Gale, Esq.

C & C: 2 services in English.

I & C: incumbent not resident: curate, who resides in the parish, has stipend of £80.

3   Chapel Hill Parish.
Area: 820 acres. *Popn.* 265 males, 280 females: total 545.

(3)   CHAPEL HILL PARISH CHURCH.
Space: free 78; other 90.
Usual number present: morn. 50; aft. 50.
> *Informant:* Chas Davis.

[Informant's form.]
[Endorsed: See letter.]

Lewis: perpetual curacy; net income £60; patron and impropriator, Duke of Beaufort.

C & C: 2 services in English.

I & C: incumbent not resident: curate, who resides at St. Arvan's [576. 2. 5] 2 or 3 miles distant, has stipend of £62.

(4)   WESLEYAN CHAPEL.
Erected 1820.
Space: free 80; other 40; standing 'in the Isle and Porch 29'.
Present: morn. 8; even. 60.
Average (12 *months*): morn. 12; even. 60.
> Henry Richard.   Society Steward.

[The parish is given as 'Tintern Abbey Parish': and this return is therefore wrongly numbered and should come under 576. 2. 2].

(5)   BIBLE CHRISTIANS.
Erected before 1800 (i.e. a dwelling house).
Present: morn. 9; aft. 14; even. 29.
Average (12 *months*): morn. 14; aft. 20; even. 30.
Remarks: [on a separate sheet] Near this place of worship there are residing 68 persons and 42 children upwards of a mile and a quarter from the Parish Church, and in consequence of having no chapel, we as a religious body of people have no Sabbath School we have had Preaching in the Neighbourhood about 25 years and should have Built a Chapel but Could not obtain a site of Land but still continue our Services in a dwelling House.
> Thomas Highley.   Steward.

4 Penterry Parish.
Area: 479 acres. *Popn.* 17 males, 17 females: total 34.

(6) PENTERRY PARISH CHURCH.
Endowed: Information under this head will be given by letter if requested.
Space: free 62; other 3.
Present: morn. 36.
Average: morn. 20; aft. 42.
Remarks: There is no Sunday School in the parish. The number of children above 5 and under 14 is 4. The return now made gives perhaps 5, but the home of the fifth is Birmingham. The average for the last 7 years has not exceeded three. The Sunday School at Chapel Hill supplies in great degree the deficiency being distant only a mile and a quarter.

Davies Jones. Perpetual Curate.

Lewis: perpetual curacy: patrons, Bishop, Archdeacon and Chapter of Llandaff: tithes commuted for £55: net income £65.

C & C: 1 service in English.

I & C: incumbent not resident.

5 St. Arvans Parish.
Area: 2,309 acres. *Popn.* 198 males, 234 females: total 432.

(7) ST. ARVANS PARISH CHURCH.
Endowed: rent £44; tithe £10.
Remarks: Perpetual Curacy of St. Arvans worth 54 per annum. Further particulars may be known at Llandaff and space available for Public Worship of the Churchwardens also from them an Answer to Instruction 7 [number present].

William Francis Cresswell.

Lewis: perpetual curacy; net income £53; patron and impropriator, Duke of Beaufort; about 50 acres of land in other parishes belong to the curacy.

C & C: 2 services in English.

I & C: incumbent not resident.

E.R.C.R.: 300 sittings.

(8) INDEPENDENT.
Erected 1849.
Space: free 84; other 16.
Present: morn. no service; aft. 48; even. no service.
Average congregation: 80.
Remarks: No Sunday School.

The Rev. Thomas Rees of Chepstow. Minister.
Henry Smith. Deacon.
Prospect Cottage, Crossway Green, Chepstow.

6   Chepstow Parish.

Area: 1,282 acres. *Popn.* 2,132 males, 2,220 females: total 4,332.

(9)   CHEPSTOW PARISH CHURCH.
Space: free 600; other 1,000.
Present: morn. 419 + 167 scholars; even. 469 + 54 scholars.
Remarks: The evening congregation includes many who have not attended in the morning and vice versa, so that the attendance for the day is nearly 1,000.

J. B. Gabriel.   Vicar.

Lewis: discharged vicarage; valued at £6. 16. 8; in the alternate patronage of Edward Bevan, Esq. and family of Burr: vicarial tithe commuted for £124. Church restored in 1841 chiefly by the efforts of the Bishop of Llandaff.
C & C: 2 services in English.
I & C: incumbent resident: curate has stipend of £100.
ICBS: grant of £550 in 1838.

(10)   BEAULAH CHAPEL, WELSH STREET.   INDEPENDANT.
Erected 1835.
Space: free 100; other 200; standing 40.
Present: morn. 52; even. 74.
Average (12 *months*): morn. 70; even. 120.
Remarks: Sunday Scholars returned on a separate paper by the Teacher.

The Rev. Thomas Rees [Absent]—Minister
of the above Chapel.
Henry Smith.   Deacon.
Prospect Cottage, Crossway Green, Chepstow.

(11)   ST. MARY'S ROMAN CATHOLIC CHAPEL.
Erected about 1830.
Space: free 28; other 42; standing 20 besides Benches for 30 children.
Present: morn. 100; even. 80.
Average: morn. 90; aft. 24 scholars; even. 60.
Remarks: I beg to remark that the Congregation belonging to this Chapel (including children) amounts to at least 200, but many of them being located at some distance in the country cannot attend but once a month.

P. Millea.   Roman Catholic Priest.

(12)   WESLEYAN METHODIST.
Erected 1807.
Space: free 150; other 150.
Present: morn. 114 + 35 scholars; aft. 75 scholars; even. 150 + 18 scholars.
Average (12 *months*): morn. 150 + 30 scholars; aft. 70 scholars; even. 200 + 20 scholars.

Henry Lougher.   Wesleyan Minister.
High Street, Chepstow.

(13) THE CHURCH ON HAWKERS HILL. CATHOLIC AND APOSTOLIC CHRISTIANS.
Erected 1837.
Space: free 160.
Present: morn. 50.
Average (12 *months*): morn. 50.
Remarks: III [Denomination]. This title is not used in an exclusive sense. We protest against being classed under any sectarian name, or among dissenters from the Church of England.

> William Smith. Priest.
> Upper Church Street

(14) BAPTIST CHAPEL.
Erected 1816.
Space: free 130; other 100.
Present: morn. 110 + 60 scholars; even. 150.

> Thomas Jones. Baptist Minister.

7   Mounton Parish.

Area: 407 acres. *Popn.* 31 males, 36 females: total 67.

(15) MOUNTON PARISH CHURCH.
Space: free 38; other 36.
Usual number present: morn. 20; aft. 20.

> *Informant:* Chrs. Davis.

[Informant's form.]
[Endorsed: See letter.]

Lewis: perpetual curacy: net income £87; patron, W. Hollis, Esq.; impropriator, T. Lewis, Esq.; tithes commuted for £55.

C & C: 1 service in English.

I & C: incumbent not resident: curate, who resides at Matherne [765. 2. 8] 1 mile distant, has stipend of £80.

8   Matherne Parish.

Area: 3,281 acres. *Popn.* 238 males, 213 females: total 451.

(16) MATHERN PARISH CHURCH.
Space: free 78; other 150.
Usual number present: morn. 35; aft. 40.

> *Informant:* Chrs. Davis.

[Informant's form.]
[Endorsed: See letter.]

Lewis: discharged vicarage: valued at £6. 3. 6½; in the patronage of the Dean and Chapter of Llandaff.

C & C: 2 services in English.

I & C: incumbent resident.

(17)   WESLEYAN CHAPEL.
Erected: Dec. 1832.
Space: free 84; other 36.
Present: morn. 7 scholars; aft. 50; even. 40.
Richard Pain. Chapel Steward.

9   St. Pierre and Runstone Parish

Area: 591 acres. *Popn.* 40 males, 25 females: total 65.

(18)   ST. PIERRE PARISH CHURCH.
Space: free 24; other 48.
Usual number present: morn. one Sunday 15; aft. next Sunday 15.
Informant: Chrs. Davis.

[Informant's form].
[Endorsed: See letter.]

Lewis: St. Pierre: discharged rectory; valued at £3. 12. 3½; patron, Mr. Lewis; tithes commuted for £119; glebe of one acre. Ruston, church of an ancient parish, demolished; for parochial purposes connected with St. Pierre and for ecclesiastical purposes with Mathern [576. 2. 8(16)] to the vicar of which the tithes are payable.

C & C: 1 service in English.

I & C: sub: Porthskewett with St. Pierre and Sudbrooke: incumbent resident.

[10]   Tidenham Parish, co. Gloucester.

[End of Chepstow Subdistrict and end of Chepstow District]

577 MONMOUTH (District)

Area of the District within Wales: 60,750 acres. *Popn. of same:* 6,987 males, 7,067 females: total 14,054.

[1 **COLEFORD (Subdistrict)**   entirely within co. Gloucester.]

2 **DINGESTOW (Subdistrict)**
   Area of the Subdistict within co. Monmouth: 27,038 acres. *Popn.* of same: 1,819 males, 1,608 females: total 3,427.

[1-6]: all parishes within co. Hereford: the returns for Welsh Bicknor [577. 2. 1] and Welsh Newton [577. 2. 4] give the county as Monmouth-shire, but the census places both in co. Hereford.

7 Skenfrith Parish.
Area: 4,720 acres. *Popn.* 320 males, 299 females: total 619.

(12) St. Bridget Skenfrith Parish Church.
Endowed: glebe £15; tithe rent charge £155; fees £2.
Space: free 220; other 90.
Present: Morn. 70 + 60 scholars; aft. 39 + 31 scholars.
Average (3 months): morn. 100 + 80 scholars; aft. 50 + 40 scholars.
Remarks: It is worthy of remark that March 30, 1851, was the day called here *Mothering Sunday* (or Mid-Lent) when the farmers, lower orders, etc., visit their parents or nearest relatives and dine etc. together, seldom attending church as usual, hence the congregation was below the average.
Stephen Cattley Baker.   Vicar.

Lewis: discharged vicarage; valued at £5. 16. 10½d.; patron, Mrs. S. Pugh; endowed with portion of the impropriate tithes; incumbent's tithe commuted for £115; glebe of 17 acres.

C & C: 2 services in English.

I & C: resident.

(13) St. Mary's Church, Coedangryd.   Roman Catholic.
Erected 1846.
Space: free 100; other 120; standing 50.
Present: morn. about 40; aft. about 13.
Average (12 months): morn. 40 or 50; aft. 12 to 20.
Thomas Abbot, M.A.   Roman Catholic Priest.
Coedangryd Cottage, Skenfrith.

(14)   NORTON SKENFRITH PARTICULAR BAPTISTS.
Erected 1845.
Space: free 156.
Present: morn. 60; even. 110.
Average: morn. 60; even. 150.
Remarks: It is useless for me to attempt to have a Sunday School in winter owing to the distance the children have to come. All the sittings are very large.

Thomas Richards.   Baptist Minister.
Great Llanlliweth, New Castle.

8   St. Maughan's Parish.
Area: 1,304 acres. *Popn.* 101 males, 92 females: total 193.

(15)   ST. MAUGHAN'S PARISH CHURCH.
Space: free 34; other 90.
Present: aft. 62.

William Vaughan Yarworth.
Officiating Minister.

[Endorsed: See letter.]

Lewis: vicarage, annexed to that of Llangattock-Vibon-Avel [577. 2. 9(16)]: tithes of the whole commuted for £58. 8. 4, of which £108 payable to the vicar.

C & C: 1 service in English.

I & C: see Llangattock Vibon Avel below.

9   Llangattock-Vibon-Avel Parish.
Area: 4,194 acres. *Popn.* 283 males, 235 females: total 518.

(16)   LLANGATTOCK VIBON AVEL PARISH CHURCH.
Space: free 105; other 85.
Present: morn. 48 + 20 scholars.
Remarks: The Church of Llangattock Vibon Avel is in a bad state of repair and is about to be rebuilt.

William Vaughan Yarworth.
Officiating Minister.

[Endorsed: See letter.]

Lewis: discharged vicarage, with that of St. Maughan's [577. 2. 8(15)] annexed; valued at £6. 18. 11½d.; patron, Jervan Perry, Esq.; impropriators, representatives of the late T. Phillips, Esq.: great tithes commuted for £168, and vicarial for £209; glebe of 5½ acres.

C & C: 1 service in English.

I & C: not resident; curate has stipend of £35.

ICBS: grant of £35 in 1852.

(17) Llanvenair Chapel.   Church of England.
Endowed: some £60, but not known precisely: land, two small farms.
Space: free 20 benches; other 25 in pews.
Present: morn. 30.
Average (3 months): about 35.
Remarks: No Day or Sunday School. The aforesaid is a chapel of ease to
Llangattock Vibon Avel. Services morning and afternoon on Sundays
alternately–without cure of souls. The attendance may be considered good
taking into account the few houses there and the scattered population.

Robert Chatto, A.M.   Curate.

Lewis: *sub* Llanvanner: chapel of ease, endowed with two farms, purchased by
grant from Queen Anne's Bounty and now let for £70 per annum.

C & C: 1 service in English.

I & C: not resident.

10   Llanvihangel-ystern-Llewern Parish.
Area: 1,864 acres. *Popn.* 100 males, 71 females: total 171.

(18) Llanvihangel Ystern Llewern Parish Church.
Endowed: tithe £210; glebe £50.
Space: free 90.
Average attendants (12 months): morn. 45 + 12 scholars;   aft. 40 + 6
scholars.

A. O. Crawley.   Curate.

Lewis: rectory, valued at £9. 8. 4; patron, the Earl of Abergavenny: tithes commuted
for £200; glebe of 80 acres.

C & C: 2 services in English.

I & C: incumbent not resident: curate, who resides in the glebe-house, has stipend
of £80.

(18) Ebenezer Chapel.   Baptist.
Erected 1842.
Space: free 150.
Present: morn. 27 + 10 scholars;   aft. 18 scholars;   even. 33.
Average (12 months): morn. 30 + 14 scholars;   aft. 20 scholars;   even. 70.

Thomas Cobner.   Minister.

11   Llantillio-Crossenny Parish.
Area: 5,951 acres. *Popn.* 44 males, 34 females: total 78.

(20)   LLANTILIO CROSSENNY PARISH CHURCH.
Endowed: tithe £213; glebe £25; fees £3.
Space: free 100; other 150.
Present: morn. 80 + 30 scholars.
Average: morn. 115 + 40 scholars.

David Davies.   Minister.

Lewis: vicarage, with that of Penrose [599. 1. 12(23)] annexed: valued at £10. 10. 5; patrons and appropriators Bishop, Archdeacon and Chapter of Llandaff: net income £270; glebe of 10 acres and glebe-house.

C & C: 1 service in English.

I & C: incumbent resident.

(21)   LLANFAIR CHAPEL.   CHURCH OF ENGLAND.
An additional church in the Upper division of Llantilio.
Consecrated 1850.
Erected partly by donation of £100 from the Church Building Society, and partly by subscriptions. Total cost £650.
Space: free 168.
Present: aft. 50.
Average: aft. 70.
Remarks: The chapel is endowed with Ten Pounds per annum from the Chapter at Llandaff and three Pounds 14/8 being the Interest of money invested in the Three Per Cent Consols.

David Davies.   Vicar of Llantilio
Crossenny.

Lewis: chapel of ease, erected by subscription in 1842, at Llanvair-gil-Coed.

C & C: 1 service in English.

ICBS: no entry: but see Penrose [577. 2. 12(23)].

(22)   ROSE COTTAGE CHAPEL.   PRIMITIVE METHODIST.
Erected 1842.
Space: free 70; other 50.
Present: morn. 45; even. 70.
Average (6 months): morn. 50 + 30 scholars; even. 80 + 36 scholars.

James Jones.   Minister.

12   Penrose Parish.
Area: 2,695 acres. *Popn.* 385 males, 350 females: total 735.

(23)   PENROSE PARISH CHURCH.
The church is very old, but in the year 1848 it was renewed and thoroughly repaired and many additional sittings gained.

Cost defrayed by Parochial Rate £38. 18*s.*, subscriptions £355; total cost £393. 18*s.*
Endowed: tithe £95; glebe £30.
Space: free 200.
Present: morn. 64 + 25 scholars.
Average (12 *months*): morn. 100 + 30 scholars; aft. 120 + 30 scholars.
Remarks: Yesterday being Midlent or 'Mothering' Sunday the Congregation was considerably less than usual.

> Arthur Montagu Wyatt.   Vicar.

Lewis: vicarage, annexed to that of Llantilio Crossenny [577. 2. 11(20)]: glebe of 50 acres.

C & C: 1 service in English.

I & C: incumbent not resident.

ICBS: grant of £100 in 1842.

13   Tregare Parish.

Area: 2,387 acres. *Popn.* 166 males, 159 females: total 325.

(24)   Tregare Parish Church.
Endowed: tithe £113; glebe £10.
Present: even. 66.
Remarks: March the 30 being Midlent Sunday, few persons attended the Church.

> Thomas Morgan.   Vicar.
> Dingestow Vicarage.

Lewis: annexed to the vicarage of Dingestow [577. 2. 14(25)]: glebe of about 10 acres.

C & C: 1 service in English.

I & C: sub. Dingestow.

ICBS: grant of £35 in 1850.

14   Dingestow Parish.

Area (with [15] Grace Dieu Park): 1,930 acres. *Popn.* 114 males, 101 females: total 215.

(25)   St. Mary Dingestow Parish Church.
Endowed: tithe £106; glebe £20.
Present: morn. 58; aft. 61.
Remarks: Very few persons attended Church on the 30 in consequence of its being Midlent or Mothering Sunday on which day there is a custom of visiting among relatives.

> Thomas Morgan.   Vicar.

Lewis: discharged vicarage with that of Tregare [577. 2. 13(24)] annexed; valued at £4. 10*s*; net income £244; patrons and appropriators the Bishop, Archdeacon and Chapter of Llandaff; glebe of 24 acres: great tithes commuted for £87. 14. 6, and the vicarial for £106.

C & C: 2 services in English.

I & C: incumbent resident.

15   Grace Dieu Park extra parochial.
Popn. 4 males, 3 females: total 7.
[No returns]

16   Rockfield Parish.
Area: 1,993 acres. *Popn.* 153 males, 138 females: total 291.

(26)   ROCKFIELD PARISH CHURCH.
Endowed: land £28; tithe £9. 15. 6; interest on £200 in Bounty Funds; fees about 15*s*; no house.
Space: whole chancel free; other 20 pews: a small gallery; supposed total sittings 170.
Present: aft. 70 + 35 scholars.
Average (3 *months*): morn. and aft. in alternation 80, exclusive of Sunday Scholars.
Remarks: The *Parochial* Sunday and Day School has been opened only on the 15th ultimo. From the gross amount [of income] must be deducted two pounds on an average for poor, Highway and Church rates exclusive of gates and on the glebe land.

Robert Chatto, A.M.,   Vicar.

Lewis: discharged vicarage, valued at £4. 3. 1½: patron and impropriator, Rev. J. Harding: great tithes commuted for £198. 4. 0., and the vicarial for £19. 15. 6.: net income £43.

C & C: 1 service in English.

I & C: incumbent resident.

[*End of Dingestow Subdistrict*]

3 MONMOUTH (Subdistrict)
Area: 7,268 acres. *Popn.* 2,797 males, 3,170 females: total: 5,967.

1   Dixton Newton Parish.

(1)   DIXTON PARISH CHURCH.
Endowed: tithe £223; glebe 25 acres; fees £2.
Space: free 70; other 120.
Present: morn. 104 + 52 scholars; aft. 80 + 50 scholars.
Remarks: The above is no criterion of the number of persons in the parish

attending public worship, as members of the Church, from the circumstances of the Church being inconveniently situated and not affording sufficient accommodation, from the scattered nature of the population and from many residing near to other parish churches.

James Lister Dighton.   Vicar.

Lewis: discharged vicarage; valued at £7. 3. 1½; net income £223; patron, Edward Machen, Esq.: impropriator, the Duke of Beaufort, Miss Griffin and others; glebe of 12 acres.

C & C: 2 services in English.

I & C: incumbent resident.

2   Monmouth Parish and Borough.

Area: 3,420 acres. *Popn.* 2,445 males, 2,744 females: total 5,189.

(2)   SCHOOL ROOM BELONGING TO JONES'S CHARITY.
Space: free 80; other 20.
Present: aft. 97.
Remarks: The Lectureship was endowed 200 years ago to afford week day administration and a Lecture on Sunday to the inmates of Jones's almshouses.

Charles Augustus Halson.   Lecturer.

(3)   CHAPEL OF THE UNION HOUSE.   For use of the Inmates of Monmouth Union House.
When Consecrated or Licenced: I have not been able to ascertain the time.
Endowed: £30 per annum paid by the Board of Guardians.
Space: It will contain about 100.
Present: aft. 51 + 47 scholars.

J. B. Bourne.   Chaplain.

(4)   CHURCH OF ST. THOMAS.
An ancient Saxon Structure, but whether originally a Parish church or otherwise is not known. It was in a dilapidated state and had not been used for many years. It was restored in 1831 and opened for divine service in 1832.
Endowed: permanent endowment £50; pew rents £10; fees £2; other sources £30.
Space: free 250; other 230.
Present: morn. 200 + 57 scholars; even. 250 + 20 scholars.
Average (3 months): morn. 250 + 70 scholars; even. 200 + 20 scholars.

Joseph Fawcett Beddy, M.A.   Minister.

Lewis: sub Monmouth; St. Thomas Over-Monow, perpetual curacy; net income £90; patron, the vicar of St. Mary's. Church restored and fitted up for divine service in 1832, partly at the expense of the Duke of Beaufort and partly by subscription.

C & C: 2 services in English.

ICBS: grant of £180 in 1830.

(5) St. Mary's Parish Church, Monmouth.
Erected: two distinct periods—about the fifteenth century: and about one hundred and fifty years back.
Space: free 360; other 750.
Usual number of attendants: morn. 500 + 150 scholars; aft. 50 scholars; even. 600.

Edw. F. Arney.   Vicar.

[Informant's form.]

Lewis: discharged vicarage; valued at £9. 2. 3; net income £270; patron and impropriator, the Duke of Beaufort.

C & C: 3 services in English.

I & C: vacant.

(6) Chapel in the County Goal.
Erected: 'A new one erected about one or two years ago.'
Space: 110.
Usual number attending: average number from 85 to 90.

Informant: Edward Johnson Gosling, M.A.
Chaplain.

[Informant's form.]

(7) Glendower Street.   Independent Chapel.
Erected 1832.
Sittings: free 100; other 500.
Present: morn. 250 + 50 scholars; even. 200.
Average (12 *months*): morn. 200 + 50 scholars; even. 180.

William Major Paull.   Minister.

(8) Wesleyan Free Church Meeting Room.   Wesleyan Methodist
(Reformer)
Space: free 200; standing 30.
Present: morn. 50; even. 105.
Average (12 *months*): morn. 70; even. 170.

William Higgins.   Manager.
Monnow Bridge, Monmouth.

(9) Monnow Street Primitive Methodist Meeting House.
Erected 1835.
Space: free 100.
Present: aft. 53; even. 64.
Average (12 *months*): aft. 40; even. 60.

George Grigg.   Superintendant.
Dry Bridge Street, Monmouth.

(10) MONNOW STREET BAPTIST CHAPEL.
Erected 1820.
Space: free 50; other 150; standing 50.
Present: morn. 63; aft. 40 scholars; even. 100.
Average: morn. 80; aft. 50 scholars; even. 130.
Remarks: The congregation on this day far below usual.

                                         Henry Clark. Minister.

(11) ST. JAMES STREET. WESLEYAN METHODIST CHAPEL.
Erected 1837.
Space: free 600; other 100.
Present: morn. 50 + 40 scholars; even. 200.
Remarks: Divine Service has been held in this town for more than 60 years. The present chapel is a new erection and some untoward circumstances have made against the congregation. Perhaps not more than half the inhabitants of the town attend any place of worship on the Sabbath day.

                                         William Baker. Minister.
                                       St. James's Street, Monmouth.

(12) ROMAN CATHOLIC CHAPEL.
Erected 1794.
Space: free 40; other 40.
Present: morn. 180.

                                Thomas Burgess. Catholic Priest.
                                St. Mary's Street, Monmouth.

(13) PRIMITIVE METHODIST (BRANCH) MEETING HOUSE.
Erected 1846.
Space: free 53.
Present: none.
Average (12 *months*)*:* morn. 40.

                                George Watkins. Steward.
                                Wye Bridge, Monmouth.

(14) BUCKHOLT PRIMITIVE METHODIST MEETING HOUSE.
Erected 1850.
Space: free 50; standing 25.
Present: aft. 20; even. 45.
Average (9 *months*)*:* aft. 24; even. 40.

                                George Gregg. Superintendant.
                                Dry Bridge Street, Monmouth.

[End of Monmouth Subdistrict]

4 TRELLECK (Subdistrict)
Area: 2,644 acres. *Popn.* 2,371 males, 2,289 females: total 4,660.

1 Wonastow Parish.
Area: 1,599 acres. *Popn.* 79 males, 62 females: total 141.

(1) WONASTOW PARISH CHURCH.
Endowed: tithe £105; glebe 6 acres.
Space: free 50; other 60.
Present: morn. 50; aft. 80.
Average (6 months): morn. 55; aft. 60.

Robert Jackson.   Rector.

[Letter attached, dated from Wonastow Rectory April 2.]
Dear Sir,
I send you the return respecting my little Rectory. The School and Sunday
School are in the neighbour parish of Dingestow; so I do not return them
I have the honour to be Dear Sir   Yrs very truly   Robert Jackson.

Lewis: discharged vicarage; valued at £4. 15s. 5d.; net income £95; patron and
impropriator, Sir W. Pilkington, Bart.

C & C: 2 services in English.

I & C: incumbent resident.

(2) PROVIDENCE CHAPEL.   PRIMITIVE METHODIST.
Erected 1850.
Space: free 78; other 32; standing room 30.
Present: morn. 26 + 14 scholars; aft. 11 scholars; even. 37.
Average (3 months): morn. 30 + 15 scholars; aft. 15 scholars; even. 45.

Thomas Conney.   Trustee.
Cunder Mill Street, Monmouth.

2 Mitchel Troy Parish.
Area: 2,000 acres. *Popn.* 185 males, 175 females: total 360.

(3) ST. MICHAEL'S PARISH CHURCH.
Space: free 60; other 140.
Present: morn. 59 + 18 scholars.
Average: morn. 60 + 22 scholars; aft. 100.

H. G. Talbot.   Rector.

Lewis: rectory with living of Cwmcarvan [577. 4. 8(23)] annexed: patron, the Duke
of Beaufort; tithes commuted for £221. 10s.; glebe 60 acres.

C & C: 1 service in English.

I & C: incumbent resident.

(4) Ebynezzer Chapel.   Wesleyan.
Erected 1843.
Space: free 20; other 2.
Present: aft. 51.
Average: general congregation about 50.

William Baker.   Minister.
St. James's Street, Monmouth.

3   Penalt Parish.
Area: 2,284 acres. *Popn.* 244 males, 223 females: total 467.

(5) Parish Church.
Endowed: tithe commuted for £156.
Present: morn. 37 + 50 scholars; aft. 78 + 38 scholars.

William Oakeley.   Curate.

Lewis: vicarage endowed with rectorial tithes and annexed to that of Trelleck [577. 4. 5(13)].

C & C: 2 services in English.

I & C: see *sub* Trelleck.

(6) Dwelling House.   Primitive Methodist.
Erected 1839.
Present: aft. 25; even. 35.

William Richards.   Society steward.

(7) Baptist Chapel.
Erected 1821.
Space: free 100.
Present: morn. 6; even. 21.
Average (6 *months*): morn. 6; even. 30.
Remarks: The above chapel has been without a minister for nearly four years; an attempt (according to the date VIII) (sic) is now being made with the view (if possible) to revive the Baptist cause at Penalt amongst a large, scattered and poor population.

Joseph Moore.   Minister.

[Endorsed: See letter.]

4   Llandogo Parish.
Area: 1,843 acres. *Popn.* 253 males, 318 females: total 571.

(8)   LLANDOGO PARISH CHURCH.
Endowed: land £45; £30 per annum dividends of consols; fees £2.
Space: free 100; other 102.
Present: morn. 82 + 47 scholars; aft. 81 + 43 scholars.
Average (6 months): morn. 80 + 40 scholars; aft. 130 + 45 scholars.
Remarks: The endowment above mentioned is that which belongs to ye
perpetual curacy. The impropriate tithes which belong to ye Rector have
been commuted for £151. 13s. 5d.

Thomas Langley, B.A.   Perpetual Curate.

Lewis: perpetual curacy; net income £72; patron, the prebendary of Caire in the
Cathedral of Llandaff; tithes commuted for £168; glebe 20 acres and glebe-house.

C & C: 1 service in English.

I & C: incumbent resident.

(9)   THE CHAPEL OF THE HOLY TRINITY, WHITEBROOK.
Licensed 1835, consecrated 1845. A chapel of ease to the Parish Church
which is 2½ miles distant.
Erected by private subscription, total cost £790. 12s.
Endowed: £15. 16s. 10d. per annum interest of 3 per cent consols.
Space: free 150; other 20.
Present: aft. 129 + 28 scholars.
Average (6 months): morn, 80 + 40 scholars; aft. 130 + 35 scholars.

Thomas Langley, B.A.   Minister.

Lewis: church erected in the hamlet of Whitebrook in 1835 by subscription.

C & C: 1 service in English.

(10)   HEPZIBAH CHAPEL.   BAPTIST.
Erected 1824.
Present: even. 11.

William Madby.   Clerk.

(11)   BEULAH CHAPEL.   BAPTIST.
Erected 1819.
Space: free 200.
Present: no service.
Average: aft. 25.

James Dale.   Deacon.
New Mills, Monmouth.

(12)   PENWERN CHAPEL.   WESLEYAN METHODIST.
Erected 'near 1800'.
Space: about 200.
Present: morn. 30.

Richard White.
Local preacher occasionally.
Kingcoed, Nr. Ragland.

5 Trelleck Parish.

Area, excluding Trelleck Grange [576. 2. 1]: 5,287 acres. *Popn.* 551 males, 477 females: total 988.

(13) TRELLECK PARISH CHURCH.
Endowed: land £50; tithe £311; glebe £38; fees £2 .10s.
Space: free 145; other 240.
Present: morn. 20 + 76 scholars; aft. 30.
Average (12 *months*): morn. 40 + 50 scholars; aft. 50.
Remarks: Many parishioners residing some miles distant from the Parish Church attend other churches in their vicinity; others are Dissenters.

Charles A. F. Kuper, M.A.   Vicar.

Lewis: vicarage with the living of Penalt [577. 4. 3(5)] endowed with rectorial tithes; valued at £8; patron, Crown in right of Duchy of Cornwall; net income £430.

C & C: 2 services in English.

I & C: incumbent resident: curate has stipend of £100.

(14) PARKHOUSE CHAPEL.   WESLEYAN METHODIST.
Erected 1835.
Space: free 94; other 16; standing room 20.
Present: aft. 60.
Average (12 *months*): aft. 100.
Remarks: We were 40 deficient on account of Middle-lent Sunday this day.

Henry Prichard.   Trustee.
Abbey Tintern.

(15) SILOAM CHAPEL.   BIBLE CHRISTIANS.
Erected 1829.
Space: free 80.
Present: aft. 38 + 24 scholars.
Average: 50 + 30 scholars.

Samuel Morgan.   Manager.

[Endorsed: See letter.]

(16) ZION CHAPEL, CATBROOK.   PRIMITIVE METHODIST.
Erected: Nov. 1844.
Space: free 20; other 2; standing room 60.
Present: 'from 80 to 100'; morn. 10½ (sic); aft. 2½ (sic).
Average: general congregation 80 to 100.

. William Milton.   Steward.

(17) EBENEZEAR CHAPEL.   BIBLE CHRISTIANS.
Erected 1838.
Space: free 16; other 5.
Average (12 *months*): aft. 30.

John Kemyes.   Manager.

(18)   LLANISHEN PARISH CHURCH, NEAR CARDIFF.
[This return is misplaced: see below 581. 1. 10 (26).]

6 Llanishen Parish.
Area: 1,742 acres. *Popn.* 177 males, 174 females: total 351.

(19)   LLANISHEN PARISH CHURCH.
Endowed: land sexaginta et octo; permanent endowment octo; fees, duo;
other sex.
Space: free about 80; other 40.
Present: none.
Average (12 *months*): morn. 50 to 60; aft. 80 to 100.
Remarks: A small old church and very damp. Mar 30 1851 was mid-Lent
Sunday and many people of this parish *absent themselves from Church and
visit their friends that day*. There is no Convenient place in the little church
for Sunday Scholars.

> Henry Warrilow.   Incumbent minister.

Lewis: perpetual curacy; net income £64; patron and impropriator, the Duke of
Beaufort; tithes commuted for £120; glebe 87 acres.

C & C: 1 service in English.

I & C: incumbent resident.

ICBS: grant of £30 in 1852.

(20)   BETHEL.   BIBLE CHRISTIANS.
Erected 1842.
Space: free 132.
Present: morn. 26; even. 60.
Average (12 *months*): morn. 30; even. 80.

> William Edwards.   Chapel Steward.
> Glynn Farm, Llanishen.

(21)   WESLEYAN METHODIST.
Erected 1820.
Space: free 70.
Present: 40 + 30 scholars; aft. 60 + 30 scholars.
Average (12 *months*): morn. 40 + 30 scholars; aft. 60 + 30 scholars.

> Mark Dowler.   Steward.

7 Llangoven Parish.
Area: 1,889 acres. *Popn.* 74 males, 55 females: total 129.

(22) LLANGOVEN PARISH CHURCH.
Endowed: land about £50; tithe £10; permanent endowment about £7.
Space: free 14; other 77.
Present: (no entry).
Average (12 *months*): (no entry).
Remarks: The entire population, with only two exceptions, attend the Parish Church, when Service is held alternately morning and afternoon.

James Farquhar.   Perpetual curate.

[Endorsed: See Letter.]

Lewis: perpetual curacy with Pen-y-Clawdd [577. 4. 9(26)] annexed; valued at £3. 7s. 1d.; net income £120; patrons and appropriators, Bishop, Archdeacon and Chapter of Llandaff, whose tithes are commuted for £170.

C & C: 1 service in English.

I & C: incumbent resident.

8 Cwmcarvan Parish.

Area: 2,875 acres. *Popn.* 173 males, 161 females: total 334.

(23) CWMCARVAN PARISH CHURCH.
Space: free 40; other 155.
Present: aft. 67 + 5 scholars.
Average: morn. 40; aft. 80.

Henry George Talbot.   Rector.

Lewis: living annexed to the rectory of Mitchel Troy [577. 4. 2(3)]; tithes commuted for £193 of which £20 payable to the Bishop of Llandaff; glebe of 10 acres belonging to the rector.

C & C: 1 service in English.

I & C: see *sub* Mitchel Troy.

(24) CWMCARVAN HILL.   WESLEYAN METHODIST.
Dwelling house erected before 1800.
Space: free 30.
Present: morn. 25; aft. 40.
Remarks: Divine service in part of the house more than 50 years.

William Edwards.   Steward.

(25) BIBLE CHRISTIANS CHAPEL HOUSE.
Erected 1842.
Average attendance: morn. 12.
Not a separate and entire building. Not used exclusively as a place of worship.

John Howells.   Steward.
Cwmcarvan Hill.

9   Pen-y-Clawdd Parish.
Area: 614 acres. *Popn.* 24 males, 18 females: total 42.

(26)   Pen-y-clawdd Parish Church.
Endowed: land about £50; tithe £10; permanent endowment about £7.
Space: free 25; other 45.
Average attendance (12 *months*): morn. 18.
Remarks: The entire population attend the Parish Church when service is
held alternately morning and afternoon.

James Farquhar. Perpetual Curate.

[Endorsed: See Letter.]

Lewis: perpetual curacy annexed to that of Llangoven [577. 4. 7(22)]: tithes belong
to Bishop, Archdeacon and Chapter of Llandaff, commuted for £50.

C & C: 1 service in English.

10   Ragland Parish.
Area: 4,083 acres. *Popn.* 452 males, 428 females: total 880.

(27)   Raglan Parish Church.
Endowed: tithe, £300; glebe £43; fees £2.
Space: free 70; other 160.
Present: morn. 106 + 36 scholars; even. 76 + 30 scholars.
Average: morn. 120 + 40 scholars; even. 120 + 40 scholars.
Remarks: The school children's sittings are not included in the number of
sittings. The general attendance at church on Mid lent Sunday is less than
average from the custom of families going to visit their relations on that
day.

William Powell, B.D.   Vicar.

Lewis: discharged vicarage; valued at £4. 6s. 3d.; patron and impropriator,
Duke of Beaufort; vicarial tithes commuted for £30; glebe of 25 acres.

C & C: 2 services in English.

I & C: incumbent resident: curate's stipend not stated.

(28)   Ebenezer Chapel.   Baptist.
Erected 1820.
Space: free 150.
Present: morn. 69 + 22 scholars; even. 73.
Average (12 *months*): morn. 100 + 41 scholars; aft. 41 scholars; even. 150.
Remarks: There is a day and Sunday School conducted in it (the building).

John Jones.   Baptist minister.

(29) ZION CHAPEL. INDEPENDENT OR CONGREGATIONAL.
Erected 1842.
Space: free 149; other 28; standing room for about 20.
Present: morn. 40; aft. 20 scholars; even. 60.
Average (12 *months*): morn. 25 + 15 scholars; aft. 20 scholars; even. 100.

Charles Norward.   Deacon.

11 Llandenny Parish.

Area: 2,228 acres. *Popn.* 199 males, 198 females: total 397.

(30) LLANDENNY PARISH CHURCH.
Endowed: £10 from the Duke of Beaufort; £30 from land.
Sittings: free 37; other 140.
Present: morn. 33 + 12 scholars; aft. 63.
Average: morn. 40; aft. 60.
Remarks: There is no other endowment except the above mentioned. The
whole value of the living is £40 per annum. There are no pew rents, dues,
Easter offerings, etc. Fees for burying, marriages, etc. may amount to £2
per annum on the average.

Augustin Williams.   Curate.

Lewis: perpetual curacy; valued at £5. 15s. 5d.; net income £50; patron and
impropriator, Duke of Beaufort, whose tithes are commuted for £330.

C & C: 2 services in English.

I & C: incumbent not resident: curate has stipend of £80.

(31) KINGCOED CHAPEL. BAPTIST.
Erected 1845.
Space: free 100.
Present: aft. 19.
Average (12 *months*): aft. 30.

John Jones.   Baptist minister.
Ragland.

(32) PRIMITIVE METHODIST CHAPEL.
Erected 1828.
Space: free 93.
Present: morn. 19; even. 50.

Thomas Giles.   Minister.
Abersychan, Pontypool.

[End of Trelleck Subdistrict and end of Monmouth District]

Area, excluding the Hamlet of Fwthog, co.Hereford (578. 2. 8): 86,095 acres. *Popn.* 31,682 males, 27,427 females: total 59,109.

1 LLANARTH (Subdistrict)
Area: 11,061 acres. *Popn.* 963 males, 946 females: total 1,909.

1   Bettws-Newydd Parish.
Area: 1,122 acres. *Popn.* 71 males, 70 females: total 141.

(1)   Bettws Newydd Parish Church.
Endowed: land £13; tithe £51; glebe £3. 12s.
Space: free 59; other 53.
Present: morn. 84 + 12 scholars.
Average (12 *months*): morn. 60; aft. 80.
Remarks: service alternately morning and afternoon.

William Price.   Minister.
Raglan.

Lewis: perpetual curacy annexed to the vicarage of Llanarth [578. 1. 3(3)]; vicarial tithes commuted for £51. 6s.; glebe of 3 acres.

C & C: 1 service in English.

I & C: see *sub* Llanarth.

2   Bryngwyn Parish.
Area: 1,484 acres. *Popn.* 159 males, 154 females: total 313.

(2)   Bryngwyn Parish Church.
Endowed: tithe (gross) £164; glebe, rent £46; fees £1.
Space: free 85; other 97.
Present: morn. 72 + 22 scholars; aft. 90 + 8 scholars.
Average (12 *months*): morn. 66 + 24 scholars; aft. 105 + 10 scholars.

William Crawley.   Rector.

Lewis: discharged rectory; valued at £4. 8s. 9d.; incumbent's tithes commuted for £164; glebe of 39 acres; impropriator's tithes of five farms commuted for £66.

C & C: 2 services in English.

I & C: incumbent resident.

[3-4] Llanarth Parish, consisting of [3] Llanarth and [4] Clytha Hamlet.
Area of the whole: 3,793 acres. *Popn.* 300 males, 310 females: total 610.

3 Llanarth Parish.
Area: 1,952 acres. *Popn.* 128 males, 142 females: total 270.

(3) LLANARTH PARISH CHURCH.
Endowed: tithe £213; glebe £75.
Space: free 40; other 190.
Average attendance (12 *months*): morn. 180 + 30 scholars; even. 110.
Remarks: The 30th of March having been this year Midlent or mothering Sunday the congregation of adults and children was far below the average attendance. I have therefore given no return lest it should lead to an erroneous impression.

William Pain. Minister.

Lewis: discharged vicarage with living of Bettws Newydd [578. 1. 1(1)] attached; valued at £10. 3s. 4d.; patrons and appropriators, Bishop, Archdeacon and Chapter of Llandaff; vicarial tithes commuted for £211; glebe of 62 acres.

C & C: 2 services in English.

I & C: incumbent resident: curate has stipend of £40.

(4) ST. MARY'S CATHOLIC CHAPEL.
Erected before 1800.
Space: free 210.
Present: morn. 130; aft. 60.

Samuel Fisher. Roman Catholic Priest.

4 Clytha Hamlet.
Area: 1,841 acres. *Popn.* 172 males, 168 females: total 340.
[No returns]

Lewis: vicarial tithes commuted for £115; glebe 2 acres.

5 Llanvair-Kilgidin Parish.
Area: 1,801 acres. *Popn.* 140 males, 128 females: total 268.

(5) LLANVOYER KILGEDDINE PARISH CHURCH.
Endowed: tithe (commuted) £276. 2s.; glebe £71; permanent endowment £46. 3s. 8d. (interest on £1,539. 11s. 4d. £3 per cent).
Space: free 50; other 150.
Present: morn. 62 + 10 scholars; even. 44 + 9 scholars.
Average (12 *months*): morn. from 70 to 90 + 12 scholars; even. from 40 to 60 + 12 scholars.

Remarks: In a Country Church it is not well possible to give a correct average Return of the number of the Congregation which varies weekly from the weather, illness, distance of the church from the chief part of the population.

Francis Lewis.   Rector.

Lewis: rectory, valued at £5. 1s. 10½d.; in gift of Sir Charles Morgan, Bart.; tithes commuted for £255; glebe 84 acres.

C & C: 2 services in English.

I & C: incumbent resident.

6   Llanvihangel-nigh-Usk Parish.
Area: 385 acres. *Popn.* 71 males, 68 females: total 139.

(7)   LLANVIHANGEL-BY-USK PARISH CHURCH.
Endowed: tithe £83; glebe £36.
Sittings: free 75; other 24.
Present: aft. 86.
Average (12 months): morn. 60 + 15 scholars; aft. 80 + 15 scholars.
Remarks: Service morning and afternoon alternately.

William Price.   Minister.

Lewis: discharged rectory; valued at £3. 8s. 9d.; in gift of Sir Samuel Fludyer, Bart.; tithes commuted for £82; glebe 26 acres.

C & C: 1 service in English.

I & C: incumbent not resident: curate, who resides in the parish, has stipend of £50.

(8)   MOSERAH CHAPEL.   CALVINISTIC METHODIST.
Erected 1837.
Space: free 42; other 84.
Present: morn. 40 + 27 scholars; even. 85.
Average: morn. 30 + 20 scholars; even. 80.

Robert Thomas.   Minister.
Longwilim Cottage, Ragland.

7   Llansaintfraed Parish.
Area: 289 acres. *Popn.* 14 males, 22 females: total 36.

(6)   ST. BRIDGET'S PARISH CHURCH.
Endowed: land and tithe £80.
Space: free about 20; other about 40.
Present: morn. 21.

Remarks: The services alternately morning and afternoon. 4 houses only in the parish. 2 occupied by Romanists.

[name omitted]   Curate.

Lewis: discharged rectory; valued in king's book at £2. 13s. 11½d.; patron, John Jones, Esq.; glebe 66 acres.

C & C: 1 service in English.

I & C: incumbent not resident: curate (William Gray), who resides at Llanthewy-Rhytherch, has stipend of £40.

[Note: the returns of this parish and of the previous one have been misplaced.]

8 Llanthewy-Rhytherch Parish.

Area: 2,187 acres. *Popn.* 208 males, 194 females: total 402.

(9) LLANTHEWY RHYTHERCH PARISH CHURCH.
Endowed: land about £20 per annum; tithe about £195; glebe house rated at £10 per annum.
Space: [no entry for free sittings]; other about 150 or 160.
Present: morn. 40 to 50 + 20 to 25 scholars; aft. 80 to 100.
Average (4 *months*): morn. 40 to 50 + 20 to 30 scholars, aft. 80 to 100.
Remarks: No school in the afternoon on Sundays. I have been resident curate in this parish only four months.

Rees Jones.   Licensed curate.

Lewis: discharged vicarage; endowed with moiety of rectorial tithes; valued at £7. 15s. 5d.; in the patronage of Crown; impropriators of the remainder of the rectorial tithes, Trustees of the Free School, Abergavenny; vicarial tithes commuted for £195; impropriated tithes for £85; glebe of 13 acres and glebe-house.

C & C: 1 service in English.

I & C: incumbent not resident: curate, who resides in the glebe-house, has stipend of £70.

(10) LLANTHEWY CHAPEL.   PARTICULAR BAPTIST.
Erected 1826.
Space: free 100; other 100.
Present: morn. 80; aft. 35 scholars; even. 200.
Remarks: Divine service is always held here both morning and evening, the Sabbath School always in the afternoon.

Thomas Lewis.   Minister.

[End of Llanarth Subdistrict]

2 LLANVIHANGEL (Subdistrict)

Area: 18,429 acres. *Popn.* 936 males, 901 females: total 1,837.

1 Llanvapley Parish.

Area, excluding the Hamlet of Fwthog: 819 acres. *Popn.* 64 males, 74 females: total 138.

(1) LLANVAPLEY PARISH CHURCH.
Endowed: tithe £150; glebe 50 acres, about £80.
Space: free 40; other 60.
Present: morn. 26 + 19 scholars; aft. 60.
Average (12 *months*): morn. 32 + 18 scholars; aft. 70.
Remarks: Sunday March 30th being Midlent or as it is called 'Mothering Sunday' is ill chosen for Counting the Congregation at Church as on that day all farm servants are permitted to visit their homes and many of them attend no church while their absence keeps other members of the masters' family at home. My congregation was smaller than usual on that day.

Thomas Williams.   Rector.

Lewis: rectory; valued at £10. 5s. 2½d.; in gift of the Earl of Abergavenny; tithes commuted for £150; glebe 54 acres.

C & C: 2 services in English.

I & C: incumbent resident.

(2) PROVIDENCE CHAPEL.   INDEPENDENT.
Erected 1810.
Space: free 100; standing room for 30.
Present: morn. 25 + 8 scholars; even. 47.
Average (12 *months*): morn. 30 + 12 scholars; even. 52.

Thomas Farmer.   Occasional minister.

[578. 5. 1(15) to 578. 5. 1(22), though correctly numbered, are inserted here in the bound volume of returns.]

2 Llanthewy Skirrid Parish.

Area: 1,060 acres. *Popn.* 53 males, 48 females: total 101.

(3) LLANTHEWY SKIRRID PARISH CHURCH.
Endowed: land £100; tithe £140.
Space: 'sufficient'.
Present: morn. 10; aft. 10; even. 10.
Remarks: The church was rebuilt about the year 1813 and consecrated

about that year at least the one part was rebuilt by parochial rate. The average attendants morning and evening about thirty more or less.

William Marston. Curate.

Lewis: rectory; valued at £7. 10s. 2½d.; in gift and incumbency of Rev. M. H. Jones; tithes commuted for £147; glebe of 109 acres and glebe-house.

C & C: 1 service in English.

I & C: incumbent not resident: curate, who resides in the glebe-house, has stipend of £80.

3   Llanvetherine Parish.

Area: 2,153 acres. *Popn.* 134 males, 97 females: total 231.

(4)   Llanvetherine Parish Church.
Endowed: tithe £296; glebe £60.
Space: free 36; other 100.
Present: morn. 63 + 22 scholars; aft. 23.

F. C. Steel, M.A. Rector.

Lewis: rectory; valued at £14. 17s. 8½d.; in gift of the Earl of Abergavenny; tithes commuted for £300; glebe 51½ acres.

C & C: 2 services in English.

I & C: incumbent resident.

4   Llangattock Lingoed Parish.

Area: 1,926 acres. *Popn.* 110 males, 117 females: total 227.

(5)   Llangattock Lingoed Parish Church.
Endowed: tithe £170; glebe £21. 10s.
Space: free (no entry); other 24.
Present: aft. 32 + 23 scholars.
Average (12 months): morn. 50 + 46 scholars; aft. 86 + 46 scholars.

John Price. Curate.

[Endorsed: See Letter]

Lewis: discharged vicarage; in gift of the Crown; endowed with the great tithes; valued at £5. 6s. 5½d.; net income £172; glebe 17½ acres and glebe-house.

C & C: 1 service in English.

I & C: incumbent not resident: curate, who resides at Llanvihangel Crucorney, 3 miles distant, has stipend of £100 for two parishes.

[5-6] Llanvihangel Crucorney Parish, consisting of [5] Llanvihangel Crucorney and [6] Penbiddle Hamlet.
Area of the whole: 3,264 acres. *Popn.* 215 males, 239 females: total 454.

5   Llanvihangel Crucorney Parish.
Popn. 162 males, 180 females: total 342.

(6)   LLANVIHANGEL CRUCORNEY PARISH CHURCH.
Endowed: tithe £255; glebe £26.
Space: free 1; other 24 pews and a gallery.
Present: morn. 55 + 23 scholars.
Average (12 *months*): morn. 60 + 45 scholars; aft. 90 + 45 scholars.

John Price.   Curate.

Lewis: discharged vicarage; endowed with a portion of the rectorial tithes; valued at £5. 19s. 7d.; patron, the Queen; net income £281; impropriators of the remainder of the rectorial tithes, the governors of Abergavenny school; glebe 40 acres: church partly rebuilt in 1835.

C & C: 1 service in English.

I & C: incumbent not resident: curate, who resides in the glebe-house, has stipend of £120.

6   Penbiddle Hamlet.
Popn. 53 males, 59 females: total 112.

(7)   ZOAR CHAPEL.   PARTICULAR BAPTIST.
Erected 1837.
Space: free 27; 'there is accomodation for 200 persons'.
Usual number of attendants: morn. 60; even. 120.

(*Informant*) Edwin Thomas.
[Informant's Form.]

[7-10]   Cwmyoy Parish, consisting of [7] Cwmyoy Upper Division, [8] Fwthog Hamlet (co. Hereford), [9] Cwmyoy Lower Division, and [10] Bwlch Trewyn.
Area of the whole: 10,366 acres. *Popn.* 398 males, 361 females: total 759.

7   Cwmyoy Parish Upper Division.
Popn. 117 males, 109 females: total 226.

(8)   LLANTHONY CHAPEL.   Ancient chapelry in the parish of Cwmyoy.
Endowed: tithe £54; permanent endowment £12. 12s. 6d.; from the Llanthony estates £5; aggregate amount £71. 12s. 6d.
Sittings: free 32; other 30.

Present: even. 26.
Average: morn. 40.
Remark: Service morning and evening on alternate Sundays.
George Griffith.   Officiating minister.
Abergavenny.

C & C: sub Cwmyoy: 1 service in English.

I & C: incumbent not resident: curate, who resides at Cwmyoy, 3 miles distant,
has stipend of £30.

8   Fwthog Hamlet, co. Hereford.

Area: 2,081 acres. *Popn.* 61 males, 59 females: total 120.
[This hamlet in the parish of Cwmyoy is placed in Herefordshire by the
Census. It contained one place of worship, as follows:]

(10)   TABERNACLE CHAPEL.   BAPTIST.
Erected 1838.
Space: free 150.
Present: morn. 40.
Average (12 *months*): 55 + 40 scholars.
Morgan Lewis.   Minister.

[Its county is given as Hereford.]

9   Cwmyoy Parish, Lower division.

Area: 7,650 acres. *Popn.* 161 males, 142 females: total 303.

(9)   BETHLEHEM CHAPEL.   CALVINISTIC METHODIST.
Erected 1839.
Space: free 16 pews.
Present: morn. 40; aft. 30 scholars; even. 60.
Average: morn. 50; aft. 40 scholars; even. 70.
John Jones.   Minister.

[For (10), missing here, see under Fwthog Hamlet above.]

(11)   ST. MARTIN'S PARISH CHURCH.
Endowed: permanent endowment £5.
Space: free 48; other 102.
Present: morn. 20.
Average (12 *months*): morn. 40; aft. 50.
Remarks: The services in the above church are morning and afternoon
alternately.
Peter Jones Lewis.   Incumbent.

Lewis: perpetual curacy: net income £68: patron, R. Powell, Esq.

C & C: 1 service in English.
I & C: incumbent resident.

(12)　HENLLAN CHAPEL.　BAPTIST.
Erected 1840.
Space: free 100.
Present: even. 97.
Average (12 *months*): aft. 50; even. 100.
Remarks: Divine Service is held at this place of worship three Sundays in the month in the afternoon and one Sunday in the month at 6 in the evening and the general congregation as stated already.

Morgan Lewis.　Minister.

[Endorsed: See Letter.]

10　Bwlch Trewyn Hamlet (formerly in co. Hereford).

Area: 635 acres.　*Popn.* 59 males, 51 females: total 110.
[No returns]

Lewis: tithes commuted for £32. 2s., payable to the perpetual curate of Cwmyoy; £24. 4s. 9d. to the incumbent of Oldcastle [578. 2. 11(13)]; £12. 14. to the incumbent of Llancillo [co. Hereford].

11　Oldcastle Parish.

Area: 922 acres.　*Popn.* 23 males, 24 females: total 47.

(13)　ST. JAMES PARISH CHURCH.
Endowed: land £22; tithe £48. Burials and marriages few.
Space: free 4; other 26 pews.
Average:　morn. 10; scholars none.

Theophilus Morgan.　Incumbent.

[Endorsed: See Letter.]

Lewis: perpetual curacy; net income £73; patron, Edmund Higginson, Esq.; impropriator, Theophilus Morgan, Esq.; tithes commuted for £48. 4s. 6d.; glebe 123 acres.

C & C: 1 service in English.

I & C: incumbent not resident.

[End of Llanvihangel Subdistrict]

3 ABERGAVENNY (Subdistrict)
Area: 10,674 acres. *Popn.* 3,885 males, 4,057 females: total 7,942.

[1-2] Llantillio Pertholey Parish, consisting of [1] Citra Division and [2] Ultra Division.
Area of the whole: 6,859 acres. *Popn.* 436 males, 412 females: total 848.

1   Citra Division.
Popn. 199 males, 176 females: total 375.

(1)   LLANTILLIO PERTHOLEY PARISH CHURCH.
Endowed: tithe £264. 15s.; glebe £60; fees £4.
Space: total 400.
Present: aft. 110 + 34 scholars.
Remark: Not an average congregation.

Thomas Morgan.   Curate.

Lewis: discharged vicarage; valued at £8. 3s. 9d; patrons and appropriators, the Chapter of Llandaff: great tithes commuted for £370, vicarial tithes for £252. 10s.; glebe of 66 acres and glebehouse.

C & C: 1 service in English.

I & C: incumbent not resident: curate, who resides in the parish, has stipend of £100.

(2)   SALEM CHAPEL.   CALVINISTIC METHODIST.
Erected 1816.
Space: free 14 pews.
Present: morn. 40 scholars; aft. 70; even. 80.
Average: morn. 50 scholars; aft. 80; even. 100.

John Jones.   Minister.
Forest Chapel.

2   Ultra Division.
Popn. 237 males, 236 females: total 473.

(3)   BETTWS CHAPEL.
Licensed for public worship by the Bishop of Llandaff in 1829 as a chapel of ease to the Parish Church of Llantillio Pertholey.   Erected partly by Parliamentary grant and partly by Private Subscription.
Sittings: free 150; other 165.
Present: morn. 42.
Remark: By no means an average number of attendants as the Services vary alternately.

Thomas Morgan.   Curate.

C & C: 1 service in English; curate performs 1 service in Welsh per month.

ICBS: grant of £30 in 1829.

[3-5] Abergavenny Parish, consisting of [3] Abergavenny (including the town of Abergavenny), [4] Lloyndu Hamlet, and [5] Hardwicke Hamlet.
Area of the whole: 4,229 acres. *Popn.* 2,646 males, 2,860 females: total 5,506.

3   Abergavenny
Popn. 2,507 males, 2,697 females: total 5,204.

(4)   TRINITY CHURCH.
Built for 8 cottagers who live in tenements built for them by the Founder of the Church, and it is free for any who chance to come to it especially the Poor of the Town of Abergavenny. Consecrated November 6th 1840, as an additional church under the circumstances stated above. Erected by the private benefaction of Miss Rachel Herbert.
Endowed: Repair Endowment Fund, £1,200; other permanent endowment £2,000 vested in Trustees and a house.
Space: free 528; other 72.
Present: morn. 200; aft. 250.
Average: morn. 200 + 40 scholars; aft. 350 + 40 scholars.
Thomas Williams.   Incumbent.

Lewis: patroness Miss Rachel Herbert for life, afterwards the Bishop; endowed with £3,000.
C & C: 2 services in English.
I & C: incumbent resident.

(5)   ABERGAVENNY PARISH CHURCH.
An ancient parish church formerly belonging to the Priory but given by Henry the 8th at the Dissolution of the Priory to the Parish when he [illegible] the old church of St. John to his [illegible] endowed Grammar School.
Endowed: tithe £500; Q.A. Bounty £19; fees, dues and Easter offerings about £40.
Space: free 546, other 1,060.
Present: 700 + 160 scholars; even. 650 + 65 scholars.
Average (12 *months*): morn. 750 + 160 scholars.
Remarks: Out of this gross sum I have had to pay in Poor and other Rates at least £50 a year and for Collection £30 and for house Rent £40, which I have now paid for nearly 50 years.
William Powell, B.D.   Vicar.

Lewis: discharged vicarage, valued at £10. 0. 7½d.; patron, C. Bailey, Esq.; impropriator Mrs. Bagot. Body of church and aisles taken down and rebuilt in 1828, and galleries added.
C & C: 2 services in English.
I & C: incumbent resident: curate's stipend not stated.
ICBS: grant of £500 in 1829.

(6) TABERNACLE CHAPEL. PRIMITIVE METHODIST.
Erected 1850.
Space: free 78; other 106.
Present: morn. 36 + 32 scholars; aft. 44 scholars; even. 90.
Average (9 months): morn. 36 + 25 scholars; aft. 35 scholars; even. 100.
Remarks: Nine months is the time that this place of Worship has been opened for Publick Service.

> William Tinney. Local preacher,
> Leader, Steward, S.S. Superintendant.
> Grofield, Abergavenny.

(7) FROGMORE STREET CHAPEL. BAPTIST.
Erected 1815.
Space: free 250; other 250.
Present: morn. 220; even. 300.
Average: even. 350.

> Micah Thomas. Pastor.

(8) ST. MICHAEL'S ROMAN CATHOLIC CHURCH.
Erected 1835.
Space: free 60; total 240.
Present: morn. 223; aft. 71.
Average (12 months): general congregation about 220.

> James Millward. Catholic Priest.

(9) WELSH BAPTIST CHAPEL.
Erected 1769.
Space: 'the whole of the sittings are free' 150.
Present: aft. 64.
Average (12 months): aft. 70.

> John Michael. Deacon.
> Monte Street, Abergavenny.

[Endorsed: See letter.]

(10) PROVIDENCE CHAPEL, LION STREET. BAPTIST.
Erected 1828.
Space: free 180; gallery 150.
Present: morn. 57; even. 82.
Remark: Strictly speaking all our sittings are free. Persons who pay for their seats do so voluntarily and nothing is demanded of other parties who regularly attend but are unable or unwilling to contribute. 32 seats in the bottom of the chapel capable of holding 180, free space for benches 40, forms with backs in the gallery 150, total 370.

> John Poole. Minister.

(11)   CASTLE STREET CHAPEL.   INDEPENDENT.
Erected 1786.
Space: free 280; other 270.
Present: morn. 149; even. 189.

> W. H. Woodhall.   Deacon.
> Tea Dealer, Abergavenny.

(12)   CASTLE STREET CHAPEL.   WESLEYAN METHODIST.
Erected 1829.
Space: free 200; other 400.
Present: morn. 80 + 40 scholars; even. 300.
Average: 80 + 40 scholars; even. 300.

> Thomas Rogerson.   Minister.

4 Lloyndu Hamlet.
Popn. 87 males, 103 females: total 190.
[No returns]

5 Hardwicke Hamlet.
Popn. 52 males, 60 females: total 112.
[No returns]

6 Llangattock-nigh-Usk Parish.
Area: 1,613 acres. *Popn.* 95 males, 83 females: total 178.

(13)   LLANGATTOCK-NIGH-USK PARISH CHURCH.
Endowed: tithe £190; glebe £120.
Space: free 20; other 100.
Present: morn. 26 + 7 scholars.
Average (12 *months*): morn. 30 + 10 scholars; aft. 40 + 10 scholars.
Remarks: Divine Service is celebrated once each Sunday morning and afternoon alternately.

> Henry Peake, B.A.   Curate.
> Westgate House, Abergavenny.

Lewis: rectory; valued at £11. 7s. 3½d.; patron, Earl of Abergavenny; tithes commuted for £215; glebe 95 acres.

C & C: 1 service in English.

I & C: Incumbent not resident: curate who resides in Abergavenny, adjacent parish, has stipend of £80.

7 Llanover Parish. Lower Division.
Area: 1,877 acres. *Popn.* 175 males, 167 females: total 342.

(14) Llanover Parish Church.
Endowed: tithe £250; glebe £42.
Space: free 50; other 200.
Present: morn. 62 + 14 scholars; aft. 56.
Average (12 *months*): morn. 80 + 20 scholars; aft. 56.

John Evans. Vicar.

Lewis: discharged vicarage with livings of Mamhilad [579. 1. 3(45)] and Trevethan [579. 1. 2(7)] united; valued at £15. 3s. 6½d.; patrons and appropriators, Bishop, Archdeacon and Chapter of Llandaff; net income £591; great tithes commuted for £145; smaller tithes for £247; glebe of 16 acres.

C & C: 2 services, of which one performed in Welsh.

I & C: incumbent resident.

(15) Hanover Chapel. Independents or Congregationalists.
Erected 1839.
Space: free 194; other 85; standing room 80.
Present: morn. 119; aft. 164.
Average: morn. 130; aft. 80 scholars; even. 220.
Remark: The first Hanover Chapel was erected in the year 1744 and is now converted into a dwelling house.

Robert Thomas. Minister.

[For the remainder of Llanover parish see 578. 4. 3 below.]

8 Llanellen Parish.
Area: 2,536 acres. *Popn.* 180 males, 188 females: total 368.

(16) Llanellen Parish Church.
Endowed: tithe £133; glebe £24; fees £1.
Space: free 40; other 106.
Present: morn. 26 + 17 scholars; aft. 36 + 20 scholars.
Average (3 *months*): morn. 60 + 20 scholars; aft. 70 + 20 scholars.

William Jones. Vicar.

Lewis: discharged vicarage; endowed with moiety of rectorial tithes; valued £8. 10s. 7d.; net income £105; impropriators of remainder of rectorial tithes, trustees of Abergavenny School.

C & C: 2 services in English.

I & C: incumbent not resident: curate, who resides in the parish, has stipend of £80.

9   Llanwenarth Parish, Citra Division.
Area: 2,860 acres. *Popn.* 132 males, 122 females: total 254.
[No returns]

Lewis: rectory; valued at £26. 6s. 3d.; patron, Earl of Abergavenny; tithes of Llanwenarth Citra commuted for £460; glebe 45 acres.

[For the remainder of Llanwenarth Parish see 578. 4. 2. below.]

10   Llanfoist Parish.   First Part.
Area: 790 acres. *Popn.* 221 males, 225 females: total 446.

(17)   LLANFOIST PARISH CHURCH.
Space: free 90; other 27.
Present: morn. 120; aft. 135.

                              William Corfield.   Rector.

Lewis: rectory; valued at £7. 4s. 4½d.; patron, Earl of Abergavenny; tithes commuted for £280; glebe 30 acres.

C & C: 2 services in English.

I & C: incumbent resident.

[For Llanfoist, Second Part, see 578. 4. 1 below.]

[*End of Abergavenny Subdistrict*]

4 BLAENAVON (Subdistrict)
    Area: 7,933 acres. *Popn.* 2,079 males, 2,776 females: total 5,855.

1   Llanfoist Parish.   The Second Part.
Area: 2,588 acres. *Popn.* 553 males, 454 females: total 1,007.

(1)   WESLEYAN METHODIST CHAPEL.
Erected 1839.
Space: free 300; other 500.
Present: morn. 200 + 180 scholars; aft. 200 scholars; even. 40 + 50 scholars.

                              James Brown.   Society steward.
                              Blaenavon.

[For the remainder of this parish see 578. 3. 10 above.]

2 Llanwenarth Parish. Ultra Division.
Area: 2,480 acres. *Popn.* 1,184 males, 1,064 females: total 2,248.

(2) GOVILON CHAPEL OF EASE.
Licensed August 10, 1848 as an additional Chapel of Ease. Erected by public subscription, total cost £800.
Space: free 150.
Present: morn. 48 + 25 scholars; aft. 30 scholars; even. 80.
Average: morn. 50 + 30 scholars; aft. 30 scholars; even. 80.
Remark: Licensed August 10, 1848. Erected by public subscription, total cost £800.

William Hughes. Minister.

Lewis: see above 578. 3. 9(9).

C & C: 2 services in English.

ICBS: grant of £90 in 1847.

(3) BAPTIST CHAPEL.
Erected 1695.
Space: free 162; other 90.
Present: morn. 262; aft. 164 scholars; even. 371.
Average (12 *months*): morn. 650; aft. 160 scholars; even. 650.
Remarks: The members and hearers reside in Llanwenarth Ultra, Llanwenarth Citra, Llanelly, Llanfoist, Llanelen, Lanover, Abergavenny. Many of those do not attend but once a month. This will account for the apparent discrepancy in the Average column.

Francis Hiley. Minister.
Govilon Post Office.

(4) WESLEYAN METHODIST CHAPEL (GARNDDYRRIS).
Erected 1829.
Space: free 200.
Present: morn. 45 scholars; aft. 45 + 32 scholars; even. 55.
Average: morn. 50 scholars; aft. 50 + 30 scholars; even. 60.

John Lashford. Steward.
Garnddyrris.
[Rightly numbered, but misplaced in bound volume of returns, after 578. 4. 3(12).]

(5) EBENEZER CHAPEL. PARTICULAR BAPTIST.
Erected 16 Dec. 1844.
Present: morn. 40 + 40 scholars; even. 61 + 40 scholars.
Average: morn. 40 + 40 scholars; even. 60 + 40 scholars.

William Williams. Minister.
Garndyris.

(6) PWLLDU. CHAPEL OF EASE FOR THREE SECTS, BAPTISTS, INDEPENDENTS AND METHODISTS.
Erected 1820, rebuilt 1850.
Space: 200.
Present: morn. 94 scholars; aft. 142 + 93 scholars; even. 123 (prayer meeting).
Average: morn. 94 scholars; aft. 93 scholars; even. 123.

                          James Davies. Deacon.
                          Collier.

[For the remainder of this parish see 578. 3. 9. above.]

3 Llanover Parish. Upper Division.

Area: 2,865 acres. *Popn.* 1,342 males, 1,258 females: total 2,600.

(7) CAPEL NEWYDD. DONATIVE.
Endowed: land £80.
Space: free 50.
Present: none.
Average: aft. 30.
Remark: The church is only served during the summer months, the situation being too stormy for winter service. The church is but of little use since the building of Blaenafon Church.

                          John Jones. Perpetual curate.
                          Blaenafon Parsonage.

Lewis: see above 578. 3. 7(14).

C & C: 1 service in Welsh from Easter to Michaelmas.

I & C: incumbent not resident: curate who resides at Blaenavon, 2 miles distant, has stipend of £20 for summer duty.

(8) BLAENAFON CHAPEL OF EASE.
Endowed: land £20; Queen Anne's Bounty £87.
Space: free 383; other 138.
Present: morn. 131 + 189 scholars; even. 269.
Average (3 months): morn. 200 + 200 scholars; even. 420.
Remarks: Consecrated 1805. Built and consecrated for the accommodation of the workmen of the Blaenafon Iron and Coal Company. Erected at the sole expense of Messrs. Thomas Hill and Samuel Hopkins, Proprietors of the Blaenafon Company; total cost probably about £3,000.

                          John Jones. Perpetual curate.
                          Blaenafon Parsonage.

Lewis: perpetual curacy; net income £114; partons, the Blaenavon Company.

C & C: 2 services in English.

I & C: incumbent resident.

(9) EBENEZER CHAPEL. BAPTIST. (BLAENAVON IRON WORKS).
Erected 1825.
Space: free 316; other 119.
Present: morn. 156; aft. 90 scholars; even. 350.
Average: morn. 160; 80 scholars; even. 360.

Owen Michael. Minister.

(10) BETHLEHEM CHAPEL, BLAENAVON. INDEPENDENTS.
Erected: The present chapel was built in 1840, the old in 1820.
Present: morn. 177; aft. scholars 135; even. 214.
Average (12 *months*): general congregation 250 to 300; scholars 130 to 140.
Remarks: The present chapel was built in lieu of the old but not on the site of the old, nor in the same parish. The old was in the Parish of Trevethin, the present in the parish of Llanover. The congregation last Sunday were under the average. The communicants are a little short of 200. The congregation the proceeding Sunday was upwards of 300.

Thomas Griffiths. Minister.

(11) PENUEL CHAPEL. WELCH CALVINISTIC METHODIST.
Erected 1819.
Space: free 226; other 340.
Present: morn. 155; aft. 137 scholars; even. 211.
Average (12 *months*): morn. 175; aft. 137 scholars; even. 241.
Remarks: In column the 8th (those present) we made an addition of 20 more in the morning and in the evening 30 more. Sometimes the Chapel cramd quite full. Sunday Scholars is put under the word afternoon, the middle column. [Added on a separate sheet in the same hand.] The first chapel that we had was Erected in the year 1799 which was known by the name of Rock Chapel, and Sunday School was established about the year 1804 and so the Cause was carrid on in this til we had a new chapel which is mentioned in the Return. The Rock Chapel was situate in the Parish of Lanwenarth in the County of Monmouth.

David Jones. Deacon.
Coal miner.

(12) BLAENAVON CHAPEL. PRIMITIVE METHODIST.
Erected 1829.
Space: free 200; other 30.
Present: morn. 90 + 100 scholars; aft. 140 scholars; even. 230.

William Harvey. Minister.
Low-Hill, Pontypool.

(13)   ENGLISH BAPTIST CHAPEL.   BLAENAVON.
Erected 1847.
Space: free 300; other 50.
Present: morn. 101 + 70 scholars; aft. 174 scholars; even. 200.
Average: morn. 100 + 70 scholars; aft. 150 scholars; even. 230.
Remark: The Chapel is called the English Baptist Chapel because there is
no other English Baptist Chapel in the place.

Griffith Havard. Minister.

(14)   HOREB CHAPEL, BLAENAVON.   BAPTIST.
Erected 1807.
Space: free 250; other 140; standing room for 100.
Present: morn. 230 + 30 scholars; even. 300 + 40 scholars.
Average: morn. 250 + 30 scholars; even. 330 + 40 scholars.
Remarks: The expression 'Sunday Scholars' is understood to refer to those
only who attend Divine Service and not to the entire number of Scholars.
If it refers to the number attending the School it should be Morning 100
and Afternoon 133. There were great many of the members unable to
attend on the 30th of March on account of a prevaling Illness.

Daniel Morgan.   Minister.

[End of Blaenavon Subdistrict]

5 ABERYSTRUTH (Subdistrict)

Area: 11,788 acres. *Popn.* 7,994 males, 6,389 females: total 14,383.

1 Aberystruth Parish.
Area and Popn: as for the Subdistrict.

(1)   NANTYGLO SCHOOL ROOM
Licensed for the performance of Divine Service. I am not able to say
positively, but I think it was licensed in 1837. It was licensed in consequence
of the distance from the parish church for the benefits of the inhabitants
of Nantyglo. Erected by Messrs. Bailey, Proprietors of the Nantyglo
Ironworks. Endowed by a grant from the Ecclesiastical Commissioners.
Space: free 150.

David Morgan. Vicar.

Lewis: sub Aberystwith: Church district formed in 1844: living in gift of Crown
and Bishop of Llandaff alternately.

C & C: 3 services, 1 Welsh, 2 English.

I & C: incumbent resident.

(2)   ST. PETER, commonly called Aberystruth or Blaen Gwent is a chapel of
Ease to Llanwenarth, the mother church.

Endowed: tithe commuted for £300; other permanent endowment £16; fees from £30 to £40.
Space: free 318; other 82.
Present: morn. 126 + 52 scholars; aft. 160; even. 142.

Daniel Rees.
Minister or P[erpetual] Curate.

Lewis: perpetual curacy; endowed with nearly whole of rectorial tithes: patron, the Earl of Abergavenny: impropriate tithes commuted for £5. 10s. and those of the incumbent for £300. Church erected in 1827.

C & C: 3 services, 1 in Welsh, 2 in English performed by the incumbent and curate.

I & C: incumbent resident; curate has stipend of £100.

ICBS: grant of £140 in 1827.

(3)   BETHEL.   WELSH WESLEYAN METHODIST ABERYSTRWYTH.
Erected 1827.
Space: free 415; other 200; standing 120.
Present: morn. 174; even. 288.
Average (3 *months*): morn. 250; aft. 200 scholars; even. 500.

William Roberts.   Wesleyan Minister.
Brynmawr near Abergavenny.

(4)   HERMON CHAPEL.   PARTICULAR BAPTIST.
Erected 1820.
Enlarged in 1830; rebuilded in 1850.
Space: free 500; other 500.
Present: general congregation about 1,000.
Average (5 *months*): general congregation about 1,000.
Remarks: Measure of the Chapel is 56 by 48 in the clear in which there is 100 rented pews accomodated 5 persons each. The rest is free space, filled with Benches. (Gallery on three parts of it.)

Samuel Williams.   Minister.
Nant y Glo.

(5)   SALEM.   CALVINISTIC METHODIST (WELSH).
Erected 1818; rebuilt 1833.
Space: free 350; other 200; standing 100.
Present: aft. 152 + 150 scholars; even. 80 + 70 scholars.
Average (3 *months*): aft. 180 + 160 scholars; even. 140 + 120 scholars.
Remarks: In this district a great number of the men are employed in the manufacture of Iron and obliged to work on the Sabbath, consequently are unable to attend Public Worship. The Sunday School is held at 10 o'clock in the forenoon.

W. Williams.   Secretary and one of the Deacons.
Nantyglo.

(6) BEREA. INDEPENDENT,
Erected 1841.
Space: free 370; other 18.
Present: morn. 296 + 261 scholars; aft. 261 scholars; even. 380.
Average: morn. 500; aft. 410 scholars.
Remarks: New chapel in course of erection 56 by 40 inside the Walls.
Meetings held occasionally at Abertillery.

> Thomas Davies.   Deacon.
> Miner.
> Berea, Nr. Nant y Glo.

(7) BLAENAU GWENT. BAPTIST.
Erected 1715.
Space: free 120; other 156.
Present: morn. 155; aft. 114 scholars; even. 215.

> John Lewis.   Minister.
> Abertillery tin works near Newport.

(8) PRIMITIVE METHODIST CHAPEL, CWMTILEREY.
Erected 1848.
Space: free 80; other 50.
Present: morn. 66 scholars; aft. 50; even. 70.

> Thomas Preese.   Steward.
> Cwmtilery.

(9) ENGLISH BAPTIST CHAPEL.
Space: free about 20; other about 50.
Usual number present: morn. 80; aft. 150 scholars; even. about 200.
Remarks: It was erected by the Welsh Independents and they sold it to
build a large Chapel and it has been rented lately by the English Baptists.

> William Roberts.   Baptist Minister.
> Blaena Works.
> *Informant.*

[Informant's form.]

(10) BLAENAU GWENT. BAPTIST.
Erected 1715, re-erected 1819.
Space: free 178; other 130.
Usual number present: morn. 150; aft. 100 scholars; even. 208.

> *Informant:* John Lewis.   Baptist
> Minister.
> Abertillery.

[Endorsed: Duplicate.]
[This is a duplicate of 578. 5. 1(7) submitted on an Informant's form by
the minister.]

(11)   SALEM BAPTIST CHAPEL.
Erected 1848.
Space: free 500; other 450.
Usual number present: morn. 60 scholars at 9 o'clock; about 300 general congregation at ½ past 10; aft. 190 scholars; even. about 600.

> *Informant:* William Roberts. Baptist
> Minister.
> Blaena.

[Informant's form.]

(12)   PRIMITIVE METHODIST CAHEPL.
Erected 1848.
Building used for Public Worship, Sunday School & Day School.
Space: free 60; other 54.
Present: morn. 50 + 23 scholars; even. 90.
Average: morn. 100 + 50 scholars.

> Llewellyn Walkley. Steward.
> Cwm Celyn and Blaena Ironworks.

(13)   HOPE CHAPEL.   WELSH CALVINISTIC METHODIST.
Erected 1845.
Space: free 222; other 218.
Present: morn. 56 + 150 scholars; even. 40 + 118 scholars.
Average: No regular account kept, but the above may be taken as an Average.
Remarks: (*a*) In 1840 the first chapel of this Congregation was built, but in the year mentioned it was undermined and fell and the present Building was erected by the Free Contributions of the Congregation assisted by neighbouring Congregations.
(*b*) In nearly the whole of the Welsh Congregations most of the Adult members (as well as children) attend the Sunday School to an advanced age and form Bible Classes.

> Edward Jones. Secretary.
> British School, Blaina.

(14)   BEAUFORT CHURCH.
Licensed as an additional Church, 24th day of Decr. 1842.
Erected by private Benefaction.
Endowed by the Ecclesiastical Commissioners £130.
Space: free 180; other 120.
Present: morn. 82 + 54 scholars; aft. 68 scholars; even. 90.

> William H .James. Minister.
> Ebbw Vale.

Lewis: church district formed in 1846; in the gift of the Crown and the Bishop of Llandaff alternatively.
C & C: 2 services of which 1 Welsh taken by incumbent and curate.
I & C: incumbent not resident.

(15)   EBENEZER CHAPEL.   CALVINISTIC METHODIST.
Erected 1851.
Space: free 324; other 360.
Usual number present: morn. 183 scholars; aft. 420; even. 420.

> *Informant:* John Evans.
> Grocer.
> Ebbw Vale.

[Informant's form.]

(16)   ENGLISH WESLEYAN METHODISTS CHAPELL, BLAINA.
Erected 1844.
Space: free 164; other 324.
Usual number present: morn. 230 + 80 scholars; aft. 150 scholars; even. 450.

> *Informant:* Thomas Hinton.
> Blaina Ironworks.

[Informant's form. This is the same as 578. 5. 1(19) below.]

(17)   LATER DAY SAINTS TABERNACLE, BLAINA IRON WORKS.
Erected 1849.
Space: free 100.
Usual number present: morn. 60 + 40 scholars; aft. 60; even. 80.
Remarks: [Building used for] Weekly School also.

> *Informant:* Thomas Parry.
> Mine Agent.
> Blaina.

[Informant's form.]

(18)   SALEM.   BAPTIST CHAPEL.
Erected 1848 (in lieu of another that was built in 1835).
Space: free 520; other 350.
Present: morn. 283; aft. 170 scholars; even. 498.
Average (12 *months*): morn. about 350; aft. 170 scholars; even. about 600.
Remarks: We have often from 750 to 800 on Sunday evening, but the general average is about 600, that is to say the average of attendances. We may reasonably calculate about 100 or 150 more belonging to our place of worship for the number that must stop at home in each family may be reckoned about the 5th or the 6th part of the whole. This remark is applicable to all denominations in this neighbourhood, I believe.

> William Roberts.   Minister.
> Blaina Works.

(19)   ENGLISH WESLEYAN METHODISTS CHAPEL, BLAINA IRONWORKS.
Erected 1844.
Space: free 186; other 312.
Present: morn. 185 + 130 scholars; even. 443.
Average (6 *months*): morn. 190 + 130 scholars; even. 450.

> Thomas Hinton, Trustee and Steward.
> Blaina Iron Works.

[This is the same as 578. 5. 1(16) above.]

(20)   MORIAH.   WELSH WESLEYAN.
Erected 1842.
Space: free 250.
Present: morn. 35 scholars; aft. 40; even. 38.
Remarks: There are a few of our members which are not well and others
which do live far off.

> William Thomas.   Steward.
> New Wesleyan Chapel, Blaina Iron
> Works.

(21)   EBENEZER CHAPEL.   CALVINISTIC METHODIST.   EBBW VALE.
Erected 1850.
Space: free 240; other 360; standing 168.
Present: aft. 79 + 100 scholars; even. 160 + 125 scholars.
Remarks: Many of the workmen employed in the Iron Works are obliged to
work on the Sabbath. They are consequently unable to attend any place of
worship. The Sunday School is held in the Chapel at 10 o'clock in the
forenoon.

> John Evans.   Elder.
> Grocer,
> New Town, Ebbw Vale.

(22)   PRIMITIVE METHODIST CHAPEL, NEWTOWN.
Congregation including Sunday Scholars: morn. 100; even. 150.

> Signed.   Joseph Williams.
> Dated. 16 Sept. 1852.

[Special query.]

[Note: 578. 5. 1(15-22) are correctly numbered but wrongly bound between
578. 2. 1(2) and 578. 2. 2(3).]

[The three returns which follow are wrongly numbered and bound among
the returns for Aberystwyth District, co. Cardigan.]

597. 2. 2(6).
SALEM, ABERYSTRUTH.   ENGLISH PARTICULAR BAPTIST.
Erected 1833.
Space: free 78; other none; standing 200.
Present: morn. 30 + 20 scholars; aft. 60 scholars; even. 70.
Average: morn. 40 + 30 scholars; aft. 70 scholars; even. 80.
Remarks: The English cause was commenced in the old Welsh Chapel
October 1849.

> William Hiley.   Deacon.
> Grocer & draper, Blaina, Nr. Newport.

597. 2. 2(7)
ENGLISH WESLEYAN CHAPEL, NANTYGLO.
Erected 1823.
Space: free 150; other 150; standing 40.
Present: morn. 200; even. 180.

> James Emery.   Wesleyan Minister.
> Brynmawr.

597. 2. 2(15)
ZION, EBBW VALE, PARISH OF ABERYSTRITH DISTRICT.
Of 'Tredegar as far as I know.'
Erected 1847.
Space: free 100; other 112; standing, 'including aisles and lobby 106'.
Present: morn. no service; aft. 70 + 27 scholars; even. 100 + 14 scholars.
Average (12 *months*): aft. 120 + 30 scholars; even. 150 + 30 scholars.

> Geo. Price.
> Primitive Methodist Minister.

[End of Aberystruth Subdistrict]

6 TREDEGAR (Subdistrict)

Area, including the Subdistrict of [7] Rock Bedwelty: 16,210 acres.
Popn. of Tredegar Subdistrict alone: 13,434 males, 11,110 females:
total 24,544.

[1-2] That part of the Parish of Bedwelty consisting of [1] Manmoel Hamlet and [2] Ushlawrcoed Hamlet.

Area and popn. as for the Subdistrict.

1 Manmoel Hamlet.

Popn. 5,083 males, 4,037 females: total 9,120.

(1) St. Georges Church (in the town of Tredegar).
A District Church built under the provisions of the 16 Section of an Act
passed in the 59 year of the reign of His Majesty King George the Third.
An additional Church, consecrated in 1836. It was erected partly by a grant
from the Incorporated Society for building of Churches and Chapels. What
was the actual cost I have no means to ascertain.
Endowed: Permanent endowment £19. 10; pew rents £45; fees £25;
Easter offerings £15; other sources all voluntary.
Space: free 570; other 570.
Average attendance: The sittings are generally well filled.
Remarks: There are two licensed school rooms in the District besides the
Church where Divine Service is held three times every Sunday and once in
the week. The Congregation in them average 200.

William Jones.   Incumbent.

Lewis: living in the gift of the incumbent of Bedwellty [578. 7. 1(1)]: church built
by grant of £1000 from the Parliamentary Commissioners, £450 from the Incorporated Society, and upwards of £600 by private subscription.

C & C: *sub* Bedwellty; 3 services, 1 Welsh, 2 English, the Welsh service performed
by the incumbent and curate.

I & C: incumbent resident: 2 curates have stipends of £100 each P.A.S.

ICBS: grant of £450 in 1833.

(2) Rhymney Church—District Parish
Erected under the Provisions of a Private Act of Parliament 2nd
Vict Sessions 1839. Received Royal assent May 14th 1839 to enable
the Rhymney Iron Co. to erect and endow a Church in the Parish of
Bedwellty in the County of Monmouth and Diocese of Llandaff.
Situated in the north Western Division of the Parish of Bedwellty; conse-
crated July 14th 1843 as an additional church. The Parish Church of
Bedwellty, being nearly seven miles distant and there being in the district
at the time above 8,000 souls without a place of worship provided by the
Church of England. Erected by the Rhymney Iron Co. and other well
wishers to the cause of the Church, at a total cost of £5,303. 16. 1.
(£2,234. 15. was collected by subscription, inclusive of a grant from the
Incorporated Society for Building and Repairing of Churches of £400;
contributed by the Rhymney Iron Co. £3,069. 1s.).
Endowed: glebe £15; permanent endowment £100; pew rents £30; fees
£20.
Space: free 575; other 272. This is the number put up on a board in
Church but it is supposed there are sittings for 100 more.
Present: morn. 9 o'clock 96, 11 o'clock 301; aft. 340 scholars; even. 756.
Average (12 *months*): morn. 9 o'clock 110, 11 o'clock 340; aft. 356 scholars;
even. 800.

Remarks: The Pew rents are appropriated to defray current expences such as cleaning and heating the Church—clerk's salary etc.

> Lodwick Edwards.   Minister.

C & C: sub Bedwelty: 3 services, 1 Welsh, 2 English, the Welsh service performed by the incumbent and curate.

ICBS: grant of £450 in 1840.

(3)   EBBW VALE SCHOOL ROOM.
Licensed in 1842 for the the accomodation of persons living 3 or 4 miles from the District Church. Erected by the Ebbw Vale Iron Company and used as their day school.
Space: free for 200 or thereabouts.
Present: morn. 123 + 118 scholars; even. 185.
Average: morn. 123 + 118 scholars; even. 185.
Average: The school room always well filled and usually more attending than the number of sittings.
Remarks: There is no encouragement given to the children to attend worship as they wd. occupy all the room now apportioned for adults. This is the only Church accomodation for a population of 7,000 souls.

> L. Charles Lewis.   Minister.

(4)   JERUSALEM CHAPEL, RHYMNEY.   PARTICULAR BAPTIST.
Erected 1841.
Space: free 288; other 308.
Present: morn. 311 + 116 scholars; even. 358.
Average (12 *months*): morn. 350 + 108 scholars; aft. 162 scholars; even. 400.
Remarks: No School on the afternoon of the 30th.

> Henry Harries.   Deacon.
> House Agent, Rhymney Iron Works.

(5)   MORIAH INDEPENDENT CHAPEL, RUMNEY.
Erected 1840.
Space: free 6 pews; other 75 pews; all the gallery free, accomodation for 500.
Present: morn. 301; aft. 250 scholars; even. 508.
Average (12 *months*): morn. 480; aft. 250 scholars; even. 500.

> E. C. Jenkins.   Minister.

(6)   MORMONITES (UCHLAWREVED).
Part of a dwelling house. Converted in a place of worship 12 months since.
Present: morn. 49; aft. 75; even. 70.

> David Jones.   Minister.
> Mount Pleasant Row, Rumney.

(7)   ENGLISH WESLEYAN METHODIST CHAPEL.
Erected 1839.
Space: free 70; other 155.
Present: morn. 87 + 45 scholars; even. 161 + 50 scholars.
Average (12 *months*): morn. 7,280 + 2,340 scholars; even. 9,360 + 2,600 scholars.
Remarks: The average [corrected to 'aggregate'] for the last 12 months as far as can be ascertained is the amount specified below including Sunday Scholars for 52 Sundays. The average attendance morning service 140 + 45 scholars; even. 180 + 50 scholars.

> John Holliday.   Steward.
> William Rees.   Leader.
> No. 360 Forge Row, Rhymney.

(8)   CWM SHON MATHEW, RHYMNEY IRON WORKS.
Branch of the Welsh Wesleyan Cause at Twyn Carno. Inhabited Dwelling House, used for the purpose of religious worship from 6 March 1851.
Dimensions of Accomodation: 13ft. by 13ft. 7ft. in height.
Present: aft. 32; even. 11.
Average (1 *month*): morn. 32; aft. 11.

> Rowland Hughes.   Wesleyan Minister.
> Merthir Tidvil.

(9)   GOSHEN, INDEPENDENT CHAPEL.
Erected 1847.
Space: free 200; other 250.
Present: morn. 226 + 80 scholars; aft. 150 scholars; even. 320.

> William Watkins.   Minister.
> Maesteg, Bridgend, Glam.

(10)   PARAN CALVINISTIC METHODIST CHAPEL, MANMOEL.
Erected 1828.
Space: free 200; standing 200.
Present: morn. 30; aft. 25 scholars; even. 60.
Average (12 *months*): morn. 70 + 30 scholars.

> Thomas Phillips.   Minister.
> Chapel Street, Tredegar Iron Works.

(11)   TABERNACL WESLEYAN METHODIST, RUMNEY.
Erected 1837.
Space: free 204; other 146.
Present: morn. 211; aft. 213 scholars; even. 286.
Average: morn. 240; aft. 210 scholars; even. 290.

> Rowland Hughes.   Minister.
> Merthyr Tydfil.

(12)   SION INDEPENDENT, RUMNEY.
Erected 1837.
Space: free 400; other 400; standing about 50.
Present: morn. 311 + 128 scholars; aft. 245 scholars; even. 375 scholars.
Average: morn. 320 + 135 scholars; aft. 250 scholars; even. 380.

> William Davies.   Supplying the pulpit.
> Brecon College.

(13)   PENUEL PARTICULAR BAPTIST.
Erected 1838.
Space: free 450; other 400.
Present: morn. 690; even. 780.
Average (12 months): general congregation 800; scholars 390.

> Isaac Price.   Secretary.
> Builder, Rhymney Iron Works.

(14)   EBENEZER.   CALVINISTIC METHODIST.
Erected 1806.
Space: free 360; other 346; standing 100.
Present: morn. 456; aft. 308 scholars; even. 562.
Average (12 months): morn. 476; aft. 330 scholars; even. 580.

> Thomas Elias.   Secretary.
> Rhymney Iron Works.

(15)   BETHEL INDEPENDENT CHAPEL.   AUGUSTA STREET, VICTORIA IRON WORKS.
Erected 1838.
Space: free 51; other 10.
Present: morn. 122 + 75 scholars; even. 261.

> John Hughes.   Minister.
> Victoria Iron Works.

(16)   PRIMITIVE METHODIST CHAPEL.   AUGUSTA STREET, VICTORIA.
Part of a dwelling house, room used exclusively for Religious Worship.
Present: aft. 26; even. 45.
Average (12 months): aft. 25; even. 45.

> William Powell.   Steward.
> Victoria Iron Works.

(17)   CAERSALEM WELSH BAPTIST CHAPEL, VICTORIA IRON WORKS.
Erected 1839.
Space: free 400; other 200.
Present: morn. 168; aft. 187 scholars; even. 252.
Remarks: The average every Sunday is estimated nearly the same through the year.

> Jenkin Rees.   Minister.

(18)   SHARON INDEPENDENT OR CONGREGATIONAL CHAPEL.
Erected 1837.
Space: free 832; other 338.
Present: morn. 500; aft. 309 scholars; even. 700.
Remarks: I have been unable to ascertain the exact number of Sunday
Scholars attending Divine Service.
Thomas Jeffreys. Independent Minister.
Briery Hill, Ebbw Vale.

(19)   ZION INDEPENDENT CHAPEL.
Erected 1843.
Space: free 176; other 87; standing 48 feet.
Present: morn. 70; aft. 86 scholars; even. 100.
Remark: We have no School at Evening, but Morning and Afternoon.
Thomas Jeffreys. Independent Minister.
Briery Hill, Ebbw Vale.

(20)   ZION PARTICULAR BAPTIST CHAPEL.
Erected 1846.
Space: free 190; other 80.
Present: morn. 40; aft. 151 scholars; even. 93.
Average (12 *months*): morn. 50; aft. 120 scholars; even. 110.
Henry Morgan.   Minister.
Briery Hill, Ebbw Vale.

(21)   PENUEL WELSH CALVINISTIC METHODIST CHAPEL, EBBW VALE.
Erected 1825.
Present: morn. 449; aft. 340; even. 557.
Average (12 *months*): morn. 550; aft. 380; even. 660.
James Griffiths.   Secretary.
Builder.
Ebbw Vale.

(22)   ENGLISH WESLEYAN CHAPEL.
Erected 1825.
Space: free 190; other 264.
Present: morn. 150 + 100 scholars; aft. 300 + 140 scholars; even. 300 +
60 scholars.
Miles Meyrick.   Steward.
Ebbw Vale.

(23)   NEBO CHAPEL.   PARTICULAR BAPTIST.
Space: free 1,018; other 182.
Present: morn. 700; aft. 258 scholars; even. 822.
Average (12 *months*): general congregation 700 to 800; scholars 300.
Thomas Evans.   Minister.
Ebbw Vale.

(24)   BETHCAR WELSH WESLEYAN METHODIST.
Erected 1830.
Space: free 225; other 125.
Present: aft. 202 + 122 scholars; even. 230.
Average (12 *months*): general congregation 300; other 142.
> Benjamin James.   Chapel Steward.

(25)   PRIMITIVE METHODIST CHAPEL, SIRHOWY.
Established 1844.
Space: free 350.
Present: aft. 110 + 22 scholars; even. 205 + 30 scholars.
Average (12 *months*): aft. 150 + 40 scholars; even. 230 + 30 scholars.
> George Price.   Minister.
> High Street, Tredegar.

(26)   PENUEL CHAPEL, TREDEGAR.   CALVINISTIC METHODIST.
Erected 1809.
Space: free 310; other 320.
Present: morn. 580; even. 150.
Average (12 *months*): morn. 600; even. 150.
Remark: Sunday Scholars with Congregation.
> Isaac Edwards.   Deacon.
> Tredegar.

(27)   SILOH PARTICULAR BAPTISTS (WELSH).
Erected 1800.
Space: free 579; other 525.
Present: morn. 445; even. 559.
Average (12 *months*): 'as above'.
Remarks: The space allowed for each sitting is 17 inches. The Sunday
Scholars do not attend Divine Service together but with their friends.
> William James.   Deacon.
> Grocer.
> Tredegar Iron Works.

(28)   WELSH WESLEYAN CHAPEL, TREDEGAR.
Built 1810; rebuilt 1836.
Space: free 205; other 115; standing 400.
Present: morn. 145; aft. 175; even. 290.
Average: general congregation 300; scholars 160.
> Daniel Lewis.   Local Preacher.
> Castle Street, Tredegar.

(29)   SHARON.   INDEPENDENT CHAPEL.
Erected 1819.
Space: free 9 pews; other 60 pews; standing 600.
Present: morn. 400 + 150 scholars; aft. 367 scholars; even. from 800 to
900.

Average (6 *months*): general congregation from 650 to 750; scholars from 320 to 380.

David Evans.   Minister.

(30)   WESLEYAN CHAPEL (ENGLISH), TREDEGAR.
Erected 1825.
Space: free 250; other 210; standing 40.
Present: morn. 170 + 70 scholars; aft. 70 scholars; even. 435.
Average (6 *months*): general congregation 300; scholars 70.

Thomas Pugh.   Trustee and Circuit Steward.
Draper.

(31)   EBENEZER PRIMITIVE METHODIST CHAPEL, TREDEGAR.
Erected 1846.
Space: free 100; other 150; standing includes aisles and lobby 140.
Present: morn. 51 + 32 scholars; even. 103 + 25 scholars.
Average (12 *months*): morn. 60 + 48 scholars; even. 180 + 20 scholars.

George Price.   Minister.
High Street, Tredegar.

(32)   ADULAM CHAPEL, TREDEGAR.   INDEPENDENT OR CONGREGATIONAL.
Erected 1848.
Space: free 266; other 252; standing 100.
Present: morn. 143; even. 215.
Average: morn. 160; aft. 111 scholars; even. 230.

William Williams.   Minister.

(33)   ENGLISH BAPTIST CHAPEL, CHURCH STREET. TREDEGAR.
Erected 1829.
Space: free 140; other 110.
Present: morn. 120 + 10 scholars; aft. 'no service'; even. 140.
Average (12 *months*): morn. 129 + 10 scholars; even. 140.

William Morgan.   Deacon.

(34)   SALEM CHAPEL, TREDEGAR.   CALVINISTIC METHODIST.
Erected 1840.
Space: free 100; other 150.
Present: morn. 120; even. 150.
Average (12 *months*): morn. 130; even. 160.

David Morgan.   Deacon.

2   Ushlawrcoed Hamlet.
Popn. 8,351 males, 7,073 females: total 15,424.

[End of Tredegar Subdistrict]

7   7 ROCK BEDWELLTY (Subdistrict)
Area: (included under Tredegar Subdistrict [578. 6]: *Popn.* 1,391 males, 1,248 females: total 2,639.

1   Hamlet of Islawrcoed (part of Bedwellty Parish):
Popn. as for the Subdistrict.

(1)   BEDWELLTY PARISH CHURCH.
According to tradition it was erected in the seventh century.
Space: free 400; other 200.
Usual number present: from 80 to 100. Morn. 'once a month the Duty is held': aft. 90; even. nil.
Remark: No Sunday School at present.
                                        Informant: Evan Jones.

[Informant's form]

Lewis: no entry.

E.R.C.R. perpetual curacy: patron and appropriator, the Bishop of Llandaff: net income £68. *Tithes* 1844: appropriated tithes commuted for £320. 16. 4.

C & C: 1 service in Welsh taken by the incumbent.

I & C: incumbent resident.

(2)   CWM Y GELLY EPISCOPAL CHAPEL.
Erected 1841.
Space: free 80; other 40.
Usual number present: from 60 to 80; morn. 70; aft. nil; even. 'occasionally'.
Remark: No Sunday School held here.
                                        Informant: Evan Jones.
[Informant's form]

C & C: 2 services, of which 1 in Welsh taken by the incumbent.

(3)   ARGOED CHAPEL.   BAPTIST.
Erected 1817.
Space: free 170; other 55; standing 135.
Present: morn. 149; even. 265.
Average (12 *months*): morn. 150; even. 260.
                        John Jarman.   Minister.

(4)   LATTER DAY SAINTS.
Private House.
Space: standing 100.
Present: morn. 30 scholars; aft. 60; even. 45.
Average (5 *months*): general congregation 50; scholars 30.
                        Evans Evans.   Elder.
                        Coal Miner, near the Rock, Blackwood.

(5) ROCK CHAPEL.   WELSH CALVINISTIC METHODIST.
Erected 1839.
Space: free 90; other 50; standing 50.
Present: aft. 70; even. 60.
Average (12 *months*): aft. 80; even. 70; scholars 'in the above'.

> Evans Jones.   Elder.
> Blackwood.

(6) BLACKWOOD WESLEYAN CHAPEL.
Erected 1828.
Space: free 60; other 75.
Present: morn. 60; even. 81.
Average (12 *months*): scholars 30.
Remarks: The Chapel is 24 ft. 6 ins wide by 28 ft 6 ins long. Afternoon
School, 30 children, attends every Sunday.

> John Waters.   Superintendant of the
> School.
> Seedsman.
> Blackwood.

(7) REHOBOTH PRIMITIVE METHODIST.
Erected 1843.
Space: free 81; other 52. 'We accomodate over floor with seats'.
Present: aft. 34 + 15 scholars; even. 58 + 12 scholars.
Average (12 *months*): aft. 50; even. 70.

> William Hallwood.   Steward.
> Blackwood.

(8) LIBANUS BAPTIST CHAPEL.
Erected 1833.
Space: free 110; other 28; standing 100.
Present: morn. 75; even. 94.
Average (12 *months*): morn. 80; even. 100.

> William Jenkins.   Deacon.
> Blackwood.

(9) SALEM.   INDEPENDANTS.
Erected 1829.
Space: free 19 pews; other 16 pews.
Present: morn. 200; aft. 88 scholars; even. 240.
Average (12 *months*): morn. 250; aft. 90 scholars; even. 300.

> Benjamin Lewis.   Minister.
> Pontmaenpengam, near Blackwood.

(10)   BRYMESAR BAPTIST CHAPEL, PONTMAENPENGAM.
Erected 1828.
Space: all free sittings 200.
Present: aft. 90 scholars; even. 131.
Average (6 *months*): general congregation, evening average 130; scholars average per Sunday 90.

> James Davies His Mark, by authority
> from John Jenkins, Hengoed.

(11)   RHIW AMROTH CHAPEL.   PARTICULAR BAPTISTS.
Erected 1839.
Space: free 70; other 56.
Average (12 *months*): morn. 60; even. 100.

> Edmund Evans.   Deacon.
> Blackwood.

[End of Rock Bedwellty Subdistrict and end of Abergavenny District]

579   PONTYPOOL (District)

Area: 51,429 acres. *Popn.* 14,563 males, 13,430 females: total
27,993.

1 PONTYPOOL (Subdistrict)
Area: 20,434 acres. *Popn.* 10,690 males, 9,924 females: total 20,614.

1   Llanhilleth Parish.
Area: 2,013 acres. *Popn.* 509 males, 390 females: total 899.

(1)   CRUMLIN CHURCH OF ENGLAND LICENSED SCHOOLROOM.
Licensed 1846.
Cost defrayed: by parliamentary grant £150; voluntary subscription £200.
Space: free 80.
Present: even. 30 + 20 scholars.
Average (2 months): even. 40 + 15 scholars.

James Hughes.   Licensed Minister.

(2)   LLANHILLETH PARISH CHURCH.
Space: free 50; other 15.
Present: morn. 14 + 31 scholars; aft. 12.
Average (3 months): morn. 18 + 25 scholars; aft. 10.

James Hughes.   Rector.

Lewis: discharged rectory, valued at £7. 15. 7½; patron, the Earl of Abergavenny;
tithes commuted for £22 to an impropriator and £75 to the rector: glebe of 85
acres.

C & C: 2 services, 1 in Welsh performed by the incumbent.

I & C: incumbent resident: curate has stipend of £70.

(3)   WESLEYAN CHAPEL.
Erected 1850.
Space: free 70; other 2.
Present: morn. 16; aft. 14.
Average: same.

Henry Crook.   Local Preacher.
Mellon Square, Commercial Street,
Newport.

(4)   EBENEZER BAPTIST CHAPEL.
Erected 1838.
Space: free 500.
Present: morn. 123; even. 210.

William Morgan.   Secretary.

2   Trevethin Parish (with Pontypool)
Area: 11,329 acres. *Popn.* 8,720 males, 8,144 females: total 16,864.

(5)   ST. JAMES' CHAPEL.
A Chapel of Ease consecrated 1821 in lieu of a previously existing one.
Erected partly by private Subscription, partly by Society for Building and
Enlarging Churches. Total cost £1,100.
Endowed: parliamentary grant £61. 16. 2.
Space: free 350.
Present: morn. 160; even. 320.
Average: morn. 180; even. 300.

George Jones.   Curate.

Lewis: separate incumbency at Pont-y-pool.

C & C: 2 services in English.

I & C: incumbent resident.

ICBS: grant of £350 in 1818.

(6)   TALYWAUN, ABERSYCHAN.   A CHURCH OR CHAPEL OF ABERSYCHAN.
It is called 'church' by the Commissioners for Building new Churches; it
is called Chapel in the Gazette publishing the assignment of a District by the
Queen in Council.
Consecrated Novr. 10th 1832 as a new Church, there having been no Church
previously in the District. The Revd. David Jones, then Curate of Treve-
thin exerted himself greatly in obtaining subscriptions. Mr. E. Haycock,
Architect, John Lane, Builder.
Cost defrayed by Church Building Society £1,000; Parochial Rate nil;
Subscriptions £600, Total £1,600.
Endowed: permanent endowment £84 per annum; pew rents £9. 2. 6; fees
£8.4; other sources £40.
Space: free 334; other 166.
Present: morn. 98 + 92 scholars; aft. 146 scholars; even. about 300 or
upwards.
Remarks: On Question 5 [how endowed] the £40 is by annual grant and may
be withdrawn at Easter. On Question 6 [*space*] I have calculated some free
seats and pews to hold 5 on which 6 sometimes are seated and others are
10 which will hold 12. This would increase the number of free sittings to
400, other sittings 588.

[Note attached]   As it bears on the general subject of the population of the

District I think it right to add a few words on the answer on the second division of No. VII [average attendance]. Yesterday's attendance at Church was less than usual even at the time of the year as on Mid Lent Sunday there is a Custom of visiting their parents and this was the case with some families yesterday causing their absence. As many of the congregation come from the distance the attendance is not so large in winter as in summer. Another circumstance which would account for the difference in number is the present depression in the Iron Trade. Not long since there were 12 Blast Furnaces working in this District, now there are only 7 and this according to the common computation would mean a difference of from two to three thousand persons in the District, including workmen and their families.

Thomas Bluett, B.A. Perpetual Curate.

Lewis: patron, the incumbent of Trevethin.

C & C: 2 services, both English.

I & C: incumbent not resident.

(7)   TREVETHIN PARISH CHURCH.
It is right to remark on this Enquiry [when consecrated] that this Parish Church was entirely rebuilt in the year 1847 at a cost of £2,700, by a Parish Rate of £220, and £200 from the Incorporated Society, the rest of the money voluntarily subscribed.
Endowed: tithe £566; fees £30; Easter offerings £6.
Space: free 600; other 266.
Present: morn. 400 + 200 scholars; aft. 250 scholars; even. 500 in a licensed Schoolroom.
Remarks: In the morning and afternoon Divine Services are performed at the Parish Church, but in the evening at a licensed schoolroom in the town of Pontypool, but all the Congregations are those of the Church of England. The above return shows also an annual income of nearly £600, but the deduction by way of Money Rates, Taxes, Curate's stipend and Interest and Instalment upon money under Gilbert's Act to build a Parsonage House to nearly £300 per annum.

Thomas Davies, M.A.
Incumbent Minister.

Lewis: perpetual curacy, in the gift of the Bishop of Llandaff: church rebuilt in 1846.

Tithes 1844: £56. 10. 10. to appropriators, £566. 17. 2. to the incumbent, and £53. 11. 9. to lay impropriators.

C & C: 1 service in English.

I & C: incumbent resident.

ICBS: 1st grant of £100 in 1827, 2nd. grant of £200 in 1845.

(8)   PONTNEWYNYDD DISTRICT PARISH under the provisions of 6 and 7 Victoria c.37. An additional church consecrated November 1844. Erected by Private Subscription; total cost £950.
Endowed: permanent endowment £60; pew rents £12; fees £2.
Space: free 350; other 60.
Present: morn. 300 + 70 scholars; even. 380 + 25 scholars.
Average: morn. 300 + 80 scholars; even. 380 + 20 scholars.

Owen T. H. Phillips.
Incumbent Minister.

C & C: 1 chapel, 2 services both in English.

I & C: incumbent resident.

(9)   SCHOOL ROOM, HIGH STREET, PONTYPOOL.   CHURCH OF ENGLAND.
Erected in summer 1838.
Space: All free sittings and accomodation for 500 people, adults and children, is provided, and it is generally as full as it can well hold.
Uusual number present: Always full to overflow with very rare exception as on very wet days.
Remarks: There is no morning service but always used for the Sunday School both morning and afternoon. As said above it is always crowded. The morning attendance is rather uncertain, much depending on the state of the weather, but the average number may be stated at about 160 boys and girls, but the afternoon often double that of the morning.

Informant: Thomas Davies, M.A.
Incumbent of Trevethin Parish and also the officiating Minister at the Town School room which is *not* a church but only a licensed room for Divine Worship.

[Informant's form]

(10)   PONTNEWYNYDD.   CHURCH OF ENGLAND.
Erected in 1840.
Space: free 60; other 340.
Usual number present: morn. 280 + 100 scholars; even. 360 + 30 scholars.

Informant: Owen T. H. Phillips.

[Informant's form.]

(11)   ENGLISH WESLEYAN CHAPEL, PONTYPOOL.
Erected 1814.
Space: free 210; other 190; standing 100.
Present: morn. 160 + 50 scholars; even. 350 + 50 scholars.
Remark: I say English Wesleyan Chapel because there is a Welsh Wesleyan Chapel in this Town of Pontypool.

George Burgess.   Trustee and Steward.

(12) TABERNACLE CHAPEL, PENYGARN, PONTYPOOL.   PARTICULAR BAPTIST.
Erected 1835.
Space: free 498; other 132.
Present: morn. 200 + 40 scholars; aft. 118 scholars; even. 320.
Remark: This church was formed in the 17th Century and in 1727 a chapel
was built about ½ mile out of Town called Penygarn. In consequence of the
distance the present place was erected in Town the old chapel still remaining
with a large burying ground attached.

> Benjamin Jones.   Senior Deacon.
> Grocer etc.
> Trosnant, Pontypool.

(13) SARDIS, TROSNANT, PONTYPOOL.   INDEPENDENT CHAPEL.
Erected before 1800; rebuilt 1823.
Space: free 140; other 70.
Present: morn. 160 + 30 scholars.

> Herbert Daniel.   Minister.
> Cefn-y-crib, near Pontypool.

(14) NODDFA CHAPEL, TREFETHIN.   BAPTIST.
Erected 1846.
Space: free 250; other 40.
Present: morn. 174; even. 174.
Average (12 *months*): morn. 274 + 200 scholars; even. 274 + 200 scholars.
Remarks: The reason for the disproportion between the average attendance
at "Noddfa" Chapel and the attendance on 30th March 1851 is the present
stagnation of Abersychan Iron Works and the consequent poverty of the
population and the removal of others to their localities.

> Edward Roberts.   Minister.
> Talywaen, near Pontypool.

(15) REHOBOTH, CRANES STREET.   WELSH CALVINISTIC METHODIST.
Erected about the year 1821.
Space: free 230; other 63; standing 157.
Present: morn. 116; aft. 105 scholars; even. 136.
Average: general congregation 158; scholars 125.
Remarks: The services are held in Welsh (except occasionally in English).
One sermon in the morning Sunday School at 2 and another sermon at 6
o'clock with two services in the week regularly and more occasionally.
P.S. A prayer meeting at 7 o'clock in the Sunday morning.

> William Brown.   Minister.
> Penytranch, Pontypool
> to be left at John Morgan, Grocer, Pontypool.

(16) TABERNACLE, GARNDDIFFAETH. CALVINISTIC METHODIST.
Erected 1827.
Space: free 102; other 90; standing 452.
Present: morn. 138; even. 250.
Average: general congregation 250; scholars 180.

>Thomas Jones. Trustee Stewart.
>Cwmfroodbaileg.

(17) SARDIS, GARNDIFFETH. INDEPENDENT CHAPEL.
Erected 1827.
Space: free 200; other 170.
Present: morn. 184 + 100 scholars; aft. 126 scholars; even. 243.
Remarks: The attendance on Sunday March 30th is a fair average of general
Congregation and Sunday Scholars for several years past.

>Morris Jones. Minister.
>Garndiffeth

(18) WESLEYAN METHODIST CHAPEL, PONTNEWYNYDD.
Erected 1850.
Space: free 180; other 80; standing 120.
Present: morn. Sunday School; aft. 100; even. 200.

>William Fleetwood. Trustee.

(19) WESLEYAN METHODIST CHAPEL, ABERSYCHAN.
Erected 1829.
Space: free 284; other 344; standing 200.
Present: morn. 450 + 249 scholars; even. 560.

>James Morgan. Chapel Steward.
>Abersychan.

(20) GARNIFFAITH WESLEYAN METHODIST CHAPEL.
Erected 1840.
Space: free 406; other 344; standing 250.
Present: morn. 300 + 200 scholars; even. 500 + 200 scholars.

>Meshach Cook. Trustee and Steward.
>Garndiffaeth.

(21) ENGLISH WESLEYAN CHAPEL.
Erected 1823.
Space: free 130; other 146; standing 120.
Present: morn. 150; aft. Sunday School; even. 270.
Average: general congregation 150; scholars 165.
Remarks: I mentioned English because there is a Welsh Chapel of the
same denomination.

>John Vipond. Trustee and Steward.
>Varteg Hill.

(22) BAPTIST CHAPEL, CRANE STREET, PONTYPOOL.
Erected 1847.
Space: free 100; other 200.
Present: morn. 110 + 30 scholars; aft. no service; even. 152.
Average (12 *months*): morn. 120 + 30 scholars; even. 200.
Remarks: The smallness of Congregation on 30th March is to be accounted for on account of the stated Pastor being absent that day. I have therefore given the general average for the twelve months in the under column.
P.S. the evening attendance included children above 12 years or thereabouts say about one 8ths. The School does not attend in the evening as such.

> Charles Davies. Deacon.
> Ironmonger, Pontypool.

(23) ST. ALBAN'S CATHOLIC CHURCH, PONTYPOOL.
Erected 1846.
Space: free 240; standing 60.
Present: morn. 280; aft. 50.
Average: morn. 300.

> William L. Woollett. Catholic Priest.

(24) WELSH WESLEYAN METHODIST CHURCH.
Erected 1839.
Space: free 230; other 20.
Present: morn. 16; aft. 44 scholars; even. 69.
Average: morn. 25; aft. 24 scholars; even. 60.

> William Rosser. Trustee and Steward.

(25) WELSH WESLEYAN METHODIST CHAPEL, VARTEG.
Erected 1829.
Space: free 160.
Present: morn. 57; aft. 60 scholars; even. 40.
Average (12 *months*): morn. 40; aft. 60 scholars; even. 40.

> David Williams. Steward.
> Garnddiffaeth.

(26) PROVIDENCE CHAPEL, GEORGE STREET, PONTYPOOL. INDEPENDENTS.
Erected 1833.
Space: free 270.
Present: morn. 84 + 46 scholars; aft. 97 scholars; even. 86.
Average: morn. about 80 + 40 scholars; aft. 70 scholars; even. 150.
Remarks: Being Middle Lent Sunday a much less congregation than usual. A day of visiting friends.

> Jonas Reddle. Pastor.
> Glanant Cottage, Pontypool.

(27)   SALEM PRIMITIVE METHODIST CHAPEL, HIGH STREET, PONTYPOOL.
Erected 1849.
Space: free 99; other 141.
Present: morn. 80 + 35 scholars; aft. 40 scholars; even. 200.

> William Harvey.   Minister.
> Sow Hill, Pontypool.

(28)   BETHEL CHAPEL, GARNDIFFAITH.   PRIMITIVE METHODISTS.
Erected 1849.
Space: free 110; other 140.
Present: morn. 110 scholars; aft. 110 + 109 scholars; even. 200.
Average (12 *months*): morn. 120 scholars; aft. 145 scholars.

> William Harvey.   Minister.
> Sow Hill, Pontypool.

(29)   PRIMITIVE METHODIST CHAPEL, ABERSYCHAN.
Erected 1832.
Space: free 162; other 88.
Present: morn. 100 + 140 scholars; aft. 151 scholars; even. 250.

> Thomas Giles.   Minister.
> Abersychan, Pontypool.

(30)   TROSNANT CHAPEL, PONTYPOOL.   BAPTIST.
Erected 1776.
Space: free 186; other 192.
Present: morn. 266 + 60 scholars; aft. 103 scholars; even. 290.
Remark: There is another Sunday School in connecton with this Chapel held at the Race, in the parish of Panteague: number of scholars on March 30, morn. 116, aft. 163. Also a Vestry in connection with the chapel not specified in VII [Space available]. The galeries will hold 250.

> David Lloyd Isaac.   Minister.

(31)   ZION CHAPEL, TROSNANT.   BAPTIST.
Erected 1844.
Space: free 380; other 140.
Present: morn. 250 + 80 scholars; aft. 130 scholars; even. 350.
Average (6 *months*): morn. 250 + 80 scholars; aft. 130 scholars; even. 300.
Remarks: Believing the principles of Nonconformists to be in accordance with the New Testament we hail their progress and dissemination and cannot refrain expressing an opinion that the Union of Church and State forms a barrier thereto.

> Joseph Davies.   Trustee.
> Albion Road, Pontypool.

(32) CAPEL-YR-YNYS CHAPEL.   INDEPENDENT.
Erected 1832.
Space: free 81; other 32; standing 30.
Present: morn. 61; aft. 63 scholars; even. 80.
Average: morn. 80; aft. 63 scholars; even. 120.

Herbert Daniel.   Minister.
Cefn y crib near Pontypool.

(33) BIBLE CHRISTIANS, PONTNYMYNYDD.
Space: free 100.
Present: morn. 21; even. 40.

William Gilbert.   Minister.
At Mr. Hodges' Grocer, Pontypool.

(34) BAPTIST CHAPEL.
Erected 'since 1800'.
Space: free 150; other 150.
Present: aft. 64 + 92 scholars.
Average (12 *months*): aft. 30 + 70 scholars.

Llewellyn Thomas. Son of the Minister.
Baptist College, Pontypool.

(35) EBENEZER CHAPEL, PONTYPOOL.   INDEPENDENT.
Erected 1742.
Space: free 245; other 139; standing 'only in the Alleys'.
Present: morn. 202; aft. 121 scholars; even. 205.
Average (12 *months*): aft. 100 scholars.
Remarks: N.B. Sittings on the gallery are all free, and 62 on the floor,
allowing 18 inches for each, 245 in all free. It is very difficult to state the
exact number of the attendants for many do attend in the morning only. I
think that about one third of the evening congregation do not attend the
morning service if not above that number generally. I do not wish to be
above the mark.

Evan Rowlands.   Minister.

(36) ABERSYCHAN CHAPEL.   ENGLISH BAPTIST.
Erected 1827.
Space: free 200; other 100. Standing 130.
Present: morn. 147; even. 270.
Remarks: Dimensions of Chapel. Ground floor in the clear 30 feet by 40.
Galary 13 feet by 30. Vestry 15 feet by 30.

Stephen Price.   Minister.
Abersychan.

(37)   WESLEYAN METHODIST CHAPEL, ABERSYCHAN.
Erected 1827.
Space: free 284; other 344; standing 200.
Present: morn. 450 + 249 scholars; aft. 'Sunday School'; even. 560.

> James Morgan.   Chapel Steward.
> Abersychan.

(38)   SILOH INDEPENDENT CHAPEL, ABERSYCHAN.
Erected 1837.
Space: free 45; other 18.
Present: morn. 35 + 30 scholars; aft. 40 scholars; even. 40.
Remarks: Minister apsent.

> Thomas Williams.   Deacon.

(39)   INDEPENDENTS ROOM, ABERSYCHAN.
Began Jan. the 6, 1850.
Present: morn. 30 scholars; aft. 55 + 38 scholars; even. 70 scholars.

> Benjamin Nicholas.   Superintendant.
> British Iron Works.

(40)   VARTEG CHAPEL.   WESLEYAN METHODIST.
Erected 1829.
Space: free 108.
Present: morn. 57; even. 21.
Average (12 *months*): morn. 40 + 45 scholars; aft. 50 scholars; even. 50.

> David Williams.   Society Steward.
> Garnddiffaith.

(41)   PISGAH.   PARTICULAR BAPTISTS.
Erected 187.
Space: free 457; other 215; standing 240.
Present: morn. 314; aft. 216 scholars; even. 480.
Average: morn. 450; even. 600.
Remarks: The reason of the falling off in our Congregation is the depression that has been [in] the Iron Trade. 4 of the furnaces in the British Works going out of blast.

> William Thomas.   Minister.
> Talywaun.

(42)   ENGLISH PARTICULAR BAPTIST CHAPEL, ABERSYCHAN.
Erected 1827.
Space: free 250; other 100; standing 100.
Usual number present: morn. 150 + 120 scholars; even. 270.
Remarks: A day school has also been kept in the Vestry.

> *Informant:* Rev. Stephen Price.
> Baptist Minister.
> Abersychan.

[Informant's form.]

(43) PROVIDENCE CHAPEL, PONTYPOOL. ENGLISH INDEPENDENTS.
Erected 1833.
pace: free 200; other 100.
Usual number present: morn. 60 + 60 scholars; even. 150.
                              Informant: J. Keddle, V.D.M.
[Informant's form.]

(44) ENGLISH WESLEYANS, SOWHILL.
Erected 1814.
Space: free 237; other 163.
Usual number present: 150 + 70 scholars; aft. 100 scholars; even. 250
scholars.
                              Informant: George Kevern.
[Informant's form.]

3 Mamhilad Parish.

Area: 1,987 acres. *Popn.* 147 males, 150 females: total 297.

(45) MAMHILAD PARISH CHURCH.
Space: [information] refused.
Usual number of attendants: morn. 18 to 20; aft. 30 to 40. No Sunday
School.
Remarks: The incumbent refused to give any information but from enquiry
I understand the attendants at the Church are as above, the parish being
very small.
                              Informant: [illegible] Registrar.
[Informant's form.]
Lewis: perpetual curacy, lately united to the vicarage of Llanover [578. 3. 7(14)].
C & C: 1 service in English.
I & C: incumbent not resident.

4 Llanfihangel Pontymoil Parish.

Area: 1,651 acres. *Popn.* 99 males, 106 females: total 205.

(46) LLANFIHANGEL PONTYMOIL PARISH CHURCH.
Endowed: Queen Anne's Bounty £78; tithe in lieu of £8. 8; fees 15s.
Space: total 120.
Present: morn. 29.
Average: morn. 25 to 30.
Remarks: The parish is very thinly inhabited there is no other place of
worship in it than the Parish Church in which Divine Service is held every
Lord's Day.
                         Christopher Cook. Curate.
Lewis: perpetual curacy, net income £87: patron, Capel Hanbury Leigh, Esq.
C & C: 1 service in English.
I & C: incumbent not resident.

5   Panteague Parish.
Area: 3,454 acres. *Popn.* 1,215 males, 1,134 females: total 2,349.

(47)   PANTEAGUE PARISH CHURCH.
Endowed: glebe £30; tithe rent charge £339; fees £15 [? 15*s.*].
Space: total 270.
Present: morn. 170.
Average: morn. 172.
Renarks: There is another place within my Parish at which I officiate every
Sunday and Wednesday evenings, the average number attending which is
about 200.

David Jones.   Rector.

Lewis: discharged rectory, valued at £7. 10. 2½: patron, Capel Hanbury Leigh,
Esq: tithes commuted for £331; glebe of 34 acres.

C & C: 1 service in English.

I & C: incumbent legally not resident.

(48)   IVY CHAPEL, PANTEG.   CHURCH OF ENGLAND.
Space: 250.
Present: even. 150.
Remarks: This building was used formerly as a meeting house by the
Quakers. It is now rented by the patron, Capel Hanbury Leigh, Esq.

David Jones.   Officiating Minister.

[Endorsed: See letter.]

Lewis: chapel situated at Pant-y-moile, formerly belonging to the Society of Friends.

[Note: Lewis also names a chapel at Pen-yr-heol built by Capel Hanbury Leigh,
Esq.]

(49)   NEW INN CHAPEL.   INDEPENDENTS.
Built 1756; rebuilt 1823.
Space: free 150; standing 'we have no such place in our chapel'.
Present: morn. 85; aft. 50 scholars; even. 88 [? 33].
Remarks: God save the Queen. No popery.

David Davies.   Minister.

(50)   KEMEYS COMMANDER PARISH CHURCH.
Endowed: land £49; permanent endowment £11.
Space: total 50.
Present: morn. 11 + 5 children.

J. P. R. Shepard.   Minister.

[This schedule has been wrongly numbered. It should be 579. 3. 6. Details
of the Parish are given below under 579. 3. 6(13).]

[End of Pontypool Subdistrict]

2 LLANGIBBY (Subdistrict)
Area: 12,635 acres. *Popn.* 1,934 males, 1,664 females: total 3,599.

[1-2] Llanvrechva Parish, consisting of [1] Upper Division and [2] Lower Division.

Area of the whole: 4,320 acres. *Popn.* 1,342 males, 1,160 females: total 2,502.

1 Llanfrechfa Parish, Upper Division.
Popn. 855 males, 662 females: total 1,517.

(1) BETHEL CHAPEL. INDEPENDENT.
Erected 1837.
Space: free 124; other 40; standing 96.
Present: morn. 100 + 50 scholars; aft. 62; even. 150.
Average (12 *months*): morn. 110 + 45 scholars; aft. 70 scholars; even. 150.
Remarks: The inserted chapel has been purchased in 1837 for the sum of £220 which has been paid by a gent. named Edward Wrench from the same place and the annual expence towards suporting the cause is £76. 0. 0. beside other incidentary expense.

> Edward Williams.   Minister.
> Bron Heulog, Cwmbran.

(2) SILOAM CHAPEL, CWMBRAN.   BAPTIST.
Erected 1838.
Space: free 150; other 35.
Present: morn. 120; even. 150.

> Ebenezer Philip Williams.
> Baptist Minister.
> Cwmbrân.

(3) GREN-MEADOW-ROOM.   WESLEYAN METHODIST.
Erected 1850.
Space: free 50.
Present: morn. 40; aft. 52; no school.
Average: general congregation about 50.

> George Thomas.
> Hugh Carter, Wesleyan Minister.
> Pontypool.

[Endorsed: See letter.]

2 Llanfrechfa Parish.   Lower Division.
Popn. 487 males, 498 females: total 985.

(4)   LLANVRECGVA PARISH CHURCH.
Endowed: land £80; tithe £12; glebe £17; gross total 109.
Space: free 140; other 14.
Average attendants: morn. 90.
Remarks: The number of children attending the two schools amounts to about 55 or 60.

William Howell.   Incumbent.

[Endorsed: See letter.]

Lewis: perpetual curacy; net income £85; patrons and appropriators, the Chapter of Llandaff: tithes commuted for £348. 3; glebe of 6 acres.
C & C: 1 service in English.
I & C: incumbent not resident.
ICBS: grant of £60 in 1828.

(5)   PRIMITIVE METHODIST CHAPEL, CWMBRAN.
Erected 1844.
Space: free 74; other 26.
Present: morn. 32 scholars; aft. 37 scholars; even. 40.
Remarks: It is also let for a day school.

Elijah Filer.   Steward.
Square, Cwmbran.

(6)   PONTRHYDYRUN CHAPEL.   BAPTIST.
Erected 1815.
Space: free about 200 to 250; other about 200 to 250.
Present: morn. 160; even. 212.
Remarks: The Sunday Scholars do not sit separate from the Congregation and were therefore included with them.

David D. Evans.   Minister.
Pontrhydŷrun Works.

(7)   SION CHAPEL.   BAPTIST.
Erected about the year 1803.
Space: free 237; other 88; standing 57 ft. by 3 ft.
Present: morn. 200; even. 350.
Remarks: Size of Sunday School Room 50ft by 12ft about 7ft high. We have no day school belonging to Sion Chapel.

Reese Griffiths.   Minister.
Ponterw, Nr. Cairlion.

(8)   GREEN MEADOW CHAPEL.   WESLEYAN.
Erected 1850; a room in a dwelling house.
Space: all free; standing 30.
Present: morn. 40; aft. 50.
Average: general congregation 50; scholars none.

David Jones.   Steward.

[This is probably the same as (3) above.]

3 Llanthewy-vach Parish.
Area: 1,350 acres. *Popn.* 100 males, 85 females: total 185.

(9) LLANTHEWY-VACH PARISH CHURCH.
Endowed: Queen Anne's Bounty £69; tithe, in lieu of, £8; fees 8s.
Space: total 80.
Present: aft. 40.
Average: morn. from 25 to 30.
Remarks: The population being very small, the Church is the only place of worship in the Parish.

Christopher Cook.   Curate.

Lewis: perpetual curacy; patrons, Jesus College, Oxford: net income £77: appropriator, the Bishop of Llandaff: tithes commuted for £90.
C & C: 1 service in Welsh.
I & C: incumbent not resident: curate, who resides in Pontypool, has stipend of £30.

4 Llandegveth Parish.
Area: 789 acres. *Popn.* 64 males, 50 females: total 114.

(10) LLANDEGVETH PARISH CHURCH.
Endowed: tithe £120; glebe £40.
Space: free 40; other 40.
Present: morn. 40 + 10 scholars.

P. A. Williams.   Rector.
Caerleon.

Lewis: discharged rectory, valued at £4. 4. 9½; patron W. A. Williams, Esq.; tithes commuted for £120; glebe of 26 acres.
C & C: 1 service in English.
I & C: incumbent resident.

5 Llangibby Parish.
Area: 4,443 acres. *Popn.* 281 males, 255 females: total 536.

(11) LLANGIBBY PARISH CHURCH.
Endowed: tithe £400; glebe £85.
Space: free 56; other 138.
Present: morn. 76 + 30 scholars; aft. 40.
Average (6 months): morn. 83 + 40 scholars; aft. 32.
Remark: There is another newly finished school in the above parish containing 60 scholars who attend Sunday Scripture readings in the School room joined by a considerable congregation, the Church connected with it being not yet finished.

Charles A. Williams.   Rector.

Lewis: rectory, valued at £19. 10. 10: patron, W. A. Williams, Esq.; tithes commuted for £504. 7. 6; glebe of 75 acres.
C & C: 2 services in English.
I & C: incumbent resident.

(12) MAESLLECH CHAPEL.   CONGREGATIONAL OR INDEPENDENT.
Erected: No date.
Space: free 90; standing 30.
Present: morn. 26 + 10 scholars; even. 41.
Average (12 *months*)*:* general congregation from 25 to 50 morning, from 50 to 100 sometimes 120 Evenings when fine weather. Scholars from 16 to 20.
Remarks: There is 16 Scholars now belonging to Sabbath School, but only 10 in attendance on 30th. I cannot give an exact description of the average congregation, sometimes thin, at others chapel filled, have seen on some occasions upwards of 150 attending divine service.

Henry Kiddle.   Pastor.

(13) BETHEL CHAPEL.   CALVINISTIC BAPTIST.
Erected 1837.
Space: free 68; other 52; standing 80.
Present: morn. 50; even. 80.

Josiah Domoney.   Minister.
Bethel Chapel House, Llangibby.

6   Glascoed Hamlet being part of the Parish of Usk [579. 3. 1-2].
Area: 1,733 acres. *Popn.* 147 males, 115 females: total 262.

(14) GLASCOED CHAPEL OF EASE.
Consecrated on the 16th August 1849 by the Rt. Rev. E. Copleston Bishop of Llandaff as an additional Church. Erected by private benefaction at a total cost of £350.
Present: aft. 96.
Average: aft. 80.
Remarks: Tradition says an ancient chapelry existed here but there are no remains. There are 12*a.* Or. 13*p.* of glebe land and £92 10*s* rent charge in the possession of laymen, viz. His Grace the Duke of Beaufort and Mr. Davies of Stourbridge.

William Evans.   Vicar of Usk.

[End of Llangibby Subdistrict]

3 USK (Subdistrict)
Area: 18,360 acres. *Popn.* 1,939 males, 1,851 females: total 3,780.

[1-2] Part of the parish of Usk, consisting of [1] Usk, and [2] Gwehellog Hamlet.
Area of the whole: 2,223 acres. *Popn.* 903 males, 873 females: total 1,776.

1 Usk.
Area: 404 acres. *Popn.* 738 males, 714 females: total 1,452.

(1) St. Mary's Church, Usk.
Endowed: land £9; tithe £285; glebe £2.
Space: free 300; other 450.
Present: morn. 250 + 70 scholars; even. 550.
Average: morn. 250 + 70 scholars; even. 550.
Renarks: [Income] subject a variation according to corn averages which this year is 3¼ per cent below £100. The School children do not attend in ye evening.

William Evans. Vicar.

Lewis: discharged vicarage, valued at £10. 10; patron, W. Addams Williams, Esq.: impropriator, the Duke of Beaufort: net income £250.

C & C: 2 services in English.

I & C: incumbent not resident.

(2) St. Francis Xavier's Catholic Church, Usk.
Erected 1846.
Space: other sittings; the Porch.
Present: morn. 130; aft. 160.

Argius (Joseph Alexander). Priest.
[The schedule is dated 29 March.]

Lewis: opened in 1847.

(3) The Twyn Chapel. Independent.
Erected before 1800.
Space: free 30; other 85; standing 20.
Present: morn. 45 + 20 scholars; even. 50 + 20 scholars.
Average (12 months): morn. 45 + 20 scholars; even. 50 + 20 scholars.

Evan Jones. Deacon and Manager.
Bridge Street, Usk.

(4) Baptist Chapel, Usk.
Erected 1842.
Space: free 150; other 120.
Present: morn. 61 + 12 scholars; even. 96 + 12 scholars.
Average (6 months): morn. 60 + 20 scholars; even. 100 + 20 scholars.

John Jones. Minister.
Bank, Usk.

(5) Wesleyan Chapel, Middle Street.
Erected 1817.
Space: free 120; other 80.
Present: morn. 45; aft. 'school'; even. 70.

John Creese. Steward.

2 Gwehellog Hamlet.
Area: 2,819 acres. *Popn.* 165 males, 159 females: total 324.

(6) WESLEYAN CHAPEL, GWEHELOG.
Erected 1822.
Space: free 126.
Present: morn. 18; aft. 80.
Average (6 *months*): morn. 15; aft. 75.

> James Hughes. Steward.
> Trostrey.

3 Llanbaddock Parish.
Area: 3,465 acres. *Popn.* 216 males, 202 females: total 418.

(7) LLANBADDOCK PARISH CHURCH.
Endowed: land £70; fees £1.
Space: free 20; other 110.
Present: morn. 30.
Average (12 *months*): general congregation about 50.

> Incumbent. Arthur Williams.

Lewis: perpetual curacy; valued at £5. 8. 9; net income £72: patron, Rev. T. A. Williams; impropriator, the Duke of Beaufort.

C & C: 1 service in English.

I & C: incumbent not resident.

(8) GLASCOED CHAPEL, LANBADOCK. BAPTIST.
Erected 1821.
Space: free 200.
Present: morn. 41 + 25 scholars; even. 100.
Average (12 *months*): morn. 50 + 25 scholars; aft. 45 scholars; even. 150 + 40 scholars.
Remarks: The chapel is situated in the parish of Lanbaddock will contain about 200 persons and it is generally filled with hearers on Sunday evenings and we have also a school morning and evening. We have scholars† from this and from other adjoining parishes.

†hearers, attendants, and members.

> Joseph Lewis, Assistant Preacher
> for Revd. Rees Rees, Minister.

4 Monkswood. Extra Parochial.
Area: 1,030 acres. *Popn.* 85 males, 85 females: total 170.

(9)   MONKSWOOD CHAPEL.
Supposed to be a chapel planted by the Monks of Tintern Abbey though there are no data to establish it.
Endowed: land £68; permanent endowment £17.
Space: total 98.
Present: aft. 30 + 12 'children'.

J. P. R. Shepard.   Minister.

Lewis: perpetual curacy: net income £69; patron and impropriator, the Duke of Beaufort.

C & C: I service in English.

I & C: incumbent not resident.

5   Goytrey Parish.
Area: 3,332 acres. *Popn.* 300 males, 254 females: total 554.

(10)   GOYTREY PARISH CHURCH (ST. PETERS).
Erected 1846. (The old church was taken down and the new one erected in this year.)
Space: free 200; other 170.
Usual number present: morn. average 100; even. 70 to 100.

Informant: Charles Elias Bird.
Churchwarden.

[Informant's form.]

Lewis: discharged rectory; valued at £4. 7. 6; patron, the Earl of Abergavenny: tithes commuted for £295; glebe of 3 acres.

C & C: 2 services, 1 English entire.

I & C: incumbent resident.

ICBS: grant of £140 in 1845.

(11)   SARON BAPTIST CHAPEL, GOITRE.
Erected 1826.
Space: free 395; other 5.
Present: morn. 52; aft. 23 scholars; even. 109.
Average (12 *months*): morn. 60 to 70; aft. 60 scholars; even. 150.

John Jones.   Minister.
Goitre Wharf, Nr. Abergavenny.

[Endorsed: See letter.]

(12)   ED. CALVINISTIC METHODIST CHAPEL.
Erected 1808.
Space: free 150; standing 157.
Present: morn. 12 scholars; aft. 50.
Average: morn. 15 scholars; aft. 60.

Roger Thomas.   Minister.
Llangwilim Cottage, Ragland.

[i.e. Capel Ed, Goytre.]

6   Kemeys Commander Parish.

Area: 500 acres. *Popn.* 43 males, 42 females: total 85.

(13)   Kemeys Commander Church.
Space: free 14; other 28.
Average congregation: morn. from 12 to 25; aft. from 16 to 30; even. no
service.

Signed. J. P. R. Shepard.
Dated. 4th September 1852.

Note: for the original return, see 579. 1. 6(50), below. This schedule is
the return to a request for information; signed by the incumbent of
Monkswood.]

Lewis: perpetual curacy: patrons and impropriators, the family of Gore: tithes
commuted for £84; glebe of about 30 acres.

C & C: 1 service in English.

I & C: incumbent not resident.

7   Trostrey Parish.

Area: 1,255 acres. *Popn.* 79 males, 97 females: total 176.

(14)   Trostrey Parish Church.
Endowed: land £67; tithe rent £10; fees £1.
Space: free 50; other 70.
Present: aft. 56 + 11 scholars.
Average (12 *months*): general congregation 120 to 130.
Remarks: The 30th March is Mid Lent Sunday in this country called
'Mothering Sunday' when the people go to visit their mothers, so that the
congregation was far less than usual.

S. W. Gardiner.   Perpetual Curate.

Lewis: discharged perpetual curacy; valued at £3. 8. 11½: net income £72: patron
and impropriator, Sir S. Fludyer, Bart: tithes commuted for £202. 10s.

C & C: 1 service in English.

I & C: incumbent resident.

8   Gwernesney Parish.

Area: 543 acres. *Popn.* 29 males, 24 females: total 53.

(15)   Gwernesney Parish Church.
Present: morn. 18.
Average: morn. 20.

James Blower.   Curate.

Lewis: discharged rectory; valued at £2. 18. 6½: net income £112: patron, the
Duke of Beaufort.

C & C: 1 service in English.

I & C: incumbent not resident: curate, who resides in the glebe-house, has
stipend of £40.

9 Langeview Parish.
Area: 1,545 acres. *Popn.* 83 males, 99 females: total 182.

(16) LANGEVIEW PARISH CHURCH.
Present: morn. 25.
Average: morn. 30.

James Blower. Incumbent.

Lewis: perpetual curacy: net income £81: patron, incumbent, and impropriator, Rev. J. Blower.

C & C: 1 service in English.

I & C: incumbent not resident.

10 Llanllowell Parish.
Area: 796 acres. *Popn.* 44 males, 48 females: total 92.

(17) LLANLLOWELL PARISH CHURCH.
Endowed: tithe £105; glebe 50.
Space: free 10; other 40.
Present: even. 40 + 15 scholars.

J. A. Williams. Rector.

Lewis: discharged rectory; valued at £2. 13. 1½: parton and incumbent, Rev. J. A. Williams: tithes commuted for £205. 10; glebe of 22 acres.

C & C: 1 service in English.

I & C: incumbent resident.

11 Llantrissent Parish.
Area: 2,762 acres. *Popn.* 157 males, 117 females: total 274.

(18) LLANTRISSENT PARISH CHURCH.
Space: free 70; other 150.
Present: aft. 30 + 15 scholars.
Average (5 months): morn. 40.

Arthur Williams. Curate.

Lewis: discharged vicarage, with the perpetual curacy of Llantillio Pertholey [578.3. 1(1)] annexed: valued at £6. 8. 9: net income £131: patron, Rev. R. Davies.

C & C: 2 services in English.

I & C: incumbent resident: curate, who resides at Penhow, 1½ miles distant, has stipend of £70.

[End of Usk Subdistrict and end of Pontypool District]

Area: 110,255 acres. *Popn.* 22,594 males, 20,878 females: total 43,472.

1 CAERLEON (Subdistrict)
Area: 51,398 acres. *Popn.* 3,212 males, 3,156 females: total 6,368.

1   Llanvaches Parish.
Area: 2,108 acres. *Popn.* 161 males, 130 females: total 291.

(1)   Llanvaches Parish Church.
Endowed: tithe £194; glebe £20.
Space: total 90.
Present: aft. 53.
Average (6 *months*): morn. 45; aft. 33.
Remarks: Divine Service is held once a day morning and afternoon alternately.

> Edward [Griffiths].   Licensed Curate.

Lewis: discharged rectory; valued at £10; net income £194: patron, Sir Charles Morgan, Bart.

C & C: 1 service in English.

I & C: incumbent not resident: curate, who resides at Penhow [580. 1. 2.], 1½ miles distant, has stipend of £70.

(2)   Tabernacle Independent Church.
Erected 1800.
Space: free 150.
Present: morn. 45; even. 51.

> David Thomas.   Minister.
> Llanvaches.

(3)   Bethany Baptist Chapel.
Erected 1814.
Present: morn. total 58.

> Thomas Leonard
> Baptist Minister.

(4)   Gilgal Chapel, Llanvathas.   Bible Christians.
Erected 1828.
Space: free 2 pews; other 12 pews.
Present: aft. 38.

> David [illegible] His Mark. Steward.

2 Penhow Parish.

Area: 1,784 acres. *Popn.* 150 males, 129 females: total 279.
[No returns]

Lewis: discharged rectory, valued at £5. 4. 9½; patron, John Cave, Esq: tithes commuted for £180; glebe of 28 acres.

C & C: 2 services in English.

I & C: incumbent (R. J. Smith) resident.

3 Llanmartin with Llandevaud Parish.

Area: 941 acres. *Popn.* 108 males, 93 females: total 201.

(5) LLANDEVAUD.
An ancient chapelry rebuilt 1846.
Space: free 45; other 20.
Average number of attendants: aft. 50.

Signed. B. Samuel.   Registrar.

[Registrar's MS return]   Dated 12th January 1852.

Lewis: perpetual curacy; valued at £5; income £40: patron, the Prebendary of Warthacwm in the Cathedral of Llandaff. The chapel is in ruins and the inhabitants attend Llanmartin church.

C & C: 1 service in English.

I & C: incumbent not resident: curate has stipend of £80.

ICBS: grant of £60 in 1843.

(6) LLANMARTIN PARISH CHURCH.
Endowed: tithe £112; glebe £18.
Space: total 13.
Present: even. total 14.
Remarks: Llanmartin is served alternately with Wilcrick morning and evening.

John Callowhill.   Minister.

Lewis: discharged rectory with that of Wilerick [580. 1. 6(10)] annexed: valued at £4. 6. 10½; net income £208: patron, Thomas Perry, Esq.: tithes of Llanmartin commuted for £110; glebe of 20 acres.

C & C: 1 service in English.

I & C: incumbent resident.

(7) BETHEL CHAPEL.   CALVINISTIC METHODIST.
Erected 1838.
Space: free 120; other 80.
Present: morn. 50 + 20 scholars; even. 120.

B. Samuel.   Deacon.
Bishton Castle.

4 Llanwern Parish.
Area: 701 acres. *Popn.* 10 males, 19 females: total 29.

(8) LLANWERN PARISH CHURCH.
Endowed: glebe 16 acres; permanent endowment, 8 acres. Queen Anne's Bounty.
Space: total 100. All in pews.
Present: morn. 60.
Remarks: The Congregation consists of individuals from the adjoining parishes as in the parish the Mansion House and one cottage are the only dwellings.

Charles Salusbury.   Rector.
Llanwern House.

Lewis: discharged rectory; valued at £4. 0. 10.: patron, Sir Charles Salusbury, Bart.: tithes commuted for £82. 8s.: glebe of 16½ acres.

C & C: 1 service in English.

I & C: incumbent resident.

5 Bishton Parish.
Area: 1,211 acres. *Popn.* 114 males, 104 females: total: 218.

(9) BISHOPSTONE PARISH CHURCH.
Endowed: 'cannot say'; fees 10s.
Space: free 15; other 40.
Present: aft. 36 + 14 scholars.
Remarks: As Curate I am unable to give the requisite information with respect to the Endowment.

Thomas Williams.   Minister.

Lewis: perpetual curacy, in the patronage of the Archdeacon of Llandaff.

C & C: 1 service in English.

I & C: incumbent not resident: curate, who resides at Langstone, 1½ miles distant, has stipend of £50.

6 Wilcrick Parish.
Area: 406 acres. *Popn.* 13 males, 15 females: total 28.

(10) WILCRICK PARISH CHURCH.
Endowed: tithe £40; glebe £10; permanent endowment £22.
Space: total 5.
Present: no service.
Average (12 *months*): general congregation, total 6.

Remarks: Wilcrick is served every Sunday alternately with Lanmartin morning and evening.

John Callowhill.   Minister.

Lewis: sub. Wilerick: discharged rectory, annexed to that of Llanmartin [580. 1. 3(6)], valued at £2. 10. 2¼: tithes commuted for £38; glebe of 13 acres.

C & C: 1 service in English.

[8-9] Magor Parish, consisting of [8] Magor, and [9] Redwick Chapelry.

Area of the whole: 10,514 acres. *Popn.* 353 males, 346 females: total 699.

8 Magor.

Area: 2,720 acres. *Popn.* 210 males, 208 females: total 418.

(11)   MAGOR PARISH CHURCH.

Space: free 132.

Present: morn. 60 + 30 scholars.

Average: morn. 80 + 30 scholars; aft. 90.

David Jones.   Curate.

Lewis: discharged rectory, valued at £7. 1. 0½: net income £285; patron and impropriator, the Duke of Beaufort.

C & C: 1 service in English.

I & C: sub. Magor with Rodwick: incumbent resident: curate has stipend of £120.

(12)   EBENEZER CHAPEL.   BAPTIST.

Erected 1816.

Used also as a day school.

Space: free 160; other 32; standing 30.

Present: morn. 50; even. 175.

Average: general congregation 175.

Thomas Leonard. Minister.

9 Redwick Chapelry.   Part of the Parish of Magor.

Area: 7,794 acres. *Popn.* 143 males, 138 females: total 281.

(13)   REDWICK PARISH CHURCH.

Space: free 84.

Present: aft. 27 + 12 scholars.

Average: 30 + 10 scholars; aft. 30 + 10 scholars.

D. Jones.   Curate.

Lewis: vicarage annexed to that of Magor [580. 1. 8(11)]: glebe of one acre.

C & C: 1 service in English.

I & C: see Magor above.

(14) Salem Chapel. Baptist.
Erected 1832.
Present: morn. 21 + 13 scholars; even. 68.

> Thomas Leonard. Baptist Minister.

10 Witson, or Whitson Parish.
Area: 1,073 acres. *Popn.* 43 males, 33 females: total 76.

(15) Witson Parish Church.
Space: free 30; other 4.
Usual number present: morn. 6.

> *Informant:* B. Samuel. Registrar.

[Registrar's form.]

Lewis: sub. Witston: discharged vicarage; valued at £6. 7. 8½: alternate patrons, Chapter of Llandaff and Provost of Eton College, the impropriators of the great tithes: net income £180.
C & C: 1 service in English.
I & C: incumbent not resident.

11 Goldcliff Parish.
Area: 14,262. *Popn.* 132 males, 131 females: total 263.

(16) Goldcliff Parish Church.
Space: 20 pews.
Average number present: alternate morning and afternoon 47; Sunday School 17.

> B. Samuel. Registrar.
> Dated: 12th January 1852.

[Registrar's MS return.]

Lewis: discharged vicarage, valued at £13. 2. 6: patrons and impropriators, Provost and Fellows of Eton College: great tithes commuted for £18, and the vicarial for £17. 5. 6.
C & C: 2 services in English.
I & C: incumbent not resident.

(17) Bethesda Church. Independent.
Erected about 1835.
Space: free about 82; other about 18.
Present: morn. 30; even. 35.
Average: general congregation [? Sunday School, aft.] about 20.
Remarks: In consequence of difficulties in way the above place has not been so well attend as in former years.

> Thomas Jones. Minister.
> Pegwelly.

(18) WESLEYAN.
Erected 1812. Not a separate building ["room" inserted].
Present: even. 38.
Average (12 *months*)*:* even. 40.

John Seys.

12 Nash Parish.
Area: 3,563 acres. *Popn.* 155 males, 156 females: total 311.

(19) NASH PARISH CHURCH.
Space: free 50.
Congregation including Sunday Scholars: 30 morning and afternoon alternative.

B. Samuel.
Dated. 9th September 1852.

[Form of Enquiry, dated 9 September 1852.]

Lewis: discharged vicarage, valued at £9. 15s.: income, £80: patrons and impropriators, Provost and Fellow of Eton College: great tithes commuted for £30, the vicarial for £26: glebe of 1½ acres.
C & C: 1 service in English.
I & C: incumbent not resident.

(20) BAPTIST CHAPEL.
Erected about the year 1822.
Space: free 93; other 45.
Present: morn. 38 + 36 scholars; even. 86.

Tom Jordan Thomas. Minister.

13 Christchurch Parish, including the Hamlet of Caerleon-ultra-Pontem.
Area: 5,757 acres. *Popn.* of Christchurch: 634 males, 662 females: total 1,396.
Popn. of Caerleon-ultra-Pontem: 179 males, 177 females: total 350.
Popn. of the whole: 813 males, 833 females: total 1,646.

(21) CHRISTCHURCH PARISH CHURCH.
Space: free 135; other 50.
Usual number of attendants: morn. 120; aft. 56.

Informant: B. Samuel.

[Informant's form.]

Lewis: discharged vicarage, valued at £13. 4. 2: in the patronage of Eton College; impropriate tithes commuted for £150, and the vicarial for £265; glebe of 90 acres, and glebe-house.
C & C: 2 services both in English.
I & R: incumbent resident.

(22)   CAERLEON VILLAGE CHAPEL.   INDEPENDENTS.
Erected 1840.
Space: free 100.
Present: even. 20.
Average: morn. 15; even. 20.
Remarks: No stated Pastor.

> John Miles.   Deacon.
> Priory Cottage, Christchurch.

14   Llangstone Parish.

Area: 1,314 acres. *Popn.* 124 males, 109 females: total 233.

(23)   LANGSTONE PARISH CHURCH.
Endowed: tithe £133; glebe £40; fees £1. 10.
Space: free 40; other 40.
Present: morn. 50 + 10 scholars.

> Thomas Williams.   Minister.

Lewis: discharged rectory, valued at £4. 1. 0½: net income £158: patrons, family of Gore: glebe of 50 acres.

C & C: 1 service in English.

I & C: incumbent resident.

15   Kemeys Inferior Parish.

Area: 1,676 acres. 54 males, 61 females: total 115.

(24)   KEMEYS INFERIOR PARISH CHURCH.
Space: free 30; other 5.
Average number attending divine service: morn. 18; aft. 25.

> Signed: B. Samuel.
> Dated: 12th January 1852.

[Registrar's MS return.]

Lewis: discharged rectory, valued at £16. 10. 5: patron, Rev. W. C. Risley: net ineome £130.

C & C: 1 service in English.

I & C: incumbent resident.

16   Tredunnock Parish.

Area: 1,393 acres. *Popn.* 88 males, 69 females: total 157.

(25) TREDUNNOCK PARISH CHURCH.
Space: free about 145; other 18.
Usual number of attendants: morn. 18; aft. 25.
                                    Informant: Edward Williams.
[Informant's form.]
Lewis: rectory, valued at £10. 0. 5; patron, Capel Hanbury Leigh, Esq.: tithes
commuted for £180; glebe of 46 acres.
C & C: 1 service in English.
I & C: incumbent resident: curate, who resides in the parish, has stipend of £50.

17 Llanhennock Parish.
Area: 1,506 acres. *Popn.* 109 males, 113 females: total 222.

(26) LLANHENOG PARISH CHURCH.
Endowed: land £36; tithe[?]; stipend £16.
Present: morn. 80 + 30 scholars.
                                    Incumbent: William Howell.
Lewis: perpetual curacy: net income £64: patrons and appropriators, Chapter of
Llandaff: tithes commuted for £150; glebe of 3½ acres.
C & C: 1 service in English.
I & C: incumbent resident.

[18-19] Llangattock Parish, consisting of [18] Llangattock, and [19] the town of Caerleon.
Area of the whole: 2,937 acres. *Popn.* 750 males, 789 feamles: total 1,539.

18 Llangattock Parish.
Popn. 128 males, 130 females: total 258.
[No returns]

19 Town of Caerleon.
Popn. 622 males, 659 females: total 1,281.

(27) CAERLEON CHURCH, IN THE TOWN OF CAERLEON.
Endowed: land £70; tithe £229; permanent endowment £17; fees etc.
£5.
Space: total 596.
Present: morn. 100 + 107 scholars; even. 180 + 87 scholars.
Average (12 months): morn. 120 + 107 scholars; even. 200 + 90 scholars.
                         David Jones. Minister.
Lewis: discharged vicarage, valued at £8. 1. 5½: net income £296: patrons and
appropriators, Bishop and Chapter of Llandaff.
C & C: 2 services in English.
I & C: incumbent resident.

(28) BAPTIST CHAPEL, CASTLE STREET, CAERLEON TOWN.
Erected 1764, enlarged 1821.
Space: free 130; other 220; standing 30 to 40.
Present: morn. 300; aft. 66 scholars; even. 320.
Average: morn. 310; aft. 79 scholars.

James Evans.   Minister.

(29) REHOBOTH.   PRIMITIVE METHODIST.   TOWN OF CAERLEON.
Erected 1844.
Space: free 60; other 40.
Present: morn. 35 + 10 scholars; aft. 12 scholars; even. 70 scholars.

Richard Jones.   Steward.

(30) WESLEYAN METHODIST.
Erected 1814.
Space: free 90; other 70; standing 30.
Present: morn. 60 + 30 scholars; aft. school.
Average (March): 60 + 30 scholars.
Remarks: We believe this to be a correct *act* of Congregation and School as far as can be ascertained at the present March 30 1851 [Signed] Wm. Jones, Jn. Green.

Wiliam Jones.   Chapel Steward.
Bootmaker.

[End of Caerleon Subdistrict]

2 NEWPORT (Subdistrict)

Area: 3,854 acres. *Popn.* 10,536 males, 9,743 females: total 20,279.

[1-2] St. Woollos Parish, consisting of [1] St. Woollos and [2] the Borough of Newport.
Area and *Popn.* as for the Subdistrict.

1 St. Woollos.
Popn. 270 males, 299 females: total 569.

(1) ST. WOOLLOS PARISH CHURCH.
Usual number of Attendants: 200.

(Unsigned).

[Informant's form.]

Lewis: discharged vicarage, with the perpetual curacy of Bettws [580. 3. 12(24)] annexed: valued at £7. 3. 11½: patron, Bishop of Gloucester and Bristol: great tithes commuted for £281, and the vicarial for £200.

C & C: 2 services in English.
I & C: incumbent resident: curate has stipend of £80.
ERCR: accom. 900.
ICBS: grant of £170 in 1819.

(2) PILLGWENLLY SCHOOL ROOM (DISTRICT OF ST. PAUL).
Used as a temporary place of worship in connection with the Church of
England.
Erected by Rowley Lascelles, Esq. [No date.]
Space: free 160.
Present: morn. 50 + 75 scholars; even. 160.
Average: morn. 50 + 69 scholars; even. 150.
Remarks: This small School room is to be replaced shortly with a church to
hold 660 people.
                              Henry Wybrow.
                              Perpetual Curate of St. Pauls.

ICBS: grant of £350 in 1851.

(3) WESLEYAN CHAPEL, PILLGWENLLY.
Erected 1828.
Space: free 290; other 350.
Present: morn. 152 + 51 scholars; even. 244.
                              Frederick Payne.   Minister.

(4) BAPTIST CHAPEL, COMMERCIAL ROAD.
Erected 1843.
Space: free 350; other 400.
Present: morn. 200; even. 300.
Average (12 *months*): morn. 200 + 117 scholars; even. 300 + 117 scholars.
                              David Edwards.   Minister.

(5) BIBLE CHRISTIAN CHAPEL.   COMMERCIAL ROAD.
Erected 1840.
Space: free 50; other 180.
Present: morn. 71; even. 84.
                              James [illegible].   Trustee.
                              No. 6 Portland Street.

(6) WESLEYAN REFORMERS.   PILLGWENLLY.
Erected 1850. Not used exclusively as a place of worship.
Space: free 225.
Present: morn. 65 + 110 scholars; even. 160 + 50 scholars.
Remarks: This Congregation consists mainly of Wesleyans who have been
expelled for disputing about matters of Discipline in Methodism.
                              John Cole.   Local Preacher and Tenant.
                              Pillgwenlly.

(7) Trinity Chapel, Pillgwenlly.   English Independents.
Erected 1844.
Space: free 48; other 106.
Present: morn. 15 + 32 scholars; even. 30 + 15 scholars.
Average (12 *months*): morn. 20 + 22 scholars; even. 26 + 11 scholars.
Alexander Bowman.   A member.
No. 10 Portland Street.

(8) Church of Jesus Christ of Latter Day Saints held at Sunderland Hall, Llanarth Street.
Rented from 3rd October 1847.
Space: Benches all free.
Present: morn. 60; aft. 200; even. 400. No scholars.

Jacob Jones.   President.
Thos. Roberts,
Shoemaker,
Top of Caroline Street,
Newport.

(9) Ebenezer Chapel, Commercial Street.   Welsh Calvinistic Methodist.
Erected 1839.
Space: free 150; other 80; standing 200.
Present: morn. 260; aft. 98; even. 201.
Remarks: above is an average.
Phillip John.   Deacon.
169 Commercial Street

(10) English Baptist Chapel, Commercial Street.
Erected 1829.
Space: free 250; other 324.
Present: morn. 350 + 82 scholars; aft. 183 scholars; even. 550.
Remarks: The attendance of the Sunday School very small on March 30th, only 183, whilst on March 23rd it was 221, and the average for the whole month including March 30th 196 ¾ and average afternoon attendance for the Qr ending March 30 is 208.
Mothering Sunday, a Welsh festival or custom *causes a smaller attendance today*.
William Allen.   Minister.
Storr Hill.

2 Newport Borough, Parish of St. Woollos.
Popn. 9,879 males, 9,444 females: total 19,323.

(11) ST. PAUL DISTRICT CHURCH.
Consecrated 1836 to supply the spiritual want of an increasing population.
Erected by the inhabitants of Newport and neighbourhood and Her
Majesty's Commission for building churches in populous places, at a total
cost of about £7,000.
Enwoed: permanent endowment £30; pew rents £220; fees £30.
Space: free 745; other 631.
Present: morn. 756 + 100 scholars; aft. 128; even. 660.
Average: morn. 770 + 130 scholars; aft. 150; even. 800.

Henry Wybrow.   Perpetual Curate.

Lewis: sub. Newport: net income £150: patron, Bishop of Llandaff.

C & C: 3 services in English.

I & C: incumbent resident: two curates have stipend of £90 each.

ICBS: grant of £500 in 1835.

(12) HOPE CHAPEL, COMMERCIAL STREET. CONGREGATIONAL INDEPENDENT.
Erected originally before 1810; in its present form in 1814.
Space: free 112; other 226.
Present: morn. 170 + 117 scholars; aft. 189 scholars; even. 210.

John Barfield, B.A.   Minister.
20 Llanarth St.

(13) [No name or title] Place: 34 LLANARTH STREET.

"CHRISTIANS", (simply). Acts XI. 26; 2 Cor. V. 17; 1 Cor. 1. 10-13;
Protestants.
Building not used exclusively as a place of worship.
Space: free 60.
Present: morn. 19; even. 19.
Average (12 *months*): morn. 18; aft. 3; even. 18.
Remarks: In some parts of England we are known by the designation
"Brethren".

John Skinner.   An Elder.
[The preliminary List gives (13) as Plymouth Brethren.]

(14) TABERNACLE CHAPEL.   CONGREGATIONAL OR INDEPENDENT.
Erected 1822.
Space: free 327; other 505.
Present: morn. 278 + 85 scholars; aft. 148 scholars; even. 513.

Thomas Gillman.   Minister.
No. 5 Great Dock Street.

(15)   Mariners' Church, Canal Side, Newport, used by all Dissenting Denominations.
Erected 1827.
Space: free 400.
Present: aft. 20.
Average (12 *months*): aft. 50.
Remarks: The place is fitted up entirely with benches, all free sittings, and the ministers of the various congregations alternately and gratuitously.

Thomas Turner.   Secretary.
Commercial Road.

(16)   M.ll Streel Chapel.   Independents.
Erected more than 200 years ago.
Space: free 150; other 50.
Present: morn. 14 + 6 scholars; even. 40 + 10 scholars.
Average (6 *months*): morn. 8 + 6 scholars; even. 25 + 10 scholars.
Remarks: There is no stated minister at present.

Lewis Edwards.   Deacon.
Bro-dawel, Nr. Newport.

(17)   St. Marie's Catholic Church.   [St. Woollos]
Erected 1839.
Space: free 300; other 600; standing 100.
Present: morn. Mass 400, 2 Do 900; aft. 200; even. 700.

Dominick [?Martin].   Parish Priest.
[The number of the parish is given as 1—i.e. St. Woollos.]

(18)   Wesleyan Methodist Chapel, Commercial Street. (St. Woollos)
Original building erected 1808; present building on same site 1850.
Space: free 300; other 900.
Present: morn. 240 + 40 scholars; even. 390.

Edward William Jones.
Chapel Steward.
Glan Môr.
[The number of the parish is given as 1—i.e. St. Woollos.]

(19)   Mount Zion Chapel, Hill Street, Newport.   Independent.
Erected 1835.
Present: morn. 156; aft. 78 scholars; even. 189.
Average (12 *months*): general congregation 186; scholars 88.

Griffith Griffiths.   Minister.

(20) WELSH BAPTIST CHAPEL, CHARLES STREET, NEWPORT.
Erected 1817.
Space: free 400; other 200; no standing except in the aisles.
Present: morn. 280; aft. 150 scholars; even. 300.
Remarks: The Congregation on the preceding Sunday (March 30) being considerably less than usual the average number must be something more.

William Thomas. Minister.

(21) WESLEYAN CHAPEL OF THE FREE CHURCH OR REFORM WESLEYANS, HILL STREET.
Erected in the year 1832 and undergoing enlargement at the present time.
Space: free 200; other 250; standing 500.
Present: morn. 145; aft. 70 scholars; even. 249.
Remarks: This Congregation is one formed of persons who have been expelled from the old Wesleyan body in consequence of their disapproval of the acts of the Conference in the year 1849 and also of persons who have retired with them together with such as have since joined them.

James Ewins. Senior Local Preacher
and Class Leader.
13 High Street.

(22) LATTER DAY SAINTS CHAPEL.
Not a separate and entire building.
Space: free 300.
Usual number: morn. 100 + above 30 scholars; aft. 100; even. 160 + about 30 scholars.

Informant: no signature.
[Informant's form. Endorsed: See letter.]

[End of Newport Subdistrict]

3 ST. WOOLLOS (Subdistrict)
Area: 29,962 acres. *Popn.* 4,069 males, 3,690 females: total 7,759.

1 St. Bride Wentllooge Parish.
Area: 3,594 acres. *Popn.* 141 males, 126 females: total 267.

(1) ST. BRIDE'S WENTLLOOGE PARISH CHURCH.
Endowed: land £30; tithe £40; glebe £2.
Space: free 140.
Present: aft. 24.
Average (12 *months*): morn. 49; aft. 49.

Remarks: The church is situated in the Moors, consequently it is almost inaccessible on wet weather which accounts for the fewness of the congregation on the present occasion.

Morgan Powell.   Minister.

Lewis: vicarage, with the living of Coedkernew [580. 3. 4(9)] united; valued at £4. 18. 1½: patron and appropriator, Bishop of Llandaff: impropriate tithes commuted for £62. 4, and the vicarial for £41. 19: glebe of one acre.

C & C: 1 service in English.

I & C: incumbent resident.

(2)   REHOBOTH BAPTIST CHAPEL, ST. BRIDES.
Erected 1837.
Space: free 72; other 12; standing 100.
Present: morn. 60 + 30 scholars; even. 90.
Average: morn. 50 + 25 scholars; even. 80.

Daniel Jones.   Deacon.

(3)   PROVIDENCE INDEPENDENT CHAPEL, SAINT BRIDES.
Erected 1826.
Space: free 96.
Present: morn. 38 + 47 scholars; even. 83 + 16 scholars.
Average (12 *months*): morn. 49 + 41 scholars; aft. 35 + 37 scholars; even. 80 + 46 scholars.
Remarks: Afternoon service every other Sunday. Attendants at Divine Service and Sunday School more or less according to the weather owing to the overflowing of the water.

Isaac Harries.   Minister.

2   Peterstone Parish.

Area: 3,234 acres. *Popn.* 70 males, 81 females: total 151.

(4)   PETERSTONE WENTLLWG PARISH CHURCH.
Endowed: land £33; tithe £21; permanent endowment £8.
Space: free 45; other 18.
Present: aft. 9.
Average: aft. 6.

Samuel Evans.   Curate.

Lewis: perpetual curacy: net income £57: patrons and appropriators, Dean and Chapter of Bristol: great tithes commuted for £130, and those of the incumbent for £25: appropriate glebe of 63 acres.

C & C: 1 service in Welsh taken by the curate.

I & C: incumbent not resident.

3 Marshfield Parish.
Area: 1,270 acres. *Popn.* 271 males, 255 females: total 526.

(5) MARSHFIELD PARISH CHURCH.
Endowed: land £63; tithe £35; fees 10*s.*
Space: 3 family pews (30 sittings).
Present: morn. 26 + 9 scholars.
Average: morn. 20 to 30 + 9 to 15 scholars.

Samuel Evans.   Curate.

Lewis: discharged vicarage, valued at £6. 2. 6: patrons and appropriators, Dean
and Chapter of Bristol: great tithes commuted for £175, and vicarial for £48;
vicarial glebe of 27 acres, and glebe-house.
C & C: 1 service, Welsh and English alternately, performed by the curate.
I & C: incumbent resident.

(6) SALEM. PARTICULAR BAPTISTS.
Erected 1807.
Space: free about 500; other 108; standing about 300.
Present: morn. 350 + 90 scholars; even. 640 + 56 scholars.

John Davies.   Secretary.
Castletown.

(7) SION. CALVINISTIC METHODIST.
Erected 1836.
Space: free 300; other 156; standing about 100.
Present: morn. 18 + 15 scholars; even. 50 + 12 scholars.
Average (12 *months*): general congregation from 50 to 60.

Edward Cosslett.   Steward.
Castletown.

(8) LOFT NEAR THE MILL, CASTLETOWN. WESLEYAN.
Building erected before 1800: not used exclusively as a place of worship.
Present: aft. 20; even. 50.
Average: morn. 52 scholars; aft. 24; even. 60.

Thomas Maule.   Steward.
near the coach and horses, Castletown.

4 Coedkernew Parish.
Area: 765 acres. *Popn.* 83 males, 78 females: total 161.

(9) ALL SAINT PARISH CHURCH, COEDKERNEW.
Endowed: land £50, tithe £20; permanent endowment £13.
Space: free 100.
Present: morn. 65 + 17 scholars.

Remark: The Church is situated in a very wet locality, the path leading to it being through ploughed field renders it almost inaccessible at present, which fully accounts of the small number of the congregation on 30 March.

Morgan Powell.   Minister.

Lewis: united to the vicarage of St. Bride's, Wentlloog [580. 3. 1(1)]: appropriate tithes commuted for £84, and the vicarial for £20.

C & C: 1 service in English.

Bassaleg Parish, consisting of the hamlets of [5] Duffryn, [6] Graig, and [7] Rogerstone.
Area: 6,955 acres. *Popn.* 1,095 males, 1,067 females: total 2,159.

5   Duffryn Hamlet.
Popn. 135 males, 139 females: total 274.
[No returns]

6   Graig Hamlet.
Popn. 321 males, 315 females: total 636.

(10)   Bassaleg Parish Church, dedicated to St. Basil, an ancient parish church to which the hamlets [i.e. of Duffryn, Graig, and Rogerstone] belong.
Endowed: tithe commuted at £392. 10*s*; house and land, gross value £40; fees £12.
Space: free 17; other 280; in gallery for children 50.
Present: morn. 150 + 57 scholars; even. 119.
Average: morn. 130 + 42 scholars; even. 70.
Remarks: A few of the senior Sunday school scholars attend the evening service and are included in the number of the general evening congregation as given above, both in the attendance on 30th March and the average attendance.

Hugh Williams.   Vicar.

Lewis: discharged vicarage, valued at £14. 13. 6½: patron, Bishop of Llandaff: tithes commuted £864. 18, of which £509. 19. belong to the bishop: glebe of about one acre.

C & C: 2 services in English.

I & C: incumbent resident.

(11)   Wesleyan Methodist Chapel.
Erected 1842.
Space: free 60; other 30.
Present: aft. 54; even. 84.
Average (12 *months*): aft. 40; even. 80.
Remarks: Sunday Scholars are included with the Congregation.

Thomas Rowland.   Class Leader.
Shoemaker, Py corner.

(12) BETHEL, GRAIG HAMLET. PARTICULAR BAPTISTS.
Erected 1825.
Space: free 259; other 128; standing 300.
Present: morn. 126 + 5 scholars; even. 170 + 25 scholars.
Average (12 *months*): morn. 150 + 12 scholars; aft. 180 + 30 scholars.
Remarks: There is at present no stationed minister in consequence of which
the Congregation is less in number this last 3 months.

> William Treharne Rees.   Deacon.
> Holly House, Nr. Newport.

7   Rogerstone Hamlet.
Popn. 636 males, 613 females: total 1,249.

(13) BETHESDA. BAPTIST CHAPEL.
Erected before 1800.
Space: free 412: vestry which is open to chapel 100; rented sittings 212;
standing in the alleys up and down which are full on some occasions 100.
Present: morn. 212; aft. 116 scholars; even. 300.
Average: morn. 300; even. 400.
Remarks: Our neighbourhood at present is visited with fever and scarletina
which prevents our members and hearers from attending divine worship as
usual to a great extent.

> Timothy Thomas.   Minister.
> Bassaleg.

(14) EBENEZER. INDEPENDENTS.
Erected 1832.
Space: free 25; other 40.
Present: morn. 20; aft. 27 + 50 scholars; even. 40.
Remarks: The state of the cause is rather low, the finances are not adequate
to its support.

> Evan Pryse.   Manager.
> Pye Corner, Bassaleg.

[8-9]   Michaelstone-y-vedw Parish, consisting of [8] Michaelstone-y-vedw, and [9] Llanvedw (Glamorgan).
Area of the whole: 3,433 acres. *Popn.* 286 males, 258 females: total 544.

8   Michaelstone-y-vedw.
Area: 1,134 acres. *Popn.* 111 males, 105 females: total 216.

(15)   MICHAELSTONE Y VEDW PARISH CHURCH.
Endowed: tithe £499; glebe £80.
Space: free 200; other 30.
Present: morn. 58; aft. 35.
Average (12 *months*): morn. 50; aft. 30.

George Brind.   Churchwarden.

Lewis: rectory, valued at £7. 10. 2½: net income £400: patron, C. Kemeys Tynte, Esq.
C & C: 2 services in English.
I & C: incumbent resident.

9   Llanvedw Hamlet (co. Glamorgan).
Area: 2,299 acres. *Popn.* 175 males, 153 females: total 328.
[No returns]

10   Risca Parish.
Area: 1,877 acres. *Popn.* 1,091 males, 953 feamles: total 2,044.

(16)   THE CHURCH OF AN ANCIENT CHAPELRY. There are no legends to know when consecrated or licensed.
Endowed: land £8 [?£80]; tithe £54; fees £5.
Space: free 162.
Present: morn. 49 + 15 scholars; even. 93.

David Davies.   Incumbent.

Lewis: perpetual curacy; net income £102: patron, the Vicar of Bassaleg [580. 3. 6. (10)]; appropriator, the Bishop of Llandaff: great tithes commuted for £80, and those of the incumbent for £49.
C & C: 2 services in English.
I & C: incumbent not resident.

(17)   PARAN.   WELSH INDEPENDENTS.
Erected 1843.
Space: free 97; standing 80.
Present: morn. 85; aft. 49 scholars; even. 91.
Average: general congregation 86 or 90; 50 scholars.
Remarks: The hours of public worship in the chapel are half past ten morning and six in the evening. Sunday School at 2 o'clock, two church meetings every week. The number of members on the register Book are 42, no stated minister. The cause is suported by neighbouring ministers etc at the annual expense of £25 per annum and that contributed by the friends of the cause by voluntary means.

Ll. Griffiths.   Deacon.
Agent Chemical Works.

(18) SOAR. WELSH CALVINISTIC METHODIST.
Erected 1810.
Space: free 28; other 80; standing 100.
Present: morn. 70; aft. 54 scholars; even. 106.
Average (12 *months*): general congregation 100; 50 scholars.

> Thomas Evans. Minister.
> Walnut Tree House, Risca.

(19) MORIAH CHAPEL. BAPTISTS.
Erected 1818; rebuilt 1836.
Space: free upwards of 200; other upwards of 200.
Present: morn. 247; aft. 100 scholars; even. 415.
Average: 'as above'.
Remarks: Be it observed that all the services are conducted almost exclusively in the Welsh language.

> James Rowe. Minister.
> Risca.

(20) WESLEYAN METHODIST CHAPEL.
Erected 1835.
Space: free 253; other 142.
Present: morn. 155 + 40 scholars; even. 250 + 69 scholars.
Average: general congregation 390; 90 scholars.

> Samuel Bateman. Steward.
> Grocer,
> Risca.

11 Henllis Parish.
Area: 2,622 acres. *Popn.* 147 males, 118 females: total 265.

(21) HENLLYS PARISH CHURCH.
Endowed: land £35. 11*s.*; permanent endowment £8. 6. 4.
Space: free 100.
Present: aft. 50 + 14 scholars.
Average: aft. 60 + 20 scholars.

> Howell Williams. Minister.

Lewis: perpetual curacy: patron, the Vicar of Bassaleg [580. 3. 6(10)]: tithes commuted for £58 payable to the incumbent, £60 to the Bishop of Llandaff, and £33 to an impropriator.

C & C: 1 service, Welsh and English on alternate Sundays.

I & C: incumbent not resident.

(22) SOAR. BAPTIST.
Erected 1836.
Space: free 119; other 79; standing 120.
Present: morn. 70; even. 100.
Average (12 *months*): morn. 80; even. 120.

John Lloyd.
William Jones } Deacons.
Henllis Vale.

(23) WESLEYAN METHODIST.
Dwelling house not used exclusively for public worship.
Space: free 40.
Present: even. 23 + 12 scholars.
Remarks: Several of the neighbours who generally attend being from home made the congregation less on March 30th than the average given below.

Uriah Barnell.   Leader.
Hansons Incline Henllis.

12   Bettws Parish.
Area: 1,132 acres. *Popn.* 52 males, 35 females: total 87.

(24) BETTWS PARISH CHURCH.
Space: free 60.
Usual number of Attendants: aft. 5. No service morn. and even.; no scholars.

Informant: John Cocker.
Farmer, Bettws.

[Informant's form.]

Lewis: annexed to the vicarage of St. Woollos [580. 2. 1(1)]: incumbent's tithes commuted for £42, and the great tithes, appropriated to the Bishop of Gloucester, for £82. 10.

C & C: 1 service in English.

ICBS: grant of £30 in 1829.

13   Malpas Patish.
Area: 988 acres. *Popn.* 153 males, 174 females: total 327.

(25) ST. MARY'S PARISH CHURCH.
Rebuilt and consecrated in 1850, cost defrayed by parochial rate £600, and subscriptions £640.
Endowed: land £78; permanent endowment £18; fees £5.
Space: free 150; other 100.

Present: morn. 80 + 40 scholars.
Average: morn. 40; aft. 40.
Remarks: The whole of the incumbents income derivable from every source
is about one hundred a year.

Incumbent: William Deacon Isaac.

Lewis: perpetual curacy; net income £60: patron and impropriator, Sir C. Morgan,
Bart.

C & C: the church was closed for repairs when the return was made.

I & C: incumbent not resident.

ICBS: grant of £85 in 1847.

14   Llanfihangel Llantarnum Parish.

Area: 4,092 acres. *Popn.* 683 males, 545 females: total 1,228.

(26)   LLANVIHANGEL LANTARNUM PARISH CHURCH.
Endowed: land £24; tithe £96; fees £4.
Space: free 114; other 12.
Present: even. 69 + 14 scholars.

David Davies.   Incumbent.

Lewis: perpetual curacy: patrons and impropriators, E. Blewitt, Esq., and family
of Wood: great tithes commuted for £90, and those of the incumbent for £101.

C & C: 2 services in English.

I & C: incumbent resident.

(27)   THE FORGE ROOM, LANTARNAM.   BAPTIST.
Erected 1849, not used exclusively as a place of worship.
Space: free 80; standing 6.
Present: morn. 32 + 22 scholars; aft. 56 scholars; even. 65.
Average (9 months): morn. 30 + 35 scholars; aft. 60 scholars; even. 80.

Thomas Morgan.   Manager.
Pudler Cwmbran Iron Works.

(28)   ELIM CHAPEL.   INDEPENDENTS.
Erected 1844.
Space: free 146; other 146; standing 64ft by 30ft.
Present: morn. 150; even. 300.
Average (12 months): morn. about 300.
Remarks: We have no day School belonging to Elim chapel.

John Jones.   Deacon.
St. Diats Farm, Llantarnum.

(29) WESLEYAN METHODIST.
Erected: no date given. Not used exclusively as a place of worship.
Present: even. 30.
Average (late months): even. 40.
Remarks: This is a house which has been used about five years by the
Wesleyans for public worship, otherwise a private dwelling.

                              Charles Birkett.   Local Preacher.
                              51 Commercial Street, Newport.

(30) PENYWAIN CHAPPEL.   INDEPENDENT.
Erected 1819.
Space: free 300; other 20.
Present: morn. 45; even. 67.
Average (12 *months*): morn. 100; even. 200.

                              William Waters.   Deacon.

[*End of St. Woollos Subdistrict*]

4 MYNYDDISLWYN (Subdistrict)

Area: 25,311 acres. *Popn.* 4,777 males, 4,289 females: total 9,066.

[1-3] Mynyddislwyn Parish, consisting of the Hamlets of [1] Clawr-plwyf, [2] Mynyddmaen, and [3] Penmain.

Area: 15,938 acres. *Popn.* of the whole parish: 3,157 males, 2,837 females:
total 5,994.

1 Clawrplwyf Hamlet.

Popn. 1,089 males, 1,007 females: total 2,096.

(1) CELYNEN CHAPEL.   ANGLICAN.
Space: free 80.
Usual number of attendants: morn. 60 + 40 scholars; aft. 60 scholars; even.
40.

                              Informant: David Jones.   Registrar.
[Informant's form.]

(2) MYNYDDISLWYN PARISH CHURCH.
Space: free 200.
Usual number of attendants: morn. 25 + 17 scholars; aft. 30 + 20 scholars.
                              Informant: David Jones.   Registrar.
[Informant's form.]

Lewis: perpetual curacy: patron and appropriator, the Bishop of Llandaff: net
income £150: appropriate tithes commuted for £580; glebe of 36 acres.
C & C: 1 service in Welsh performed by the incumbent.
I & C: incumbent resident: curate has stipend of £70.

(3) SILOH CHAPEL.   CALVINISTIC METHODIST.
Erected 1813.
Space: free 200; standing 50.
Present: morn. 55; aft. 43 scholars; even. 58.
Average (12 *months*): morn. 70; aft. 46 scholars; even. 90.

> Henry Edmunds.   Elder.
> Gelligroes, Blackwood.

(4) GELLY HOVE, MONYTHISLOYNE.   WESLEYAN METHODIST.
Erected: 1846.
Space: free about 40; other about 60; standing very little.
Present: morn. 45 + 29 scholars; even. 39 + 9 scholars.
Average: 'Don't know'.

> Aaron Brain.   Secretary.

(5) DWELLING HOUSE, GARMON TIPPING, MYNYDDYSLWYN.
WESLEYAN REFORMERS.
Present: morn. 29; even. 14.

> Garmon Tipping.
> Flowerdeluce, Blackwood.

(6) NEW BETHEL, MYNYDDISLWYN, INDEPENDENTS.
Erected 1765.
Space: free 250.
Present: morn. 294; aft. 157 scholars; even. 205.
Average: morn. 321; aft. 140 scholars; even. 250.
Remarks: Free sittings are large seats and will contain ten persons in each seat. The support of the cause in the place is entirely by voluntary contribution. In 1849 a large school room was built in connection with the said chapel where day school is kept and £100 debt remains.

> Moses Ellis.   Minister.

(7) BABELL WELSH CALVINISTIC METHODIST.   MYNYDDYSLWYN.
Erected 1827.
Space: free 84; other 80; standing none, the chapel being fully seated.
Present: morn. 45 + 20 scholars; aft. 64 scholars; even. 50 + 40 scholars.
Average (12 *months*): morn. 70 + 30 scholars; even. 80 + 40 scholars.
Remarks: Several of the Congregation were confined at home this Sunday by sickness.

> Morgan Thomas.   Elder.
> Ynysddu.

(8) TWYN GWYN, MYNYDDISLWYN.   BAPTIST.
Erected 1829.
Space: free 200; standing 100.
Present: morn. 94; aft. school; even. 135.

Average (12 *months*): morn. 100; even. 160.
Remarks: Those of the Sunday Scholars that attended are included in the
General Congregation. Their attendance at Divine Service is irregular, so
that a close average could not be made.

David Williams.   Deacon.
Pantycelyn, near Blackwood.

2   Mynyddmaen Hamlet.
Popn. 822 males, 697 females: total 1,519.
[No returns]

3   Penmain Hamlet.
Popn. 1,246 males, 1,133 females: total 2,379.

(9)   HOREB CHAPEL, TONTREBEL, MYNYDDISLWYN.   INDEPENDENT.
Erected about the year 1828 or 1829.
Space: free 96.
Present: morn. 61; aft. 61 scholars; even. 92.
Average (12 *months*): general congregation 1,126; scholars 660.
Remarks: The Chapel is in length 26 feet 5 inches. Breadth 16 feet 1 inch
within the walls.

Thomas Lewis.   Minister.
Tontrebel, Crumlin.

(10)   CAPEL Y GARN, ABERCARN.   INDEPENDENTS.
Erected 1847.
Space: free 54; other 108; standing 450.
Present: morn. 72; aft. 39 scholars; even. 113.
Remarks: The Congregation being a branch of Bethel Mynyddislwyn, the
annual expences therof is nearly £40 which are defrayed by voluntary
contributions.

Benjamin Mathews.   Deacon.
Abercarn.

(11)   NAZARETH.   WELSH CALVINISTIC METHODIST.
Erected 1841.
Space: free 29 by 33.
Present: morn. 53 scholars; aft. 60 scholars; even. 58 scholars.
Average: general congregation 60; scholars 49.

William Stephen. [Office not specified.]
Evan Edwards.
Abercarne.

(12) CYMREIGYDDION HALL, ABERGWYDDON. PARTICULAR BAPTISTS.
In February last the Room was fitted up for use of the Particular Baptists.
[It is] regularly [used] as a Day School and for the general purposes of
Public Meeting.
Space: All free Room. 300.
Present: morn. 200 + 266 scholars; even. 226.
Average (3 months): general congregation 200; scholars 266.

> David ap Rhys Stephen. Minister.
> of Abergwyddon.

(13) READING ROOM, ABERCARNE. WESLEYAN METHODIST.
Erected: before 1800.
Present: morn. 23 + 21 scholars; aft. 30 scholars; even. 45.
Average (2 months): general congregation 68; scholars 50.
Remarks: The room which we hold meetings in of Sundays is made use of
in the week days for school. We only use it on Sundays.

> George Hawkins. Class Leader.
> No. 133 Abercarne.

(14) COURT Y BELLA. A LICENSED SCHOOL ROOM [ANGLICAN].
Licensed for public worship, March 1846.
Erected by a grant from the Privy Council, £700, and by private benefac-
tion, Sir Thomas Phillips, £700.
Space: free 300.
Present: morn. 130 + 7 scholars; even. 120 + 9 scholars.

> Incumbent: Rees Jones.
> Penmain. Blackwood.

(15) PENMAIN CHAPEL. INDEPENDENTS.
Erected 1694; rebuilt 1820.
Space: free 322; other 210.
Present: morn. 235; aft. 140 scholars; even. 338.
Remarks: Our seats and alleys are wide and when the chapel is full of
persons standing and sitting as sometimes is the case in annual meetings,
etc. it is calculated that it will hold about 1,500.

> Ellis Hughes. Minister.
> Penmain. Blackwood.

(16) JERUSALEM. INDEPENDENTS.
Erected 1840.
Space: free 66; other 180; standing 100.
Present: morn. 92; aft. 74 scholars; even. 120.
Average: morn. 105; aft. 74 scholars; even. 140.

> John Morgan Thomas. Minister.
> ['Independent' crossed out]
> Blackwood.

(17)   BETHEL CHAPEL OR MEETING HOUSE.   BABTIST.
Erected 1809 and 1810.
Space: free 352; other 111.
Present: morn. 270; aft. 140 scholars; even. 425.
Remarks: Chapel admeasurements in the clear between the Walls 44 feet
by 36 feet, that is for the ground floor. Galleries: 35 by 11; ditto 36 by 11
and ditto 22 by 7.
Note. Some Sundays the Meeting House is quite full when we consider the
Congregation to be from 600 to 700.

Charles Turner.   Member.
Carpenter.   Newbridge.

**[4-5]   Part of Bedwas Parish, consisting of the Hamlets of [4] Lower
Bedwas and [5] Upper Bedwas.** [For the remainder of the parish see
581. 1.7.]
Area: 4,207 acres.   *Popn.* 480 males, 444 females: total 924.

4   Lower Bedwas.
Popn. 225 males, 191 females: total 416.

(18)   BEDWAS PARISH CHURCH.
Space: free 162; other 12.
Present: morn. 30; aft. 33.
Average (3 *months*): morn. 30 + 17 scholars; aft. 35.
Remarks: There has been no Sunday School during the last two months
for the want of a teacher. If the said church has been erected in a more
central part of the parish it would have been better attended.

Watkin Watkins.   Rector.

Lewis: rectory, with the living of Ruddry [581. 1. 6( )] annexed: valued at
£10. 14. 19½: patron, the Crown: appropriator, the Bishop of Llandaff, whose
tithes commuted for £187. 12. 6: bishop has glebe of 100 acres.

C & C: 1 service in Welsh taken by the curate.

I & C: incumbent (Bishop of Llandaff) not resident: curate, who resides in the
glebe-house, has stipend of £120.

(19)   HEPHZIBAH.   BAPTIST.
Erected 1840.
Space: free 70; other 39; standing 91.
Present: morn. 80; aft. 59 scholars; even. 149.
Average (12 *months*): morn. 88; aft. 49 scholars; even. 150.

Owen E. Jones.   Pastor.
Bedwas.

(20) TABOR. INDEPENDENT.
Erected 1829.
Space: free 200; other 60.
Present: morn. 120; aft. 95 scholars; even. 260.
Remarks: The whole Chapel is free except 10 Seates which will contain 6
persons each.

> John Morgan Thomas. Minister.
> Blackwood.

5 Upper Bedwas Hamlet.
Popn. 223 males, 223 females: total 446.
[No returns]

[6-8] Machen Parish, consisting of the Hamlets of [6] Lower Machen, [7] Upper Machen and [8] Rhydgwen, the latter in the county of Glammorgan.
Area: 4,460 acres. *Popn.* 1,172 males, 1,038 females: total 2,210.

6 Lower Machen.
Popn. 547 males, 457 females: total 1,004.

(21) MACHEN PARISH CHURCH.
Endowed: tithe £469. 7.; glebe £3; fees £9.
Space: morn. 127 + 42 scholars; aft. 35 + 27 scholars.
Remarks: The presence of measles in the parish at the time will account for
the small attendance of children.

> Augustus Morgan.   Rector.

Lewis: rectory valued at £10. 16. 5½: patron, Sir Charles Morgan, Bart.: impropriate
tithes commuted for £14, and the rectorial for £469. 3. 9; glebe of one acre, and
glebe-house.

C & C: 2 services in English.

I & C: incumbent resident, curate has £80.

(22) PROVIDENCE. PRIMITIVE METHODIST.
Erected 1846.
Space: free 140; other 60.
Present: morn. 40 + 96 scholars; aft. 98 scholars; even. 87.
Average (12 *months*): morn. 50 + 110 scholars; aft. 110 scholars; even.
120.

> Thomas Giles. Minister.
> Abersychan.

(23)   EBENEZER.   WESLEYAN.
Erected 1851.
Space: free 96; other 72; standing 50.
Present: aft. 70; even. 150.

> Joseph Beeston.
> George Young.
> Grocer.
> Machen.

7   Upper Machen.

Popn. 529 males, 492 females: total 1,021.

(24)   CAPEL UCHA.   WESLEYAN METHODIST (WELSH).
Erected 1830.
Space: free 180; other 72.
Present: morn. 28 + 30 scholars; even. 33.
Average (12 *months*): morn. 30 + 30 scholars; even. 60.

> Thomas Price.   Chapel Steward.
> Bedwas.

(25)   SILOAM.   BAPTIST.
Erected 1820.
Space: free 312; other 211.
Present: 'no service'.
Average (12 *months*): morn. 150; aft. 70 scholars; even. 200.

> Thomas Williams.   Deacon.
> Gellifiniog, Machen.

[Endorsed: See letter.]

(26)   ADULLAM.   UPPER MACHEN, NEAR THE FOUNTRY.   INDEPENDENTS.
Erected before 1846.
Present: morn. 80 + 32 scholars; aft. 'School'; even. 200.

> Evan Jones.   Deacon.
> Dyer.
> Pandy, Machen.

(27)   CAPEL Y GROES.   CALVINISTIC METHODIST.
Erected 1843.
Space: free 60; other 15; standing 40.
Present: morn. 30 scholars; aft. 47; even. 37.

> Hugh Lumley.   Leader.
> Pandy Machen.

8 Rhydgwern Hamlet, co. Glamorgan.
Popn. 96 males, 89 females: total 185.

(28) DRAETHON. ROOM OR PLACE OF WORSHIP IN HAMLET OF RHYDY-GWERN. WESLEYAN METHODIST.
Erected 1825. Building not used exclusively as a place of worship.
Space: standing 60.
Present: even. 39.
Average (12 *months*): general congregation 44.
Remarks: Religious service in the place is held in a dwelling house occupied by James Howells. Wesleyan Methodists commenced preachin in the above Place the year 1835.

> Signed by Mark: James Howell.
> Leader of the Society.
> Mason,
> Dreathon.

[End of Mynyddislwyn Subdistrict, and of Newport District and end of Monmouthshire Registration County]

ADDENDA

Welsh parishes in English Districts.

348   HEREFORD District

6 HEREFORD (Subdistrict)

9   Grosmont Parish.
Area: 6,838 acres. *Popn.* 367 males, 317 females: total 684.
( )   GROSMONT PARISH CHURCH.
Endowed: tithe £201: house and garden £17; glebe £1. 10s; fees £2. 11s.
Space: free 126; other 293.
Present: gen. cong. morn. 102, aft. 51: School 21.
Average (6 *months*)*:* gen. cong. 120; aft. 60; School 25.

William Walwyn Trumper.   Minister.

Lewis: discharged rectory, valued at £2. 15. 10. : patron, J. L. Scudamore, Esq.: tithes commuted for £77. 14.

C & C: 1 service in English.

I & C: incumbent not resident.

10   Llangua Parish.
Area: 695 acres. *Popn.* 63 males, 45 females: total 118.

( )   LLANGUA PARISH CHURCH.
Endowed: tithe £74; Bounty £34.
Space: free 50.
Present: gen. cong. morn. 16.
Average: morn. 40.

W. E. Lellow.   Rector.
Rentchurch.

Lewis: discharged rectory, endowed with the small tithes only: valued at £6. 5. 2½: patron, the Crown: net income £118.

C & C: 1 service in English.

I & C: incumbent not resident: curate has stipend of £40.

43 SOUTH WALES

Area: 2,816,599 acres. *Popn.* 301,492 males, 305,964 females: total 607,456.

GLAMORGAN

Area: 606,780 acres. *Popn.* 125,087 males, 115,008 females: total 240,095.

581   CARDIFF (District)

Area: 117,797 acres. *Popn.* 24,902 males, 21,589 females: total 46,491.

1 CAERPHILLY (Subdistrict)
Area: 27,164 acres. *Popn.* 4,217 males, 2,419 females: total 8,121.

1-5   Parish of Eglwysilan, consisting of the Hamlets of [1] Energlyn, [2] Park, [3] Hendredenny, [4] Glyntaff, and [5] Rhydyboithan.
Area of the whole parish: 13,619 acres. *Popn.* 2,691 males, 2,419 females: total 5,110.

1   Energlyn Hamlet.
Popn. 467 males, 485 females: total 952.

(1)   St. Martin's. Ancient Chapelry, now a consolidated district.
Consecrated 1822 in lieu of previously existing one.
Endowed: land £123; tithe £40; permanent endowment £21. 19s.
Space: free 90; other 60.
Present: morn. 55 + 24 scholars.

Judah Jones.   Perpetual Curate.
Caerphilly

Lewis: sub Eglwysilan: perpetual curacy, with portion of land attached.

C & C: no entry.

I & C: resident.

ICBS: Grant of £100 in 1821.

(2)   Schoolroom licensed for public worship.
Licensed 1849 for Welsh Duty in the evening.
Present: even. 34.
Remark: The above Room is private property which the Proprietor allows to be used as a schoolroom for public worship.

J. Jones.   Minister.
Caerphilly

(3)   EGLWYSILAN PARISH CHURCH.
Endowed: tithe £140; glebe £12; fees £10.
Space: free 225.
Present: aft. 17.
Average (12 *months*): morn. 20; aft. 40; even. 50.
Remark: The Church is served alternately in the morning and afternoon.
When the service is in the morning there is a service in the evening also.
The church is situated on the brow of a hill far apart from the population.
In the summer the Congregation average from 50 to 100.

> William Leigh.   Vicar.
> Eglwysilan, Pontypridd

Lewis: discharged vicarage with that of Llanvabon annexed, rated at £6. 13. 1½;
patron and impropriator the Bishop and Chapter of Llandaff; net income £140;
glebe house and glebe of 10 acres.

C & C: 2 services, both entirely in Welsh, taken by the incumbent.

I & C: incumbent resident: curate has stipend of £80.

(3A)   NANTGARW.   SCHOOLROOM.   CHURCH OF ENGLAND.
Licensed for Divine Service October 8, 1845, for the convenience of the
population of the Village and neighbourhood, they being far from the Parish
Church.
Erected by public subscriptions and grants from the National Society and
the Privy Council.
Endowed: Parliamentary grant £75, National Society £70, subscriptions
£149. 15; total £294. 15.
Space: free 132.
Present: morn. 8 + 16 scholars; even. 35.
Remarks: The average congregation is about 40.

> William Leigh.   Vicar of Eglwysilan.

(4)   TABOR CALVINISTIC METHODIST.
Erected: 1843.
Space: free 80; other 136.
Usual number of attendants: morn. 85 scholars; aft. 250; even. 250.

> David Morgan, his mark.   Deacon.
> Taffs Well Lock, near Tongwinlais.

[Informant's form]

(5)   TABOR.   CALVINISTIC METHODIST.
Erected 1843.
Space: free 36; other 102; standing 23 feet by 17 feet.
Present: morn. 75; aft. 150; even. 161.

Average number: morn. 300; aft. 600; even. 644.

> Thomas Williams.
> William Christopher.
> Deacons.
> Taffs Well

[Note: second entry for the same chapel.]

(6) EBENEZER. CAERPHILLY. WESLEYAN METHODIST.
Erected 1815.
Present: aft. 22.
Average (12 *months*): aft. 30.

> Thomas Price.   Leader.
> Police Officer.
> Caerphilly

[Endorsed: Duplicate, *and* See letter.]

(7) THE WESLEYAN CHAPEL. CAERPHILLY.
Erected 1815.
Space: 37 feet by 22 feet all free.
Present: aft. 22.
Average (12 *months*): aft. 30.

> Thomas Price.   Leader of the Society.
> police officer.

[Note: second entry for the same chapel.]

(8) BETHEL CHAPEL. CAERPHILLY. WELSH INDEPENDENT.
Erected 1848.
Space: free 150; other 146.
Present: aft. 29 scholars; even. 111.
Average (12 *months*): aft. 40 scholars; even. 120.

> John Rowland.   Deacon.
> Malster.
> Caerphilly

(9) WATFORD INDEPENDANT CHAPEL.
Erected: not known.
Space: free 45; standing 'benches for 42'.
Present: morn. 20; even. 30.
Average: morn. 20; even. 35.

> Stephen Evans.   Deacon.
> Tailor, Caerphilly.

(10) TONYVELYN. CAERPHILLY. BAPTIST.
Erected 1800.
Space: free 450; other 86; standing 40.
Present: morn. 300; aft. 129 scholars; even. 409.

> Richard Evans.   Deacon.

(11) ROCK CHAPEL. CAERPHILLY. WELSH CALVINISTIC METHODIST.
Erected 1800.
Space: free 5; other 165; standing '12 feet by 10 feet. 120'.
Present: morn. 23; aft. 23 scholars; even. 22.
Average: general congregation 40; scholars 26.

> David Williams. Deacon.
> Butcher.
> Caerphilly

(12) CARMEL. UPPER BOAT. WELSH CALVINISTIC METHODIST.
Erected Anno Domini 1839.
Space: free 15; other 120; standing length 16 feet, breadth 12 ditto.
Present: morn. 36; aft. 63 scholars; even. 69.
Average: morn. 50; aft. 63 scholars; even. 120.
Remarks: Our congregation was less than usual in consequence of having no ministry, but Prayer Meeting. Size of the Chapel is 28 feet by 28 do.

> Thomas John. Steward.
> Collier. Nantgarw.

(13) NANTGARW MEETING HOUSE. INDEPENDENTS.
Erected 1825.
Space: free 300.
Present: aft. 110 scholars; even. 264.
Average: general congregation 264; scholars 110.
Remarks: The Length 30ft. The Breadth 21ft.

> John Thomas. Local Preacher.
> Nantgarw.

(14) AINON. BAPTIST. TONGWYNLAIS.
Erected 1832, enlarged 1850.
Space: free 200; other 264; standing 60.
Present: morn. 260; aft. 120 scholars; even. 540.
Average (12 *months*): morn. 300; aft. 140 scholars; even. 560.
Remarks: Our Meeting House will hold about 700 when crammed which is the case often on Sunday evening. We have no service in the afternoon except Sunday School. but when the ordinance of Baptism is administered which was the case this Sunday afternoon in the presence of about 800 persons, the service conducted by the River Taff and the candidate *immersed* in the River.

> William Lewis. Minister.

(15) WHITECROSS. INDEPENDENTS.
Erected before 1800 about the year 1723 or 1724.
Space: free 196; other 350; standing 'a free place which is a corner. It will accomodate about 50'.
Present: morn. 200; aft. 59 scholars; even. 150.

Average (12 *months*): morn. from 250 to 450; even. from 150 to 200.
Remark: Our evening Congregation is almost always smaller than the morning for our church holds service in four different places in the evening. We got 4 Sunday Schools every afternoon.

Moses Rees.   Minister.

(16)   WESLEYAN [CHAPEL—struck out] METHODIST ROOM, UPPER BOAT.
Erected 1840, not used exclusively as a place of worship.
Space: free 25; standing 10.
Present: morn. 10.
Average (2 *months*): morn. 15.

John Workman.   Minister.
Pontypridd.

[Note: this volume of schedules has been repaired and rebound, and Lisvane Parish Church inserted here and numbered (16B) and Lanedern Parish Church as (16C).]

(17)   EBENEZER.   INDEPENDENT.
Erected 1846.
Space: free 120; other 100; standing 160.
Present: morn. 100; aft. 54 scholars; even. 172.
Average: general congregation 242; scholars 82.

Thomas Thomas.   Secretary.
Rhydyfelen.

(18)   BETHLEHEM.   BAPTIST.
Erected 1847.
Space: free 120; other 36; standing 80.
Present: morn. 30; aft. 18 scholars; even. 65.
Average (12 *months*): general congregation 80; scholars 30.

David Moses.   Diacon.
Rhydfelan.

(19)   GLYNTAFF.
A district Church consecrated 29 October 1839 as an additional church to meet the spiritual wants of the lay population of the District.
Erected by public subscription and grants from the Incorporated Society and from the Commissioners for building and repairing of churches.
Cost: I have no means of ascertaining the items.
Endowed: permanent endowment, £400; pew rents £30; fees £4.
Space: free 750; other 250.
Present: morn. 306; aft. 200 scholars; even. 260.

John Griffiths.   Perpetual Curate.

Lewis: 'A very handsome church has been built in the hamlet by public subscription . . .; it is endowed with £400, by the Hon. R. H. Clive and J. Bruce Pryce, Esq.

jointly, and was opened for divine service on Sunday the 22nd of April 1838, by the Rev. W. Leigh, vicar of the parish, by virtue of a license from the Lord Bishop of Llandaf, who subsequently consecrated it with the churchyard on October 29th, 1839: it will afford accomodation for 1,000 persons.'

ICBS: Grant of £400 in 1836.

2   Park Hamlet.
Popn. 76 males, 64 females: total 140.
[No returns]

3   Hendredenny Hamlet.
Popn. 299 males, 257 females: total 556.
[No returns]

4   Glyntaff Hamlet.
Popn. 1,097 males, 953 females: total 2,050.
[No returns]

5   Rhydyboithan Hamlet.
Popn. 752 males, 660 females: total 1,412.
[No returns]

6   Ruddry Parish.
Area: 2,639 acres. *Popn.* 174 males, 168 females: total 342.

(20)   RUDREY.
The chapelry at Rudry is commonly called a 'District Chapelry' to the mother church at Bedwas. The name given to it as its consecration is not agreed upon.
Endowed: fees 'nothing to signify'.
Space: free 100.
Present: morn. 16 + 16 scholars.
Average (3 *months*): morn. and aft. alternatly, 25 + 20 scholars.

David Jones.   Curate.

Lewis: Living consolidated with the rectory of Bedwas [580. 4. 4(18)], co. Mon.: tithes, payable to the Bishop of Llandaf, commuted for a rent-charge of £100, subject to rates, averaging £16: glebe of 2 acres valued at £2.

C & C: 1 service in Welsh taken by the curate.

I & C: vide sub Bedwas, 580. 4. 4(18), above.

(21) EBENEZER. INDEPENDENTS.
Erected 1821.
Space: free 386.
Present: 53; aft. 33 scholars; even. 105.
Average (12 *months*)*:* morn. 150; aft. 35 scholars; even. 200.
Remark: The reason that the general congregation being greater in the average is that fortnightly I do attend the church.

John Jones. Ind. Minister.
Rhudry.

7 Van Hamlet, part of Bedwas Parish [580. 4. 4].
Area: 825 acres. *Popn.* 32 males, 30 females: total 62.
[No returns]

8 Lisvane Parish.
Area: 1,338 acres. *Popn.* 115 males, 105 females: total 220.

(22) LISVANE PARISH CHURCH.
Endowed: land £15; tithe £10; glebe £46.
Present: morn. 20.
Remark: There is no school belonging to the Church, but there is a school belonging to the Anna Baptists and a many assembled from many Parishes.

Benjamin Jones. Officiating Minister.

Lewis: Perpetual curacy endowed with £1,000 royal bounty, and £200 parliamentary grant; in the alternate patronage of the Earl of Plymouth and C. K. Kemeys Tynte, Esq., the impropriators. Net income £60.

C & C: 1 service in Welsh taken by the curate.

I & C: not resident.

ERCR: accomodation 100.

(23) DERWENDEG (FAIR OAK) BAPTIST CHAPPEL, LLYSVAEN.
Erected before 1800.
Space: free 200.
Present: morn. 100 + 24 scholars; even. 104 + 38 scholars.

William Williams. Minister.
Llysvaen

9 Llanedarn Parish.
Area: 2,636 acres. *Popn.* 187 males, 151 females: total 338.

(24)   LLANEDARN PARISH CHURCH.
Space: all free.
Endowed: land £15; tithe £50.
Present: aft. 21.
Average: aft. 30.
Remark: The reason why the Congregation was so small on March the 30
in the above Church might be attributed to the uncertainty of having service
in the Church on account of the incumbent being ill.

> Edward Jenkins.   Vicar.

Lewis: Discharged vicarage united to that of St. Mellon's, co. Mon. [581. 2.
1(1)]; rated at £5. 8. 1½; impropriation vested in Chapter of Llandaf.
C & C: 1 service in Welsh taken by the incumbent.
I & C: sub St. Mellons: resident.
ERCR: accommodation. 600.

(25)   PEN Y GROES SCHOOL ROOM.   CALVINISTIC METHODIST.
Erected 1840.
Space: free 100.
Present: aft. 35 + 6 scholars.

> John Morgan.   Deacon.
> Llanedarn.

10   Llanishen Parish.
Area: 2,915 acres. *Popn.* 193 males, 195 females: total 388.

(26)   LLANISHEN PARISH CHURCH.
Space: Gallery 25; free 18 seats with room for 8 in each; other 2 seats
with room for 8 in each; standing 25; total 185.
Usual number of attendants: morn. between 60 and 70; aft. about 40
scholars.

> *Informant:* Benjamin Jones,
> Perpetual Curate.

[Informant's form. For the original return by the incumbent see below.]

Lewis: perpetual curacy, endowed with £200 private benefaction, and £800 royal
bounty; net income £46: patrons, Earl of Plymouth and C. K. Kemeys Tynte,
alternately, who are also the impropriators: tithes, let for £70 per annum, and
subject to an annual payment of £10 to the perpetual curate.
C & C: 1 service, alternately English and Welsh, taken by the incumbent.
I & C: resident.

[The original return, bound in 577. 4. 6(18) is as follows:]
LLANISHEN PARISH CHURCH, NEAR CARDIFF.
Endowed: land £25; tithe £10; permanent endowment £35.
Space: all free.
Present: morn. 49 + 30 scholars.
Average: morn. 70 + 30 scholars.

> Benjamin Jones.   Officiating [Minister].

(27) WESLEYAN METHODISTS.
Building not used exclusively as a place of worship.
Space: free 21 feet by 15 feet.
Present: even. 20.
Average (12 *months*)*:* even. 18.

> Charles Tucker.   Minister.
> Cardiff.

(28) CAPPEL GWILYM.   BAPTIST.
Erected 1831.
Present: even. 30.
Remark: no morning service here, nor Sunday School.

> Thomas Jones.   Deacon.
> Deri Du, Llanishen.

11 Whitchurch Parish.

Area: 3,192 acres. *Popn.* 825 males, 836 females: total 1,661.

(29) WHITCHURCH PERPETUAL CURACY.
An ancient chapelry, built as a chapel of Ease to Llandaff Parish but now a
Parish Church.
Endowed: with the yearly payment of £80 from the Ecclesiastical Com-
missioners for England.
Space: free about 50; other about 200.
Present: morn. [MS torn] even. 10.

> E. P. Thomas.   Perpetual Curate.

Lewis: Living annexed to that of Llandaf: tithes commuted for a rent-charge of
£493, of which £133 is payable to the Bishop, Archdeacon, and Chapter of Llandaf,
and the remainder divided equally between the Bishop, and the Precentor of the
Cathedral, Prependaries of Fairwell and Fairwater.

C & C: 2 services, 1 in Welsh, taken by the incumbent.

I & C: resident.

(30) PENLAN CHAPEL OR MELINGRIFFITH.   WESLEYAN METHODIST (WELSH)
Erected about 1800 in lieu of another room used exclsively as a place of
worship.
Space: free 33 feet by 17 feet.
Present: even. 125.
Average (12 *months*)*:* even. 120.

> Henry Wilcox.   Wesleyan Minister.
> Cardiff.

(31) Penylan Chapel generally called Melingriffith. Wesleyan Methodists (English).
Erected about 1800 in lieu of another room. Used exclusively as a place of worship.
Space: free 33 feet by 17 feet.
Present: aft. 110.
Average (12 *months*): aft. 100.

Charles Tucker. Wesleyan Minister.
2 Wellington Terrace, Cardiff.

[The same room as 581. 1. 11(30) and (35).]

(32) Ebenezer Chapel. Calvinistic Methodist.
Erected 1810.
Space: free 100; other 68; standing 100.
Present: morn. 57; aft. 21 scholars; even. 60.
Average (12 *months*): morn. 70; aft. 40 scholars; even. 76.
Remark: Some Sundays the Congregation has been 160 or 200 and scholars have been in number 60.

John Dew. Steward.
Whitchurch.

(33) Ararat. Wauntroda. Baptist.
Erected 1824.
Space: free 307; other 130.
Present: morn. 140; aft. 64 scholars; even. 300.

David Davies. Minister.
Wauntroda.

(34) Beulah. Dissenters.
Erected 1848.
Space: free 60; standing 40.
Present: aft. 80; even. 60.
Average (12 *months*): aft. 80; even. 60.

John Jones. Minister.
Rhudry.

(35) Penylan Chapel. Wesleyan Methodist.
Erected about 1810.
Space: free 200; standing 33 by 17.
Present: morn. 130 scholars; aft. 103; even. 125.
Average (12 *months*): morn. 120 scholars; aft. 100; even. 150.

John Thomas. Sunday School
Secretary.
Job's Row, Whitchurch.

[Endorsed: See letter. Cf. 581. 1. 11(30) and (31).]

[*End of Caerphilly Subdistrict*]

2 CARDIFF (Subdistrict)
Area: 26,543 acres. *Popn.* 12,696 males, 10,389 females: total 23,085.

1 St. Mellons Parish, co. Monmouth.
Area: 2,574 acres. *Popn.* 324 males, 313 females: total 637.

(1) St. Mellons Parish Church.
Endowed: land £36; tithe £80; fees £1. 5.
Space: free 60.
Present: morn. 27.
Average: morn. 35.

Edward Jenkins.   Vicar.

Lewis: discharged vicarage with that of Llanedarn [581. 1. 9 (24)] annexed: valued at £10. 1. 5: in the alternative patronage of the Bishop and Chapter of Llandaff and the Dean and Chapter of Bristol, who are together the appropriators: net income £160.

C & C: 2 services, 1 in Welsh taken by the incumbent.

I & C: resident.

(2) Bethania.   Calvinistic Methodist.
Erected 1820.
Space: Platform and gallery free; other 29.
Present: morn. 109; aft. 70; even. 141.
Average: morn. 120; aft. 90 scholars; even. 170.

Philip Roberts.   Deacon.
Mill Farm.

(3) Soar.   Independent.
Erected 1837.
Space: free 50; other 72; standing 50.
Present: morn. 31; aft. 30 scholars; even. 50.
Average: morn. 50; aft. 30 scholars; even. 60.
Remark: The average number of attendants at Soar during the 12 months preceding the return to the best of my judgment including Sunday Scholars is about 100.

Thomas Jones.   Minister.

(4) Caersalem Baptist.
Erected 1830.
Space: free 184; other 45; standing 100.
Present: morn. 90 + 60 scholars; even. 200.

David Evans.   Minister.

2 Rumney Parish, co. Monmouth.

Area: 3,375 acres. *Popn.* 161 males, 147 females, total 308.

(5) Rumney Parish Church.
Endowed: land £52; tithe £35; glebe £5. 10; permanent endowment £4; fees 10s; other sources £3.
Space: free 140; other 10.
Present: morn. 32 + 10 scholars; aft. 16 + 8 scholars.
Average (12 *months*): morn. 14 + 6 scholars; aft. 5.
Remarks: Probably many more than usual attended the Church service on this day, the 30th March, inst. at this church, being desirous to show themselves to be Protestant Church people especially in opposition to Roman Catholic dangerous errors.

William Jones. Minister.

Lewis: discharged vicarage, valued at £5. 10. 7½: patrons and appropriators, the Dean and Chapter of Bristol: great tithes commuted for £195 and the small tithes for £45; net income £86: vicar has glebe of 3 acres.
C & C: 1 service in Welsh taken by the incumbent.
I & C: resident: curate has stipend of £90.

(6) Gilead. Wesleyan Methodist.
Erected 1845.
Space: free 70; other 24.
Present: morn. 39; even. 34.
Average (12 *months*): morn. 30 + 20 scholars; even. 50.

Edward Thomas. Chapel Steward.
Gardener.

3 Roath Parish.

Area: 3,500 acres. *Popn.* 138 males, 174 females: total 312.

(7) Roath Parish Church.
Endowed: land £37. 12; tithe £75; Q A B £6. 13. 2.; dues on the average about £10.
Space: free 154.
Present: morn. 28 + 6 scholars; aft. 29 + 8 scholars.
Average: morn. 35 + 10 scholars; aft. 30 + 9 scholars.
Remarks: The soldiers living in the Long Cross Barracks in this parish always attend divine service in the Town of Cardiff, the distance nearly the same as to Roath Church. Sunday March 30, 1837 a sermon was preached on behalf of a Charity School in S. Mary's Church Cardiff by the Lord Bishop of Llandaff. Many of the inhabitants of Roath attended.

Charles C. Williams. Churchwarden.
Roath Court, Cardiff.

Lewis: Vicarage not in charge, endowed with £800 royal bounty; net income £106:

tithes commuted for £307. 10., of which £160 is payable to the Dean and Chapter of Gloucester, £72. 10. to the Marquis of Bute, who is also patron of the benefice, and £75 to the vicar. Vicar has 12 acres of land in the parish of Bedwas, and 10 acres in the parish of St. Woollos, co. Monmouth.

C & C: 2 services both in English.

I & C: resident.

4 Cardiff. Parishes of St. John and St. Mary.

Area: 2,321 acres. *Popn.* 10,286 males, 8,065 females: total 18,351.

(8) St. John the Baptist, Cardiff. Parish Church.

Endowed: Being only the curate I cannot tell correctly.
Space: free 200; other about 700; children 150.
Present: Impossible to say.
Remark: Having made no provision to ascertain the foregoing information, my return would probably be erroneous.

J. Stacey. Curate.

I & C: not resident: curate, who resides in the glebe-house has stipend of £150.

(9) St. Mary the Virgin.
Consecrated 6 Nov. 1845 as a new Parish Church in lieu of the old one destroyed by a flood some two hundred years ago.
Erected by grants and voluntary contributions, total cost £7,000.
Endowed: Houses £60; tithe £61. 12.; pew rents £100; Easter offerings offerings uncertain.
Space: free 1,200; other 600.
Present: morn. 900 + 268 acolars.
Remark: In the evening there is a service also in the School Room 100 to 150. In the afternoon there is service also in a boat house for sailors 70. In the evening there is service also on board ship—cannot tell the number, it depends upon the size of the vessel.

U. Leigh Morgan. Vicar.

Lewis: The two livings of St. John and St. Mary are discharged vicarages consolidated. St. John's rated at £13. 4. 6½, and St. Mary's at £4. 5. 10: present net income £260 with a glebe and house: patrons and impropriators, the Dean and Chapter of Gloucester. St. Mary's erected 1843, by private subscription, the patrons, public subscriptions, and aid of Church Building Society.

C & C: St. John's, 2 English services. St. Mary's 3 services, 1 in Welsh, taken by the incumbent.

I & C: resident: curate has stipend of £110.

ICBS: grant of £500 in 1840.

(10) WESLEY CHAPEL. ENGLISH WESLEYAN METHODIST.
Erected 1850 in lieu of one erected before 1800.
Space: free 420; other 800.
Present: morn. 600 + 112 scholars; even. 1,000.
Average (6 *months*): morn. 600 + 100 scholars; even. 900.
Remarks: The average attendance is only given for six months that being the time the new chapel has been opened in lieu of the old one.

> Charles Tucker. Minister.
> 2 Wellington Terrace, Cardiff.

(11) BETHEL. *Welsh* WESLEYAN METHODIST.
Erected 1838.
Space: free 50; other 116.
Present: morn. 67 + 20 scholars; even. 104.
Average (12 *months*): morn. 60 + 10 scholars; even. 100.

> Henry Wilcox. Minister.

(12) Name of Place of Worship: 'None but Barracks'.
LATTER DAY SAINTS.
Not used exclusively as a place of worship.
Present: morn. 50; aft. 200; even. 250.

> James Ellis. Elder.
> No. 36 Tredegar Place, Cardiff.

(13) ZION CALVINISTIC METHOIDIST.
Erected 1827.
Space: free 140; other 366.
Present: morn. 340 + 27 scholars; even. 392 + 60 scholars.
Average (3 *months*): morn. 328 + 24 scholars; even. 376 + 52 scholars.

> Thomas Davies. Elder.
> 1 East Terrace, Cardiff.

(14) BETHEL. BUTE DOCK. BAPTIST.
Erected 1849.
Space: free 268.
Present: morn. 74 + 77 scholars; aft. 54 + 74 scholars; even. 114.

> William Jones, Wharton St.
> and
> Andrew Gunton Fuller,
> Nelson Terrace,
> Cardiff, Ministers.

(15)   St. David's Roman Catholic Church.
Erected 1842.
Space: 400 + 362 free; other 180.
Present: 1st. 450, 2nd. 750; aft. 150 scholars; even. 100.
Remark: I have marked 1st and 2nd because there are two services in the
morning except once a month.

> Thomas Cody.   Roman Catholic Priest.
> David St., Cardiff.

(16)   St. Davids' Roman Catholic Church.
Erected: 1842.
Space: free 362; other 30; standing about 400.
Present: 1st. 450; 2nd. 750; aft. 150 scholars; even. 100.
Remark: I have marked 1st and 2nd because there are two services in the
morning except once a month.

> Thomas Cody. Roman Catholic Priest.

[Endorsed: Duplicate. i.e. of previous return.]

(17)   Bethany Chapel. Baptist.
Erected 1807.
Space: free 468; other 440. Lecture room attached for week day services;
free seats for 230.
Present: morn. 301 + 136 scholars; aft. at school 205 scholars; even. 570.

> William Jones and
> Andrew Gunton Fuller.   Ministers.
> Nelson Terrace, Cardiff.

(18)   English Independents.
Space: free 100; other 250.
Usual number of attendants: morn. 120.

> [no signature]

[Informant's form. This schedule is wrongly bound into 601.1.]

(?19)   Ebenezer Street Chapel.   Welsh Independents.
Space: free 200.
Usual number of attendants: morn. 200.

> [no signature]

[Informant's form. This schedule is wrongly bound into 601.1.]

(?20)   Tabernacle.   The Hays, Cardiff.   Baptist.
Erected 1821.
Present: morn. 419 + 124 scholars; aft. 218 scholars; even. 700.
Average (12 *months*): morn. 419 + 124 scholars; aft. 218 scholars; even.
850.

Remarks: The Vestry adjoining capable of seating 200 persons—all free. About 150 less this evening than the *average* attendance owing to our minister being from home.

> William Owen.   Deacon.
> Printer and Publisher.

[This schedule is wrongly bound into 601.1.]
[Note: (39) below should be included here.]

5.   Llandaff Parish.
Area: 4,352 acres. *Popn.* 893 males, 928 females: total 1,821.

(21)   CATHEDRAL OF LLANDAF.
Endowed: tithes—small tithes; no land; no glebe.
Space: free about 150, + stalls.
Present: morn. 90 to 100; aft. 70 to 80.
Remark: The questions are not very applicable to the state of things.

> Richard Prichard.   Senior Vicar.

Lewis: The cathedral, as parochial church, is united with the adjoining parish of Whitchurch [581. 1. 11(29)], and two priest-vicars officiate alternately in the two churches. The great tithes of both parishes are the property of the chapter, the senior and junior vicars each receiving an annual stipend in lieu of the small tithes, the former of £214, the latter of £76. The Bishop, who is Dean of St. Paul's, has the patronage of all the dignities of the church, and of 7 benefices, with an income of £1,000 per annum. The Chapter has the patronage of the two minor canonries, and 17 benefices, and 1 other alternately, with a net revenue of £700.

I & C: sen. vicar resident.

(22)   EBENEZER OR ELY CHAPEL.   WESLEYAN METHODIST.
The present chapel built in the year 1843 in lieu of the old one built about the year 1800.
Space: free 64; other 70.
Present: morn. 20 scholars; aft. 20; even. 40.
Average (12 *months*): morn. 40 + 20 scholars; even. 50.

> Henry Wilcox.   Minister.

(23)   WESLEYAN METHODIST CHAPEL, CITY OF LLANDAFF.
Rebuilt in the year 1839 in lieu of an old one which was built in 1813.
Space: free 100; other 78.
Present: morn. 10 scholars; aft. 46; even. 40.
Average (12 *months*): morn. 10 scholars; aft. 40; even. 50.
Remark: The 75 [other sittings] represent sittings in the pews that are let quarterly for a certain sum per sitting.

> Henry Wilcox.   Minister.

(24) WESLEYAN METHODIST.
Name: 'none. It was a Cottage'.
Erected 1843.
Present: even. 50.
Average: even. 50.

Charles Tucker.   Minister.

[Endorsed: Dwelling house.]

(25) PARTICULAR BAPTISTS.
A room, 'erected' 1826.
Present: morn. 11; even. 54.

John Thomas.   Deacon.
Ely Road.

[Endorsed: room]

6   **Parish of Radyr.**
Area: 1,530 acres. *Popn.* 221 males, 196 females: total 417.

(26) RADYR PARISH CHURCH, DEDICATED TO ST. JOHN.
Endowed: tithe £75; permanent endowment £60, augmented by money charged on Patron's Estate; fees £1. 10.
Space: free 40; other 40.
Present: morn. 32 + 23 scholars; aft. 34.
Average (3 *months*): morn. 20 + 20 scholars; aft. 25.

David Jones.   Curate.

Lewis: Vicarage, endowed with £60 per annum private benefaction, and £200 royal bounty; net income, £59; patron and impropriator, Earl of Plymouth; tithes commuted for £113. 9., of which £38. 9. is payable to the impropriator, and £75 to the vicar, the latter subject to rates, averaging £5.

C & C: 1 service, alternately Welsh and English, taken by the curate.

I & C: not resident: curate, who resided at St. Fagan's, has stipend of £60.

(27) BETHEL.   CALVINISTIC METHODIST.
Erected 1842.
Space: free 30; other 168; standing 60.
Present: morn. 88 scholars; aft. 70; even. 74.
Average: general congregation 150; scholars 105.

William Hugh.   Deacon.

7   **Parish of St. Fagan.**
Area: 2,241 acres. *Popn.* 262 males, 253 females: total 515.

(28)   St. Fagan's Parish Church.
Space: free 250.
Usual number of attendants: 120 including scholars.
                                    Informant: [no signature]
[Informant's form]
Lewis: Rectory with Llanillterne [581. 4. 4(6)] annexed; rated at £14. 9. 7; patron, Earl of Plymouth; tithes commuted for £383, with glebe of 74 acres, valued at £110, and a parsonage built in 1795 by the incumbent.
C & C: 1 English service.
I & C: resident; curate has stipend of £40.

(29)   Tabernacle, St. Ffagan.   Welsh Calvinstic Methodist.
Erected before the year 1780, removed in 1837 to the present chapel erected on another spot.
Space: free 30; other 204; standing 100 feet.
Present: morn. 100; aft. 44 scholars; even. 300.
Average (12 *months*): morn. 150; aft. 40 scholars; even. 300.
Remark: The morning service differs from the evening because it is rather early, being at 9 o'clock.
                          Thomas Phillips.   Secretary.
                          Scuborfawr, St. Ffagans.

(30)   Wesleyan Methodists.
Erected in the year 1822.
Space: free 18 feet by 14 feet.
Present: aft. 40.
Average: aft. 36.

                          Charles Tucker.   Minister.

8   Cairau Parish.
Area: 746 acres. *Popn.* 42 males, 38 females: total 87.

(31)   Caerau Parish Church.
Space: free 40.
Usual number of attendants: morn. 10.
                                    Informant: [no signature]
[Informant's form]
Lewis: The parish constitutes a prebend in the cathedral church of Llandaf, valued at £3. 10. 7½, and endowed with the tithes of the parish as also the tithes of the parishes of Penterry [577. 4. 4(10)] and Llandogo [576. 2. 4(6)], co. Monmouth. Living a perpetual curacy, endowed with £1,000 royal bounty; net income, £60; patron, Prependary of Caerau. Tithes have been commuted for £154, of which £4 are payable to the Bishop of Llandaf, and £150 to the Prependary, who has also a glebe of 20 acres, valued at £23 per annum.
C & C: 1 Welsh service taken by the incumbent.
I & C: not resident.

9 Leckwith Parish.

Area: 1,302 acres. *Popn.* 56 males, 58 females: total 114.

(32   LECKWITH PARISH CHURCH.
Endowed: tithe £107.
Space: free 20; other 50.
Present: aft. 17 + 10 scholars.
Remark: service is alternate morning and afternoon.

James Evans.   Rector.

Lewis: Consolidated discharged rectory, with Llandough and Cogan [581. 2. 11(34) and 581. 2. 13(38)], rated at £8. 8. 4.; patron, Marquess of Bute. For tithe commutation, see Llandough (11) below. Church dedicated to St. James.

C & C: 1 service, alternately Welsh and English, taken by the incumbent.

I & C: resident.

ERCR: accommodation 100.

10   Michaelstone-le-Pit Parish.

Area: 790 acres. *Popn.* 45 males, 42 females: total 87.

(33)   MICHAELSTONE LE PIT PARISH CHURCH.
Space: free 100.
Usual number of attendants: morn. 20 including scholars; aft. do.; even. do.

Informant: [no signature]

[Informant's form]

Lewis: Discharged rectory, rated at £4. 10. 7½, endowed with £200 royal bounty, and £200 parliamentary grant; net income, £65; patron, T. B. Rouse, Esq., Courtyrala.

C & C: 1 service in English.

I & C: not resident.

11   Llandough-juxta-Penarth Parish.

Area: 689 acres. *Popn.* 67 males, 68 females: total 135.

(34)   LANDOUGH PARISH CHURCH.
Endowed: tithe £84.14; glebe £8.
Space: free 70.
Present: morn. 27 + 25 scholars.
Remark: Service is alternate morning and afternoon.

James Evans.   Rector.

Lewis: Discharged rectory, with the rectory of Leckwith [581. 2. 9 (32)] and the vicarage of Cogan [581. 2. 13 (38)] annexed: rated at £8. 8. 4; patron, Marquess of Bute; tithes, with those of Leckwith and Cogan, commuted for £240, subject to rates, which average £34; glebe of 33 acres, valued at £30 per annum.

C & C: 1 service, alternately Welsh and English, taken by the incumbent.

I & C: resident.

(35)   BAPTIST.
Erected: 'It was a dwelling house rented about the year 1839 for religious worship exclusively.'
Space: free 150.
Present: morn. 22; even. 50.

William Jenkins.   Deacon.

12   Penarth Parish.
Area: 1,507 acres. *Popn.* 53 males, 53 females: total 105.

(36)   PENARTH PARISH CHURCH.
Endowed: tithe £58; glebe £5; permanent endowment £60; fees 10*s.*
Space: other 60.
Present: aft. 35 + 10 scholars.
Remark: The service is alternate morning and evening.

E. W. Evans.   Curate.

Lewis: Discharged rectory, with that of Lavernock [581. 2. 14(27)] annexed; endowed with a rent-charge of £50 by Thomas Lewis, in 1716; patron, Earl of Plymouth: net income £136.

C & C: 1 service, alternately Welsh and English, taken by the curate.

I & C: not resident: curate, who resides at Llandough, 4 miles distant, has stipend of £80.

14   Lavernock Parish.
Area: 1,014 acres. *Popn.* 39 males, 42 females: total 81.

(37)   LAVERNOCK PARISH CHURCH.
Emdowed: fees 5*s.*
Space: other 30.
Present: morn. 9.
Remark: The service is alternate morning and afternoon.

E. W. Evans.   Curate.

Lewis: Rectory not in charge consolidated with that of Penarth: church dedicated to St. Lawrence.

C & C: 1 service, alternately Welsh and English, taken by the curate.

I & C: Vide Penarth, 581. 2. 12(36).

13   Cogan Parish.
Area: 602 acres. *Popn.* 20 males, 13 females: total 33.

(38) COGAN PARISH CHURCH.
Endowed: tithe £52. 12.; glebe £28.
Space: free 70; other 24.
Remark: The church is desecrated and in ruins, the inhabitants attending divine service in the adjoining parish church of Llandough to which Cogan is united.

James Evans.   Rector.

Lewis: With the livings of Llandough and Leckwith, a consolidated rectory; rated at £8. 8. 4. For tithes and net income, see under Leckwith [581. 2. 9(32)].

C & C: with Leckwith, 1 service, alternately Welsh and English, taken by the incumbent.

(39) CHARLES STREET, CARDIFF, SOCIETY OF FRIENDS.
Estimated number of persons capable of being seated: about 200 if closely seated.
Present: morn. 5, average attendance about 7; aft. 3 only; even. none.
Remark: When the meeting house was first erected we sat down on 1st day morning to the number of 30 to 35 since which time some have been removed by death and others (whole families at a time) removed to other Places.

Samuel Beavington.

[Note: this, and the previous two returns, are out of order.]

[*End of Cardiff District*]

3. ST. NICHOLAS (Subdistrict)
Area: 30,865 acres. *Popn.* 2,315 males, 2,257 females: total 4,572.

1 Sully Parish.
Area: 2,167 acres. *Popn.* 77 males, 60 females: total 137.

(1) SULLY PARISH CHURCH.
Endowed: tithe £277; glebe 28 acres; fees about £3; total about £300.
Space: 80 sittings. Practically the sittings are all free.
Present: morn. 17 + 19 scholars; aft. 35 + 16 scholars.

George Woods.   Rector.

Lewis: Discharged rectory, rated at £11. 9. 9½: net income £250. Patroness, Mrs. Thomas of Sully House.

C & C: 2 English services.

I & C: Resident.

(2) WESLEYAN METHODISTS (ENGLISH).
Building not used exclusively as a place of worship.
Occupied since 1849.
Space: 18 feet by 18 feet.
Present: even. 40.
Average: even. 35.

Charles Tucker.   Minister.

2   Cadoxton-juxta-Barry Parish.
Area: 1,028 acres.   *Popn.* 129 males, 143 females: total 272.

(3) CADOXTON-JUXTA-BARRY PARISH CHURCH.
Endowed: tithe £112; glebe £30.
Space: free 78.
Present: aft. 25 + 22 scho.ars.
Average (12 *months*): morn. 35 + 25 scholars.
Remark: Service is performed alternate Sundays in the morning at 11 o'clock and at 2½ in the afternoon. The church will accomodate about 78 persons. All free sittings.

William Jenkins.   Curate.

Lewis: discharged rectory, rated at £5. 2. 1; net income £100. Patron, R. F. Jenner, Esq.

C & C: 1 service taken by incumbent and curate. Welsh occasionally.

I & C: resident: curate's stipend £40.

(4) TABOR BABTIS CHAPEL.
Erected 1811.
Usual number present: morn. 50; even. 70.

Informant: Ll. Morgan.   Registrar.

[Informant's form]

(4A) PHILADELPHIA BAPTIST.
Erected 1817.
Space: free 78.
Present: morn. 39; even. 54.

John Morgan.   Deacon.
St. Andrews.

(5) BETHEL. WESLEYAN METHODIST.
Erected 1814.
Space: free 80; standing 40.
Present: morn. 41; even. 42.
Average: general congregation 70.

John Williams.   Local Preacher.

(6) SION. WELSH CALVINISTIC METHODIST.
Space: free 100; other 66; standing 100.
Present: morn. 45; aft. 30 scholars; even. 160.
Average (12 *months*)*:* general congregation 150; scholars 30.

Job Thomas. Elder.
Pencotry.

3 Merthyr Dovan Parish.
Area: 1,396 acres. *Popn.* 82 males, 70 females: total 152.

(7) MERTHIR DOVAN PARISH CHURCH.
Endowed: land £20; tithe £115.
Space: total sittings 14.
Present: morn. 22.
Average: morn. 10.

William Spickett Warden.
Clerk of the above.

Lewis: discharged rectory, rated at £4. 17. 3½., endowed with £200 royal bounty.
Net income £109. Patron, R. F. Jenner, Esq.

C & C: 1 Welsh service, taken by the curate.

I & C: rector not resident: curate resides at Bonvilstone, [581. 3. 11 (21)] 4 miles
distant, and receives sipend of £50.

4 Highlight. Extra parochial.
Area: 390 acres. *Popn.* 10 males, 9 females: total 19.

Lewis: Highlight is an extra-parochial district, for ecclesiastical purposes attached
to the parish of Merthyr Dovan, the inhabitants attending divine service at the
parish church.

5 Barry Parish.
Area: 835 acres. *Popn.* 39 males, 35 females: total 74.

(8) BARRY PARISH CHURCH.
Endwed: tithe £34; glebe 31 acres; Queen Anne's Bounty £9. 1. 6.
Space: free 36; other 12.
Present: morn. 15; aft. and even. 'no service'.
Remark: I have no remark to make.

Paul Ashmore. Rector.

Lewis: rectory not in charge, united to the rectory of Porthkerry; net income £87;
patrons, the six sons of the late Sir Samuel Romilly.

C & C: 1 service in English.

I & C: vide sub Porthkery [581. 3. 6(9)].

6 Porthkerry Parish.
Area: 1,131 acres. *Popn.* 67 males, 79 females: total 146.

(9) PORTHKERRY PARISH CHURCH.
Endowed: tithe £180 per annum; glebe 63 acres.
Space: free 40; other 18. Room for 44 school children in addition.
Present: morn. no service; aft. 26 + 21 scholars; even. no service.
Remark: I have no remarks to make.

Paul Ashmore.   Rector.

Lewis: discharged rectory, to which Barry is united; rated at £7. 8. 1½.; patrons, the sons of Sir Samuel Romilly; tithes commuted for rent-charge of £123. 13., subject to rates averaging £16; glebe of 60 acres valued at £65 per annum.

C & C: 1 service in English.

I & C: not resident; curate occupies glebe house, and receives stipend of £80.

7 Penmark Parish.
Area: 3,395 acres. *Popn.* 243 males, 252 females: total 495.

(10) PENMARK PARISH CHURCH.
Space: free about 150; other 50.
Usual number of attendants: morn. about 60, including 30 scholars; aft. about 25, including 10 scholars; even. service at Aberthaw chapel [same parish], 2 miles from parish church, about 30 attendants.

Informant: John Alexander.

[Informant's form]

Lewis: vicarage, rated at £8. 13. 4.; patrons, Dean and Chapter of Gloucester. Tithes commuted for a rent-charge of £558. 0. 3., of which a sum of £347. 5. is payable to the Dean and Chapter; and glebe of 13 acres valued at £16 per annum; rent-charge and glebe subject to rates averaging £55. 2. 6. per annum: £210. 15. 3., subject to rates averaging £28. 7., payable to the vicar, who has a glebe of 100a. 2r. 26p. valued at £135. 10. and a house. The chapels Aberthaw and Rhôs . . . have long since fallen into decay.'

C & C: 2 services, both in English.

I & C: resident.

(11) RHOOSE BAPTIST.
Erected before 1800.
Space: 12 feet by 18 feet.
Present: aft. 30.
Average: morn. 30.

Morgan Morgan.   Steward.
Rhoose.

[Endorsed: See letter]

(12) NURSTON. INDEPENDENT.
Space: free 100; standing 30.
Present: morn. 15; even. 111.

> Dacor Robert Peers.
> Morgan Morgan.   Minister.

(13) SARDIS CHAPEL. CALVINISTIC METHODIST.
Erected 1832.
Space: free 300; other 16.
Present: morn. 100; aft. 16 scholars; even. 150.
Average (12 *months*): morn. 200; aft. 20 scholars; even. 300.

> Thomas Mathews.   Deacon.
> Fontigary.

8 Llancarvan Parish.

Area: 4,500 acres. *Popn.* 359 males, 303 females: total 662.

(14) LLANCARVAN PARISH CHURCH.
Endowed: tithe commuted at £245; glebe, land house £46; fees £2.
Space: free 150; other 100.
Present: morn. 120 + 25 scholars; even. 40 + 10 scholars.

> David Morgan.   Vicar.

Lewis: discharged vicarage, rated at £8. 13. 9., in the patronage of the crown; appropriators, Dean and Chapter of Gloucester: tithes commuted for £570. 10. 2., of which £325. 10. 2 is payable to the appropriators, subject to rates averaging £41. 5., and £245, subject to rates averaging £33, to the vicar who also has glebe of 12 acres, valued at £33. 5. per annum.

C & C: 2 services, one in Welsh and one in English, taken by the incumbent.

I & C: legally not resident.

(15) BETHLEHEM, LANCARVAN. BAPTIST.
Erected 1823.
Space: free 300; other 168.
Present: morn. 200; even. 450 + 40 scholars.
Average: morn. 190; even. 560 + 60 scholars.

> Edmund Thomas Bassett.   Minister.
> [?Bassett Edmund Thomas]

(16) ZOAR, LANCARVAN. CALVINISTIC METHODIST.
Erected 1831.
Space: free 200; other 16.
Present: aft. 40 scholars; even. 38.

> Thomas Edwards.   Deacon.
> Leech Castle, Bonvilstone.

(17)   CARMEL, LANCARVAN (LIEGECASTLE).   INDEPENDANT.
Space: free 'none'; other 'none'; standing 400.
Present: morn. 60; even. 200.
Average: general congregation 100.

> Jonathan Measey.   Deacon.
> Wood Carter,
> Pen yr heoel, Bonvilstone.

(18)   EBENEZER, LANCARVAN VILLAGE.   WESLEYAN.
Erected 1835.
Space: free 110; standing 300.
Present: morn. 56; aft. 75; even. 94.
Average (6 *months*): morn. 60, 'total' [?scholars] 60; even. 80.

> William Griffith, Jnr.   Deacon.

9   Llantrithyd Parish.
Area: 1,391 acres. *Popn.* 100 males, 101 females: total 201.

(19)   LLANTRITHYD PARISH CHURCH.
Endowed: tithe, gross £136; glebe, gross £80.
Space: free 71; other 79.
Present: morn. 50 + 28 scholars; even. 26 + 24 scholars.
Average (6 *months*): morn 50 + 36 scholars; even. 30 + 25. scholars.

> M. J. Tyler.   Minister.

Lewis: discharged vicarage, rated at £8. 13. 4; patron, Sir T. D. Aubrey, Bart.:
tithes commuted for £132. 17. 9; glebe of 52 acres, valued at £80, and glebe-house.
C & C: 2 services, one in Welsh and one in English, taken by the incumbent.
I & C: [no entry].
ICBS: grant of £25 in 1839.

10   Welsh St. Donats Parish.
Area: 2,175 acres. *Popn.* 147 males, 144 females: total 291.

(20)   WELSH ST. DONATTS PARISH CHURCH.
Space: total 120.
Usual number of attendants: average 20.
Remark: There is no school in the parish.

> *Informant:* Llewellyn Morgan.
> Registrar.

[Informant's form]

Lewis: perpetual curacy, annexed to the vicarage of Llanblethian [583. 3. 22(36a)]:
impropriators, Dean and Chapter of Gloucester; impropriate tithes commuted for
£116. 9. 11, subject to rates averaging £10, and the vicarial tithes for £50.
C & C: 1 service, alternately English and Welsh, performed by the curate.
I & C: *vide sub* Llanblethian.

11 Bonvilston Parish.
Area: 1,178 acres. *Popn.* 145 males, 149 females: total 294.

(21) BONVILSTONE (ST. MARY'S) PARISH CHURCH.
Endowed: land £5; tithe £40.
Space: free 45; other 75.
Present: morn. 51; even. 30.
Average: morn. 76; even. 35.
Remark: The morning service is alternate with another Church at 11 o'clock in the morning and 2 o'clock on the afternoon.

Lewis Thomas.   Curate.

Lewis: perpetual curacy, rated at £6. 9. 2, endowed with £14 per annum principally out of the small tithes, and £200 private benefaction, £200 royal bounty, and £500 parliamentary grant; net income £83; patron and impropriator, Richard Basset, Esq.: the great tithes commuted for a rent-charge of £80, and those payable to the perpetual curate, for one of £54.
C & C: 1 service in English.
I & C: incumbent not resident; curate, who resides in the parish, has stipend of £65.

12 Llanvithin.   Ex. paroch.
Area: 466 acres. *Popn.* 14 males, 15 females: total 29.

13 St. Nicholas Parish.
Area: 2,104 acres. *Popn.* 205 males, 209 females: total 414.

(22) ST. NICHOLAS PARISH CHURCH.
Endowed: land including glebe £55; tithe £210.
Space: free 35; other 19, independent of gallery which will hold 40.
Present: morn. 50 + 40 scholars; even. 10.
Average (12 months): morn. 50 + 40 scholars; even. 9.

William Morgan.   Curate.

Lewis: discharged rectory, rated at £11. 10.; patron, John Bruce Pryce, Esq.: tithes commuted for £210, subject to rates averaging £23. 7. 9. per annum; glebe of 56 acres, valued at £59.
C & C: 2 services, one in Welsh, taken by the incumbent.
I & C: resident.

(23) TREHILL CALVINISTIC METHODIST.
Erected before 1800.
Space: free 120.
Present: morn. 60; even. 110.
Average: morn. 50 + 28 scholars.

Edward Jones.   Elder.

(24) Croes y Parc. Particular Baptist.
Erected 1777.
Space: free 180.
Present: morn. 130 + 32 scholars; even. 150.
David John.   Deacon.
Peterston Bridge.

14   St. Lythans Parish.
Area: 1,248 acres. *Popn.* 74 males, 61 females: total 135.

(25) St. Lythan's Parish Church.
Endowed: land and glebe £40; tithe £140.
Space: free 96.
Present: morn. 8 + 8 scholars; aft. 30 + 12 scholars.
Average (12 *months*): morn. 5 + 8 scholars; aft. 32 + 12 scholars.
William Morgan.   Curate.

Lewis: discharged vicarage, endowed with the great tithes, rated at £6. 1. 3.; net income, £199, with a glebe house; patron, Archdeacon of Llandaf: tithes commuted for a rent-charge of £140, subject to rates averaging £14 per annum; glebe contains 40 acres, valued at £40.

C & C: 2 services, one in Welsh taken by the incumbent and curate.

I & C: incumbent not resident; curate resides in the glebe house, and receives stipend of £80.

15   Wenvoe Parish.
Area: 2,955 acres. *Popn.* 231 males, 244 females: total 475.

(26) Wenvoe Parish Church.
Endowed: tithe and glebe £365.
Space: other 140.
[Remainder of form blank. No signature.]

Lewis: rectory, rated at £13. 7. 1; net income £326; patron, Mr. Jenner: glebe-house.

C & C: 2 services in English.

I & C: not resident: curate, who resides in the glebe-house, has stipend of £100.

(27) Twyn'r odyn. Particular Baptist.
Erected 1823.
Space: free 200; other 36 rented seats; free benches; standing 200 men.
Present; morn. 78; aft. 72 scholars; even. 213.
Remark: Here is the average number of our Congregation during the last 12 month. About 90 in the morning and about 250 in the evening and about 60 in the Sunday School at 2 o'clock.
Robert Owen.   Minister.
Twynyrodyn, Wenvoe.

(28) ZOAR. CALVINISTIC METHODIST.
Erected 1832.
Space: free 55; other 65; standing 130.
Present: morn. 60; even. 95.

> Benjamin Richards. Secretary.
> Smith.
> Wenvoe.

16 St. Andrew Parish.
Area: 3,149 acres. *Popn.* 250 males, 238 females: total 488.

(29) ST. ANDREW PARISH CHURCH.
Usual number of attendants: morn. 8; aft. 8.

> *Informant:* L. Morgan. Registrar.

[Informant's form]
Lewis: rectory, rated at £13. 14. 1½: in the patronage of the crown: tithes com-
muted for £355, subject to rates averaging £24: glebe of 75 acres, valued at £96
and rectory-house built by the Rev. Windsor Richards.
C & C: 2 services, one in Welsh, performed by the curate (the benefice being
vacant).
I & C: vacant.
ERCR: accom. 200.

(30) EBENEZER. CALVINISTIC METHODIST.
Built about the year 1760 and rebuilt about the year 1839.
Space: free 200; other 30 seats rented.
Present: morn. 50; aft. 142 + 40 scholars; even. 50 + 35 scholars.
Average: morn. 960; aft. 840; even. 1,440 [whole line crossed out].
Remark: The scholars in morning and evening for the 12 calendar months
are included in the general congregation.

> Thomas John. Deacon.

17 Michaelston-super-Ely Parish.
Area: 299 acres. *Popn.* 26 males, 22 females: total 48.

(31) MICHALESTON SUPER ELY PARISH CHURCH.
Endowed: tithes commuted at £60; glebe 45.
Space: free 3 pews; other sittings open without pews; total 49.
Present: morn. 6; aft. and even. no service.
Average (12 months): morn. 9; aft. and even. no service.
Remarks: There is a school in the adjoining parish of St. Georges provided
for the Sunday scholars of Michaelston super Ely, and St. Brides and for
Day Scholars.

> David Thomas. Curate.

Lewis: discharged rectory with the rectory of St. Bride's super Ely [581. 4. 1(1)]
consolidated, rated at £8. 6. 8; net income £100; patron, Llewelyn Traherne,

Esq.: tithes commuted for £60, subject to rates averaging £5. 3. 6; glebe of 28 acres, valued at £36.

C & C: 1 service in Welsh taken by the curate.

I & C: incumbent resident; curate's stipend £40.

18 St. George Parish.
Area: 1,058 acres. *Popn.* 117 males, 123 females: total 240.

(32) ST. GEORGES PARISH CHURCH.
Space: free 20; other 120.
Present: morn. 27 + 79 scholars.
Average (12 *months*): morn. from 35 to 40 + 70 scholars; aft. from 35 to 40 + 76 scholars.
Remark: I do not know the value of the Benefice.

L. A. Nicholls.   Curate.

Lewis: discharged rectory, rated at £7. 5. 7½; net income £140, with a glebe house; patron, Rev. John Montgomery Traherne.

C & C: 1 service, alternately Welsh and English, taken by the curate.

I & C: incumbent resident. Curate's stipend £40.

[End of St. Nicholas Subdistrict]

4 LLANTRISAINT (Subdistrict)
Area: 33,225 acres. *Popn.* 5,674 males, 5,039 females: total 10,713.

1 St. Brides-super-Ely Parish.
Area: 676 scres. *Popn.* 58 males, 57 females: total 115.

(1) ST. BRIDES SUPER ELY PARISH CHURCH.
Endowed: tithe commuted at £104; glebe £20.
Space: other 80.
Present: aft. 45.
Average (12 *months*): morn. 30; aft. 30.
Remark: The children who reside in this parish resort to the School in the adjoining parish of St. George. The School at St. Georges is for the instruction of the children of St. Georges, St. Brides and Michaelstone super Ely.

S. A. Nicholls.   Rector.

Lewis: discharged rectory, consolidated with the rectory of Michaelston-super-Ely [581. 3. 17(31)], net income £117, with a glebe house.

C & C: 2 services, of which 1 in Welsh, taken by the incumbent.

I & C: incumbent resident; curate's stipend £40.

2 Peterstone-super-Ely Parish.
Area: 2,010 acres. *Popn.* 114 males, 108 females: total 222.

(2) PETERSTONE SUPER ELY PARISH CHURCH.
Endowed: land £25; tithe, commuted at £250; Easter offerings £5.
Space: free 100; other 50.
Present: morn. 9; aft. 30.
Average (12 *months*): morn. 8; aft. 24.
Remark: The Glebe House, or as it is called Parsonage House, has lately been sold to the S. Wales Railway Company, and none as yet has been built for the Minister to reside which is a great detriment to Parish.

David Thomas.   Curate.

Lewis: rectory, rated at £7. 12. 8½; net income £228; patrons, Sir T. D. Aubrey and Col. Wood.
C & C: 2 services, of which 1 in Welsh taken by the curate.
I & C: incumbent not resident; curate lives in glebe house, and receives stipend of £80.

(3) EBENEZER.   INDEPENDENT.
Erected 1834.
Space: free 'none'; other 'none'.
Present: morn. 60; aft. 12 scholars; even. 109.
Average (6 *months*): morn. 360; aft. 120; even. 600.

Thomas Griffiths.   Deacon.

3 Pendoylan Parish.
Area: 3,504 acres. *Popn.* 196 males, 167 females: total 363.

(4) PENDOYLAN PARISH CHURCH.
Space: free 8; other [blank]; total 84.
Usual number of attendants: morn. 84; aft. 80.

Informant: [blank]

[Informant's form]
Lewis: discharged vicarage, rated at £8. 13. 4; net income £112; patron and appropriators Archdeacon and Chapter of Llandaf.
C & C: 1 service, alternately Welsh and English, taken by the incumbent.
I & C: incumbent not resident.

(5) CLAWDDCOCH.   CALVINISTIC METHODIST.
Erected 1820.
Space: standing 400.
Present: morn. 250 + 80 scholars; aft. 250 + 88 scholars; even. 300.

William Bassett.   Secretary.
Caewiga, Pendoylan.

4   Llanilterne Parochial Chapelry.
Area: 1,080 acres. *Popn.* 69 males, 68 females: total 137.

(6)   LLANILLTERNE.   An ancient Chapelry in the parish of St. Fagans.
Endowed: fees about 10s.
Space: other 50.
Present: aft. 10.
Average (5 *months*): morn. 12; even. 20.
Remark: The Rent charge of this Chapelry, belongs to the Rector of St.
Fagans. There are no emoluments attached to it but the surplice fees.

L. A. Nichols,
Officiating Minister.

Lewis: living consolidated with the rectory of St. Fagan's [581. 2. 7(28)].
I & C: vide sub St. Fagan's.

(7)   LLANILTERN CHAPEL.   TAIHIRION.   INDEPENDENTS.
Erected about 1761.
Space: free 203.
Present: morn. 37 + 36 scholars; even. 60 scholars.
Average (12 *months*): morn. 70 + 40 scholars; even. 120.

Evan Williams.   Deacon.

5   Pentyrch Parish.
Area: 3,975 acres. *Popn.* 682 males, 717 females: total 1,599.

(8)   PENTYRCH PARISH CHURCH.
Space: free 80; other 40.
Usual number of attendants: morn. 50; aft. 75.

Informant: H. James Thomas.
Vicar of Pentyrch.

[Informant's form]

Lewis: discharged vicarage, rated at £8. 3. 1½.; endowed with £200 royal bounty;
net income £113; patrons and appropriators, Archdeacon and Chapter of Llandaf.
C & C: 1 service, alternately Welsh and English, taken by the incumbent.
I & C: resident.

(9)   PENUEL.   BAPTIST.
Erected 1838.
Space: free 72; other 12; standing 21 feet by 6.
Present: morn. 51 + 21 scholars; aft. 'school time'; even. 160 + 29
scholars.
Average: morn. 57 + 30 scholars; even. 160 + 29 scholars.

William James.   Deacon.
Pencoed, Nr. St. Fagans.

(10) WESLEYAN READING ROOM.   Part of a dwelling house.
Space: free 60.
Present: aft. 60; even. 500.
Average (6 months): aft. 60; even. 50.

John J. Workman.   Minister.
Pontypridd.

(11) HOREB.   CALVINISTIC METHODIST.
Erected 1839.
Space: free 120; other 170.
Present: morn. 120 + 85 scholars; aft. 118; even. 50.
Average (12 months): morn. 160 + 86 scholars; aft. 160; even. 120.

Thomas Hopkin.   Deacon.
[signed by mark]   Nant y Cassar, Pentyrch.

(12) BETHLEHEM.   INDEPENDENT.
Erected 1830.   Used also as a day school.
Space: free 13 benches = 78; other 25 pughs = 150; standing 100.
Present: morn. 194 + 131 scholars; aft. school; even. 179.
Average (12 months): morn. 250 + 131 scholars.

George Pike.   Deacon.
Pentyrch Iron Works.

6 Llantrisaint Parish.

Area: 16,669 acres. *Popn.* 2,200 males, 1,981 females: total 4,181.

(13) TALYGARN. A Chapel of Ease without cure of souls, repaired from a
ruin about 40 years ago by an individual (Dr. Lisle) upon purchasing an
estate called Talygarn.
Endowed: land £24 by Queen Anne's Bounty: permanent endowment
Bounty Office £13; stipend paid by Jesus College £10.
Space: free 60; other 5.
Present: aft. 12.
Remark: The Congregation very small, particularly when the Family are
not in residence at the Mansion House. The services are alternate Sundays
morning and evening. The evening is best attended when the Family are
absent. I cannot average them.

Francis Taynton.   Incumbent.
Cowbridge.

Lewis: vide sub Llantrissent; living is a perpetual curacy, endowed with £1,000
royal bounty; net income £30; patrons and impropriators, Principal and Fellows
of Jesus College, Oxford: chapel recently repaired.
C : C: 1 service in English.
I & C: incumbent not resident.

(14A)   St. John's Chapel of Ease.
Endowed: land £35; permanent endowment £60.
Space: free 20; other 128. One free seat containing 20; Sixteen containing eight each.
Present: aft. 15.
Average: aft. 35.

J. Williams.   Officiating Minister.

Lewis: vide sub. Llantrissent: perpetual curacy, endowed with £200 private benefaction, £1,000 royal bounty, and £1,000 parliamentary grant; patron, Mrs. Pritchard; net income £95.

C & C: 1 service, alternately English and Welsh, performed by the curate.

I & C: incumbent resident.

(14B)   Llantrisant Parish Church.
Space: free 118; other 152.
Average congregation including Sunday Scholars: morn. 250; aft. 200; even. no service.

Signed: Robert Cooke.
Dated: 26 June 1852.

[This is a MS return requested urgently by the Registrar.]

Lewis: vicarage, rated at £26. 14. 2.; endowed with the vicarial tithes of the parishes of Aberdare [582. 4. 2(5)], Llantwit-Vairdre [581. 4. 7(25)], Llanwonno [582. 1.1(1)], and Ystrad-Dyfodwg [582. 4. 3(25)]; net income £555, with a glebe-house; patrons and appropriators, Dean and Chapter of Gloucester.

C & C: 2 services, one in Welsh, taken by the incumbent.

I & C: resident; curate's stipend £50.

(15)   Cymmar Chapel.   Independent.
Erected before 1800.
Space: free 496; other 104.
Present: morn. 224 + 241 scholars; even. 332.
Average (12 *months*): morn. 450 + 260 scholars; even. 500.

Joshua Evans.   Minister.

**(16)   Zorobabel, Swan Street, Llantrissaint.
Wesleyan Methodist.**
Erected 1813.
Space: free 30 feet by 19 feet.
Present: aft. 30; even. 50.
Average (12 *months*): aft. 25; even. 40.

Charles Tucker.   Minister.
2, Wellington Terrace, Cardiff.

(17) BETHLEHEM, LANTRISSANT. CALVINISTIC METHODIST.
Built 1775, rebuilt 1825.
Space: free 472; other 236; standing 300.
Present: morn. 100 + 60 scholars; aft. 38 scholars; even. 200.
Average: morn. from 500 and upwards + 102 scholars.
Richard Morgan.

(18) BETHEL, BLUE STREET, LLANTRISAINT. INDEPENDENT.
Erected 1809.
Space: free 300.
Present: morn. 80; aft. 41 scholars; even. 300.
Average (12 *months*): general congregation 200; scholars 50.
John Davies.   Deacon.
Mason
Cefn Mably, Llantrisaint.

(19) CROSS VANE. CALVINISTIC METHODIST.
Erected 1837. Building also used for a day school.
Space: free 200.
Usual number of attendants: morn. 95 scholars; aft. 150; even. 180.
Informant: Morgan Morgan.
Crofta, Llantrisaint.

[Informant's form]

(20) SION, LLANTRISANT. CALVINISTIC METHODIST.
Erected 1829.
Usual number of attendants: morn. 150 + 120 scholars; even. 200.
Informant: Richard Evans.
Maes y gelin, Llantrisant.

[Informant's form]

(21) BAPTIST CHAPEL.
Erected 1826.
Space: free 300.
Present: morn. 28; even. 37.
William Thomas.   Local Preacher.
Gwen y Mol Farm, Llantrisant.

(22) EBENEZER, LLANTRISANT (DINAS). CALVINISTIC METHODIST.
Erected 1829.
Space: free 138; other 172; standing 103.
Present: morn. 155 + 50 scholars; even. 185 + 70 scholars.
Average (3 *months*): morn. 220 + 80 scholars; aft. 220 + 80 scholars;
even. 220 + 80 scholars.
Thomas Thomas.   Elder.
Dinas Colliery, Nr. Pont y pridd.

(23)   Tonyrevil Chapel, Lantrisant.   Welch Calvinistic Methodist.
Erected about 1793.
Space: free 60; other 145; standing 200.
Present: morn. Sunday School, 80 scholars; aft. 83 + 22 scholars; even.
204 + 119 scholars.
Average (12 *months*): morn. Sunday School time; aft. 150 + 50 scholars;
even. 310 + 120 scholars.

> Evan Thomas.
> Superintendant and Deacon.

(24)   Capel Castellau, Llantrissant.   Independent.
Erected 1843. Not used exclusively as a place of worship.
Space: free 300; other 102.
Present: even. 93.
Average: morn. 130.
Remark: The Sunday School is every morning except once every month.

> Joshua Evans.   Minister.
> Cymmar.

[Endorsed: See letter]

7 Llantwitvairdre Parish.
Area: 5,311 acres. *Popn.* 2,155 males, 1,941 females: total 4,096.

(25)   Lantwit Vairdre Parish Church.
Space: free 180; other 200.
Usual number of attendants: morn. 45; aft. 55.

> *Informant:* H. James Thomas.
> Perpetual Curate.

[Informant's form]

Lewis: perpetual curacy; endowed with £1,000 royal bounty, and £1,400 parliamentary grant; net income £100; patron, vicar of Llantrissent [581. 4. 6(14b)]
who owns vicarial tithes: impropriators Dean and Chapter of Gloucester: lately
repaired.

C & C: 1 service, alternately English and Welsh, performed by the incumbent.

I & C: not resident.

(26)   Salem, Llantwit Vairdre (Cross Inn).
Calvinistic Baptists.
Erected about 1841.
Space: free 100.
Usual number of attendants: morn. 90 + 40 scholars; even. 100 + 40
scholars.

> *Informant:* John Williams.
> Cross Inn, Llantwit Vairdre.

[Informant's form]

(27) SARON, LLANTWIT VARDRE. CALVINISTIC METHODISTS.
Erected A.D. 1848.
Space: free 560; other 140.
Present: morn. 142; aft. 109 scholars; even. 203.
Average (12 *months*): morn. 135; aft. 100 scholars; even. 160.

Morgan Roberts. Steward.
Gwern y Garwn, Pontypridd.

(28) LIBANUS, TREFOREST. BAPTISTS.
Erected 1841.
Space: free 150; other 320; standing 60.
Present: morn. 133; aft. 168 scholars; even. 233.
Remark: The above estimation is very near to what the usual congregation are here.

Owen Williams. Minister.
Treforest.

(29) BRINTIRION. CALVINSTIC METHODIST.
Erected April 26th 1791.
Space: free 100; standing 200.
Present: morn. Sunday School 57; aft. 78; even. 99.
Average (6 *months*): morn. Sunday School 60; aft. 700 (sic); even. 100.

Noah Edwards. Treaserer.
Bryntirion Near Llantrisant.

[Endorsed: See letter]

(30) SARDIS CHAPEL, PONTYPRIDD. INDEPENDENT.
Erected 1834.
Space: free 460; other 80.
Present: morn. 410; aft. 182 scholars; even. 514.
Average: morn. 400; aft. 180 scholars; even. 450.

David Powell. Deacon.
Draper. Pontypridd.

(31) TABERNACLE. INDEPENDENT.
Erected 1844.
Space: free 200; standing 200 men. The whole of the building will contain about 300 persons.
Present: morn. 62; aft. Sunday School 53; even. 93.
Remark: The number attending each service during the twelve months passed is near the same as been stated allready for March the 30th 1851.

William Lewis. Deacon.
Iron Miner.
Efail Isha, Landwitwardre.

(32) WESLEYAN CHAPEL.   WESLEYAN METHODIST.
Erected 1830. Building also used for a day School.
Space: free 300; standing 50.
Present: aft. 220 + 55 scholars; even. 210.
Average (6 *months*): aft. 200 + 70 scholars; even. 200.

Charles Bassett.   Trustee.
Pontypridd.

[End of Llantrisant Subdistrict and end of Cardiff District]

Area: 112,886 acres. *Popn.* 41,425 males, 35,379 females: total 76,804.

1 GELLIGAER (Subdistrict)
Area: 34,955 acres. *Popn.* 4,819 males, 4,166 females: total 8,985.

1 Llanwonno Parish.
Area: 13,013 acres. *Popn.* 1,703 males, 1,550 females: total 3,253.

(1)   LLANWONNO PARISH CHURCH.
Space: free 35; other 45.
Usual number of attendants: from 25 to 35 at Present; morn. 25; no Sunday School at present.

Informant: Thomas Williams.
Gellibech

[Informants' form. For the incumbent's return, see (8) below.]

Lewis: perpetual curacy, endowed with £1,000 royal bounty, and £1,600 parliamentary grant; net income £95; patron, vicar of Llantrissent.

C & C: 1 service in Welsh, taken by the curate.

I & C: incumbent not resident; curate resides at Llanvabon, 4 miles distant; curate's stipend £70.

(2)   MOUNTAIN ASH.   PARTICULAR BAPTISTS.
Erected 1840.
Space: free 40; other 72.
Present: morn. 70; aft. 45 scholars; even. 112.
Average: morn. 70; aft. 45; even. 112.
Remark: The chapel is now too small, the congregation require a larger.

Thomas Price.   Minister.
Rose Cottage, Aberdare.

(3)   VANHAYLY CHAPLE.   CALVINISTIC METHODIST.
Erected 1786.
Space: free 4; other 6; standing 100.
Present: morn. 40 scholars; aft. 65; even. 95.
Average: morn. 35 scholars; aft. 80; even. 100.

George Davies.   Deacon.
New House, Llanwonnos,
Nr Pont-y-Pridd.

(4)   ENGLISH WESLEYAN CHAPEL, PONTYPRIDD.
Erected 1848.
Space: free 120; other 110; standing 60.
Present: morn. 100 + 40 scholars; aft. 73; even. 180.
Average (6 *months*): morn. 80 + 50 scholars; aft. 70; even. 200.

> Charles Bassett.   Trustee.
> Pontypridd.

(5)   PENUEL, TAFF STREET, PONTYPRIDD.   WELSH CALVINISTIC METHODIST.
Erected about the year 1815.
Space: free 282; other 168.
Present: morn. 256; aft. 267 scholars; even. 400.

> Noah Morgan.   Deacon.
> Near High Bridge, Pontypridd.

(6)   TEMPERANCE HALL OR LECTURE ROOM, NEWBRIDGE.   PRIMITIVE METHODIST.
Erected 1850.
Space: free 120; standing 20 persons if wanted.
Present: morn. average 35 to 40; even. 57.
Average (6 *months*): morn. 40; even. 45 to 50.

> John Edwards.   Local Preacher.
> Mill Street, Pontyprith.

(7)   CARMEL CHAPEL.   BAPTIST.
Erected 1810; rebuilt and enlarged 1831.
Space: free 218; other 194.
Present: morn. 270; aft. 210 scholars; even. 385.
Average (12 *months*): morn. 270; aft. 180 scholars; even. 385.
Remark: The most scrupulous care has been taken to make a true and correct return. Two competent persons were appointed to take the number one by one as the Congregation was assembling. Children from nine years of age down were not counted and are not returned.
If the same scrupulous care be taken generally the Religious Census will be almost perfect and the Government will secure its most commendable aim.

> James Richards.   Minister.
> Pontypridd.

(8)   LLANWONNO PARISH CHURCH.   HOME HAMLET.
Endowed: land £40; tithe £10; permanent endowment £46.
fees about £7.
Space: free 150.
Present: morn. 56.

Remark: The church being at a considerable distance from the Bulk of the inhabitants of the parish causes the attendance to be smaller than it should.

William Davies.   Minister.
Ponty Pridd

[This duplicates (1) above.]

[Note: 582. 1.3(21) and (22) below, i.e. Siloam and Zoar, Llanwonno, should follow here.]

2   Llanfabon Parish.

Area: 5,369 acres. *Popn.* 1,042 males, 883 females: total 1,925.

(9)   LLANFABON PARISH CHURCH.
Lately rebuilt at a total cost of £889; cost defrayed by parliamentary grant £50; parochial rate £54; subscriptions £785.
Endowed: tithe £73. 5s; fees £6.
Space: free 180.
Present: morn. 39; aft. 100.

William Morgan.   Curate.

Lewis: consolidated with the vicarage of Eglwysilan [518. 1. 1 (3)]: tithes commuted for £270, of which a sum of £200 is payable to the Bishop, Archdeacon, and Chapter of Llandaf, and £70 to the vicar.
I & C: vide sub Eglwysilan.
ICBS: grant of £50 in 1846.

(10)   YSTRAD CHAPEL, LLANVABON.   METHODIST.
Space: free 54; other 42.
Usual number of attendants: morn. 40 + 30 scholars; even. 40.

Informant: William Walter.
Gelligaer.

[Informant's form, endorsed: See letter.]

(11)   HOREB, LLANVABON.   WESLEYANS.
Erected 1840.
Space: free 30; other 70.
Usual number of attendants: morn. 20 + 30 scholars; even. 15.

Informant: William Morgan.
[Signed by a mark]

[Informant's form]

(12)   LIBANUS.   INDEPENDENT.
Erected 1833.
Space: free 260; other 49.
Usual number of attendants: morn. 160 + 160 scholars; even. 350.

Informant: Daniel Hughes.

[Informant's form. This return duplicates 582. 1. 2(31) below.]

(13) Zoar. Independents.
Erected 1830.
Space: standing 3,500.
Present: morn. 30 + 30 scholars; even. 35.
Average (12 *months*): general congregation 100; scholars 50.

> Thomas Thomas. Deacon, the Minister being absent.
> Lechwen, Quakers Yard.

(14) Berthlwyd. Baptist.
Erected 1841.
Space: free 92; other 93; standing 115.
Present: morn. 96 + 55 scholars; even. 157.
Average (12 *months*): general congregation about 220; scholars 61.

> William Davies. Diacon.
> Berthlwyd, Quakers Yard.

[Note: 582. 1. 3(23), i.e. Ebenezer, Llanfabon, should follow here.]

3-7 Gelligaer Parish, consisting of the Hamlets of [3] Brithdir, [4] Ysgwyddgwyn, [5] Garth-gynyd, [6] Cefn, and [7] Hengoed.
Area of the entire parish: 16,573 acres. *Popn.* of the entire parish: 2,074 males, 1,733 females: total 3,807.

3 Brithdir Hamlet.
Popn. 1,313 males, 1,049 females: total 2,362.

(15) Brithdir Chapel of Ease.
Endowed: tithe 40.
Space: free 60.
Present: morn. 8.

> Thomas Williams, his mark.
> Chapel Warden.

Lewis: perpetual curacy, annexed to the rectory of Gelligaer (27), below.
C & C: 1 service in Welsh taken by the curate.
I & C: *vide sub* Gelligaer.

(16) Bethlehem. Welsh Calfinistick Methodist.
Erected 1838.
Space: free 50; other 53; standing 140.
Present: morn. 198 scholars; aft. 400; even. 300.
Average (12 *months*): morn. 217 scholars; aft. 350; even. 300.
Remarks: Sunday School in the morning at 10 o'clock, and Preaching at 2 in the Afternoon and at 6 in the Evening.

> Evan Evans. Secretary.
> Rhymney Iron Works.

(17)   PRIMITIVE METHODIST, PONTLOTYN VILLAGE.
Erected 1850.
Space: free 50; other 72; standing 30.
Present: aft. 40 + 8 scholars; even. 70 + 9 scholars.

> George Price.   Minister.
> High Street, Tredegar.

(18)   LONG ROOM, PONTABER BARGOED.   INDEPENDENTS.
Space: free 100; standing 100.
Present: aft. 23.

> Thomas Thomas.   Deacon.
> Flower, Bedwellty.

(19)   HOREB.   PARTICULAR BAPTIST.
Erected 1848.
Space: free 130; other 60; standing 200.
Average: general congregation. 210; scholars 60.
Remark: The congregation requires a larger chapel.

> John David Williams.   Minister.
> Cwmbach, Aberdare.

(20)   HENGOED BAPTIST.
Erected 1710.
Space: free 126; other 108.
Present: morn. 147; aft. 54 scholars; even. 75.
Average (12 *months*): general congregation. 300; scholars 50.
Remark: The average of attendants are taken at 300 every Sunday throughout the year.

> John Jenkins.   Minister.
> Hengoed, Maesycwmer.

(21)   SILOAM, LANWYNO.   CALVINIST METHODIST.
Erected 1849.
Space: free 40; other 150; standing 500.
Present: morn. 200 + 150 scholars; aft. 'servis'; even. 'Do'.
Average: aft 300; even. 400.

> Evan James.   Steward.
> Nr Pontypridd.

[This return is wrongly placed and numbered: it should be 582. 1.1.]

(22)   SOAR LONG ROOM, LLANWONO.   INDEPENDENTS.
Erected 1849.
Space: free 90.
Present: morn. 60 + 50 scholars; even. 60 + 50 scholars.
Average: morn. 60 + 50 scholars; even. 60 + 50 scholars.

> Richard Williams.   Superintendent.
> P'pridd.

[Wrongly numbered and placed.]

(23)　EBENEZER, LLANVABON.　CALVINIST METHODIST.
Erected 1831.
Space: free 144; other 90; standing 400.
Present: morn. 51 + 59 scholars; even. 43.
Average: morn. 80 + 60 scholars.

> Thomas Williams. Deacon (the Minister being absent).
> Heolfain, Nelson.

[This return wrongly placed and numbered: it should be 582. 1. 2.]

(24)　SOAR, PONTLOTYN VILLAGE, GELLYGAER.　WELSH BAPTIST.
Erected 1837.
Space: free 138; other 228; standing 100.
Present: morn. 450; aft. 276 scholars; even. 500.
['from 450 to 500' written across column VII.]
Average (12 *months*): morn. 400; aft. 227 scholars; even. 500.

> William Williams.　Deacon.
> Bookseller, Rhymney Iron Works.

(25)　SALEM, CWM VELIN, GELLYGARE.　WELSH BAPTIST.
Erected 1830.
Space: free 48; standing 100.
Present: morn. 30 + 10 scholars; even. 30 + 10 scholars.
Average: morn. 30 + 10 scholars; even. 30 + 10 scholars.

> William Simons.　Deacon.
> Blacksmith, Cwmvelin.

(26)　CRAIG BARGOED.　INDEPENDENTS.
Erected 1715.
Space: free 90; other 80.
Present: morn. 140; aft. 30 scholars; even. 160.
Average (12 *months*): morn. 150 + 25 scholars.

> James Evans.　Independents Minister.
> Craig Bargoed, Near Merthyr Tydfil.

(27)　GELLIGAER PARISH CHURCH.
Endowed: tithe £669; fees £5.
Space: free 200; others 150.
Present: morn. 28 + 22 scholars; aft. 11 + 5 scholars.
Average (12 *months*): morn. 27 + 10 scholars; aft. 9 + 4 scholars.

> Edward Price.　Minister.

Lewis: rectory, with Brithdir [582. 1. 3(15)] annexed; rated at £20. 7. 11; patron, Marquess of Bute; tithes commuted for £669. 3. 1., and there is a glebe house.

C & C: 2 services, one in Welsh, taken by the curate.

I & C: incumbent not resident; two curates with stipends of £40 and £110 respectively, the latter occupying the glebe house.

(28)   WESLEYAN METHODIST, CEFN OR CENFIG HILL.
No date for erection: 'part of a house'.
Space: free about 30.
Present: aft. 35.

> J. S. Spencer Jones. Wesleyan Minister.
> Bridgend.

[This return is wrongly placed: it should come under 583. 3. 15, i.e. under Tythegston Parish in Bridgend Subdistrict of the Bridgend Union.]

(29)   METHODIST CHAPEL, YSTRAD.
Erected before 1800.
Space: free 75; other 40; standing 140.
Present: morn. 18 scholars; aft. 23; even. 16.
Average (12 *months*): general congregation 140; scholars 18.

> Thomas Roberts, his mark.

[This return is wrongly numbered but correctly bound in with Llanfabon Parish.]

(30)   HOREB, QUAKERS YARD.   WESLEYAN.
Erected 1839.
Space: free 50; other 30; standing 100.
Present: morn. 40 scholars; even. 44.
Average: general congregation 60; scholars 40.

> William Morgan.   Deacon.
> Berthlwyd, nr. Quakers Yard.

[This return is the same as 582. 1. 2(11), above. It is wrongly numbered but correctly bound in with Llanfabon Parish.]

(31)   LIBANUS.   INDEPENDANTS.
Erected about the year 1833.
Space: free 280; other 36.
Present: morn. 174 + 40 scholars; even. 307 + 50 scholars.

> David Edwards.   Sacretary.

[This return is the same as 582. 1. 2(12), above. It is wrongly numbered but correctly bound in with Llanfabon Parish.]

[End of Gelligaer Subdistrict]

2 LOWER MERTHYR RYDFIL (Subdistrict)

Area: 15,244 acres. *Popn.* 12,170 males, 10,977 females: total 23,147.

1   Part of the Parish of Merthyr Tydfil.

Area and *popn.* as for Lower Merthyr Tydfil Subdistrict.

(1)   St. David's Church, Chapel of Ease.

Consecrated Septr 8th 1847 as an additional church for English service.

Erected by Private Benefaction or subscription aided by parliamentary grant: Parliamentary grant £1,000; private benefaction £2,592; total £3,592.

Endowed: permanent endowment £50; pew rents £84.

Space: free 600; other 600.

Present: morn. 232 + 80 scholars; even. 289 + 60 scholars.

Average: About the same, the evening cong[regation] larger in winter and smallest at this season.

Remark: All the expences connected with the repair of Church, services etc. are paid out of the pew rents amounting on an average to about £45 a year. The Curate's salary is made up by me to £100 a year.

James C. Campbell.   Rector.

C & C: 2 services, both in English.

I & C: as for the Parish Church. (2) below.

ICBS: grant of £700 in 1840.

(2)   Merthyr Tydfil Parish Church.

Endowed: tithe £312. 9; glebe £48. 9. 3; fees £80; Easter Offerings £12.

Space: free 860.

Present: morn. 'not known, about 400'; aft. 76; even. 605.

Average: morn. 400; aft. from 70 to 90; even. 700.

Remark: In giving the value I have deducted the burdens from the tithe and glebe. I have not deducted the income tax, nor the curate's salary of £150, nor the tenths which amount to £2. 1. I have not deducted the interest of mortgage to Queen Anne's Bounty for house which was last year £53. 9. 3. The afternoon congregation is English, the other Welsh. The majority of English congregation removed to St. Davids on its consecration. There is a congregation in a licensed room in the parish with a congregation averaging from 90 to 100.

J. C. Campbell.   Rector.

Lewis: rectory, rated at £20. 5. 7½; net income £675, with glebe-house: patron, Marquess of Bute.

C & C: 3 services, 2 in Welsh, taken by the curate.

I & C: incumbent resident; curate's stipend £150.

ICBS: grant of £150 in 1820.

(3)   A school room licensed in the district of Cyfarthfa formed under Sir R. Peel's Act, licensed since 1846, there being no church for the New District. A church is badly wanted *if Parliament will make a grant.*
Space: free 200; other 4.
Present: morn. about 50; even. about 70.
Average: morn. 50 + 30 scholars; even. 90 + 15 scholars.

John Nowell.   Minister.
Cyfarthfa.

C & C: 3 services, 2 in Welsh, taken by the incumbent in licensed room; Chapel net yet built.

I & C: incumbent resident.

(4)   PENHEOLGERRIG CHAPEL.   INDEPENDENTS.
Erected 1837.
Space: free 13 benches.
Present: morn. 115 scholars; aft. 120 scholars; even. 226.
Average (12 *months*): morn. 120 scholars; aft. 130 scholars; even. 260.
Remark: Space of the chapel, 24 feet by 19 feet.

Daniel Jones.   Minister, Bethesda
Chapel.

(5)   SHILOH.   WESLEYAN.
Erected 1811.
Space: free 157; other 363.
Usual number of attendants: morn. 152; aft. 184 scholars; even. 355.

Informant: William Watkins.
Tramroad Side near St. David's
Church.

[Informant's form]

(6)   BETHEL, GEORGE TOWN.   BAPTIST.
Erected 1809.
Space: free 700; other 300.
Usual number of attendants: morn. at eleven 300; at nine 170 scholars; aft. at two 190 scholars; even. 400.

Informant: John Lloyd.   Baptist
Minister.

[Informant's form]

(7)   *Endorsed:* No place at all [?Troed-y-rhyw].
Remark: We as Wesleyans have no *Proper* place of Worship at Troed-y-Rhyw, nor any Society at present, attempts are being made to form a society but as yet none in existence.

Informant: Hugh Carter.
Wesleyan Minister.
Merthyr.

(8) ADULLAM. INDEPENDENTS.
Erected 1831.
Space: 32 by 34; 17 6; free 68.
Usual number of attendants: morn. 150 + 56 scholars; aft. 140 scholars; even. 345 + 67 scholars.

> *Informant:* Rev. Levi Lawrence.
> Adullam, Merthyr Tydfil.

[Informant's form]

(9) CARMEL, CLWYD-Y-FAGWYR. CALVINISTIC METHODIST.
Erected August 1840.
Space: free 80; standing 20.
Present: morn. 10 + 70 scholars; even. 12 + 60 scholars.
Average (12 *months*): morn. 10 + 70 scholars; even. 12 = 60 scholars.
Remark: The Sunday School is held in the chapel in the Afternoon.

> John Price. Elder.
> Clwydyfagwyr.

(10) SILO, PENTREBACH OR ABERCANAID. CALVINISTIC OR PARTICULAR BAPTIST.
Erected in 1840 or 1841.
Space: free 150 may sit on benches on the gallery; other 55 pews; standing 200.
Present: morn. 226; aft. 200 scholars; even. 305.
Average (12 *months*): general congregation 500 adults and children; scholars 250.
Remarks: School attendace at 9 o'clock a.m. and at 2 o'clock, p.m. every Sunday. Divine Service at 11 o'clock a.m. and at 6 o'clock, p.m. every Sunday. At present we have no fixed minister, but the place is regularly supplied by some of our neighbouring ministers.

> Morgan Joseph. Civil Engineer (retired)
> for the congregation being one of the deacons,
> Mount Pleasant.

(11) GRAIG CHAPEL. CALVINISTIC METHODIST.
Erected 1848.
Space: free 190; other 51.
Present: aft. 177; even. 110.
Average (12 *months*): general congregation 185; scholars 90.
Remark: School attendance at 10 o'clock in the morning. Divine Service at 2 o'clock and at 6 o'clock in the evening.

> Thomas Scurry. Elder.
> Graig Chapel House.

(12) ENGLISH WESLEYAN METHODIST.
Erected 1797.
Space: free 142; other 218.
Present: morn. 101 + 29 scholars; even. 160.
Average (12 *months*): morn. 150 + 60 scholars; even. 240.

Joseph Fletcher. Minister.

(13) SOAR HIGH STREET. INDEPENDENT.
Erected 1803.
Space: free 457; other 962.
Present: morn. 791 + 300 scholars; aft. 406 scholars; even. 1,378.

Benjamin Owen. Minister.

(14) PENNSYLVANIA OR PONTMORLAIS. WELSH CALVINISTIC METHODIST.
Erected 1793; enlarged 1834.
Space: free 504; other 638; standing 462.
Present: morn. 346 + 150 scholars; aft. 'no service'; even. 438 + 200 scholars.
Average (12 *months*): morn. 400 + 150 scholars; aft. 'no service. School';
even. 650 + 200 scholars.

Evan John. Elder.
Pontmorlais Chapel House.

(15) INDEPENDENT CHAPEL, THOMAS STREET, MARKET SQUARE, HEOL-
WORMWOOD.
Erected 1841.
Space: free 100; other 600.
Present: morn. 170 + 70 scholars; aft. 110 scholars; even. 180.

J. D. Hill. Minister.
Tydfil's Well.

(16) HIGH STREET CHAPEL. BAPTIST.
Erected 1840 and 1841.
Space: free 250; other 430.
Present: morn. 320 + 78 scholars; even. 430 + 75 scholars.
Average (12 *months*): morn. 325 + 80 scholars; even. 450 + 70 scholars.

Thomas Davies. Baptist Minister.

(17) ZION. BAPTIST.
Erected 1789.
Space: free 408; other 606. '68 free sittings in the gallery, 101 paid sittings
on the ground floor'.
Present: morn. 1,000 + 200 scholars; aft. 300 scholars; even. 1,500.
Average: morn. 1,000 + 200 scholars; aft. 300 scholars; even. 1,500.
Remark: The dimension of the chapel are 70 ft by 52 ft over the walls.

John Jones. Minister.

(18) SARON, TROEDYRHIW. INDEPENDENT.
Erected 1835.
Space: free 128; other 210.
Present: morn. 140 scholars; aft. 200 scholars.
Average (12 *months*): general congregation 238[?]; scholars 200.
Remark: The Sunday School commenced 1822 in a private dwelling house and continued so untill the chapel was build in 1835.

> William Morgan. Secretary.
> Saron Troedyrhiw.

(19) SOAR, TROEDYRHIW. BAPTIST.
Erected 1850.
Space: free 100; other 200.
Present: morn. 150 + 56 scholars; aft. 70 scholars; even. 250.
Average (6 *months*): morn. 200 + 66 scholars; aft. 80 scholars; even. 300.

> David Williams. Minister.
> Troedyrhiw.

(20) WESLEYAN METHODIST.
A hired room.
Erected; 'about the year of 1830'; not used exclusively as a place of worship.
Space: free 42.
Present: aft. 20; even. 36.

> James Jones. Steward.
> Brickmaker.

(21) CYMREIGYDDION HALL OR WHITE LION INN HALL. LATTER DAY SAINTS.
Erected 'after 1800'.
Space: free 1,000.
Present: morn. 107 + 50 scholars; aft. 180 + 293 scholars.

> William Phillips. Elder.
> 14 Castle Street.

(22) YNYSGAU, BRIDGE STREET. PROTESTANT DISSENTERS.
Erected before 1800.
Space: free 205; other 40.
Present: morn. 226; aft. 233 scholars; even. 402.
Remark: The Chapel is connected with the Independents but as the Deed of the Chapel designates it "Protestant Dissenting Chapel" it was deemed best to enter it so.

> Morgan Jones. Deacon.
> at Dal Williams, Castle Street.

(23) TEMPERANCE HALL. WESLEYAN METHODIST REFORMED.
Erected: 'not known'. Building not used exclusively as a place of worship.
Space: free 120.
Present: morn. 40; aft. 44 scholars; even. 80.

> Thomas Maddy.   Local Preacher.
> Pontmorlais.

(24) SHILOH CHAPEL, HEOLWERMOD. WESLEYAN.
Rebuilt 1828.
Space: free 157; other 363.
Present: morn. 149; aft. 181 scholars; even. 360.

> Thomas Williams.   Society Steward.
> Victoria Street.

(25) SYNAGOGUE, VICTORIA STREET. MERTHYR JEWISH CONGREGATION.
Erected 1848.
Space: free 10; other 30.
Present: morn. 34; aft. 21; even. 23.
Average (6 *months*): morn. 25; aft. 20; even. 20.

> Joseph Barnett.   President.
> Victoria Street.
> Moses Lewis Isaacs.   Secretary.

(26) UNTARIAN CHAPEL.
Erected 1821.
Space: free 100; other 200.
Present: morn. 80 + 70 scholars; aft. 115 scholars; even. 120.

> George Lunn.   Minister.

(27) SOAR. BAPTIST.
Erected 1850.
Space: free 120.
Usual number of attendants: morn. 80; aft. 50 scholars; even. 200.

> *Informant:* David Williams.   Minister.
> Troedyrhiw.

[Informant's form. Endorsed: a duplicate of No. 19. This relates to the same place of worship as 582. 2. 1(19), and is in the same handwriting, that of the minister, but the information supplied is not identical.]

(28) EBENEZER, PLYMOUTH STREET. BAPTIST.
Erected 1793.
Space: free 500; other 500; standing 200.
Present: morn. 755 + 214 scholars; aft. 219 scholars even. 1,060.
Average: morn. 800 + 260 scholars; aft. 260 scholars; even. 1,000.
Remark: The Sunday School begins in the morning at 9 o'clock and divine service at 11 o'clock.

> John Lloyd.   Minister.

[End of Lower Merthyr Tydfil]

3 UPPER MERTHYR TYDFIL (Subdistrict)
Area: 2,500 acres. *Popn.* 12,558 males, 10,673 females: total 23,231.

1   Part of the Parish of Merthyr Tydfil.
Area and *popn.* as for Upper Merthyr Tydfil Subdistrict.

(1)   DOWLAIS PARISH CHURCH, in the heart of the town of Dowlais, a separate parish in all ecclesiastical matters. Consecrated 27th Nov. 1827, and is the only church in the parish of Dowlais.
Erected by the Dowlais Iron Company.
Cost all defrayed by the Dowlais Company.
Endowed by 1/5 of the tithe and glebe of Merthyr Tydfil; fees from £30 to £60; Easter offerings from £5 to £12.
Space: all free to the Welsh congregations 240; about half the pews rented to the English Congregation 240. Total sittings 480.
Present: morn. (English) 258 + 112 scholars; aft. (Welsh congregation) 200; even. (English) 170 + 70 scholars.
There is a Welsh service in the Church every Sunday Evening after the English. Present on March 30th 1851, 427.
Remarks: There is in the Parish of Dowlais a School room where divine service is performed twice every Sunday in Welsh. *Present:* morn. 70; even. 100.

E. Jenkins.   Rector.

[For the schoolroom, *vide* (8) below.]

Lewis: rectory not in charge, in the gift of the Marquess of Bute.

C & C: 4 services, 2 in Welsh, taken by the incumbent and curate.

I & C: incumbent not resident; curate's stipend £80.

(2)   WESLEYAN REFORMED.
Occupying a room in a building not used exclusively as a place of worship.
Space: standing 40.
Present: even. 35.
Remark: We cannot give an average number of attendants for 12 months as we have only begun separate services on February the 9th 1851. Our preaching place is a dwelling house.

Henry Davies.   Steward.
Grocer.
Penywern, Dowlais.

(3)   HEBRON, CAE HARIS, DOWLAIS.   BAPTIST.
Erected 1841.
Space: free 2 downstairs; other 58; standing 40 feet by 8.
Present: morn. 500 + 100 scholars; even. 600 + 140 scholars.

Average: morn. 550 + 120 scholars; even. 670 + 150 scholars.
Remark: The gallery is all free sittings except the front. We have three places for Sunday Schools and Prayer meetings with exception to the one in the Chapel one are the Gwernddu one at Pantywaen one at Long town **great** many of which are not able to attend the Chapel in the winter.

> Thomas Mathews.   Secretary.
> Rail inspector.
> Dowlais.

(4)   CAERSALEM, WELL STREET, DOWLAIS.   PARTICULAR BAPTISTS.
Erected in 1820; re-erected in 1832.
Space: free 600; other 400; standing about 100.
Present: morn. 800 + 200 scholars; aft. 'school'; even. 1,000 + 331 scholars.
Average (6 *months*): morn. 750 + 200 scholars; even. 1,000 + 330 scholars.

> Edward Evans. Minister.

(5) BETHANIA CHAPEL, DOWLAIS. INDEPENDENTS.
Erected 1824.
Space: free 593; other 540; standing 300.
Present: morn. 692; aft. 550 scholars; even. 900.
Average (12 *months*): morn. 1,000; aft. 700 scholars; even. 1,400.
Remark: As Bethania Chapel was too small for the Congregation a new chapel was erected last year in connexion with it and about 5 hundred of the Congregation two sittings in the new as it is to be seen on another schedule.

> [no signature]

[See (11) below.]

(6) BUTE ARMS ROOM, DOWLAIS. LATTER DAY'S SAINTS.
Building not used exclusively as place of worship but temporary room. Building erected since 1800.
Present: 83, general congregation 209 + 40 scholars, total 332; aft. 110; even. 112.

> William Thomas.
> Later Day's Saints.

7.   BRYN SION CHAPEL. INDEPENDENTS.
Erected about 1834; rebuilt and enlarged in 1844.
Space: free 244; other 427; standing 150.
Present: morn. 495; even. 526.
Average (12 *months*): morn. 600; aft. 700.

> Daniel Roberts. Minister.

(8)   GELLYFAELOG.   DOWLAIS.   ANGLICAN.
Space: free 170.
Present: morn. 70 + 60 scholars; aft. 112 scholars; even. 100.
Average: morn. 60 + 80 scholars; aft. 100 scholars; even. 80.

> John Morgan.   Curate of Dowlais.
> Gwernllwyn.

[See (1) above.]

(9)   PRIMITIVE METHODIST CHAPEL, DOWLAIS.
Erected 1846.
Space: free 60; other 182; standing 150.
Present: morn. school; aft. 80; even. 130.
Average (3 *months*): average congregation 130; scholars 30.

> William Prosser.   Local Preacher.
> Ivor Street, Dowlais.

(10)   PRIVATE HOUSE.   BAPTIST.
Erected 9th of Febry 1851.
Space: free 42.
Present: aft. 42 scholars.
Average (1 *month*): morn. 22 scholars; even. total 22.

> Robert Davies.   Local Preacher.
> High Street, Dowlais.

(11)   GWERNLLWYN CHAPEL, DOWLAIS.   INDEPENDENT.
Erected 1850.
Space: free 244; other 427; standing 150.
Present: morn. 505; even. 709.

> Joseph Hughes.   Minister.

[See (5) above.]

(12)   ST. DETUTUS' CHAPEL.   ROMAN CATHOLIC.
Erected 1844.
Space: free 300; standing 300.
Present: morn. 600; aft. 40 + 110 scholars.

> James Dawson.   Roman Catholic Priest.
> Dowlais.

(13)   HERMON CHAPEL. HAMLET OF HEOLWERMOOD. WELSH CALVINISTIC
METHODIST.
Erected 1827; rebuilt 1840.
Space: free 1,000; other 500.
Present: morn. 599 scholars; aft. 1,022; even. 1,044.
Average (12 *months*): morn. 650 scholars; aft. 1,300; even. 1,300.

> Robert Frederick.   Deacon.
> Grocer, Dowlais.

(14)   ENGLISH WESLEYAN CHAPEL.
Erected about 1827.
Space: free 100; other 210.
Present: morn. 100 + 24 scholars; even. 160 + 25 scholars.

> Frederick Atkins.
> Chapel and Society Steward.
> Bethania Street, Dowlais.

(15)   SHILO.   WELSH WESLEYAN METHODIST, DOWLAIS.
Erected 1831.
Space: free 153; other 219.
Present: morn. 110; aft. 130 scholars; even. 170.
Average: general congregation 240; scholars 120.

> Thomas Price.   Class Leader and Local
> Preacher.
> Tailor.
> Horse Street, Dowlais.

(16)   PANTSCALLOG.   INDEPENDENTS.
A dwelling house; preaching commenced here in 1844.
Space: all free; standing 100.
Present: morn. 30; aft. 52 scholars; even. 50.

> John Thomas.   Minister.
> Bethlehem, Dowlais.

(17)   ELIM BAPTIST CHAPEL, PENDARREN.
Erected 1843.
Space: free 300; other 300; standing 100.
Present: morn. 300 + 233 scholars; even. 455.
Average (6 *months*): morn. 400 + 220 scholars.

> David Hughes.   Deacon.
> Tea Dealer.

(18)   HOREB INDEPENDENT CHAPEL, PENYDARREN.
Erected 1839.
Present: morn. 500; aft. 544; even. 544.
Average: morn. 500 + 300 scholars.

> John Morgan.   Deacon.

(19)   LATTER DAY SAINTS, PENDAREN.
Not used exclusively as a place of worship.
Present: morn. 40 + 30 scholars; aft. 50 + 30 scholars; even. 50 + 30 scholars.
Average (6 *months*): morn. 45 + 30 scholars.

Remark: The room where the Latter-day Saints hold their meetings in Pendaren, in Merthyr Tydfil is adjoining the Mason's Arms which is also the Club room.

John Jones. Elder.
care of Mr Thomas Griffiths, Baker,
Gellifaelog Bridge.

(20) New Inn Room. Latter Day Saints.
Space: all free sittings: standing 200.
Present: morn. 77 + 46 scholars; aft. 96; even. 132.

Thomas Llewellyn. Elder.
High Street, Pendaren.

(21) Bethesda Chapel, Gafael y Garth. Independents or Congrega-
tionalists.
Erected 1811.
Space: free 204; other 534; standing 'in all a space for 140'.
Present: morn. 782 + 473 scholars; aft. 480 scholars; even. 847.
Average (12 *months*): morn. 780 to 800 + 470 scholars; even. 840 to 900 +
604 scholars.
Remark: The space of our chapel is down stairs 49 feet by 38; gallery 26 by
18 feet.

David Jones. Minister.

(22) Tabernacle, Bryant & Field. Baptist.
Erected 1835.
Space: free 1,000; other 600.
Present: morn. 700; aft. 340 scholars; even. 1,000.
Average (12 *months*): morn. 900; aft. 350 scholars; even. 1,600.

John Roberts. Minister.

(23) Mount Moriah. Primitive Methodist.
Erected about the year 1847 or 1848.
Space: free 90; other 128; standing about 30 each side.
Present: morn. 89 + 53 scholars; aft. 92 scholars; even. 146.
Average (12 *months*): morn. 90; even. 150; total morn. 4,680; even. 7,800.
Remark: The Congregation have been on the decrease today March 30th.
The school today have been on the increase to the amount 15.

David Thomas. Local Preacher.
43 Cyfarthfa Rowe.

(24) Bethlehem Pant-tywyll, Caepant tywyll.
Calvinistic Methodist.
Erected 1841.
Space: free 250; other 400; standing 40.

Present: morn. 147 + 100 scholars; aft. 'Sunday School'; even. 80 + 110 scholars.

Average (12 *months*): morn. 100 + 108 scholars; aft. school; even. 110 + 130 scholars.

James Morris. One of the Trustees.

2 Vainor Parish. Co. Brecon. Diocese of St. David's.
Area: 6,597 acres. *Popn.* 1,360 males, 1,307 females: total 2,667.

(25) CEFN COED CYMMER LICENSED SCHOOLROOM.
Licensed in 1833 for the convenience of the inhabitants, the distance of the place from the Mother Church being about 3 miles.
Erected by private subscription altogether at a total cost of £150.
Endowed: It has not been endowed. The Curate is supported by the Local Aid Society. The grant is £100.
Space: benches 35 (total sittings 210).
Present: morn. 112; aft. 'school' 123; even. 202.
Average: morn. 130; aft. school 150; even. 230.

William Roberts. Curate.
Gwernllwyn, Dowlais.

(26) VAYNOR PARISH CHURCH.
Endowed: tithes commuted at £260; glebe 27 acres.
Space: free 42; other 72.
Present: morn. 80; aft. 'school' 14; even. 90.
Average: morn. 100; aft. 33; even. 130.
Remarks: Church attendance at this time of the Year is never good, the farmer being more engaged than usually, their Cattle requiring more care this time of the year than any other time.

Rees Williams. Rector.

Lewis: rectory, rated at £8. 3. 11½, and in the patronage of the crown; gross income £292, arising from tithes producing £260, and glebe land £32.

C & C: 1 service in Welsh performed by the incumbent.

I & C: incumbent resident; curate's stipend £90.

(27) LATTER DAY SAINTS ROOM, CEFN COED Y CYMER.
Taken on rent March 13 1848.
Space: standing 200.
Present: morn. scholars 63; aft. 120; even. 135.

William Richards. President.
Miner.
Cefncoed-y-cymmer.

(28)   CAE CHAPEL, CEFN COED Y CYMER.   CALVINISTIC METHODIST.
Erected A.D. 1807.
Space: free 110; other 215; standing 232.
Present: morn. Sunday School; aft. 152 + 106 scholars; even. 140 + 110 scholars.

> John Llewellyn.   Deacon.
> Grocer.
> Cefncoedycymmer.

(29)   THE OLD MEETING HOUSE.   UNITARIAN.
Erected before 1800.
Space: 23 seats each one contain 7 persons; standing, gallery will contain 200.
Present: morn. 113; even. 84.
Average (12 *months*): morn. 120; even. 100.
Remark: The Sunday Scholars are included in account.

> Owen Evans.   Minister.
> Cefn.

(30)   CARMEL.   PARTICULAR BAPTIST.
Erected 1844.
Space: free, galleries; other 32 in no. let Quarterly; standing 20.
Present: 142 + 40 scholars; even. 173 + 153 scholars.
Average: morn. 148 + 40 scholars; even. 150 + 142 scholars.

> John Morgan.   Deacon.

(31)   EBENEZER, CEFN COED Y CYMMAR.   INDEPENDENT OR CONGREGATIONALIST.
Erected 1838.
Space: The whole chapel is free except the 41 pews paid for; standing see page [i.e. column] 9.
Present: morn. 195; even. 352 + 201 scholars.
Average (12 *months*): morn. 250; even. 336 + 190 scholars.
Remark: The Chapell in side measures 30 feet by 29 feet 10 inches. The whole is accomodated with seats or pews, except 2 ailes measuring 7 ft 10 inches wide including the back by 15 ft 7 long, and a piece on the middle 18 ft by 7 ft 4 inches and that is accomodated with benches. The galary is all seated and will hold 153 persons.

> Henry Thomas.   Manager.
> Cooper.

(32)   BETHLEHEM, VAYNOR.   INDEPENDENTS.
Erected 1828.
Space: free 12; other 48; standing 200.
Present: aft. 50; even. 25 scholars.

> John Thomas, Minister,
> Bethlehem, Dowlais.

(33) TABOR, COED Y CYMMER. INDEPENDENTS.
Erected 1845.
Space: free 84; other 110; standing 40.
Present: morn. 70 + 20 scholars; aft. 'school'; even. 100 + 30 scholars.
Average (12 months): morn. 90 + 18 scholars; aft. 'school'; even. 120 +
30 scholars.

William Moses. Minister.
Tydfil's Well.

(34) ADULAM, TRAMROAD. MERTHYR TYDFIL. INDEPENDENT.
Erected 1831.
Space: free 209; other 185; standing 106.
Present: morn. 293 + 108 scholars; aft. 198: even. 397.

Levi Lawrence. Minister.

[This return is wrongly placed, and should come under 582. 3. 1.]

(35) BETHEL, GEORGETOWN, MERTHYR, GLAMORGAN. BAPTIST.
Erected before 1800.
Space: free 300; other 200; standing 200.
Present: morn. 140 scholars; aft. 600 + 159 scholars.
Average: morn. 176 scholars; aft. 640 + 176 scholars.
Remark: The Sunday School begins at one o'clock in the afternoon, and
divine service at 3 o'clock.

John Lloyd. Baptist Minister.

[This return is wrongly placed, and should come under 582. 2. 1.]

[*End of Upper Merthyr Tydfil Subdistrict*]

4 ABERDARE (Subdistrict)
Area: 53,590 acres. *Popn.* 10,518 males, 8,256 females: total 18,774.

1 Penderyn Parish, co. Brecknock, Diocese of St. David's.
Area: 12,765 acres. *Popn.* Lower Penderyn 877 males, 686 females: total
1,552: Upper Penderyn 112 males, 113 females: total 225.

(1) PENDERYN PARISH CHURCH.
Endowed: tithe £305; land £10; fees £10.
Space: free 150; other 28.
Present: morn. 65 + 30 scholars.

Charles Maybery. Rector.

Lewis: Rectory, rated at £9. 3. 11½; patron William Winter, Esq., M.D.: tithes
commuted for £305; glebe of 4½ acres valued at £5. 6. 3.
C & C: 1 service in Welsh performed by the incumbent.
I & C: incumbent resident.

(2) TABERNACLE, PENDERIN. LATTER DAY SAINTS.
Erected 1838; building not used exclusively as a place of worship.
Space: free 500; standing 50.
Present: Welsh Meeting, morn. 62; aft. 68; even. 83. English Meeting, morn. 12; aft. 17; even. 24. Scholars: morn. 40; aft. 48; even. 30.
Average: Welsh Meeting, morn. 22; aft. 20; even. 53. English Meeting, morn. 12; aft. 17; even. 24. Scholars: morn. 40; aft. 48; even. 30.

> Morgan Evans.
> George Rogers, English.
> John Davis, Welsh.
> Hirwaun.

(3) SILOAM. PARTICULAR BAPTIST.
Erected about 1823.
Space: free 150; other 4.
Present: morn. 60 + 51 scholars; even. 105.

> Daniel Evans.   Minister.
> Penderin.

(4) BETHEL. BAPTIST.
Erected before 1800; building not used exclusively as a place of worship.
Space: free 48; other 72; standing 40.
Present: morn. 40; aft. 26 scholars; even. 54.

> David Davies.
> Abernant.

2 Aberdare Parish.   co. Glamorgan, diocese of Llandaf.
Area: 16,310 acres. *Popn.* 8,403 males, 6,596 females; total 14,999.

(5) ST. JOHN THE BAPTIST PARISH CHURCH, ABERDARE.
Endowed: land £23; tithe £10; glebe house and garden; permanent endowment £150; fees £68; total gross £251.
Space: free none; other 176.
Present: morn. full; aft. Welsh full; Sunday Scholars 'no assigned space'.
Average (any number of months): morn. full; aft. Welsh full; even. full.
Remark: Two new churches to be built this year; one already contracted for to hold 750; the other to be built in the course of the summer to hold 600. Total church room 1,426.

> John Griffith. Vicar.

Lewis: perpetual curacy, endowed with £600 royal bounty, and £1,800 parliamentary grant; net income £108: patron, Vicar of Llantrissaint [581. 4. 6(14b)], who receives the vicarial tithes.
C & C: in the parish church: 3 services of which 1 in Welsh taken by the rector: in a licensed room at Hirwaun; 1 service alternately English and Welsh taken by the curate: in a licensed room at Aberaman; 1 service in English.
I & C: incumbent resident; curate's stipend £100.
ICBS: grant of £400 in 1850 (for St. Elvan's), and £400 in 1851 (for St. Fagan's).

(6)   A chapel school, Cardiff Street, Aberdare.
Authorised for Divine Service in *Welsh* by the Bishop of Llandaff. Welsh
service at 6 pm every Sunday. Authorised by the bishop, October 1850, to
supply a want, that is to give the *Welsh* a service at 6 pm., the parish church
being then occupied by the English.
Endowed: The clergyman is supported by 'The *London* Curates Aid
Society'.
Space: free 150.
Present: even. officiating clergyman ill; no duty.
Average: even. 150.
Remark: When the new Church now building is complete this congrega-
tion will occupy the Ancient Parish Church.

John Griffith.   Vicar.

(7)   Chapel School, Cwmbach, Aberdare.
Authorised by the Bishop Jan. 1, 1851, for two services to the *Welsh* at
11 am and 6 pm.
Erected by voluntary contributions; total cost £600.
Endowed: The Clergyman supported by 'The *Diocesan* Curates Aid
Society'.
Space: free 200.
Present: morn. 71; aft. 'School'; even. 86.
Average: morn. 70; aft. 'School'; even. 100.

John Griffith.   Vicar.

(8)   Bryn Sion, Cwmbach.   Independents.
Erected 1846.
Space: free 100; standing 100.
Present: morn. 59 + 20 scholars; aft. 31 scholars; even. 75.
Average: morn. 50 + 30 scholars; aft. 60 scholars; even. 80.
Remark: There is a place for about 100 to sit and also free. There is a
place for 50 also to stand.

John Lloyd.   Minister.

(9)   Particular Baptists, Abernant y groes.
Erected 1840.
Space: free 200; other 100; standing 210.
Present: no information.
Average: general congregation 450; scholars 120.
Remark: The parcel of ground on which the chapel is built has been
bequeathed to the church by William Thomas Davies.

John David Williams.   Minister.
Cwmbach.

(10)   MOUNTAIN OF ZION.   INDEPENDENT.
Part of a dwelling house, 'erected' 1851.
Space   free 45; standing 35.
Present: aft. 10 + 35 scholars.

> Daniel Rowland.   Deacon.
> Mountain Ash.

(11)   MORIAH, LLWYDCOED.   CALVINISTIC METHODIST.
Erected 1839.
Space: free 16; other 72; standing 150.
Present: morn. 135; aft. 111 scholars; even. 148.
Average (2 months): morn. 140; aft. 115; even. 140.

> Edward Pugh (His mark).   Deacon.
> Farmer.
> Llwydcoed.

(12)   ENGLISH WESLEYAN METHODIST.
Erected 1841.
Space: free 68; other 48.
Present: aft. 44 + 1 scholars; aft. 61 + 2 scholars.
Average (12 months): aft. 40; even. 76.

> George Walls.   Chapel Steward.

(13)   WELSH WESLEYAN CHAPEL.
Opened for religious worship Jan 4th 1850.
Space: free 370; other 280.
Present: morn. 95; aft. 85 scholars; even. 170.

> Evan Evans.   Trustee.
> Weigher,
> Aberaman.

(14)   CARMEL, PEN-Y-POUND.   PARTICULAR BAPTISTS.
First erected in 1812, enlarged to present size in 1832 on the present site.
Space: free 250; others 500; standing 110.
Present: morn. 707 + 157 scholars; aft. school 230; even. 840.
Average (12 months): morn. 707 + 158 scholars. aft. 170 scholars; even.
840.
Remark: Our chapel is now much too small to contain the congregation. We
are now erecting a new chapel and a large and comodious school room which
will contain more than double the number of free and other sittings. We
shall occupy the new chapel and school room on 30 Sept. 1851. The cost of
erection will be £1,200.
On the afternoon of March 30th we had our Quarterly Meeting of the Sunday
School which gave rather more than the average number.

> Thomas Price.   Minister.
> Rose Cottage, Aberdare.

(15)   LATTER DAY SAINTS.
Building not used exclusively as a place of worship.
Space: free 200.
Present: morn. 110 + 65 scholars; aft. 178; even. 186.
Average (12 *months*): morn. 100 + 40 scholars; aft. 150; even. 160.
Remark: This is a spacious room, adjoining another Building, but not used
exclusively as a place of Worship but on Sundays and Week Evenings and
will not contain more than about 200 seated.

> William Sims.   Elder.

(16)   GWAWR CHAPEL, ABERGWAWR.   BAPTISTS.
Erected 1849.
Space: unfinished.
Present: morn. 100 + 30 scholars; aft. 60 scholars; even. 450.
Average (12 *months*): morn. 250 + 40 scholars; aft. 80 scholars; even. 450.

> Dewi Bevan Jones.   Minister.
> Aberamman.

(17)   LIBANUS, ABERAMAN.   WELSH CALVINISTIC METHODISTS.
Erected 1847.
Space: free 180; other 330; standing 190.
Present: morn. 200; aft. 229 scholars, including teachers; even. 200.
Remark: I consider the day's return to be a fair average of constant
attendants both of Congregations and of Sunday Scholars as well as actual
numbers attending this day. We have been Keeping the Sunday School in
dwelling houses for some months previous to erecting chapel. See dates of
each.

> William Morgan.   Secretary.
> Aberaman Colliery.

(18)   SALEM.   INDEPENDENTS.
Erected 1842.
Space: free 12; other 276.
Present: morn. 94 + 41 scholars; even. 91 + 80 scholars.
Average: morn. 100 + 50 scholars; even. 100 + 80 scholars.

> John Harrison.   Elder.
> Gadlys.

(19)   SILOA.   CONGREGATIONALIST.
Erected 1844.
Space: free 235; other 265.
Present: morn. 331 + 162 scholars; aft. 224 scholars; even. 430.

> David Price.   Minister.

(20) Nebo, Hirwaun. Independent.
Erected 1821.
Space: free 105; other 540; standing 420.
Present: morn. 433 + 260 scholars; aft. 280 scholars; even. 500.

> David Evan Williams. Deacon.
> 'Bristol House', Hirwaun.

(21) Soar, Hirwain. Wesleyan.
Erected before 1825.
Space: free 240; other 180; standing 80.
Present: morn. 70 scholars; aft. 111; even. 120.
Average (6 months): morn. 70 scholars; aft. 150; even. 180.

> Lewis Davies. Chapel Steward.
> Hirwain.

(22) Ramoth [Hirwain]. Baptist.
Erected 1825.
Space: free 213; standing 210.
Present: morn. 275; aft. 220 scholars; even. 340.

> Benjamin Evans. Minister.
> Hirwain.

(23) Carmel. Welsh Calvinistic Methodist.
Erected 1829.
Space: free 150; other 250; standing 100.
Present: morn. 296; aft. 240 scholars; even. 347.
Average (12 months): general congregation 300; scholars 220.

> Evan Griffith. Deacon.
> Grocer.
> Hirwain.

(24) Bethel, Hirwaun. Calvinistic Methodist.
Erected 1823.
Space: free 160; other 183; standing 57.
Present: morn. 213 scholars; aft. 271; even. 258.
Average (12 months): general congregation 271; scholars 230.

> Morgan Davies. Elder.
> Grocer.

3-6 Ystradyfodwg Parish: consisting of the Hamlets of [3] Rhigos, [4] Middle, [5] Home, and [6] Clydach.
Area of the whole parish: 24,515 acres. *Popn.* of the whole parish: 1,137 males, 861 females: total 1,998.

3 Rhigos Hamlet.
Popn. 664 males, 403 females: total 1,047.

(25) YSTRADYFODWG PARISH CHURCH.
Endowed: land £35; tithe £10.
Space: free 132.
Present: morn. 10.

> D. W. Williams. Vicar.
> Dinas Colliery.

Lewis: perpetual curacy, endowed with £600 royal bounty and £800 parliamentary grant; net income £85: patron, Rev. J. B. Williams; impropriators, Dean and Chapter of Gloucester.

C & C: 1 service in Welsh.

I & C: incumbent resident.

ICBS: grant of £50 in 1844.

4 Middle Hamlet.
Popn. 119 males, 128 females: total 247.

(26) LIBANUS, BLAENYCWM. PARTICULAR BAPTIST.
Erected 1839.
Space: free 48; other 30; standing 20.
Present: morn. 67 + 23 scholars; even. 78.
Average: morn. 200 + 54 scholars; even. 200.

> Howell Lewellyn. Deacon.

5 Home Hamlet.
Popn. 174 males, 136 females: total 310.

(27) SOAR, DINAS. BAPTIST.
Erected 1831-32.
Space: free 150; other 130; standing 140.
Present: morn. 163; aft. 113 scholars; even. 240.
Average (6 months): morn. 180; aft. 95 scholars; even. 330.
Remark: The afternoon column is filled with the number of scholars in the Sunday School which is held at that time.

> William Lewis. Minister.

(28) YNYSFACH. BAPTIST.
Erected 1786.
Space: free 120; other 45; standing 100.
Present: morn. 65; aft. 40 scholars; even. 84.
Average (6 *months*): morn. 70; aft. 38 scholars; even. 80.

John Morgan.   Secretary.
Ynysfach, Ystrad-dyfodwg.

6 Clydach Hamlet.
Popn. 200 males, 194 females: total 394.
[no returns]

[End of Aberdare Subdistrict and end of Merthyr Tydfil District]

Area: 109,511 acres.   *Popn.* 11,789 males, 11,633 females: total 23,422.

1 MAESTEG (Subdistrict)
Area: 43,164 acres. *Popn.* 3,863 males, 3,625 females: total 7,488.

1-3 Llangynwyd Parish, consisting of the Hamlets of [1] Middle Llangynwyd, [2] Lower Llangynwyd, and [3] Cwmdu.
Area of the whole parish: 15,460 acres. *Popn.* 2,914 males, 2,565 females: total 5,479.

1   Middle Llangwynwyd Hamlet.
Area: 3,076 acres. *Popn.* 173 males, 156 females: total 329.

(1)   LLANGYNWYD PARISH CHURCH.
[Prefatory note attached to the schedule] The parish of Llangynwyd (often nicknamed Llangonoyd, Langonoyd) in the County of Glamorgan and Diocese of Llandaff contains 15,461 acres, 1r. 27p.; and is divided into four Hamlets *Baidan* (called in the Poor Law documents Llangonoyd Lower), *Llangynwyd Middle, Cwmdû* and *Llangynwyd Higher.*
Baiden Hamlet per se contains 2,279 a. 3r. 17p. The central point of this portion of the parish is distant 2¼ miles from the Parish Church. There is a dilapidated Chapel in this.
Llangynwyd Middle, per se, contains 2,526 a. In this hamlet is situate, on the top of a hill, the Parish Church.
Cwmdu Hamlet, per se, contains 4,110 a. 3r. The central point of this portion of the parish (in which is located a numerous population) is distant 2 miles from the Parish Church. In this Hamlet is a room, licensed by the Bishop, for divine service in connection with the Church of England. For this room £9 per ann. are paid,—it is very inadequate to the wants of the place and may contain 140 to 150 sittings. The above 3 portions of the parish are situated in the *Bridgend and & Cowbridge Union.*
Llangynwyd Higher (in the Neath Union) *per se* contains 6,544a. 1r. 13p. The central point of this portion of the Parish is distant 3½ miles from the Parish Church. Some portions of this Hamlet are distant 7 miles, or more, by the nearest Parish road, from the Parish Church. One of the Church-wardens of the Parish resides in this Hamlet, and his residence is, by the nearest parish road, 5¾ miles distant from the Church! ! So that, to and fro

of a Sunday morning, he has nearly 12 miles to travel to church! ! There is, in this Hamlet, a Schoolroom built for their Workmen's children, by the Llynvi Iron Co., which room is kindly lent for divine service, in accordance with the Rites and Ceremonies of the Church of England, and which for this purpose, in November last, was licensed by the Bishop of the Diocese. This room may contain 80 or 90 sittings. The population of this Hamlet increases wonderfully. A Church ought to be built there, indeed, there ought to be a separate Church in each Hamlet of this large Parish, for three of the Hamlets are not only very distant from the Parish Church but the roads thereto are most mountainous and miserable. Those, or their successors, who appropriated and misapplied the Rectorial Tithes of this large parish ought *now* to make some amends. There were entered on the Parish Registers in the year 1850: 40 Baptisms; 52 Marriages, 86 Burials.

> Richard Pendrill Llewelyn, M.A.
> Vicar of Llangynwyd Parish,
> Glamorganshire.

[The above note is not in the same hand as the signature.]

[Return]
LLANGYNWYD, but spelt by ignoramuses & asses Llangonoyd, Langonoyd, etc. The parish church of four Hamlets. Situated in the Village of Llangynwyd.

Consecrated before 1800, probably for the good of his own soul by *Mr* Cynwyd, or, it may be, from a feeling that property has its duties as well as its rights.

How or by whom erected: Said to be built originally by a gentleman called Cynwyd, a great man in his day.

Cost, how defrayed: Some say out of Mr Cynwyd's private purse.

Endowed: tithe net £138; glebe 3 cots, Vicarage house and garden; fees, average £14.

Space: free 145; other 22.

Present: morn. Welsh, 70 + 17 scholars; aft. English 11.

Remark: There are in the Hamlet in which the Church is situate, only three families (and my own family is one of the three) capable of understanding an English service.

> R. P. Llewelyn, M.A.   Vicar.

[The return is not in the same hand as the signature.]

Lewis: discharged vicarage, rated at £19. 5.; net income £135, with a glebe house: patron and impropriator, L. W. Dillwyn, Esq. In the township of Bayden was formerly a chapel of ease, now in ruins.

C & C: 1 Welsh service, taken by the incumbent, in the parish church: 2 services, of which 1 in Welsh, in a licensed room at Maesteg, taken by the curate.

I & C: incumbent resident.

(2) PABELL, LLANGYNWYD VILLAGE.   CALVINISTIC METHODIST.
Erected: present building in 1843.
Space: free 80; standing, below 22 feet by 12 feet, gallery 13 ft by 7ft.
Present: aft. 66.
Remark: All in Welsh Language.

> Evan Evans.   One of the members.
> Llangynoyd Village.

(3) BETHESDA, LLANGONOYD.   INDEPENDENT.
Erected 1799.
Space: free 80; other 1; standing 513 square feet.
Present: aft. 75; even. 70.
Average: aft. 100; even. 80.
Remark: All Welsh.

> William Morgan.
> Independent Minister.
> Langonoyd Vilage.

2 Lower Llangynwyd Hamlet.

Area: 2,027 acres. *Popn.* 160 males, 144 females: total 304.

(4) BETHANIA, LLANGYNOYD.   WELSH BAPTIST.
Erected 1832.
Space: free 372; other 318; standing 60 men.
Present: morn. 302; aft. scholars 236; even. 700.
Average: general congregation 400; scholars 255.

> Edward Williams.   Secretary.
> Temple Street, Maesteg.

(5) MOUNT SION, TONDU.   BABTIST.
Erected 1848.
Space: free 120 men.
Present: morn. 12 men; even. 33 men. No school held today.

> Thomas William.   Deacon.
> Fuller, Pontcoytrahen

3 Cwmdu Hamlet.

Area: 3,813 acres. *Popn.* 1,736 males, 1,614 females: total 3,350.

(6) MAESTEG LICENSED ROOM, MAESTEG.   CWMDU HAMLET.
Licensed August 1845, to meet the increasing population. The Room is
distant from the Parish Church 2 miles. Originally a private house, but
converted and hired for Church purposes at £9 per annum.
Endowed: Pastoral Aid Society £100.
Space: free 145.

Present: morn. (English) 67 + 38 scholars; even. (Welsh) 47 + 7 scholars.
Average (6 months): morn. (English) 64 + 30 scholars; even. (Welsh) 50 + 15 scholars.
Remark: Additional services are very much called for by the Inhabitants of this Hamlet.

Thomas Jones.   Licensed Curate.

[This return is in the hand of 583. 1. 1(1) above.]

(7)   ENGLISH BAPTIST CHAPEL, BOWRINGTON STREET, MAESTEG. FREE COMMUNION OR GENERAL BAPTIST.
Erected 1850.
Space: free 130.
Present: morn. 69; aft. 38 scholars; even. 92.

Job Hurley.   Deacon.

(8)   CARMEL, LANGONOYD.   INDEPENDENT.
Erected 1827, rebuilt 1830, do. 1850.
Space: 2,313 ft; free 250; other 500.
Present: morn. 300; aft. 'school' 282 scholars; even. 500 ;
Average: (10 *months since reopened*): morn. 400; aft. 200; scholars; even. 700.

William Morgan.   Minister.
Llangynoyd.

(9)   WESLEYAN METHODIST, MAESTEG, LLANGOYNYD.
Erected about 1829.
Space: free 250; standing 50.
Present: morn. 30; aft. 50; 'no school'.
Average (12 months): general congregation about 80; scholars, none.
Remark: The place of worship referred to in the paper was originally built by the Welch Calvinistic Methodists, but it becoming too small for them was sold to the Wesleyans about 1845.

William Rowe.   Society Steward.
Maesteg.

(10)   TABOR, CWMDU, LANGONOYD.   CALVINISTIC METHODIST.
Erected 1840.
Space: free 192; other 162; standing 20 superficial feet.
Present: morn. 398; aft. 243 scholars; even. 367.
Average: morn. 260 scholars; aft. 500; even. 500.
Remark: Service is generally kept thus; morning—school; afternoon public worship; evening do.

David Bowen.   Abraham Williams.
Maesteg Iron Works.

(11) ZOAR, MAESTEG. CONGREGATIONALISTS.
Erected 1841.
Space: free 10; other 255; standing 24 feet by 13, also a gallery over about ¾ of the chapel.
Present: morn. 185.
Average (three months): morn. 180; aft. 160 scholars; even. 250.
Remarks: No Sunday School as we were going to the Babtist Chapel for the evening.
Size of the Chapel, 42 by 44 in the clear.

James Jones. Deacon.
[Herbert?] Place, Maesteg.

(12) SARON, MAESTEG. INDEPENDENT.
Erected 1840.
Space: free 220; other 330.
Present: morn. 80 + 20 scholars; aft. 75 scholars; even. 140 + 30 scholars.

William Watkins.
Independent Minister.

4   Bettws Parish.
Area: 5,086 acres. *Popn.* 204 males, 217 females: total 421.

(13) BETTWS CHAPELRY.
Space: free 22.
Congregation: morn. 20; aft. 43.

Signed: David [?] James.
Dated: 13th October 1852.

[MS return]
Lewis: perpetual curacy, annexed to the vicarage of Newcastle [583. 3. 9(11)], which is endowed with the rectorial tithes.
C & C: 2 services, of which 1 in Welsh, taken by the curate.
I & C: See under 583. 3. 9(11) below.

(14) BETTWS CHAPEL. PARTICULAR BAPTISTS.
Erected 1831.
Space: free 200.
Present: morn. 80 + 20 scholars; even. 100.
Average: morn. 80 + 20 scholars; even. 100.

Hopkin Jenkins.
Officiating Minister.
Pantdyfodwg, Bridgend.

(15)   City Chapel, Bettws.   Unitarian.
An old place connected with Newcastle Meeting House.
Rebuilt in 1845.
Present: general congregation. aft. 8 to 10.

John Jones.
Dissenting Minister.
Bridgend.

5   Llangeinor Parish.
Area: 6,710 acres. *Popn.* 172 males, 178 females: total 350.

(16)   Llangeinor Parish Church.
Endowed: permanent endowment about £70.
Space: total 180.
Present: morn. 30; even. 16.
Average: morn. 40 to 50; even. 15 to 20.

Thomas Jones.   Curate.

Lewis: perpetual curacy, endowed with £600 royal bounty, and £200 parliamentary grant; net income £71; patron and impropriator, C. R. M. Talbot, Esq.
C & C: 1 service in Welsh, taken by the curate.
I & C: incumbent resident.

(17)   Graig Wen, Cwmgarw, Langinor.   Particular Baptist.
Erected 1831.
Space: free 150.
Present: morn. 24 scholars; aft. 82; even. 80.
Average (12 *months*): morn. 90 + 30 scholars; aft. 78; even. 96.

Jenkin Thomas.   Deacon.
Lliest, Langinor.

6   Llandyfodwg Parish.
Area: 6,508 acres. *Popn.* 140 males, 144 females: total 284.

(18)   Llandyfodog Parish Church.
Endowed: tithe £60; glebe £16; permanent endowment £10.
Space: other 280.
Present: aft. 30.
Average: aft. 30 to 40.

Thomas Jones.   Minister.

Lewis: discharged vicarage, rated at £8. 13. 4., and endowed with £200 royal bounty; net income £89: patron, R. T. Turberville, Esq.; impropriator, C. R. Talbot, Esq.
C & C: 1 service in Welsh, taken by the curate.
I & C: incumbent not resident, curate, living at Bridgend 3 miles distant, has a stipend of £84.

(19) PARAN, LANDEVODWG. BAPTIST.
Erected 1817.
Space: All free; no other.
Present: morn. 86 + 30 scholars; even. 107.

> Hopkin Jenkins.   Minister.
> Paran, Blackmill.

(20) GLYNOGWR, LANDEFODOG. CALVINISTIC METHODIST.
Erected 1819.
Space: free 30; other 126.
Present: morn. 86 + 82 scholars; even. 100.
Average (12 *months*): 150.

> Thomas Jenkins.   Deacon.
> Cae-Rosser, Landefodog.

(21)   (This return is missing)
[According to the Registrar's preliminary check list, this chapel was Independent. 583. 1. 13(32) should possibly be included here.]

7 Llanharan Parish.
Area: 3,050 acres. *Popn.* 171 males: 159 females: total 330.

(22) LLANHARAN CHAPELRY.
Endowed: tithe £193. 5.
Space: total 60.
Present: morn. 25 + 15 scholars.
Average (12 *months*): morn. 20 + 17 scholars: Service alternate with Llanilid morning and afternoon.
Remark: Llanharan is a Chapelry under Llanilid in the gift of the Lord Chancellor.

> Thomas Morgan Davies.   Rector.

Lewis: rectory consolidated with the rectory of Llanilid [583. 1. 8(22)].

C & C: 1 service in Welsh taken by the incumbent.

I & C: see under 583. 1. 8(23) below.

8 Llanilid Parish.
Area: 1,574 acres. *Popn.* 94 males, 91 females: total 185.

(23) LLANILID PARISH CHURCH.
Endowed: tithe £136. 5.; glebe £12. 11.
Space: free 8; other 54.
Present: morn. 35 + 12 scholars.

Average (12 *months*): morn. 30 + 10 scholars: services alternate with Llan-haran morning and afternoon.

Remark: Llanilid with the Chapelry of Llanharan is a benefice in the gift of the Lord Chancellor. The services morning and afternoon are performed alternately in each.

Thomas Morgan Davies. Rector.

Lewis: discharged rectory with the rectory of Llanharan consolidated, rated at £7. 15. 7½.; in the patronage of the crown; present net income £253, with a glebe house.

C & C: 1 service in Welsh taken by the incumbent.

I & C: incumbent resident.

9-12   Coychurch Parish, consisting of the Hamlets of [9] Higher Coychurch, [10] Pencoed, [11] Lower Coychurch, and [12] the Chapelry of Peterstone.

Area of the whole parish: 9,105 acres. *Popn.* 663 males, 593 females: total 1,256.

9   Higher Coychurch Hamlet.

Area: 3,910 acres. *Popn.* 153 males, 143 females: total 296.

(24) BETHEL.   INDEPENDANT.

Erected about the year 1818.

Space: free 80; standing 40.

Present: morn. 10 scholars; aft. 55; even. 42.

Average (12 *months*): morn. 65 + 30 scholars; aft. 60 + 20 scholars; even. 50.

Remark: This meeting house was first built by subscription and has lately been repaired at about £33 cost.

Owen Owens.   Minister.
Brynmenyn.

10   Pencoed Hamlet.

Area: 2,045 acres. *Popn.* 260 males, 250 females: total 490.

(25) SALEM.   CALVINISTIC METHODIST.

Erected in the year 1775, recuilt in 1830.

Space: free 600; other 200; standing 200.

Present: morn. 150 + 50 scholars; even. 175 + 50 scholars.

Average (6 *months*): The number being just as above stated.

John Howell.   Elder.
Bryncwttyn Bridgend.

11   Lower Coychurch Hamlet.
Area: 1,090 acres. *Popn.* 142 males, 143 females: total 285.

(26)   Coychurch Parish Council.
Endowed: tithe £465; glebe £44; fees £5.
Space: free 75; other 230.
Present: morn. 70 + 31.
Remark: The above includes the amount of rent charge of the four hamlets
of which the parish is made up.

Samuel Jones.   Curate of Coychurch.

Lewis: rectory, rated at £21. 1. 8.; present net income £446 with a glebe house:
patron, Earl of Dunraven: tithes of Lower Coychurch commuted for £130, subject
to rates, averaging £15 per annum: glebe of 36 acres, with appendages, worth
£54. 10. per annum. Chapel of Ease at the hamlet of Peterston [583. 1. 12(28)].
C & C: 1 service in Welsh taken by the curate.
I & C: incumbent not resident: curate, resident in the glebe house, has a stipend
of £100.

(27)   Weslean Chappel, Coychurch.
Erected 1828.
Present: aft. 40; even. 28 scholars.
Average (12 *months*): aft. 50; even. 15 scholars.

Rees Jenkin.   By Mark.   Manager.

12   Peterstone Chapelry.
Area: 2,060 acres. *Popn.* 108 males, 77 females: total 185.

(28)   Peterstone super Montem Chapel.
Consecrated in 1833, instead of the old church which was taken down.
Erected by Mr E. Davies Tregroes, at a total cost of £250.
Space: total 130.
Present: aft. 45 + 32 scholars.
Average: aft. 40 + 25 scholars.
Remark: This Hamlet Chapel is annexed to Coychurch.

Samuel Jones.   Curate.

Lewis: Chapel dedicated to St. Peter, and annexed to the rectory of Coychurch:
tithes commuted for a rent-charge of £75, subject to rates, averaging £9. 1. 8.
C & C: 1 service in Welsh taken by the curate.

(29)   Bethlehem Llanharan.   Independents.
Erected before 1800.
Space: free 40; standing 100.
Present: morn. 120; aft. 60 scholars; even. 300.
Average (12 *months*): morn. 200; aft. 70 scholars; even. 400.

William Griffiths.   Minister.
Llanharan, Llantrisant.

13-14   St. Brides Minor Parish, consisting of [13] St. Brides Minor and [14] Ynysawdre Hamlet.
Area of the whole: 2,215 acres. *Popn.* 350 males, 329 females: total 679.

(30)   ST. BRIDES MINOR PARISH CHURCH.
Endowed: tithe £150; glebe £20.
Space: free 50; other 100.
Present: morn. 30; aft. 250.

Edward Roberts.   Rector.

Lewis: discharged rectory, rated at £5. 3. 6½.; net income £176, with a glebe house: patron, Earl of Dunraven.
C & C: 1 service in Welsh taken by the incumbent.
I & C: incumbent resident.

(31)   BETHARAN, BRYNMWYN, ST. BRIDES MINOR.   INDEPENDENT.
Erected 1806.
Space: free 30.
Present: morn. 384; aft. 90 scholars; even. 199.

Owen Owens.   Minister.

(32)   BETHANIA, LANDEVODUCK. INDEPENDENT.
Erected 1846.
Space: free 90.
Present: morn. 30 + 20 scholars; aft. 38; even. 50.
Average (12 *months*): morn. 28 + 18 scholars; aft. 39; even. 45.

Morgan Williams.   Deacon.

[This return is wrongly numbered and wrongly placed. It should probably be under 583. 1. 6.]

[End of Maesteg Subdistrict]

2 COWBRIDGE (Subdistrict)
Area: 32,939 acres. *Popn.* 3,205 males, 3,311 females: total 6,516.

1   Llangan Parish
Area: 1,175 acres. *Popn.* 132 males, 129 females: total 261.

(1)   LANGAN PARISH CHURCH.
Endowed: tithe £160; glebe £100.
Space: free 100.
Present: morn. 12; aft. 25.
Average (1½ *months*): morn. 20; aft. 25.
Remark: This parish for the last 8 or 10 years almost wholly given up to

Dissent is chiefly Welsh. For the last two months or nearly so 2 services have been performed in this church by order of the Diocesan.

Thomas Davies. Curate.

Lewis: discharged rectory, rated at £12. 16. 0½., and the alternate patronage of the Earl of Clarendon and the Earl of Dunraven; net income £244; glebe of about 60 acres, with glebe house: tithes commuted for £152. 10., subject to rates averaging £25.

C & C: 1 service in Welsh taken by the curate.

I & C: incumbent not resident; curate, who resides in the glebe house, has stipend of £40.

(2)   SARON, IN THE VILLAGE OF TREEOS. INDEPENDENTS.
Erected 1830.
Space: free 84; other 138; standing 60.
Present: morn. 140; aft. 91; even. 300.
Average (12 *months*): morn. 200; aft. 70; even. 350.

William Griffith. Minister.
Llanharan.

2   St. Mary Hill Parish.
Area: 1,404 acres. *Popn.* 125 males, 122 females: total 247.

(3)   ST. MARY HILL PARISH CHURCH.
Endowed: land £20. 14; tithe £70. 5.
Space: total 80.
Present: morn. 35 + 47 scholars.
Average: morn. 40 + 25 scholars.
Remark: The average of the Sunday School scholars in the school room is 75.

John Griffiths. Vicar.

Lewis: discharged vicarage, rated at £5. 11. 3., and endowed with £200 royal bounty; net income £90; patron and impropriator, Sir T. D. Aubrey, Bart.

C & C: 1 service in Welsh taken by the incumbent.

I & C: incumbent not resident; curate, resident in the glebe house, has stipend of £40.

3   Llanhary Parish.
Area: 1,554 acres. *Popn.* 128 males, 133 females: total 261.
(4)   LLANHARRY PARISH CHURCH.
Endowed: tithe £206; glebe £35.
Space: free 37; other 38.
Present: morn. 13 + 8 scholars; aft. 35 + 13 scholars.

William Williams. Curate.

[Endorsed: See Letter]

Lewis: discharged rectory, rated at £5. 12. 8½; net income £120; patron Richard Hoare Jenkins, Esq.

C & C: 1 service in Welsh taken by the incumbent.

I & C: incumbent not resident.

(5) PENIEL. INDEPENDENTS.
Erected in 1825, rebuilt 1850.
Space: free 120; other 68.
Present: morn. 40; aft. 25 scholars; even. 160.
Average (12 *months*): morn. 50; aft. 40 scholars; even. 160.

> John Evans.   Minister.
> Maendy, Nr. Cowbridge.

4   Ystradowen Parish.
Area: 1,494 acres. *Popn.* 116 males, 105 females: total 221.

(6)   YSTRADOWEN PARISH CHURCH.
Endowed: land, *enhanced* by Queen Anne's Bounty £26; permanent
endowment purchased £15. 4. 6.; Bounty Office £9.
Space: free 64; other 14.
Present: morn. 11.
Remark: I cannot average the congregation, not knowing that it would be
required I have taken no account. The services are alternate Sundays
mornings and afternoons, the afternoon is generally considered the largest.

> Francis Taynton.   Incumbent.

Lewis: perpetual curacy, endowed with £1,200 royal bounty, and £200 parliamentary grant; net income £41; patrons and impropriators, Chapter of Llandaf.

C & C: 1 service, alternately Welsh and English.

I & C: incumbent not resident.

5   Llansannor Parish.
Area: 1,798 acres. *Popn.* 102 males, 106 females: total 208.

(7)   LANSANNOR OR THAWE PARISH CHURCH.
Endowed: tithe £191. 6.
Space: total 60.
Present: aft 29 + 14 scholars.
Average: general congregation 30; scholars 15.

> John Griffith.   Rector.

Lewis: discharged rectory, rated at £7. 15. 7½; net income £120, of which £10 are
paid as a modus for the Llansannor House demesne; patron J. Bailey, Esq.

C & C: 1 service, alternately Welsh and English.

I & C: incumbent not resident.

6   Penlline Parish.
Area: 1,784 acres. *Popn.* 160 males, 178 females: total 338.

(8) LLANFRYNACH.
Endowed: Return made in Chapel Return.
Remark: The church is far apart from the inhabitants consequent[ly] not used for public services except in summer months on alternate Sundays in the afternoon when the congregation may average about forty persons.

William Llewellyn.   Vicar.

C & C: sub Llanfrynach: Church served only occasionally; being inconveniently situated, people attend the parochial chapter of Penlline.

I & C: vacant

(9) PENLLYNE CHAPEL.
Consecrated about 1700, because the church is situated far apart from the residences of the inhabitants.
Endowed: land £14; tithe £62; glebe £1. 5.; permanent endowment £19. 19; fees £1.
Space: all.
Present: morn. 30 + 15 scholars; aft. Welsh 6.
Average (12 *months*): morn. 60 + 20 scholars; aft. 10 Welsh.
Remark: A portion of parishioners who are Church attendants from home at present. The Welsh congregation would be more numerous were they not deterred by great echo of Chapel which I hope to find [have?] remedied shortly.

William Llewellyn.   Minister.

Lewis: sub Penllyne: discharged vicarage, rated at £4. 15. 2s., and endowed with £600 royal bounty; patron and impropriator, Earl of Dunraven: tithes commuted for £161. 19., of which £100 are payable to the impropriator, subject to rates averaging £15. 16. 3., and £61. 19., subject to rates that average £10. 3. 1., to the vicar; glebe of quarter of an acre, valued at 5s per annum

C & C: 1 service in English, occasionally in Welsh, by the curate.

I & C: sub Penlloyne: vacant.

(10) NEBO. CALVINISTICK METHODIST.
Erected October 1831.
Space: free 400; other 48; standing 400.
Present: aft. 120; even. 100.
Average: general congregation 100.

David Reynolds.   Elder.
Shoe Maker, Penlline.

7 Cowbridge Parish.
Area: 96 acres. *Popn.* 515 males, 551 females: total 1,066.
Consecrated 1850.
Endowed: tithe £17; fees £7; Easter offerings £11.
Space: free 258; other 387.

Present: morn. 173 + 20 scholars; even. 192 + 20 scholars.
Remark: In December last the church was repewed the provision of church room previously to the alteration was 440 of which number 39 were free.

Thomas Edmondes.   Minister.

Lewis: no distinct incumbency: originally a chapel of ease to the church of Llanblethian, it is served by the vicar of that parish: rectorial tithes commuted for a rent-charge of £17. 3.
C & C: 2 services in English taken by the incumbent.
I & C: see *sub* Llanblethian [583. 2. 22] below.
ICBS: grant of £150 in 1849.

(12)   ENGLISH WESLEYAN CHAPEL.
Erected 1850.
Space: free 31; other 128.
Present: morn. 32 + 14 scholars; even. 31 + 18 scholars.
Average: morn. 60 + 20 scholars.

John Parsons, Chapel Steward.

(13)   WELSH WESLEYAN CHAPEL.
Erected 1780.
Space: free 60; other 77; standing 39.
Present: morn. 21; even. 94.
Average: general congregation 60 to 90.

John Rees.   Minister.
Cowbridge.

(14)   SION CHAPEL LIMES.   CALVINISTIC METHODIST.
Erected 1825.
Space: free 120; other 290; standing 200.
Present: morn. 150; aft. 'school'; even. 350.
Average: general congregation 560; scholars 82.

Thomas Williams.   Deacon.
Flannel Mannefactor.

(15)   RAMOTH BAPTISTS CHAPEL.   PARTICULAR BAPTISTS.
Erected 1816 but rebuild and enlarged 1828.
Space: free 250; other 230; standing 200 between the sittings.
Present: morn. 100; even. 250.
Average (12 *months*): morn. 150 to 200; aft. school; even. 500.
Remark: A prayer meeting we had yesterday, the minister had to be in another place, which will account for the congregation being less. The average for 12 months is not to much. I have seen a 1,000 in the chapel in the evening before now.

John Evans.   Minister.

8   St. Hilary Parish.
Area: 1,200 acres. *Popn.* 82 males, 75 females: total 157.

(16) SAINT HILARY PARISH CHURCH.
Endowed: tithe £30; Queen Anne's Bounty £67 per annum.
No other incomes.
Space: free 60; other 80.
Present: morn. 40 + 33 scholars.
Average: morn. always between 70 and 80.
Remark: Only morning service and the attendance of the children is always the same.

George Traherne. Vicar.

Lewis: discharged vicarage, rated at £5. 14. 4¼., and endowed with £200 private benefaction and £1,000 royal bounty; patrons and impropriators, the Bishop, Archdeacon, and Chapter of Llandaf: great tithes commuted for £91, with a glebe of 72*a.* or. 28*p*, valued at £118 per annum, and the vicarial for one of £33; vicar the lessee of the great tithes and glebe under the appropriators.
C & C: 1 service in English taken by the incumbent.
I & C: incumbent resident; curate's stipend £40.

9 St. Mary Church Parish.
Area: 727 acres. *Popn.* 54 males, 50 females: total 104.

(17) ST. MARY CHURCH PARISH CHURCH.
Endowed: tithe £100; glebe £36; fees £1; Easter offerings 10*s.*
Space: total 'cir' 60.
Present: morn. 30 + 16 scholars; even. 50.
Average (12 *months*): morn. 'Cir' 40; even. 'cir' 50.
Remark: This parish and Llandough (which adjoins) are consolidated.

Edward Doddridge Knight. Rector.

Lewis: discharged rectory, united with that of Llandough [583. 2. 21(36)] rated at £5. 6. 8.
C & C: 1 service in Welsh taken by the incumbent.
I & C: incumbent resident.

10 Flemingston Parish.
Area: 672 acres. *Popn.* 41 males, 38 females: total 79.

(18) FLEMINGSTONE OR ST. MICHAEL ON THE HILL PARISH CHURCH.
Endowed: tithe, gross £68; glebe £39.
Space: free 28; other 35.
Present: morn. 8.
Average: morn. 12 or 14.

Thomas Powel. Curate.

Lewis: discharged rectory, rated at £4. 18. 9.; net income £196; patron, Earl of Dunraven.
C & C: 1 service, alternately Welsh and English.
I & C: incumbent not resident: curate resident in Llanblethian [583. 2. 22(36a)] (3 miles distant), and paid stipend of £100 for two parishes, this and Llanvihangel [583. 2. 20(35)].

11   Eglwys-Brewis Parish.
Area: 367 acres. *Popn.* 10 males, 7 females: total 17.

(19)   Eglwys brewis (St. Brise) Parish Church.
Endowed: tithe £75; glebe £42. 5.; fees 2s.
Space: free about 12; other 15.
Present: aft. 14.
Average: aft. 12.
Remark: There is but one service each Sunday which service is in the afternoon regularly.

John Davies.   Churchwarden.

Lewis: discharged rectory, rated at £3. 18. 6½; tithes commuted for £75: patron, John Dillwyn Llewellyn, Esq.
C & C: 1 service alternately Welsh and English.
I & C: incumbent not resident.

12   St. Athan Parish.
Area: 1,771 acres. *Popn.* 177 males, 199 females: total 376.

(20)   St. Athans Parish Church.
[This return is missing.]
Lewis: rectory, rated at £15. 9. 7.; net income £369, with a glebe house; patron, W. Rayer, Esq.
C & C: 2 services in English.
I & C: incumbent resident: curate's stipend £50.

(21)   Hope Chapel.   Calvinistic Methodist.
Erected 1845.
Space: free 200; other 100.
Present: aft. 56; even. 40.

William Stephens.   Chapel Steward.

(22)   Wesleyan Methodist Chapel.
Erected 1811.
Space: free 170; other 30.
Present: morn. 30 scholars; aft. 46 + 18 scholars; even. 59 + 22 scholars.

Samuel Hammett.   Chapel Steward.

(23)   Bethel Welsh Wesleyan Chapel.
Erected 1811.
Space: free 117; standing 112.
Present: aft. 50; even. 90.
Average: general congregation 90 to 100.

John Rees.   Minister.

13   Gileston Parish.
Area: 496 acres. *Popn.* 28 males, 37 females: total 65.

(24)   GILESTON PARISH CHURCH.
Remark: I beg leave to decline making any return relative to the Living at
Gileston or to the state of public worship or education in that parish believing such information to be unauthorised by Parliament and not calculated to
be of any general utility to the Country.

Frederic F. Edwardes.
Patron and Rector.

Lewis: discharged rectory, rated at £5. 13. 0½; endowed with £200 private benefaction and £400 royal bounty; net income £80; patron and incumbent, son of
John Edwardes who married heiress of the Willis family, proprietor of the manor.

C & C: 2 services, both in English.

I & C: incumbent not resident.

14   Llanmaes Parish.
Area: 1,085 acres. *Popn.* 102 males, 81 females: total 183.

(25)   LANMAES PARISH CHURCH.
Endowed: tithe £259. 6; glebe £100.
Space: free 180.
Present: monr. 20; aft. 40.

John Williams.   Church warden.

Lewis: rectory, rated at £10. 2. 3½; net income £294: patron, Marquess of Bute;
72 acres of glebe.

C & C: 2 services, both in English.

I & C: incumbent resident; curate's stipend £80.

15   Llantwit Major Parish.
Area: 5,298 acres. *Popn.* 513 males, 564 females: total 1,077.

(26)   LANTWIT MAJOR PARISH CHURCH.
Endowed: tithe £220.
Space: free 100; other 250.
Present: morn. 80 + 27 scholars; aft. 10.

Edward W. Vaughan.   Vicar.

Lewis: discharged vicarage, with the rectory of Llysworney [583. 1. 23(39)] annexed,
rated at £14. 13. 9.; net income £410; patrons, Dean and Chapter of Gloucester:
tithes commuted for £771. 7. 11, of which £481. 7. 11., subject to rates averaging
£67. 14. 4 per annum, payable to the Dean and Chapter, who also have a glebe of 12
acres, valued at £25 annually; £220 are the property of the vicar, subject to rates,
averaging £5. 10., and £70 belongs to an impropriator, also subject to rates averaging £10 per annum.

C & C: 2 services, both in English.

I & C: incumbent resident.

(27) Wesleyan Chapel, Lantwit.
Space: free 140; other 120.
Present: morn. 50 + 8 scholars; even. 100 + 14 scholars.
Average: general congregation 90; scholars 30.

Robert Price.   Steward.

(28) Bethel.   Particular Baptists.
Erected 1830.
Space: free 4 large pews free, benches with backs free; standing, walking
allies or space between benches and pews.
Present: morn. 55; aft. 20 children in school; even. 180.
Average (12 *months*): morn. 65 + 30 scholars; aft. 'no service'; even. 250.
Remark: Yesterday being the first Sunday after Communion Sunday, the
attendants always less in number.

Jabez Lawrence.   Minister.

(29) Bethesda.   Independent.
Erected 1806.
Space: all free; standing about 200.
Present: morn. 75 + 30 scholars; aft. school; even. 30.
Average (12 *months*): general congregation 3,460; scholars 1,560.

Morgan Morgan.   Minister.

(30) Wesleyan Chapel, Llanillyd Fawr.
Erected 1847.
Space: free 78; other 89; standing 50.
Present: morn. 50; even. 110.
Average: general congregation 000; scholars 30.

John Rees.   Minister.

(30a) Tabernacle Calvinistic Methodist.
Erected about 1822.
Space: free 290; other 79; standing 135.
Present: morn. 30 + 10 scholars; aft. 8 + 40 scholars; even. 136 + 10
scholars.
Remarks: Morning prayer meeting; afternoon school; evening sermon.

E. Bassett.   Elder.

16 Llandow Parish.
Area: 1,086 acres. *Popn.* 67 males, 67 females: total 134.

(31) Landow Parish Church.
[This return is missing.]
Lewis: discharged rectory, rated at £7. 4. 4½, in the patronage of Jesus College,

Oxford: tithes commuted for £197. 12., subject to rates averaging £14. 12. 3, with a glebe of 60*a*. 2*r*. 12*p*. valued at £80. 12. 6. per annum, and a glebe house.

C & C: 1 service, mixed Welsh and English, taken by the curate.

I & C: incumbent not resident: curate, resident at Brufter, 2 miles distant, has stipend of £75.

17 St. Donats Parish.

Area: 1,018 acres. *Popn.* 65 males, 67 females: total 132.

(32) ST. DONATS PARISH CHURCH.
Endowed: land £51; tithe £85; glebe £5; fees £1.
Space: free 100.
Present: aft. 43.

John Williams. Vicar.
Marcross Rectory.

Lewis: discharged vicarage, rated at £3. 14. 4½.; endowed with £200 royal bounty; net income £131: patron, Thomas Tyrwhitt Drake, Esq.

C & C: 1 service alternately Welsh and English. taken by the curate.

I & C: incumbent not resident.

18 Marcross Parish.

Area: 1,041 acres. *Popn.* 50 males, 42 females: total 92.

(31) MARCROSS PARISH CHURCH.
Endowed: tithe £151; glebe £55; fees £1.
Space: free 60; other 20.
Present: morn. 32.

John Williams. Rector.

Lewis: discharged rectory, rated at £9. 10. 10., and in the patronage of the Archdeacon and Chapter of Llandaf; tithes commuted for £151. 7., with glebe-land; net income £216. 7; parsonage-house built under Gilbert's Act.

C & C: 1 service alternately Welsh and English.

I & C: incumbent resident.

19 Monknash Parish.

Area: 1,584 acres. *Popn.* 66 males, 44 females: total 110.

(34) MONKNASH PARISH CHURCH.
[This return is missing.]

Lewis: perpetual curacy, endowed with £200 royal bounty, and £200 parliamentary grant; net income £70; patron, John Bruce Pryce, Esq: tithes commuted for £189, of which £142 is paid to the impropriator, and £47 to the perpetual curate, both amounts subject to rates averaging £7. 9. 1 and £2 per annum respectively.

C & C: 1 service alternately Welsh and English.

I & C: incumbent not resident; curate, who has a stipend of £90, resides 1 mile away in adjoining parish.

20   Llanmihangel Parish.
Area: 586 acres. *Popn.* 18 males, 19 females: total 37.

(35)   LLANMIHANGLE PARISH CHURCH.
Endowed: tithe £13; glebe £42.
Space: free 20; other 40.
Present: aft. 3.
Present: aft. 7 or 8 .

Thomas Powel.   Curate.
Cowbridge.

Lewis: rectory not in charge; net income £142, with a glebe house: patron, Earl of Dunraven.

C & C: 1 service alternately Welsh and English taken by the curate.

I & C: incumbent not resident: curate, who has a stipend of £100 for two chapelries, resides at Llanblethian, 1 mile distant.

21   Llandough Parish.
Area: 683 acres. *Popn.* 53 males, 60 females: total 113.

(36)   LLANDOUGH (ST. DOCHWY) PARISH CHURCH.
Endowed: tithe £80; glebe £65; Easter offerings £1. 10.
Space: free 12; other about 50.
Present: aft. 40 + 1 scholars.
Average (12 *months*): morn. about 35; aft. about 53.
Remark: This parish and St Mary Church are consolidated. The services are alternately in the morning and afternoon in this church.

Edward Doddridge Knight.   Rector.

Lewis: discharged rectory with that of St. Mary-church [583. 2. 9(17)] united, rated at £4. 18. 9.; net income £263, with a glebe house: patron, C. R. M. Talbot, Esq.

C & C: at Llandough, 1 service in English: at St. Mary church 1 service in Welsh taken by the incumbent.

I & C: incumbent resident.

22   Llanblethian Parish.
Area: 3,148 acres. *Popn.* 361 males, 406 females: total 767.

[(36A)]   LLANBLETHIAN (ST. JOHNS). Vicarage with the annexed parishes of Cowbridge and Welsh St. Donats.
Endowed: tithe £145; glebe £80; fees £3; Easter offerings £4. 10.
Space: free 67; other 113.
Present: aft. 49.

Remark: The Church is situated at one extremity of a Parish 4 miles long. I have been told that the number was as above. I was myself ill at home. The duties are alternately at 11 a.m. and 3 p.m.

Thomas Edmondes.   Minister.

[This lacks a final number and is bound in between (40) and (41).]

Lewis: discharged vicarage, with the perpetual curacies of Cowbridge [583. 2. 7(11)] and Welsh St. Donatt's [581. 3. 10(20)] annexed, rated at £10. 3. 4.;   net income £279;   patrons and impropriators, Dean and Chapter of Gloucester;   tithes of Llan-blethian commuted for £412. 6. 5., of which a sum of £271. 6. 5. is payable to the Dean and Chapter and £141 to the incumbent, who also has a glebe of 55 acres valued at £80 per annum.

C & C: 1 service in English.

I & C: incumbent resident;   curate's stipend £40.

(37)   ABERTHYN CHAPEL.   CALVINISTIC METHODIST.
Erected 1749, rebuilt 1780.
Space: free 200;   standing 100.
Present: morn. Sunday School;   aft. 100;   even. no service.

Richard Thomas.   Deacon.

(38)   MAENDY.   INDEPENDENTS.
Erected 1802, rebuilt 1842.
Space: free 300.
Present: morn. 150;   aft. 60 scholars;   even. 160.
Average (12 *months*): morn. 140;   aft. 80 scholars;   even. 180.

John Evans.   Minister.

23   Llysworney Parish.
Area: 897 acres. *Popn.* 91 males, 93 females: total 184.

(39)   LISWORNEY PARISH CHURCH.
Endowed: tithe £190.
Space: free 20;   other 80.
Present: morn. 40 + 17 scholars.

Edward W. Vaughan.   Rector.
Llantwit Major.

Lewis: discharged vicarage, annexed to that of Llantwit-Major [583. 2. 15(26)], rated at £4. 7. 3½, and endowed with the great tithes of the parish;   tithes commuted for £190, subject to rates averaging £33. 5. 8;   glebe of about 3/4 acre, valued at £1. 10. per annum.

C & C: 1 service in English.

I & C: incumbent resident.

(40) EBENEZER. PARTICULAR BAPTISTS.
Erected 1843.
Space: free 100; other 8; standing 50.
Present: aft. 50; even. 80.
Average: aft. 50 to 60; even. 100 to 150.
Remark: The Sunday School is sometimes in the Morning and on other
Sundays in the afternoon but it is general larger in the afternoon than in the
morning. And we have seen the congregation in evening more than 200—
but general this is correct.

> John Evans. Minister.

26 Colwinstone Parish.
Area: 1,760 acres. *Popn.* 140 males, 130 females: total 270.

(41) COLWINSTONE (ST. MICHAEL'S) PARISH CHURCH.
Endowed: land £32; tithes, commuted, £88. 2; glebe £7; permanent
endowment £6. 10; fees about £2; aggregate annual amount £135. 12.
Space: free about 30; other about 80.
Present: morn. 49 + 15 scholars.
Average (12 *months*): morn. 35 + 15 scholars; aft. 70 + 15 scholars.
Remark: There is but one service on each Sunday which service is
alternately morning and evening.

> Richard Bassett. Minister.

Lewis: discharged vicarage, rated at £6. 6. 8., endowed with £200 private benefaction, and £400 royal bounty; net income £130; patron, David Thomas, Esq., who
is also the impropriator: impropriate tithes commuted for £124, subject to rates
averaging £10 per annum, and the vicarial tithes for £88, with a glebe of 2½ acres,
valued at £3. 2. 6. per annum.

C & C: 1 service alternately Welsh and English.

I & C: incumbent resident.

[End of Cowbridge Subdistrict]

3 BRIDGEND (Subdistrict)
Area: 33,408 acres. *Popn.* 4,721 males, 4,697 females: total 9,418.

1 St. Andrew Minor Parish.
Area: not stated. *Popn.* 4 males, 12 females: total 16.
[No returns.]

Lewis: sinecure rectory in the patronage of T. Franklin, Esq., of Clementston who,
as proprietor of that estate, pays the minister a modus of £5.
I & C: vacant.
ERCR: accomodation 200.

2 Wick Parish.
Area: 1,370 acres. *Popn.* 195 males, 209 females: total 404.
[No returns.]

Lewis: living consolidated with the vicarage of St. Brides Major [583. 3. 3.(?)].

ERCR: accomodation 150.

C & C: 1 service in English, with one Welsh service in addition every other Sunday, performed by the curate (of St. Bride's Major).

[3-5] St. Brides Major Parish, consisting of the Hamlets of [3] St. Brides, [4] Lampha, and [5] Southerndown.
Area of the whole parish: 6,402 acres. *Popn.* 393 males, 414 females: total 807.

3 St. Brides Hamlet.
Popn. 171 males, 205 females: total 376.

(1) PENYLAN ST. BRIDES. CALVINSTIC METHODIST.
Erected 1828.
Space: free 100; other 12; standing 100.
Present: morn. 69; aft. 60 + 40 scholars; even. 100.

Average (12 *months*): general congregation 100; scholars 40.

David Yorwerth.
Southerndown.

[There is no return for the parish church.]

Lewis: vicarage, with the perpetual curacy of Wick [see under 583. 2. above], rated at £9. 16. 5½: net income £176, with glebe-house: patron, R. Turberville Esq: impropriator, C. Talbot, Esq.

ERCR: accomodation 200.

C & C: 2 services, 1 in English and 1 in Welsh, performed by the incumbent.

I & C: not resident: residence and stipend of curate not stated.

ICBS: grant of £75 in 1851.

4 Lampha Hamlet.
Popn. 89 males, 71 females: total 160.
[No returns.

5 Southerndown Hamlet.
Popn. 133 males, 138 females: total 271.
[No returns.]

6 Ewenny Parish.
Area: 1,975 acres. *Popn.* 144 males, 128 females: total 272.

(2) Soar. Welsh Calvinistic Methodist.
Erected 1832.
Space: free 142; other 58.
Present: morn. 45; aft. 53 scholars; even. 92.

> David Arthur. Deacon.
> Corntown.

(3) Baptist.
Present: morn. 60; even. 120.
Average: general congregation 50; scholars 30.

> Edward Moore.

[7-9] Coyty Parish, consisting of the Hamlets of [7] Higher Coyty, and [8] Lower Coyty.
Area of the whole parish: 4,571 acres. *Popn.* 1,113 males, 1,191 females: total 2,304.

7 Higher Coyty Hamlet.
Area: 2,911 acres. *Popn.* 273 males, 252 females: total 525.

(4) Nolton Chapel of Ease to Coyty Parish.
Consecrated August 1836, in lieu of an old Chapel called by the same name. Not an additional church.
Endowed: fees £5; dues £1; Easter Offerings £1.
Space: free 72.
Present: aft. 140.

> J. Harding. Rector of Coyty.

(5) Coyty Parish Church, with Nolton Chapel.
Endowed: tithe £550; fees £8.
Space: 90 (all free save one pew).
Present: morn. 44 + 34 scholars; aft. no service; even. no service.
Average: [crossed out].

> David Evans. Assistant Curate.

Lewis: rectory with the chapel of Nolton annexed [583. 3. 7.(4)], rated at £21. 12. 3½; patron, Earl of Dunraven: tithes of the Higher Hamlet commuted for £250, and those of Lower Hamlet for one of £300.

C & C: at the parish church, 1 service in Welsh: at Nolton, 2 services in English.

I & C: incumbent resident: curate's stipend £100.

ICBS: grant of £325 to Nolton in 1835.

(6) GILEAD. INDEPENDENT.
Erected 1826.
Space: free 130; standing 90.
Present: aft. 65 + 23 scholars; even. 106 + 36 scholars.

> John David Williams. Minister.

(7) TABERNACLE. INDEPENDENT.
Erected 1805-7.
Space: free 290; other 200.
Present: morn. 150 + 50 scholars; even. 350 + 67 scholars.
Remarks: The congregation to some extent fluctuating—some times it is not
quite so large, and sometimes it is considerably larger.

> John David Williams. Minister.

8 Lower Coyty Hamlet.

Area: 1,660 acres. *Popn.* 840 males, 939 females: total 1,779.

(8) THE HOPE, BRIDGEND. ENGLISH BAPTIST CHAPPEL.
Erected 1850.
Space: They are all as yet free.
Present: morn. 75 + 10 scholars; even. 151 + 8 scholars.
Remarks: The Chappel has had only three services in it previous to that it
has been held in the Vestry Room. Average number of hearers is from 80
to 100.

> Thomas Lewis. Deacon.
> Brewer.

[For (9), Magalene Church, see under 583. 3. 18 below.]

(10) BETHESDA, OLDCASTLE, BRIDGEND. CALVINISTIC METHODIST.
Erected before 1800.
Space: free 300; other 39; standing 300.
Present: morn. 200 + 50 scholars; aft. school; even. 400 + 120 scholars.
Average (12 *months*): morn. 200 + 30 scholars; aft. school; even. 400 +
100 scholars.
Remarks: The 38 sittings in No. 7 [i.e. other sittings] are capable of holding
180 persons.

> Walter Hibbert.
> Bridgend.

[9-10] Newcastle Parish, consisting of [9] Higher Newcastle, and [10] Lower Newcastle.

Area of the whole parish: 2,870 acres. *Popn.* 760 males, 776 females: total
1,536.

9   Higher Newcastle Hamlet.

Popn. 425 males, 397 females: total 822.

(11)   NEWCASTLE CHURCH.
Rebuilt 1850.
Space: free 121; other 94.
Usual number of attendants: morn. 150 + 100 scholars; even. 190 + 40 scholars.

> *Informant:* [sig. illegible.]

[Informant's form.]

Lewis: discharged vicarage, with Bettws [583. 1. 4.(13)], Laleston [583. 3. 11, no return], and Tythegston [583. 3. 14. no return] annexed, rated at £7. 7. 3½., in the patronage and impropriation of the Crown; net income £197, with a glebe house.

C & C: at Newcastle 2 services, both in English: at Bettws Chapel 2 services of which 1 in Welsh; at Laleston Chapel 1 service in Welsh; at Tythegston Chapel 1 service in Welsh once a month, otherwise in English. Services at Bettws and Tythegston taken by the curate.

I & C: incumbent resident; 2 curates receive stipends of £40 each.

ICBS: grant of £150 in 1850.

[The returns for Laleston Chapel, and Tythegston Chapel are missing, and not accounted for in the Registrar's preliminary list.]

(12)   TRINITY CHAPEL, ABERKENFIG.   CALVINISTIC METHODIST.
Space: free 45; other 125; standing 100.
Present: morn. 67 scholars; aft. 48; even. 63.
Average (12 *months*): general congregation 80; scholars 75.

> David Lewis.   Manager.
> Blacksmith, Aberkenfig.

(13)   PENEVAY CHAPEL, PENEVAY VILLAGE.   BAPTIST.
Erected 1718.
Present: morn. 80; aft. 42 scholars; even. 200.
Average (12 *months*): general congregation. 220; scholars 50.

> Morgan Thomas, Deacon.
> Miller, Aberkenfig.

[See also (23) below which should be included here.]

10   Lower Newcastle Hamlet.

Popn. 335 males, 379 females: total 714.
[No returns.]

[11-12] Laleston Parish, consisting of [11] Higher Laleston Hamlet and [12] Lower Laleston Hamlet.
Area: 1,631 acres. *Popn.* of the whole parish: 266 males, 272 females: total 538.
[Laleston Church is missing, and does not appear on the registrar's preliminary list.]

Lewis: living consolidated with the vicarage of Newcastle.

ERCR: accomodation 109.

For *C & C* and *I & C:* see under Newcastle, 583. 3. 9(11) above.

(16) LALASTON CHAPEL, LALASTON. WELSH CALVINISTIC METHODIST.
Erected 1831.
Space: free 125; other 17.
Present: morn. 64 + 20 scholars; even. 53 + 41 scholars.
Average (12 *months*): morn. 120 + 45 scholars; aft. 100 + 40 scholars; even. 120 + 45 scholars.

> John Howells. Steward.
> Whitney, Merthyr Mawr.

[Note: this return is mis-numbered, being placed under Newton-Nottage.]

13 Merthyr Mawr Parish.
Area: 2,590 acres. *Popn.* 78 males, 76 females: total 154.
[No returns.]

Lewis: perpetual curacy, endowed with £200 private benefaction and £800 royal bounty; net income £69; patron, Sir John Nichol; appropriator, Archdeacon of Llandaff.

ERCR: accomodation 200.

C & C: 1 service in English.

I & C: not resident; curate, who resides at Newton, 3½ miles distant, has stipend of £50.

[14-15] Tythegston Parish, consisting of the Hamlets of [14] Tythegston Upper and [15] Lower Tythegston.
Area of the whole parish: 2,871 acres. *Popn.* 633 males, 519 females: total 1,152.
[The return for Tythegston Church is missing, and does not appear in the registrar's preliminary list.]

Lewis: the living is annexed to the vicarage of Newcastle.

ERCR: accomodation 80.

For *C & C* and *I & C:* see under Newcastle, 583. 3. 9(11) above.

(17) NEBO, CEFN CRIBBWR. PARTICULAR BAPTIST.
Erected 1849.
Space: free 100.
Present: morn. 49 scholars; aft. 140; even. 100.
Average (12 *months*): morn. 140 + 44 scholars; aft. 140 + 44 scholars.

> Rees Davies. Minister.
> Penevay

(18) ELIM, KENFIG HILL. INDEPENDANTS.
Erected 1847.
Space: free 250; other 250. The whole space is free.
Present: morn. 200 + 20 scholars; aft. school; even. 100 + 30 scholars.
Average (12 *months*): morn. 140 + 30 scholars; aft. school; even. 140 + 30 scholars.
Remark: Division VII [i.e. space available]. There are no fitted sittings placed in it, only some moveable Benches, to which any person is intitled to have free access.

> Griffith Jones. Minister.
> Kenfig Hill, Pyle.

[Note: 582. 1. 3(28) should be included here.]

16 Newton Nottage Parish.
Area: 3,877 acres. *Popn.* 492 males, 467 females: total 959.

[For Newton Nottage Parish Church, see (19) below).]

(14) NOTTAGE CHAPEL, NOTTAGE. GENERAL BAPTIST.
Erected before 1800.
Space: free 200. Standing room: the Building will accomodate above 200.
Present: morn. 100 + 35 scholars; even. 160.

> Titus Lloyd. Minister.

(15) HOPE CHAPEL, NEWTON NOTTAGE. INDEPENDENT.
Erected 1827.
Space: free 100; other 150.
Present: morn. 70; aft. 40 scholars; even. 200.

> John Hopkins Minister.

[See also (24) below, which should be included here.]

(19) NEWTON NOTTAGE PARISH CHURCH.
Endowed: tithe about £320; glebe £8; fees about £6.
Space: about 190.
Present: morn. 118; aft. about half the number generally.
Remark: In the summer or in fine weather the congregation is generally much larger.

> Robert Knight, Rector.

[This return is misplaced and wrongly numbered:]

Lewis: rectory, rated at £17. 4. 7., in the patronage of the lords of the manor; net income £375.

C & C: 2 services, both in English.

I & C: incumbent not resident; curate's stipend £30.

17 Pyle Parish.

Area: (with that of Kenfig) 5,251 acres. *Popn.* of Pyle alone 500 males, 491 females: total 991.

(20) PYLE PARISH CHURCH.
Endowed: see return for Kenfig Church.
Space: free 34; other 140.
Present: morn. 56 + 6 scholars.
Average (12 *months*): morn. 60.
Remarks: The services are morning and afternoon alternately in the churches of Pyle and Kenfig.

William Williams.   Vicar.

Lewis: discharged vicarage, consolidated with that of Kenfig. [For details, see under Magdalene Church, 583. 3. 8(9) below, which is misplaced and wrongly numbered.]

C & C: 1 service in Welsh taken by the incumbent.

I & C: incumbent resident.

(21) CORNELLY CHAPEL, PYLE.   WELSH CALVINISTIC METHODIST.
Erected 1788.
Space: 90; other 540; standing 604.
Present: morn. 303 + 30 scholars; even. 410 + 60 scholars.

Morgan Rees.   Deacon.
Postmaster.

18 Kenfigg Parish.

Area: (with that of Pyle) 5,251 acres. *Popn.* 143 males, 142 females: total 285.

(9) MAGDALENE CHURCH, KENFIG: mother church of the consolidated parishes or Hamlets of Pyle and Kenfig.
Endowed: land £30; tithe £50; permanent endowment £26, fees £4.
Space: free 18; other 96.
Present: aft. 63.
Average (12 *months*): aft. 60.

Remark: The services are morning and afternoon alternately in the Churches of Pyle and Kenfig. The net income of the living of Pyle and Kenfig is £94.

William Williams. Vicar.

Lewis: discharged vicarage with that of Pyle consolidated, rated at £4. 8. 11¼., endowed with £800 royal bounty and £800 parliamentary grant net income £95; in the patronage of the Crown; impropriator, C. R. M. Talbot, Esq.

C & C: 1 service in Welsh.

I & C: incumbent resident.

[This form is wrongly numbered and placed.]

583. 1.[?]
584. 1.[?] (?22)   Llangonyd, Maesteg.
English Wesleyan Methodist.
Erected about 1829.
Space: 200.
Present: morn. 30; aft. 50.

William Rowe. Society Steward.

[This return has been bound in right to left—i.e. reversed. The printed pagination is correct, but there is no reference in the top right-hand corner. The references 583. 1 and 584. 1 are on the bottom left-hand corner, indicating a doubt in the mind of the checker. Probably, it should come under 584. 1. 2.

3.   0.   (23)   English Wesleyan Methodist, Bridgend.
Erected 1842.
Space: free 200; other 200; standing room, none except the aisles.
Present: morn. 50 + 29 scholars; even. 150 + 30 scholars.

Philip Price. Steward.
Bridgend.

[This return is misplaced and should come under 583. 3. 9-10.]

3. 0.   (24)   Wesleyan Preaching Room, Porthcawl, Western District.
Erected about the year 1830.
Space: free 90.
Present: aft. 42 + 56 scholars; even. 46 + 31 scholars.
Remark: On the 30th March I preached morning and afternoon at this place. The services are generally held afternoon and eveing.

J. Spencer Jones. Minister.
Bridgend.

[This return should be under 583. 3. 16 (Newton Nottage Parish).]

[*End of Bridgend Subdistrict, and end of Bridgend District*]

584 NEATH (District)

Area: 162,817 acres. *Popn.* 24,208 males, 22,263 females: total 46,471.

1 MARGAM (Subdistrict)
Area: 32,902 acres. *Popn.* 7,962 males, 6,732 females: total 14,697.

1 Margam Parish.
Area: 18,725 acres. *Popn.* 2,558 males, 2,189 females: total 4,747.

[(1): this return is marked 'Duplicate'.]
ST. MARY'S MARGAM (PERPETUAL CURACY).
Restored in 1809 at the expence principally of Mr Talbot the Lay Impropriator.
Cost defrayed by Parochial Rate: [this entry is ticked]
Permanent endowment £40 p.an.; fees 'no account of'; other sources £34. 6. 8; the Lay Impropriator £60.
Space: other 500.
Present: morn. 54 + 20.
Average (12 *months*): 64 + 20.
Remark: The Incumbent received £60 per annum from the Lay Impropriator in addition to the endowment. Service is performed in Welsh & English every alternate Sunday morning. The service was performed this day in Welsh, which is usually not so well attended as the English Service.

> H. Ll. Prichard. Church Warden.
> Tir Caradoc, Taibach.

[(2): this return is marked 'Duplicate']
MARGAM CHAPEL OF EASE, TAIBACH.
Consecrated September 1827 as an additional Church or Chapel of Ease to Margam Church.
Erected by Grants from the Society for Enlargement and Endowment of Churches and by private Subscription. Cost defrayed by Private Benefaction or from other sources, £1,500.
Endowed: £400 in the 3p.c. Consults.
Space: free 430; other 160.
Present: aft. 92 + 53 scholars;
Average (12 *months*: 92 + 53 scholars.

> Wm. Llewellyn Powell. Chapel Warden.

(1)   St. Mary's Parish Church, Margam.
Endowed: permanent endowment from the Impropriator £40; fees about
£8; parliamentary grants £810. 3. 1.
Space: other 510.
Present: morn. 54 + 20 scholars.
Average (12 *months*): morn. 70 + 20 scholars.

Richard Evans.   Perpetual Curate.

(2)   Margam Chapel of Ease.
Consecrated as an additional Church, 1821.
Erected by Subscription.
Cost defrayed by private subscription and a grant from the Society for
promoting the enlargement of Churches and Chapels.
Endowed: permanent endowment £400 Private Benefaction: fees £7.
Space: free 430; other 70.
Present: morn. 92 + 55 scholars.
Average: 92 + 55 scholars.

Richard Evans.   Perpetual Curate.

Lewis: perpetual curacy, endowed with £1,600 parliamentary grant; net income
£121; patron and impropriator, C. R. M. Talbot, Esq.
At Taibach a chapel of ease was erected in 1827; principal contributors, C. R. M.
Talbot, Esq., the English Copper Company, John Reynolds, Esq., and Robert
Smith and Co., assisted by a grant from the Incorporated Society for Building and
Enlarging Churches and Chapels; a gallery has since been erected at a cost of £100.

C & C: 1 church and 1 chapel, 1 service in Welsh and 1 in English taken by the
incumbent.

I & C: incumbent resident.

ICBS: grant of £400 in 1824.

(3)   Beulah, Groes, Margam.   Welsh Calvinistic Methodist.
Erected 1838.
Space: free 72; other 198; standing 60.
Present: morn. 28 + 12 scholars; aft. 200 + 35 scholars.
Average (12 *months*): aft. 150 + 50 scholars.

Howell Griffith.   Diacon.
Margam, Taibach.

(4)   Soar, Penybryn.   Calvinistic Methodist.
Erected 1849.
Space: free 105; other 95; standing 100.
Present: even. 115 + 35 scholars.
Average (12 *months*): aft. 130 + 35 scholars.

Edwin Thomas.   Steward.
[Rees Griffiths Penybryn crossed out].
Penybryndu, Nr. Pyle.

(5) DYFFRYN, TAIBACH. CALVINISTIC METHODIST.
Erected 1842.
Space: free 250; other 409.
Present: morn. 434 + 220 scholars; even. 659.
Average: general congregation 500; scholars 220.

> Edward Daniel. Senr. Secretary.
> Taibach.

(6) VELINFACH, MARGAM. CALVINISTIC METHODIST.
Erected 1836.
Space: free 100.
Present: morn. 45.

> Evan Williams. Deacon.
> Tyn y ffarm, Margam.

2   Higher Llangynwyd Hamlet (part of Llangynwyd parish)
Area: 6,544 acres. *Popn.* 845 males, 641 females: total 1,496.

(7) THE SPELTER LICENSED SCHOOL ROOM.
Licensed 16th of November 1850. The central point of this hamlet is $3\frac{1}{2}$
miles distant from the parish Church & to meet the increasing population the
Bishop has licensed this small room.
Erected by the Llynvi Iron Company as a School room.
Endowed: £100 Pastoral Aid with Maesteg.
Space: free 95.
Present: aft. (Welsh): 38 + 15 scholars.
Average (3 *months*): aft. (Welsh): 70 + 18 scholars.
Remark: Additional services & a resident Curate are much called for by the
inhabitants of this Hamlet.

> Thomas Jones. Officiating Minister.
> Maesteg.

[For remainder of this parish, see 583. 1. 1(1) above.]

(8) CHAPEL OF EASE, LLANGONOYD HIGHER.
Space: free 96.
Usual number of attendants: morn. 100 scholars; aft. 50.
Remark: Formerly an engine house. Altered two years.

> [unsigned]

[Informant's form]

(9) SALEM, SPELTER WORKS. BAPTIST.
Erected before 1846.
Space: free 520; other 180.
Present: morn. 90; aft. school; even. 114.

Average: morn. 90 + 120 scholars.
Remark: Hon. Sir, Our place of worship at present to hold Divine Worship is an old Store belonging to the Llynfi Co. but we have taken a lease for to build a chapel thereon close to this neighbourhood.

> Howell Davies.   Minister.
> Maesteg.

(10) SILOH, MAESTEG.   INDEPENDENT.
Erected about 1842.
Space: all free.
Present: morn. 120; aft. 100 scholars; even. 146.
Remark: Hon. Sir, As Remarks on this Return ther is nothing Particular— except that our place of worship is to small to contain the general Congregation on Sunday, the Cause of the Lord do increase. In July 1849 the Members of the Church belongs to this place of worship was not above 30 in number, but now thank God about 130; the general Congregation then about 40 to 50 but now in general about the number that is mentioned in the other column and mostly over.

> Henry Prichard.   Minister.

[See also 583. 3. 18(?22) below.]

3 Aberavon Parish.
Area: 2,598 acres. *Popn.* 1,234 males, 1,146 females: total 2,380.

(11) ABERAVON PARISH CHURCH.
Endowed: tithe £50.
Space: free 20; other 42, each sitting holding four persons [i.e. 80 free and 164 other].
Present: aft. 52; even. 150.
Average (3 months): morn. 100 to 130 + 40 scholars; aft. 40 to 50; even. 130 to 200.
Remark: The same remark is applicable to the difference in the number of attendants in Aberavon Church as in Baglan.

> D. O. James.   Curate.

Lewis: discharged vicarage, endowed with the great tithes, with Baglan [584. 2. 1(1)], annexed rated conjointly at £9. 4. 9½.; patron, Rev. Davies Rees; tithes commuted for £190.

C & C: 2 services, of which 1 in Welsh taken by the incumbent.

I & C: incumbent resident.

(12)   WESLEYAN METHODIST, ABERAVON.
Erected 1842.
Space: free [2 crossed out] 16; other 20; standing 60.
Present: morn. 25; aft. 37 scholars; even. 42.
Remarks: The two free sittings are capable of holding sixteen adults.

> Richard Roberts.   Elder.
> Lower Row, Michaelstone-super-avon.

(13)   WERN CHAPEL, NEW STREET.   INDEPENDENTS.
Erected 1849.
Space: free 49; other 53.
Present: morn. 144 scholars; aft. 283; even. 256.
Average: aft. 280; even. 300.

> Daniel Richards.   Secretary.
> Tailor.
> To the Care of Mr D. Morgans
> Aberavon.

(14)   ZION.   BIBLE CHRISTIAN.
Erected 1851. 'The Chapel may be considered a separate building though there is a dwelling house for the Minister attached to it'.
Used exclusively as 'a place of worship only at present about to raise a Sabbath School'.
Space: free 40; other 100.
Present: no information.
Average: even. 120.
Remark: The cause at present in this place is in its infancy. We have not had time to bring things into a proper Way of Working. We expect a Sabbath School will soon be formed which will contain at least 60 children.

> Samuel Jory.   Minister.
> Care of T. Hobbs, Aberavon.

(15)   CARMEL.   CALVINISTIC METHODIST.
Erected 1810.   Rebuilt 1844.
Space: free 312; other 204; standing 222.
Present: morn. 252; aft. 123 scholars; even. 397.
Average (1 *month*): morn. 260; aft. 150 scholars; even. 400.

> Emanuel Griffiths.   Deacon.
> Grocer, High Street.

(16)   TABERNACLE.   INDEPENDENTS.
Erected 1822.
Space: ffee 166; other 28 (private property); standing 100.
Present: morn. 68 scholars; aft. 100; even. 90.

> David Williams.   Minister.

(17)   EBENEZER, CATTLE STREET.   BAPTIST.
Erected 1835.
Space: free 288; other 215; standing 60.
Present: morn. 150; aft. 154 scholars; even. 300.
Average (12 *months*): morn. 200; aft. 200 scholars; even. 400.

John Rhys Morgan.   Minister.

(18)   MORRIA SHAPEL, ABRAVON.   LATER DAY SINTES.
Space: all free; standing 40.
Present: morn. 23; even. 23.
Remark: Formerly a Baptist Chapel but of late rented to the Latter Day Saints. [Signed] George Lewis, Registrar.

Wm. Howell.   Elder.

(19)   [This return is missing; Mormonite according to the Registrar's preliminary list.]

[4-5]   Michaelstone-super-Avon Parish, consisting of the Hamlets of [4] Lower Michaelstone, and [5] Upper Michaelstone.
Area of the whole parish: 5,035 acres. *Popn.* 3,325 males, 2,749 females: total 6,074.

4   Lower Michaelstone Hamlet.
Area: 915 acres. *Popn.* 2,965 males, 2,456 females: total 5,421.
(20)   MICHAELSTONE-SUPER-AVON PARISH CHURCH.
Space: free 223; other 132.
Present: morn. 150 + 236 scholars; aft. 83; even. 115 + 127 scholars.
Remarks: Parish Church under Repairs, and present place of worship incapable of accomodating more persons. We have four Services on the Sabbath at different hours of the day. Services performed by two Curates.

Richard Walker, M.A., Curate.
John Morgan, Curate.
Cwmavon Works.

Lewis: perpetual curacy, endowed with £800 royal bounty and £800 parliamentary grant; net income £112; patron, J. Coke, Esq.
C & C: 2 services, of which 1 in Welsh, taken by the curate.
I & C: incumbent resident.
ICBS: grant of £100 in 1850.

(21)   ROCK CHAPEL, PWLLYGLAW, CWMAVON.   INDEPENDENT.
Erected 1839.
Space: free gallery; other 33 let; standing 4 benches.
Present: morn. 550; aft. 90 scholars; even. 650.
Average (12 *months*): morn. 800; aft. 200; even. 900.

William Thomas.   Minister.

(22) ZION CHAPPEL. INDEPENDENT.
Erected 1822.
Space: free 406; other 464.
Present: morn. 424; aft. 44 + 282 scholars; even. 610.
Average (8 months): 600 aft.

> Edward Roberts. Minister.

(23) PENUEL, CWMAFAN. BAPTIST.
Erected 1844.
Space: free 212; other 197; standing 200.
Present: morn. 350; aft. 194 scholars; even. 459.

> David Thomas. Minister.
> Aberavan.

(24) ENGLISH WESLEYAN CHAPEL.
Erected 1849.
Space: free 40; other 79.
Present: morn. 50; aft. 51 scholars; even. 120.
Average (8 months): morn. 40; aft. 60 scholars; even. 150.

> Wm. Williams. Minister.
> Neath.

(25) TABERNACLE. WELSH CALVINISTIC METHODIST.
Erected 1837 & 8.
Space: free 126; other 180; standing 140.
Present: morn. 196; aft. 161 scholars; even. 271.
Average: morn. 250; aft. 200 scholars; even. 320.
Remark: Respecting Congregation on 30 March beeing smaller, there was
Two Monthly Meeting Held by the Denomination in their district Else-
where.

> David Davies. Elder.
> Church Square, Cwmavon.

(26) DWELLING HOUSE, PELLY STREET, CWMAVON. PRIMITIVE METHODIST.
Erected 1848. Formerly dwelling house.
Space: free 10 benches: [60].
Present: morn. 25; even. 35.
Average (6 months): general congregation 30; scholars 80.

> John Pryor. Deacon.
> Pelly Street, Cwm Avon.

5 Upper Michaelstone Hamlet.
Area: 4,120 acres. *Popn.* 360 males, 293 females: total 653.

(27) PONTRHYDYFEN CHAPEL. CALVINSTIC METHODIST.
Erected 1826.
Space: free 738; other 338.
Present: morn. 160; aft. 190 scholars; even. 280.
Average: general congregation 350; scholars 222.

> John Williams. Manager.
> Pontrhydyfen Chapel House.

[End of Margam Subdistrict]

2 NEATH (Subdistrict)
Area: 20,183 acres. *Popn.* 5,000 males, 5,065 females: total 10,065.

1-2 Baglan Parish, consisting of the Hamlets of [1] Lower Baglan and [2] Higher Baglan.
Area of the whole parish: 6,479 acres. *Popn.* 263 males, 295 females: total 558.

1 Lower Baglan Hamlet.
Popn. 176 males, 208 females: total 384.

(1) BAGLAN PARISH CHURCH.
Endowed: tithe £140.
Space: free 129; other 4, each sitting holding four persons.
Present: morn. 120; aft. 40.
Remark: The English services having been attended to will easily account for the small attendance in the afternoon Welsh service.

> D. O. James. Curate.
> of Aberavon and Baglan.

Lewis: consolidated vicarage with that of Aberavon [584. 1. 3(11)], both of which are endowed with the great tithes; in the patronage of Rev. Edward Thomas.

C & C: 1 service alternately Welsh and English.

I & C: see Aberavon above.

2 Higher Baglan Hamlet.
Popn. 87 males, 87 females: total 174.
[No Returns].

3   Briton Ferry Parish.
Area: 1,593 acres.   *Popn.* 897 males, 840 females: total 1,737.

(2)   ST. MARY'S PARISH CHURCH, BRITON FERRY.
Endowed: land £124; permanent endowment £10.
Space: other about 140. All else Pews.
Present: morn. 60; even. 40.
Remark: The attendance was thinner than usual an Sunday the 30th March 1851. The Church is generally filled up.

Evan Thomas.   Minister.

Lewis: perpetual curacy, endowed with £400 private benefaction, and £600 royal bounty; net income £124: patron and impropriator, Earl of Jersey.
C & C: 2 services, both in Welsh.
I & C: incumbent resident.

(3)   WESLEYAN PREACHING ROOM.
Dwelling house appointed as a Preaching Room.   Separate building used exclusively as a place of worship.
Space: free 100.
Present: even. 60 + 40 scholars.

Wm. Williams.   Minister.
Neath.

(4)   BETHEL.   WELSH CALVINISTIC METHODIST.
Erected 1848.
Space: free 170; other 240; 'Free Space of standing room: 17 ft by 15 ft. down floor; 40 ft by 36 ft.; Gallery 40 ft by 20 ft.'
Present: morn. 185; aft. 164 scholars; even. 242.
Average (6 *months*): 'the above being a fair average'.

William Williams.   Deacon.
Agent.   Briton Ferry.

(5)   BETHESDA INDEPENDENT.
Erected 1848.
Space: free 166; other 196; standing 160.
Present: morn. 192; aft. 141 scholars; even; even. 250.

Griffith Lewis.   Elder.
Labourer.   Giants Grave.

[? sign. by mark]

(6)   REHOBOTH.   PARTICULAR BAPTIST.
Erected 1848.
Space: free 190; other 60; standing none.
Present: morn. 100; aft. 82 scholars; even. 170.
Average (12 *months*): general congregation 10; scholars 70.

Titus Jones.   Minister.

4   Neath Parish.
Area: 1,121 acres. *Popn.* 2,799 males, 2,979 females: total 5,778.
(7)   ST. THOMAS PARISH CHURCH.
Space: free 150; other 500.
Usual number of attendants: morn. 350; aft. 400.

Informant: Sankey Gardner.
Churchwarden.

[Informant's form]

Lewis: rectory with Lantwit [584. 2. 7(23)], annexed rated at £16. 2. 3½.; net income £353, with a glebe house; patron, H. J. Grant, Esq.

C & C: 2 services, both in English.

I & C: incumbent resident.

(8)   TABERNACLE, WATER STREET.   PARTICULAR BAPTIST.
Erected 1841.
Space: free 224; other 88.
Present: morn. 80; aft. 45; even. 130.
Average (12 *months*): general congregation 180; scholars 55.

Titus Jones.   Minister.

(9)   ENGLISH WESLEYAN METHOIST CHAPEL.
Erected 1814.
Space: free 70; other 500.
Present: morn. 170 + 45 scholars; aft. 100 scholars; even. 200.

Wm. Williams.   Minister.

(10)   ENGLISH INDEPENDENT OR CONGREGATIONALIST.
Erected 1849.
Space: free 50; other 250.
Presnt: morn. 52; even. 100.
Average (12 *months*): morn. 70; even. 150.

E. S. Hart, M.A.   Minister.

(11)   TABERNACLE, FOXHOLE.   BAPTIST.
Erected 1829.
Space: free 50.
Present: aft. 39; even. 45.

John Matthews.
Agent.
Foxhole, Nr. Swansea.

[This return is wrongly numbered and placed. The chapel is correctly returned as 584. 6. 1(8) below.]

(12) LATTERDAY SAINTS.
Name or title: 'Nonne'.
Whether separate or entire building: No.
Whether used exclusively as a place of worship: Yes.

> William Harris. Elder.

(13) ZOAR. INDEPENDENT.
Erected 1828-9.
Sp ce: free 476; other 383; standing 274.
Present: morn. 495; aft. 123 scholars; even. 711.
Remarks: N.B. Several Sunday Schools attached to Zoar Chapel in different localities where Members of the above place of worship resides. The acc. of which (regarding their names) you will find in the 'Reports on the state of Education' in Wales. Page 6 of the copy forwarded to each minister in 1848 trusting that a true acct. of each of the above schools will be returned from each locality.

> John Mathews, Minister.
> Eastgate Terrace, Neath.

(14) UNITARIAN CHAPEL, GREEN STREET.
Erected about 1817.
A room underneath let for a school room.
Space: free 15; other 120.
Present: morn. 80; even. 125.
Average: morn. 55; even. 100.
Remarks: This chapel had been closed for eight years previous to August 1850. Sunday Scholars not bound to attend the chapel; and those who come sit with their parents or friends.

> Rupert Lant Carpenter, B.A.

(15) SUMMERFIELD CHAPEL, GREEN STREET. INDEPENDENTS.
Erected about 1772.
Space: free 270; other 114.
Present: morn. 206; aft. 104 scholars; even. 288.

> Peter Davies. Secretary of the Sunday School.
> New Market Street.

(16) BETHANY. BAPTIST.
Erected: 1805.
Space: free 150; other 170.
Present: morn. 111 + 50 scholars; even. 210 + 40 scholars.
Average (12 months): morn. 150 + 60 scholars; even. 250 + 45 scholars.

> Rees Evans. Minister.

(17) BETHLEHEM GREEN. CALVINISTIC METHODIST.
Erected 1810.
Space: free 270; other 264; standing 100.
Present: morn. 203 + 138 scholars; even. 273.
Average (12 *months*)*:* general congregation 290; scholars 150.

> David Davies.
> Joiner.
> Chapel House, Neath.

(18) QUAKER.
Registered 7 m (July) 14th in the 41st year of George 3rd about 1801.
Admeasurement in superficial feet; floor 696 ft., galleries 264ft.
Space: 154 Persons capable of being seated.
Present: morn. 40; aft. 16.
Remarks: For 8 months meeting at 10 and 3 o'clock. For 4 mon. 10 and 6
o'clock. Average attendance for 12 months say 37 morning, say 18 afternoon
or evening.

The Gallery is partitioned off by shutters and used as a meeting for Discipline
when required.

> [?Thom^s] Rees.

[The remark about the gallery is written on the top right hand corner of the
return, with a neat drawing of the gallery, with dimensions, underneath.]

**[5-7] Lantwit-juxta-Neath Parish, consisting of the Hamlets of [5]
Resolven, [6] Clyne, and [7] Lower Lantwit.**
Area of the whole parish: 10,990 acres. *Popn.* 1,041 males, 951 females:
total 1,992.

5 Resolven Hamlet.
Area: 4,560 acres. *Popn.* 329 males, 301 females: total 630.

(19) RESOLVEN PARISH CHURCH.
Erected May 1850.
Space: free 200.
Usual Number of Attendants: morn. 40 + 20 scholars.

> *Informant:* Samuel Jenkins.
> Churchwarden.

[Informant's form]

Lewis: Chapel of ease to the parochial church.

(20) Ynysfach, Lantwit. Calvinistic Methodist.
Erected 1821.
Space: free 24; other 120.
Present: even. 70.

Thomas Davies.   Elder.
Shoemaker, Ynysfach.

(21) Baptist, Ynysfach.
Erected 1821.
Space: free 7; standing 'none'.
Present: morn. 42; aft. 39 scholars; even. 85.

Ebenezer Morgan.   Minister.
Glyn Neath.

(22) Melin Court Chapel. Congregationalists.
Erected before 1800.
Space: free 138; other 48; standing 50.
Average (6 months): general congregation 180; scholars 60.
Remarks: Some of the same persons attends morning, afternoon and even-
ing. But they are only one congregation.

John Thomas.   Minister.
Glyn Neath.

6 Clyne Hamlet.
Area: 2,164 acres. *Popn.* 63 males, 68 females: total 143.
[No returns]

7 Lower Lantwit Hamlet.
Area: 4,266 acres. *Popn.* 637 males, 582 females: total 1,219.

(23) Llantwit by Neath Parish Church.
Endowed: tithe rent charge £220; glebe £18; fees £3; Easter Offerings
£2.
Space: free 40; other 80.
Present: aft. 61.
Average (2 months): aft. 320.

Matthew Whittington.   Churchwarden.
Tonna, Neath.

Lewis: consolidated with the rectory of Neath [584. 2. 4(7)].

C & C: 1 service, alternately Welsh and English, performed by the incumbent.

I & C: resident.

[End of Neath Subdistrict]

3 YSTRADFELLTEY (Subdistrict)
Area: 39,039 acres. *Popn.* 1,482 males, 1,383 females: total 2,865.

[1-3] Cadoxton Parish: that part of the parish consisting of the Hamlets of [1] Neath, [2] Middle Neath, and [3] Upper Neath.
Area: 8,770 acres. *Popn.* 904 males, 811 females: total 1,715.

1 Lower Neath Hamlet
*Popn.*103 males, 116 females: total 216.

(1)   Aberpergwm Chapel of Ease.
Space: free 140; other 32 (private).
Present: morn. (Welsh) 30; aft. (English) 30.
Remarks: For the fifth question [i.e., endowments] see the return of the Revd. D. H. Griffith, Vicar of Cadoxton.

> Howel Price. Curate.
> Ynys-yr-allor, Glyn Neath.

Lewis: chapel of ease to the parochial church, in the grounds of Aberpergwm house.

C & C: 2 services, of which 1 in Welsh, taken by the curate, occasionally by the incumbent [of Cadoxton].

2 Middle Neath Hamlet.
Popn. 119 males, 117 females: total 236.
[No returns]

3 Upper Neath Hamlet.
Popn. 682 males, 581 females: total 1,263.

(2)   Addoldy Glyn Neath, Glynneath Chapel, Cadoxton uxta Neath, Llangatock. Independents.
Erected 1839.
Space: free 560.
Present: morn. 320; aft. 137 scholars; 360.
Average (12 *months*): morn. 390 incl. 137 scholars; even. 420.
Remarks: The Sunday Scholars are included in the average number of the Congregation. The greater part of those that attends in the morning are also present in the Evening. Prayer meetings are kept in the evening at certain remote places by members of the congregation.

> John Thomas. Minister.

(3) BETHEL, GLYN NEATH. BAPTIST.
Erected 1846.
Space: free 42; other 11; standing 100.
Present: morn. 72; aft. 76 scholars; even. 96.
Average: morn. 80 + 20 scholars; even. 120 + 30 scholars.

> Ebenezer Morgan. Minister.

(4) EBENEZER, PONTNEATH VAUGHAN. CALVINISTIC METHODIST.
Erected 1822.
Space: free 102; other 108; standing 100.
Present: morn. 105 scholars; aft. 220; even. 150.
Average: general congregation 190; scholars 110.

> Richard Evans. Manager.

[4-5] **Glyn-corrwg Parish, consisting of [4] the Hamlet of Glyn-corrwg, and [5] the Chapelry of Blaengwrach.**
Area of the whole parish: 11,294 acres. *Popn.* 217 males, 222 females: total 439.

4 Glyn-corrwg Hamlet.
Area: 8,262 acres. *Popn.* 41 males, 52 females: total 93.

(5) GLYNCARWG PARISH CHURCH.
Space: free 100; other 10.
Present: aft. 4 to 6.

> *Informant:* Philip Davies. Registrar.

[Informant's form]

Lewis: perpetual curacy with that of Blaen-Gwrach [584. 3. 5(8)] annexed: endowed with £600 royal bounty, and £200 parliamentary grant; net income £89; patron, Nash Vaughan Edwards, Esq.

C & C: 1 service in Welsh, taken by the curate.

I & C: incumbent not resident; curate, who has a stipend of £60, resides at Llantwit, ½ mile distant.

(6) CYMAR. INDEPENDENT.
Erected before 1800.
Space: free 13.
Present: morn. 23; aft. 253; even. 48.
Average: morn. 30; even. 55 + 20 scholars.

> David Henry. Independent Minister.
> Maesteg.

5   Blaengwrach Chapelry.
Area: 3,032 acres. *Popn.* 176 males, 170 females: total 346.

(7) Blaengwrach Chapel.   Presbyterian.
Erected before 1800.
Used also as a Day School.
Space: all free.
Present: morn. 12 to 15.
Average: morn. 13.

Evan Lewis.   Minister.
Blaengwrach, Glyn Neath,

(8) Blanegwrach Chapel.
Erected: about 200 years old.
Space: free 50; other 12.
Usual Number of Attendants: even. 10 to 30.

Informants: Philip Davies.
Registrar.

[Informant's form]
Lewis: perpetual curacy, annexed to that of Glyn-Corwg, endowed with £800
royal bounty.
C & C: 1 service in Welsh, taken by the curate.

**6   Ystradvelltey Parish, co. Brecon, diocese of St. Davids, consisting
of Upper and Lower parts.**
Area: 19,025 acres. *Popn.* 361 males, 350 females: total 711.

(9) Ystradfellte Parish Church.
Endowed: tithe £100; fees £5.
Space: other 200.
Present: morn. 40.

Charles Maybery.   Curate.
Penderyn Rectory, Merthyr Tydfil.

Lewis: living consolidated with that of Devynock [600. 2. 6(16)]; tithes commuted
for a rent-charge of £270, divided in three equal parts between the impropriators,
the Bishop of Gloucester and Bristol, and the vicar of Devynock.
C & C: 1 service in Welsh performed by the curate.
I & C: curate has stipend of £50.

(10) Penuel Chapel.   Calvinistic Methodist.
Erected 1808.
Space: free 48; other 108; standing 40.
Present: morn. 40; aft. 43 scholars; even. 55.
Average (12 *months*): morn. 40; aft. 45 scholars; even. 65.

David Powell.   Elder.
Goitre, Ystradfellte.

(11) HERMON, YSTRADFELLTY. INDEPENDENTS.
Erected before 1800.
Space: 24ft by 18ft.; free 12; other 22.
Present: morn. 60 + 15 scholars; even. 40.
Average (12 *months*): morn. 60 + 15 scholars; even. 40.

> Thos. Price. Deacon.
> Ystradfellty.

[End of Ystradfellte Subdistict]

4 YSTRADGUNLAIS (Subdistrict)
Area: 34,504 acres. *Popn.* 4,183 males, 3,804 females: total 7,987.

1 Ystradgunlais Parish, co. Brecon, diocese St. David's.
Area: 21,954 acres. *Popn.* 1,986 males, 1,772 females: total 3,758.

(1) YNIS CHAPEL, YSTRADGYNLAIS. CALVINISTIC METHODIST.
Erected 1850.
Space: free 50; standing 60.
Present: aft. 82 + 20 scholars.
Average: aft. 60 + 20 scholars.

> John Walters. Minister.

(2) SARDIS. INDEPENDENT.
Erected 1841.
Space: free 60; other 64.
Present: morn. 414; aft. 407 scholars; even. 447.

> Henry Rees. Minister.

(3) AINON. BAPTIST.
Erected 1848.
Space: free 16; other 28.
Pressnt: morn. 87; aft. 42 scholars; even. 96.

> Morgan Morgans. Deacon.
> Ystradfawr, Ystradgynlais.

(4) YORATH CHAPEL, CWMGIEDD. CALVINISTIC METHODIST.
Erected 1806.
Space: free 188; other 200; standing 110.
Present: morn. 300 + 125 scholars; even. 400 + 113 scholars.
Average (12 *months*): morn. 300 + 200 scholars; even. 450 + 100 scholars.

> John Walters. Minister.

(5)   Ystradgynlais Parish Church.
Endowed: land £72; fees £10-£15.
Space: 280.
Present: morn. (Welsh) 161; aft. (English) 61; even. (Welsh) 101.
Remarks: The Congregation on Sunday March 30 were rather smaller than usual. The Church is situated at the extreme corner of a Parish consisting of 1,200 acres and therefore beyond the reach of a considerable portion of the population.

> Walter Jones Williams.   Rector.

Lewis: rectory, rated at £9. 10. 7½, in the patronage of the proprietor of the Yniscedwin estate: tithes commuted for £372.

C & C: 3 services, of which 2 in Welsh, performed by incumbent and curate.

I & C: incumbent resident; curate's stipend £110.

(6)   Tynycoed, Ystradgynlais.   Independent.
Erected before 1800. Cost defrayed by private benefaction etc. £800.
Space: 416.
Present: morn. 124; even. 123.
Average: morn. 250 + 120 scholars; even. 300 'in the neighbourhood'.

> James Williams.
> Independent minister.

[Entered on a Church of England schedule.]

(7)   Nantyffin, Ystradgunlais.   Baptist.
Erected 1811.
Space: free 340.
Present: morn. 88; aft. 22 scholars; even. 120.
Average: morn. 120 + 25 scholars; even. 120.

> William Lumley Evans.   Minister.
> Nantyfin.

(8)   Coelbren District Chapel, Upper Ystradgynlais.
Endowed: land £72; fees £1.
Space: free 60.
Present: aft. 22.
Average: about the same.
Remarks: The chapel of Coelbren is situated in an outlandish part of the country, where the population are few and it is not accessible to everybody on all weathers.

> Evan Jenkins.   Curate.
> Glantawe, Ystradgynlais.

Lewis: formerly a chapel of ease to the parish church endowed as a perpetual curacy; net income £45: in the patronage of the rector: rebuilt in 1799 almost wholly at the expense of Walter Price, Esq., of Glynllech.

C & C: 1 service in Welsh, performed by the curate.

I & C: incumbent not resident; curate, who resides in the parish, has stipend of £50.

2 Llanguick Parish, co. Glamorgan, diocese St. David's.

Area: 12,550 acres. *Popn.* 2,197 males, 2,032 females: total 4,229.

(9) LLANGUICK PARISH CHURCH.

Endowed: land £32; tithe £10; permanent endowment £15; fees £3. 15s. Out of this Curate's salary is to be deducted £30.

Space: free 240; other 9.

Present: aft. 191 + 55 scholars.

Average: aft. 216 + 45 scholars.

> Wm. Thomas.   Perpetual Curate.
> Pontardawe.

Lewis: perpetual curacy, endowed with £600 royal grant and £1,200 parliamentary grant; in the patronage of Mrs. Leach, the impropriator; net income £103; tithes commuted for £300.

C & C: 1 service in Welsh performed by the curate.

I & C: incumbent not resident; curate's stipend not stated.

(10) GURNOS CHAPEL.   WESLEYAN METHODISTS.

Erected 1839.

Space: free 80; other 70; standing 60.

Present: morn. 30; even. 50.

Average (12 *months*): morn. 40; even. 60.

> John Bowen.   Society Steward.
> Yniscedwyn Works, Nr. Swansea.

(11) BULA CHAPEL, CWMTWRCH.   CALVINISTIC BAPTIST.

Erected 1833.

Space: free 250; other 168; standing 20.

Present: morn. 200 + 60 scholars; even. 240 + 80 scholars.

Average (12 *months*): general congregation 120; scholars 80.

> Lewis Rees.   Deacon.
> Cwmtwrch.

(12) PANT-TEG, LLANGUKE.   INDEPENDENTS.

Erected 1820.

Space: free 201; other 580; standing 250.

Present: morn. 500; aft. 407 scholars; even. 609.

Average (12 *months*): morn. 500; aft. 400 scholars; even. 700.

> Phillip Griffiths.   Minister.
> Alltwen.

(13) SOAR, YSTALYFERA. CALVINISTIC BAPTISTS.
Erected 1847.
Space: free 96; other 124; standing 50.
Present: morn. 90; even. 101.
Average (12 *months*): general congregation 160.
Remarks: Of the numbers said here to attend divine worship about 40 on the average from the Sunday Scholars.

> William Nicholas. Deacon.
> Ystalyfera.

(14) TRINITY CHURCH, GALLTYGRYG.
Space: free 140; other 60.
Present: morn. [MS torn]; even. 88 + 15 scholars.
Average: morn. 65 + 90 scholars; even. 80 + 20 scholars.
Under what circumstances licensed or consecrated: Means to endow cannot be obtained from the Ecclesiastical Commission.

> Thomas Rogers. Curate.
> Ystalyfera Iron Works.

Lewis: no entry: the church was erected in 1845 as a chapel of ease to Llan-giwg Parish Church.

C & C: 1 service partially in Welsh, performed by the curate.

I & C: see under Llanguick [584. 4.2(9)] above.

(15) SARON RHYDYFRO. INDEPENDENTS.
Erected 1843.
Space: free 130; standing 70.
Present: morn. 160; aft. 105 scholars; even. 102 scholars.
Remark: Generally from 140 to 180 attend on Sunday Morning; Evening from 80 to 120; a prayer Meeting on Monday neight. Society on Thursday night. Prayer Meeting on Saturday Night in the neighbourhood:- weekly sermons occasionally duly attended.

> William Hopkin. Deacon.
> Gotregarth.

(16) CWMLLYNFELL, CAEGURWEN DISTRICT, LLANGUKE.
INDEPENDENT DISENTERS [or congregationalists—crossed out]
Erected before 1800.
Space: free 65; standing 30.
Present: morn. 425 + 398 scholars; even. 300.
Average (6 *months*): general congregation 600; scholars 447.

> John Herbert. Deacon.
> [R. Pryce, Independent Minister—
> crossed out]

(17) CARMEL, HAMLET OF CAEGURWEN, LLANGUICK. INDEPENDENTS.
Erected 1771; rebuilt 1830.
Space: free 192; other 140.
Present: morn. 190 + 105 scholars; aft. 160; even. 230.
Remark: The seats are all free. There are down 28 seats which will afford an average of 6 in each to sit and five which will 12 in each. The gallery will contane about 140 to sit.

> David [?Jones]. Deacon.
> Farmer.
> Llwynhen, Llanguick.

[*End of Ystradgynlais Subdistrict*]

5 CADOXTON (Subdistrict)
Area: 27,304. *Popn.* 3,392 males, 3,189 females: total 6,581.

[1-6] Cadoxton Parish: that part of the parish consisting of the Hamlets of [1] Blaenhonddan, [2] Dyffryn-Clydach, [3] Coedfrank, [4] Ynis-y-mond, [5] Upper Dylais, and [6] Lower Dylais.
Area of this part of the parish: 23,290 acres. *Popn.* of the same part: 2,889 males, 2,710 females: total 5,599.
For the remainder of the parish see above 584. 3. 1-3.

1 Blaenhonddan Hamlet.
Popn. 654 males, 687 females: total 1,341.

(1) MOUNT ZION. BAPTIST.
Erected 1842.
Space: other 300.
Present: morn. 80; even. 144.
Average (6 *months*): morn. 150; even. 200.
Remarks: The want of a stated minister for the last few weeks accounts for the fact that our attendance today is so far below average.

> Danl. Griffiths. Secretary.
> East Terrace, Neath.

(2) CADOXTON-JUXTA-NEATH PARISH CHURCH.
Space: free 350; other 150.
Usual number of attendants: morn. 100 - 150 + 120 scholars; even. 200 - 300.*
Remark: *This is quite a different congregation from the morning, being entirely in Welsh and the morning all English.

> D. H. Griffith. Vicar.

[Informants' form]

Lewis: vicarage, rated at £5. 11. 10½, endowed with £200 royal bounty, and £800 parliamentary grant; net income £240; patron and impropriator, Capel Hanbury Leigh, Esq. 2 chapels of ease at Crynant [584. 5. 5(12)] and Aberpergwm [584. 3. 1(1)].

C & C: 2 services, of which 1 in Welsh, performed by the incumbent.

I & C: incumbent resident: 2 curates with stipends of £100 and £80 respectively.

(3) ABERDULAIS. BAPTIST.
Erected 1850.
Space: free 72; other 284.
Present: morn. 139; aft. 75 scholars; even. 150.

Joseph Davies.   Deacon.

2 Dyffryn-Clydach Hamlet.
Popn. 506 males, 491 females: total 997.

(4) SKEWEN PARISH CHURCH.
Church of a new Parish under the provisions of 6 & 7 Vict. c. 37.
Situated in the District Parish of Skewen in Cadoxton Juxta Neath.
Consecrated Nov 28th. 1850.
Erected by Parliamentary Grant and Private subscription. Cost defrayed by Parliamentary Grant—£275, other sources £793.
Endowed: permanent endowment £150.
Space: free 247; other 72.
Present: morn. 112; even. 65 + 35 scholars.

George Griffiths.   Minister.
Neath.

C & C: no entry.
I & C: incumbent resident.
ICBS: grant of £150 in 1848.

(5) EBENEZER, CADOXTON. WESLEYAN METHODIST.
Erected 1836.
Space: free 100; other 80; standing 100.
Present: morn. 36; even. 36.
Average (12 *months*): morn. 30; aft. 40 scholars; even. 70.

John Hussey.   Society Steward.
Neath Abbey Ironworks.

3 Coedfrank Hamlet.
Popn. 879 males, 849 females: total 1,728.

(6) Sion, Cadoxton.   Calvinistic Methodist.
Erected 1843.
Space: free 205; other 210; standing 70.
Present: morn. 153 + 182 scholars; aft. 246; even. 236.

> David Davies. Deacon.
> Skewen. Joiner.

(7) Salem Chapel, Cadoxton.   Independents.
Erected 1842.
Space: free 100; standing 150.
Present: aft. 77 scholars; even. 56.
Remark: Salem Chapel is a Branch of Summerfield chapel in the Borough Town of Neath.

> David Davies.   Elder.
> Neath Abbey.

(8) Bethleham, Cadoxton.   Independant Dissentters.
Erected 1839.
Space: free 170; other 144; standing 60.
Present: morn. 250; aft. 206 scholars; even. 374.

> Thomas Jenkins.   Deacon.
> Joiners Arms, Skewen.

4   Ynis-y-mond Hamlet.
Popn. 171 males, 173 females: total 344.

(9) Sion Chapel, Glaish.   Independents Calvinist.
Erected 1840.
Space: free 171 [standing gallery 150—deleted]
Present: morn. 100 + 64 scholars; even. 92.

> John Rees.   Minister.
> Canaan Chapel, Swansea.

5   Upper Dylais Hamlet.
Popn. 494 males, 330 females: total 824.

(10) Onllwyn Chapel, Onllwyn.   Independent.
Erected 1848.
Space: free 200.
Present: morn. 98 + 65 scholars; aft. 72 scholars; even. 150.
Average: morn. 120 + 70 scholars; even. 180 + 60 scholars.

> Evan Davies.   Minister.
> Onllwyn Iron Works.

(11)   GODRE RHOS, CADOXTON.   INDEPENDENT.
Erected before 1800.
Space: free 240.
Present: morn. 160; aft. 200 + 100 scholars; even. 100.

> Henry Rees.   Minister.
> Ystradgynlais.

(12)   CROYNANT CHAPEL OF EASE.
Space: free 75.
Usual number of attendants: morn. from 20 to 30 + 30 scholars.
Remark: Neither the Vicar nor the curate can answer the 2nd query. It appears to be as old as the parish Church. Signed: Wm. Morfa Jones. Registrar.

> *Informant:* E. Thomas.   Curate.

[Informant's form]

Lewis: chapel of ease, called Crynant chapel.

I & C: see under Cadoxton Parish Church [584. 5. 1(2))].

C & C: 1 service in Welsh performed by the curate.

6   Lower Dylais Hamlet.
Popn. 185 males, 180 females: total 365.
[No returns]

7   Killybebill Parish.
Area: 4,014 acres. *Popn.* 503 males, 479 females: total 982.

(13)   KILYPEBYLL PARISH CHURCH.
Endowed: land £4; tithe, after deducting all taxes £63; glebe at £1 per acre £4. 15*s*; permanent endowment £6. 15*s*; fees £1. 5*s*. Curate's salary to be deducted £30.
Space: free 75; other 15.
Present: morn. 73 + 30 scholars.
Average: norn. 97 + 27 scholars.
Remarks: Sunday Scholars at the Church schoolroom March 30th 1851: males 37; females 20, total 58; Sunday scholars at Church 30: total 88.

> Wm. Thomas.   Rector.

Lewis: discharged rectory rated at £4. 6. 8., augmented by £268. 4. 4. parliamentary grant; in the patronage of the crown: net income £120: tithes commuted for £115; glebe of nearly 12 acres, valued at £10 per annum.

C & C: 1 service, mixed English and Welsh, performed by the incumbent.

I & C: incumbent resident; curate's stipend £30.

ICBS: grant of £30 in 1837.

(14) ALLTWEN. INDEPENDANT CALVINISTICAL.
Erected before 1800.
Space: free 450; other 276.
Present: morn. 350 + 144 scholars; aft. 429; even. 300.
Average (12 *months*)*:* general congregation 545; scholars 150.

> Rd. Hopkins. Deacon.
> Alltwen Uchaf, Pontardawe.

[End of Cadoxton Subdistrict]

6 LLANSAMLET (Subdistrict)
Area: 8,835 acres. *Popn.* 2,189 males, 2,087 females: total 4,276.
1 Llansamlet Parish. Diocese of St. David's.
Area and *popn.* as for the Subdistrict.

(1) LLANSAMLET PARISH CHURCH.
Endowed: tithe £46. 13. 4*d*; fees £20; other sources £121.
Space: free 150; other 250.
Present: morn. 150 + 30 scholars; aft. 48.
Average: morn. 156 + 30 scholars; aft. 50.
Remarks: A new Church, called Kilvey Church, in the district of Foxhole
about 3 miles from the parish church was built through my exertions in
1843. It is only licensed for Divine Service. It will contain about 400. My
curate is supported by a Grant from the C.P.A. Society aided by private
Subscriptions. Built entirely by private subscriptions. Cost about £1,200.
Average Attendance 150.

> Morgan Rice Morgan.
> Perpetual Curate.

Lewis: perpetual curacy, endowed with £800 royal bounty, net income in 1835 £94;
augmented in 1841 by the Ecclesiastical Commissioners with £24 per annum out
of the fund raised by the suspension of certain canonries and prebends: patron and
appropriator, Bp. St. David's.
C & C: 2 services, partially in English and Welsh, performed by the incumbent.
I & C: incumbent not resident: 2 curates with stipends of £140 and £80
respectively.
ICBS: grant of £20 in 1840.

(2) KILVEY CHURCH CHAPEL OF EASE. DIOCESE OF ST DAVID'S.
Licensed in 1843 as an additional church.
Erected by private subscription at a cost of about £1,350.
Endowed: pew rents about £15. 10*s*.; other sources £160.
Space: free 202; other 144.
Present: morn. 113 + 113 scolars; aft. 95 + 98 scholars; even. 119.

> Thomas Walters. Minister.
> Kilvey Parsonage.

C &-C: 2 services in English.

(3) BETHEL, VILLAGE OF TAI YR YSGOL, LLANSAMLET. INDEPENDENT.
Erected 1818; re-erected 1850.
Space: free 125; other 494; standing 200.
Present: morn. 275; aft. 111; even. 324.
Remark: The return as to space available is given in a manner that the congregation may have easy access. The chapel held the day of opening from 900 to 1,000.

Robert James.   Secretary.
Schoolmaster.
Nr. Travellers' Rest, Llansamlet.

(4) EBENEZER, LLWYNBIWYDIA, LLANSAMLET. WELSH CALVINISTIC METHODIST.
Erected 1834.
Space: free 60; other 198; standing 60.
Present: morn. 100 + 80; aft. school; even. 115 + 71 scholars.
Average (3 *months*): morn. 120 + 80 scholars; even. 140 + 70 scholars.

Hezeciah Thomas.   Deacon.
Lon Lase, Llansamlet.

(5) SALEM.   CALVINISTIC METHODIST.
Erected 1782.
Space: free 100; other 640; standing 300.
Present: morn. 305 scholars; aft. 593; even. 643.
Average (2 *months*): morn. 284 scholars; aft. 608.

Evan Jenkins.   Deacon.

(6) ADULAM MEETING HOUSE.   BAPTIST.
Erected 1848.
Space: all free.
Present: morn. 76; even. 71.

David Thomas.   Baptist Minister.
Adulam Meeting House.

[Denomination is giving as 'Welsh Preaching'.]

(7) CANAAN.   INDEPENDENTS.
Erected 1839.
Space: other 342; standing 40.
Present: morn. 148; aft. 124 scholars; even. 389.
Remark: The reason for the difference in the attendance Morning and evening is that many of the copper men work from Saturday morning until Sunday Morning; consequently they cannot attend until the evening.

John Rees.   Minister.
Canaan Cottage, Foxhole.

(8)   TABERNACLE, FOXHOLE.   BAPTIST.
Erected 1829.
Space: free 33.
Usual number of attendants: morn. 24 scholars; aft. 35; even. 49.

Informant: Jenkin Jenkin.
Foxhole.

[Informant's form. The correctly completed return is 584. 2.4(11) above.]

[End of Llansamlet Subdistrict and End of Neath District]

585   SWANSEA (District)

Area: 103,769 acres. *Popn.* 22,763 males, 24,144 females: total 46,907.

1 LLANDILO-TALYBONT (Subdistrict)
Area: 34,706 acres. *Popn.* 2,503 males, 2,498 females: total 5,001.

1-3 Llangafelach Parish: that part of the parish consisting of [1] the Hamlet of Rhyndwy-Clydach, [2] the Hamlet of Mawr, and [3] the Hamlet of Penderry (including the village of Llangafelach).
Area of the whole Parish (including the Hamlet of Clase in the Subdistrict of Llangafelach): 27,305 acres. *Popn.* (excluding the Hamlet of Clase): 1,802 females, 1,791 males: total 3,593.
[For the remainder of this parish see 585 2. 1. below.]

1 Rhyndwy-Clydach Hamlet.
Popn. 789 males, 789 females: total 1,578.

(1) St. John's. A new District Parish Church, erected under 6 & 7 Vict. c. 37 (Sir R. Peels' Act).
Situated at Clydach in the Parish of Llangyfelach.
Consecrated June 24th 1847 as an additional church.
Erected by subscription.
Endowed: by the Ecclesiastical Commissioners £150.
Cost defrayed: by Church Building Society £200: Incorporated Society £150: Local Subscription £1,000: total £1,350.
Space: free 180; other 180.
Present: morn. 100 + 30 scholars; even. 150.
Average (12 *months*): morn. 200 + 40 scholars; even. 250.

Enoch Rees. Incumbent.

Lewis: no entry.
C & C: 2 services, morn. in English, even. in Welsh, performed by the incumbent.
I & C: incumbent resident.
ICBS: grant of £50 in 1845.

(2) Hebron. Clydach. Independent.
Erected 1810.
Space: free 162; other 444; standing 50.
Present: morn. 350; even. 404.
Average ([?] *years*): morn. 350; aft. 290 scholars; even. 410.

Thomas Thomas. Minister.
High Street, Swansea.

(3) BETHANIA. LLANGYFELACH OR CLYDACH. BAPTISTS.
Erected 1841.
Space: free 106; standing 150.
Present: morn. school; aft. 120; even. 100.

David Davies. Minister.
Treboeth.

(4) THE QUAR, CLYDACH. GENERAL BAPTISTS.
Erected 1816.
Space: free 84.
Present: morn. 60.
Average: morn. 100 to 120.

David Jones. General Baptist Minister.
Foxhole.

(5) GELLI-ONNEN. UNITARIAN.
Erected 1692; re-erected 1801.
Space: free 500; other 300.
Present: morn. 64.
Average (12 *months*): morn. 100 to 150.

John Jones. Presbyterian Minister.
Fardre, Nr. Swansea.

(6) ADULAM OF PONTARDAWE. PARTICULAR BAPTIST.
Erected 1844.
Space: free 96.
Present: morn. 30; even. 70.
Average: morn. 40; even. 56.

Charles Williams. Minister.
Thomas John. Deacon.

(7) TABERNACLE, PONTARDAWE. CALVINSTIC METHODIST.
Erected 1842.
Space: free 180.
Present: aft. 80 + 60 scholars.
Average: aft. 80 + 60 scholars.

John Walters. Minister.
Ystradgynlais.

(8) HOREB, PONTARDAWE. WESLEYAN METHODIST.
Erected 1845.
Space: free 17; other 93; standing 30.
Present: morn. 60 scholars; aft. 50; even. 68.
Average (12 *months*): morn. 60 scholars; aft. 80; even. 60.

Isaac Jones. Steward.

(9) BARAN. INDEPENDENT.
Erected 1805.
Space: other 23 will take 6 men in each; standing 190.
Present: morn. 110; aft. 40 scholars; even. 70.
Average (6 *months*): morn. 200; aft. 56.
Remarks: The Galary is all free made in three seats from one end to the other which will contain the no set in the column Free space [i.e. standing].

> John Howell. Deacon.
> Nantmole, Pontardawe.

(10) SALEM, LLANGAFELACH. INDEPENDENT BAPTIST.
Erected 1774.
Space: free 180.
Present: morn. 100; aft. 70 + 30 scholars.

> W. Morgan Rees. Diacon.
> Salem, Llangafelach.

[The sign. in a different hand.]

2 Mawr Hamlet.

Popn. 405 males, 405 females: total 810.

(11) FELINDRE CHAPEL, LLANGAFELACH. INDEPENDENT.
Erected 1821.
Space: free 60; other 90.
Usual number of attendants: morn. 90 + 25 scholars; aft. 25 scholars; even. 100.

> *Informant:* Richard Jenkins.
> Gellifeddau, Llangafelach.

[Informant's form. 585. 2. 1(3) is a duplicate of this.]

(12) GARNSWLLT, LLANGEFELACH. INDEPENDENT PAPTIST.
Erected 1842.
Space: free 546.
Present: even. 100.
Remar': No morning service.

> William Jenkins. Deacon.
> Caemain, near Pontardulais.

(13) GERAZIM, LLANGEFLEACH. INDEPENDENT BAPTIST.
Erected 1811.
Space: all free.
Present: morn. 60.
Remark: No evening service.

> William Jenkins. Diacon.
> Caemain.

3 Penderry Hamlet.

Popn. 597 males, 608 females: total 1,205.

(14) BETHLEHEM, PENDERY LOWER. INDEPENDENT.
Erected 1840.
Space: free 255; other 156.
Present: morn. 220; aft. school; even. 250.
Average (12 *months*): 300.

> William Humphreys. Minister.
> Cadley, Penllergare.

(15) GORSEINION CHURCH IN THE PARISH OF LLANGYFELACH.
Consecrated in 1839, but not endowed as an additional church.
Erected by J. Llewelyn, Esq., Penllergare.
At a cost of upwards of £2,000.
Space: free 190.
Present: morn. (English) 41 + 87 scholars; aft. (Welsh) 55.
Average: morn. (English) 52 + 110 scholars; aft. (Welsh) 90.
Remark: This church is not *regularly* consecrated—a deed of consecration
was sent over to Penllergare when a child of J. D. Llewelyn was to be buried.

> Thos. Lewis. Minister.

Lewis: no entry.
C & C: 2 services, English in the morning, Welsh in the afternoon, performed by
the curate.
I & C: no entry.

(16) MYNYDD-BACH CHAPEL. WELSH INDEPENDENTS.
Erected 1762.
Space: free 320 running; other 56; standing 50 superficial fee.
Present: morn. 239; aft. 105 scholars; even. 250.
Average (12 *months*): gen. cong. 250; scholars 120.
Remarks: The assemblage of this congregation have taken place about the
year 1700 or previous and upwards of 12 churches have been established as
branches of this place.

> William Rees. Deacon.
> Cadley.

(17) CAERSALEM NEWYDD, PENDDERY. BAPTIST.
Erected 1839.
Space: free 108; other 468.
Present: morn. 206; aft. 128 scholars; even. 265.
Average (7 *months*): morn. 250; aft. 140 scholars; even. 300.

> John Jones. Minister.

4 Landilo-Talybont Parish.

Area: 7,401 acres. *Popn.* 712 males, 696 females: total 1,408.

(18) LLANDILOTALYBONT CHURCH.
Endowed: tithe £140; land £30; fees £1. 5s.
Space: free none; other 260.
Present: morn. 60 to 70; aft. 40 to 50 incl. 25 scholars; even. 120 incl. 20 scholars.
Average: morn. 70 to 90; aft. 40 to 50 incl. 24 to 30 scholars; even. 70 to 100 incl. 30 scholars.
Remarks: Note, The old parish Church of Llandilotalybont is most awkwardly situated on the verge of the river Loughor, surrounded by vast Marches, which are often overflown by Tides and floods 3 or 4 feet deep over the paths leading thereto so as to render it impossible for the people to attend at such times.
Afternoon and evening services are performed by License in the National Schoolroom at the Village of Pontarddulais. The afternoon service is performed in *English*, and the Evening in *Welsh*, till the New Church now Building is Consecrated.

Thomas Clarke. Vicar.

Lewis: discharged vicarage, rated at £4. 14. 7.; net income £172, including glebe valued at £32 per annum: patron and impropriator John Edwards Vaughan, Esq.
C & C: 1 service in Welsh performed by the incumbent.
I & C: legally not resident.

(19) ST. JAMES' CHAPEL OR GOPPA-FACH. CALVINISTIC METHODISTS.
Erected 1775, rebuilt in 1843.
Space: free 162; other 258; standing 24 feet in Length 10 feet in Breadth.
Present: morn. 150; aft. 61 scholars; even. 200.
Average (4 months): morn. 100; aft. 50 scholars; even. 140.
Remark: NB. The congregation is smaller during four months in the winter winter when the day is short, as it is seen in the return.

John Jones. Secretary.
Cwm-y-llech.

(20) CARMEL CHAPEL, GWENLAIS. BAPTIST.
Erected 1835.
Space: free 300.
Present: No service at the Chapel.
Average (12 months): general congregation 100; scholars 42.
Remark: As the Chapel is now Rebuilding, the Congregation and School are interupted. The Chapel when finished will be much Enlarged and more Commodious.

John Lewis. Deacon.
Goldengrove.

(21) Trinity Chapel. Wesleyan Methodist.
Erected 1811.
Space: free 57; other 92; standing 60.
Present: morn. 50; aft. 48 scholars; even. 110.
Average (12 months): morn. 55; aft. 30 scholars; even. 37.

> Robert Williams. Minister.
> Pleasant Row, Swansea.

(22) Brynteg Chapel. Independents.
Erected final in 1815.
Space: free 200; other 220.
Present: morn. 400 + 80 scholars.
Average (12 months): morn. 450 + 90 scholars.

> Isaac Williams. Minister.
> Brynteg, Loughor, Nr. Llanelly.

[*End of Llandilo-Talybont Subdistrict*]

2 LLANGAFELACH (Subdistrict)
Area: 11,856 acres. *Popn.* 5,551 males, 5,704 females: total 11,255.

1   Clase Hamlet, in the parish of Llangafelach.
Popn. 3,616 males, 3,686 females: total 7,302.
[For the remainder of this parish see 585. 1. 1-3 above.]

(1) St. John's Chapel of Ease, Morriston.
Endowed: land £40; permanent endowment £40.
Space: All the sittings are free; total sittings 108.
Present: aft. 43 + 15 scholars; even. 74 + 17 scholars.
Average (12 months): 100 + 15 scholars; even. 130 + 20 scholars.

> David [H] Jones, Sunday School
> Teacher.
> Bath, Morriston.

Lewis: perpetual curacy; net income £85; patron and impropriator Sir John Morris.
C & C: 2 services, morn, in English, even. in Welsh, performed by the curate.
I & C: incumbent not resident; curate, resident in the parish, has stipend of £70.

(2) LLANGYFELACH PARISH CHURCH.
Endowed: tithe £210; fees £20.
Space: free 600; other 100.
Present: morn. 150 + 40 scholars.
Average: morn. 160 + 46 scholars.

Thomas Edwards.   Curate.

Lewis: vicarage, rated at £9. 14. 9½.; in the patronage of the Bishop who, as Dean of the College of Brecknock, is impropriator: tithes commuted for a rent-charge of £1,050, of which sum £845 are payable to the Bishop, and £205 to the vicar.

C & C: no return.
I & C: incumbent resident.
ICBS: grant of £40 in 1812.

(3) FELINDRE, LLANGYFELACH. INDEPENDENT.
Erected 1821.
Space: all free.
Present: morn. 200; even. 210.

John Davies.   Minister.
Cwmamman.

[This return duplicates 585. 1. 2(11) above.]

(4) SILOH, LANDORE. INDEPENDENTS.
Erected 1829.
Space: free 150; other 454.
Present: morn. 268; aft. 362 scholars; even. 469.
Average (12 *months*): morn. 310; aft. 360 scholars; even. 521.

Thomas Thomas.   Minister.
103, High Street, Swansea.

(5) ZOAR, ZOAR STREET, MORRISTON. BAPTISTS.
Erected 1850.
Space: free 200.
Present: morn. 54; aft. 60 scholars; even. 82.
Average (12 *months*): morn. 50; aft. 67 scholars; even. 70.

Philip Morgan.   Minister.

(6) LIBANUS, MORRISTON. INDEPENDENT.
Erected before 1800.
Space: free 150; other 452.
Present: morn. 471; aft. 341 scholars; even. 621.
Remarks: The Chapel being too small for the Congregation it is intended to enlarge it.

Thomas Jones.   Minister.

(7) WELSH WESLEYAN METHODIST, MORRISTON.
Not a seperate and entire building: not used exclusively as a place of
worship.
Space: free 50.
Present: morn. 15; even. 15.
Average (4 *months*): morn. 19.

> William Istance. Society Steward.
> Tallow Chandler.
> Morriston.

(8) MORRISTON MARKET ROOM. WESLEYAN METHODIST.
Erected 'since 1800'.
Space: free 88.
Present: aft. 30 scholars; even. 40.

> Joseph Faull. Steward.
> Tyr Cenol, Morriston.

(9) PHILADELPHIA CHAPEL, MORRISTON. CALVINISTIC METHODIST.
Erected 1802.
Space: free 102; other 576; standing 262.
Present: morn. 359; aft. 406 scholars;* even. 610.
Remark: *Including Branch School and Teachers.

> Edwd. Daniel. Junr. Secretary.

(10) DINAS NODDFA. PARTICULAR BAPTIST.
Erected 1823.
Space: free 150.
Present: morn. 85 scholars; aft. 150; even. 140.

> Benjn. Watkins. Minister.
> Morriston.

(11) HOREB CHAPEL, BATH, MORRISTON. INDEPENDENTS.
Erected 1843. 'And a Gallery put in it in 1845'.
Space: free 64; other 280; standing 120.
Present: morn. 150; aft. 138 scholars; even. 234.
Average: morn. 160; aft. 190 scholars; even. 300.
Remark: There being on the Church Register above 270 members in actual
communion.

> Thomas Davies. Minister.

(12) ZION. PARTICULAR BAPTIST.
Erected 1847.
Space: free 260; other 240; standing 150.
Present: morn. 80 + 25 scholars; even. 120 + 30 scholars.
Average (6 *months*): Morn. 120 + 25 scholars; even. 140 + 35 scholars.

Remark: Many of the Scholars being Members are mixed up with the General Congregation, which accounts for scholars being so few out of the number attending the School in the afternoon.

> Benjn. Watkins.   Minister.
> Morriston.

(13)   BETHEL, CLASE.   CALVINISTIC METHODIST.
Erected 1809.
Space: all free excepting 5 seats or pews; standing 60.
Present: morn. 42 scholars; aft. 130.
Average: morn. 42 scholars; aft. 130.

> Thos. Thomas.

2   Llanrhidian Higher Division: part of Llanrhidian parish.
Area: 9,106 acres. *Popn.* 682 males, 761 females: total 1,443.
[For the remainder of this parish see 5854 17 below.)

(14)   LLAN-NEWYDD.   A Chapel of Ease, time immemorial.
Consecrated Decbr. 1850, by the Bishop of St. David's.
Erected by the humble exertions of the Ch. Warden of Llanrhidian Higher.
Cost defrayed: private benefaction or subscription £300; total cost £700.
And regrets to observe that he has been left missing £400, and that the Incorporated building Society for promoting and building Churches refused its aid on the plea of not being applied before the Church had been erected. Although substantially built with the best materials—such a rule has highly invonvenienced this Churchwarden.
Space: free 125; other 125.
Present: morn. 200; aft. 125.
Average: morn. 230; aft. alternate service 200.
Remarks: Whereas it appears evident by this document that the Government is desirous to get information, I beg to observe that it would be well for the spiritual well-being of this Kingdom were the Government to divide long and large Parishes. This Parish being about 11 miles long, How is it possible for a Clergyman to attend the spiritual requirements of such a Parish?

> P. Evans.   Churchwarden.

C & C: sub Llanrhidian: 1 service, partially in English and Welsh, performed by the curate.

(15)   THREE CROSSES CHAPEL.   INDEPENDENT.
Erected 1788; re-erected and enlarged 1831.
Space: free 240; other 260.
Present: morn. 500 + 40 scholars; aft. school.
Average (12 *months*): general congregation 500 to 600; scholars 60.

> John Evans.   Minister.
> 3 Crosses.

(16) BETHEL, PENCLAWDD. INDEPENDANTS.
Erected: not known.
Space: free 108; other 240.
Present: 260 + 120 scolars; even. 300.

> John Evans. Minister.
> Three Crosses.

(17) TABERNACLE, PENCLAWDD. WELSH CALVINISTIC METHODIST.
Erected 1836.
Space: free 140; other 100.
Present: morn. 50 + 30 scholars; even. 150 + 50 scholars.

> William Williams. Minister.
> Penclawdd.

(18) MOUNT HERMON, PENCLAWDD. BAPTIST.
Erected 1807.
Space: free 60; standing 50.
Present: morn. 20; aft. 25 scholars; even. 22.
Average (12 *months*): general congregation 30 to 40; scholars 20 to 30.

> John Williams. Minister.
> Penclawdd.

(19) PENUEL. WELSH CALVINISTIC METHODIST.
Erected 1844.
Space: free 100.
Present: aft. 60 + 30 scholars.

> William Williams. Minister.
> Penclawdd.

3 St John near Swansea Parish.
Area: 431 acres. *Popn.* 600 males, 615 females: total 1,215.

(20) SILOAM, PENTRE ESTYLL CHAPEL. INDEPENDANTS.
Erected 1839.
Space: free 'Eight Yeards Square'; other 58.
Present: morn. 350 + 202 scholars; even. 400.
Average (6 *months*): morn. 350 + 200 scholars; even. 400.

> Thomas Davies. Minister.
> Pentre Estyll.

[For the Parish Church, see 585. 3. 1(6) below.]

4   Swansea Higher Division;   part of the Parish of Swansea.

Area: 2,319 acres. *Popn.* 653 males, 642 females: total 1,295.

(21)   BABELL, CAE BABELL.   CALVINISTIC METHODIST.
Erected 1838.
Space: free 8.
Present: aft 91 scholars; even. 117.

> Thomas Thomas.   Elder.
> Cwmdu.

[End of Llangafelach Subdistrict]

3 SWANSEA (Subdistrict)

Area: 6,710 acres. *Popn.* 11,244 males, 12,363 females: total 23,607.

1   Swansea Town and Franchise: part of the Parish of Swansea.

Area: including SWANSEA LOWER [2] and ST. THOMAS [3]: 6,710 acres.
Popn. (including 53 Military in Barracks) 10,260 males; 11,326 females:
total 21,586.

(1)   ST. MARY'S.   THE PARISH CHURCH, SWANSEA.
Endowed: land £42; tithe £90; fees £90. Two curates kept salary £120
& £100 p.an. respectively.
Space: free 418, 212 being for children; other 953.
Present: morn. 743 + 101 scholars; even. 596.
Average (12 *months*)*:* morn. 950 + 100 scholars; even. 800.
Remarks: Of these 953 'other sittings' in this Church the whole of the North
Aisle which contains 120 sittings is *claimed by one individual*. The North
Gallery containing 150 sittings is private property. The Chancel containing
150 sittings is the property of the Lay Rector. So that out of 953 sittings
424 are not under the control of the Church-wardens and those parts of the
Church are comparatively empty while many of the Parishioners are
applicants for sittings in vain.

> Edward B. Squire.   Vicar.

Lewis: discharged vicarage, rated at £7. 14. 4½.; endowed with £200 private
benefaction, £200 royal bounty, and £800 parliamentary grant: net income £291:
patron and impropriator, Sir John Morris, Bart. Tithes commuted for rent-charge
of £424, of which two thirds belong to the impropriator, and one third to the vicar.

C & C: 2 services in English.

I & C: incumbent resident: 2 curates have stipends of £100 and £90 respectively.

(2) TRINITY CHURCH, SWANSEA.
Built under the 40 years Act, with no District assigned, but wholly independent of any other Church being held from the Patrons of Vicarages of Swansea.
Consecrated October 26th 1843, as an additional Church.
Erected by subscription, at a cost of £4000 including purchase of ground.
Endowed: Sources of Income from Pew Rents and Easter Offerings alone, from which after paying all necessary expences there remains about £50 per annum.
Space: free 450; other 700.
Present: morn. 255 + 91 scholars; even. 290.
Average: morn. 300 + 100 scholars; even. 400.
Remarks: I have given ye Average Attendance so far as I cd. judge, but it is so very irregular from the character of the place that I can little more than make a rough estimate. The income also is very fluctuating, and nothing could be strictly determined or returned.

> George Ackloms.   Incumbent.
> Trinity Vicarage.

C & C: 2 services in English.
I & C: incumbent resident.

(3) WAENWEN SCHOOLROOM, WAENWEN.   INDEPENDANTS.
Erected 1843.
Space: free 150.
Usual number of attendants: aft. 90 scholars; even. 100.

> *Informant:* Abraham Bevan.
> Collier, Waenwen.

[Informant's form]

(4) TRADES HALL, HIGH STREET, SWANSEA.   LATTER DAY SAINTS.
Erected 1840.
Space: all free.
Usual number of attendants: morn. 50; aft. 70; even. 200.

> *Informant:* David Davies.
> Clarks Court.

[Informant's form]

(5) LADY HUNTINGDONS CHAPEL, ADELAIDE PLACE.
Countess of Huntingdon's Connexion.
Erected 1791.
Space: free 50; other 600.
Usual number of attendants: morn. 300 + 150 scholars; even. 560 + 40 scholars.

> *Informant:* Thomas Dodd.   Minister.
> 11 Nelson Terrace, Swansea.

[Informant's form]

(6)   St. John's-juxta-Swansea Parish Church.
Endowed: land £67; Parly. Grants £20 7*s.* 4*d.*; fees £15; other sources, patrons £5.
Space: free 700; other 800.
Present: aft. 450 + 30 scholars; even. 150 + 20 scholars.
Average: aft. 500 + 50 scholars; even. 150 + 40 scholars.

> Morgan Rice Morgan.
> Perpetual Curate.
> Pengwern.

Lewis: perpetual curacy, endowed with £600 royal bounty, and £1,400 parliamentary grant; net income £87: patron and impropriator Sir John Morris. Church taken down and rebuilt in 1824, the cost being defrayed by a grant of £575 from the Incorporated Society, and by private subscription.
"The parochial church of *St. John juxta Swansea* is also situated within the town, and, from the service being performed in it in the Welsh, as well as the English, language, is of considerable benefit to the inhabitants of this part of the town, who are mostly of the poorer class, and speak only Welsh, and also in a great degree compensates for the deficiency of sittings in the church of St. Mary."

C & C: 2 services, both in Welsh performed by the incumbent and curate.

I & C: incumbent not resident: curate has stipend of £80 for this and Llansamlet.

ICBS: grant of £575 in 1824.

(7)   Bethany Chapel (English), Edward Street.   Calvinistic Methodist.
Erected 1847.
Space: free 200; other 450; standing 200.
Present: morn. 200 + 80 scholars; even. 250 + 50 scholars.
Average: morn. 250 + 80 scholars; even. 350 + 50 scholars.

> William Rosser.   Deacon.
> Pier Street, Burrows, Swansea.

(8)   St. David's Church.   Roman Catholic.
Erected 1847.
Space: free 200; other 12; standing 200;
Present: morn. 300; even. 200.
Average (12 *months*): general congregation 350; scholars 200.

> Charles Kavanaugh. Roman Catholic Priest.
> Rutland Street, Swansea.

(9)   Trinity Chapel, Park Street.   Welsh Calvinistic Methodist.
Erected 1829.
Space: free 300; other 700.
Present: morn. 478; even. 507.

> William John.   Deacon.
> Heathfield Street, Swansea.

(10) THE SYNAGOGUE, WATERLOO STREET. JEWS.
Erected before 1800.
Space: free 30; other 42.
Present: morn. Saturday 36; aft. Saturday 15; even. Friday 29.
Average (6 *months*): morn. Saturday 44; aft. Saturday 16; even. Friday 32.

Isaac Jacob. President.
Castle Street.

(11) WESLEYAN CHAPEL, NEWTON. WESLEYAN METHODISTS.
Erected 1825.
Space: free 60.
Average: even. 50.

W. Bytheway. Minister.
Union Street.

(12) BAPTIST CHAPEL, HEATHFIELD STREET. PARTICULAR BAPTIST.
Erected 1826.
Space: free 300; other 500; standing 200.
Present: morn. 284 + 20 scholars; even. 497 + 124 scholars.
Average (12 *months*): morn. 345 + 45 scholars; even. 556 + 124 scholars.

John Roberts. Secretary.
23 Princes Street.

(13) CAPEL SION, HIGH STREET. WELSH CALVINISTIC INDEPENDANTS.
Erected 1849.
Space: free 500; other 350; standing 500.
Present: morn. 214; aft. 108 scholars; even. 550.
Average: morn. 250; aft. 90 + 120 scholars; even. 600.
Remarks: This Place of Worship was commenced in Victoria rooms, Oxford Street, Swansea 1841 and was removed to a Chapel wich was Built in High Street 1843 and sold to the South Wales Railway Company 1849 where their station is and the present Chapel was Built in the same year and called Capel Sion.

David Davies. Deacon.
Castle Street.

(14) TOWER LANE CHAPEL, HIGH STREET. PRIMITIVE METHODIST.
Erected 1838.
Space: free 140; other 160.
Present: morn. 100 + 50 scholars; even. 260.
Average (12 *months*): morn. 100 + 50 scholars; even. 260.

John Rees Brenton. Steward.
26 Goat Street.

(15) EBENEZER CHAPEL, EBENEZER STREET. INDEPENDENTS.
Erected 1826.
Space: free 300; other 620.
Present: morn. 362; aft. 247 scholars; even. 481.
Average: morn. 400; aft. 280; even. 550.
Remarks: As for Sunday scholars in No. 8 most of those who attend the Sunday school attend the other services with the exception of those who are too young. We generally overate our congregation. Most people would suppose we had 800 people last evening by viewing the assembly, but when numbered they were found short of 500.

> Elijah Jacob. Minister.

(16) TABERNACLE. WESLEYAN METHODIST.
Erected 1812.
Space: free 82; other 214; standing 50.
Present: morn. 70; aft. 91 scholars; even. 170.
Average (12 *months*): morn. 60; aft. 87 scholars; even. 200.

> Robert Williams. Minister.
> Pleasant View.

(17) BETHESDA, BETHESDA STREET. BAPTISTS.
Erected 1830.
Space: free 300; other 450.
Present: 300 + 50 scholars; aft. 224 scholars [deleted]; even. 550 + 100 scholars.
Average (12 *months*): morn. 350 + 50 scholars; aft. 100 scholars [deleted]; even. 600 + 50 scholars.

> Daniel Davies. Minister.
> No 2 Nelson Place.

(18) GREENHILL CHAPEL. WELSH CALVINISTIC METHODIST.
Erected 1799.
Space: free 400.
Present: aft. 140.
Average: aft. 140 about.
Remark: The School is held here in the morning. No service kept in the Evening, they attend another place or places of worship.

> William Johns. Deacon.
> Heathfield.

(19) SOAR, HIGH STREET. CALVINISTIC INDEPENDENTS.
Erected 1849.
Space: free 106; other 187.
Present: morn. 135; aft. school; even. 360.

Average (6 *months*): general congregation 350; scholars 150.
Remark: A new interest commenced in March 1848 with only 6 Church
Members.

Rees Rees.   Minister.

(20)   BETHLEHEM, GROFT.   PARTICULAR BAPTIST.
Erected about 1850.
Space: free 50; standing 80.
Present: morn. 30.
Average: morn. 30.

Richard Thomas.   Deacon.
Chapel Street, Greenhill.

(21)   SILOAM.   BAPTIST.
Erected 1830.
Space: free 120; other 96; standing 'on the Gallery 90 feet of benches
with waggon room on the floor'.
Pressent: morn. 60 + 20 scholars; even. 100.
Average: morn. 100 + 25 scholars.
Remark: The congregation being less last Sunday than usual.

John Pugh.   Pastor of the Church.

(22)   BETHEL NEWEDD, SKETTY.   INDEPENDENTS.
Erected 1770, or before 1800.
Space: free 100; other 300 (75 pews).
Present: morn. 240; aft. 130 scholars; even. 260.
Average (12 *months*): morn. 280; aft. 150 scholars; even. 300.
Remark: Sunday scholars at Bethel Newedd Chapel—80.
At Rhydydefaid school being a branch school—20.
At Crocket being a branch school—20
being amt returned 130.

Samuel Rosser.   Deacon
Sketty.

(23)   UNITARIAN, HIGH STREET.
Erected before 1800.
Space: 400.
Present: morn. 157; aft. 50 scholars; even. 121.
Average (6 *months*): morn. 180; even. 120.
Remarks: The Church was rebuilt and enlarged 1848. No particular sittings
are *free* or otherwise;—poor persons who cannot afford to contribute to the
maintenance of the Church have sittings provided for them wherever there
is un-preoccupied sitting-space. The Sunday school is held in a separate
building and the scholars are not required to attend at the church. Some of
them do.

Geo. Browne Brock.   Minister.

(24) CASTLE STREET MEETING HOUSE OR CHAPEL. INDEPENDENT OR
CONGREGATIONAL.
Erected about 1815.
Space: free 300; other 500.
Present: morn. 216 + 69 scholars; even. 373 + 53 scholars.
Average (12 *months*): morn. 400; even. 500.

> William Jones. Minister.
> 11 Gower Street.

(25) WESLEY CHAPEL, GOAT STREET. WESLEYAN METHODIST.
Erected before 1800.
Space: free 300; other 700.
Present: morn. 402; even. 494.
Average (12 *months*): morn. 450; even. 550.

> Thomas Evans. Steward.
> 10 High Street.

(26) YORK PLACE, YORK STREET. BAPTIST.
Erected 1828.
Space: free 200; other 368.
Present: morn. 352; even. 465.

> David Evans. Minister.
> 5 Northampton Place.

(27) WESLEYAN CHAPEL, SKITTY. WESLEYAN METHODISTS.
Erected 1842.
Space: free 60; standing 12.
Present: even. 55.
Average: even. 56.

> W. Bytheway. Minister.
> Union Street.

(28) SAILORS CHAPEL ON THE QUAY. BRITISH AND FOR[EIGN] SAILORS SOCIETY·
Erected before 1800. Used also as a sailors' Reading Room.
Space: free 150.
Present: aft. 130.
Remarks: This Chapel is rented by the Committee of the Swansea aux.
Sailors Society and is gratuitously supplied by 8 dissenting ministers of the
town.

> Ths. Dodd. Secty. to the Society and
> occasional minister.
> Nelson Terrace

(29) MISSING.
[According to the preliminary list this place of worship belonged to the
Church of England.]

(30)   MEETING HOUSE OF THE SOCIETY OF FRIENDS, HIGH STREET.
Erected before 1800.
Admeasurement in superficial feet: floor 1,120; galleries 532.
Space available: floor 168; galleries 27.
Present: morn. 22, aft. 13.

> Henry Knight.
> Llwyn Derw.

[End of Swansea Subdistrict]

4 GOWER (Subdistrict)
Area: 50,497 acres. *Popn.* 3,465 males, 3,579 females: total 7,044.

1 Oystermouth Parish.
Acres: 5,194 acres. *Popn.* 834 males, 1,004 females: total 1,938.

(1)   OYSTERMOUTH PARISH CHURCH, dedicated to All Saints.
Situated about the Center of the Parish.
Supposed to have been Consecrated Centuries ago, but Age unknown.
Under what circumstances consecrated or licensed: The Minister cannot
tell save & except its being consecrated to the Worship of Almighty God &
dedicated to his Service.
Endowed: [Added on a sheet bound in with the return]:

Land produces	£32.	7.	0.
Rent from Lay Rector	16.	0.	0.
3 Per Cents	33.	18.	10.
Total	£87.	5.	10.

Space: free 200; other 400.
Present: morn. 158 + 50 scholars; aft. 'no service till after Easter'.
Average (12 *months*): morn. general. congregation 300; scholars 100; aft.
'no service from Ms. to Easter'.
Remarks: The congregation fluctuates from 200 to a full Church. The
service from Easter to November are Morn. 11;—aft. 3., from November
to Easter 11 in the morning.

> Samuel Davies.   Perpetual Curate.
> The George, Oystermouth.

Lewis: perpetual curacy, endowed with £200 royal bounty and £1,000 parliamentary grant; net income £85; patron and impropriator, Colonel Perrott.

C & C: 2 services in summer, 1 in winter, in English.
I & C: incumbent resident.
ICBS: grant of £60 in 1833.

(2)   BETHANY, NORTON.   BAPTIST.
Erected 1850.
Space: free 160; other 20.
Present: aft. 80 scholars; even. 200.
Average: aft. 80 scholars; even. 100.

John Evans.   Deacon.
Newton.

(3)   WESLEYAN CHAPEL.   WESLEYAN METHODIST.
Erected 1817.
Space: free 108.
Present: aft. 10 scholars; even. 50.

[unsigned]

(4)   PARACLITE CHAPEL.   INDEPENDENTS.
Erected 1818.
Space: all free.
Present: morn. 130; aft. 70 scholars; even. 200.

John Marks Evans.
Independent Minister.
Newton.

(5)   MOUNT SION, DUNS, OYSTERMOUTH.   INDEPENDENT.
Erected 1850.
Space: all free.
Present: morn. 100 + 20 scholars; even. 280.

William Clement.
Independent Methodist Minister.
Mumbles.

(6)   TABERNACLE.   INDEPENDENT,
Erected 1831.
Space: all free.
Present: aft. 72.

John Marks Evans.   Minister.
Mumbles.

(7)   PRIMITIVE METHODIST CHAPEL.
Erected 1846.
Space: free 150.
Present: morn. 20; even. 100.
Average (12 *months*): morn. 20; even. 100.

John Rees Brentin.   Steward.
26 Goat Street, Swansea.

2   Bishopston Parish.
Area: 2,387 acres. *Popn.* 272 males, 241 females: total 513.

(8) BISHOPSTON PARISH CHURCH.
Situated in the centre of the parish.
Endowed: tithe £236; glebe £40.
Space: free 30; other 370.
Present: morn. 250 + 47 scholars.
Average (12 *months*): morn. 250 + 47 scholars; aft. 330 + 47 scholars.

David Jones.   Rector.

Lewis: rectory, rated at £9. 6. 8.; net income £242, with a glebe house: patron,
Bishop of Llandaf.
C & C: 1 service in English.
I & C: incumbent resident.
ICBS: grant of £25 in 1831, and of £70 in 1852.

(9) PROVIDENCE. INDEPENDENT.
Erected 1804.
Space: free 142.
Space: free 142.
Present: morn. 30; aft. 40.

John Williams.   Minister.

(10) MURTON WESLEYAN CHAPEL. WESLEYAN METHODIST.
Erected 20 years.
Space: free 60.
Present: even. 68.

Francis Morgan.   Local Preacher.

3 Pennard Parish.
Area: 2,292 acres. *Popn.* 183 males, 165 females: total 348.

(11) PENNARD PARISH CHURCH.
Space: free 30; other 100.
Usual number of attendants: morn. 90; aft. 130.

Informant: David Jones.   Minister.

[Informant's form]

Lewis: discharged vicarage, rated at £3. 16. 8.; endowed with £600 royal bounty;
net income £79; patrons and impropriators, Warden and Fellows of All Souls'
College, Oxford.
C & C: 1 service in English.
I & C: incumbent not resident: curate, who resides in Bishopston, 1½ miles away,
has stipend of £60.

(12) [PENNAR]D PARISH CHURCH.
Space: free 20; other 300.
Present: morn. [MS torn]; aft. 300.
Average: morn. 200; aft. 300.

David Jones.   Vicar.

[This return is for the same church]

4　Ilston Parish.

Area: 2,879 acres. *Popn.* 174 males, 182 females: total 356.

(13)　ILSTON PAROCHIAL CHURCH.　An antient Rectory, in the Patronage of the Crown. Dedicated to St. Iltidus, or Iltid. Hence the name Ilston, or Iltid's Town. In Welsh Llaniltid.

Space: The sittings are all now free or open sittings: it having been newly pewed about four years ago: with open seats instead of square double pews, which were allocated by one or two Farm Houses. Now they are all free to the Parishioners in general, tho they nicely keep to old stations. Total sittings 120.

Present: morn. 50 + 15 scholars; aft. 'no service alternate service'.

Average (12 *months*): morn. 45 + 17 scholars; aft. 70 + 15 scholars.

Remarks: The Service is alternately morning and afternoon. The hour in the morning being half past 10, in the afternoon half past two. The Congregation is much better in the afternoon than in the morning: nearly double. On the March the 23 being afternoon service, there were 80 persons present.

> John Collins.　Rector.
> Ilston Rectory.

Lewis: rectory, rated at £9. 6. 8., in the patronage of the Crown: net income £200 with a glebe house.

C & C: 1 service in English.

I & C: rector not resident: curate resides in glebe-house, and has stipend of £50.

(14)　MOUNT PISGAH, PARK MILL.　INDEPENDENT.

Erected 1822.

Space: free 200.

Present: morn. 36.

Average: morn. 30; aft. 60 scholars; even. 150.

Remark: Public Worship only once on every Sabbath, morning and evening alternately.

> William Johnson Ford.　Minister.
> Immanuel Chapel House, Paviland,
> Gower.

5　Penmaen Parish.

Area: 1,538 acres. *Popn.* 61 males, 53 females: total 114.

(15)　PENMAEN PARISH CHURCH.

Endowed: land £35; tithe £101; glebe 50 acres; fees 'trifling'.

Space: free 20; other 83.

Present: morn. 32 + 22 scholars.

Average: morn. 40 + 30 scholars; aft. 55 + 30 scholars.

Remarks: I would remark that there is a hamlet of this parish called Paviland situate about 7 miles distant, the inhabitants there never attend divine service in this church in consequence of the distance. They average from 30 to 40 people.

Edward K. James. Rector.

Lewis: discharged rectory, rated at £4. 10., endowed with £200 private benefaction, and £200 royal bounty: in the patronage of the Crown: net income £210, with a glebe house.

C & C: 1 service in English.

I & C: no return.

(16) IMMANUEL CHAPEL, HAMLET OF PAVILAND. INDEPENDENT.
Erected 1821.
Space: free 180; other 20.
Present: aft. 48 scholars; even. 150.
Average (12 *months*): morn. 60; aft. 50 scholars; even. 150.
Remarks: Divine service held every alternate Sabbath in the morning and on the opposite Sabbath in the Evening. School kept every Sabbath afternoon.

William Johnson Ford. Minister.
Immanuel Chapel House, Paviland,
Gower.

6 Nicholaston Parish.
Area: 731 acres. *Popn.* 56 males, 76 females: total 132.

(17) NICHOLASTON PARISH CHURCH.
An antient Church and a Rectory, consecrated with the adjoining Rectory of Oxwich, in the patronage of C. R. M. Talbot, Esq., Lord Lieutenant if the County of Glamorgan. Church dedicated to St. Nicholas. Hence its name is derived. Nicholas's Town or Nicholaston.
Space: The sittings are now considered free & open it being filled with open seats four or six years ago; tho many still keep to their old sittings. The old Pews were simple ones & mostly attached to Farm Houses. It is a very small Parish. Total Sittings 60.
Present: aft. service.
Average: morn. 30; aft. 50 alternate service.
Remarks: The Services of the Churches in the Deanery of Gower are alternately in the morning at half past 10 and the afternoon at half past two. There is generally double the number of attendants in the afternoon, to what there is in the morning. Most of the Clergy in the Deanery of Gower serve two Churches.

John Collins, M.A. Rector.
Rural Dean of West Gower.

Lewis: discharged rectory, with that of Oxwick [585. 4. 8(20)] annexed, rated at £5. 11. 0½.; net income £224 with a glebe house: patron, R. C. M. Talbot, Esq.
C & C: 1 service in English.
I & C: incumbent not resident: curate has stipend of £40 for this and Oxwich.

7   Penrice Parish.
Area: 2,248 acres. *Popn.* 198 males, 200 females: total 398.

(18)   PENRICE PARISH CHURCH.
Space: free about 12; other, enclosed pews, 100.
Present: morn. 45 + 22 scholars.
Average (12 *months*): morn. 40 to 50 + 30 scholars; aft. 60 to 80 + 30 scholars.
Remarks: The service is alternately as in the whole of the Deanery, in the morning at ½ part 10, in the afternoon at ½ past 2. Nearby double the number in the morning attend in the afternoon.

> John Lloyd.   Rector of Rhossilly and Officiating Minister.

Lewis: perpetual curacy, endowed with £800 royal bounty; net income £53: patron and impropriator, Earl of Jersey.

C & C: 1 service in English.

I & C: incumbent not resident.

(19)   HORTON CHAPEL, HORTON.   WESLEYAN METHODIST.
Erected 1815.
Space: free 132.
Present: morn. 70; even. 140.
Average: scholars 60.

> William Tucker.   Local Preacher.
> Horton.

8   Oxwich Parish
Area: 1,602 acres. *Popn.* 172 males, 197 males, 197 females: total 369.

(20)   OXWICH PARISH CHURCH.
Space: free 130; other, Rectory Pew, 4.
Present: aft. 80 + 17 scholars.
Average (12 *months*): morn. 50 to 60 + 50 scholars; aft. 80 to 100 + 50 scholars.
Remarks: The service is alternately in the morning at ½ past 10; in the afternoon at ½ past 2. Nearly double the number in the afternoon of that in the morning.

> John Lloyd.   Rectory of Rhossilly and Oxwich.

Lewis: discharged rectory, united with that of Nicholaston [585. 4. 6(17)], and rated at £9. 9. 2.

C & C: 1 service in English.

I & C: incumbent resident: curate has stipend of £40 for this and Nicholaston.

(21) PRIMITIVE METHODIST CHAPEL. PRIMITIVE METHODIST.
Erected 1838.
Space: free 110; standing 50.
Present: even. 120.
Average (12 *months*): even. 5160. [?aft. 5, even. 160.]

> Joseph Hibbs. Itnerant Preacher.
> 4 Clifton Street, Swansea.

(22) OXWICH CHAPEL. WESLEYAN METHODIST.
Erected 1806.
Space: all free; standing 20.
Present: morn. 50; even. 90.

> William Tucker. Class Leader.
> Berry Hall, Nr. Swansea.

9 Port Eynon Parish.
Area: 1,136 acres. *Popn.* 179 males, 172 females: total 351.

(23) PORT EYNON CHURCH.
Space: free 190.
Usual number of attendants: morn. 80 + 30 scholars; aft. 160 + 30 scholars.

> *Informant:* John Davies. Minister.

[Informant's form]

Lewis: rectory, rated at £9. 5. 10.; in the patronage of the Crown: net income £121 with a glebe-house.
C & C: 1 service in English.
I & C: incumbent not resident: curate, who has stipend of £50, resides at Reynoldston [585. 4. 11(24)], 2½ miles distant.

10 Knelston Parish.
Area: 537 acres. *Popn.* 60 males, 67 females: total 127.
[No returns]

11 Reynoldston Parish.
Area: 1,047 acres. *Popn.* 151 males, 164 females: total 315.

(24) REYNOLDSTON CHURCH.
Space: free 130.
Usual number of attendants: morn. 40; aft. 80.

> *Informant:* John Davies. Minister.

[Informant's form]

Lewis: discharged rectory, rated at £5. 11. 0½; in the gift of C. R. M. Talbot, Esq.: tithes commuted for a rent-charge of £102; glebe of 41a 1r 13p, valued at £27. 5. per annum.
C & C: 1 service in English.
I & C: incumbent resident.

12 Llandewy Parish.
Area: 1,853 acres. *Popn.* 97 males, 77 females: total 174.

(25)   LLANDDEWI PARISH CHURCH.
Endowed: land £31. 10*s*; tithe £42. 19*s*; permanent endowment £6. 10*s*.
Space: free 35; other 80.
Present: aft. 87 + 15 scholars.
Average: morn. 40 + 10 scholars; aft. 85 + 13 scholars.
Remarks: I commenced as new vicar the duties of this parish on the 1st of December last. The figures in the 4th and 5th Columns of Division 7 [i.e. average attendants morn. and aft.] must be understood as giving the average number of attendants from that time up to the 30th March 1851. The Sunday Scholars are principally, if not entirely from a parish whose Church is in ruins and of which parish I have the oversight.

Charles P. M. Williams.   Clergyman.

Lewis: discharged vicarage, rated at £3. 3. 4., and endowed with £800 royal bounty; net income £71: patron and impropriator, Bishop of St. David's. Vicar receives a small additional stipend from the Chapter of St. David's as compensation for additional duties connected with parish of Knelston [585. 4. 10] whose church is in ruins.
C & C: 1 service in English.
I & C: no return.

13 Rhoscilly Parish.
Area: 2,470 acres. *Popn.* 175 males, 192 females: total 367.

(26)   RHOSSILEY PARISH CHURCH.
Space: free 6; other 114.
Present: even. 51.
Average (12 *months*)*:* morn. 40 + 6 scholars; aft. 50 + 6 scholars.
Remarks: The Service is alternately as in the whole of the Deanery, in the morning at ½ past 10, and in the afternoon at ½ past 2. The afternoon congregation varies from 50 to 90.

John Lloyd.   Rector.

Lewis: rectory, rated at £9. 6. 8.; net income £104: in the patronage of the Crown.
C & C: 1 service in English.
I & C: incumbent resident.

(27)   WESLEYAN CHAPEL.   WESLEYAN METHODIST.
Erected 1835.
Space: free 160.
Average: even. 140 + 40 scholars.

Willm. Bytheway. Wesleyan Minister.
Union Street, Swansea.

(28) PITTON CHAPEL.   WESLEYAN.
Erected 1833.
Space: all free.
Present: aft. 112.
Average: general congregation. 100; scholars 60.

George Beynon.   Chapel Steward.
Pitton, Rhoscilly.

14   Llangennith Parish.
Area: 1,479 acres. *Popn.* 208 males, 190 females: total 398.

(29) LLANGENYDD PARISH CHURCH.
Present: morn. about 100; aft. 100.
Average (12 *months*): morn. about 100; aft. 100.

Elisha Gordon.   Churchwarden.
Burry Green.

Lewis: discharged vicarage, rated at £5. 16. 8.; endowed with £400 royal bounty; net income £51; patrons and impropriators, Warden and Fellows of All Souls College, Oxford: glebe-house.

C & C: 1 service in English.

I & C: incumbent not resident; curate, who has stipend of £48, resides at Fairy Hill, 2 miles distant.

(30) BETHESDA CHAPEL.   CALVINISTIC METHODIST.
Erected 1813.
Space: free 400.
Present: morn. 70; even. 130.
Average (12 *months*): morn. 90; even. 140.
Remarks: 80 communicants belong to the chapel when all are together.

William Griffiths.   Minister.
Burry Green.

15   Llanmadock Parish.
Area: 6,727 acres. *Popn.* 127 males, 142 females: total 269.

(31) LLANMAYDOCK OTHERWISE LLANFADOG OTHERWISE LLANMADOCK PARISH CHURCH.
Endowed: tithe £56. 10*s*; glebe £61. 10*s*; surplus fees £1.
Space: other 12.
Present: aft. 70 + 20 scholars.
Average (6 *months*): morn. 50 + 20 scholars.
Remarks: In this parish of Llanmadock, County Glamorgan, a single

service is performed every Sunday and this an alternate service—the service being one Sunday in the morning, the next Sunday in the afternoon.

Prosser Pearce.   Rector of Llanmadock.

Lewis: rectory, rated at £9.; net income £112: in the patronage of the Crown. Church rebuilt in 1748.

C & C: 1 service in English.

I & C: incumbent resident.

ERCR: accomodation 100.

(32) TRINITY CHAPEL.   CALVINISTIC METHODISTS.

Erected 1816.

Space: free 200.

Present: aft. 120.

Average (12 *months*): morn. 130 + 60 scholars.

William Griffiths.   Minister.
Burry Green.

(33) LLANMADOCK CHAPEL.   PRIMMITIVE METHODIST.

Erected 1838.

Space: free 60; other 20.

Present: morn. 30; aft. 50; even. 60.

Average: morn. 60.

John Jenkins.   Manager.

16   Cheriton Parish.

Area: 1,419 acres. *Popn.* 135 males, 177 females: total 312.

(34) CHERITON PARISH CHURCH.

Endowed: tithe £113; glebe £55; fees £1.

Space: free 144.

Present: morn. 59 + 8 scholars.

Average: morn. 60 + 14 scholars; aft. 100 + 14 scholars; even. 110 + 14 scholars.

Remarks: The undersigned was Curate of Cheriton up to the middle of October 1850 and has again resumed the duties since the 16th of the present month. It is therefore to be observed that the figures in the 4th, 5th and sixth columns of Division 7 [i.e. average number of attendants, morn. aft. and even.] signify the average number of attendants during the 12 calendar months preceding the 13th of October 1850.

Charles Prytherch Middleton Williams.
Minister.
Scurlage House, Llanddewi.

Lewis: rectory, rated at £9. 7. 3½.; net income about £160; in the patronage of the Crown.

C & C: 1 service in English.

I & C: incumbent not resident: curate, who resides in the glebe-house, has stipend of £80.

17   Llanrhidian Lower: part of the parish of Llanrhidian.

Area: 12,958 acres. *Popn.* 283 males, 280 females: total 563.
[For the remainder of ths parish see 585. 2. 2. above.]

(35) LLANRHIDIAN PARISH CHURCH.
Endowed: land £23; tithe £10; Queen Anne's Bounty £64. fees £5.
Space: free 400.
Present: aft. 300 + 40 scholars.
Average (3 *months*): aft. 200 to 300 + 40 to 50 scholars.
Remarks: I preach alternately at Llanrhidian and Penclawdd on the morn-
ing and afternoon of every Sabbath. The return from Penclawdd will be
made by the Church warden.

George Rees.   Vicar.

[For the Penclawdd return see 585. 2.2(14) above.]

Lewis: discharged vicarage, rated at £12. 13. 4.; endowed with £400 royal bounty,
and £1,600 parliamentary grant; in the patronage of Trustees of G. Morgan, Esq.;
net income £99.

C & C: at Llanrhidian, 1 service in English: at Llan-newydd [585. 2. 2(14)] 1
service partially in English and Welsh, performed by the curate.

I & C: no return.

(36) OLD WALLS CHAPEL, LLANRHYDIAN.   CALVINISTIC METHODIST.
Erected 1813.
Space: free 350.
Present: even. 160, average attendance.
Remark: No service held on March 30th 1851.

William Griffiths.   Minister.
Burry Green.

*[End of Gower Subdistrict and end of Swansea District
and end of Glamorgan Registration County]*

CARMARTHENSHIRE

Area: 497,776 acres. *Popn.* 45,519 males, 49,153 females: total 94,672.

Area: 73,451 acres. *Popn.* 11,618 males, 11,889 females: total 23,507.

1 LOUGHOR (Subdistrict)
Area: 24,458 acres. *Popn.* 1,799 males, 1,783 females: total 3,582.

1 Loughor Parish, co. Glamorgan.
Area: 3,999 acres. *Popn.* 563 males, 539 females: total 1,099.

(1)   LOUGHOR PARISH CHURCH.
Endowed: tithe £211. 10s.; glebe £30; fees £1. 10s.
Space: free 150.
Present: morn. 50 + 37 scholars; even. 50.
Average (12 *months*): morn. 60 + 37 scholars; even. 50.
Remarks: As to the *Endowment* I give the gross commuted value of the tithe without deducting the outgoings. As to Attendance I have to add that the congregations are quite distinct—the morning service being Welsh and the evening English.

> J. Powell Jones.   Rector.

Lewis: rectory, rated at £9. 10. 5., in the patronage of the Crown: tithes commuted for £210; glebe of 8 acres, with a glebe-house.

C & C: 2 services, morn. in Welsh, even. in English, performed by the curate.

I & C: incumbent resident; curate has stipend of £80.

(2)   MORIAH, LOUGHOR BOROUGH.   CALVINISTIC METHODIST.
Erected 1822.
Space: free 12; other 270; standing 'Middle of the Chapel and the Gallory except the Front'.
Present: morn. 74 scholars; aft. 200; even. 261.
Average: general congregation 301; scholars 120.

> David Harry.   Elder.

(3)   PENUEL.   BAPTISTS.
Erected 1843.
Space: all free.
Present: morn. 100; aft. 40 scholars; even. 150.

> James James.   Minister.
> Three Crosses, Swansea.

2 Llangennech Parish, co. Carmarthen.

Area: 2,394 acres. *Popn.* 475 males, 490 females: total 965.

(4) LLANGINNECH PARISH CHURCH.
Endowed: land £76; glebe £15.
Space: free 155; other 45.
Present: morn. 80 + 50 scholars; aft. 240.
Average: morn. 90 + 60 scholars; aft. 270.

　　　　　　　　　　　　　　Thomas Morgan.　Perpetual Curate.

[Endorsed: See letter]

Lewis: perpetual curacy, endowed with £200 royal bounty; patron and impropriator Edward Rose Tunno, Esq., of Llangennech Park, who augmented the income of the benefice, previously £82 per annum, with a farm producing £40 per ann.

C & C: 2 services, alternately English and Welsh, performed by the incumbent.

I & C: incumbent resident.

ICBS: grant of £180 in 1852.

(5) [illegible ? Bethel]. INDEPENDENT.
Erected 1811.
Present: even. 180.
Average: general congregation 196.

　　　　　　　　　　　　　　John Joseph.　Minister.
　　　　　　　　　　　　　　Llangennech.

(6) SALEM. BABTIST.
Erected 1840.
Space: free 180.
Present: morn. 130; aft. 40 scholars; even. 110.
Average: general congregation 120; scholars 40.

　　　　　　　　　　　　　　Daniel Jones.　Minister.
　　　　　　　　　　　　　　Salem Allt Llangenech.

3 Berwick Hamlet. Part of Llanelly Parish.

Popn. 764 males, 754 females: total 1,518.

(7) BRYN, LLANELLY. INDEPENDENT.
Erected 1841.
Space: free 500.
Present: morn. 300; aft. 342 scholars; even. 550.

　　　　　　　　　　　　　　John Williams.　Deacon.
　　　　　　　　　　　　　　[Pen]llwyngwyn, Llangennech.

(8) SOAR, LLWYNHENDY. BAPTIST.
Erected 1850.
Space: free 60; standing '48 by 42 within the walls'.
Present: morn. 560; even. 580.
Average (3 *months*): general congregation morn. 500 to 600; scholars 200 to 240.
Remarks: We have an old chapel but it was to small for the congregation and we Built a New Chapel on another piece of Ground close by the other and the new cost us £800. And we intend to make the old Chapel a school house for dayly school.

> Morgan Jones. Minister.
> Llwynhendy.

[End of Loughor Subdistrict]

2 LLANELLY (Subdistrict)

Area of the whole parish, including the Hamlet of Berwick [586. 1. 3], the Borough of Llanelly [586. 1], and the Hamlets of Hengoed [2] and Westfa [3]: 18,075 acres. *Popn.* of the whole parish, excluding the Hamlet of Berwick: 6,032 males, 6,113 females: total 12,145.

1 Llanelly Borough.

Popn. 4,194 males, 4,221 females: total 8,415.
(1) LLANELLY PARISH CHURCH.
Endowed: land £80; glebe £25; permanent endowment £11. 13. 4.
Space: 650.
Present: morn. 700 + 130 scholars; aft. 800 + 130 scholars; even. 600.
Average: morn. 650 + 125 scholars; aft. 780 + 130 scholars; even. 600.
Remarks: There are four services regularly performed in this Church. And the Church is generally well filled.

> Ebenezer Morris. Vicar.

Lewis: discharged vicarage, rated at £6. 6. 8., net income £96; tithes commuted for £270, with a glebe of 40 acres worth £80 per annum; vicar has also a glebe and glebe house worth £20 per annum: patron and impropriator, Rees Goring Thomas, Esq.: two lectures in the week, one in Welsh, one in English.

C & C: 4 services alternately Welsh and English, performed by the incumbent.

I & C: incumbent resident.

ICBS: grant of £200 in 1845.

(2) SILOAH, LLANELLY. INDEPENDENTS.
Erected 1840.
Space: free 82; other 484.
Present: morn. 150 + 134 scholars; even. 156 + 246 scholars.
Remarks: Several absent, some on sea, some engaged in copper smelting and some on account of illness.

David Davies.   Minister.

(3) BETHEL CHAPEL. PARTICULAR BAPTIST.
Erected 1840.
Space: free 455; other 275; standing 'the Aisles only where about 100 may stand'.
Present: morn. 271; aft. 215 scholars; even. 346.
Remarks: The Chapel is 63 feet long by $41\frac{1}{4}$ feet wide. Has 80 seats on the ground floor = 440 sittings; gallery 58 seats = 290 sittings; total 730 exclusive of standing room in the aisles only for say 100 : 830.

William Hughes.   Minister.

(4) SEA SIDE WESLEYAN CHAPEL. WESLEYAN METHODIST.
Erected 1838.
Space: free 126; other 20.
Present: morn. 25; aft. 29; even. 25.

Thomas Harding.   Minister.

(5) CAPEL ALS. INDEPENDENT.
Erected 1780.
Space: free 220; other 630.
Present: morn. 800; even. 850.
Average: morn. 700 to 800; even. 850.
Remarks: [in Column 1]: In times of yore there was an old dame of the name of Alice living on the spot where the chapel is built at the corner of whose house there was a well over which the chapel is, which was called Alice's Well and when the place was occupied by the chapel it was called very naturally Capel Alice abreviated Capel Als.
[in Column IX] The congregation was not counted on March 30 but judging from the available spaces it was as given. It should be also understood that great many of the people are obliged to work on the Sabbaths in copper works and other works which require to be kept in order so that *all* the worshippers are never at the same time in any of the chapels in this place. There are at least 1,300 who are in the habit of frequenting this chapel which is always crammed in the evening. Most of the Sunday School attend to worship in the chapel and most of the congregation belong to the Sunday School.

David Rees.   Minister.

(6)   MORMONITES CHAPPEL OR LATER DAY SAINTS.
Erected 1847.
Space: free 160.
Present: morn. 50 + 30 scholars; aft. 150; even. 200.
Remarks: President of the Llanelly Branch Benjamin Jones.

> Officers—Elders 13
> do   —Prists 8
> do   —Preachers 9
> do   —Deacons 9

> officers total 39

The members of the whool saints within this Branch the total 216.

> Joseph Evans.   Elder of the later day saints.

(7)   PARK STREET CHAPEL.   INDEPENDENT.
Erected 1839.
Space: free 100; other 350; standing about 50.
Present: morn. 139; even. 160.
Remarks: There are about 300 [?200] persons who are in the habit of attending this chapel. But the average attendance does not exceed 160. This is an English Chapel. The English population is very scattered. There is a morning school, average attendance 60.

> Thomas Roberts.
> Independent Minister.

(8)   SION CHAPEL.   BAPTISTS.
Erected 1821.
Space: free 670; other 130.
Present: morn. 400; even. 750.
Average (12 *months*): morn. 400; aft. 363 scholsrs; even. 750.

> James Spencer.   Baptist Minister.

(9)   CAPEL NEWYDD.   CALVINISTIC METHODIST.
Erected 1809, re-erected 1840.
Space: free 90; other 738; standing 250.
Present: morn. 450 + 150 scholars; aft. 275 scholars; even. 900 + 200 scholars.
Average: morn. 600 + 150 scholars; aft. 275 scholars; even. 1,000 + 200 scholars.
Remarks: The Congregation being less the Sunday March 30 1851 in consequence of not having a popular Minister. The Congregation being less morning than evening owing to servants not being at liberty to attend. The Congregation before the reerection average morning 150, evening about 100, Sunday school about 50.

> John Bowen.   Minister.

(10)   Wesleyan Methodist.   Wesleyan Methodists.
Erected 1792, re-built in 1828, enlarged in 1834.
Space: free 100; other 200.
Present: morn. 96; even. 152.

Samuel Bevan.   Chapel Steward.
Ironmonger.

(11)   Adulam. Felinfoel.   Baptist.
Erected: First in the year 1709, Rebuilt in 1840.
Space: all free.
Present: morn. 900; even. 800.
Average: aft. 250 scholars.
Remarks [in Column VI]: Worship Morning and Evening, School in the
Afternoon.
There is a large Burying Ground attached to the Chapel, on a lease 999 years.
Length of the Chapel out side of the walls 61 feet, width 57. Galeries at
both ends and the midle—seated on the whole flore and the galeries.

Daniel Jones.   Minister.
Felinfoel.

(12)   Horeb.   Particular Baptist.
Erected 1832.   Also used as a Day School.
Space: free 105.
Present: morn. 77; aft. 62 scholars; even. 95.
Average: morn. 120; aft. 80 scholars; even. 150.

Jeremiah Griffiths.   Deacon.
Upper Lodge, Nr. Horeb.

(13)   Mount Selen.   Baptist.
Erected before 1800.
School in the week days, the average number in attendance is from 20-30.
Average: morn. 20 to 25 scholars; aft. 40 to 50.

Daniel Jones.   Minister.

(14)   Parish Church of St. Paul, Llanelly.
Consecrated [MS torn]13th. 1850 as an additional Church.
Erected by grant from Her Majesty's Commissioners for Building
New Churches, from the Incorporated Society for Building
New Churches, and Voluntary Subscriptions.
Cost defrayed by Grants £510, by Private Subscription, etc.
say £2,300. Total Cost (say) £2,810. 0. 0.
Endowed: Permanent Endowment under the provisions of 6 & 7
Victoria c. 37, £150. Fees (say) £5.
Space: free 503.

Present: morn. generally full—150 scholars; even. generally full.
Remarks: There are two large and respectable congregations worshipping
at this Church: namely—Welsh and English.

David Edward Williams.
Perpetual Curate.

C & C: 2 services, English at 11 a.m., Welsh at ½ p. 6 p.m., performed by the
incumbent.
I & C: incumbent resident.
ICBS: grant of £260 in 1848.

(15)   CAPEL IFAN CHURCH, LLANNON DISTRICT, LLANELLY.
Congregation including Sunday Scholars 56.
Attendance: morn. aft. even.: About 56 at each period.
Free seats: 56.

Signed: William Davies.
Dated: 4 August 1852.

[Inquiry form]
Lewis: sub Llanelly: recently rebuilt by the patron, with provision for the maintenance of a clergyman.
[This schedule is wrongly numbered and consequently misplaced: it should
come under 586. 4. 2.]

2   Hengoed Hamlet.
Popn. 873 males, 803 females: total 1,776.
[no returns]

3   Westfa Hamlet.
Popn. 566 males, 528 females: total 1,094.
[No returns]

[End of Llanelly Subdistrict]

3 PEMBREY (Subdistrict)
Area: 31,905 acres. *Popn.* 2,394 males, 2,564 females: total 4,958.

1   Pembrey Parish.
Area: 26,735 acres. *Popn.* 1,622 males, 1,688 females: total 3,310.

(1)   LLANDDURY, LLANDURY.
When erected: cant say.
Accomodation: free 200.
Usual number of attendants: aft. 65.

Informant: Bryn Williams.

[Informant's form]

(2) St. Mary.
When erected: cannot be ascertained.
Accomodation: free None; Appropriated about 500.
Usual number of attendants: general congregation: 40 to 70. aft. about 40;
even. none.
School irregularly attended, sometimes not exceeding 6 children.

Informant: John Thomas.

[Informant's form]

(3) Pembrey.
When erected: two or three hundred years.
Accomodation free about 700.
Usual number of attendants: general congregation: about 700, scholars 35;
aft. 40.

Informant: Benjn. Williams.

Lewis: discharged vicarage,with Llandury [586.3.1.] benefice annexed, endowed with
£600 royal bounty, and £1,400 parliamentary grant; net income £69, with a glebe-
house; patron and impropriator, Earl of Ashburnham: tithes commuted for a rent-
charge of £700. Church dedicated to St. Illtyd. At Llandury Hamlet a commodious
chapel of ease, where where devine service is performed regularly in the afternoon.

C & C: Pembrey with Llandyry: 3 services in 2 Sundays at Pembrey, 1 service a
fortnight at Llandyry: Welsh services alternately in the afternoon, and every Sunday morning with the exception of 3 Sundays.

I & C: incumbent resident.

(4) Gusgam, Pembrey. Baptist.
Erected 1839.
Space: free 120.
Present: morn. 46 scholars; aft. 79; even. 43.
Average (12 *months*): morn. 48 schol; aft. 120; even. 43.

David Rogers. Deacon in Chapel.
Achildu Ucha Farm.

[Endorsed: See letter]

(5) Ebenezer. Wesleyan Methodists.
Erected 1832.
Space: free 28; other 106.
Present: morn. 23 + 5 scholars; aft. 91 + 21 scholars; even. 80 + 20
scholars.
Average (12 *months*): morn. 22 + 4 scholars; aft. 103 + 26 scholars;
even. 90 + 25 scholars.

Remarks: Divine services performed in this chapel are as follows.

  7 o'clock in the morning — prayer meeting
  2   do.   afternoon — preaching
  6   do.   evening — prayer meeting.

N.B. On the 30th March the services were performed by a local preacher in the absence of the minister.

> Alexander Davis.   Chapel Steward.
> Red Lion, Pembrey.

(6)   BETHEL.   CALVINISTIC METHODIST.
Erected 1812.
Space: free 30; other 250: standing 100.
Present: morn. school; aft. 94 + 40 scholars.
Average (6 *months*): morn. school; aft. 280 + 70 scholars; even. 291 + 76 scholars.

> John Williams.   Steward.
> [?] Tarvincanal, Pembrey.

(7)   JERUSALEM.   INDEPENDENT DISSENTERS.
Erected 1812.
Space: free 175; other 174.
Present: aft. 168 + 60 scholars; even. 197 + 70 scholars.
Average (12 *months*): aft. 230 + 70 scholars; even. 280 + 70 scholars.

> Henry Edmunds.   Deacon.

(8)   SARDIS.   INDEPENDENT.
Erected 1831.
Present: morn. 72 scholars; aft. 170; even. 80.
Average: morn. 195 + 79 scholars.

> David Jones.   Minister.

(9)   REHOBOTH, PENBRE.   INDEPENDENT.
Erected 1827.
Space: free 120; other 54; standing 30.
Present: aft. 121; even. 97.
Remark: No service in the morning Except once a Month, the attendance then will average the number 200.

> Henry Evans.   Minister.
> Rehoboth, Pembrey.

(10)   BETHLEHEM, POOL BEMBREY.   BAPTIST PARTICULAR.
Erected 1835.
Space: free 72.
Present: morn. 61 + 40 scholars; even. 75 + 50 scholars.
Average (12 *months*): general congregation 94 average.

> Daniel Ungoed.   Deacon.
> Pool Pembrey.

(11) CARMEL. INDEPENDENT DISSENTERS.
Erected 1827.
Space: free 100; other 208.
Present: morn. 180 + 20 scholars; even. 100 + 30 scholars.
Average (12 *months*): morn. 250; even. 150.

John Williams. Deacon.
Pantachddy.

2 St. Mary Parish, Kidwelly.

Area: St. Mary Within 2,637 acres. *Popn.* 640 males, 715 females: total 1,355.
St. Mary Without 2,533 acres. *Popn.* 132 males, 16 females: total 293.

(12) KIDWELLY PARISH CHURCH.
Endowed: [MS torn] land [£]; tithe [?]. 5. 9½; permanent endowment [£]; Easter Offerings £1. 0s. 10d.
Space: free 724; other 110.
Present: morn. (Welsh) [?]; aft. (English) about 700.
Average: No statement can be made in this particular as not sufficient notice have been taken as to the attendance so as to state numbers.
Remarks: [MS torn] . . . Lords day in this Town is but very little regarded as a day for spiritual worship [pub]lick houses are allowed to be open, and frequented during Divine Service. Publick [hou]ses are very numerous in this place, and even the Town Clerk keeps a . . . publick house. Often times on the Lord's day we are not only hear cursing and . . . once swearing in our streets, but frequently we see most brutal fighting, and . . . [n]otice taken thereof by the authority of the Town. This is the cause why places [of wor]ship are so little frequented and religion so little appreciated and professed at Kidwelly.

Thomas Griffiths. Vicar.

Lewis: discharged vicarage, rated at £7. 10., net income £97; in the patronage of the Crown; impropriators, G. R. and H. Maliphant, Esqrs., and their sisters.
C & C: 2 services, alternately Welsh and English, morn. and even. performed by the incumbent.
I & C: legally not resident.

(13) BETHESDA. WESLEYAN METHODISTS.
Space: free 100; other 91.*
Usual number of Attendants: morn. about 40; aft. about 50; even. about 50.
*See letter.

Informant: Benjamin Williams.
Tyisha, Pembrey.

[Informant's form]

(14) BETHESDA. WESLEYAN METHODISTS.
Erected 1816.
Space: free 60; other 174.
Present: morn. 30; even. 150.

Joseph Jones.   Wesleyan Minister.

[This is for the same place of worship as the previous return.]

(15) CAPEL NEWYDD, BOROUGH OF KIDWELLY. CALVINISTIC METHODIST.
Erected 1830.
Space: free 130; other 190; standing 150.
Present: morn. 64 scholars; aft. 250; even. 250.
Average (12 *months*): general congregation 300; scholars 82.

David John.   Elder.
Shoemaker.
Lady Street, Kidwelly.

(16) CAPEL SUL, TOWN AND BOROUGH OF KIDWELLY.   INDEPENDENTS.
Erected 1787; re-erected and enlarged 1831.
Space: free 220; other 330.
Present: morn. 240; aft. 60 scholars; even. 130.
Average (12 *months*): morn. 365; aft. 85 scholars; even. 158.
Remarks: There are many attending this place of worship from the adjoining parishes of St. Ismael and Llandevilog and Pembrey.

David Jones.   Minister.

(17) SILOAM, TOWN OF KIDWELLY. BAPTIST.
Erected 1821.
Space: free 165; other 30.
Present: morn. 71; aft. 23 scholars; even. 72.

John Evans.   Deacon.
Cordwainer.
Bridge Street.

(18) HOREB, BOROUGH OF KIDWELLY. CALVINISTIC METHODIST.
Erected 1841.
Space: free 13; other 7.

David Evans.
Mynyth y Garreg.

[End of Pembrey Subdistrict]

4 LLANNON (Subdistrict)
Area: 17,078 acres. *Popn.* 1,792 males, 1,890 females: total 3,682.

1 Glyn Hamlet, part of Llanelly Parish.
Popn. 399 males, 461 females: total 860.
[No returns]

2 Llannon Parish.
Area: 11,446 acres. *Popn.* 851 males, 845 females: total 1,696.

(1) Llannon Parish Church.
Endowed: land £95.
Space: free; other 53.
Present: aft. 130 + 50 scholars.

       James Whitworth. Curate.

Lewis: perpetual curacy, endowed with £800 royal bounty, and £1,200 parliamentary grant; net income £86: patron and impropriator, Rees Goring Thomas, Esq., whose tithes have been commuted for £775, subject to rates averaging £75 per annum. Church rebuilt in 1841, and contains 606 sittings of which 326 are free.

C & C: 2 services, morn. in English, aft. in Welsh. performed by the curate.

I & C: incumbent not resident: curate resident in the parish and has stipend of £112 for this and Llandarog [589. 1. 1(1)].

ICBS: grant of £200 in 1839.

(2) Bethania, Glyn Hamlet. Independent.
Erected 1800.
Space: free 250; standing 250 square feet.
Present: morn. 203; aft. 159 scholars; even. 120.
Average (12 *months*): morn. 303; aft. 180 scholars; even. 150.

       Henry Davies. Minister.
       Near Pontardulas.

(3) Pentwyn Chapel. Welsh Calvinistic Methodists.
Erected 1824.
Space: free 300; standing 100.
Present: morn. 97 scholars; aft. 123; even. 99.
Average (12 *months*): general congregation 250; scholars 124.

       David Davies. Manager.
       Llwydcoedfawr, Llannon.

(4) Llwunteg, Goitre Hamlet. Independents.
Erected 1845.
Space: free 6; other 162.

Present: morn. 133; aft. 57 scholars; even. 139.
Average (12 *months*): general congregation 160; scholars 78.

Henry Davies. Minister.
Near Pontardulas.

(5) HERMON. CALVINISTIC BAPTIST.
Erected 1850.
Space: free 270; standing 250;
Present: morn. 218; aft. 56 scholars; even. 210.
Average (12 *months*): morn. 112; aft. 65 scholars; even. 120.

Daniel Jones. Minister.
Llanelly.

[Note: 586. 2. 1.(15) should be included under this parish.]

3 Llanedy Parish.

Area: 5,632 acres. *Popn.* 542 males, 584 females: total 1,126.

(6) LLANEDY PARISH CHURCH.
Endowed: land £42; tithe £308; glebe £12.
Space: free 6; other 150.
Present: aft. 70.
Remark: I have no Sunday School at present, the room being in sad
Repair; but, mean soon to remedy this, and commence School again.

Henry Williams. Minister.

Lewis: rectory, rated at £8, and given by George IV to St. David's College; net
income £360. Church repaired and enlarged by a gallery at the west-end, affording
additional 120 sittings, towards which the Society for the enlargement of churches
and chapels gave £100.

C & C: 2 services in summer, 1 in winter, performed in Welsh by the curate.

I & C: incumbent resident.

ICBS: grant of £100 in 1829.

(7) BETHESDA PONTHENRY. BAPTISTS.
Erected 1838.
Space: all free; standing 50.
Present: morn. 27 scholars; aft. 90; even. 50.
Average: general congregation 90; scholars 35.
Remark: The 10 pews and the gallery are all free sittings.

David Jones. Minister.
Brynygroesfach, Llanelly.

(8) LLANEDI. INDEPENDANTS.
Erected 1712.
Space: free 204.
Present: morn. 160; aft. 30 scholars; even. 45.*
Average (12 *months*): morn. 294; aft. 40 scholars; even. 50.
Remark: *Prayer Meeting.

> John Joseph.   Independant Minister.
> Llanedi.

(9) EBENEZER.   CALVINSTIC METHODIST.
Erected 1836.
Space: free 84; standing 100.
Present: morn. 65; aft. 49 scholars; even. 67.
Average (3 *months*): morn. 70 + 45 scholars; aft. 90 + 70 scholars; even.
120.

> John Francis.
> Grocer.
> Llanedi.

(10) SARDIS. BAPTIST.
Erected 1812.
Present: morn. 79; aft. 50 scholars; even. 110.
Average (12 *months*): morn. 140; aft. 50 scholars.

> John Rees. Assistant Minister.
> Llangennech.

[*End of Llannon Subdistrict and end of Llanelly District*]

587   LLANDOVERY (District)

Area: 154,572 acres. *Popn.* 7,268 males, 7,787 females: total 15,055

1 LLANDDAUSAINT (Subdistrict)
Area: 10,307 acres. *Popn.* 416 males, 435 females: total 851.

1   Llanddausaint Parish.
Area and *Popn.* same as for the Subdistrict.

(1) LLANDDAUSANT PARISH CHURCH, CONSOLIDATED TO LLANGADOCK, SITUATED IN THE HAMLET OF BLAENSAWDDE.
Endowed: tithe rent charge £60; fees £2.
Space: free about 300.
Present: aft. 60 [?+] 100 scholars.
Average (6 *months*): aft. 60 to 80 + 100 to 120 scholars.

> David Davies.   Curate.
> Gwynfe.

Lewis: annexed to the vicarage of Llangadock [587. 2. 1(1)] : tithes commuted for £180, of which £80 are paid to the Bp. of St. David's £40 to the Prepandary of Llanvynydd, and £60 to the vicar.

C & C: 1 service in Welsh performed by the [?] curate.

I & C: see under Llangadock [587. 2. 1(1)].

(2) TWYN LLANAR.   CALVINSTIC METHODIST.
Erected 1790.
Space: other 54; standing 50.
Present: morn. 349; aft. 42 scholars.
Average (6 *months*): morn. 380; aft. 50 scholars; even. 250.

> Owen Lewis.   Minister.
> Penyrhyn, Llanddausant.

[End of Llanddausaint Subdistrict]

2 LLANGADOCK (Subdistrict)
Area: 15,642 acres. *Popn.* 1,365 males, 1,455 females: total 2,820.
[1-3] Llangadock Parish, consisting of [1] Above Sawdde Hamlet,

[2] Dyffryn Cidrich Hamlet, and [3] Gwynfe Quarter Bach.
Area and *Popn.* of the whole Parish as for the Subdistrict.

1 Above Sawdde Hamlet.
Popn. 385 males, 440 females: total 825.

(1) LLANGADOCK VAWR PARISH CHURCH.
Endowed: tithe Rent Charge £183; glebe £15; fees about £5; other sources £17.
Space: free about 300.
Present: morn. (English) 109 + 101 scholars; aft. (Welsh) 67 + 98 scholars; even. (Welsh) 73.
Average (6 months): morn. (English) 120 + 80 scholars; aft. (Welsh) 80 + 80 scholars; even. (Welsh) 88.

> Thomas Davies. Vicar.

Lewis: vicarage, with Llanddausaint annexed [587. 1. 1(1)], rated at £9; net income £181 with a glebe-house; patron, Bp. of St. David's: tithes commuted for £549.8.9., of which £244. 3. 5½ is payable to the Bp. £122. 2. 1½ to the Prependary of Llanvynydd, and £183. 3. 2 to the vicar; glebe of 5 acres, valued at £3.
C & C: 2 services, alternately Welsh and English.
I & C: incumbent resident; curate has stipend of £40.

(2) GOSHEN. CALVINISTIC METHODIST.
Erected 1792; re-erected 1840.
Space: free 87; other 268.
Present: morn. 98; aft. 103 scholars; even. 200.

> Benjamin David Thomas. Minister.

(3) EBENEZER CHAPEL. WESLEYANS.
Erected 1808.
Space: free 50; other 105; standing 100.
Present: aft. 32; even. 33.
Average: general congregation 50; scholars 30.

> Henry Evans. Class Leader.

(4) PROVIDENCE. INDEPENDENT.
Erected 1840.
Space: free 150; other 150.
Present: morn. 168; aft. 102 scholars; even. 221.

> John Williams. Minister.

2 Dyffrun Cidrich Hamlet.
Popn. 318 males, 362 females: total 680.

(5) BETHLEHEM. INDEPENDENT.
Erected 1800.
Space: free 294; other 204.
Present: morn. 250; aft. 200 scholars; even. 350.
Average (12 months): morn. 300; aft. 180 scholars; even. 360.

> David Jones. Minister.

(6) SION, CAREG LLAWDDE. CALVINISTIC BAPTIST.
Erected 1807.
Space: other 42; standing 200.
Present: morn. 24.
Average: 35.

Rees Evans. Minister.

3 Gwynfe Quarter Bach.
Popn. 662 males, 653 females: total 1,315.

(7) JERUSALEM. INDEPENDENTS.
Erected before 1800.
Space: free 397; standing 164.
Present: morn. 337; aft. school; even. 238.
Average (12 *months*): general congregation 315; scholars 308.

D. Lewis. Deacon.

(8) GIBEA, LANGADOCK. INDEPENDENT.
Erected 1843.
Space: free 400; standing 120.
Present: morn. 302; aft. 201 scholars; even. 331.

Hopkin Herbert. Deacon.
Aman Iron Works, Nr. Llandilo.

(9) GWYNFE CHAPEL, an ancient chapelry.
Endowed: land £98; permanent endowment £2; fees £1. 10 .
Space: free about 100; other about 38.
Present: morn. 45; aft. 25.
Average (6 *months*): morn. 50 to 60; aft. 25 to 30.

David Davies. Curate.

Lewis: formerly a chapel of ease to Llangadock [582. 2. 1(1)], now an independent
perpetual curacy without a district annexed: endowed with £1,000 royal bounty and
£800 parliamentary grant; net income £107; patron, vicar of Llangadock.

C & C: 1 service in Welsh performed by the curate.

I & C: incumbent resident.

[End of Llangadock Subdistrict]

3 LLANSADWRN (Subdistrict)
Area: 11,505 acres. *Popn.* 822 males, 877 females: total 1,699.

1   Llansadwrn Parish.
Area: 7,064 acres. *Popn.* 539 males, 588 females: total 1,127.

(1) LLANSADWRN PARISH CHURCH.
Endowed: land £27; tithe £85; glebe £3; fees £1. 10s.
Space: free 184; other 42.
Present: aft. 50 + 6 scholars; even. 40 + 5 scholars.
Average: aft. 70; even. 25.

John Jones.   Vicar.

Lewis: discharged vicarage, with the perpetual curacy of Llanwrda [587. 3. 2(7)]
annexed; rated at £6. 10., and in the gift of Lady Foley; net income £165 with a
glebe-house: tithes commuted for £351. 15. of which £263. 14. 9 are payable to the
impropriator, and £87. 18. 3 to the vicar, both subject to rates, averaging £10;
glebe of 3 acres, and £15 allowance from the impropriator.

C & C: 1 service in Welsh performed by the incumbent.

I & C: incumbent resident.

(2) CHAPEL, LLANSADWRN MOUNTAIN.
Not consecrated or licensed.
Built by subscription.
Space: free 100.
Present: aft. 55 + 11 scholars.
Average: aft. 60; even. 40.
Remark: There are no pews in this chapel, only free benches in the middle
of it and round about the walls.

John Jones.   Vicar of Llansadwrn.

(3) EBENEZER.   INDEPENDANT.
Erected 1830.
Space: free 6; other 156; standing 50.
Present: morn. 85; aft. 106 + 97 scholars; even. 105.
Average (2 months): general congregation 100; scholars 70.

Morgan Williams.   Deacon.

(4) CARMEL.   INDEPENDENTS.
Erected 1828.
Space: 204.
Present: morn. 68; aft. 66 scholars; even. 70.
Average: morn. 100; aft. 60 scholars; even. 80.

David Jones.   Diacon.
Eskem, Nr. Llangadock.

(5) LIBANUS. CA(L)VINIST BAPTIST.
Erected 1788.
Space: other 228; standing 100.
Present: morn. 57 [? +] 50 scholars; aft. 60.
Average (12 *months*): general congregation 70; scholars 55.

> David Price.   Deacon.
> Blaenywain.

(6) CAPEL SION. CALVINISTIC METHODIST.
Erected 1797 or 1798; rebuilt 1846.
Space: free 30; other 282; standing 200.
Present: morn. 43 scholars; aft. 118.
Average (3 *months*): morn. 50 scholars; aft. 150.
Remarks: A prayer meeting held at 6 in the evening and about 60 present.
The internal measure of Capel Sion: 29¼ft by 30ft.

> John Davies.   Steward.
> Myrtle Hill, Llansadwrn Village.

2 Llanwrda Parish.
Area: 4,441 acres. *Popn.* 283 males, 289 feamles: total 572.

(7) LLANWRDA PARISH CHURCH.
Endowed: tithe £52. 10s.; glebe £6; permanent endowment £6. 10s;
fees £1.
Space: free 176; other 48.
Present: morn. 46 + 20 scholars; even. 64 + 18 scholars.
Average (12 *months*): morn. 60 + 15 scholars; even. 65 + 18 scholars.
Remark: The congregation was less than usual.

> John Jones.   Vicar.

Lewis: annexed to the vicarage of Llansadwrn [587. 3. 1(1)]: tithes commuted for
£210, one-fourth of which belongs to the vicar, the remainder being the property
of the impropriator, Mr Hughes: glebe of 3 acres, valued at £5. 12.
C & C: 1 service in Welsh performed by the incumbent.
I & C: as for Llansadwrn [587. 3. 1(1)].

(8) TABOR. INDEPENDENT.
Erected 1792.
Space: free 90; other 123.
Present: morn. 131; aft. 25 scholars; even. 96.
Average: general congregation 200.

> Thomas Evans.   Deacon.
> Bwlchygwynt, Llanwrda.

[End of Llansadwrn Subdistrict]

4 MYDDFAI (Subdistrict)
Area: 11,914 acres. *Popn.* 520 males, 549 females: total 1,069.

[1-2] Myddfai Parish, consisting of [1] Lower Myddfai Hamlet, and [2] Upper Myddfai Hamlet.
Area of the parish: 11,914 acres.
Area and *popn.* of the whole parish, as for the Subdistrict.

1 Lower Myddfai Hamlet.
Popn. 293 males, 308 females: total 601.

(1) MOTHVEY PARISH CHURCH.
Endowed: tithe £140; glebe £10; permanent endowment £6; fees £3.
'The taxes and other expences are deducted from the above'.
Space: free 90; other 420.*
Average (12 *months*): morn. about 140 + 52 scholars; even. about 70 + 30 scholars.
Remarks: It is not long since the regular evening service was commenced. There are some church families in the parish who from convenience attend other churches which are nearer.

Thomas Thomas.   Curate.

*See Letter.

Lewis: discharged vicarage, rated at £6. 6.8., endowed with £200 royal bounty; net income £115; tithes commuted for £419. 14., of which £280 are payable to the Bp. of St. David's, patron, subject to rates averaging £32. 10., and £139, 14. to the vicar, subject to rates averaging £16. 5.; glebe of about $5\frac{1}{2}$ acres, valued at £10, and a house.

C & C: 1 service, partially in Welsh in the morn., wholly in Welsh in the evening, performed by the incumbent curate.

I & C: incumbent not resident, curate, resident in the glebe-house, has a stipend of £55.

(2) SION. INDEPENDENTS.
Erected 1823; re-erected 1844.
Space: free 52; other 250.

Average (1 *month*): general congregation 200; scholars 80.

John Williams.   Minister.

2 Upper Myddfai Hamlet.
Popn. 227 males, 241 females: total 468.

(3) SARDIS. INDEPENDENTS.
Erected 1792; rebuilt 1827.
Space: free 106; other 125.
Average (6 *months*): general congregation 100; scholars 25.

John Williams.   Minister.

(4) SALEM. CALVINISTIC METHODIST.
Erected 1822.
Space: free 6; other 138; stnading 200.
Present: morn. 61 scholars; aft. 105; even. 36.
Average: morn. 61 scholars; aft. 120.

David Davies. Elder. Deacon.

(5) MOTHVEY CHURCH.
Space: free 100; other 500.
Usual number of attendants: morn. 123 + 43 scholars; even. 65 + 30 scholars.
Remarks: There was a return for Mothvey Church . . . time this year. The number of seats at the above Church is 79, of which 13 are double seats.

Informant: Thomas Thomas. Curate.

[Informant's form. For the original return, see 587. 4. 1(1).]

[End of Myddfai Subdistrict]

5 LLANDINGAT (Subdistrict)

Area: 8,107 acres. *Popn.* 1,178 males, 1,364 females: total 2,542.

[1-4] Llandingat Parish, consisting of [1] Llandovery Borough, [2] Telych Hamlet, [3] Forest Hamlet, and [4] Ystrad Hamlet.
Area and *Popn.* as for the Subdistrict.

1 Llandovery Borough.
Popn. 885 males, 1,042 females: total 1,927.

(1) LLANDINGAT PARISH CHURCH.
Endowed: tithes (net) £193. 13. 4; Glebe £40; permanent endowment £46. 5. 4: total £279. 18. 8. Deduct Rates & Taxes & curates salary £49. Total £230. 18. 8. Fees £5. Total £235. 18. 8.
Space: free 148; other 279.
Present: morn. 292 + 36 scholars; even. 314.
Remarks: The morning congregation being English and the evening congregation being Welsh—should be reckoned together to give a correct estimate of the attendance, as they are for the most part distinct. That would give us 642. The above answer to Question V includes the endowment of Llanfair ar y bryn—as they form one Benefice.

Joshua Hughes. Vicar.

Lewis: vicarage with that of Llanfair-ar-y-bryn [587. 6. 1(1)] annexed; rated at £7; net income £254: tithes of Llandingat commuted for £650, of which £520, or three-fourths, are payable to the precentor and chapter of St. David's, and £130, or one-fourth, to the vicar, who also has a glebe of 23 acres, and a house, valued at £82.

C & C: 2 services, of which the morn. in Welsh, performed by the curate.

I & C: incumbent resident [no mention of a curate].

ICBS: grant of £150 in 1850.

(2) EBENEZER CHAPEL. PARTICULAR BAPTIST.
Erected 1844.
Space: free 100; other 200; standing 40.
Present: morn. 86; even. 90.
Average: general congregation 80; scholars 53.
Remarks: Attended at the Llandovery Union Workhouse at 2 o'clock to preach and examine the children.
Present 54.

John Morgan. Minister.
Tallog, Nr. Llandovery.

(3) WESLEYAN CHAPEL, CASTLE STREET. WESLEYAN METHODIST.
Erected 1808.
Space: free 20; other 100; standing 40.
Present: morn. 81; even. 90.
Average: 90.

William Williams.
Grocer, etc., Llandovery.

(4) TABERNACLE CHAPEL, QUEEN STREET. CALVINISTIC METHODIST.
Erected about 1800.
Space: free 200; other 600.
Present: morn. 450; aft. 526 scholars; even. 572.
Average (12 *months*): 'Nearly as above'.
Remarks: A great portion of our Congregation consists of Farmers and their families, of a circuit of about 2 miles around the Town.

Rees Jones. Deacon.
High Street.

(5) SALEM INDEPENDENT CHAPEL. INDEPENDENT.
Erected 1799.
Space: free 165; other 484; standing 220.
Present: morn. 440; aft. 342 scholars; even. 529.
Remarks: The congregation is formed of the Inhabitants of the Town and the Immediate neighbourhood.

D. Thomas. Deacon.
High Street.

2 Telych Hamlet.
Popn. 97 males, 96 females: total 193.
[No returns]

3 Forest Hamlet.
Popn. 117 males, 130 females: total 247.
[No returns]

4 Ystrad Hamlet.
Popn. 79 males, 96 females: total 175.
[No returns]

[End of Llandingat Subdistrict]

6 LLANFAIRARYBRYN (Subdistrict)
Area: 23,457 acres. *Popn.* 834 males, 871 females: total 1,705.

[1-4] Llanfairarybryn Parish, consisting of [1] Rhandir-Isaf Hamlet, [2] Rhandir-Canol Hamlet, [3] Rhandir-Uchaf Hamlet, and [4] Rhandir-Abbot Hamlet.
Area and *popn.* of the whole parish as for the Subdistrict.

1 Rhandir-Isaf Hamlet.
Popn. 210 males, 242 females: total 452.

(1) LLANFAIR AR Y BRYN PARISH CHURCH.
[Endorsed: See Llandeingat].
John James. Curate.

Lewis: vicarage, annexed to that of Llandingat, endowed with £1,000 parliamentary grant: tithes commuted for £600, of which £444. 16. are payable to the Precentor and Chapter of St. David's, £111. 4. to the vicar, and £44 to the impropriator (not stated).

C & C: 1 service in Welsh.

I & C: see under Llandingat [587. 5. 1(1)].

(2) YSTRADFFYN CHAPEL OF EASE, LLANFAIR AS Y BRYN.
Consecrated before 1800.
Endowed: fees £1. 'I am only Curate. I can't say what the value is. Incumbent Rev. J. Jones Llansadwrn Llandovery South Wales'.
Space: free 90.
Present: morn. 25 scholars; aft. 48.
Average (12 *months*): morn. from 25 to 30; aft. from 70 to 90.

Remarks: This Chapel stands in such isolated place that a large congregation can't be expected And the population much scattered.

John Williams. Curate.

Lewis: sub. Llanvair-ar-y-bryn: the chapel is called Nant-y-Bai, situated in the township of Rhandi Ystrad-Ffin: perpetual curacy, endowed with £200 private benefaction, and £1,000 royal bounty; net income £59; patron, Earl of Cawdor.

C & C: 1 service in Welsh performed by the curate.

I & C: incumbent not resident: curate resides at Cilycwm, 6½ miles distant, and has stipend of £45.

[This schedule is misplaced: it should be with 587. 6. 4.]

(3) CAPEL CYNFAL SCHOOLROOM, LLANFAIR AR Y BRYN.
Licensed in 1849, by the Bishop.
Erected by subscription & grants from the Committee of Council & National Society.
Endowed: nil.
Space: free 120.
Present: even. 86.

John Jones. Curate.

(4) PENTRE TY GWYN. INDEPENDENT.
Erected 1749.
Space: free 90; other 240.
Present: morn. 200; aft. 181 scholars; even. 154.

William Jones. Minister.

[Note: (7) should be included here.]

2 Rhandir-Canol Hamlet.

Popn. 162 males, 149 females: total 311.

(5) GOSEN. CALVINISTIC METHODIST.
Erected 1844.
Space: other 264.
Present: morn. 90 scholars; aft. 150; even. 105 scholars.
Average (12 *months*): morn. 80 scholars; aft. 150; even. 100 scholars.

*Thomas Morgans. Deacon.
Rees Evans.
Llanchinfa.

[*signed with a mark]

(6) SALEM. CALVINISTIC METHODIST.
Erected 1829 in lieu of another.
Space: free 126; standing 100.
Present: morn. 147; aft. 121 scholars; even. 161.
Average (12 *months*): morn. 160; aft. 121 scholars.

William Jenkins. Minister.
Llansawel, Nr. Llandovery.

(7) BETHEL.   INDEPENDENT.
Erected 1841.
Space: free 126; other 128.*
Average: morn. 160.

Wm. Rees.   Minister.

[Endorsed: see letter]
[Note: this schedule is misplaced.]

3 Rhandir-Uchaf Hamlet.
Popn. 137 males, 136 females: total 273.
[No returns]

4 Rhandir-Abbot.
Area: 7,618 acres. *Popn.* 325 males, 344 females: total 669.
[No returns]

[End of Llanfairarybryn Subdistrict]

7 LLANWRTYD (Subdistrict).   Co. Brecon.
Area: 14,555 acres. *Popn.* 317 males, 367 females: total 684.

1 Llandulas in Tyr Abbot Parish.
Area: 3,220 acres. *Popn.* 64 males, 67 females: total 131.

(1) LLANDULAS PARISH CHURCH OR NEW CHURCH IN TYR ABBOT.
Consecrated before 1800.
Endowed: land £44; permanent endowment £6. 10. of money fm. Queen
Anne's Bounty.
Space: free 80; other Reading Room 50.
Present: morn. 27.
Average (12 months): morn. 35.
Remarks: The service is always morning in Winter & alternately on times
in the Summer Months & better attended in Summer being as the locality
is so high and mountainous.

Henry Morgan.   Perpetual Curate.

Lewis: sub. Newchurch in Tir Abbot, otherwise Llandulas, co. Brecon: perpetual
curacy, endowed with £1,000 royal bounty, and with £200 in money, and £20 per
annum by Sackville Gwynne, Esq.: patron, Col. Gwynne of Glanbrân, the
impropriator; net income £47.

C & C: 1 service in Welsh performed by the incumbent.

I & C: not resident.

ICBS: grant of £100 in 1830.

[2-3]   Llanwrtyd Parish, consisting of [2] Clawdd-madog Hamlet, and [3] Llechweddor Hamlet.
Area of the whole parish: 11,335 acres. *Popn.* 253 males, 300 females: total 553.

2   Clawdd-madog Hamlet.
Popn. 116 males, 137 females: total 253.

(2)   Llanwrtyd Parish Church, commonly called Llanwrtyd Church.
Endowed: tithe £60.
Space: free 250.
Present: morn. 17 scholars; aft. 9.
Average: morn. 50 + 20 scholars.
Remarks: The Parish Church is in a sequestered place being 1¼ Mile from the Village so that in Winter few attend but in the Summer months the Attendants average from fifty to sixty.

> William Jenkins.   Vicar.
> Llangammarch.

Lewis: annexed to the vicarage of Llangammarch [599. 1. 3(6)].

C & C: 1 service in Welsh performed by the incumbent.

I & C: see under Llangammarch.

(3)   Gelynos Chapel.   Independents.
Erected before 1800.
Space: free 288; standing 50.
Present: morn. 103; aft. 37 scholars; even. 46.
Average (12 months): general congregation 150; scholars 62.
Remarks: I am of the opinion that the said Chapel will accomodate sitting Room for 276 in the said 48 pews and also Forms or Seats for the accomodation of 150—also free space or standing Room for 50 with moveable Forms insomuch that the sd. Chapel will contain in all 476 that is accomodation for so many.

> John Griffiths.   Minister.
> Llanwrtyd.

3   Llechweddor Hamlet.
Popn. 137 males, 163 females: total 300.

(4)   Bethesda Chapel.   Calvinistic Methodist.
Erected 1808.
Space: free 100; other 220; standing 200.
Present: morn. 140; aft. 143 scholars; even. 130.
Average: general congregation 150; scholars 140.

Remarks: The Sunday School had Commenced before the present Chapel. The Total of the Congregation 200. The Total number also of the Sunday School. 163.

John Winston. Deacon.
Llanwrtyd.

[End of Llanwrtyd Subdistrict]

8 CILYCWM (Subdistrict)
Area: 17,300 acres. *Popn.* 721 males, 766 females: total 1,487.

1 Cilycwm Parish.
Area and *popn.* as for the Subdistrict.

(1) LLANFIHANGEL CILYCWM PARISH CHURCH.
Endowed: fees £3.
Space: free 59.
Present: morn. 198 + 204; even. 122.
Average (12 months): morn. 100 to 220 + 70 to 100 scholars; even. 110 to 130.
Remarks: The parish is unfortunately about 17 miles in length and the parishioners from the extreme points cannot be expected to attend the parish church.

John Williams. Vicar.

Lewis: sub Kilycwm: perpetual curacy, net income of £142, of which £10 derived from tithes and remainder from land and QAB: patron, Thynne Howe Gwynne, Esq.
C & C: 1 service partially in Welsh performed by the incumbent.
I & C: no return.

(2) SOAR CHAPEL. CALVINISTIC METHODIST.
Erected 1740.
Space: free 200; other 68; standing 200.
Present: morn. 65 scholars; aft. 274; even. 86.
Average: morn. 65 scholars; aft. 274; even. 86.

William Jones. Elder.
Shoemaker.

(3) SMYRNA. PARTICULAR BAPTIST.
Erected 1828.
Space: free 12; other 126.
Present: morn. 60; aft. 41 scholars; even. 81.
Average (12 months): morn. 65; aft. 43 scholars; even. 80.

John Williams. Minister.
Llandovery.

(4) CWMSARNDDU CHAPEL.   PARTICULAR BAPTIST.
Erected 1812.
Space: free 36; other 126; standing 12 or 15.
Present: morn. 28 + 75 scholars; aft. 75 scholars; even. 48 + 75 scholars.
Average (12 *months*): morn. 94 + 70 scholars; aft. 70 scholars; even. 94 + 70 scholars.

David Jones.   Minister.
Cnwchdeiliog.

(5) BWLCHYRHIW.   PARTICULAR BAPTIST.
Erected before 1800.
Space: morn. 33 + 39 scholars.
Average (12 *months*): morn. 50 + 44 scholars.
Remarks: This chapel is very old it is erected about the year 1711 and there is a worship in it ever since. But the congregation is very uncertain because it is situated among the Mountains, some time of the year it is Populous and some time not, at the present time it is very little because the weather is cold and wet.

David Jones.   Deacon.
Bwlchyrhiw Chapel.

(6) SION CHAPEL.   PARTICULAR BAPTIST.
Erected 1829.
Space: free 150; standing 100.
Present: aft. 84 + 65 scholars.
Average (12 *months*): aft. 120 + 70 scholars.

Morgan Lewis.   Deacon.

[End of Cilycwm Subdistrict]

9 CONWIL-CAYO (Subdistrict)
Area: 41,785 acres. *Popn.* 1,095 males, 1,103 females: total 2,198.

1 Conwil-Cayo Parish.
Area and *popn.* as for the Subdistrict.

(1) CRUGYBAR, CAYO.   INDEPENDENT.
Erected before 1800, re-erected 1837.
Space: free 72; other 348.
Present: morn. 222; aft. 66 scholars; even. 133.
Average: morn. 200; aft. 60 to 70 scholars; even. 120.

Evan Jones.   Minister.
Nr. Llandovery.

(2) CAYO PARISH CHURCH.
Endowed: fees £5.
Space: free 180; other 120.
Present: even. 50.
Average (12 *months*): even. 60 to 100.

> Benj. Miasden. Minister.
> Pumpsaint.

Lewis: vicarage with that of Llansawel [588. 1. 1(3)] annexed; rated at £5; in the patronage of the crown: net income £224, with a glebe-hous; impropriate tithes commuted for £400, subject to rates, averaging £12. 13. 10½: vicarial tithes commuted for a rent-charge of £142. 10., subject to rates averaging £6. 6.; glebe of 50 acres, valued at £30.

C & C: 1 service in Welsh performed by the curate.

I & C: incumbent not resident: curate resides in the glebe-house and has stipend of £150.

(3) TYNEWYDD ALIA[S] CAYO CHAPEL. CALVINISTIC METHODIST.
Erected before 1800.
Space: free 72; other 67.
Present: morn. 197; aft. 43 scholars; even. 102.
Average (12 *months*): morn. 290; aft. 67 scholars; even. 110.

> Daniel Williams. Local Preacher.
> Cayo.

(4) SALEM. BAPTIST.
Erected 1828.
Space: free 112; other 87; standing 50.
Present: morn. 60; aft. 125.
Average (12 *months*): general congregation 145; scholars 55.

> Timothy Jones. Minister.
> Ffinnant, Pumpsaint.

(5) BETHEL. BAPTIST.
Erected 1834.
Space: free 150; other 160; standing 50.
Present: morn. 244 + 56 scholars.
Average (12 *months*): morn. 200 + 80 scholars.

> Timothy Jones. Minister.

(6) SARON. CALVINISTIC METHODIST.
Erected 1838.
Space: free 250; other 10.
Present: morn. 10.
Average (12 *months*): morn. 80 + 30 scholars.

> David Harry. Deacon.
> Gellynewydd. Pumpsaint.

(7) CWRT. CALVINISTIC METHODIST.
Erected before 1800.
Present: morn. 80 scholars; aft. 130.
Average (6 *months*): morn. 60 scholars; aft. 120.

> David Evans. Steward.
> Glanmeddyg, Pumpsaint.

[End of Cayo Subdistrict and end of Llandovery District]

588   LLANDILOFAWR (District)

Area: 97,207 acres. *Popn.* 8,651 males, 9,317 females: total 17,968.

1 TALLEY (Subdistrict)
Area: 17,184 acres. *Popn.* 1,019 males, 1,037 females: total 2,056.

1 Llansawel Parish.
Area: 10,017 acres. *Popn.* 535 males, 516 females: total 1,051.

(1) LLANSAWEL CHAPEL.   CALVINISTIC METHODIST.
Erected before 1800.
Space: free 157; other 57; standing 250.
Present: aft. 303; even. 300.
Average: morn. 250. 163 scholars; aft. M 100; even. F 63.

> James Davies.   Deacon.
> Troesgotta, Nr. Llandilo.

[Signed with a mark]

(3) LLANSAWEL PARISH CHURCH, HAMLET OF GENOL.
Endowed: tithe £105; glebe £5.
Space: Gallery free; other on pews 30 x 6 = 180.
Present: morn. 55.
Average (12 *months*): morn. 70 to 75.

> Benj. Mensden.   Minister.
> Pumpsaint.

Lewis: vicarage, annexed to that of Gayo [587. 9. 1(2)]; tithes commuted for £334, of which £232 are payable to the impropriator, subject to rates averaging £6. 4. 6., and £102 to the vicar, subject to rates averaging £4. 15. 5.; glebe of 4 acres, valued at £4.

C & C: 1 service in Welsh performed by the curate.

I & C: see *sub* Conwil-Cayo [587. 9. 1(2))].

[The above follows 588. 1. 2(1), having been wrongly bound and numbered.]

2 Talley Parish.
Area: 7,167 acres. *Popn.* 484 males, 521 females: total 1,005.

(2)   St Michaels Tally Parish Church.
Endowed: land £120; tithe £8; permanent endowment £8.
Space: free 115; other 250.
Present: morn. 70 + 60 scholars; even. 40.
Remarks: The weather being very raw and cold the attendance on 30th was below average.

David Lewes Jones.   Curate.

Lewis: perpetual curacy, endowed with £800 royal bounty, and £1,000 parliamentary grant; net income £127: patron, Rev. William Thomas Nicholl, heir of the late Ven. Thomas Beynon, Archdeacon of Carmarthen, who purchased the tithes and advowson of the living from the family of Abermarles: impropriate tithes commuted for £299. 15., subject to rates averaging £9. 10; glebe of 3½ acres, valued at £11. 3. 6. All sittings except 2 belong to the rate-payers; the seats in the gallery are free.

C & C: 2 services, partially in Welsh in the morn., wholly in Welsh in the even., performed by the curate.

I & C: incumbent not resident: curate, who resides in the parish, has stipend of £75.

[Return wrongly bound in with Llansawel parish.]

(4)   Eskernant Chapel.   Calvinistic Methodists.
Erected before 1800.
Space: free 42; other 240.
Present: morn. 276 scholars; aft. 300.

David Walters.   Elder.
Pantyresker, Nr. Talley.

(5)   Providence Cwmdu Chapel.   Particular Baptists.
Erected 1789; rebuilt and enlarged un 1839.
Space: free 24; other 324; standing 98.
Present: morn. 200; aft. 55 scholars; even. 150.
Average (12 *months*): morn. 286; aft. 55 scholars; even. 200.
Remarks: The attendants having lately decreased through the want of a minister being elected by the chapel.
[Signed: T.J.]

Thomas Griffiths.   Secretary.
Ffosyhwyad, Nr. Llandilo.

[End of Talley Subdistrict]

2 LLANFYNYDD (Subdistrict)
Area: 11,790 acres. *Popn.* 742 males, 798 females: total 1,540.

1 Brechfa Parish.
Area: 530 acres. *Popn.* 55 males, 52 females: total 107.

(1) St Teilo Brechfa Parish Church.
Endowed: land £90; tithe £21.
Space: free 100; other 10.
Present: aft. 123.
Remarks: The Service in the Church at Brecgfa is held alternately morning and afternoon. The Fees (surplice) are those received during the 12 months next preceeding the 30th March.

> Joshua Davies. Officiating Minister.

Lewis: rectory not in charge, endowed with £600 royal bounty; net income £72: patrons, alternately George Morgan, Esq., and the representative of the late Mrs. Elizabeth Hughes.
C & C: 1 service in Welsh performed by the curate.
I & C: vacant.
ICBS: grant of £50 in 1848.

(2) Brechfa Chappel. Methodists.
Erected before 1800.
Space: free 6; other 170; standing 150.
Present: morn. 102; even. 24 scholars.
Average (12 *months*): morn. 120; even. 40 scholars.

> David Thomas. Deacon.
> Gilfach Llanegwedd.

[Sign. in a different hand.]

2 Llanfynydd Parish.
Area: 10,744 acres. *Popn.* 659 males, 717 females: total 1,376.

(3) Llanfynydd Parish Church.
Endowed: Eccles. Comm. grant £17; tithe £121. 13. 4*d.* Queen Anne's Bounty £11. 10. 8*d.*
Space: other 300.
Present: morn. 98.
Average (12 *months*): morn. 100.
Remarks: While I am engaged in doing duty at another church, the members have a prayer meeting at the schoolroom at 4 o'clock.

> William Harris. Vicar.

Lewis: prepend in the Collegiate Church of Brecknock, annexed to the precentorship,

and rated at £18. The living is a discharged vicarage, rated at £6. 13. 4.;
endowed with £384. 14. 5 parliamentary grant; net income £121; patron, the Bp.:
tithes commuted for £365, of which £243. 6. 8 or two-thirds are payable to the
prependary, and £121. 13. 4 or one-third to the vicar.

C & C: 1 service in Welsh, performed by the incumbent.

I & C: incumbent resident.

(4) SPITE. CALVINISTIC METHODIST.
Erected 1771; rebuilt 1838.
Space: free 72; other 246.
Present: morn. 127; aft. 94 scholars; even. 103.
Average (12 *months*): morn. 150; aft. 70; even. 120.
Remarks: Space available for Public Worship is 29 feet by 34 feet in the
clear. Number of sittings already Provided Including Free and other Sit-
tings 53. and are adapted to Contain 6 persons in each seat for sitting.

David Williams.   Deacon.

(5) AMOR, IN THE VILLAGE OF LLANFYNYDD. CALVINISTIC BAPTISTS.
Erected 1830.
Space: free 24; other 156.
Present: morn. 45 scholars; aft. 90.
Average (12 *months*): morn. 40 scholars; aft. 90; even. 60.
Remarks: Space available for public worship: Number of Sittings already
provided Including Free and other Sittings 30 and are adapted to contain
six persons in each seat (or sittings).

David Jones.   Deacon.
Hafodforgan.

(6) CARMEL. CALVINISTIC METHODISTS.
Erected 1850.
Space: free 28; other 76.
Present: morn. 40 scholars; aft. 70; even. 40.
Average: morn. 50 scholars; aft. 90; even. 40.
Remarks: Space available for Public Worship is 20 feet by 20 feet in the
clear. Number of Sittings already Provided Including Free and other sittings
is 26 and are adapted to contain 4 persons in each seat for sittings.

Thomas Thomas.   Deacon.

[Returns (4), (5), (6) are in the same hand except for the signs.]

3 Llanfihangel-Cilfargen Parish.
Area: 516 acres. *Popn.* 28 males, 29 females: total 57.

(7) LLANFIHANGEL VACH KILFARGEN PARISH CHURCH.
Endowed: land £76; tithe £32. 1*s.*; glebe 10*s.*
Present: aft. 15.
Average (12 *months*): aft. about 20 sometimes more.
Remarks: This Parish is about the smallest in the Diocese. Its population at the last Census 65. The poor and road-rates and property tax average about £7. 10*s* or £8 a year.

W.Th.Nicholls. Minister.

Lewis: discharged rectory, rated at £1. 6. 8; endowed with £200 private benefaction and £600 royal bounty: patron, Earl Cawdor: tithes commuted for £32; glebe of a little more than an acre, valued at £1. 7. 6 per annum: net income £116. Church rebuilt about 1822 at the sole expense of Rev. Thomas Beynon, a former rector: pewed and all sittings appropriated.

C & C: 1 service in Welsh performed by the incumbent.

I & C: incumbent not resident.

[End of Llanfynydd Subdistrict]

3 LLANGATHEN (Subdistrict)
Area: 17,843 acres. *Popn.* 1,434 males, 1,609 females: total 3,043.

1 Llanegwad Parish.
Area: 12,330 acres. *Popn.* 945 males, 1,063 females: total 2,008.

(1) LLANEGWAD, an ancient Parish Church of the Norman Gothic style, & rebuilt on the same foundations & in the same style, 1849.
Situated in the Hamlet of Egwad, Llanegwad.
Endowed: tithe £299. 5*s.* 4*d.*
Space: free for the poor 141; free 169. Besides Benches in the Chancel.
Present: morn. 210 + 40 scholars; even. 160.
Average (12 *months*): morn. about 250; even. about 270.
Remarks: The Church will contain when perfectly full about 500, & the appearance of the congregation is more than two thirds full. There are three Schools in different Parts of the Parish in connection with the Established Church.

Eleazer Evans. Vicar.

Lewis: vicarage, rated at £8. 13. 4.; patron, the Bp.: tithes commuted for £626. 2., of which £326. 16. 8 are payable to the impropriator, T. D. Berington, Esq., and £299. 5. 4. to the vicar.

C & C: 2 services in Welsh performed by the incumbent.

I & C: incumbent resident.

ICBS: grant of £54 in 1847

(2)   Horeb Chapel, Hamlet of Miros.   Independents.
Erected 1830.
Space: free 60; other 80.
Present: aft. 66 + 25 scholars; even. 35 + 25 scholars.
Average (12 *months*): aft. 10 + 40 scholars; even. 55 + 25 scholars.
Remarks: The 'Free Space' is furnished with benches for Accomodation.
The attendance on March 30th was much less than usual owing to the
Inclemency of the weather.

> John Richards.   Deacon.
> Penrhiwgale, Llanegwad.
> At the King's Arms, Carmarthen.

(3)   Pont yr Ynyswen Chapel, Lechgron Hamlet.   Calvinistic
Methodist.
Space: free 60; other 95; standing 60.
Present: aft. 86 + 20 scholars; even. 80 + 16 scholars.
Average (12 *months*): even. 60 + 90 scholars.

> Rich. Thomas.   Steward.
> Waingranod, Llanegwad.

(4)   Cwmbran.   Wesleyan Methodist.
Erected 1812.
Space: free 10; other 110.
Present: morn. 80; aft. 30 scholars; even. 120.
Average: morn. 71; aft. 30; even. 115.

> Joseph Jones.   Wesleyan Minister.

(5)   Siloam.   Independent Society dissenting party.
Erected 1826.
Space: free 250 [deleted]; other 45; gallery free.
Present: morn. 180; even. 198 + 90 scholars.

> David Williams.   Daecon.
> Llwchgwyn.

2   Llangathen Parish.
Area: 5,513 acres. *Popn.* 489 males, 546 females: total 1,035.

(6)   Llangathin Parish Church.
Endowed: tithe £130.
Space: free 390.
Present: morn. 90 + 27 scholars.
Average (12 *months*): morn. 110 + 35 scholars.

> David Evans.   Vicar.
> Broad Oak.

Lewis: discharged vicarage, rated at £6. 13. 4., endowed with £200 parliamentary grant; patron and appropriator, Bishop of Chester: tithes commuted for £390, of which £260 are payable to the Bishop, subject to rates averaging £5. 6. 8., and £130 to the vicar, subject to rates averaging £2. 13. 4.

C & C: 1 service in Welsh performed by the curate.

I & C: incumbent not resident: curate, who resides in the parish, has a stipend of £70.

(7) ELIM CHAPPEL.   BABTIST.
Erected 1817.
Space: free 56; other 144; standing 150.
Present: morn. 90; aft. 37 scholars; even. 98.
Average (12 months): general congregation 130; scholars 80 to 90.
Remarks: A day school and Sunday School has lately been arisen in the Neighbourhood within half a Mile.

> John Davies.   Minister.
> Penllwyne.

(8) COLLEGE.   CALVINISTIC METHODIST.
Erected before 1800.
Space: other 25.
Present: morn. 150; aft. 81 scholars; even. 200.
Average (12 months): morn. 150; aft. 81 scholars; even. 200.

> William Morgan.   Deacon.

(9) CROSS INN.   CALVINISTIC METHODISTS.
Erected 1792; re-erected 1830 [deleted].
Space: free 200; other 60.
Present: morn. 177 scholars; aft. 231.
Remarks: Cross Inn Chaple is Situated near the Confines of the parishes of Llangathen and Llanegwad, nearly half the congregation from each parish.

> David Simpson.   Steward.
> Glantowy.

(10) CARTHENDY CHURCH, LLANGARTHEN.
Erected 1836.
Space: free 100; other 8.
Usual number of attendants: morn. 100 + 40 scholars; aft. 80 + 40 scholars.

> *Informant:* Wm Morgan.

[Informant's form]

Lewis: built by Rev. George Wade Green, of Court Henry, at his own expence for the accomodation of his own family and neighbourhood.

[End of Llangathen Subdistrict]

4 LLANDILO (Subdistrict)
Area: 20,909 acres. *Popn.* 2,215 males, 2,597 females: total 4,812.

1 Llandyfeisant Parish.
Area: 1,551 acres. *Popn.* 119 males, 128 females: total 247.

(1) LLANDIFEISANT PARISH CHURCH.
Endowed: Queen Anne's Bounty £6.
Average (12 *months*): aft. 60.

Griffin Williams.   Minister.

Lewis: sub Llandeveyson: donative, endowed with £200 private benefaction, and £1,000 royal bounty; net income £51: patron and impropriator, Earl Cawdor, whose tithes have been commuted for £150, and who also has a glebe of 30 acres valued at £9 per annum.

C & C: 1 service, Welsh and English on alternate Sundays.

I & C: incumbent resident.

2 Part of Llandilofawr Parish, including Llandilo Town.
Area: 19,358 acres. *Popn.* 2,096 males, 2,469 females: total 4,565.

(2) ST. TEILO; LLANDILO-FAWR PARISH CHURCH.
Endowed: tithe £512.
Space: free (for adults) 293; (for children) 244; other 294.
Present: morn. 173 + 109 scholars; aft. 136 + 27 scholars; even. 173.

J. W. Pugh.   Vicar.

Lewis: vicarage, endowed with one-third of all the tithes, rated at £16; patron, the Bp; impropriator of the remainder of the tithes, D. J. Parker, Esq.: tithes commuted for £1,536. 12., of which £1,024. 8. is payed to the impropriator, and £512. 4. to the vicar.

C & C: 2 services, in Welsh in the aft., performed by the curate.

I & C: incumbent resident: 2 curates with stipends of £100 and £120 respectively.

ICBS: grant of £220 in 1847.

(3) TRINITY CHAPEL, COMMONLY CALLED TALIARIS.
Consecrated before 1800.
Endowed: land £51; permanent endowment £56.
Space: free 48; other 16.
Present: morn. 50 + 30 scholars.
Remarks: Many of the scholars sit in the North part of the Church on benches provided for them.

John Williams.   Minister.
Taliaris Parsonage.

Lewis: sub Llandilo-fawr: chapel enlarged by the late Lord Robert Seymour, and endowed by him with a house and 8 acres of land; minister entitled to an annual salary of £11 out of the estate of Taliaris, and other chapel expences provided for out of the same bequest.

C & C: 1 service, partially in English and Welsh, performed by the incumbent.

I & C: incumbent resident.

(4) BRYN AMMAN CHURCH SCHOOL.
Bryn Amman is only a schoolroom with a day school and a Sunday School.
Sunday Scholars 50 to 60.
Day Scholars 100 to 120.

[No sign.]

[Endorsed: Church of England]

(5) TABERNACLE, FAIRFACH NEAR LLANDILOFAWR. INDEPENDENTS.
Erected 1817; re-erected 1839.
Space: free 172; other 235.
Present: morn. 218; even. 319.
Remarks: The figures crossed out in the sittings columns [i.e. 27 and 48] was in consequence of my filling the Columns with No. of Pews in the first instance and not sittings.

James Thomas. Secretary.
Grocer, Llandilo.

(6) LLWYNYRONEN, HAMLET OF TREGIB. WESLEYAN METHODISTS.
Erected 1810; re-erected 1850.
Space: free 100; other 110.
Present: morn. 75; aft. 37 scholars; even. 95.
Average: morn. 95; aft. 40 scholars; even. 95.

Rees Davies. Steward.
Maesyffynon.

(7) ONNENFAWR, TREGIB. UNITARIANISM.
Erected 1840.
Space: free 100; standing about 50.
Present: morn. 50.
Average (12 *months*): morn. 45.

Titus Evans. Minister.
King Street, Carmarthen.

(8) BETHEL, PONTBRENARAETH. BAPTIST.
Erected before 1800.
Space: free 80; other 135; standing 80.
Present: morn. 80; aft. 88 scholars; even. 106.
Average: general congregation 100; scholars 50.

Thomas Lloyd. Minister.
Cwmifor.

(9) HERMON. INDEPENDANTS.
Erected 1812.
Space: 35 pews and large Galary; standing 200.
Present: morn. 400; aft. school; even. from 400 to 450.
Average: general congregation 450; scholars 77.
Remarks: 200 members belonging to this place of worship.

David Williams.   Deacon of Hermon.
Chappel, Penhill, Nr. Llandilo.

(10) SALEM. INDEPENDANTS.
Erected 1830.
Space: free 145; other 148; standing 120.
Present: morn. 166; aft. 88 scholars; even. 142.
Average: morn. 166; aft. 88 scholars; even. 142.

David Jones.   Minister.
Pantarfon.

(11) CWMIFOR. BAPTIST.
Erected before 1800.
Present: morn. 140; aft. 89 scholars; even. 160.

John Morgans.   Deacon.
Maesgwastad.

(12) SILO, PENYBANK INDEPENDANTS OR CONGREGATIONALISTS.
Erected: Built 1848 in Lew of Building 181[?].
Space: free 150; other 162; standing 72.
Present: morn. 80; aft. 72 scholars; even. 103.
Remarks: The Religious Denomination is Independants or Congregation-
alishts as it is down in the column also built 1848 in lew of building 1820.
I thought it proper to rite these above lest the writing in the colums should
be missed understood.

William Harries.   Deacon.
Llandilo Post Office, Glanmyddyfi.

(13) EBENEZER. BAPTIST.
Erected 1829.
Space: free 40.
Present: morn. 61; even. 111.

Z. Davies.   Minister.

(14) WESLEYAN CHAPEL. WESLEYAN.
Erected before 1800.
Space: free 80; other 200; standing 30.
Present: morn. 73; even. 195.

Thomas Williams.   Society Steward.

(15) SALEM. CAL[VINISTIC] METHODISTS.
Erected before 1800.
Space: free 98; other 197.
Present: morn. school; aft. 208; even. 187.
Average (12 *months*): morn. school; aft. 210; even. 250.

> Benjamin Davies Thomas. Minister.

(16) CAPEL ISAAC. INDEPENDENT.
Erected: 1846 in lieu of a building of 1790 which was built on the site of one of 1672.
Space: free 143; other 216; standing 50.
Present: morn. 214; aft. 159 scholars; even. 239.
Remarks: The 159 Sunday Scholars Comprises the Children of all the branches of the Sunday School belonging to the Congregation.

> William Thomas. Minister.

[End of Llandilo Subdistrict]

5 LLANDEBIE (Subdistrict)
Area: 19,481 acres. *Popn.* 2,341 males, 3,276 females: total 6,517

1 Part of Llandilofawr Parish.
Area: 6,250 acres. *Popn.* 614 males, 579 females: total 1,193.

(1) CHRIST CHURCH CWM AMMAN.
The District attached to Llandilofawr made up of parts of Five different Parishes viz. Llandilofawr, Llandybie, Bettws, Llanguick and Llangadock.
Consecrated 1842. This Church was consecrated for the new District Distant from the nearest Church about 5 miles.
Erected by grant from Her Majesty's Com. £400

    Incorporated Society   300

    Lord Dynevor   500

    Subscription   800

    Total cost for Church and house £2,000
Endowed: land £25; tithe £125; glebe £10; fees £5.
Space: free 499; other 46.
Present: morn. 210 + 60 scholars; even. 106.
Remarks: The congregation in the evenings is always smaller during the short days because we have no proper access to the Church, being situated between two rivers.

> James Richard Griffiths. Incumbent.

Lewis: [no details of endowments given.]
C & C: 3 services, always in Welsh except in the morn., performed by the incumbent.
I & C: incumbent resident.
ICBS: grant of £300 in 1841.

(2) LLANDYFÂN.

This Chapel no doubt belonged to the Established Church originally, but afterwards fell into the hands of the Unitarians, and in the year 1840 or 1841 restored again to the Church.

There is no District attached to this place.

Licensed about ten years ago, as an additional place of worship.

How or by whom erected: I cannot say.

There is no endowment attached to Llandyfân.

Space: free 150.

Present: aft. 106 + 47 scholars.

> James Richard Griffiths.
> Officiating Minister.

Lewis: annexed to the church of Llandilo-fawr through the munifiscence of Lord Dynevor.

(3) BETHEL, CHRIST CHURCH, LLANDILO. INDEPENDENT.

Erected 1773.

Space: free 500; standing 1500.

Present: morn. 349; aft. 83 scholars; even. 259.

Average (12 *months*): morn. 500; even. 250.

> John Davies. Minister.
> Cwmamman.

(4) TABERNACL. CALVINISTIC METHODIST.

Erected 1841.

Space: free 250; other 300; standing 380.

Present: morn. 75 scholars; aft. 137; even. 59.

Average (12 *months*): morn. 900; aft. 1860; even. 720.

> Francis Francis. Deacon.
> Cwmaman.

2 Llanfihangel-Aberbythych Parish.

Area: 6,036 acres. *Popn.* 397 males, 436 females: total 860.

(5) LLANFIHANGEL ABERBYTHICK PARISH CHURCH.

Rebuilt at the expence of the Earl of Cawdor. Total cost unknown.

Endowed: land £50; tithe £8; Queen Anne's Bounty £28; stipend £10.

Space: free 210.

Present: aft. 114 + 45 scholars.

> Geo. Griff Williams. Officiating Minister.

Incumbent's name is Rev. D. H. J. Williams, Llwynhelyg, Llandilo.

Lewis: perpetual curacy, endowed with £200 private benefaction, £400 royal bounty, and £800 parliamentary grnat: patron and impropriator, Earl Cawdor, whose tithes have been commuted for a rent-charge of £207. 10: repaired in 1763.

C & C: 1 service in Welsh performed by the incumbent.

I & C: incumbent not resident.

(6) CEFNBRACH CHAPPEL. CALVINISTIC METHODIST.
Erected 1749.
Space: free 24; other 138. '4 long benches for Poor people, 23 pews'.
Present: morn. 41 scholars; aft. 92; even. 59.
Average: morn. 50 scholars; aft. 110; even. 90.

> David Davies. Elder.
> Bryn Martyn, Nr. Llandilo.

(7) MILO. INDEPENDENT.
Erected 1830; re-erected 1850.
Space: about half free. 27 Pews Private Individuals.
Present: morn. 134; aft. 100; even. 156.
Average: general congregation 140; scholars 89.

> Thomas Jenkins. Officiating Minister.
> Penygroes, Llandybie.

(8) CHARMEL. BABTIST. LLANVIHANGELABERTHICK.
Erected 1833.
Space: all free space.
Present: morn. school; aft. 20; even. 86.
Average: general congregation 108; scholars 30.

> Benjamin Thomas. Officiating Minister.

(9) [illegible]RCH CWMAMMAN.
Consecrated 1843.
Space: free 545; other 499.
Usual number of attendants: morn. 150 to 200 + 70 to 100 scholars; even.
100 to 150.

> *Informant:* William Jones.

[Informant's form: this might be a duplicate of 588. 5. 1(1).]

3 Llandebie Parish.

Area: 10,710 acres. *Popn.* 1,406 males, 1,479 females: total 2,885.

(10) LLANDEBIE PARISH CHURCH.
Endowed: tithe £175. 0. 10*d*; glebe £10.
Space: free 300; other 300.
Present: morn. 300; even. 350.
Average (4 months): morn. about 300; even. about 350.

> Lewis Morgan. Vicar.

Lewis: discharged vicarage, rated at £4; endowed with one-third of all the tithes, and £200 parliamentary grant; net income £99, with a glebe-house: patron, the Bp: impropriators of the remainder of the tithes, Precentor and Chapter of St. David's, whose tithes have been commuted for a rent-charge of £525, subject to rates averaging £12. 14.

C & C: 1 service partially in Welsh, performed by the curate.

I & C: incumbent resident: curate has stipend of £60.

(11) EBENEZER, CROSS INN. BAPTIST.
Erected 1850-1.
Space: free 60; other 138; standing 50.
Present: morn. 60; even. 100.
Remarks: Sunday School to be commenced immediately on the completion of the Building.

> John Thomas. Secretary.
> Railway Station, Cross Inn.

(12) CROSS INN INDEPENDANT CHAPPEL.
Erected before 1800.
Present: morn. 280; aft. 172 scholars; even. 226.
Average: morn. 330; aft. 166 scholars.

> Morgan Morgans. Deacon.
> Parkhenry, Llandebie.

(13) SOAR, LLANDEFAIN. BAPTIST.
Erected 1808.
Space: free 90; other 162; Free Space 14 ft by 6 ft.
Present: morn. 250; even. 200 + 50 scholars.
Average (6 *months*): general congregation 200; scholars 50.
Remarks: Rebuilt 1849.

> Thomas Thomas. Secretary.
> Pistill, Nr. Llandebie.

(14) WAENLLAN CHAPEL. WELSH WESLEYAN METHODIST.
Erected before 1810.
Space: free 5; other 105.
Present: morn. 45 scholars; aft. 60; even. 30.
Average (12 *months*): morn. 50 scholars; aft. 85; even. 32.

> Rees Morris. Secretary.
> Cilcoll, Nr. Llandebie.

(15) LLANDEBIE CHAPEL. CALVINISTIC METHODIST.
Erected 1829.
Space: free 5; other 100.
Present: morn. 46 scholars; aft. 38; even. 19.
Average (12 *months*): morn. 40 scholars; aft. 80; even. 20.

> George Griffiths. Secretary.
> Draper & Grocer, Llandebie.

(16) HENDRE CHAPEL. CALVINISTIC METHODIST.
Erected 1812.
Space: free 108; other 114; standing 250.
Present: morn. 118; aft. 103 scholars; even. 157.

Average (12 *months*): morn. 200; aft. 120 scholars; even. 300.

John Morris. Secretary.
Dderwn, Llandebie.

(17)   [This return, for an Independent chapel, is missing.]

(18)   PENYGROES.   INDEPENDENT.
Erected 1825.
Space: free 454; standing 26 large sittings, large gallery, large standing room.*
Present: morn. 147; aft. 104 scholars; even. 158.
Average: morn. 200; aft. 134 scholars; even. 210.

John Evans. Deacon.
Near Llandebie.

[*See letter]

(19)   SARON, BLINOG HAMLET.   BAPTIST.
Erected 1814.
Space: all free.
Present: morn. 137; aft. 30 scholars; even. 78.
Remarks: Last Sunday we had no preacher, prayer meetings morning and evening. Our average about from 160 to 200.

Benjamin Thomas. Officiating Minister.
Tyrplasgwyn, Llandebie or otherwise
B. Thomas, Baptist Minister, Saron.

4   Bettws Parish.

Area: 6,465 acres. *Popn.* 824 males, 755 females: total 1,579.

(20)   BETTWS PARISH CHURCH.
Endowed: land £54; tithe £10; permanent endowment £34; fees £2.
Space: free 181.
Present: morn. 25 + 20 scholars; aft. 36.
Average (5 *months*): morn. 25; aft. 60.
Remarks: On the 30th March there was a Collection in the Church in behalf of the Society for the Propogation of the Gospel in Foreign. The afternoon congregation was much below the average on this account.

Richard Bowcott. Perpetual Curate.

Lewis: perpetual curacy, annexed to the vicarage of Llandebie [588. 5. 3(10)]; endowed with £800 royal vounty, and £1,000 parliamentfiry grant; net income £98.

C & C: 1 service in Welsh performed by the curate.

I & C: incumbent not resident; curate has a stipend of £60.

(21)   WESLEYAN METHODIST, PONTAMMAN.
Erected about 1840.
Space: free 72.
Present: morn. 35; even. 35.

N. Morris. Steward.
Pontamman Works, Nr. Llandilo.

(22)   SION CHAPEL.   WELSH CALVINISTIC METHODIST.
Erected before 1800.
Space: free 86; standing 120.
Present: morn. 101; even. 111.
Average (2 *months*)*:* general congregation 150; scholars 133.

William Evans.   Elder.
Weaver.
Bettws, near Cross Inn.

(23)   BETHESDA, CWAMMAN.   PARTICULAR BAPTIST.
Erected 1843.
Space: free 174; standing 200.
Present: morn. 256; aft. 54 scholars; even. 264.
Average (12 *months*)*:* morn. 240; aft. 54 scholars; even. 246.

David Jones.   Manager.

(24)   LATTER-DAY SAINTS, CWMAMMAN.
Space: free 100.
Present: aft. 3 + 15 scholars; even. 18 + 20 scholars.

John Griffith.   Elder.
Nr. Prince Albert Inn, Cwm Amman.

[End of Llandebie Subdistrict and End of Llandilofawr District]

Area: 172,546 acres. *Popn.* 17,982 males, 20,160 females: total 38,142.

1 LLANGENDEIRNE (Subdistrict)
Area: 48,501 acres. *Popn.* 4,288 males, 4,693 females: total 8,981.

1   Llanddarog Parish.
Area: 4,501 acres. *Popn.* 500 males, 536 females: total 1,036.

(1)   LLANDDAROG PARISH CHIRCH.
Endowed: land £90.
Space: other 54.
Present: morn. 150.
Remarks: The service in the Church is Morning and Afternoon alternately.

James Whitworth.   Curate.
Llannon, Near Llanelly.

Lewis: prebend in the collegiate church of Brecknock; rated at £10; patron, the Bp.; the living a perpetual curacy, endowed with £200 private benefaction, £400 royal bounty, and £1,200 parliamentary grant; net income £81; patron and appropriator, Prebendary of Llanddarog, whose tithes have been commuted for £319, subject to rates averaging £22. 14. 10½; glebe of 4 acres valued at £10. 13.

C & C: 1 service in Welsh.

I & C: incumbent not resident: curate, who resides at Llanon, 6 miles distant, has a stipend of £112 for this and Llanon.

(2)   CAPEL NEWYDD.   CALVINISTIC METHODIST.
Erected 1795.
Used also as a Day School.
Space: free 80; other 240; standing 80.
Present: aft. 84 scholars; even. 215.
Average: aft. 84 scholars; even. 213.

Richard Jones.   Elder.
Lodge, Llanddarog.

(3)   BETHLEHEM, PORTHYRHYD.   BAPTIST.
Erected 1817; re-erected 1842.
Space: free 44 by 34. Gallery except the front seats. Other, Floor except the large seats.
Present: morn. 165; aft. 75 scholars; even. 161.

Henry Davies.   Deacon.
Wernfraith, Llandarog.

(4) SOAR. CALVINISTIC METHODIST.
Erected 1834.
Space: free 120; standing 100.
Present: morn. 62; aft. 52 scholars.
Average (12 *months*): general congregation morn. 95; scholars, morn. 60.
Remarks: The cause was established in this district in 1776.

> Moses Gelly. Diacon.
> Manachlog.

(5) CHAPPEL SION, LLANDDROG. INDEPENDANT.
Erected before 1800.
Space: other 300; standing 400.
Present: morn. 250; aft. 103 scholars; even. 168.
Average (12 *months*): morn. 300; aft. 100 scholars; even. 200.

> John Anfield. Secretary.

2 Llanarthney Parish.

Area: 10,994 acres. *Popn.* 997 males, 1,079 females: total 2,076.

(6) LLANARTHNEY PARISH CHURCH.
Endowed: tithe [illegible]; glebe £1.
Space: free 170; other 70.
Average (6 *months*): morn. 170 + 60 scholars.
Remarks: There is an evening service held in the Summer months.

> George Griffith Williams. Curate.
> Llanddarog Cottages.

Lewis: prebend in the collegiate church of Brecknock, rated at £15; patron, the Bp.: living a discharged vicarage, valued at £8, and endowed with £200 royal bounty: net income £170.

C & C: 1 service in Welsh, save 1 a month [? in English].

I & C: with Llanllian Chapelry incumbent not resident; curate, who resides at Ynyslas, 2 miles distant, has stipend of £150.

[Note: there is no return for Llanllian Chapel]

(7) PENRHIWGOCH, LLANARTHNEY. PARTICULAR BAPTISTS.
Erected 1797.
Space: free 200; other 170; standing 60.
Present: morn. 300; even. 150.
Average (12 *months*): morn. 350.

> Benjamin Thomas. Minister.
> Penrhiwgoch.

(8) DALE CHAPPEL. CALVINIST METHODIST.
Erected 1814.
Space: free 100; other 37; standing about 100.
Present: morn. 105 scholars; aft. 132; even. 121.
Average: general congregation 130; scholars 100.

> Thomas Jones. Steward.
> Danyrallt.

(9) CAPPEL DEWI CHAPEL. CALVINISTIC METHODISTS.
Erected 1811.
Space: free 20; other 80; standing 1/6 of the Chapel.
Present: morn. 30 + 45 scholars; even. 28 + 24 scholars.

> John Evans. Deacon.
> Penddantwyn fawr.

(9A) NEW LLANLLUAN. CALVINISTIC METHODISTS.
Erected 1840.
Space: other 174; standing 18 feet by 6.
Present: morn. 106; aft. 108 scholars; even. 100.
Average: morn. 190; aft. 108 scholars; even. 100.

> William Stephens. Deacon.
> Dullgoed ucha.

3 Llangunnor Parish.
Area: 5,795 acres. *Popn.* 578 males, 579 females: total 1,157.

(10) LLANGUNNOR PARISH CHURCH.
Situated on Llangunnor Hill at the extremity of the Parish abutting on the
Towy River to the North.
Erected: The Nave of the Church was rebuilt about the year 1814. The
cost was defrayed by money borrowed at the time on credit of the Church
Rate, £400 of which including Principal and interest remains unpaid. Cost
defrayed, by Parochial rate, £800.
Endowed: land £1. 10s; tithe £225. 15. 3d; glebe £40; fees £2.
Space: free 250.
Present: morn. 180.
Average: aft. 60.
Remarks: There is no Sermon given at the Afternoon Service at four o'clock.
The Sunday School is kept between the hours of two and four every Sunday.
The children and adults remain during the Service.

> James Griffiths. Vicar & Officiating
> Minister.

Lewis: discharged vicarage rated at £3; endowed with £200 private benefaction,
£200 royal bounty; net income £225: patron, the Bp.: impropriator, Sir G. G.
Williams, Bart. Rebuilt about 1806.
C & C: 2 service, Welsh in the morning, partially in Welsh in the even. performed
by the incumbent.
I & C: incumbent resident.

(11) BABELL. WELSH CALVINISTIC METHODIST.
Erected 1834.
Space: free 200.
Present: even. 150.
Average (12 *months*): even. 160.
Remarks: The Building is too small for the present congregation & school.
There are two other services held at this place during the week: viz:-
including Monday & Friday evening.

James Lloyd.   Superintendant.

(12) PHILLADELPHIA. INDEPENDENT.
Erected 1809.
Space: free 120; other 264.
Present: morn. 350; aft. 212 scholars; even. 173.
Average: general congregation 400; scholars 238.

Evan Evans.   Minister.
Plasymynydd.

4 Llangendeirne Parish.

Area: 11,810 acres. *Popn.* 1,140 males, 1,283 females: total 2,423.

(13) LLANGENDEIRNE PARISH CHURCH.
Endowed: land £50; tithe £11. 13. 4*d*; permanent endowment (parl.
grant) £12. 11. 6*d*; fees £3. 10*s*.
Space: free 800.
Present: morn. 120 + 30 scholars; aft. 40 + 10 scholars.
Average (12 *months*): morn. 120 + 30 scholars; aft. 40 + 10 scholars.

Daniel Jones.   P. Curate.
Cwmafel.

Lewis: perpetual curacy, endowed with £600 royal bounty, and £1,200 parliamentary grant; net income £88; patron and impropriator, Rees Goring Thomas,
Esq.

C & C: 2 services in Welsh, performed by the incumbent and curate.

I & C: incumbent not resident: curate has stipend of £80 for this and Llandefailog [589. 1. 5(23)].

(14) DWELLING HOUSE AT LLANDRE, LLANARTHNEY. INDEPENDENT.
Erected: Part of a dweling house unknown when erected, but by the cause
or Society begun four years ago. Used as a dwelling house.
Space: free 80; standing 80.
Present: morn. 36 scholars; aft. 44.
Average (12 *months*): morn. 26 + 30 scholars; aft. 55 to 60.
Remarks: The cause of our worshipping in private house is that the land

proprietors in the neighbourhood have refused the rent of a spot of ground for the erection of a house of worship. A petition was drawn up and signed by the Congregation (to apply for a convenient spot for purchase) and then sent to the different land Proprietors—all refused. One offered a spot for four times the value of the Rent. We accepted this disadvantageous offer, and drew up the lease, but after all he refused to fulfill his promise. We would feel glad were there a law to authorize us to demand a convenient spot for the erection of a house of worship.

> David Griffith. Deacon.
> Dryslwyn fawr, Llangathen.

[This should be bound in with 589. 2.]

(15) BETHEL. LLANGEDEIRNE. BABTIST.
Erected before 1800; re-built 1810.
Space: free 3.
Present: morn. 250; aft. 70 scholars; even. 150.
Average (12 *months*): morn. 300; aft. 80 scholars.

> John Evans. Manager.
> Alltyfedw.

(16) SALEM. CALVINISTIC METHODIST.
Erected 1809.
Space: free 300; standing 60.
Present: morn. 120 scholars; aft. 250; even. 150.
Average (12 *months*): morn. 127 scholars; aft. 260.

> William Davies. Deacon.
> Llangendeirne Village.

(17) EBENEZER. INDEPENDENT.
Erected 1830.
Space: all free.
Present: morn. 100; aft. 60 scholars; even. 100.

> Daniel Evans. Minister.
> Nazareth. Nr. Llanelly.

(18) TRALLWN CHAPEL. WESLEYAN.
Erected 1814.
Space: free 50; standing 52.
Present: morn. 20.
Average (3 *months*): morn. 13.

> William Harries. Chapel Steward.
> Gwendraeth. Llanelly.

(19) CAERSALEM. INDEPENDENT.
Erected 1816.
Space: free 306.
Present: morn. 90 scholars: aft. 140; even. 150.
Average: general congregation 200; scholars 107.

> Jacob Davies. Diacon.
> [?'Tailor]

(20) NAZARETH, GLYN HAMLET. INDEPENDENT.
Erected 1803.
Space: all free.
Present: morn. 300; aft. school; even. 300.
Remarks: Great many of our Congregation come from Llanelly parish.
Note: The congregation usual are 300 more or less according to the whether
because the whether make a difference in the Country.

> Daniel Evans. Minister.

(21) SOAR, MINKAU. HAMLET GLYN. PARTICULAR BAPTIST.
Erected 1837. Also used as a Day School.
Space: free 114; standing 40.
Present: morn. 40 scholars; aft. 150; even. prayer meeting at 6, 50.
Average (12 *months*): morn. 70 scholars; aft. 180; even. prayer meetings
in general, 50.

> David Thomas. Deacon.
> Van.

5 Llandefeilog Parish.

Area: 7,320 acres. *Popn.* 621 males, 700 females: total 1,321.

(22) RAMA. INDEPENDENT.
Erected 1841.
Space: free 200.
Present: morn. 68; aft. 58 scholars; even. 83.
Average (12 *months*): morn. 180; aft. 90 scholars; even. 190.

> John Rees. Deacon.
> Placegwyn.

(23) LLANDEFEILOG PARISH CHURCH.
Endowed: land £40; tithe £11. 13. 4*d*; glebe £7. 10*s*; permanent endow-
ment (parl. grant) £6. 15*s*; fees £1. 10*s*.
Present: morn. 30 + 30 scholars; aft. 40 + 10 scholars.
Average (12 *months*): morn. 120 + 30 scholars; aft. 40 + 10 scholars.
Remarks: As English is always performed on the *last* Sunday in the Month

at Llandefeilog Church in the morning, the Welsh who do not understand the Language do not attend, which was the cause that so few attended March 30, 1851.

Daniel Jones.   Vicar.
Cwmafel.

Lewis: vicarage, rated at £9. 13. 4; endowed with £200 royal bounty, and £1,600 parliamentary grant; net income £64: patron, —— Barker, Esq: the impropriation vested in trustees.

C & C: 2 services in Welsh, save 1 a month in English; performed by the incumbent and curate.

I & C: incumbent legally not resident: curate has stipend of £80 for this and Llangendeirne [588. 1. 4(13)].

(24) PENYGRAIG, LLANDEVILOG.   INDEPENDENTS.
Erected before 1750.
Space: all free. Floors and Galary 440.
Present: morn. 320; aft. 115 scholars; even. 210.
Average (12 *months*): general congregation 250 to 350; scholars 110 to 165.
Remarks: Chapel re-build *twice since* 1810.

David Gravell.   Elder.
Cwmfelin.

(25) LLANGENHEIDDON CHAPEL, LLANDEVEILIOG.   CALVINIST METHODIST.
Erected 1824.
Space: free 143; other 25.
Present: morn. school; aft. 51 + 8 scholars; even. 46 + 7 scholars.
Average (12 *months*): aft. 47 + 44 scholars; even. 45 + 30 scholars.
Remarks: 19 pews 5 sittings each   =   95
        1 large pew   do   25   =   25
        8 Benches with Backs do 6   =   48
                             ———
                           168
                           ———

John Evans.   Deacon.
Penymaes.

(26) LLANDEVEILOG CHAPEL, LLANDEVEILOG VILLAGE.
CALVINISTIC METHODIST.
Erected before 1800, enlarged in 1820, enlarge in 1846.
Space: free 250; standing 24 ft by 9.
Present: morn. 120; aft. school; even. 130.
Average: morn. 200; even. 240.
Remarks: The reason for the difference between the number of attendance on the 30th and the general congregation is that No Minister attended on the 30th as it seldom happens.

David Humphreys.
Nantyllan.

6   St. Ishmaels Parish.
Area: 8,081 acres. *Popn.* 452 males 516 females: total 968.

(27)   SAINT ISHMAEL'S PARISH CHURCH.
Space: free 320.
Present: morn. 60.
Remarks: Saint Ishmael being so far from any village the congregation are not so numerous in winter as summer.

Thomas B. Griffiths.   Vicar.

Lewis: discharged vicarage, rated at £7, and in the patronage of the Crown; vicarial tithes commuted for £137; glebe valued at £60; glebe-house: chapel of ease at Llansaint [(28) below].

C & C: with Llansaint chapel of ease: 1 service at St. Ishmael's partially in Welsh and English, 1 service in Welsh at Llansaint, performed by the incumbent.

I & C: no return.

(28)   LLANSAINT CHAPEL OF EASE UNDER THE PARISH CHURCH OF SAINT ISHMAEL.
Space: free 150.
Present: no service.
Average (12 *months*): morn. 120; aft. 140.
Remarks: The service is held in the chapel once every two months in the morning for the benefit of the old communicants, St. Ishmael the mother church being to far.

Thomas Griffiths.   Vicar.

(29)   ST. THOMAS' CHAPEL, FERRYSIDE.
Consecrated by the Bishop of the Diocese August 1828 as an additional Church for the benefit of Ferryside Ventris & Inhabitants.
Erected under the care of the Revd. Edward Patron of Isgoed. Cost defrayed by Parliamentary Grant and Private Benefaction and Public Subscription. Total Cost not known.
Space: free 192; other 104.
Present: aft. 80 + 20 scholars.
Average (12 *months*): aft. 100.
Remarks: The Ferryside being a sea bathing place the congregation is more numerous in summer than winter having two more churches in the Parish the service is held only once every Sunday.

Thomas B. Griffiths.   Minister.

Lewis: sub Ferryside: erected by subscription, aided by grant from the Incorporated Society: opened in 1828: perpetual curacy in the patronage of the vicar of St. Ishamel's for the time being: endowed by the late Rev. Edward Picton with £4 per annum, and £600 royal bounty; net income £23.

C & C: 1 service in English.

I & C: vacant.

ICBS: grant of £165 in 1827.

(30) CAPEL LLANSAINT. WELSH CALVINISTIC METHODISTS.
Erected 1817.
Space: free 1; other 18; standing 100.
Present: morn. 85 + 27 scholars; even. 181 + 45 scholars.
Remarks: The service is held alternately at this place of worship viz. in the
morning at 10 one Sunday, and on the other Sunday at 2 and at 6, when the
service is at 10 in the morning, the school is kept at 2 in the afternoon and
when the service is at 2 and 6 the school is kept at 10 in the morning.

> David Thomas. Steward.
> Treforis, Ferryside.

(31) FERRYSIDE BAPTIST CHAPEL.
Erected before 1800.
Space: free 72; other 104.
Present: morn. 126; aft. 26 scholars; even. 116.

> John Jenkons.
> Holewan [?] Pale, Ferryside.

[End of Llangendeirne Subdistrict]

2 ST. CLEARS (Subdistrict)
Area: 42,238 acres. *Popn.* 3,447 males, 3,866 females: total 7,313.

1 Llanstephan Parish.
Area: 6,710 acres. *Popn.* 597 males, 680 females: total 1,277.

(1) LLANSTEPHAN PARISH CHURCH.
Endowed: tithe £88; glebe £3; permanent endowment £22; fees £1; net.
£110. 14. 1*d.*
Space: free 50; other 37.
Average (12 *months*): morn. 250 + 50 scholars.

> Benjamin Evans. Perpetual Curate.

Lewis: perpetual curacy, rated at £8. 13. 4, with that of Llangunnock [589. 2. 10(29)]
annexed; endowed with £200 private benefaction, £600 royal bounty, and £1,500
parliamentary grant; net income £101, with a glebe-house: patrons, Messrs.
Morris, bankers, Carmarthen, and Miss Lloyd, who are impropriators of the tithes
which have been commuted for £529; glebe of 23 acres valued at £17 per annum.

C & C: with Llangunnock; no return.

I & C: with Llangunnock; 1 service in the church partially in Welsh and English,
performed by the incumbent.

(2) WESLEYAN METHODISTS, LLANSTEPHAN.
Erected 1808.
Space: free 35; other 65.
Present; aft. 50; even. 40.

> Henry Dawkins.
> Union Hall, Llanstephan.

(3) OLD CHAPEL, LLANYBRI. INDEPENDANT.
Erected before 1800.
Space: all free.
Present: morn. 70 scholars; aft. 120 + 70 scholars.
Average (12 *months*): morn. 110; aft. 72 scholars.

> Josiah Thomas Jones. Minister.
> Blue Street, Carmarthen.

(4) NEW CHAPEL OF LLANYBRI. INDEPENDENT.
Erected 1814.
Space: free 108; other 200; standing 108.
Present: morn. 262; aft. 61 scholars; even. 59.
Average (12 *months*): morn. 256; even. 90.

> William James. Minister.
> Llanstephan.

(5) MISPA. BAPTIST RELIGIOUS.
Erected 1833.
Space: other 11 sittings all let; standing 50.
Present: aft. 71 + 18 scholars.
Average (6 *months*): aft. 70 + 18 scholars.

> David Davies. Manager.
> Dyffryntawel.

(6) MORIA. CALVINISTIC METHODIST.
Erected 1804.
Space: free 40; other 150; stnding 50.
Present: morn. 46 scholars; aft. 54; even. 50.
Average (12 *months*): morn. 80; aft. 90 + 60 scholars; even. 70.

> John Thomas. Elder.
> [?Moele.]

2 Laugharne Parish with Laugharne Township.

Area: 14,708 acres. *Popn.* of Laugharne Parish: 259 males, 271 females:
total 530.
Popn. of Laugharne Township: 672 males, 809 females: total 1,481.
Popn. of the whole: 931 males, 1,080 females: total 2,001.

(7) St. Michail, Laugharne Parish Church.
Space: free 220; other 365.
Present: morn. 204 + 84 scholars; aft. 123 + 71 scholars.

> J. G. Mitford.   Churchwarden.
> Laugharne.

Lewis: prebend in the cathedral church of Winchester, rated at £45: vicarage, with the rectory of Llansadwrnen [589. 2. 3(12)] annexed, rated at £6; net income £411, with a glebe-house: patrons, Dean and Chapter of Winchester; impropriators, Lord Kensington and G. Watkins, Esq. Vicar has patronage of the united chapelries of Kenfig [590. 3.3(5)] and Marcos [590. 3. 6(11)].

C & C: 2 services in English, with a Welsh service once a year.

I & C: with Llansadwrnen: incumbent resident; curate has stipend of £40.

(8) Bwlchnewydd.   Baptist.
Erected 1802.
Space: free 126; other 30.
Present: morn. 34 scholars; aft. 88.
Average (12 *months*): morn. 130 + 30 scholars; aft. 100 + 32 scholars; even. 70.

> David Davies.   Minister.
> Bwlchnewydd.

(9) Providence, Cliff Street.   Independent.
Erected 1850.
Space: free 84; other 180.
Present: morn. 133; aft. 56 scholars; even. 250.
Average: general. congregation 280; scholars 68.
Remarks: Philiadelphia the old chapel was Rebuilt in 1800, but gone out of Repairs. Providence was built in cliff street by the same Denomination in 1850.

> Richard John.   Deacon.
> Smith.
> Laugharne.

(10) Tabernacle.   Calvinistic Methodist.
Erected 1833.
Space: free 100; other 200; standing about 100.
Present: morn. 57 scholars; aft. 143; even. 156.

> Rees Havard.   Minister.
> Calv. Methst. Minister, Laugharne.

(11) Wesleyan Methodist Chapel, Newbridge.
Erected 1811.
Space: free 116; other 46.
Present: aft. 45; even. 56.

> Thomas Harding.   Minister.
> Llanelly.

3 Llansadurnen Parish.

Area: 1,644 acres. *Popn.* 112 males, 105 females: total 217.

(12)   LANSADURNEN PARISH CHURCH.
Space: free 40; other 42.
Present: morn. 40.
Remarks: The rectory of Llansadurnen is annexed to the Vicarage of Laugharne and the income of the former is included in the return for Laugharne.

> J. R. Taylor.   Curate.
> Pendine.

Lewis: rectory, annexed to the vicarage of Laugharne, [589.2.2.(7)] rated at £6.
C & C: *sub* Laugharne: 1 service at Llansadurnen.
I & C: see *sub* Laugharne.

4 Llandawke Parish.

Area: 613 acres. *Popn.* 16 males, 21 females: total 37.

(13)   LLANDAWCKE PARISH CHURCH.
Endowed: [MS illlegible].
Space: free 60.
Present: aft. 22.
Average (12 *months*): morn. 22; aft. 22.

> David Thomas.   Rector.

Lewis: rectory with that of Pendine [590. 3. 5(9)] annexed: rated at £7. 10; net income, £88; patron, Col. Powell; tithes commuted for £55, subject to rates averaging £1. 18. per annum; glebe of 2 acres valued at £5 per annum.
C & C: 1 service in English.
I & C: incumbent resident.

5 Llandowror Parish.

Area: 1,783 acres. *Popn.* 200 males, 203 females; total 403.

(14)   LLANDOWROR PARISH CHURCH.
Present: aft. 100.

> Evan Rowland Thomas.   Curate.
> Mount Pleasant, St. Clears.

Lrwis: discharged rectory, rated at £6; net income £132, with a glebe-house: patron, Sir R. B. P. Phillips, Bart.
C & C: 1 service in Welsh performed by the curate.
I & C: no return.
ERCR: accommodation 350.

(15) Tabernacle, Llandowror Village.   Calvinistic Methodist.
Erected 1796.
Space: free 72; other 138; standing 60.
Present: morn. 94; aft. 62 scholars; even. 96.
Average (12 *months*): general congregation 120; scholars 79.

> Thomas Morgan.   Deacon.
> Llandowror.

6 Llanginning Parish.
Area: 3,270 acres. *Popn.* 209 males, 215 females; total 424.

(16) Llanginning Parish Church.
Space: free 10; other 14.
Usual number of attendants: morn. 40; aft. 40.

> *Informant:* John Phillip.   late clerk.

[Informant's form]

Lewis: perpetual curacy, endowed with £800 royal bounty; net income £74:
patron, J. Lewes Philipps, Esq.; tithes commuted for £200, payable to All Soul's
College, Oxford, subject to rates averaging £23. 12. per annum.

C & C: no return.

I & C: incumbent not resident; curate who resides at St. Clears, 2 miles distant,
has stipend of £40.

(17) Rhydyceisiaid, Llanginin.   Independents.
Erected 1709.
Space: free 100; other 180; standing 100.
Present: morn. 266; aft. 126 scholars.
Average: morn. 200; aft. 100 scholars.

> William Davies.   Minister.
> Rhydyceisiaid.

7 St. Clears Parish.
Area: 2,534 acres. *Popn.* 562 males, 678 females: total 1,240.

(18) St. Clears Parish Church.
Endowed: land £65; tithe £90.
Present: morn. 120.

> John Evans.   Vicar.

Lewis: discharged vicarage, rated at £4. 17. 1; endowed with £200 private benefaction, £200 royal bounty, and £600 parliamentary grant; net income £133: patron,
J. Lewes Philipps, Esq.: impropriator, Warden and Fellows of All Souls' College,
Oxford; impropriate tithes commuted for £185. 11. 4, and the vicarial for
£92. 15. 8, both subject to rates averaging £17. 15. 8½ per annum; glebe of 9 acres
valued at £11 per annum.

C & C: no return.

I & C: incumbent resident.

ERCR: accommodation 500.

(19)　BETHLEHEM CHAPEL.　INDEPENDENTS.
Erected 1764 or 1765.
Space: free 252; other 270; the passages are sometimes used as standing room.
Present: morn. 383, including scholars.
Average (12 *months*): morn. 550, including scholars.
Remarks: This chapel is a large commodious Building calculated to seat about 800 persons. It is situate at some distance from the Town, and the congregation frequently lower in numbers from the inclemency of the weather etc. etc. No service held at the chapel in the evening.

> John Williams.　Minister.

(20)　GARDDI CHAPEL.　WESLEYAN METHODIST.
Erected 1810.
Space: free 120; other 36.
Present: morn. 120; aft. school; even. 150.

> William Mason.　Deacon.
> Brick Maker.
> St. Clears.

(21)　CAPELYGRAIG.　UNITARIANS.
Erected 1826.
Space: free 66.
Present: even. 15.

> David Beynon.　Minister.
> Pwlltrap.

(22)　CAPEL MAIR OR ST. MARY'S CHAPEL, TOWN OF ST. CLEARS. INDEPENDENTS.
Erected about 35 years ago.
Space: free 216; other 36.
Present: 240 including scholars.
Average (12 *months*): about 300 including scholars.
Remarks: Service held at the Chapel at 6 o'clock in the Evening. The Sunday School at 2 in the afternoon. No Service in the Morning.

> Joseph Williams.　Minister.
> Clare Hill.

(23)　SION CHAPEL.　BAPTIST.
Erected 1848.
Space: free 60; other 180.
Present: morn. 145; aft. 91 scholars; even. 201.
Remarks: Length of the Chapel 35 feet. Breadth 32 feet. There are Furms

round the Gallery for Free Sittings and Also Round the lower Floor of the Chapel. there are 2 Rooms under the Gallery 13 feet 4 inch by 11 feet each —for free Sittings and for Sabbath School.

> David Morris. Deacon, the Minister being from home.
> Victoria House, St. Clears.

8 Llanfihangel-abercowin Parish.

Area: 5,180 acres. *Popn.* 396 males, 456 females: total 852.

(24) St. Michael, Llanfihangel Abercowin Parish Church.

Erected 1847.

Space: free 112; other 133.

Usual number of attendants: morn. 80; aft. 90.

> *Informant:* Joseph Howell.
> Churchwarden.

Lewis: annexed to the vicarage of Mydrim [589. 4. 8(24)]: tithes commuted for £506, of which £439 are payable to the Archdeacon of St. David's, and subject to rates averaging £57. 8. 10, and £67 to the impropriator, subject to rates averaging £1.

C & C: sub Mydrim; 1 service partially in English and Welsh, performed by the incumbent.

I & C: incumbent resident.

(25) Llanfihangel Chapel. Calvinistic Methodist.

Erected 1829.

Space: free 36; other 66; standing 80.

Present: aft. 105; even. 80.

Average: 70.

> Michael Davies. Steward.

(26) Bancyfelin Chapel. Calvinistic Methodists.

Erected before 1800.

Space: free 42; other 138; standing 20.

Present: morn. 250; even. 200.

Average: general congregation 250 to 300; scholars 90 to 100.

> Joshua Phillips. Minister.

(27) Salem. Baptist.

Erected 1769; re-built 1812.

Space: free 60; other 198. "No Free Space of Standing Room".

Present: morn. 132 + 40 scholars.

Average: 200 to 300.

Remarks: 7.   They are huge seats.
  8.   Sunday School in the afternoon.
  8.   General congregation including the Sunday School which is about 70.

> David Williams. Minister.

9 Llandilo-abercowin Parish.
Area: 922 acres. *Popn.* 34 males, 42 females: total 76.

(28) Llandilo Abercowin Parish Church.
Endowed: tithe £52; fees 10*s.*
Space: free 48.
Present: morn. 10; aft. 10.
Average: morn. 10; aft. 10.
Remarks: The net income £55. The population of the last Census about 80.

John Thomas.   Rector.

Lewis: perpetual curacy, endowed with £200 royal bounty; net income £54: patron, ——Hughes, Esq.: tithes commuted for £65, subject to rates averaging £4. 3. per annum.

C & C: 1 service in Welsh performed by the incumbent.

I & C: incumbent resident.

10 Llangunnock Parish.
Area: 4,879 acres. *Popn.* 390 males, 386 females: total 776.

(29) Llangynnog Parish Church.
Space: other 432.
Average (12 *months*): even. 60 + 15 scholars.
Remarks: Llangynnog being *united* to Llanstephan, the Income of both inclusive is that returned for Llanstephan.

Benjamin Evans.   Perpetual Curate.
The Parsonage, Llanstephan.

Lewis: perpetual curacy, annexed to the vicarage of that of Llanstephan [589. 2. 1(1): tithes commuted for £252.

C & C: 1 service partially in Welsh, performed by the incumbent.

I & C: no return.

(30) Bethesda, Llangynock.   Independents.
Erected 1773.
Space: all free.
Present: morn. 52; aft. 27 scholars.

Josiah Thomas Jones.   Minister.
Blue Street, Carmarthen.

(31) EBENEZER, LLANGUNNOCK.   PARTICULAR BAPTIST.
Erected 1811.
Space: free 54; other 222.
Present: morn. 200 + 55 scholars; aft. school; even. 120 + 40 scholars.
Average (12 *months*)*:* morn. 230 + 35 scholars; even. 120 + 40 scholars.

Thomas Williams.   Minister.
Llangunnock.

[End of St. Clears Subdistrict]

3 CARMARTHEN (Subdistrict)
Area: 18,563 acres. *Popn.* 6,162 males, 7,132 females: total 13,294.

1 Llangain Parish.
Area: 2,660 acres. *Popn.* 203 males, 242 females: total 445.

(1) LLANGAIN PARISH CHURCH.
Endowed: land £78; fees £10.
Average attendance: morn. 50; even. 40.
Remarks: Net income £75. The last Census of the Population are about 400.

John Thomas.   Perpetual Curate.

Lewis: perpetual curacy, endowed with £800 royal bounty net income £85: patron and impropriator, F. Bludworth, Esq., whose tithes have been commuted for £55. 18.

C & C: 1 service in Welsh performed by the incumbent.

I & C: incumbent not resident.

ERCR: accommodation 400.

(2) SMYRNA.   INDEPENDENT.
Erected 1834.
Space: free 70; other 145; standing 50.
Present: morn. 79 scholars; aft. [MS. torn].
Average: morn. 89 scholars; aft. 235; even. 120.

David Davies.   Deacon.
Porthycliniau.

2 Carmarthen, St. Peter Parish.
Area, incl. [3] Castle Green: 5,155 acres. *Popn.* of St. Peter Parish: 4,580 males, 5,591 females: total 10,171. *Popn.* of Military in Barracks 201.
Popn. of Castle Green, Ex. Paro. 106 males, 95 females: total 201.

(3)   LLANLLWCH CHURCH.
An ancient chapelry, made the Church of a District Chapelry under the 16
sec of 59 Geo 3. cap 124, in Nov 1843.
Endowed: land £99. 13s; permanent endowment £38. 3s; fees too trifling
to be named.
Space: free 150.
Present: morn. 89 + 38 scholars; even. 79 + 40 scholars.
Average (12 *months*): morn. 100 + 40 scholars; aft. 100 + 40 scholars.
Remarks: The services at Llanllwch are in the morning and afternoon, and
morning and evening every alternate Sunday.

Thomas Williams.   Minister.

Lewis: [*sub.* Carmarthen]: perpetual curacy, in the patronage of the vicar of St.
Peter's; net income £108.

C & C: 2 services, partially in Welsh, performed by the incumbent.

I & C: incumbent resident.

(4)   ST. PETER PARISH CHURCH.
Space: other 800.
Usual number of attendants: morn. (English) 50 + 60 scholars; aft. (Welsh)
130; even. (English) 700.
Remarks: No free sittings all appropriated to families in the morning and
evening at 6. The afternoon all free for the Welsh poor.

Informant: Geo. W. White.
Registrar of Births & Deaths.

[Informant's form]

Lewis: discharged vicarage, rated at £6. 13. 4., endowed with £400 private benefaction, £400 royal bounty, and £400 parliamentary grant: patron, St. David's College,
Lampeter since 1816; net income £176, with a glebe-house: impropriate tithes
commuted for £920.

C & C: 3 services, entirely English morn. and even., entirely Welsh aft.

I & C: incumbent resident, curate has stipend of £30.

(5)   A ROOM APPROPRIATED FOR DIVINE SERVICE IN THE WORKHOUSE AND
ALSO A SCHOOLROOM.
Licensed by the Bishop of the Diocese.
Erected by the Inhabitance of the District.
Cost defrayed by a Parochial Rate.
Present: morn. 60; aft. 90.
Average: morn. 60; aft. 90.

Thomas Jones.   Clergyman.
Priory Street.

(6) THE GAOL CHAPEL IN THE COUNTY PRISON AT CARMARTHEN.
Consecrated by the Bishop of the Diocese before 1800.
Endowed: County Stock £80.
Space: free 120.
Present: morn. 40 + 12 scholars; aft. 40.
Average: morn. 44 + 10 scholars; aft. 44.

> Rees T. Jones.   Chaplain.
> Priory Street.

(7) BETHEL, JOHNS TOWN.   CALVINISTIC METHODIST.
Erected 1824.
Space: free 150; standing 60.
Present: aft. 65.
Average: aft. 80.

> James Mortimer.   Trustee.
> Picton Terrace.

(8) UNION STREET CHAPEL.   INDEPENDENT.
Erected 1848.
Space: free. 150; other 410.
Present: 98 + 43 scholars; even. 117 + 53 scholars.

> William Morgan.   Minister.
> Union Street.

(9) WATER STREET CHAPEL.   CALVINISTIC METHODISTS.
Erected 1813.
Space: free 325; other 685.
Present: morn. 394 + 43 scholars; even. 470 + 42 scholars.

> Griffith Harris.   Deacon.
> Water Street.

(10) LAMMAS STREET CHAPEL.   LATTER DAY SAINTS.
Part of a house.
Erected 1848.
Present: morn. 25 + 21 scholars; aft. 49; even. 65.
Average: morn. 24 + 21 scholars; aft. 40; even. 56.

> David Evans.   Deacon.
> Lammas Street.

(11) UNITARIAN CHAPEL, TEMPLE STREET.
Erected 1839.
Space: free 40; other 210.
Present: morn. 170; even. 165.
Remarks: Average number cannot be given.

> David Lloyd.   Minister.

(12) Zion Chapel.   Near the Market Place.   Calvinistic Methodist.
Erected 1850.
Space: free 92; other 258.
Present: morn. 110 + 20 scholars; even. 175 + 15 scholars.
W. Howells. Minsister.

(13) Return missing.   [Independent Chapel]

(14) Loft over a dwelling house in Water Street.   Roman Catholic.
Space: free 120.
Present: morn. 99; even. 46.
Average (5 *months*): 90.
Remarks: The entire congregation belonging to the Chapel men women
and children 150.
Peter Lewis. R.C. Priest.
Lammas Street

(15) English Wesleyan Chapel, Chapel Street. Wesleyan Methodist
Space: free 166; other 405.
Present: morn. 156; even. 176.
Remarks: We have a Sunday School in the afternoon, but the children do
not attend the chapel.
Geo. Bagnall. Acting Trustee.

(16) Lammas Street Chapel. Independent.
Erected 1726; re-built and enlarged 1826.
Space: free 200; other 900; standing 100.
Present: morn. 640; aft. 170; even. 802.
Hugh Jones. Minister.
Union Street.

(17) Elim, Ffynonddrain. Independent.
Erected 1850.
Space: free 72; other 210.
Present: aft. 253; even. 297.
Average: general congregation 305; scholars 146.
William Howells. deacon.
Penybont, Nr. Carmarthen.

(18) Tabernacle. Baptists.
Erected 1811; re-erected 1842.
Space: free 150; other 650.
Present: morn. 400, 100 (English); aft. school; even. 600.
Average: general congregation 800; even. 600.
Hugh William Jones. Minister.

(19) EBENEZER. WELSH WESLEYAN METHODISTS.
Erected 1824.
Space: free 150; other 300; standing 150.
Present: morn. 90; aft. 60 scholars; even. 180.
Average (12 *months*): morn. 86; aft. 55 scholars; even. 182.

Thomas Jones. Minister.

(20) PENUEL, PRIORY STREET. PARTICULAR BAPTIST.
Erected before 1800.
Space: being rebuilt.
Present: no service.
Average (12 *months*): morn. 550; aft. 140 scholars; even. 800.
Remarks: The Chapel now in the course of Rebuilding. Our services held
in a room for the time being near the Slaughter House in the Town of
Carmarthen.

Nathaniel Thomas. Minister.
Priory Street.

4 Abergwilly Parish.
Area: 10,748 acres. *Popn.* 1,121 males, 1,204 females: total 2,325.

(21) ABERGWILI PARISH CHURCH.
Space: free 352; other 230.
Present: morn. 114 + 59 scholars; even. 150.
Average (12 *months*): morn. 130 + 55 scholars; even. 190.
Remarks: The average number in the summer months is much larger than
what is stated above. On several occasions in each year the Church is
completely filled (See these remarks continued on the opposite page of this
paper).
[Remarks No. VIII continued] I cannot make these returns without
expressing my decided conviction *that no reliance whatever can be placed in
the accuracy of the returns* made in great many instances and stating my
opinion that to publish them would not only tend to lead people to most
erroneous conclusions. To ensure accuracy at any future time, two conditions are absolutely necessary. The condition is that the enumeration be
entrusted to *disinterested* persons. This would prevent *wilful* exaggeration of
which I could give shameful specimens in dissenting localities, as published
in Welsh Periodicals.
The other condition referred to is that the day on which the enumeration is
to take place be not made known beforehand. This could do away with the
unseemly and irreligious plan of persons leagued together to run from
Chapel to Chapel on a particular day for the *special object* of cramming
different Chapels. By this plan, which *has been* put into operation by dissenting bodies before the 30th instant, when they have been making returns to
answer their own purposes, the same person is made to represent three or

four different persons according to the number of chapels he has attended on a particular Sunday and in this manner the numbers of dissenters are unduly multiplied.

Enoch Pugh.   Vicar.

Lewis: discharged vicarage, rated at £3. 6. 8; endowed with £200 private benefaction, and £200 royal bounty; net income in 1835, £94, since 1841 augmented by the Eccles. Commissioners with £24 per annum: patrons and impropriators, Dean and Canons of Windsor, with courtesy of presentation in the Bp. of St. David's also: impropriate tithes commuted for £700. 6., subject to rates averaging £10 per annum, and the vicarial tithes for £50, subject to rates averaging £5; glebe of 1½ acres, with glebe-house.

C & C: 2 services in Welsh, save 1 a month in English; performed by the incumbent.

I & C: not resident: curate has stipend of £80.

ICBS: grant of £250 in 1841.

(22)   Llanfihangel-uwch-Gwili Chapel of Ease: without a District assigned to it.
Endowed: land £65; permanent endowment £6. 2s; fees 8s.
Space: free 122; other 8.
Present: aft. 32.
Average (12 months): aft. 50.
Remarks: The Sunday Scholars do not attend the chapel as [illegible] body; and it is left to their discretion and choice whether they attend the services of this Chapel or some other place of Worship. The Sunday School is held on Sunday morning. (See these remarks continued on the opposite page.) [Remarks No. VIII continued.] I cannot become a party to these unauthorized returns without expressing my strong conviction that in a great many instances no reliance whatever can be placed on the accuracy of the returns made, and without entering my protest against any perons attempting to impose upon the public by publishing such fallacious statements, as the returns will doubtless [do] in hundreds of instances.

Enoch Pugh.   Incumbent.

Lewis: formerly a chapel of ease, now a perpetual curacy, endowed with £1,200 royal bounty: patron, vicar of Abergwili.

C & C: 1 service in Welsh performed by the incumbent.

I & C: incumbent resident; curate has stipend of £30.

ICBS: grant of £50 in 1844.

(23)   Ebenezer.   Independent.
Erected 1815.
Space: free 120; other 252.
Present: morn. 150; even. 230.

David Thomas.   Deacon.

(24) NANTGAREDIG CHAPEL. CALVINISTIC METHODIST.
Erected 1765.
Space: free 100; other 130; standing 15.
Present: morn. 33 + 126 scholars; aft. school; even. 23 + 86 scholars.
Average (12 *months*): general congregation. 40; scholars 140.

> William Thomas. Deacon.
> Tynewydd, Llangwad.

(25) GLANYRANELL CHAPEL, WHITE MILL. BAPTIST.
Erected 1835.
Space: free 18; other 144; standing 20.
Present: morn. 32 + 18 scholars; aft. school; even. 33 + 14 scholars.
Average (12 *months*): general congregation. 40; scholars 40.

> David Griffiths. Deacon.
> Capeldewilsha, Llanarthney.

(26) PANTTEG. INDEPENDENT.
Present: morn. 160; aft. 109 scholars.
Average: morn. 300; aft. 109 scholars.

> David Davis. Minister.

(27) SALEM. CALVINISTIC METHODIST.
Erected before 1800.
Space: free 6; other 132; standing 30.
Present: morn. 100 scholars; aft. 150; even. 120.

> Edward Edwards. One of the Deacons.
> Pantyglien Farm, Abergwilly.

(28) NEBO CHAPEL, PENYRHEOL. INDEPENDENT.
Erected 1840.
Space: free 78; other 66.
Present: morn. 52; aft. 32 scholars.
Average (2 *months*): morn. 80; aft. 32 scholars.

> Enoch Davies. Deacon.
> Penllwynionwg, Abergwilly.

(29) PENIEL. INDEPENDENTS.
Erected 1809.
Space: all free.
Present: morn. 277; aft. 280.

> David Davies. Minister.
> Pantteg.

(30)   St. David's Church, Carmarthen.
Consecrated: in the spring of 1842, after being endowed with £1,000, collected in voluntary contributions.
Erected partly by parliamentary grant, and partly by voluntary subscription.
Cost defrayed: by Parliamentary Grant   £3,000
                      Private Subscription or
                                Benefaction   £1,400
                                                              ————
                                                              4,400
Endowed: permanent endowment £140; pew rents £40; fees £10.
Space: free 508; other 560.
Present: morn. 700; even. 750.
Average (6 *months*): morn. 700; even. 750.
Remarks: The members that are connected with and attend the Church are more than are set forth above. It is also an important fact that the Morning and Evening Services are attended by totally different Congregations: viz. English in the Morning and Welsh in the Evenings. To arrive at a proper estimate of the actual attendance they must be added together which will give a total of from 1,500 to 2,000.

> D. A. Williams.   Incumbent.
> Picton Terrace.

C & C: 3 services, English at 11 a.m., Welsh at 9 a.m. and 6 p.m.

I & C: no return.

ICBS: grant of £400 in 1852.

[End of Carmarthen Subdistrict]

4 CONWIL (Subdistrict)
Area: 63,244 acres. *Popn.* 4,085 males, 4,469 females: total 8,554.

1 Llanllawddog Parish.
Area: 7,013 acres. *Popn.* 346 males, 379 females: total 735.

(1)   Llanllawddog Parish Church.
Llanllawddog Church is a single not double Church belonging to a separate Parish.
Endowed: land £70; fees £1.
Space: free 70; other 90.
free, for about 70 persons; other, said to belong to farms. Total about 150.
Present: morn. 80 + 40 scholars.
Average: The service morning and evening alternately every Sunday. School in the afternoon when no service.

Remarks: The above Church has been newly rebuilt. The Congregation are sometimes more than 120 and sometimes less and the Sunday School vary in number owing to the Church being in a Secluded Spot in the Parish.

Willm. Henry Powell. Perpetual Curate.

Lewis: perpetual curacy, with that of Llanpympsaint [589. 4. 1(3)] annexed; endowed with £800 royal bounty; net income £150: patron, vicar of Abergwili; appropriators, Dean and Canons of Windsor: tithes commuted for £200, subject to rates averaging £5 per annum.

C & C: 1 service partially in Welsh, performed by the incumbent.

I & C: not resident: resident at Llanpumpsaint.

ICBS: grant of £50 in 1849.

(2)   New Chapel, Rhydagane [?].   Calvinistic Methodist.
Erected 1817.
Space: other 84.
Present: even. 260.
Average (12 *months*): general congregation 200; scholars 50.

Edward Edwards.   Deacon Secretary.
Bookbinder.

2   Llanpumpsaint Parish.
Area: 4,079 acres. *Popn.* 268 males, 252 females: total 520.

(3)   Llanpumpsaint Parish Church.
Llanpumpsaint Church is a Small Church of a *Seperate* Parish.
Endowed: land £70; fees £1.
Space: free—'Free'; other 4 or 5 = 30 said to belong to the Farms in the Parish.
Present: aft. 80 + 30 scholars.
Average: morn. 80 + 30 scholars.
Remarks: The Above Parish Church has been Consecrated from time immemorial. It contains 13 large seats which will Contain severally about 8 persons. The Congregation are sometimes more than above but seldom much less. There is a day School kept in the Gallery of this Church as the number of Children vary—sometimes 20 and sometimes 30.

William Henry Powell.   Perpetual Curate.

Lewis: perpetual curacy annexed to that of Llanllawddog [589. 4. 1(1)]; endowed with £1,000 royal bounty;: tithes commuted for £180; appropriators, Dean and Chapter of Windsor; subject to rates averaging £5. 10. per annum.

C & C: 1 service in Welsh performed by the incumbent.

I & C: resident.

(4)   HOREB, RHYDARGAU [?].   CALVINISTIC BAPTISTS.
Erected 1783.
Space: free 120; gallery 7 Benches all free sittings.
Present: morn. 40 scholars; aft. 193.
Average (12 *months*): general congregation 80; scholars 69.

Henry Evans.   Tresurer.

(5)   LANPUMSANT CHAPEL.   CALVINISTIC METHODIST.
Erected: last building 1827.
Space: free: 'unpaid'; other: 'payment'.
Present: morn. 200; aft. 154 scholars; even. 250.
Average: 150.

Thomas Lloyd.   Deacon.

3   Newchurch Parish.
Area: 4,894 acres. *Popn.* 393 males, 478 females: total 871.

(6)   NEWCHURCH OR LLANNEWYDD PARISH CHURCH.
Endowed: land £93. 6. 11; fees £1.
Present: aft. 100 + 41 scholars.
Average: morn. 130 + 66 scholars.

Thos Williams.   Minister.
Johns Town, Carmarthen.

Lewis: perpetual curacy, endowed with £600 royal bounty and £1,400 parliamentary grant; net income £96: patron and impropriator, family of Mallock. Church entirely rebuilt in 1829.

C & C: 1 service partially in Welsh and English performed by the incumbent.

I & C: not resident.

ICBS: grant of £100 in 1830.

ERCR: accommodation 400

(7)   CWMDWYFRAN CHAPEL.   CALVINISTIC METHODIST.
Erected before 1800.
Space: free 70; other 108; standing 60.
Present: morn. 70 scholars; aft. 160; even. 151.
Average (12 *months*): morn. 90 scholars; aft. 180; even. 170.

David Richards.   Steward.
Care of the Landlord of White Horse,
Priory Street, Carmarthen.

4   Merthyr Parish.
Area: 2,218 acres. *Popn.* 139 males, 177 females: total 316.

(8) Henffwlch. Merthir. Calvineth Trefnython [i.e. Calvinistic Methodist]
Present: morn. 54.

David John.

(9) Cana. Merthyr. Independent.
Erected 1819.
Space: free 54; other 174.
Present: morn. 81 scholars; aft. 153; even. 102.
Average (12 *months*): morn. 226 [? incl.] 111 scholars; aft. 226 [? incl.] 111 scholars; even. 226.

David Phillips.   Minister.

[There is no return for the parish church, noted in *Lewis* as follows: discharged rectory, rated at £4. 17. 1; patron, the crown: tithes commuted for £165; glebe of 38 acres valued at £36 per annum.]

5   Abernant Parish.
Area: 6,321 acres. *Popn.* 416 males, 453 females: total 869.

(10)   Abernant Parish Church.
Endowed: I cannot state the amount being annexed to Conwil.
Space: free 200.
Present: 70.
Average (12 *months*): morn. 200; aft. 170.
Remarks: On account of some peculiar local circumstances the attendance on the 30th of March was unusually small.

Henry Jones Davis.   Curate.

Lewis: discharged vicarage with the perpetual curacy of Conwil in Elvet [589. 4. 6(16)] annexed; rated at £7. 13. 4; endowed with £200 royal bounty and £1,000 parliamentary grant; net income £131 with a glebe-house: patron and impropriator, Duke of Leeds. Glebe land attached is one of the most extensive in the principality.
C & C: 1 service in Welsh performed by the incumbent.
I & C: no return.

(11)   Bethania.   Baptist.
Erected 1839.
Space: free 72; other 79; standing 38.
Present: morn. 72 scholars; aft. 152; even. 40.
Average (12 *months*): morn. 70 scholars; aft. 160; even. 65.

Thomas Thomas.   Secretary.
Talog, nr. Carmarthen.

(12) ABER. INDEPENDENT.
Erected 1839.
Present: aft. 34 scholars: even. 78.
Average (12 *months*): general congregation 100; scholars 60.

> Thomas Jones. Superintendent of
> Sunday School.
> Pantyhendyisaf, Abernant.

(13) BWLCHNEWYDD. INDEPENDENT.
Erected 1746, re-built 1808, enlarged 1832.
Space: free 500; standing 150.
Present: morn. 284; aft. 138 scholars; even. 196.
Average (12 *months*): general congregation 250 to 550; scholars 100 to 150.
Remarks: As is the case frequently in Wales, the chapel is so crammed occasionally, that many more attend than are able to find room to sit and are consequently forced to stand.

> Michael D. Jones. Minister.

6 Conwil-in-Elfet parochial Chapelry.
Area: 13,153 acres. *Popn.* 819 males, 892 females: total 1,711.

(14) CONWIL PARISH CHURCH.
Endowed: I am not able to state the amount being annexed to Abernant.
Space: free 150.
Present: morn. 60.
Average (12 *months*): morn. 120; aft. 100.
Remarks: On account of some peculiar local circumstances the attendance on the 30th March was unusually small.

> Henry Jones Davis. Curate.

Lewis: perpetual curacy annexed to the vicarage of Abernant [589. 4. 5(10)]; endowed, exlcusively of Abernant, with £3 per annum, and a legacy of £8 by Mrs. Anna Warner.

C & C: 1 service in Welsh performed by the incumbent.

I & C: no return.

(15) FENNON HENRY. BAPTIST.
Erected 1731.
Space: free 198.
Present: morn. 180 + 30 scholars.

> David Evans. Baptist Minister.
> Conwil.

(16) HERMON. INDEPENDENT.
Erected 1825.
Space: free 17; standing 200.
Present: aft. 176.
Average (12 months): morn. 250; aft 91 scholars.

David Morgan   Deacon.
Llain, nr. Conwil Elvet.

(17) BLAENYCOED. INDEPENDENTS.
Erected 1807.
Space: free 136; other 240; standing 68.
Present: morn. 226; aft. 124 scholars.
Average (12 months): morn. 348; aft. 155 scholars.

John Jones.   Elder.
Drysgolgoch.

(18) BETHEL, CONWILL ELVET VILLAGE.   CALVINISTIC METHODISTS.
Erected 1792.
Space: free 60; other 100; standing 60.
Present: morn. 200; even. 150.
Average (12 months): 200.

John Jones.   Deacon.
Penddôl.

7   Treleach-ar-Bettws Parish.

Area: 11,492 acres. *Popn.* 740 males, 792 females: total 1,532.

(19) BETTWS CHAPEL OF EASE, TRELECH A'R BETTWS.
Endowed: not at all endowed.
Space: free 150.
Present: no service.
Average (12 months): aft. 130.

David Thomas Thomas.   Minister.

(20) TRELECH A'R BETTWS PARISH CHURCH.
Endowed with Land, Tithe, Glebe, and a Parliamentary Grant.
Space: free 187; other 18.
Present: morn. 159.
Average (12 months): morn. 175.

David Thomas Thomas.

Lewis: discharged vicarage, rated at £6. 13. 4; endowed with £400 royal bounty, and £1,200 parliamentary grant; net income £143: patron, the Bp.; impropriator, Earl of Lisburne and Richard Price, Esq. Church rebuilt in 1834.

C & C: 1 service a fortnight in Welsh performed by the curate.

I & C: incumbent resident.

ICBS: grant of £80 in 1834.

(21) PETERWELL. INDEPENDENT.
Erected 1808.
Space: free 192; standing 32 foot long 7 in breadth. gallery 18½ foot long
long 6½ in breadth.
Present: morn. 125; aft. 77 scholars; even. 50.
Average (12 *months*): gen. cong. 300; scholars 100.

> Evan Jones. Minister.
> Carmarthen.

(22) TYHEN. CALVINISTIC METHODIST.
Erected 1830.
Space: free 42; other 108; standing 100.
Present: even. 96.

> Theos. Howells. Deacon.
> Cefnonen, Treleach ar Bettws to be left
> at 3 samons water street Carmarthen.

(23) EYNON. BAPTISTS.
Erected 1828.
Space: free 200; standing 50.
Present: aft. 140: general congregation and scholars.
Average (12 *months*): general congregation and scholars 180.

> John Richards. Deacon.

[Note, return (26) below relates to this parish.]

8 Mydrim Parish.

Area: 6,905 acres. *Popn.* 483 males, 513 females: total 996.

(24) MYDRIM PARISH CHURCH.
Space: free 40; other 16.
Usual number of attendants: morn. 90-100; aft. 100-150; even. none.
Sunday Scholars: morn. from 50 to 60 according to the season of the year.

> *Informant:* D. F. Howells. School-
> master.

[Informant's form]
Lewis: discharged vicarage, with the perpetual curacy of Llanvihangel-Abercowin
annexed [589. 2. 8(24)]; rated at £7. 10.; endowed with £600 parliamentary grant;
net income £116; patron, Bp. of St. David's: tithes, payable to the archdeacon as
Prebendary of Mydrim, commuted for £550; glebe of 35 acces valued at £30 per
annum.

C & C: 1 service partially in Welsh performed by the incumbent.

I & C: resident.

(25) GIBEAN. INDEPENDENTS.
Erected 1841.
Space: free, all other seats free; other, 12 seats let to individuals.
Usual number of attendants: morn. 60 to 70 + 40 to 45 scholars; aft. 70 to 80; even. 30 (prayer meeting).

> David Thomas. Deacon.
> Bronhaul, Mydrim.

[Informant's form]

(26) ROCK CHAPEL, TRELECH AR BETTWS. INDEPENDENT.
Erected before 1800.
Space: free 416; other 188.
Present: general congregation morn. 381; aft. 586; even. 198. Sunday Scholars: none this day.
Average (12 months): general congregation 200-1,000 (to a great degree regulated by the weather) scholars 200 (Average of the chapel Sunday school).
Remarks: This Chapel measures within walls 34 ft x 30, to which belong 6 different sunday schools.

> Thos. Evans, Secretary. No Minister.
> Glynblewog.

[Misnumbered: this return should be under 589. 4. 7.]

(26A) MYDRIM. CALVINISTIC METHODISTS.
Erected before 1800.
Space: free 80; other 165; standing about 600.
Present: morn. 80 scholars; aft. 175; even. 62. 'Instructing the Sunday School on Religious duty'.

> John Havard. Deacon.
> Mydrim.

9 Llanwinio Parish.
Area: 7,169 acres. *Popn.* 481 males, 533 females: total 1,014.

(27) LLANWINIO PARISH CHURCH.
Endowed: land £94. 3s.
Space: free 133; other 224.
Present: morn. 50; aft. 50.
Average (12 months): morn. 70.

> Rees Griffith. Perpetual Curate.

Lewis: perpetual curacy, endowed with £400 royal bounty, and £1,600 parliamentary grant; patron and impropriator, Mr Howell: net income, £83.
C & C: one service in Welsh performed by the incumbent.
I & C: resident.

(28) Cwmbach. Calvinistic Methodist.
Erected 1765.
Space: free 114; other 168; standing 100.
Present: morn. 330; aft. 124 scholars; even. 100.
Average (12 *months*): morn. 400; aft. 100 scholars; even. 150.

        John Williams. Steward.
        Caerchedydd, Llanwinio.

(29) Moriah. Independents.
Erected 1829.
Space: free—all.
Present: morn. 69 scholars; aft. 167.
Average (12 *months*): morn. 55 scholars; aft. 155.

        J. Davies. Minister.
        Glandŵr, Sy. Clears.

(30) [Ramoth], Cwmfelin. The Baptists.
Erected before 1800.
Whether seperate etc: He was built by himself.
Space: free 276.
Present: morn. 103 scholars; aft. 132; even. 60.
Average: morn. 350; aft. 110 scholars; even. 80.
Remarks: This 30 day of March 1851 did happen on the Sabath that has the congregation smallist in the month and so this Sabath in the months through the year and the case is we held the meeting at the Afternoon.

        William Enoc Jones. Minister of the
        Gospel, Cwmfelin.

[End of Conwil Subdistrict and End of Carmarthenshire District]

PEMBROKESHIRE

Area: 366,040 acres. *Popn.* 39,620 males, 44,852 females: total
84,472.

590   NARBERTH (District)

Area :   124,903 acres.   *Popn.* 10,459 males, 11,671 female
total 22,130.

1 LLANBOIDY (Subdistrict)
Area: 26,655 acres.   *Popn.* 1734 males, 1981 females: total 3715.

1   Llanboidy Parish, co. Carmarthen.
Area: 10,666 acres.   *Popn.* 835 males, 960 females: total 1795.

(1)   Llanboidy Parish Church.
Endowed: tithe rent charge £137.17.6; glebe £20.
Space: free 200; other 300.
Present: morn. 300+ 66 scholars.
Average: morn. 350 + 70 scholars; aft. 400 + 70 scholars.

> John Evans.   Vicar.
> St. Clears.

Lewis: discharged vicarage, rated at £8, endowed with £1000 parliamentary grant;
net income £136: patron, Bp. St. David's: tithes commuted for £615, of which
£396. 12. 6 are payable to the Earl of Lisburne, £137. 17. 6 to the vicar, and £80.
10. to All Souls' College, Oxford; the whole subject to rates averaging £90. 17.
per annum.

C & C: 1 service, partially in Welsh, performed by the incumbent.

I & C: resident.

ICBS: grant of £35 in 1844.

(2)   Eglwysfair Glantaf Chapelry.
Endowed: land £62; tithe £6.
Space: free for 8 persons: others, none [242 + 8 = 250 added in another
hand].
Present: aft. 250.
Remarks: The above-named Church is in a wretched state of repair.
There are only eight sittings, but there have been placed planks round
the Church, for the people to sit on during Divine Worship.

> Samuel Jones.   Perpetual Curate.
> Llwynbrain, St. Clears.

Lewis: [*sub.* Llanboidy]; perpetual curacy, endowed with £800 royal bounty,
and £400 parliamentary grant; patron, Frederick Bludworth, Esq., who is the

impropriator of 11/14th of the tithes, the remainder belonging to the incumbent and other impropriators: net income £66.

C & C: 1 service in Welsh performed by the incumbent.

I & C: no return.

ICBS: grant of £130 in 1851.

(3) CEFN-Y-PANT. INDEPENDENTS.

Erected 1844.

Space: free 108

Present: aft. 26.

Average (12 *months*): general congregation 160; scholars 33.

Remarks: Preaching at this place on alternate Sunday afternoons.
[Endorsed: see Letter].

> John Davies. Minister.
> Glandwr, St. Clears.

(4) TRINITY CHAPEL, LLANBOIDY VILLAGE. INDEPENDENTS OR CONGRE-GATIONALISTS.

Erected before 1800.

Space: free 18; other 25.

Present: morn. 110 scholars; aft. 226.

Average (12 *months*): morn. 130; aft. 300.

> Joshua Lewis. Minister.
> Llanboidy.

(5) SOAR INDEPENDENT CHAPEL.

Erected 1836.

Day School annexed.

Space: free 10; other 43; standing 300.

Present: morn. 250; aft. 150 scholars.

Average (12 *months*): general congregation 140; scholars 130.

Remarks: The building cost about £200 School house about £80. Voluntary contributions.

> John Thomas.
> Forest.

2 Eglwysfairachyrig Chapelry (pt. of Henllan-Amgoed Parish): **co. Carmarthen.**

Area: 2618 acres. *Popn.* 129 males, 137 females: total 266.

(6) EGLWYSFAIR A CHERRYG, a Chapel of Ease under the Church of Henllan amgoed.

Endowed: tithe £70.

Space: free 50.

Present: morn. 7.

Average (12 *months*): morn. 10; aft. 30.
Remarks: The service is performed in this Chapel alternately Morning and Afternoon.

John Rees.   Officiating Minister.
Eglwysfairachyrig.

Lewis: chapel of ease to the rectory of Henllan Amgoed [595.3.1.(2)].

C & C: 1 service in Welsh performed by the curate.

I & C: see *sub*. Henllan Amgoed.

(7)   RHYD Y PARK.   UNITARIAN.
Erected before 1800.
Space: free 80; standing 70.
Present: morn. 76.
Average (12 *months*): morn. 70.

James Evans Deacon.
Fronisaf.   Eglwysfairachurig.

3 Llanglydwen Parish.   co. Carmarthen.
Area: 1834 acres.   *Popn*. 130 males, 148 females; total 278.

(8)   LLANGLWYDWEN PARISH CHURCH.
Endowed: tithe £100.
Space: free 150.
Remarks: Divine Service Morning and afternoon every other Sunday. The General Congregation about Eighty.

Job Griffiths.   Registrar, Narberth.

Lewis: discharged rectory, rated at £2. 13. 4; endowed with £200 parliamentary grant; in the patronage of the Crown; net income £96.

C & C: 1 service partially in Welsh performed by the incumbent.

I & C: not resident.

(8)   LLANGLWYDWEN CHURCH.
When erected: Immemorial.
Sittings: all in the Church.
Attendants: about 80.

Informant: Job Griffith.   Registrar by the representation of the Revd. W. Evans, the Rector.

[Informant's form: endorsed, Duplicate]

(9) HEBRON. INDEPENDENT.
Erected 1805.
Space: free 300; standing 180.
Present: aft. 315.
Remarks: The Sunday Scholars are included in the General Congregation, being mostly attendants on public worship. The internal dimensions of the house contains 1222 square feet.

> Simon Evans. Minister.
> Eglwyswen.

4   Cilymaenllwyd Parish (Part of).   co. Carmarthen.
Area: 3,505 acres.   *Popn.* 261 males, 247 females; total 508.

(10) CILYMAENLLWYD PARISH CHURCH.
Endowed: permanent endowment £120.
Space: free 135.
Present: morn. 36.
Average (12 *months*): morn. 30; aft. 50.
Remarks: A school near the ¦Church has been recently opened during the hours of Divine Service the novelty of which is not yet worn off, by the Anabaptists and has greatly interfered with the usual attendance.

> R. Bowen Jones. Rector.
> Narbeth.

Lewis: discharged rectory, rated at £6. 10.; in the patronage of the Crown: tithes commuted for £200. subject to rates averaging £20 per annum.

C & C: 1 service in Welsh performed by the incumbent.

I & C: not resident.

ICBS: grant of £100 in 1842.

[For the remainder of this parish see 590.4.4.].

(11) NEBO. INDEPENDENT.
Erected 1836.
Space: free 272; standing 140.
Present: morn. 240.
Remarks: The Sunday Scholars are included in the General Congregation, most of them attending public worship but not seated apart.

> Simon Evans. Minister.
> Egwlyswen.

(12) LOGYN. PARTICULAR BAPTISTS.
Erected 1827.
Space: free 115; other 119.

Present: aft. 63 + 40 scholars; even. 55 + 30 scholars.
Average (6 *months*): general congregation 100; scholars 50.

> David Edwards.   Deacon.
> Llanafon, Lanboidy.

5   Llanfallteg Parish: partly in co. Carmarthen and co. Pembroke.
Area of Llanfallteg in co. Carmarthen: 1,448 acres. *Popn.* of same: 106
males, 169 females: total 275. *Area* of Llanfallteg in co. Pembroke: 418
acres. *Popn.* of same: 39 males, 52 females: total 91. *Area* of whole parish:
1,866 acres. *Popn.* 145 males, 221 females: total 366.

(12A)   LLANVALLTEG PARISH CHURCH.
Endowed: land £8. 10s.   tithe £195.
Space: free 40; other 90.
Present: morn. 30.

> Richard Hughes.   Rector.
> Pentan, Narberth.

Lewis: discharged rectory, rated at £4; endowed with £200 royal bounty; net
income £144; patron, Bp. St. David's.
C & C: 1 service in Welsh performed by the incumbent.
I & C: resident.

6   Monachlogddu Parish.
Area: 6166 acres.   *Popn.* 234 males, 268 females; total 502.

(13)   MONACHLOGDDU PARISH CHURCH.
Endowed: 'As a curate I do not know the amount'.
Space: free 120.
Present: aft. 30.
Average: aft. 40.

> David Thomas.   Curate.
> Monachlogddu.

Lewis: perpetual curacy, endowed with £1000 royal bounty; net income £180;
patron, Sir R. B. P. Phillips, Bart.; tithes commuted for £52. 10. payable to the
curate, and subject to rates averaging £4. 15. 2. per annum.
C & C: 1 service in Welsh performed by the curate.
I & C: incumbent not resident; curate, who has stipend of £70, resides at
Llangolman 2½ miles distant.

(14)   BETHEL MONACHLOGDDU.   PARTICULAR BAPTIST.
Erected 1794.
Present: morn. 106 scholars; aft. 200 scholars.

> Walter Davies.   Baptist Minister.

[End of Llanboidy Subdistrict]

2 LLANDISSILIO (Subdistrict)
Area: 25,686 acres. *Popn.* 1,634 males, 1,857 females: total 3,491.

1 Llangolman Parish.
Area: 2,912 acres. *Popn.* 130 males, 161 females: total 291.

(1) LLANGOLMAN PARISH CHURCH.
Llangolman and Llandilo are consolidated. Llandilo is in ruin, no Duty
performed.
Endowed: land £30; tithe £40; permanent endowment £6. 6s; £9. 9. 4d.
Space: free 14.
Present: morn. 15.
Average: aft. 15.

> George Harries.   Cleryman.
> Maenclochog.

Lewis: perpetual curacy, with that of Llandilo [590. 2. 2(2)] annexed, endowed with
£800 royal bounty; net income £97: tithes commuted for £110, of which £76. 6. 8
are payable to the impropriator, H. W. Bowen, Esq, who is patron, and £33. 10. 4
to the vicar; both subject to rates averaging £10. 11. 1 per annum.
C & C: sub Llandilo with Llangolman: 2 services in Welsh Performed by the
incumbent.

I & C: not resident.

ERCR: accom. 260.

2 Llandilo Parish.
Area: 1,132 acres. *Popn.* 59 males, 70 females: total 129.
[No return for the parish church].

Lewis: perpetual curacy annexed to that of Llangolman: endowed with £800 royal
bounty: tithes commuted for £33, of which £22 are payable to the impropriator,
subject to rates averaging £3. 4. 1 per annum, and £11 to the vicar, subject to rates
averaging £1. 12. per annum.

ERCR: accom. 140.

(2) LLANDILO.   INDEPENDENT.
Erected before 1800; rebuilt 1845.
Space: free 12; other 26.
Present: morn. 80 scholars; aft. public worship 200; even. prayer meeting
50.
Average (12 *months*): morn. 70 scholars; aft. 300; even. 60.

> Benjn. James. Independent Minister.
> Llandilo.

3   Maenclochog Parish with the Hamlet of Vorlan.
Area: 2,754 acres. *Popn.* 212 males, 243 females: total 455.

(3)   MAENCLOCHOG PARISH CHURCH.
Endowed: land £5. 15s; tithe £40; glebe £5; permanent endowment
£6. 6. 3., £6. 11. 10.
Space: free 15.
Present: aft. 50.
Average: morn. 50.

> George Harries.
> Vicar of Maenclochog.

Lewis: discharged vicarage, endowed with £400 royal bounty and £400 parliamentary grant; net income £70: patron and impropriator Hugh Webb Bowen,
Esq.: tithes commuted for £150 of which £100 are payable to the impropriator,
and £50 to the vicar, who also has a glebe of 2 acres, valued at £2. 10. per annum.

C & C: 1 service in Welsh performed by the incumbent.

I & C: resident.

(4)   MAENCLOCHOG.   INDEPENDANT.
Erected 1791.
Space: free 58.
Present: morn. 12 scholars; aft. 100.
Average: morn. 20 scholars; aft. 200.
Remarks: The divine Service is kept Morning and Evening every other
Sunday.

> David Owen.   Minister.
> Silo, nr. Ambleston.

(5)   TABERNACLE, VILLAGE OF MAENCLOCHOG.   INDEPENDENT.
Erected 1847.
Space: free 252; other 48
Present: morn. 140; even. 47.
[Endorsed: See Letter].

> David William.   Deacon.
> Blacknuck, Parish of Henry's Moat.

4   New Moat Parish.
Area: 3,101 acres. *Popn.* 166 males, 167 females: total 333.

(6)   NEW MOAT PARISH CHURCH.
Endowed: tithe £200.
Space: free 82; other 101.

Present: aft. 45 incl. 10 scholars.
Average (2 *months*): morn. 45 incl. 10 scholars; aft. 50 incl. 12 scholars.

> Thomas Thomas.   Rector.
> Clabeston, Haverfordwest.

Lewis: rectory, rated at £2. 4. 7; patron, W. H. Scourfield, Esq: tithes commuted for £200.

C & C: 1 service partially in Welsh, performed by the incumbent.

I & C: not resident.

5 Llys-y-frân Parish.
Area: 1,466 acres. *Popn.* 78 males, 101 females: total 179.

(7)   LLYS Y FRAN PARISH CHURCH.
Endowed: tithe £95; glebe £1; permanent endowment £12.
Present: aft. 9.

> James Thomas.   Rector.

Lewis: discharged rectory, rated at £3. 0. 5; endowed with £400 royal bounty; joint patrons, Sir R. B. P. Philipps, Bart., and Col. Scourfield, the former having 2 turns and the latter one: tithes commuted for £95, glebe of 1 acre, valued at £3 per annum.

C & C: 1 service in English performed by the incumbent.

I & C: no return.

ERCR: accom. 150.

(8)   GWASTAD.   CALVINISTIC METHODIST.
Erected 1836.
Space: free 10; other 29.
Present: morn. 60 scholars; aft. 150; even. 140.
Average: general congregation 140; scholars 70.

> Thomas Phillips.   Elder.
> Southfield.

6 Clarbeston Parish.
Area: 1,588 acres. *Popn.* 79 males, 99 females: total 178.

(9)   CLARBESTON PARISH CHURCH.
Endowed: land £42; permanent endowment £30. 13.
Space: free 67; other 60.
Present: morn. 75 incl. 12 scholars.
Average: (2 *months*): morn. 90 incl. 15 scholars; aft. 100 incl. 18 scholars.

> Thomas Thomas.   Perpetual Curate.

Lewis: perpetual curacy, endowed with £800 royal bounty and £400 parliamentary grant; net income £60; patron, Rev. Thomas Thomas; impropriator, W. H.

Scourfield, Esq., the Mote; tithes commuted for £44. 10.; glebe of 48*a* 2*r* 25*p*, valued at £24. 7. per annum.
C & C: 1 service partially in Welsh, performed by the incumbent.
I & C: resident.
ICBS: grant of £50 in 1840.

(10) CARMEL. BAPTIST.
Erected 1804.
Space: all free.
Present: morn. 250 + 40 scholars; aft. 80.
Average: morn. 250.

> Henry Price. Baptist Minister.
> Carmel

7 Bletherston Parish.
Area: 2,366 acres. *Popn.* 161 males, 159 females: total 320.

(11) BLETHERSTONE PARISH CHURCH.
Erected: 'There is a monument erected in it about 200 years ago'.
Space: free 130; other 18 pews.
Usual Number of attendants: morn. 50; aft. 50.

> *Informant:* Hugh Evans. Parish Clerk.

[Informant's form]
Lewis: consolidated vicarage with Llawhaden [590. 5. 3(6)]: impropriate tithes, payable to the chancellor of St. David's, commuted for £116. 13. 4, and the vicarial for £58. 6. 8, both subject to rates averaging £17. 18. 11 per annum.
C & C: see *sub* Llawhaden.
I & C: see *sub* Llawhaden.

8 Llanycefn Parish.
Area: 2,684 acres. *Popn.* 202 males, 240 females: total 442.

(12) LLANYCEFN PARISH CHURCH.
Endowed: Queen Anne's Bounty £51.
Space: free 200.
Present: morn. 30.
Average: morn. 50.

> David Thomas. Curate.

Lewis: perpetual curacy; endowed with £1,000 royal bounty and £200 parliamentary grant; net income £51: patron and impropriator, Sir R. B. P. Philipps, Bart. Church repaired in 1841.
I & C: incumbent not resident: curate, who resides at Llangolman 2½ miles distant, has a stipend of £40.
C & C: 1 service in Welsh performed by the curate.

9 Llandissilio Parish: in co. Pembroke and co. Carmarthen.

Area in co. Pembroke: 1,748 acres. *Popn.* 183 males, 240 females: total 423.

Area in co. Carmarthen: 4,719 acres. *Popn.* 278 males, 292 females: total 570.

(13) LLANDISILIO [PARISH CHURCH].
Space: free 130; other 118.
Present: aft. general congregation 60; scholars 50.
Average: aft. general congregation 100; scholars 50.

Thomas Harries. Vicar.

Lewis: prebend in the collegiate church of Brecknock, valued at £12. 9. 4½; in the gift of the Bp. St. David's. Living a discharged vicarage, valued at £7, endowed with £400 royal bounty, in the patronage of the Bp.: tithes commuted for £385, of which £242. 18. are payable to the prebendary, subject to rates averaging £22 per annum; £132. 10. to the vicar, subject to rates averaging £12; and £9. 12. to an impropriator, subject to rates averaging £1. Church erected in 1838 by means of a rate, private subscription and a grant of £60 from the Church Building Society.

C & C: 1 service in Welsh performed by the incumbent.

I & C: resident.

ICBS: grant of £70 in 1839.

(14) BLAENCONYN. BAPTIST.
Erected 1844.
There is a day school in the Chapel until such time as we will erect a school house.
Space: free 20; other 22.
Present: morn. 127 scholars; aft. 300; even. 200.
Average (12 *months*): morn. 350 + 100 scholars; aft. 259 + 80 scholars; even. 200.
Remarks: We have divine Service morning and afternoon alternately and Sunday School in like manner, but have divine Service continually at 6 o'clock P.M.

Owen Griffiths. Baptist Minister.

(15) PISGAH. VILLAGE OF LLANDISSILIO. INDEPENDENTS.
Erected 1825.
Space: free 39.
Present: morn. 161; aft. 56 scholars.

Samuel Evans. Secretary.

(16) Rhydwilym Chapel. co. Carmarthen. Particular Baptist.
Erected 1701.
Space: free 350.
Present: morn. 275; aft. 89 scholars.
Average (12 *months*): morn. 370; aft. 105 scholars.
Remarks: A stone in the wall of the Chapel Engraved Literal as under:

IOHN EUANS O· LLWYNDWR
GOSTODD GWNEITHWR
Y· TY HWN ANNO· DOM· 1701

— — — — — — — — — —

GAN· DDUMUNO ·Y· TY HUN·
Y· USE· Y· BOBLE BYTH· SY·
N· DALA·Y· VI· GWUDDOR·
SY·N Y· VJ· OR· HEBRE· i·2·

Henry Price. Minister.

(17) Domgay Chapel. Co. Montgomery. Congregationalist.
Space: free 120; other 60.
Present: morn. 40 scholars; aft. 70 + 20 scholars; even. 150 + 30 scholars.
Remarks: At Present without a Pastor depending upon Supplies.

David Jones. Deacon.
Llandrinio, Oswestry.

[This return is misplaced: it should come under 609. 2. 11.]

10 Egremont Parish. Co. Carmarthen.
Area: 1,006 acres. *Popn.* 83 males, 78 females: total 161.

(18) Egremont Parish Church.
Endowed: land £50; tithe £3; permanent endowment, interest of £600 in
Queen Anne's Bounty.
Space: free 45; other 45.
Present: morn. 52.
Average (12 *months*): morn. 60.

John Thomas. Churchwarden.
Egremont, Nr. Narberth.

Lewis: donative curacy, endowed with £1,000 royal bounty, net income £51;
patron and impropriator, R. A. Mansel, Esq. Church rebuilt in 1839, partly by
means of a grant from the Incorporated Society.

C & C: 1 service partly in Welsh performed by the incumbent.

I & C: not resident.

ICBS: grant of £40 in 1839.

11 Grondre Hamlet (pt. of Cilymaenllwyd Parish).
Area: acres. *Popn.* 3 males, 7 females: total 10.
[For the remainder of the parish see 590. 1. 4. above]
[No returns]

[End of Llandissilio Subdistrict]

3 AMROTH (Subdistrict)
Area: 24,608 acres. *Popn.* 1,645 males, 1,718 females: total 3,363.

1 Part of Henllan-Amgoed Parish.   Co. Carmarthen.
Area: 1,033 acres. *Popn.* 85 males, 88 females: total 173.
[For the remainder see 590. 1.2.]

2 Llangan Parish, co. Carmarthen, and Llangan Hamlet, co. Pembroke.
Area of Llangan Parish: 4,758 acres. *Popn.* 280 males, 326 females: total 606.
Area of Llangan Hamlet: 194 acres. *Popn.* 9 males, 16 females: total 25.

(1) LLANGAN PARISH CHURCH.   CO. CARMARTHEN.
Endowed: tithe £100; glebe £45.
Space: free 100.
Present: aft. 20.
Average (12 *months*): morn. 20; aft. 50.
Remarks: The service is performed in this Church alternately.

> John Rees.   Curate.
> St. Clears.

Lewis: prebend in the cathedral church of St. David's, valued at £7, and in the gift of the Bp. Living a discharged vicarage, rated at £3, endowed with £400 royal bounty, and £1,200 parliamentary grant; net income £86; patron, the Bp.; prebendary has two-thirds of tithe, and the vicar one-third: part of the parish is tithe free.

C & C: 1 service in Welsh performed by the incumbent.

I & C: no return.

(2) HENLLAN-AMGOED PARISH CHURCH.   CO. CARMARTHEN.
Endowed: tithe £90.
Space: free 60.
Present: morn. 16.
Average (12 *months*): morn. 20; aft. 50.

Remarks: Divine Service is performed Morning and Afternoon alternately in this church.

Samuel Jones.   Curate.
Llwynbrain.

Lewis: discharged rectory, rated at £6. 10. 5; net income £86; patrons, the landed proprietors of the parish; impropriators, F. Bludworth, Esq., and others. For the chapelry attached see [590. 1. 2(6)].

C & C: 2 service in Welsh performed by the curate.

I & C: no return.

[Note error in parish numbering: for details see 1 above.]

(3) HENLLAN. CO. CARMARTHEN. CONGREGATIONALISTS.
Erected 1830.
Space: free 41; other 100.
Present: morn. 550; aft. 145 scholars.
Average (12 months): morn. 600; aft. 145 scholars.
Remarks: The congregation was not numbered on the 30th March, but a judicious estimate was taken. Should an partr. account be required, I should be happy to furnish it. The congregation is not very fluctuating as the difference will be very little next Sunday or the following.

Joshua Lewis.   Minister.
Henllan.

(4) NAZARETH. CO. CARMARTHEN. BAPTIST.
Erected 1849.
Space: free 250.
Present: even. 190.
Average (5 months): morn. 150; even. 250.
Remarks: This chapel was opened for Divine Service on October 1850. No Sunday School has been kept yet. We Intend to begin it, on next Sunday Being April the 6th.

Theophilus Thomas.   Minister.
Whitland, nr. St. Clears.

3 Cyffic Parish.   co. Carmarthen.
Area: 4,556 acres. *Popn.* 277 males, 243 females: total 520.

(5) CIFFIC PARISH CHURCH.
Space: free 20; other 130.
Usual number of Attendants: morn. 60; aft. 60.

[No sign.]

[Informant's form]

Lewis: perpetual curacy, consolidated with that of Marros [590. 3. 6(11)]; endowed with £8 benefaction by the vicar of Laugharne, and £800 royal bounty; net income £56: patron, vicar of Laugharne: impropriate tithes commuted for £185, and the vicarial for £40.

C & C: 1 service partially in Welsh performed by the curate.

I & C: not resident.

(6) BWLCH Y GWYNT. BAPTIST.
Erected before 1800.
Space: free 36; other 2.
Present: morn. 134; aft. 48 scholars.
Average (12 *months*): morn. 250; aft. 120.

> Theophilus Thomas.   Minister.
> Nazareth, Whiteland.

4 Eglwys-cymmin Parish.   Co. Carmarthen.
Area: 3,740 acres. *Popn.* 163 males, 150 females: total 313.

(7) ST. MARGARET'S PARISH CHURCH.
Endowed: tithe £200; glebe £3.
Space: free 30; other 103.
Present: aft. 80.

> John Rees Taylor.   Rector.
> Pendine, Nr. Laugharne.

Lewis: rectory, rated at £8, in the patronage of the Crown; net income £147, with glebe-house.

C & C: 1 service in English.

I & C: vacant.

(8) ELIM, EGLWYSCUMMIN. INDEPENDENT.
Erected 1832.
Space: free 120; other 96.
Present: morn. 136 + 44 scholars; even. 55.

> David Mathias. Independent Minister.
> Elim, nr. St. Clears.

5 Pendine Parish.   Co. Carmarthen.
Area: 1,578 acres. *Popn.* 99 males, 82 females: total 181.

(9) PENDINE PARISH CHURCH.
Endowed: tithe £67.
Space: free 130.
Present: morn. 41.
Average: morn. 41; aft. 41.

> David Thomas.   Rector.
> Llandawke.

Lewis: rectory not in charge, annexed to that of Llandawke [589. 2. 4(13)]: tithes commuted for £67, subject to rates averaging £5. 16 per annum.

C & C: 1 service in English.

I & C: resident.

(10) Chapel of the United Brethren, commonly called Moravians. Now occupied by the Welsh Calvinistic Methodists.

Erected 1810.

Space: free 120; standing 14 feet by 12 feet.

Present: aft. 54; even. 63.

> Rev. William Williams. Local Preacher.
> Pendine.

6 Marros Parish. Co. Carmarthen.

Area: 2,574 acres. *Popn.* 81 males, 74 females: total 155.

(11) Marros Parish Church.

Space: free 120; other 80.

Usual number of attendants: morn. 80 + 30 scholars. aft. 80 + 30 scholars.

> [no sign.]

[Informant's form]

Lewis: vicarage, consolidated with Kifig [590. 3. 3(5)], endowed with £8 per annum private benefaction, by the vicar of Laugharne, and £800 royal bounty; net income £65: patron, incumbent of Laugharne: tithes commuted for £88. 10., of which £72. 10. payable to the impropriators, subject to rates averaging £3. 12. 4, and £16 to the vicar, subject to rates averaging £1. 4. per annum.

C & C: 1 service in English performed by the incumbent.

I & C: not resident.

ICBS: grant of £60 in 1844.

7 Amroth Parish.

Area: 2,878 acres. *Popn.* 394 males, 442 females: total 836.

(12) Amroth Parish Church.

Endowed: Land £30; tithe £45; permanent endowment £15.

Space: free 28; other 200.

Present: morn. 160 + 50 scholars.

Remarks: The service is alternately morning and evening. The attendance is greater in the summer.

> William Phillips. Curate.

Lewis: discharged vicarage, rated at £3. 18. 6½; endowed with £600 royal bounty, and £600 parliamentary grant; net income £112,; patron and impropriator Charles Poyer Callen, Esq.

C & C: 1 service in English.

I & C: incumbent not resident: curate, who resides at Cranwear, 1½ miles distant, has stipend of £60.

ICBS: grant of £60 in 1852.

(13) ELIM. INDEPENDENT.
Erected 1850.
Space: free 150.
Present: even. 113 + 95 scholars.
Average (10 months): even. 110 + 100 scholars.
Remarks: In this Chapel the Sunday school is kept Sunday Morning and afternoon alternately, and Divine Service in the evening.

> Benjamin Rees. Trustee.
> Stepaside.

8 Crunwear Parish.

Area: 1,690 acres. *Popn.* 131 males, 158 females: total 289.

(14) CRUNWEAR PARISH CHURCH.
Endowed: tithe £105; glebe £40.
Space: free 60; other 120.
Present: even. 150.
Remarks: The service is alternately morning and evening. The congregation in the summer months is larger. The net value is of course below the statement above.

> Wm. Phillips. Rector.

Lewis: discharged rectory. rated at £6. 16. 10½; in the patronage of the Crown: net income £100.
C & C: 1 service in English.
I & C: resident.
ICBS: grant of £45 in 1846.

(15) MOUNTAIN. INDEPENDENTS.
Space: all free.
Present: morn. 50.

> William Phillips. Elder.
> Amroth.

9 Ludchurch Parish.

Area: 1,607 acres. *Popn.* 126 males, 139 females: total 265.

(16) LUDCHURCH PARISH CHURCH.
Endowed: tithe £90; glebe £8.
Present: aft. upwards of 80.
Average: morn. 80 to 100.
Remarks: The service is alternately.

> Thomas Murray. Churchwarden.

Lewis: discharged rectory, rated at £3. 14. 4½; in the patronage of the Crown; tithes commuted for £84; glebe of 10 acres valued at £10.
C & C: 2 services in English.
I & C: incumbent not resident; curate, who resides at Lampeter Velfrey, 2½ miles distant, has stipend of £50.

(17) Ebenezer.   Independent.
Erected 1844.
Space: free 25.
Present: morn. 90; even. 30.
Average (12 *months*): morn. 70.

> John Williams.   Deacon.
> Stepaside, Saundersfoot.

[End of Amroth Subdistrict]

4   NARBERTH (Subdistrict)

Area: incl. Slebech Subdistrict: 34,921 acres. *Popn.* of Narberth Subdistrict: 1,788 males, 2,071 females: total 3,859.

4   Castle Dyrran Hamlet, part of the parish of Cilymaenllwyd, co. Carmarthen.

Area: 666. *Popn.* 32 males, 38 females: total 70.
[For the remainder of the parish see 590. 1. 4.]

(1)   Castledwyran Church.
Endowed: [illegible] £45.
Space: free 60.
Present: aft. 30.
Average: aft. 30.

> N. Bowen Jones.   Rector.

Lewis: perpetual curacy united to the rectory of Cilymaenllwyd [590. 1. 4(10)].
C & C: 1 service in Welsh performed by the incumbent.

I & C: not resident.

[Note: error in numbering of the above.]

1   Crinow Parish.

Area: 352 acres. *Popn.* 30 males, 39 females: total 69.

(2)   Crinow Parish Church.
Space: free 30; other 40.
Present: aft. 20.
Average: morn. 45; aft. 30.
Remarks: The Children of this parish have the privilege of going to either of the schools in the two adjoining parishes, where they are required to attend the Sunday Schools.

> D. Jones.   Minister.
> Llanddewivelfrey.

Lewis: rectory not in charge, endowed with £600 royal bounty; in the patronage of the Crown; net income £79: tithes commuted for £49. 16, with glebe of 1 acres valued at £3.

C & C: 1 service partially in Welsh performed by the curate.

I & C: not resident.

ICBS: granto of £12 in 1840.

2 Lampeter-Velfrey Parish.

Area: 5,667 acres. *Popn.* 464 males, 536 females: total 1,002.

(3) LAMPETER VELFREY PARISH CHURCH.
Endowed: tithe £475; glebe £60.
Space: free 150; other 286.
Present: morn. 130 + 14 scholars.
Average (12 *months*): morn. 140 + 14 scholars.

William Hatton. Rector.

Lewis: rectory, rated at £10; in the patronage of the Crown, net income £409, with a glebe-house.

C & C: 2 services in English.

I & C: no entry.

ICBS: grant of £150 in 1837.

(4) GLYNYRHYD CHAPEL. PARTICULAR BAPTISTS.
Erected first 1811, rebuilt 1835.
Space: free 30; other 14.
Present: morn. 250; aft. 74 scholars; even. 80.*
Average (5 *months*): general congregation 400; scholars 100.†
Remarks: We have but one congregation each part of the day.
*This Lord's day we have our School in the Afternoon. The next in the Morning.
† The average each Sunday during those months.

John Edwards. Minister.

3 Llanddewi Velfrey Parish with Henllan Hamlet.

Total area: 4,022 acres. *Popn.* of the parish: 365 males, 374 females: total 739. *Popn.* of the Hamlet: 19 males, 19 females: total 38.

(5) LLANDEWI VELFREY PARISH CHURCH.
Space: free 100; other 200.
Present: morn. 250 + 60 scholars; aft. 60 scholars.
Average: morn. 200 + 60 scholars; aft. 200 + 50 scholars.

D. Jones. Minister.

Lewis: rectory and vicarage: sinecure rectory, rated at £8; in the patronage of the impropriators, St. David's College, Lampeter: net income, £130: discharged vicarage, rated at £7. 9. 4½; in the gift of the Crown; net income £197, with a glebe-house. Vicarage-house rebuilt under Gilbert's Act.

C & C: 1 service partially in Welsh performed by the incumbent.

I & C: resident.

(6) BETHEL, LLANDDEYVELFREY. INDEPENDENTS.
Erected 1824; rebuilt 1849.
Space: free 11; other 41.
Present: aft. 145 + 80 scholars; even. 30 + 30 scholars.
Average (12 *months*): general congregation 160; scholars 80.
Remarks: The Sunday School is always held in the morning. Preaching in the afternoon and a prayer Meeting in the Evg.

> Thomas Thomas. Deacon.
> Gwindy, Narberth.

(7) FFYNNON CHAPEL, LANDEWY VELFREY. PARTICULAR BAPTISTS.
Erected before 1800. Rebuilt near the old site in 1850.
Space: free 40; other 17; standing 'None with the exception of the Iles.
Present: morn. 57 scholars; aft. 300 + 57 scholars; even. 60 + 30 scholars.
Average (5 *months from April*): general congregation about 600: scholars 100.*
Remarks: We have but one congregation each part of the day. This Sunday we have our School in the Morning. The next in the afternoon, etc. etc.
*The average for each Sunday during those months.

> John Edwards. Minister.

(8) CAVAN. INDEPT.
Erected 1787.
Space: free 67: 40 ft by 32, 21 high.
standing room; 4 ft wide round the galary at bac and to ends as pasage dito down staires. 2 pasiges from front to bac 3 ffeet wide.
Present: morn. 500; aft. 350.
Average: 135.

> David Phillips. Minister.

[Note: this is wrongly numbered and should be under 590. 4. 2.]

5 Narberth North: part of Narberth Parish.
Area: incl. Narberth South [590. 5. 1]: 6,084 acres. *Popn.* 878 males, 1,063 females: total 1,941.

(9) TABERNACLE. INDEPENDENT.
Erected 1815.
Space: free 140; other 290; standing 120.
Present: morn. 380 + 50 scholars; even. 320.
Average: morn. 380 + 50 scholars; even. 320.

> John Lewis. Deacon.
> Draper.

(10) NEBO. CALVINISTIC METHODIST.
Erected 1843.
Space: free 72; other 116; standing 30 x 4 feet.
Present: aft. 61 + 7 scholars; even. 37 + 8 scholars.
Average: general congregation 76; scholars 10.
Remarks: The School is kept in the morning.

> John Evans. Manager.

(11) BETHESDA, HIGH STREET, NARBERTH. PARTICULAR BAPTIST.
Erected 1837.
Space: free 150; other 600.
Present: morn. 150 scholars; aft. 350; even. 400.
Average: morn. 150 scholars; aft. 360; even. 400.

> Benjn. Thomas. Minister.
> Whitley, nr. Narberth.

(12) WESLEYAN CHAPEL, SHEEP STREET. WESLEYAN METHODIST.
Erected 1811.
Space: free 40; other 93.
Present: morn. 71 + 57 scholars; even. 58 + 26 scholars.
Remarks: The congregation was unusually small at the Evening Service.

> Joseph Davies. Chapel Steward.
> Currier.

(13) ST. ANDREW'S PARISH CHURCH. NARBERTH WESTEND.
Space: free 202; other 258.
Present: morn. 224 + 137 scholars; even. 166 + 41 scholars.
Remarks: V [i.e. endowments]. The queries herein will be answered with
all particulars hereafter if required.

> Wm. Lloyd. Rector.

Lewis: rectory, with Robeston Wathen [590. 5. 2(3)] annexed; rated at
£25. 10. 10; in the patronage of the Crown: net income £417: tithes commuted
for £550, with glebe of 60 acres, valued at £60 per annum. Church lately rebuilt,
partly by grant of £150 from the Incorporated Society, and partly by a rate upon the

inhabitants amounting to one third of the costs. New rectory-house erected at a cost of £913 raised by a mortgage on the living under Gilbert's Act.

C & C: 2 services in English.

I & C: resident; curate has stipend of £75.

ICBS: grant of £150 in 1821.

[End of Narberth Subdistrict]

5 SLEBECH (Subdistrict)

Area (incl. under Narbeth Subdistrict): *Popn.* 1,634 males, 1,863 females: total 3,497.

1 Narbeth South: part of Narberth parish.

Area (incl. under Narberth North [590. 4. 5.]: *Popn.* 399 males, 482 females: total 881.

(1) INDEPENDANTS, TEMPLETON.
Erected 1819.
Space: free 30; other 30.
Present: aft. 129 + 45 scholars; even. 112 + 68 scholars.
Remarks: Our services are morning and afternoon alternateley.

> William Thomas. Deacon.
> Templeton.

(2) MOLESTON. P. BAPTISTS.
Erected 1763, rebuilt on the site 1842.
Space: free 140; other 240; standing 160 feet.
Present: morn. 350 + 87 scholars.
Average (10 *months*): morn. 350-400 + 80-100 scholars.
Remarks: We have returned the sittings as sited for individuals both free and other sittings.

> David Phillips. Baptist Minister.
> Malerton.

2 Robeston Wathen Parochial Chapelry.

Area: 1,345 acres. *Popn.* 195 males, 227 females: total 422.

(3) ROBESTON WATHON CHURCH.
Ancient Parish Church attanched to the Rectory of Narberth.
Space: free 70; other 80.
Present: aft. 80 + 30 scholars.
Remarks: Particulars [regarding endowments] herein will be given hereafter if necessary.

> Wm. Lloyd. Rector.

Lewis: consolidated with the rectory of Narberth [590. 4. 5(13)]. Church lately rebuilt at a cost of £330, of which £70 was raised by a rate, £90 from the Church Building Society, and the remainder by subscription from the landed proprietors and the rector.

C & C: 1 service in English.

I & C: see *sub* Narberth.

ICBS: grant of £95 in 1840.

3   Llawhaden Parish.

Area: 4,490 acres. *Popn.* 321 males, 348 females: total 669.
(4)   GOSHEN.   CALVINISTIC METHODIST.
Erected 1840.
Space: free 125.
Present: morn. 103 + 25 scholars; even. 54 + 14 scholars.
Average: 102 + 36 scholars.
Remarks: Sunday School Scholars Average 60.

> John Lewis.   Elder.
> Portyslade.

(5)   BETHESDA.   INDEPENDENTS OR CONGREGATIONALISTS.
Erected 1797; rebuilt 1848.
Space: free 350.
Present: morn 275; aft. 96 scholars; even. 167.

> Samuel Thomas.   Minister.

(6)   LLAWHADEN PARISH CHURCH.
Endowed: tithe commuted at £105; glebe 17 acres.
Space: free 108; other 160.
Present: aft. 110 + 19 scholars.

> Daniel Jones.   Vicar.

Lewis: prebend in the cathedral church of St. David's, rated at £17. 17. 1: discharged vicarage, with the perpetual curacy of Bletherston [590. 2. 7(11)] annexed, rated at £8. 18. 6½; net income £152, with glebe-house: tithes commuted for £315, of which £210 are payable to the Chancellor of St. David's, who also has a gleb e of 170 acres valued at £160 per annum, and £105 to the vicar, who has a glebe of 45 acres valued at £50 per annum: rates on the whole average £25. 15. 1. per annum.

C & C: 1 service partially in Welsh.

I & C: resident.

5   Slebech Parish.

Area: 4,586 acres. *Popn.* 168 males, 185 females: total 353.

(7) SLEBECH PARISH CHURCH.
Erected in January 1848 in lieu of old Parish Church.
Endowed: land £95; tithe £48; permanent endowment (Queen Anne's Bounty) £6. 6s.
Space: 100.
Present: aft. 60.
Remarks: Service alternately morning and afternoon. Plenty of sittings. *In Summer* the congregation is generally about 130, weather permitting.

W. D. Landon. Perpetual Curate.

Lewis: perpetual curacy, endowed with £200 private benefaction, and £800 royal bounty: patron and impropriator, Baron de Rutzen: net income £50. New building in course of construction by the patron at estimated cost of £5-£6,000.

C & C: with Minwear returned as 'out of repair'. 1 service in English

I & C: resident.

(8) ZION'S CHAPEL.
Erected 1833.
Space: free 20; standing 30.
Present: aft. 127 + 38 scholars;
Average (11 *months*): morn. 120 + 68 scholars.
Remarks: The Services are held morning and afternoon alternately and likewise the school.

David Jenkins. Minister.
Dollaston Wiston Parish.

6 Mounton Parish.

Area: 330 acres. *Popn.* 17 males, 15 females: total 32.
[No returns]

Lewis: consolidated with the rectory of Narberth [590. 4. 5(13)]: the church now a chapel of ease: impropriator, the Callen family.

C & C: no entry.

I & C: no entry.

7 Minwere Parish.

Area: 1,957 acres. *Popn.* 48 males, 46 females: total 94.
[No returns]

Lewis: perpetual curacy, endowed with £200 private benefaction, £400 royal bounty and £200 parliamentary grant: net income £50: patron and impropriator, Baron de Rutzen.

C & C: no entry.

I & C: no entry.

8 Martletwy Parish.

Area: 3,551 acres. *Popn.* 381 males, 448 females: total 829.

(9) MARTLETWY PARISH CHURCH.
Endowed: land £15; tithe £80. 4. 5; glebe £6.
Space: free 172; other 62.
Present: aft. 75.
Average (6 *months*): morn. 100; aft. 100.
Remarks: There is divine service once only on each Sunday morning and afternoon alternately.

> Edmund Edward Allen.
> Officiating Minister.

Lewis: discharged vicarage, rated at £4; endowed with £200 royal bounty and £400 parliamentary grant: patron and impropriator, Hon. Capt. Greville: tithes commuted for £180, of which £100 are payable to the impropriator and £80 to the vicar who also has a glebe of 4 acres valued at £5 per annum; net income £100. Church contains between 700 and 800 sittings, half of which are free.

C & C: 1 service in English.

I & C: not resident; curate, who resides at Yerbeston 3 miles distant, has a stipend of £50.

ICBS: grant of £40 in 1849.

9 Coedcanlass Parish

Area: 1150 acres. *Popn.* 81 males, 86 females: total 167.

[No returns]

Lewis: donative, annexed to the vicarage of Martletwy [(9) above]: minister has stipend of £2 paid by the impropriator, Sir John Owen, Bart., who repaired the years a few years since.

C & C: No return.

I & C: No return.

(10) HOREB CHAPEL. INDEPENDANT.
Erected before 1830; rebuilt 1842.
Space: free 120; other 80; standing 100.
Present: morn. 67.
Average: morn. 100.

> J. W. D. Thomas.　Deacon.
> Camp's Hill.

(11) MARTLETWY CHAPEL. PARTICULAR BAPTISTS.
Erected before 1830.
Space: free 160; other 40; standing 100.
Present: morn. 197.
Average (12 *months*): morn. 200.

> Thomas Davies.　Deacon.
> Martletwy House, Haverfordwest.

(12) Burnett's Hill Chapel. Welsh Methodist.
Erected 1810.
Space: free 170; other 18; standing 50.
Present: aft. 170.
Average (12 *months*): morn. 200.

> Thomas Owen. Elder.
> Land Shippin, Haverfordwest.

[End of Slebech Subdistrict]

6 BEGELLY (Subdistrict)
Area: 13,033 acres. *Popn.* 2,024 males, 2,181 females: total 4,205.

1 Yerbeston Parish.
Area: 1,224 acres. *Popn.* 77 males, 76 females: total 153.

(1) Yerbeston Parish Church.
Endowed: tithe £73; glebe £24.
Space: free 45; other 52.
Present: morn. 40; aft. 40.
Average (5 *months*): morn. 40; aft. 40.
Remarks: There is divine service once only on each Sunday morning and afternoon alternately.

> Edmund Edward Allen.
> Officiating Minister.

Lewis: discharged rectory, rated at £5. 3. 9; endowed with £400 private benefaction and £400 royal bounty: patron, Baron de Rutzen.

C & C: 1 service in English.

I & C: incumbent not resident: curate, who resides in the parish, has stipend of £65.

2 Loveston Parish.
Area: 1,233 acres. *Popn.* 83 males, 76 females: total 159.

(2 Loveston Parish Church.
Endowed: Bounty Rent Charge £110.
Space: free 60; other 40.
Present: morn. 14.
Average (12 *months*): morn. 12-25; aft. 15-30.
Remarks: The Services are Alternate Morning or Evening.

> James Dalton. Curate.
> St. Issell's, Tenby.

Lewis: discharged rectory, rated at £4. 5. 5; endowed with £600 royal bounty;

net income £109: patron, Earl of Cawdor: tithes commuted for £90; glebe of 2 acres, valued at £5 per annum.

C & C: 1 service in English.

I & C: incumbent not resident: curate, who resides at St. Issell's, 4 miles distant, has stipend of £50.

3   Reynoldston Parish.

Area: 525 acres. *Popn.* 49 males, 51 females: total 100.

(3)   REYNOLDSTON PARISH CHURCH.
Endowed: land £27; tithe £33; permanent endowment £15.
Space: free 70; other 35.
Present: aft. 60.
Average (12 *months*): morn. 35; aft. 60.

James Dawkins Palmour.   Incumbent.

Lewis: donative, endowed with £600 royal bounty and £200 parliamentary grant; net income £62: patron, Sir R. Phillips, Bart.

C & C: 1 service in English.

I & C: not resident.

4   Jeffreston Parish.

Area: 2,343 acres. *Popn.* 308 males, 371 females: total 679.

(4)   JEFFRESTON PARISH CHURCH.
Endowed £132.
Space: free 160; other 150.
Present: morn. 180.
Average (12 *months*): morn. 150; aft. 200.
Remarks: I have no means of knowing from what source the endowment is derived, but I have stated as nearly as I can its annual value.

John Dawkins Palmour.   Curate.

Lewis: vicarage, rated at £4. 17. 6; endowed with £200 private benefaction, £600 royal bounty and £1,000 parliamentary grant; net income, £134; patrons and impropriators, Precentor and Chapter of St. David's.

C & C: 1 service in English.

I & C: no return.

(5)   WESLEYAN CHAPEL.   WESLEYAN METHODIST.
Erected before 1820.
Space: free 78; other 12.
Present: aft. 48 + 22 scholars; even. 70.

Thomas Hat.   Leader.

(6) Cresselly.   Primitive Methodists.
Erected 1837.
Space: free 120.
Present: aft. 30-50.
Average: 60.
Remarks: The Sice of the Chapel is 30 feet by 14 feet.

George Davies.   Chappel Steward.

[The following note is attached]   This return is exceedingly inaccurate and I fear that most of the returns from Dissenting congregations are very far from the truth. This return I can state from my own personal knowledge is false. It sets down 60 as the average congregation. The truth is the congregation seldom exceeds 15 and there are only 3 persons in the Parish who call themselves Primitive Methodists.

[Signed] J. D. Palmer.
Registrar.

5   Begelly: part of the Parish of Begelly.
Area: 2,447 acres. *Popn.* 375 males, 404 females: total 779.

(7) Begelly Parish Church.
Endowed: tithe £200; glebe £20; fees £2.
Space: free 250; other 50.
Present: morn. 150 + 75 scholars.
Average (12 *months*): morn. 150 + 75 scholars; aft. 200 + 75 scholars.

Richard Burthby.   Rector.

Lewis: discharged rectory, rated at £12. 19. 2; net income £216: patron, Sir R. B. P. P. Phillip Philipps.

C & C: 1 service in English.

I & C: resident.

(8) Zion.   Calvinistic Methodist.
Erected 1828.
Space: free 150.
Present: aft. 200 + 16 scholars; even. 66 + 12 scholars.
Average (12 *months*): morn. 90 + 12 scholars; aft. 140 + 16 scholars; even. 60 + 12 scholars.
Remarks: 2. The service on March 31st was unusually large.
2. The first service each sabbath is held morning and afternoon alternately.
3. Many of the Sunday Scholars attend a school in the adjoining parish.
4. A Gallery is in the course of erection for 50 more sittings.

Thomas Ashford.   Minister.

6   Williamston Chapelry: part of the parish of Begelly.
Area: 1,431 acres. *Popn.* 270 males, 281 females: total 551.

(9)   EAST WILLIAMSTON CHAPEL OF EASE TO BEGELLY.
Space: free 40; other 60.
Present: aft. 100 + 35 scholars.
Average (12 *months*): morn. 60; aft. 100 + 35 scholars.
Remarks: The income is included in Begelly. The Chapel is a miserable place.

> Richard Burthby.   Rector.
> Begelly Rectory.

C & C: 1 service in English.

(10)   MORETON CHAPEL.   WESLEYAN METHODIST.
Erected 1850.
Space: free 100; other 30.
Present: morn. 55 scholars; aft. 130; even. 100.
Average (3 *months*): general congregation 90.

> Benjamin Owens.   Superintendant.

7   St. Issells Parish.
Area: 3,830 acres. *Popn.* 862 males, 962 females: total 1,794.

(11)   ST. ISSELLS PARISH CHURCH.
Endowed: Queen Anne's Bounty R. Charge £131; fees £2.
Space: free 80; other 270.
Present: aft. 183 + 77 scholars.
Average (12 *months*): morn. about 200 + 70 scholars.
aft. from 200-300 + 80 scholars.
Remarks: The Services are alternate Morning and Afternoon.

> James Dalton.   Vicar.

Lewis: discharged vicarage, rated at £3. 17. 6; endowed with £600 royal bounty, and £400 parliamentary grant: patrons and impropriators, Dean and Chapter of St. David's: vicarial tithes commuted for £105, subject to rates averaging £17. 12. 4, and the Chapter tithes for £140, subject to rates averaging £19. 13. 8: glebe-house, and glebe of 10 acres valued at £8 per annum.
C & C: 1 service in English.
I & C: resident.

(12)   SARDIS.   INDEPENDENT.
Erected 1808.
Space: free 160; other 120; standing, gallery 24 ft by 6: free space 24 by 18.
Present: morn. 124.
Average (12 *months*): morn. 250.

> William Thomas.   Minister.

(13) BETHESDA. CALVINISTIC METHODIST.
Erected 1826.
Space: free 150.
Present: morn. 60 + 4 scholars.
Average (12 *months*): aft. 70 + 6 scholars.
Remarks: The service is held at 10 and 2 alternately.

> Thomas Ashford. Minister.
> Begelly.

(14) BETHEL. INDEPENDENTS.
Erected 1838.
Space: free 134; other 124; standing 60.
Average (12 *months*): 250.
Remarks: The service is 10 and 6.

> William Thomas. Independent
> Minister.
> Saundersfoot.

(15) HILL CHAPEL, KINGSMOOR. PRIMITIVE METHODIST.
Erected 1837.
Space: free 120; other 80.
Present: morn. 70; even. 200.
Average (12 *months*): morn. 100; aft. 30 scholars; even. 200.

> John Maylard. Minister.
> Pembroke Dock.

[End of Begelly Subdistrict and end of Narberth District]

Area: 70,276 acres. *Popn.* 10,778 males, 12,182 females: total 22,960.

1 TENBY (Subdistrict)
Area: 29,740 acres. *Popn.* 3,983 males, 4,966 feamles: total 8,949.

1 Redberth Parish.
Area: 305 acres. *Popn.* 58 males, 79 females: total 137.

(1) REDBERTH PARISH CHURCH.   An ancient building restored.
Endowed: land £64; permanent endowment £2.
Space: free 53; other 91.
Present: morn. 41 + 37 scholars.
Remarks: The ancient Church was pulled down and the materials reconstructed at a cost of about £200.

> Gilbert N. Smith.   Curate.
> Gumfreston Rectory.

Lewis: perpetual curacy; endowed with £1,200 royal bounty and £200 parliamentary grant: patron, Bp. St. David's: net income £66: impropriation belongs to the crown. Church rebuilt and opened for public worship in August 1841, at a cost of £200 raised partly by rate, partly by private and public constributions, aided by a grant of £20 from the Church Building Society.

C & C: 1 service in English.

I & C: no return.

ICBS: grant of £20 in 1840.

(2) WESLEYAN METHODIST.
Erected 1822.
Space: free 72.
Present: even. 68.

> Thomas Howells.   Local Preacher.
> Redberth.

2 Gumfreston Parish.
Area: 1,644 acres. *Popn.* 75 males, 72 females: total 147.

(3) GUMFRESTON PARISH CHURCH.
Endowed: tithe £154; glebe £54; fees £1.
Space: free 37; other 57.

Present: morn. 23 + 18 scholars.

Gilbert N. Smith.   Rector.

Lewis: discharged rectory, rated at £9. 12. 3½; patron, Meyrick family: tithes commuted for £154; glebe of 26 acres, valued at £25. 4. per annum.

C & C: 1 service in English.

I & C: resident.

3 Tenby: St. Mary Parish.
Area: 2,242 acres. *Popn.* 1,315 males, 1,893 females: total 3,208.

(4) St. Mary's Parish Church, High Street, Tenby.
Endowed: tithes, commuted.
Space: free 340; other 688.
Remarks: The Minister cannot make a return to No. 7 [i.e. attendances] never having considered that it came within his province of ability to certify such facts.

J. N. Humphreys.   Rector.

Lewis: consolidated rectory and vicarage; rated at £26. 10. 10 (rectory) and £13. 6. 8 (discharged vicarage); glebe of 15 acres, with a house, valued at £58 per annum: tithes commuted for £236.

C & C: 2 services in English.

I & C: resident: curate has stipend of £50.

(5) Mans Hill Chapel, Tenby out-liberty.   Brethren in Christ.
Erected 1827.
Used as a dwelling.
Present: morn. 60.

George Morgan.   Leader.
Mans Hill.

(6) The Bethel Chapel.   Mixed.
Space: free 200.
Present: aft. 60.
Average: aft. 80.
Remarks: The Bethel Chapel belongs to all the Denominations in the town of Tenby. Tis an united effort to benefit the Sailors & Fisherman. One Sabbath Service and one weekly service are held—Opened only on the 1st Sabbath in '51.

(Rev) Daniel Anthony.
Occasional Supply.

(7) WESLEYAN CHAPEL.   WESLEYAN METHODIST.
Erected 1804.
Space: free 200; other 100.
Present: morn. 72 + 20 scholars; efen. 158 + 30 scholars.
Average: morn. 100 + 20 scholars; even. 200 + 40 scholars.

Thomas Rowe.   Steward.
7 Crackwell St.

(8) THE TABERNACLE CHAPEL, FROG STREET.   INDEPENDENTS.
Erected 1822.
Space: free 190; other 200.
Present: morn. 250 + 30 scholars; even. 350 + 30 scholars.

Rev. Danel Anthony.   Minister.
High Street.

(9) BAPTIST CHAPEL.
Erected 1845.
Vestry used for day school.
Space: free 84; other 170; standing 50.
Present: morn. 130; even. 200.
Average: general congregation 300; scholars 65.

William Thomas Phillips.   Baptist
Minister.
Rose Cottage, South Parade.

4 Caldy Island.   Ex. Par.
Area: 462 acres. *Popn.* 46 males, 40 females: total 86.
[No returns]

5 St. Margaret's Island.   Ex. Par.
Area: 10 acres. *Popn.* nil.
[No returns]

6 Penally Parish.
Area: 2,832 acres. *Popn.* 194 males, 204 females: total 394.

(10) PENALLY PARISH CHURCH.
Endowed: tithe by Commutation £90; glebe nine acres £10; fees on an
average £1, Easter offerings £2. I have made no deducations for Rates.
Present: no service.
Average (12 *months*): morn. 150 + 55 scholars; aft. 120 + 50 scholars.
Remarks: As the Church is now being restored I cannot state the number of
free and other sittings, but they will be considerably increased by the new
arrangements.

John Hughes.   Minister.

Lewis: discharged vicarage, rated at £4. 17. 11; endowed with £200 royal bounty; net income £77: with a glebe-house: patron, Bp. St. David's: impropriator, Sir R. B. P. Phillips, Bart. Vicarage erected by the incumbent in 1822 under Gilbert's Act.

C & C: 2 services in English.

I & C: resident.

ICBS: grant of £42 in 1850.

7   Manobier Parish.

Area: 3,493 acres. *Popn.* 317 males, 381 females: total 698.

(11)   MANOBIER PARISH CHURCH.
Endowed: land £31; tithe £30; glebe £4; permanent endowment £13; fees £1.
Space: free 70; other 170.
Present: morn. 223.
Average: morn. 240.

Henry Hughes.   Minister.

Lewis: discharged vicarage, rated at £8; endowed with £600 royal bounty, and £1,400 parliamentary grant: in the patronage of Christ's College, Cambridge, the impropriators of the great tithes. Accomodation recently augmented by the erection of a gallery.

C & C: 1 service in English.

I & C: not resident.

ICBS: grant of £40 made in 1838.

(12)   JAMESTOWN PRIMITIVE METHODIST CHAPEL.
Erected 1828.
Space: free 50; other 30; standing 20.
Present: aft. 60.
Average (3 months): aft. 60.

John Bittle.   Chapel Steward.
Jamestown.

(13)   INDEPENDENT CHAPEL, NEWTON.   INDEPENDENTS.
Erected 1822.
Space: free 100; other 60.
Present: aft. 120.
Remarks: There is ony one Service on Sunday held alternately morning and afternoon.

James Eddy.   Minister.

(14) PENUEL. PARTICULAR BAPTIST.
Erected 1850.
Space: free 100; other 80; standing 20.
Present: aft. 130; even. 200.

> William Freeman.   Deacon.
> James Cook.   Manager.
> Jamestown.

8   Hodgeston Parish.
Area: 709 acres. *Popn.* 36 males, 41 females: total 78.

(15)   HODGESTON PARISH CHURCH.
Endowed: tithe £75; glebe from the parish of Manobier £25; permanent endowment £46. no deductions for rates etc.
Space: free 8; other 40.
Present: aft. 80.
Remarks: I cannot state the average number of attendants during twelve months preceding March 30, 1851 as I was only inducted on the 26 of February last.

> Henry Hughes.   Minister.

Lewis: rectory, rated at £7. 13. 4: patrons, Sir John Owen, Bart., and Price Price, Esq.: tithes commuted for £73, with a glebe of a 20 acres valued at £26 per annum.
C & C: 1 service in English.
I & C: not resident.

9   Lamphey Parish.
Area: 1,976 acres. *Popn.* 191 males, 204 females: total 395.

(16)   LAMPHEY PARISH CHURCH.
Endowed: land £27; tithe £74. 5s; glebe £16; fees £2.
Space: free 90; other 230.
Present: morn. 160 + 25 scholars; even. 197.
Average: morn. 243 + 40 scholars; even. 230 + 10 scholars.
Remarks: There is no other place of worship in the Parish. Infants, together with habitual absentees from worship may be reckoned at 90. The church is quite often full.

> James Broff Byers.   Vicar.

Lewis: discharged vicarage, rated at £5. 8. 11½; endowed with £600 royal bounty; net income £115: patron and impropriator, Bp. St. David's: lands alienated in 16th. cent are tithe free; tithes commuted for £133, of which £60 payable to the Bp. and £73 to the vicar, who also has glebe of 4 acres, valued at £15 per annum: church restored in 1826 partly by subscription, partly by rate, and partly by gift from the Incorporated Society.
C & C: 2 services in English.
I & C: resident: curate's stipend not stated.
ICBS: grant of £100 made in 1827.

10 St. Florence Parish.

Area: 2,490 acres. *Popn.* 164 males, 191 females: total 355.

(17) SAINT FLORENCE PARISH CHURCH.
Endowed: tithe £30; glebe £20; permanent endowment £16; fees £2.
Space: free 30; other 144.
Present: aft. 80 + 39 scholars.
Average: morn. 75 + 40 scholars; aft. 75 + 40 scholars.
Remarks: Great want of Sittings.

G. W. Birkett. Vicar.

Lewis: sinecure rectory and vicarage: the rectory, rated at £16. 12. 1, in the patronage of St. John's College, Cambridge. The vicarage, discharged, rated at £4. 18. 4; endowed with £400 royal bounty; patron, the rector: the livings to be consolidated at the next appointment: rectorial tithes commuted for £160, subject to rates averaging £14 per annum, with glebe of 20 acres, valued at £35: vicarial tithes commuted for £80, with a glebe of 10 acres valued at £20 per annum.

C & C: 1 service in English.

I & C: resident.

(18) BETHEL. INDEPENDENT.
Erected about the year 1802.
Space: free 4; other 22; standing 50 (people).
Present: morn. 82; even. 75.
Average (12 *months*)*:* morn. 120.

Benjamin Evans. Minister.
Green, Pembroke.

11 Carew Parish.

Area: 5,636 acres. *Popn.* 462 males, 529 females: total 991.

(19) ST. MARY'S CAREW PARISH CHURCH.
Endowed: land £10; tithe £90; glebe £3; permanent endowment £23; fees £2; other sources £20.
Space: free 100; other 360.
Present: morn. 200; aft. 50 + 50 scholars.
Average: morn. 200; aft. 50 + 50 scholars.

John Phelps. Vicar.

Lewis: discharged vicarage, not rated, endowed with £200 private benefaction, £400 royal bounty, and £800 parliamentary grant; net income £182, with a glebe-house; patron and impropriator, Bp. St. David's: impropriate tithes commuted for £481, with a glebe of 33 acres, valued at £30 per annum; vicarial tithes commuted for £89. 15., with a glebe of 2 acres valued at £5.

C & C: 2 services in English.

I & C: resident.

ICBS: grant of £75 in 1838.

(20) LECTURE ROOM. [in other hand, 'Dissenter']
Erected 1841.
Cost: £74, defrayed by private benefaction.
Space: free 50.
Average (12 *months*): even. 1,481 [underlined].
Remarks: Service held every month.

James Rogers. Steward.
Williamston Park.

[This return is on an Established Church schedule.]

(21) PISGAH. PR. BAPTIST.
Erected 1821.
Space: free 140; other 110; standing 20.
Present: morn. 36 scholars; aft. 205.
Average: general congregation 200; scholars 36.

Thomas James. Manager.
Pisga, Carew.

(22) WESLEYAN METHODIST.
Erected 1816.
Space: free 108; other 36.
Present: aft. 100; even. 120.
Present: aft. 100; even. 120.
Average (12 *months*): aft. 130.

John Codd. Steward.
Sagiston, Nr. Pembroke.

12 Lawrenny Parish.

Area: 2,672 acres. *Popn.* 182 males, 216 females: total 398.

(23) LAWRENNY PARISH CHURCH.
Endowed: tithe £168. 10s; glebe £28. 4s.
Space: free 100; other 120.
Present: morn. 70.
Average (12 *months*): morn. 120; aft. 150.

Richard Hoon. Church warden.

Lewis: discharged rectory, rated at £13; net income £168: patron, the Barlow family.

C & C: 1 service in English.

I & C: not resident: curate, who resides at Llangum, 2 miles distant, has stipend of £50.

13   Nash Parish, with Upton Hamlet.

Area of Nash: 577 acres. *Popn.* 69 males, 63 females: total 132.
Area of Upton: 435 acres. *Popn.* 10 males, 13 females: total 26.

(24)   NASH PARISH CHURCH.
Endowed: tithe £80; glebe £60.
Space: free 63; other 70.
Present: morn. 70 + 8 scholars.
Average: morn. 80.

W. P. Evans.   Rector.

Lewis: rectory with Upton annexed, rated at £6. 12. 8½; net income £130 with a
glebe-house: patron, Rev. William Evans: tithes commuted for £80; glebe of 26
acres valued at £55 per annum.
C & C: 1 service in English.
I & C: legally not resident.
ICBS: grant of £70 in 1841.

14   Cosheston Parish.

Area: 2,440 acres. *Popn.* 265 males, 286 females: total 551.

(25)   COSHESTON PARISH CHURCH.
Endowed: tithe £247; glebe £40.
Space: free 20; other 280.
Present: morn. 94 + 48 scholars; aft. 97 + 51 scholars.
Remarks: The above is the *exact number* of Persons attending Divine Service
on Sunday March 30, 51. Yet I'll say the average number for the year is
150 (besides the Sunday Scholars)—many at the present season being
kept away by sickness. Total number of in the Book are boys 30, girls 29.

William Bowling.   Rector.

Lewis: discharged rectory, rated at £11. 12. 11; net income £160, with glebe-
house: patron, George Bonling, Esq., of Woodfield.
C & C: 2 services, partially in English and Welsh.
I & C: resident.
ICBS: grant of £100 in 1833.

(26)   NEBO.   INDEPENDENTS OR CONGREGATIONALISTS.
Erected 1836.
Space: free 130.
Present: morn. 27 scholars; aft. 55; even. 26.
Average: morn. 20 scholars; aft. 50.
Remarks: Erected by voluntary subscriptions.

William Trevent.   Deacon.

(27)   CONGREGATIONAL OR INDEPENDENT.
Space: free 40.
Present: even. 45.
Remarks: This is a place under the jurisdiction of the Independent Chapel at Pembroke for Prayer meetings Exclusively on every Sunday Evening. The Congregation is composed of members of the Church and other Denominations of Desenters which is termed Union Prayers. Consequently they will be returned from their respective places of Worship Morning and Afternoon.

John Lewis.   Deacon.

15   Pembroke St. Michael Parish.
Area: 1,817 acres. *Popn.* 603 males, 753 females: total 1356.

(28)   ST. MICHAEL'S PARISH CHURCH, TOWN OF PEMBROKE.
Almost entirely rebuilt in 1832.
Space: free 100; other 400.
Usual number of attendants: morn. 350 + 100 scholars; even. 350.

Charles Philipps.   Vicar.

[Informant's form]

Lewis: discharged vicarage, consolidated with those of St. Mary's [591. 2. 1(2)], and St. Nicholas or Monkton [591. 2. 1(3)]; rated at £9, viz., St. Michael's £4, and St. Nicholas £5, St. Mary's being not in charge: net income £439, with a glebe-house: patron and impropriator, Sir John Owen, Bart. Tithes commuted as follows:- St. Mary's, for £350, of which £187. 10. are payable to the impropriator, and £162. 10. to the vicar, subject to rates averaging £22. 10: of St. Michael's, for £325, of which £162. 10. are payable to the impropriator, and £162. 10. to the vicar, subject to rates averaging £22. 10: of St. Nicholas, for £475, of which £300 belong to the impropriator, and £175 to the vicar, subject to rates averaging £20. Cost of rebuilding St. Michael's in 1832 defrayed by a parochial rate.

C & C: 3 services in English.

I & C: resident: 2 curates have stipends of £110 and £50 respectively.

ICBS: grant of £350 in 1832.

(29)   WESLEYAN CHAPEL.
Erected 1822.
Space: free 250, other 350.
Present: morn. 300 + 108 scholars; even. 320 + 94 scholars.
Remarks: The attendance of congregation and School children of yesterday is about the average.

William Wairlowe.   Steward.

[End of Tenby Subdistrict]

2 PEMBROKE (Subdistrict)
Area: 30,991 acres. *Popn.* 5,658 males, 6,004 females: total 11,662.

1   St. Mary Parish.
Area: 3,457 acres. *Popn.* 3,542 males, 4,079 females: total 7,621.
Military in barracks: 253.

(1)   St. John's, Pembroke Dock.
New Parish under provisions 6 & 7 Vict. cap. 37.
Situated at Pembroke Dock, in the new Parish Town of Pembroke Dock.
Consecrated on 29th Sept. 1848, by Bishop of St. David's;   Mother Church, St. Mary's Pembroke.
Erected by the inhabitants.
Cost defrayed by   £500 from Admiralty
                        £3,000 Inhabitants
                        ————
                        £3,500
Endowed: Fees £10;   Easter offerings £5;   Ecclesiastical Commissioners £150.
Space: free 500; other 375.
Present: morn. 430 + 52 scholars; even. 769 + 50 scholars.
Average (12 *months*): morn. 400 + 79 scholars; even. 750 + 62 scholars.

Geoff. Fitzroy Kelly, M.A. Incumbent.

Lewis: see entry under St. Michael's Parish [591. 1. 15(28)].
C & C: 2 services in English.
I & C: residents.
ICBS: grant of £450 in 1845.

(2)   St. Mary Church.
Space: free 20; other 81.
Usual number of attendants: morn. 300; even. 300.

Informant: Jos. Lewis. Registrar.

[Informant's form]
Lewis: see entry under St. Michael Parish, 591. 1. 15(28).

[2] (3)   Monkton or St. Nicholas.
Space: free 2; other 50.
Usual number of attendants: morn. 80; even. 60.

Informant: Jos Lewis. Registrar.

[Informant's form]

[Note: this return is misplaced; it should come under 591.2.2, p.400 below]

(4)   CHAPEL OF HER MAJESTY'S DOCK YARD PEMBROKE.
Situated within the Walls of the Yard, in the Parish of St. John's.
Neither consecrated nor licensed.
Erected by Lords Commissioners of the Admiralty.
Space: 800.
Present: morn. 265; aft. 112.
Average (12 *months*): morn. 250; aft. 100.

> James H. Mallet.   Chaplain of Her
> Majesty's Dockyard.

Lewis: chapel not consecrated; in the patronage of the Admiralty.

C & C: 2 services in English.

I & C: incumbent resident.

(5)   BETHANY CHAPEL, PEMBROKE DOCK.   BAPTIST.
Erected 1818.
Space: free 170; other 441.
Present: morn. 250; aft. school; even. 300.
Average (12 *months*): morn. 300 + 108 scholars; aft. 130 scholars; even. 450.
Remarks: Sickness is very prevalent among the members and the congregation at this time. Several families were absent on that account last Lord's Day. The Sunday School attends divine worship on Sabbath mornings. The particulars given by the Superintendent.

> Henry James Morgan. Minister.
> Front Street.

(6)   BAPTIST CHAPEL.
Obtained by the Baptists in 1836.
Space: free 140; other 86; standing 50.
Present: morn. 170; even. 250.
Average (12 *months*): morn. 1,960; even. 3,250.
Remarks: The chapel was erected as a dwelling house afterwards occupied by the Wesleyan Body, and taken by us in 1836: since then it has been considerably improved.

> Thomas Morgan.   Minister.

(7)   TABERNACLE.   INDEPENDENTS OR CONGREGATIONALISTS.
Erected 1812.
Space: free 86; other 230.
Present: morn. 194; aft. 33 scholars; even. 146.
Average (12 *months*): morn. 208; aft. 30 scholars; even. 147.

> [Signature illegible]   Deacon.

(8)   PREACHING ROOM, CASTLE BACK.   PRIMITIVE METHODIST.
Fitted up for worship 1839.
Space: free 75.
Present: aft. 70; even. 70.
Average (12 *months*): aft. 60; even. 60.

John Jones.   Steward.
Main Street.

(9)   GISHOM CHAPEL [?], PEMBROKE DOCK.   CALVINISTIC METHODIST.
Erected 1838.
Space: free 140; other 360.
Present: morn. 330; 'for scholars see S. Sch' Report'. aft. school Sunday
School; even. 350; 'for scholars see S. Sch. Report'.
Average: morn. 400; even. 400.

John Adams.   Secretary.
Pembroke Dock.

(10)   BETHEL.   BAPTIST.
Erected 1844.
Space: free 90; other 450.
Present: morn. 250 + 70 scholars; aft. 81 scholars; even. 400.
Average (6 *months*): morn. 281 + 81 scholars; aft. 120 scholars; even. 490.
Remarks: The lower number in Division the VIII [i.e. Attendances] shows
increase which is accounted for by the fact of the weather being more
favourable and therefore the attendance is something larger in the Summer
season than in the autumn and winter. Some also have lately left for other
and distant places.

Evan Davies.   Minister.
Lewis Street, Pembroke Dock.

(11)   WESLEY CHAPEL, MEYRICK STREET, PEMBROKE DOCK.   WESLEYAN
METHODIST.
Erected 1848.
Space: free 346; other 574.
Present: morn. 389 + 191 scholars; even. 545 + 80 scholars.
Remarks: The Chapel and School room is one building. The School room
being underneath the floor of the Chapel but not underground.
This Chapel was built in lieu of one that was too small, not on the same site
but on a more central part of the town. The old Chapel was built in the
year 1820 and disposed of in 1849.

John Road.   Steward.
Shipwright.
Meyrick Street, Pembroke Dock.

(12)   TEMPERANCE HALL is at present used as a place of worship. A Chapel being in course of erection to be called "Meyrick Street Chapel" to contain about 500 persons and will be ready to receive them about Christmas next.

INDEPENDENT.
Space (Meyrick Street Chapel) to contain 500.
Present: morn. 151 + 80 scholars; even. 186 + 50 scholars.
Average (5 *months*): morn. 150 + 80 scholars; even. 180 + 50 scholars.

William Burdwood.   Treasurer.

(13)   ZION CHAPEL, PEMBROKE DOCK.   PRIMITIVE METHODIST.
Erected 1849.
Space: free 120; other 48.
Present: aft. 60; even. 60.
Average (12 *months*): morn. 40 scholars; aft. 150 + 50 scholars; even. 150.

John Maylard.   Minister.
Hobbs Point.

(14)   ST. MARY'S.   ROMAN CATHOLIC.
Erected four years.
Space: free 150; standing 30.
Present: morn. 110; aft. 50.

Oliver Maybury [?].   Priest.
Dimand Street, Pembroke Dock.

(15)   TABERNACLE, NORTH BREWERY STREET.   INDEPENDENT.
Erected 1824.
Space: free 36; other 516.
Present: morn. 150 + 70 scholars; even. 250.
Average (3 *months*): morn. 200 + 60 scholars; even. 300.

Charles Sumpter.   Deacon.
7 Queen Street.

(16)   BETHEL CHAPEL, WEST GATE.   CALVINISTIC METHODISTS.
Erected 1826.
Space: free 90; other 158.
Present: morn. 110 + 30 scholars; even. 160 + 20 scholars.
Average: morn. 120 + 60 scholars; even. 200 + 30 scholars.

William Powell.   Minister.

2   Monckton Within and Without Parish.

[For the parish church see 591. 2. 1. (3) above.]
Area: 4,629 acres. *Popn.* 733 males, 812 females: total 1,545.

(17) Gilead Chapel, Monkton. Calvinistic Methodists.
Erected 1844.
Space: free 80; other 39; 30-40 might stand in the places not occupied with pews or forms.
Present: aft. 95.
Average (12 *months*): aft. 100 + 40 scholars.

> John Davies. Minister.
> Mead Lodge Mews, Pembroke Dock.

(18) Ebenezer, Monktown or St. Nicholas. Independent.
Erected 1850.
Space: 30 feet by 18 all free.
Present: no service, average no. 100.
Remarks: This place is in connection with the Tabernacle Pembroke, the services are conducted by the minister and the members of that place of worship.

> William Trewent. Deacon.

(19) Hundleton Chapel. Calvinistic Methodist.
Erected 1820.
Space: free 100; other 36.
Present: aft. 86 + 20 scholars; even. 54 + 20 scholars.
Average: aft. 110 + 20 scholars; even. 80 + 10 scholars.

> William Powell. Minister.

3 St. Petrox Parish.
Area: 967 acres. *Popn.* 37 males, 49 females: total 86.

(20) St. Petrox Parish Church.
Endowed: tithe £46; glebe £60.
Space: free 40; other 45.
Present: morn. 53.
Average: morn. 60; aft. 30.
Remarks: I have answered the above questions to the best of my ability but I fear there is not much ground to build any thing upon.

> F. G. Leach. Rector.

Lewis: discharged rectory, rated at £7. 3. 9; net income £154: patron, Earl Cawdor: tithes commuted for £116, of which £70 payable to the impropriator, and £46 to the rector, who also has a glebe of 46½ acres valued at £68 per annum. Benefice united to the rectory of Stackpole-Elidur [591. 2. 4(21)] in 1839, and a portion of the tithes has been taken to augment the living of Castlemartin [591. 2. 8(24)] by act of parliament.
C & C: 1 service in English.
I & C: no return.

4 Stackpole-Elidor Parish.
Area: 2,845 acres. *Popn.* 164 males, 157 females: total 321.

(21) STACKPOLE ELIDOR PARISH CHURCH.
Endowed: tithe £207; permanent endowment £28.
Space: free 40; other 170.
Present: aft. 77.
Average (12 *months*): morn. 120.
Remarks: I beg to state that I have given the average number of attendants during the last 12 months in the morning as for particular reasons the service is performed in this Parish Church during a greater portion of the year in the morning. I beg to state also that the Church is about to be altered and there will be a large increase in free sittings given.

F. Geo. Leach.   Rector.

Lewis: rectory, in the patronage of Earl Cawdor; united in 1839 to that of St. Petrox, the glebe-lands and a portion of the tithes having been surrendered to the Earl in lieu of lands and tithes of the same value given to the vicarage of Castlemartin: rated at £15. 12. 1, and endowed with £600 royal bounty: impropriate tithes commuted for £270: glebe of 77 acres valued at £87 per annum.

C & C: 1 service in English.

I & C: no return.

5 Bosherston Parish.
Area: 1,566 acres. *Popn.* 129 males, 117 females: total 246.

(22) BOSHERSTON PARISH CHURCH.
Endowed: tithe £107; glebe £65; fees 15s.
Space: free 70; other 75.
Present: morn. 76 + 17 scholars; aft. 43 + 16 scholars.
Average (12 *months*): morn. 60 + 16 scholars; aft. 35 + 17 scholars.

William Allen.   Rector.

Lewis: rectory, rated at £11. 6. 8: patron, Earl Cawdor: tithes commuted for £110. 10: glebe of 65 acres valued at £62. 10 per annum.

C & C: 2 services in English.

I & C: resident.

6 St. Twinell Parish.
Area: 1,358 acres. *Popn.* 111 males, 99 females: total 210.
[No return for the parish church.]
Lewis: discharged vicarage; rated at £3. 17. 11: net income £150, with a glebe-house: patrons, Precentor and Chapter of St. David's: appropriators, Dean and

Chapter of Hereford: tithes commuted for £184, of which, £104 belong to the appropriators subject to rates averaging £12, and £80 to the vicar subject to rates averaging £9.

C & C: 1 service in English.

I & C: incumbent not resident: curate, who resides at Pembroke 3 miles distant, has stipend of £50.

(23) THORN. CALVINISTIC METHODIST.
Erected about 1812.
Space: free 108; other 62.
Present: morn. 90 scholars; aft. 160; even. 140.

> Evan Pervis, Minister
> Tremorgan

7 Warren Parish.

Area: 1,169 acres. *Popn.* 63 males, 61 females: total 124.
[For the returns see (26) below.]

8 Castlemartin Parish.

Area: 4,867 acres. *Popn.* 215 males, 189 females: total 404.

(24) CASTLEMARTIN PARISH CHURCH.
Endowed: land £7. 15; tithe £170; glebe £65; endowment £6. 6.; fees £1. 10.
Space: free 50; other 160.
Present: morn. 73 + 18 scholars; aft. 19 + 14 scholars.
Remarks: The items of endowment are given after making deductions for rates and taxes.

> James Allen.   Vicar.

Lewis: discharged vicarage, rated at £7. 17. 6, endowed with £400 royal bounty: patron and impropriator, Earl Cawdor, who in 1839 augmented the living with tithes and land to the value of £200 per annum, in lieu of tithes and lands surrendered to him by Stackpole-Elidor [591. 2. 4(21)]: impropriate tithes commuted for £320, and the vicarial for £80, with a glebe of 2 acres.

C & C: 2 services in English.

I & C: resident.

9 Angle Parish.

Area: 4,581 acres. *Popn.* 214 males, 223 females: total 437.

(25) St. Mary's, Angle Parish Church.

Endowed: land (Queen Anne's Bounty) £12. 10.; tithe £52. 13.; glebe £4. 4.; permanent endowment £14; Bounty £6. 10.; fees £2; Easter Offerings 10s.

Space: Free, Including all: other 31; total 31.

Present: morn. 50 to 100 + 42 scholars; aft. 100 to 120 + 42 scholars.

Average (12 *months*): morn. 100 to 160 + 42 to 45 scholars; aft. 100 to 160 + 42 to 45 scholars.

Remarks: The Parish of Angle comprises a Sinecure Rectory with a Good Glebe House & Garden, with three fourths of the tithes (Agricultural) leaving the Resident Vicar or Incumbent one fourth with 3½ acres of Glebe. No habitable House of Residence without paying a high rent to he Proprietor and the performance of the whole duties of the Parish. The Population consists chiefly of Fishermen with their families including farm labourers' families employed by the Farmers in the neighbourhood or otherwise.

Thomas Dalton.   Vicar.

Lewis: sinecure rectory and discharged vicarage; rectory rated at £10. 10, of net annual value of £157 with glebe of 20 acres and a glebe-house; vicarage rated at £3. 19. 2, endowed with £600 royal bounty, of gross annual value of £80: patron, Bp. of St. David's: one fourth of the tithes appropriated to the vicarage, and the remainder to the rectory.

C & C: 1 service in English.

I & C: legally not resident.

Warren Parish.

Area: 1,169 acres. *Popn.* 61 males, 63 females: total 124.

(26) Warren Parish Church.

Endowed: land (bounty) £31; tithe £50; glebe £12; permanent endowment £5; fees 10s.

Space: free 14, exclusive of chancel where a few Benches are occasionally placed.

Present: morn. 30-40 + 10-12 scholars; aft. 30-40 + 10-12 scholars.

Average (12 *months*): morn. 40-50 + 10-15 scholars; aft. 40-50 + 10-15 scholars.

Remarks: Warren is a small Parish consisting of Three Farms only with a few cottages tenanted by poor Labourers and families who are mostly Dissenters or Independents whose place of Worship is situated in a Neighbouring Parish although they occasionally attend the Church.

Thomas Dalton.   Vicar.

Lewis: discharged vicarage, rated at £4. 8. 1½; endowed with £400 royal bounty, and £200 parliamentary grant; net income £83: patron, Bp. St. David's: tithes commuted for £170, of which £120 are payable to the Bp., and £50 to the vicar, who also has a glebe of 4 acres valued at £12 per annum.

C & C: 1 service in English.

I & C: not resident.

[This return is wrongly bound and numbered: it should follow 591. 2. 6(23).]

(27) BAPTIST, ANGLE.
Private cottage.
Present: morn. 30; aft. 40; even. 37.
Average: morn. 40-50; aft. 40; even. 50-70.
Remarks: I am a Baptist Home Missionary having not as yet any chapel erected, therefore do preach in a cottage and in the open air. We have no Sabbath School for the want of a place to keep it in. I preach in Castlemartin hundred in ten or eleven different places week nights included.

> Thomas Harries.
> Baptist Home Missionary.
> Milford

10 Rhoscrowther Parish.
Area: 2,536 acres. *Popn.* 97 males, 104 females: total 201.

(28) RHôS CROWTHER PARISH CHURCH.
Endowed: tithe £280; glebe £80.
Space: free 50; other 82.
Present: morn. 84 + 29 scholars; aft. 30 + 20 scholars.
Average (6 months): aft. 70 + 25 scholars.

> George Scott.   Rector.

Lewis: rectory, rated at £15. 12. 11; in the patronage of the crown: tithes commuted for £280, with glebe of 75 acres valued at £112 per annum, with a glebe-house.
C & C: 1 service in English.
I & C: resident.

11 Pwllcrochan Parish.
Area: 3,016 acres. *Popn.* 100 males, 114 females: total 214.

(29) PWLLCROCHAN PARISH CHURCH.
Endowed: tithe commuted at £175; glebe commuted at £21; fees less than £1.
Space: free 160; other 7.
Present: aft. 49 + 19 scholars.
Remarks: There is only a Single Service—Morning and Afternoon alternate Sundays—This will account for no entry at VII [i.e. average number of attendants] of persons attending divine service—morning and evening.

> George Cartinel.   Rector.

Lewis: rectory, rated at £9. 12. 11, and in the patronage of the crown: tithes commuted for £175, with glebe of 9 acres valued at £9. 9. per annum, with a glebe-house.
C & C: 1 service in English.
I & C: resident.

(30) WALLASTON.   CALVINISTIC METHODIST.
Erected 1809.
Space: free 6; other 14.
Present: morn. 68; aft. 12 scholars; even. 45.
Average (12 *months*): morn. 80; aft. 20; even. 70.

> William Hale. Elder.
> Lambecth, Nr. Pembroke.

[End of Pembroke Subdistrict]

3 ROOSE (Subdistrict)
Area: 9,545 acres. *Popn.* 1,137 males, 1,212 females: total 2,349.

1 Burton Parish.
Area: 3,815 acres. *Popn.* 479 males, 500 females: total 979.

(1) BURTON PARISH CHURCH.
Endowed: tithe £120; glebe & house £60.
Present: morn. 120.

> John Brigstock.   Rector.

Lewis: rectory, rated at £15. 12. 11; patrons, Earl Cawdor for two turns, and Sir John Owen, Bart., for one: tithes commuted for £216, with glebe of 40 acres, valued at £60, and glebe-house.

C & C: 1 service in English.

I & C: no return.

(2) GALILEE. BAPTIST.
Erected 1831.
Space: free 284; other 16.
Present: morn. 160; aft. 60 scholars; even. 170.
Remarks: Remark on No. 7 space of chapel contains about 300 sittings = free but 4 which contain about 16 = other Part of the Chapel with galury free—Average congregations 280.

> Henry Evans. Baptist Minister Neyland area.
> Hobbs Point, Pembroke.

(3) SARDIS CHAPEL. BAPTIST.
Erected 1822.
Space: free about 250; other 50; standing—none specifically set apart but aften as many stand as can sit.
Present: morn. school; aft. about 150; even. prayer meeting.
Average (12 *months*): 300.
Remarks: The service here is held alternately morning one Sunday and afternoon the other. The attendance was considerably under average last Lord's Day. The congregation in this place is a very scattered one The weather etc sometimes greatly affect the attendance.

> Henry James Morgan. Minister.
> Front Street, Pembroke Dock.

(4) BURTON SCHOOL ROOM. CALVINISTIC METHODIST.
Erected after 1800.
Used exclusively as a place of worship.
Space: free 60.
Present: even. 45 + 17 scholars.

> John Davies. Minister.
> Mead Lodge, Pembroke.

(5) HERSON MOUNTAIN. METHODIST.
Erected 1815.
Space: free 30; other 3.
Present: morn. 84; even. 34.

> William Esmond. Deacon.

2 Rose-market Parish.
Area: 1,759 acres. *Popn.* 227 males, 238 females: total 465.

(6) ROSEMARKET PARISH CHURCH.
Endowed: tithe £75; glebe £25; other sources £20.
Space: free 18.
Present: aft. 21.
Average: morn. 21.
Remarks: Tithe of parish £75; Vicarage £25; farm
Service performed every alternate Sunday.

> Enoch Barrah. Churchwarden.

Lewis: sub. Rhosmarket; discharged vicarage: rated at £4; endowed with £200 royal bounty; in the patronage of the Crown: net income £106; impropriator, G. S. Roch, Esq.; the vicar, in addition to the small tithes, has the tithe of hay.

C & C: 1 service in English.

I & C: not resident.

(7)   TABERNACLE. RHOSMARKET.   INDEPENDENT DISSENTERS.
Erected before 1800.
Space: free 110; other 72.
Present: morn. 110; aft. 54 scholars; even. 75.
Average (12 *months*): general congregation 130; scholars 70.
Remarks: Average number on the morning of Mar. 30 less than usual.
Average number on the afternoon of Mar. 30 less than usual.

> Evan Thomas.   Minister.
> Studdolph, Milford Haven.

3   Llanstadwell Parish.
Area: 3,971 acres. *Popn.* 431 males, 474 females: total 905.

(8)   LLANSTADWELL PARISH CHURCH.
Endowed: land £11; tithe £109; glebe £4; fees £3.
Space: free 50; other 125.
Average (6 *months*): morn. 110 + 20 scholars.
Remarks: The service is performed morning and afternoon alternately.

> Joseph Tombs.   Minister.
> Hill Street, Haverford West.

Lewis: discharged vicarage, rated at £7. 17; endowed with £200 royal bounty and £200 parliamentary grant: patron, Rev. A. Crymes: two-thirds of the great and the small tithes are impropriate, the remaining one-third belong to the vicar, and commuted for £110, of which 10s are in lieu of Easter offerings; glebe of 7½ acres, valued at £10 per annum.

C & C: 1 service in English.

I & C: not resident.

(9)   WESLEYAN CHAPEL, WATERSON VILLAGE.
Erected 1836.
Space: free 50; other 10.
Present: aft: 30 to 40.
Remarks: I beg to observe that this Chapel is not attended Regularly by any Minister, which is the reason it was not filled up at the time the Census was taken.

> *Informant:* John Lewis.   Registrar.

[Informant's form]

(10) HONEYBOROUGH. BAPTIST.
Erected 1840.
Space: free 130; other 70.
Present: aft 73.
Average: morn. 120.

> Thomas Thomas. Minister.
> Bullford Cottage,
> Johnstone Post Office.

(11) HEBRON. BAPTIST CHAPEL.
Erected 1850.
Space: free 80; other 160; standing 40.
Present: morn. 53; aft. 70 scholars; even. 100.
Average: general congregation 76; scholars 70.

> John Edwards. Manager.
> Leading Man of Shipwrights.

(12) WESLEYAN CHAPEL. WESLEYAN METHODIST.
Erected 1850.
Space: free 70; other 87.
Present: aft. 90 + 30 scholars; even. 90 + 15 scholars.
Average: morn. 50 + 30 scholars; even. 100 + 15 scholars.
Remarks: At Present Service is held Every Sunday Evening and Morning
Alternately and Occasionally in the afternoon.

> Thomas Evans. Steward.
> Joiner.
> Neyland.

[End of Roose Subdistrict and end of Pembroke District]

Area: 170,861 acres. *Popn.* 18,383 males, 20,999 females: total 39,382.

1 MILFORD (Subdistrict)
Area: 36,186 acres. *Popn.* 4,858 males, 4,957 females: total 9,815.

1   Steynton Parish (incl. Milford).
Area: 7,275 acres. *Popn.* 1,906 males, 1,710 females: total 3,616.

(1)   STEYNTON PARISH CHURCH.
Endowed: tithe £205; glebe £30; fees £10.
Space: other 300; free 'none except the moveable benches chiefly occupied by the S. School children.'
Present: morn. 110 + 50 scholars.
Remarks: Altho' there are no Free sittings properly so called, there are several pews in the Church which are used as such, the prescriptive owners either not claiming or occupying them.

William Beach Thomas.   Vicar.

Lewis: discharged vicarage united to that of Johnston [592. 1. 13(30)]; endowed with the whole of the great and small tithes of a portion of the parish, the remainder forming part of the income of St. Mary's, Haverfordwest [592. 2. 4(10)]: vicarial tithes commuted for £58. 10., subject to rates averaging £5. 12. 11 per annum.
C & C: 1 service in English.
I & C: legally not resident: curate has stipend of £52.

(2)   ST. KATHERINE'S CHAPEL OF EASE, TOWN OF MILFORD.
Consecrated and licensed in the year 1805, as an additional church on the Petition of the Founder & Propriator, C. Greville, Esq.
Erected at his own expence, by the above names Charles Greville Esq. Total cost not known.
Endowed: Parliamentary Grant £47. 13. 4; Pew Rents £30.
Space: free 120; other 268; gallery 12.
Present: even. 200.

Thomas Brigstock.
Incumbent Minister.

Lewis: sub. Milford: erected chiefly at the expence of Hon. Charles Francis Greville, lord of the manor, and consecrated in 1808.
C & C: 2 services in English.
I & C: resident.

(3) TREISCROSS, STEYNTON. INDEPENDENT DISSENTERS.
Erected since 1800.
Space: free 115; other 45; stading 20 to 30.
Present: aft. 114; even. 50.
Remarks: The number present on Mar. 30th 1851 about an average attendance.

Evan Thomas. Minister.
Studdolph, Milford Haven.

(4) WESLEYAN CHAPEL, MILFORD HAVEN. WESLEYAN.
Erected 1832.
Space: free 200; other 150.
Present: morn. 166; even. 235.

Aaron Langley. Minister.
Milford Haven.

(5) MILFORD HAVEN. PARTICULAR BAPTIST.
Erected 1828. S. School room attached.
Space: free 168; other 164.
Present: morn. 220 + 25 scholars; even. 300 + 30 scholars.

James H. Thomas. Minister.

(6) STYNTON, MILFORD DOCK YARD. [ROMAN] CATHOLIC.
About 1844 first used as Catholic Chapel.
Space: free 14; standing about 300.
Present: no service.
Average (12 *months*): morn. 40; even. 30.

James Kinny. Minister.
Victoria Place, Milford.

(7) TABERNACLE, BACK STREET, MILFORD. INDEPENDENT.
Erected 1808.
Space: free 110; other 240.
Present: morn. 230; other 250.

Thomas Lloyd. Minister.

(8) WESLEYAN CHAPEL, HAKIN. WESLEYAN METHODIST.
Erected 1806.
Space: free 150; other 200.
Present: morn. 184; even. 264.

Aaron Langley. Minister.

2   Hubberston Parish.
Area: 1,880 acres. *Popn.* 489 males, 551 females: total 1,040.

(9)   HUBBERSTON PARISH CHURCH.
Endowed: tithe £180; glebe £24.
Space: free 60; other 23.
Present: morn. 100 incl. scholars; aft. 115 incl. scholars.

O. Leach.   Rector.

Lewis: rectory, rated at £6. 2. 8½; in the patronage of the Crown; tithes commuted for £180; glebe of 9 acres valued at £18 per annum: parsonage rebuilt in
1840's at expence of rector.

C & C: 2 services in English.

I & C: resident.

(10)   REHOBOTH.   CALVINISTIC METHODIST.
Erected 1840.
Space: free 130; other 100.
Present: morn. 134 + 12 scholars; aft. 54 scholars; even. 160 + 14
scholars.
Average: morn. 100; aft. 35 scholars; even. 110.
Remarks: Our Sunday School and congregation varies, sometimes a good
many Sailors, at other times few or none.

David Vaughan.   Elder.

3   Herbrandston Parish.
Area: 1,989 acres. *Popn.* 125 males, 130 females: total 255.

(11)   ST. MARY HERBANDSTON PARISH CHURCH.
Endowed: tithe £220; glebe £18; fees £1.
Space: free 100; other 100.
Present: aft. 24 + 49 scholars.
Average: morn. 25 + 35 scholars.
Remarks: on No. 6 [i.e. Space] There is a sufficient no. of sittings of both
Classes.

William Roch.   Rector.

Lewis: rectory, rated at £7. 13. 4; patron, the Crown; tithes commuted for £222,
with a glebe-house, and glebe of about 1 acre, valued at £40 per annum.

C & C: 1 service in English.

I & C: resident.

4   St. Ishmaels Parish.
Area: 4,167 acres. *Popn.* 235 males, 293 females: total 528.

(12) St. Ishmaels Parish Church.
Endowed: tithe £100; glebe £5.
Space: free gallery; other 33 pews; total 260.
Present: morn. 79 + 34 scholars.
Remarks: Morning and afternoon service alternately.

Samuel Walker Saunders.   Vicar.

Lewis: discharged vicarage, rated at £6. 12. 8½; endowed with £200 royal bounty; patron, the Crown: portion of the rectorial tithes impropriate in the Corporation of Tewkesbury commuted for £169; vicarial tithes commuted for £120, subject to rates averaging £18 per annum; glebe of 7¼ acres valued at £10 per annum.

C & C: 1 service in English.

I & C: resident.

(13) Tabernacle.   Independents.
Erected about 1825.
At present a day school kept in the free sittings division.
Space: free 170; other 30; standing 30.
Present: aft. 160.
Average (12 *months*): 195.
Remarks: There has been no Sunday School kept here for the last six years —there being a Charity School kept in the Village by the Established Church and the attendance of the Scholars is required in the Sunday School as a condition on which they are admitted to the day school.

Theophilus James.   Minister.
St. Ishmaels.

(14) Sandy Haven.   Baptist.
Erected 1813.
Space: free 176; other 24.
Present: even: 140.
Average (12 *months*): 140.

Thomas Davies.   Minister.

5 Dale Parish.
Area: 3,038 acres. *Popn.* 197 males, 209 females: total 406.

(15) Dale Parish Church.
Endowed: land £47; permanent endowment £13.
Space: free 60; other 130.
Present: morn. 74 + 45 scholars.
Average: morn. 80 + 45 acholars.
Remarks: morning and afternoon alternately.

J. W. Saunders.   Perpetual Curate.

Lewis: perpetual curacy, endowed with £800 royal bounty; net income £65: patron and impropriator, Mr Phillips.

C & C: 1 service in English.

I & C: not resident.

(16)   TABERNACLE.   INDEPENDENT OR CONGREGATIONALISTS.
Erected 1838.
Space: free 130; other 20; standing 24.
Present: even. 111.
Remarks: Every alternate Sunday there is service in the Established Church in the morning, in the Tabernacle in the afternoon and in the Weslean Chapel in the Evening. Every other alternate Sunday there is service in the Weslean Chapel in the morning, Tabernacle in the evening. we have a prayer meeting *every* Sunday morning at 6 a.m. with the attendance from 5 to 15, this morning 9.

Theophilus James.   Minister.

(17)   WESLEYAN METHODIST.
Erected 1809.
Space: free 114; Paid sittings 26.
Present: morn. 87.
Average: about 90.
Remarks: The chapel will comfortably seat 140. Reckoning 14 inches for a person it would seat 156.

William Spriggs.   Local Preacher and
Chapel Steward.

6   Marloes Parish.
Area: 2,478 acres. *Popn.* 260 males, 248 females: total 508.

(18)   MARLOES PARISH CHURCH.
Endowed: land £13; tithe £103; glebe £7; fees £2.
Space: free 15; other 60.
Present: even. 50.
Remarks: Number VI with reference to the "space available for public worship" has been left out in the instructions.

William Bowen Harris.   Minister.

Lewis: discharged vicarage, rated at £5; endowed woth £200 royal bounty; patron, the Crown; net income £80: impropriator, Lord Kensington.
C & C: 1 service in English.
I & C: not resident.

(19)   MARLOES.   BAPTISTS.
Erected 1821.
Space: free 144; other 74.
Present: morn. 118.
Remarks: The service being held here morning and evening alternately, the eveng. congregation once a fortnight averages about 220.

Thomas Davies.   Minister.
St. Ishmaels.

(20) M ARLAES. WESLEYAN METHODIST.
Erected about 1767, enlarged 1837.
Space: free 240; other 42.
Present: even. 165.
Average: 150 + 45 scholars.
Remarks: In stating the number of sttings I have stated the number that it will comfortably seat. Reckoning 14 inches for each person it would seat 300.

William Spriggs.   Local Preacher.
Dale

7   St. Brides Parish.

Area: 1,683 acres. *Popn.* 77 males, 97 females: total 174.

(21   ST. BRIDES PARISH CHURCH.
Endowed: tithe £195; glebe £15; fees £1.
Space: free 20; other 70.
Present: morn. 53.

William Bowen Harries.   Minister.

Lewis: discharged rectory, rated at £15. 12. 11; in the alternate patronage of Sir W. Phillips, Bart., W. Philips, Esq. and Mary Bird Allen: tithes commuted for £195.

C & C: 1 service in English.

I & C: not resident.

8   Hasguard Parish.

Area: 1,745 acres. *Popn.* 92 males, 80 females: total 172.

(22)   HASGUARD PARISH CHURCH.
Endowed: land £6; tithe £168.
Space: other 7.
Present: morn. 7.
Average: 4.

Wm. Edmunds.   Rector.

Lewis: discharged rectory, rated at £18. 6. 6; patron, the Crown: net income £170.

C & C: 1 service in English.

I & C: not resident.

9   Talbenny Parish.

Area: 1,425 acres. *Popn.* 109 males, 126 females: total 235.

(23) TALBENNY PARISH CHURCH.
Space: sufficient; free 100; other 100.
Present: morn. 21.
Average: morn. 25.
Remarks: In answer to No. 5 [How endowed] being curate I cannot say the amount of Tithe or Glebe.

> William Roch.   Curate.
> Little Haven, Haverfordwest.

Lewis: discharged rectory, valued at £9. 12. 6; patron Sir John Owen, Bart.: tithes commuted for £150; glebe of 25 acres, valued at £30 per annum.

C & C: 1 service in English.

I & C: incumbent not resident; curate, who resides at Herbrandston, 3½ miles distant, has stipend of £40.

(24) HALL, TALBENNY. WESLEYAN METHODISTS.
Erected 1830.
Space: free 120; standing 30.
Present: aft. 66.
Average: morn. 90; aft. 90.
Remarks: I have given the number attending Service March 30th and the average number although we have very frequently over one Hundred in Attendance.

> John Wathen.   Class Leader and Local Preacher.
> Middle Hall, Haverfordwest.

(25) TABERNACLE, VILLAGE OF LITTLE HAVEN. INDEPENDENTS OR CONGREGATIONALISTS.
Erected about 1812, rebuilt 1842.
Space: free 300; standing 45.
Present: even. 207.
Average (12 *months*): 280.
Remarks: For some time past we have had no Sunday School in this place there being a large School both day & Sunday with the Established Church and the attendants of the day free school are required to attend Sunday School.

> Theophilus James.   Minister.
> St. Ishmaels.

10   West Walton Parish.
Area: 1,408 acres. *Popn.* 227 males, 291 females: total 518.

(26) WALTON WEST PARISH CHURCH.
Endowed: land £14; tithe £135; glebe £8; permanent endowment £6. 6s; fees £1. 17. 6.
Space: free 52; other 51.

Present: aft. 66 + 90 scholars.
Average (12 *months*): morn. 20 + 50 scholars; aft. 45 + 70 scholars.
Remarks: The Church cannot contain more than the *sixth* part of the population; it is in a very dilapidated & dangerous state, not fit for Divine Service, and ought to be rebuilt and enlarged.

Joseph Brown. Minister.

Lewis: discharged rectory, rated at £6. 13. 4; endowed with £400 royal bounty; net income £154: patron Rev. Robert Ferrier: tithes commuted for £134. 15.; glebe of 1 acre, valued at £1. 10. per annum.

C & C: 1 service in English.

I & C: incumbent not resident; curate, who resides at Haverfordwest, 5 miles distant, has stipend of £65.

ICBS: grant of £10 in 1852.

(27) WESLEYAN METHODIST.
Erected 1835.
Space: free 84; other 80.
Present: morn. 50.
Remarks: The sittings are generally all occupied in the evening service. The average congregation is about 80.

William Spriggs. Local Preacher.
Dale

11   Walwins Castle Parish.
Area: 2,904 acres. *Popn.* 171 males, 182 females: total 353.

(28) WALWYN'S CASTLE PARISH CHURCH.
Endowed: tithe £270; glebe about 45 acres.
Space: free 100; other 100 (ample for the congregation).
Present: morn. 49; aft. 25.
Average (12 *months*): morn. 30; aft. 24.

Robert Lang, M.A. Rector.

Lewis: rectory, rated at £7. 13. 4.; in the patronage of the Crown: net income, £270, with a glebe-house.

C & C: 2 services in English.

I & C: resident.

12   West Robeston Parish.
Area: 1,100 acres. *Popn.* 73 males, 67 females: total 140.

(29) ROBESTON WEST PARISH CHURCH.
Endowed: tithe £180; glebe £5.
Space: sittings 5.

Present: morn. 2.
Average: morn. about 6; even. about 6.

William Edwards. Officiating Minister.

Lewis: rectory, rated at £6. 6. 8; in the patronage of the Crown; net income £169.
C & C: 1 service in English.
I & C: no return.

13 Johnston Parish.

Area: 1,293 acres. *Popn.* 134 males, 129 females: total 263.

(30) JOHNSTON PARISH CHURCH.
Endowed: tithe £105; glebe £23.
Space: free, including those occupied by the S. School about 70; other 50.
Present: aft. 30 + 40 scholars.
Average: aft. 30 + 40 scholars.
Remarks: Having two Churches, viz. Steynton and Johnston, I am obliged
to have the Service in the afternoon at the Latter, excepting on the 1st.
Sunday in the morn, & I have therefore entered the average attendance
under the afternoon column.

W. B. Thomas.   Rector.

Lewis: discharged rectory, consolidated with that of Steynton [592. 1. 1(1)]; rated
at £2. 0. 5.; endowed with the rectorial tithes; in the patronage of the Crown:
net income £322, with a glebe-house.
C & C: 2 services in English.
I & C: legally not resident; curate has stipend of £52.

(31) HOREB, POPE HILL. BAPTIST.
Erected 1817.
Space: free 170; other 30.
Present: morn. 190 [?100] + 80 scholars; aft. 80 scholars; evn. 100.
Average: morn. 150; even. 100.
Remarks: No accomodation for Sunday scholars during divine service.
The public service is one Sunday in the morning and the other in the after-
noon and a meeting for prayer every Sunday evening.

Thomas Thomas. Minister.
Bullford Cottage.

14 Llangwm Parish.

Area: 2,434 acres. *Popn.* 442 males, 486 females: total 928.

(32) LLANGWM PARISH CHURCH.
Endowed: tithe £150; glebe £40.
Space: free 128; other 78.

Present: aft. 191.
Average: morn. 150; aft. 200.

Thomas Williams.   Rector.

Lewis: discharged rectory, rated at £7. 12. 11.; endowed with £200 parliamentary grant; endowed with £200 parliamentary grant: patrons alternately Sir John Owen, Bart., and Mrs. Owen Barlow: tithes commuted for £190, subject to rates averaging £23. 15. 2 per annum; glebe of 35 acres, valued at £36 per annum, with a glebe-house.

C & C: 1 service in English.

I & C: resident.

ICBS: grant of £70 in 1837.

(33)   Llangum Chapel.   Wesleyan.
Erected 1822.
Space: free 168;   other 18;   standing 20.
Present: morn. 101;   even. 78.
Average (12 *months*): morn. 180.

John Styrme.   Steward.

15   Freystrop Parish.
Area: 1,637 acres. *Popn.* 322 males, 358 females: total 679.

(34)   Freystrop Parish Church.
Space: free 70;   other 50.
Present: morn. 68.
Average (9 *months*): 90.
Remarks: I know nothing of the Endowment. The service is Morning and Afternoon alternately.

D. W. Adams.   Curate.

Lewis: discharged rectory, rated at £5. 13. 9; endowed with £200 royal bounty; in the patronage of the Crown: tithes commuted for £121. 10.; glebe of 18 acres, valued at £41.18. per annum.

C & C: 1 service in English.

I & C: not resident; curate, who resides at Haverfordwest, 2½ miles distant, has stipend of £30.

(35)   Bethel, Middle Hill.   Independent.
Erected 1818;   rebuilt 1840.
Space: other 9.
Present: morn. 64 scholars;   aft. 111.
Average (12 *months*): general congregation 200-250; scholars 60-70.
Remarks: This chapel was rebuilt in 1840, being too Small to hold the Congregation. No Sittings in it formerly which were paid for, but now there are 9.

Nathaniel Harries.   Minister.
Merlin's Bridge.

(36)   SOCIETY OF FRIENDS MEETING-HOUSE, CROSS STREET, MILFORD.
Erected 1807.
Admeasurement: floor area 32 x 22; gallery none.
Space: 60.
Present: morn. 5.

G. Starbuck.

[This return is out of order, and is endorsed 592. 1. 1. 36.N.2.]

[*End of Milford Subdistrict*]

2 HAVERFORDWEST (Subdistrict)
Area: 40,059 acres. *Popn.* 5,603 males, 6,773 females: total 12,376.

1   Harroldston St. Issells Parish.
Area: 1,150 acres. *Popn.* 167 males, 164 females: total 331.

[13]   (1)   HAROLDTON WEST PARISH CHURCH.
Endowed: land £18; tithe £98; glebe £12.
Space: free 24; other 60.
Present: morn. 17.
Aveage: morn. 25; aft. 25.
Remarks: There is only one Service on each Sunday alternately morning
and evening.

Francis Thomas.   Minister.

[Note: This return is out of order, having been correctly numbered by
parish but wrongly bound in with Harroldston St. Issells, for which see
(32) below.]

Lewis: perpetual curacy, endowed with £400 royal bounty; patrons, Pembroke
College, Oxford, to whom it was presented along with that of the adjoining living of
Lambston [592. 2. 12(31)], by Sir John Philipps of Picton Castle: tithes commuted
for £120, subject to rates averaging £9. 13. 1¾.; glebe of 15 acres, arising from the
bounty, valued at £14 per annum.

C & C: 1 service in English.

I & C: legally not resident.

(2)   WESLEYAN CHAPEL, HAROLDSTON ST. ISSELS.   WESLEYAN METHODIST.
Erected 1829.
Space: free 87; other 8.
Present: even. 46 + 31 scholars.

John Morgan.   Minister.
Court House, Haverfordwest.

(3) SALEM. INDEPENDENT.
Erected 1837.
Space: free 8.
Present: even. 40.
Average (12 *months*): aft. 20 scholars; even. 60.
Remarks: With regard to the Sunday School in the above chapel about 20
is the average number of Scholars on Sunday afternoons.
Preaching is always on Sunday evening, about 60 attend, sometimes more
sometimes less. Prayer meeting held on Wednesday evening.

> Nathaniel Harries.   Minister.
> Merlins Bridge.

(4) WESLEYAN CHAPEL, HAROLDSTON ST. ISSELS.
Erected 1829.
Space: free 87; other 8.
Present: even. 46 + 31 scholars.

> John Elliott.   Local Preacher.
> Merlins Bridge.

[This duplicates 592. 2. 1(2).]

2 Haverfordwest, St. Thomas Parish.
Area: 1,016 acres. *Popn.* 667 males, 912 females: total 1,579.

(5) ST. THOMAS PARISH CHURCH.
Endowed: I do not know the particulars; easter offerings £3.
Space: free 83; other 140.
Average (6 *months*): morn. 156; aft. 71.
Remarks: There is no sermon after the Afternoon Service.

> Joseph Tombs.   Minister.
> Hill Street.

Lewis: rectory not in charge; in the patronage of the Crown; net income £31;
with a glebe-house: tithes commuted for £180; glebe of 14 acres valued at £76. 3,
and other buildings valued at £44. 7. per annum.
C & C: 2 services in English.
I & C: resident.
ICBS: grant of £50 in 1819.

(6) MACPELAH. BAPTIST.
Erected 1842.
Space: free 120.
Present: aft. 76.

> David Davies.   Minister.

(7) ALBANY CHAPEL. BEFORE IT WAS REBUILT IN THE YEAR 1841 CALLED THE GREEN MEETING HOUSE. INDEPENDENT.
Erected before 1800. Originally used as a place of Public Worship since 1720. [Built about 1701—crossed out.]
Space: free 154; other 257. Also 150 feet of free sittings in School Room connected.
Present: morn. 450; even. 425.
Average (12 *months*): morn. 300; even. 300.
Remarks: The free sittings measure 256 feet in length. The sittings paid for measure 444 feet 8 ins in length which amounts being divided by 20 inches the space being considered enough for a sitting give the number of sittings as entered in VII. s. 495.

James Williams.   Minister.

(8) MORAVIAN CHAPEL, ST. THOMAS GREEN. THE UNITED BRETHREN.
Space: free 200.
Present: morn. 74 + 16 scholars; aft. 24; even. 173.
Average (10 *months*): morn. 65; even. 160.

Henry O. Essex.   Minister.
St. Thomas Green

(9) ST. THOMAS.
Name: None.
Denomination: Mixed.
Erected: 1838.
Present: morn. 89; even. 89.
Remarks: 4 Clergy man attend one each Sunday—Wesleyan, Baptist, Presbaterian, Independent. No Chaplain being appointed to the Workhouse.

William Thompson.
Master of the Workhouse.

3   Furzy Park and Portfield.   Ex. Parochial
Area: 820 acres. *Popn.* 92 males, 103 females: total 195.
[No returns]

4   St. Mary Parish, Town and County of Haverfordwest.
Area: 30 acres. *Popn.* 668 males, 992 females: total 1,590.

(10) ST. MARY PARISH CHURCH.
Endowed: land £21; tithe £58. 10*s*; permanent endowment £20; fees £15; other sources £16. 10*s*.; Easter Offerings: Quite uncertain.
Space: free 294; other 506.
Present: morn. 333 + 81 scholars; even. 495.
Remarks: No Notice was given the Sunday *proceding* the 30th March that

the number attending Divine Service on that day would be taken down for the purpose of being inserted in this Return.

Tho. Watts.   Minister.
Goat Street.

Lewis: vicarage, endowed with £20 per annum chargeable on the tithes of the parish of Tremaen [593. 3. 3(7)], co. Cardigan, £200 royal bounty, and £200 parliamentary grant: in the patronage of the Corporation, who are the impropriators of the tithes, and pay the incumbent a stipend of £100 per annum.

C & C: 2 services in English.

I & C: resident.

ICBS: grant if £150 in 1844.

5   St. Martin Parish, Town and County of Haverfordwest.

Area: 1,955 acres. *Popn.* 924 males, 1,163 females: total 2,087.

(11)   ST. MARTIN PARISH CHURCH.

Endowed: land £40; permanent endowment £46; fees £1. 10s.

Space: free 130; other 200.

Present: aft. 141.

Remarks: There is, in addition to the 130 free sittings, space reserved for the accomodation by form sitting for sixty sunday school children, but as the children of St. Martin's parish go every Sunday to St. Mary's Church, the central church of the Town, in company with the National School children of the parishes in the Township the space is now made available for that purpose. Divine Service is performed alternately morning and afternoon and the general congregation of each of such services averages about 150.

Amos Crymes.   Perpetual Curate.

Lewis: perpetual curacy, endowed with £1,200 royal bounty, and £1,200 parliamentary grant; net income £80: patron and impropriator, Hugh Webb Bowen, Esq.

C & C: 1 service in English.

I & C: not resident.

ICBS: grant of £100 in 1839.

(12)   PRENDERGAST PARISH CHURCH.

Endowed: tithe (Gross Value) £222. 0. 6d; glebe £8; permanent endowment QAB £6. 10s; fees £1. 10s: easter offerings £1.

Space: free 50; other 300.

Present: morn. 120.

Average (12 *months*): morn. 120; aft. 120.

Remarks: The Sunday Scholars assemble at St. Mary's Church Haverfordwest.

William Watts Harris.   Minister.

Lewis: discharged rectory, rated at £9. 14. 9; endowed with £200 royal bounty: patron, the crown: net income £183.

C & C: 1 service in English.

I & C: not resident.

[This return is misplaced and should be under 592. 2. 6. below.]

(13) WESLEYAN CHAPEL. WESLEYAN METHODIST.
Erected before 1800.
Space: free 520; other 680.
Present: morn. 380 + 50 scholars; even. 499.

> John Morgan. Minister.
> Court House, Haverfordwest.

(14) BRIDGE STREET, ST. MARTIN'S PARISH.
LATTER DAY SAINTS.
Erected before 1800. Separate building wholly for public worship.
Space: all free; standing 100.
Present: morn. 20; aft. 30; even. 60.
Average (12 *months*): as above.

> John Griffiths. Elder.
> Bridge St.

(15) TABERNACLE CHAPEL. INDEPENDENT.
Erected 1774.
Space: free 200; other 500. Standing: 2 Passages.
Present: morn. 700 + 116 scholars; aft. 222.
Average (12 *months*): morn. 700 + 116 scholars; aft. 222 scholars.
Remarks: Chapel closed being under repairs since January 1st 1851.

> Thos. Beynon. Secretary and Deacon.

(16) BETHESDA. BAPTIST.
Erected 1788.
Space: free 310; other 440.
Present: morn. 480; even. 645.

> David Davies. Minister.

(17) WESLEYAN CHAPEL. WESLEYAN METHODIST.
Erected about 1835.
Space: free 60; other 45.
Present: morn. 51 scholars; aft. 52 + 50 scholars.

> John Morgan. Minister.
> Court House.

6 Prendergast Parish.
Area: 1,104 acres. *Popn.* 659 males, 814 females: total 1,473.
[For the Parish Church see (12) above.]

(18) WESLEYAN CHAPEL. WESLEYAN METHODIST.
Erected 1835.
Space: free 96.
Present: 42; even. 96.

> John Morgan. Minister.
> Court House.

(19) PRIMITIVE METHODISTS.
Erected about 1836.
Not used exclusively as a place of worship.
Space: free 100.
Present: aft. 30; even. 60.

> William Allen. Class leader.
> Bootmaker.

7 Uzmaston Parish.
Area: 2,070 acres. *Popn.* 307 males, 376 females: total 683.

(20) UZMASTON PARISH CHURCH.
Endowed: land £55; permanent endowment £41; fees, dues, easter offerings £1.
Space: free 161; other 119.
Present: morn. 80 + 91 scholars.
Average (12 *months*): morn. 100 + 70 scholars; aft. 140 + 70 scholars.
Remarks: For the last eight years there has been a service every fortnight on a Sunday afternoon in a barn not licensed but permitted by the Bishop. (Average number of attendants 80). This has been interrupted since Michaelmas 1850 by my having the temporary charge of another parish.

> Samuel Owen Meares.
> Perpetual Curate.

Lewis: perpetual curacy, endowed with £600 royal bounty, and £400 parliamentary grant; net income £117: patrons and impropriators, Precentor and Chapter of St. David's, whose tithes have been commuted for £205, subject to rates averaging £18. 11. 8.
C & C: 1 service in English.
I & C: resident.
ICBS: grant of £75 made in 1836, and a second grant of £25 in 1843.

(21) CARTLETT CHAPEL OF EASE TO UZMASTON CHURCH.
Licensed 7 April 1841.
How Consecrated: The room was fitted to meet the needs of a large number of the parisioners above a mile distant from the parish church of Uzmaston.
How or by whom erected: The room was fitted up by the exertions principally of

> James Mayler, Esq.
> George Harvey, Esq. of Haverfordwest
> George Phillips, Esq.

Total Cost: about £50.
Space: free 120.
Average number of attendants: Service only on Wednesdays regularly; 60.

> Samuel Owen Meares.
> Perpetual Curate.

8   Boulston Parish.
Area: 1,822 acres. *Popn.* 101 males, 123 females: total 224.

(22)   BOULSTON PARISH CHURCH.
Endowed: land £12.
Space: free 56; other 43.
Present: aft. 70.
Average: morn. 70; aft. 70-90.
Remarks: Sir, I regret cannot give a more detailed account.

James Philipps.   Incumbent.

Lewis: donative; net income £25: patron and impropriator, Robert Innes Ackland, Esq.
C & C: 1 service in English.
I & C: not resident.

9   Wiston Parish.
Area: 7,030 acres. *Popn.* 377 males, 397 females: total 774.

(23)   PARISH CHURCH OF THE PARISH AND BOROUGH OF WISTON.
Endowed: land £64; tithe £85; permanent endowment (bounty) £6. 10s.
Space: free 70.
Present: morn. 200.
Average: morn. 200-300.
Remarks: The services are alternate morning and afternoon. The above is the gross amount, *without any deductions.*

James Philipps.   Incument.

Lewis: perpetual curacy, endowed with £800 royal bounty; net income £164: patron, Earl Cawdor; tithes commuted for £360, of which the impropriator has £275, and the incumbent £85, subject to rates averaging £7. 15. per annum.
C & C: 1 service in English.
I & C: not resident.

(24)   WISTON DHAPEL.   CALVINISTIC METHODIST.
Erected 1813.
Space: all free; standing 44 feet by 26.
Present: morn. 53 scholars; aft. 140.

James Hughes.   Elder.
Froghall, Spittal parish, Nr. Haverfordwest.

10   Rudbaxton Parish.
Area: 4,142 acres. *Popn.* 307 males, 362 females: total 669.

(25)   RUDBAXTON PARISH CHURCH.
Restored from a state of ruin by the Present Rector, who was appointed by the Lord *Chancellor in Nov.* 1844. Parsonage and school built since.

Endowed: tithe commuted at £280.
Space: free 152; other 40.
Present: morn. 33 + 22 scholars; aft. 23 + 18 scholars.
Average (12 *months*): morn. 50 + 50 scholars; aft. 50 + 50 scholars.
Remarks: The 2 Congregations do not consist of the same individuals, the Church being 2 miles from the bulk of the population. The only church way being a very narrow long lane nearly impassable the greater part of the year.

William Meyler. Rector.

Lewis: Rectory, rated at £15. 4. 2; in the patronage of the Crown: net income £199. Formerly two chapels of ease in the parish, now in ruins.
C & C: 2 services in English.
I & C: no return.
ICBS: grant of £100 made in 1845.

(26) BETHLEHEM. PARTICULAR BAPTIST.
Erected 1819.
Space: all free.
Present: morn. 247.
Average (12 *months*): 200 + 60 scholars.
Remarks: no religious service is held in the afternoon or evening.

John Lewis of Ambleston.
Deacon and Elder.

(27) CUNDALE CHAPEL. INDEPENDENT.
Erected 1837.
Space: free 15; other 7.
Present: morn. 200 + 96 scholars.

Henry Mathias. Minister.
Wolfsdale.

11 Camrose Parish.
Area: 8,129 acres. *Popn.* 610 males, 631 females: total 1,241.
[No return for the Parish Church]:
Lewis: discharged vicarage, rated at £6. 10. 5; endowed with £400 parliamentary grant: net income £127, with a glebe-house: patron and impropriator, Mr Bowen.
C & C: 1 service in English.
I & C: incumbent (W. W. W. Bowen) resident.

(28) WOLFSDALE, BETHEL CHAPEL. INDEPENDENTS.
Erected 1827.
Space: free 17; other 6.
Present: morn. 160 + 37 scholars; aft. 141; even. 126.
Average (12 *months*): morn. 160 + 37 scholars.

Henry Mathias. Minister.
Wolfsdale.

(29) LEBANON. BAPTIST.
Erected 1838.
Space: free 84; standing 30 feet by 10 feet.
Present: morn. 56; even. 62.
Average (6 *months*)*:* morn. 50; even. 80.
Remarks [on an attached sheet]*:* Our Chapel was built in 1838; the land being given by a Neighbouring Gentleman, when a few Baptist friends in and About Camrose came to the determination of Building a small Chapel for the convenience of Worship and for a publick day School. (though no Sunday School at present). the space without sittings for the school 30 feet long by 10 feet broad the other space is filled up with free sittings. We have no stated minister for the last twelve months being supplied by neighbouring Ministers with the students from the Haverfordwest Academy. the weekly school has been tried by several school masters since the errection of the Chapel but was given up for the want of scholars the schoolmaster could not find his own support by the number of Scholars attending. We live in an agriculture district, the poorer class being too poor to pay for the schooling of their children. The present school master is an old Englishman, William Rouse, being in this country for this some years he has as yet few scholars he has his maintainance chiefly by the Generosity of friends.

Henry John.   Deacon.
Delcomb, Nr.
Haverfordwest.

(30) KEYSTON CHAPEL. INDEPENDENT.
Erected 1799.
Space: free 180.
Present: morn. 180 + 20 scholars; even. 71 + 26 scholars.

James Williams.   Minister.

12   Lambston Parish.
Area: 1,761 acres. *Popn.* 141 males, 142 females: total 283.
(31) LAMBSTON PARISH CHURCH.
Space: free 50; other 55.
Usual number of attendants: morn. about 30; aft. 30.

Francis Thomas.   Perpetual Curate.

[Informant's form]

Lewis: perpetual curacy; endowed with £200 royal bounty: in the patronage of Pembroke College, Oxford: net income £164: tithes commuted for £140, subject to rates averaging £9. 1. 3; glebe of above 13 acres, valued at £10 per annum.

C & C: 1 service in English.

I & C: not resident.

13   Westharolston Parish.
Area: 1,718 acres. *Popn.* 66 males, 74 females: total 140.

(32)   HAROLDSTON ST. ISSELS PARISH CHURCH.
Endowed: land £18; permanent endowment £5; other sources £36.
Space: free 70; other 36.
Present: aft. 50.
Average (12 *months*): morn. 30; aft. 45.
Remarks: The Church is inconveniently situated about a mile and a half from
the place where the bulk of the Parishioners reside. The services Morning
and Afternoon alternately. The Congregation is generally double in the
afternoon to that it is in the Morning, but I have merely given the Average.

> D. W. Adams.   Minister.
> Hill Strett, Haverfordwest.

[This return is out of order, being correctly numbered by parish but wrongly
bound in with West Haroldston Parish. For the correct entry see above (1).]

Lewis: perpetual curacy, endowed with £600 royal bounty, and £568 parliamentary grant: net income £66. 10. 8; with a glebe of about 9 or 10 acres arising
from bounty land.

C & C: 1 service in English.

I & C: not resident.

14   Nolton Parish.
Area: 1,504 acres. *Popn.* 122 males, 123 females: total 245.

(33)   NOLTON PARISH CHURCH.
Space: free 26; other 101.
Present: aft. 48 + 14 scholars.
Remarks: I am not aware of the amount of the endowment.

> James Tasker.   Curate.

Lewis: discharged rectory, rated at £4. 2. 11; endowed with £200 royal bounty: in
the patronage of the Crown: net income £154, with glebe-house: tithes commuted
for £118, subject to rates, averaging £6. 18. 7; and glebe of nearly 30 acres valued
at £40 per annum.

C & C: 1 service in English.

I & C: not resident: curate, who resides in the glebe-house, has a stipend of £75
for this and Roch.

15   Roch Parish.
Area: 4,603 acres. *Popn.* 347 males, 416 females: total 763.

(34) ROCH PARISH CHURCH.
Space: free 50; other 174.
Present: morn. 85 + 17 scholars.
Remarks: I am not aware of the amount of endowment.

> James Tasker. Curate.
> Nolton Rectory.

Lewis: discharged vicarage, rated at £4. 13. 9; endowed with £200 royal bounty, and in the patronage of the Crown: net income £137; impropriator, George Augustus Harries, Esq.: tithes commuted for £299. 17., of which £200 are payable to the impropriator, subject to rates averaging £12. 16. 8., and £99. 17. to the vicar, subject to rates averaging £6. 8. 4.; glebe of 2½ acres, valued at £6 per annum.
C & C: 1 service in English.
I & C: not resident; curate, who resides at Nolton, 2½ miles distant, has stipend of £75 for this and Nolton.

(35) PENUEL. BAPTIST.
Erected 1822.
Space: free 215.
Present: morn. 124; even. 74.
Remarks: Average number of congregation according to the total more or less as the weather permitteth. No Sunday School at present we are visiting the sick in the afternoon. Any question deemed necessary we should be happly to answer in future.

> Elias Thomas. Minister.

(36) WESLEYAN CHAPEL. WESLEYAN METHODIST.
Erected 1834.
Space: free 109; other 58.
Present: aft. 93.

> John Charles. Leader.

16 Treffgarne Parish.
Area: 1,205 acres. *Popn.* 48 males, 51 females: total 99.

(37) TREFFGARNE PARISH CHURCH.
Endowed: land £24; tithe £20; glebe £25; permanent endowment £11. 15. 10.
Space: all free except three.
Present: morn. 21.
Average: aft. 30.
Remarks: £11. 15s. 10d. being the annual interest of Queen Anne's Bounty and Parliamentaty Grants appropriated to the said living.

> Thomas Jenkins. Rector.

Lewis: discharged rectory, rated at £1. 13. 9.; net income £60; glebe-house built by the incumbent in 1832: patron, John Evans, Esq., lord of the manor and proprietor of the whole parish.
C & C: 1 service partially in English and Welsh.
I & C: resident.

> *[End of Haverfordwest Subdistrict]*

3 ST. DAVIDS (Subdistrict)
Area: 44,524 acres. *Popn.* 3,846 males, 4,451 females: total 8,297.

1 St. Lawrence Parish.
Area: 1,751 acres. *Popn.* 108 males, 122 females: total 230.

(1)   St. Lawrence Parish Church.
Endowed: land £26; tithe £80; glebe £30; permanent endowment £18.
Space: free 60; other 24.
Present: morn. 29.
Average (12 *months*): morn. 33; aft. 60.

William Neyler.   Rector.

Lewis: discharged rectory, rated at £3. 18. 9.; endowed with £400 royal bounty:
in the patronage of the Crown: net income £103, with a glebe-house: tithes
commuted for £80, subject to rates, averaging £6. 4. 3. per annum; glebe of 30
acres, valued at £20 per annum.
C & C: 1 service, English and Welsh on alternate Sundays performed by the
incumbent.
I & C: resident.

2 Hays-Castle Parish.
Area: 4,462 acres. *Popn.* 170 males, 175 females: total 345.

(2)   Hays-Castle Parish Church.
Endowed: tithe £30; permanent endowment £54. 0. 2d.;* fees 10s.
Space: free 52; other 29.
Present: aft. 9.
Remarks: *This endowment of Fifty-four 0/2 is for the augmentation of the
Vicarage of *Brawdy with* Hays Castle being a consolidated living.

Thomas Davies.   Vicar.

Lewis: discharged vicarage, consolidated with that of Brawdy [592. 3. 6(10)]:
parish, with that of Brawdy, constitutes a prebend attached to the decanal stall in
the cathedral church of St. David's: chapel of ease in the village of Ford.
C & C: 1 service partially in English and Welsh, performed by the incumbent.
I & C: not resident.

(3)   Ford Village, Haycastle.
A chapel without any district annexed & without cure of souls.
Endowed: land purchased by Queen Anne's Bounty £70; permanent
endowment £2; bounty money interest £19. 10.
Space: free 70.
Present: aft. 35.
Average (12 *months*): aft. 50.

Remarks: Four times in the year there is a Morning Service, when the Lord's Supper is being administered.

> Peter David Richardson.
> Perpetual Curate.

Lewis: perpetual curacy: endowed with £1,200 royal bounty; net income £70: patron W. E. Tucker, Esq.

C & C: 1 service in Welsh on alternate Sundays performed by the incumbent.

I & C: not resident.

(4)   PENBONT FORD.   INDEPENDENT.
Erected 1806.
Space: all free.
Present: morn. 157; even. 69.

> Daniel Davies.   Minister.
> Hook, Ambleston.
> Haverfordwest.

(5)   HALL.   CALVINISTIC METHODIST.
Erected 1820.
Space: free 90; other 90; standing 30.
Present: morn. 66 scholars; aft. 149.
Average: gen. cong. 260; scholars 55.
Remarks: 55 this 30th day of March, but other times above 67.

> William Evans.   Deacon.
> Ford.

3   St. Edrens Parish.
Area: 916 acres. *Popn.* 57 males, 67 females: total 124.

(6)   ST. EDREN'S PARISH CHURCH.
Endowed: land £90; permanent endowment £21.
Space: free 60; other 14.
Present: aft. 14.

> William Meyler. Perpetual Curate.
> St. Lawrence, Haverfordwest.

Lewis: perpetual curacy, endowed with £800 royal bounty, and £200 parliamentary grant; net income £85; in the patronage of the Lord Chancellor having been exchanged by the Upper Chapter in the Cathedral church of St. David's for the living of St. Elvis; the impropriation remains with the Chapter.

C & C: 2 service, English and Welsh on alternate Sundays performed by the incumbent.

I & C: resident.

ICBS: grant of £70 in 1845.

(7) BLAENLLYN. BAPTIST.
Erected 1843.
Space: free 191; other 112.
Present: morn. 342; aft. 99; even. 141.

> T. E. Thomas. Minister.
> Haverfordwest.
> Trehales, St. Edrins, Trevine.

4 Llanrithan Parish.
Area: 1,719 acres. *Popn.* 88 males, 96 females: total 184.

(8) LLANRUTHAN PARISH CHURCH. (PERPETUAL CURACY).
Endowed: land £73; permanent endowment £17. 18. 2.
Space: free 40; other 10.
Present: aft. 32 scholars.
Average: from 35 to 40.
Remarks: The Divine Service is performed every other morning and after-
noon and from 35 to 40 are the attendants.

> George Mathias. Churchwarden.

Lewis: perpetual curacy, endowed with £800 royal bounty, and £200 parliamentary
grant; net income £86: patrons and impropriators, Subchanter and Vicars Choral
of the cathedral church of St. David's, whose tithes have been commuted for £102,
subject to rates averaging £1 per annum.
C & C: 1 service in Welsh performed by the incumbent.
I & C: not resident.

5 Llandeloy Parish.
Area: 1,843 acres. *Popn.* 114 males, 131 females: total 245.

(9) LLANDELOY OR LLANDELOI PARISH CHURCH.
Endowed: land £25; tithe £42.
Space: free 12; other 20 (decayed).
Remarks: The roof of the Church which has for a long time been in a state
of dilapidation now fallen in.

> John Davies. Vicar.
> Haverfordwest.

Lewis: discharged vicarage, annexed to that of Llanhowel [592.3.15.(35)]; rated
at £5, and endowed with £800 royal bounty and £200 parliamentary grant:
impropriators, Dean and Chapter of St. David's.
C & C: 1 service partially in English and Welsh performed by the incumbent.
I & C: not resident.

6 Brawdy Parish.
Area: 5,401 acres. *Popn.* 353 males, 400 females: total 753.

(10)   Brawdy Parish Church.
Endowed: tithe £70; permanent endowment £54. 0. 2*d*.; fees £1.
Space: free 40; other 80.
Present: morn. 15.
Remarks: This endowment of Fifty four pounds of *Brawdy cum Hays Castle*.
The living is consolidated.

> Thomas Davies.   Incumbent.
> Brawdy, Haverfordwest.

Lewis: discharged vicarage with that of Haycastle [592. 3. 2(2)] annexed; rated at
£3. 18. 9.; endowed with £200 royal bounty, and £1,400 parliamentary grant; net
income £115: patron and impropriator, Bp. of St. David's.
C & C: 1 service, partially in English and Welsh, performed by the incumbent.
I & C: not resident.

(11)   Penycwm.   Independents.
Erected 1826.
Space: free 70.
Present: even. 130.
Average: even. 130.

> John Thomas.   Deacon.
> Llethr House, Solva.

(12)   Rhydygella.   Calvinistic Methodist.
Erected 1821.
Space: free 180; standing 60.
Present: morn. 40 + 30 scholars; aft. alternately.
Average: morn. 60 + 30 scholars.

> David Rees.   Deacon.
> Rhydygelli, Solva.

7   St. Elvis Parish.
Area: 414 acres. *Popn.* 18 males, 11 females: total 37.

(13)   St. Elvis Parish Church.
Endowed: land £42; tithe £31.
Remarks: The Church has been in a dilapidated state many years & no
service performed there. It is annexed to the Parish of Whitchurch.

> J. P. Williams.   Rector.
> Whitchurch.

Lewis: discharged rectory, rated at £2. 10. 10; endowed with £800 royal bounty;
in the patronage of the Dean and Chapter of St. David's by an exchange with the
Crown: net income £72: tithes commuted for £31, and 10*s* Easter Offerings, subject
to rates averaging 18*s* per annum.
C & C: out of repair.
I & C: resident.

8 Whitchurch Parish.
Area: 3,138 acres. *Popn.* 554 males, 698 females: total 1,252.

(14) NATIONAL SCHOOL ROOM, SOLVA.
Licensed as a place of worship by the Lord Bishop of Saint David's in the
month of February 1841.
Circumstances of License: On account of the inconvenient distance of the
Parish Church of Whitchurch from the village of Solva, where the mass of
the population reside.
Space: free; standing 50.
Present: even. 130.
Remarks: The Vicar of the Parish of Whitchurch performs the Duty at the
School Room, & has done so for more than ten years, without any remunera-
tion beyond what he receives as Incumbent of the Parish.

> Peter Beynon.   Churchwarden.
> Solva.

(15) WHITCHURCH PARISH CHURCH.
Endowed: land £40; tithe £97. 6. 8*d*; permanent endowment £4; fees 10*s*;
gross £141. 6. 8*d*; net £90.
Space: other 120; free, none but plenty of standing space.
Present: morn. 35.
Average: morn. 50.
Remarks: Having answered the above queries according to the best of my
belief, I may perhaps be permitted to observe that with reference to the
census of the population they are quite impertinent, and not being authorized
by the Act to which they pretend to refer they are disingenuous. The
Registrar General no doubt will be able to assign a satisfactory reason why
no enquiry as to *Endowments* has been inserted in the Returns for Dissenting
Places of Worship.

> James Propert Williams.   Vicar.
> Whitchurch.

Lewis: discharged vicarage, rated at £5. 15. 7½; endowed with £200 royal bounty,
and £800 parliamentary grant; net income £101: tithes commuted for £292, of
which £146. 13. 4 are payable to the patrons, Precentor and Chapter of St. David's
cathedral, £48 to the sub-chanter and vicars-choral, and £97. 6. 8. to the vicar.

C & C: 2 services, 1 in the church, 1 in the Schoolroom at Solva; English service
at 10 a.m. at Whitchurch, and in Welsh at 2 p.m. in summer, and 6 p.m. in winter
at Whitchurch; performed by the incumbent.

I & C: resident.

(16) [Headed: Duplicate of Page 14]
NATIONAL SCHOOL ROOM.
Licensed 1841.
Erected as a School room in 1836.

Space: about 200.
Usual Number of Attendants: even. 80-100.

J. P. Williams.   Vicar of Whitchurch.
[Informant's form]

(16) TREFFGARN OWEN. INDEPENDENTS.
Erected 1686; enlarged 1753; rebuilt 1833.
Space: free 406; other 135; standing 500.
Present: morn. 301 + 59 scholars; even. 100 + 47 scholars.
Average (12 *months*): morn. 390 + 60 scholars; even. 80 + 40 scholars.

John Evans.   Sunday School Secretary.
Trefgarn Owen, Brawdy.

(17) PAVAN. INDEPENDENTS.
Erected 1841.
Space: free 80; standing 40.
Present: even. 94.
Average: even. 80.
Remarks: There is no service in the morning as those who attend the evening service at Trefgarn Independent Chapel in the morning.

B & I Griffiths.   Ministers.
Trefgarn, Solva.

(18) MIDLEMILL. PARTICULAR BAPTIST.
Erected before 1800.
Space: free 400; other 61; standing 200.
Present: morn. 310.
Average (12 *months*): morn. 520.

Thomas Morris.   Local Preacher.
Merchant.
Solva.

(19) WELSH CALVINISTIC METHODIST, SOLVA.
Erected 1823 in lieu of another building.
Space: free 180; standing 150.
Present: morn. 40 scholars; aft. 200.
Average (12 *months*): morn. 75 scholars; aft. 200.
Remarks: From the result of the memorable "Blue Books" inquiry the writer will be disappointed any favourable report of the present.

John Williams.   Steward.
Solva.

(20) WESLEYAN METHODIST.
Erected 1812.
Space: free 90; other 70; standing 40.

Present: aft. 61.
Average (12 months): aft. 100.

> Isaac Jenkins.   Minister.
> St. Davids.

(21)   OLD MEETING HOUSE, SOLVA.   INDEPENDENT.
Erected before 1800.
Space: free 240; other 140.
Present: morn. 268 + 112 scholars; even. 223 + 112 scholars.
Average (12 months): morn. 200 + 100 scholars; even. 250 + 100 scholars.

> John David Jones.   Minister.
> Solva.

(22)   SION CHAPEL, WHITCHURCH.   'PECULIAR' BAPTISTS.
Erected 1819.
Space: free 15; other 10.
Present: even. 220.
Average (12 months): morn. 300.

> Thomas Morris.   Local Preacher.
> Solva.

(33)   ZION, ST. DAVID'S.   BAPTIST.
Erected 1839.
Space: free 2; other 39.
Usual number of attendants: morn. 200 + 50 scholars; even. 200.

> *Informant:* Thomas Perkin.
> Weaver.
> St. David's.

[Informant's form]

[*Note:* the parish enumeration of this and the following return should be
9-13, i.e. the parish of St. David's.]

(24)   BETHANIA, TRELETHIDFAWR VILLAGE, ST. DAVID'S.
CALVINISTIC METHODIST.
Erected about 1836.
Space: all free.
Usual number of attendants: morn. 40 scholars; aft. 90-100.

> *Informant:* Ebenezer Williams.
> Druggist.
> St. David's.

[Informant's form]

9-13   St. Davids Parish, consisting of [9] Cylch Bychan, [10] Cylch-Gwylod-y-Wlad, [11] Cylch Mawr, and [12] Cylch-y-Dre Divisions, and [13] Ramsey Island.
Area of the whole parish: 11,185 acres. *Popn.* 1,370 males, 1,090 females: total 2,460.

(25)   Cathedral Church of St. David's.
Space: free 140, other 20.
Present: morn. 64; aft. 71.
Average (12 *months*)*:* summer: morn. 80; aft. 100. winter: morn. 48; aft. 48. average: morn. 64; aft. 74.
Remarks: English Service. The population is chiefly Welsh in the Parish of Saint David's. The Welsh Congregation in the Cathedral is entirely a distinct congregation. The congregation is much smaller in winter owing to the coldness of the Choir.

> W. Richardson.   Senior Minor Canon and Prebendary of St. Davids.
> Nathaniel Davis.   Minor Canon and Prebendary.

Lewis: the ecclesiastical establishment consists of the bishop (who is also dean), a precentor, chancellor, treasurer, four archdeacons, eight prebendaries, and six canons-cursal; a sub-chanter, four priest-vicars, four lay-vicars, an organist, six choristers, a master of the grammar school, verger, porter, sexton, and a keeper of the church during time of service. The diocese embraces 454 benefices, of which 140 have glebe-houses; 15 resident incumbents have curates; 175 curates are employed by non-resident incumbents. The Bishop has the patronage of all dignities of the church, except three canonries, and of 98 benefices, and an income of £2,500; the chapter has the partonage of 11 benefices, and a net revenue of £1,300, which is equally divided, but the precentor (who in practice is dean), the chancellor, and the treasurer, have also separate revenues, together with free residences: one of the elective canonries is suspended and its revenues paid over to the ecclesiastical commissioners.
The living is a perpetual curacy, endowed with £600 royal bounty, and £1,200 parliamentary grant, and in the patronage of the Precentor and Upper Chapel of St. David's; net income £110; tithes commuted for three respective rent-charges, one for £720 payable to the Precentor and Chapter, the second for £320 payable to the Sub-chanter and Vicars-choral, and the third for £7 payable to the Bishop. Cathedral is used as the parochial church, with four services, two in English and two in Welsh.
C & C: 4 services, 2 in English in the Choir, and 2 in Welsh in the south transept.
I & C: no return.

(Duplicate 23)
Zion, New Street, St. Davids.   Baptist.
Erected 1823.
Space: free 20; other 38.
Present: morn. 180; even. 180.
Average: aft. 60 scholars.

> William Reynolds.   Minister.
> Trevine.

(26) CARVARCHELL CHAPEL.   CALVINISTIC METHODIST.
Erected before 1800.
Space: free 17; other 28; standing 400.
Present: morn. school; aft. 115.
Average: general congregation 120; scholars 35.

> John Lewis.   Minister.
> Fishguard.

(27) BEREA.   INDEPENDENTS OR CONGREGATIONALISTS.
Erected 1834 ⎱
            1839 ⎰
Space: free 61; other 96.
Present: even. 139.
Average (12 *months*): general congregation 150.

> James Griffiths.   Minister.
> St. Davids.

(28) BETHEL.   BAPTIST.
Erected 1840.
Space: all free.
Present: morn. 47 scholars: aft. 123.
Average: morn. 60 scholars; aft. 150.

> John D. Evans.   Baptist Preacher.
> Solva.

(29) RHODIAD.   INDEPENDENTS OR CONGREGATIONAL.
Erected 1785.
Space: free 98; other 70.
Present: morn. 231.
Average (12 *months*): 250.

> James Griffiths.   Minister.
> St. Davids.

(30) BETHEL, CITY OF ST. DAVIDS.   WESLEYAN METHODISTS.
Erected 1813.
Space: free 80; other 138: standing 40.
Present: morn. 73; even. 156.
Average: morn. 90; even. 200.
Remarks: Great sickness among the members of the congregation on Sunday March 31st thereby occasioning less attendance.

> Isaac Jenkins.   Minister.
> St. Davids.

(31) TABERNACLE, CITY OF ST. DAVID'S.   WELSH CALVINISTIC METHODISTS.
Erected about 1815.
Space: free 200; other 350; standing 50.
Present: morn. 308; even. 343.
Average: The above is supposed to be about the average number.
Remarks: The services in the above named Chapel are supported by voluntary contributions. The Church and Congregation have also erected a spacious Room for a day school.

> William Morris.   Minister.
> St. Davids.

(32) EBENEZER.   CITY OF ST. DAVIDS.   INDEPENDENTS OR CONGREGATIONALISTS.
Erected 1815. ⎫
         1838. ⎭
Space: free 26; other 40.
Present: even. 209.
Average (12 *months*): morn. 170; even. 210.
Remarks: March 30 No meeting in the morning being at Rhodiad for the cenveniency of country members.

> Jno. Lloyd Jones.   Minister.
> Solva.

(33) CATHEDRAL CHURCH OF ST. DAVIDS.
The Welsh Service is perfomed in the South Transept, which has been nearly filled up for that purpose.
Endowed:
Space: free 300.
Present: morn. 201; even. 170.
Remarks: should Agriculture produce continue in the present depressed state there must be a reduction made of ¼ at least in the land.

> W. Richardson.   Perpetual Curacte.
> St. David's.

[Endorsed: See 25]

15 Llanhowell Parish.
Area: 1,381 acres. *Popn.* 96 males, 93 females: total 189.

(34) LLANHOWELL PARISH CHURCH.
Endowed: land £25; tithe £41.
Space: free 70; other 15.

Present: aft. 90.
Average: morn. 30-70; aft. 90-100.

> John Davis. Vicar.
> Solva.

Lewis: prebend in the cathedral church, rated at £19. 9. 7, annexed to the Archdeaconry of Carmarthen: discharged vicarage, with that of Llandeloy[592. 3. 5(9)] annexed; net income £120; patrons and impropriators, Dean and Upper Chapter of St. David's cathedral church.

C & C: 1 service partially in English and Welsh.

I & C: not resident.

ICBS: grant of £100 in 1834.

16   Llanrian Parish.
Area: 3,683 acres. *Popn.* 579 males, 599 females: total 1,178.

(35)   LLANRIAN PARISH CHURCH.
Endowed: tithe £101. 10. 7d; permanent endowment £10. 3. 8d.
Space: free 209; other 158.
Present: morn. 100.
Aveage: aft. 135 [for the Sunday preceding March 30th].

> Jacob Hughes. Minister.
> Trevgwr, Harverfordwest.

Lewis: discharged vicarage, rated at £19. 9. 7.; endowed with £200 royal bounty and £600 parliamentary grant; net income £105: patron, Bp. of St. David's.

C & C: 1 service partially in English and Welsh, performed by the incumbent.

I & C: not resident.

(36)   TREVINE.   CALVINISTIC METHODIST.
Erected 1786; rebuilt 1834.
Space: free 4; other 34; standing 100 persons.
Present: morn. 225; aft. 109 scholars; even. 185.
Average (12 *months*): general congregational 230; scholars 100.

> William Phillip. Deacon.
> Rhoslyn, Llanrian.

(37)   TREVINE.   PARTICULAR BAPTIST.
Erected 1843.
Space: free 7; other 13.
Present: morn. school; even. 183.

> William Mathias.   Deacon.
> Trevine.

(38) CROESGOCH, LLANRYAN.   PARTICULAR BAPTIST.
Erected 1817.
Space: free 36; other 8.
Present: morn. school; aft. 348.

> David Jones.   Deacon.
> Croesgoch.

17   Mathry Parish.
Area: 6,992 acres. *Popn.* 507 males, 545 females: total 1,052.

(39) MATHRY PARISH CHURCH.
Endowed: land £20; tithe £190; glebe £75; permanent endowment £10;
fees £2.
Space: free 60; other 108.
Present: morn. 36; even. 26.
Average (12 *months*): morn. 45; even. 33.
Remarks: The aggregate annual amount of endowment is about £97. 0. 0.

> E. D. Evans.   Minister.

Lewis: discharged vicarage, united, together with that of St. Nicholas [592. 4. 1 (1)]
to the vicarage of Granston [592. 3. 18 (41)]; rated at £4. 7. 6.; endowed with £200
royal bounty: the rectory constituted the Golden Prebend in the Cathedral Church
of St. David's, rated at £25. 14. 4½.; in the patronage of the bishop, under whom
the tithes are held on lease by Sir John Owen, Bart.
C & C: 2 services in Welsh performed by the incumbent.
I & C: resident.

(40) REHOBOTH. INDEPENDENTS.
Erected 1840.
Used exclusively as a place of worship, 'Except keeping a day school till
School Room will be ready'.
Space: free 36; other 28.
Present: morn. 180; aft. 55 scholars; even. 89.
Average (12 *months*): general congregation 220; scholars 65.

> Samuel Evans.   Minister.

18   Granston Parish.
Area: 1,639 acres. *Popn.* 90 males, 105 females: total 195.

(41) GRANSTON PARISH CHURCH.
Endowed: tithe £50; glebe £10.
Space: free 30; other 30.
Present: aft. 21.
Average (12 *months*): morn. 15; aft. 30.

> Rowland Daniel.   Vicar.
> Letterston.

Lewis: discharged vicarage, annexed to those of Mathrey [592. 3. 17(39)] and St. Nicholas [592. 4. 1(1)]; rated at £6. 8. 11½; in the patronage of the bishop of St. David's: a portion of the tithes of Granston belong to a lay impropriator, whose claim has been commuted for £17, and the portion connected to the vicarage for £50; glebe of 14 acres, valued at £7 per annum; net income £316, with a glebe-house.

C & C: 1 service in Welsh performed by the incumbent.

I & C: legally not resident.

(42) LLANGLOFFAN.   BAPTIST.
Erected before 1800.
Space: free 300; other 300.
Present: morn. 337; aft. 64* + 148 scholars; even. 287.*
Average (12 *months*): morn. 500; even. 300.
Remarks: *There are two services every Sunday Evening which are kept in two domestic houses and in the Chapel and a Domestic House alternately. The service in the afternoon is kept once a month in a Domestic House.

Thomas Williams.   Minister.

[End of St. David's Subdistrict]

4 FISHGUARD (Subdistrict)
Area: 50,092 acres. *Popn.* 4,076 males, 4,818 females: total 8,894·

1 St. Nicholas Parish.
Area: 2,141 acres. *Popn.* 166 males, 189 females: total 355.

(1) ST. NICHOLAS PARISH CHURCH.
Endowed: tithe £50.
Space: free 50; other 50.
Present: morn. 30.
Average (12 *months*): morn. 40; aft. 90.

Rowland Daniel.   Vicar.
Letterston.

Lewis: prebend in the cathedral church of St. David's, with a residence in that city attached; valued at £5. 4. 6½; in the patronage of the Bishop: the living a discharged vicarage, annexed, with that of Mathrey [592. 3. 17(39)], to the vicarage of Granston [592. 3. 18(41)]: tithes commuted for £153, of which £102 are payable to the Prebendary, subject to rates averaging £7. 4. 6, and £51, subject to rates averaging £3. 7. 11 per annum to the vicar; glebe of 36 acres valued at £25. 4. per annum.

C & C: 1 service in Welsh performed by the incumbent.

I & C: *sub.* Granston. legally not resident.

(2) RHOSYCAERAN.   INDEPENDENTS OF CONGREGATIONALISTS.
Erected before 1800.
Space: free 84.
Present: morn. 157 + 70 scholars.
Average (12 *months*): morn. 180 + 76 scholars.
Remarks: Every Sunday evening Divine Services are held in different parts of the neighbourhood and the average attendance may be calculated at about 160.

David Bateman.   Minister.
Fishguard.

2 Manorowen Parish.

Area: 1,263 acres. *Popn.* 85 males, 104 females: total 189.

(3) MANORWEN PARISH CHURCH.
Endowed: land £68. 8*s*; permanent endowment £8. 17. 7*d*.
Space: free 34; other 26.
Present: aft. 56.

A. H. Richardson.   Minister.

Lewis: vicarage not in charge, endowed with £600 royal bounty, and £200 parl. grant: net income £86: patrons and impropriators, Sub-Chanters and Vicars-Choral of St. David's: tithes commuted for £80, subject to rates of £9. 15.
C & C: 1 service in Welsh and English on alternate Sundays performed by the incumbent.
I & C: not resident.

3 Llanwnda Patish.

Area: 5,701 acres. *Popn.* 595 males, 697 females: total 1,292.

(4) LLANWNDA PARISH CHURCH.
Endowed: land £19. 4*s*; tithe £209. 11. 7*d*; permanent endowment £39. 8. 8*d*.
Space: free 72; other 30.
Present: morn. 38 + 11 scholars.
Average (12 *months*): morn. 70 + 15 scholars.
Remarks: The net sum received in lieu of Tithes after deducting the poor rate, road rate, income tax and other expences is £169. 11. 7.
N.B. The Church of Llanwnda is situated on the Northern side of the parish, the bulk of the population is at the foot of a steep hill on the Southern side.

A. H. Richardson.   Minister.

Lewis: discharged vicarage, rated at £3. 5. 2½; endowed with £200 royal bounty, and £400 parl. grant: net income £220; patrons and appropriators, Precentor and Canons of St. David's Cathedral.
C & C: 1 service partially in English and Welsh performed by the incumbent.
I & C: resident.

(5) BERACAH.   CALVINISTIC METHODIST.
Erected 1830.
Space: free 101; other 133; standing 55.
Present: morn. 99 + 15 scholars.
Average (12 *months*): morn. 200 + 25 scholars.
Remarks: The service being held on the 30th of March in the morning. But the most numerous attendance is in the afternoons and the evenings.

David Meyler.   Supplying Minister.

(6) HARMONY.   BAPTIST.
Erected 1828.
Space: free 9; other 31.
Present: morn. 79 scholars; aft. 202; even. 61.
Average (12 *months*): general. congregation 250; scholars 79.
Remarks: The Communion Sunday is more numerous as to members, and hearers. The Chapel is a station, or a Branch of the Baptists Church at Llangloffan [592. 3. 18(42)], in the Parish of Granston, Pembrokeshire.

Henry Davies.   Minister.

(7) SALEM.   INDEPENDENTS OR CONGREGATIONALISTS.
Erected 1840.
Space: free 36.
Present: even. 44 + 50 scholars.

David Bateman.   Minister.

4   Fishguard Parish.
Area: 4,208 acres. *Popn.* 977 males, 1,339 females: total 2,316.

(8) ST. MARY'S PARISH CHURCH.
Endowed: land £30. 8s; tithe £70; permanent endowment £32; fees £5;
Space: free 82; other 101.
Present: morn. 87 + 41 scholars; even. 111 + 30 scholars.
Remarks: The net income is about £115 per annum. 39 of the free sittings and 6 large pews are huddled together in the Chancel, to the back of the Pulpit. The Church is much too small; if larger, the congregation would doubtless be proportional to the accomodation.

Thomas Richardson.   Curate.

Lewis: discharged vicarage, rated at £4. 0. 5; endowed with £200 royal bounty, and £800 parl. grant: in the partonage of the Crown: net income £111: impropriator, J. Hughes, Esq; impropriate tithes commuted for £230; vicarial tithes commuted for £70, with a glebe of 12 acres, valued at £16.
C & C: 2 services partially in English and Welsh, performed by the curate.
I & C: no return.

(9) TOWER HILL CHAPEL.   CALVINISTIC METHODISTS.
Erected 1759.
Space: free 231; other 544; standing 372.
Present: aft. 574; even. 535.
Average: general congregation 872; scholars 148.
Remarks: The service in Sunday the 30th of March 1851 being in the afternoon and evening. The morning service being more numerously attended.

David Meyler.   Supplying Master.

(10) HERMON. PARTICULAR BAPTIST.
Erected 1776; rebuilt 1832.
Space: free 16, with long seats at the back for 66; other 87.
Present: morn. 308; aft. 118 scholars; even. 286.
Average: morn. 350; aft. 140 scholars; even. 400.
Remarks: During the winter when Sailors are at home Congregations are more numerous.

Richard Owen.   Minister.
Park Street, Fishguard

(11) EBENEZER, KENSINGTON STREET. BAPTIST.
Erected 1850.
Space: free 19; other 30.
Present: morn. 65 scholars; aft. 180; even. 150.
Average (6 *months*): morn. 220 + 69 scholars; aft. 200 + 69 scholars; even. 190.
Remarks: A prayer Meeting held on the evening of the 30th. A communion meeting held in the morning every month. Also a Sunday School held in the evening once a month.

James Owen.   Deacon.
Saddler.
High Street.

(12) TABERNACLE. INDEPENDENTS OR CONGREGATIONALISTS.
Erected before 1800.
Space: free 34; other 62.
Present: morn. 113 + 80 scholars; aft. 24 + 92 scholars; even. 134 + 85 scholars.
Remarks: The afternoon Service is performed in English.
The figures are rather below than above the Average attendance.

David Bateman.   Minister.

5 Llanllawer Parish.
Area: 1,202 acres. *Popn.* 53 males, 57 females: total 110.

(13) LLANLLAWER PARISH CHURCH, ANNEXED TO THE MOTHER CHURCH OF LLANYCHLLWYDOG.
Endowed: tithe commuted for £76. 17*s*; permanent endowment, not known.
Fees: only marriage fees: Easter offerings not collected: Pew rents, none.
Space: large enough for all the parishioners. Free sittings sufficient for the attendants, some of the forms are out of repair.
Present: aft. 26.
Average: The foregoing is more than the average number.

Wilkin William Thomas.   Rector.

Lewis: rectory not in charge annexed to that of Llanerchllwydog [593. 1. 1(1)].

C & C: 1 service in Welsh performed by the incumbent.

I & C: not resident.

6   Llanychaer Parish.
Area: 2,053 acres. *Popn.* 113 males, 106 females: total 219.

(14) LLANYCHAER PARISH CHURCH.
Endowed: land £6. 13*s*; tithe £56; permanent endowment £16. 1. 6*d*; fees £1.
Space: free 60; other 10.
Present: aft. 66.

William Davies.   Curate.

Lewis: discharged rectory, rated at £3. 6. 8; endowed with £400 royal bounty, and £200 parl. grant: net income £69: patron, Rev. James Williams Jones.

C & C: 1 service in Welsh performed by the incumbent.

I & C: no return.

7   Llanstinan Parish.
Area: 1,579 acres. *Popn.* 113 males, 104 females: total 1,971.

(15) LLANSTINAN PARISH CHURCH.
Endowed: land £96; permanent endowment £12.
Space: free 22; other 17.
Present: morn. 80.
Average (12 months): morn. 30; aft. 50.

W. Clement Bowen.   Perpetual Curate.

Lewis: perpetual curacy, endowed with £600 royal bounty, and £200 parl. grant; net income £100; patron, Col. Owen; appropriator, Sub-chanter in the Cathedral Church of St. Davids.

C & C: 1 service partially in English and Welsh, performed by the incumbent.

I & C: not resident.

(16)   MAINRE.   CALVINISTIC METHODIST.
Erected 1843.
Space: free 12; other 14; standing 20 persons.
Present: morn. 61; aft. 50 scholars; even. 40 scholars.

John James }
George John } Ministers in turn.
Glanafon

8   Jordanston Parish.

Area: 1,876 acres. *Popn.* 65 males, 79 females: total 144.

(17)   JORDANSTON PARISH CHURCH.
Endowed: land £17. 10*s*; tithe £86; glebe £8.
Space: free 30; other 18.
Present: morn. 17-19.
Average: morn. 12-15.
Remarks: The parish is small and the inhabitants are scattered.

Henry Halkan.   Rector.

Lewis: discharged rectory, rated at £6. 3. 9; endowed with £400 royal bounty;
net income £91: patron, G. G. Vaughan, Esq.

C & C: 1 service partially in English and Welsh performed by the incumbent.

I & C: not resident.

9   Llanfair-Nant-y-Gof Parish.

Popn. 2,597 acres. *Popn.* 133 males, 126 females: total 259.

(18)   LLANFAIR NANT Y GÔF PAROCHIAL CHAPEL.
Endowed: tithe £143: glebe £83.
Space: free 50.
Present: aft. 29.
Remarks: This is the Parish Church of Llanfair united to the Parish of
Letterston and called a Chapel.

George Harris.   Rector.
Letterston.

Lewis: annexed to the rectory of Letterston [592. 4. 10(19)]; tithes commuted for
£133, subject to rates averaging £2. 5.; glebe of 164 acres, valued at £105 per
annum.

C & C: 1 service in Chapel: see *sub* Letterston.

I & C: see *sub* Letterston.

10   Letterston Parish.

Area: 2,216 acres. *Popn.* 242 males, 316 females: total 558.

(19)   LETTERSTON PARISH CHURCH.
Endowed: tithe £150; glebe £40.
Space: free 94; other 24.
Present: morn. 60.

George Harries.   Rector.

Lewis: discharged rectory with the peretual curacy of Llanfair-Nant-y-Gove
[592. 4. 9(18)] annexed; rated at £12. 11. 0½; in the patronage of the Crown: net
income £387: tithes commuted for £150, subject to rates averaging £3. 17; glebe
of 27 acres, valued at £27 per annum.
C & C: 3 services in 2 Sundays, in Welsh at Letterston on alternate Sundays:
Welsh services performed by both incumbent and curate.
I & C: resident: curate has stipend of £40.
ICBS: grant of £50 in 1844.

(20)   SARON.   BAPTIST.
Erected before 1800.
Space: free 240; other 220.
Present: morn. 120; aft. 200; even. 104.
Average (12 *months*): morn. 250; aft. 500; even. 250 [?150].

Benjamin Owen.   Minister.
Good Hope.

(21)   WESLEYAN METHODIST CHAPEL.
Erected 1813.
Space: free 42 (7 x 6); other 24 (4 x 6); standing 40.
Present: morn. 40.
Average (12 *months*): morn. 30.

Isaac Jenkins.   Minister.
St. David's.

11   Little Newcastle Parish.
Area: 2,712 acres. *Popn.* 212 males, 221 females: total 433.

(22)   LITTLE NEWCASTLE PARISH CHURCH.
Endowed: land purchased by Queen Anne's Bounty money £70; permanent
endowment including Parliamentary grant £27.
Space: free 120; other 20.
Present: morn. 36.
Average: morn. 60; aft. 80.
Remarks: Little Newcastle is now consolidated with the adjoining Parish
of St. Dogwells [592. 4. 12(23)], for which a separate return is made—Divine
Service is performed alternately morning and afternoon at Little New-
castle.

Peter David Richardson.
Perpetual Curate.

Lewis: *sub* Newcastle (Little): perpetual curacy, endowed with £800 royal bounty, and £200 parliamentary grant; net income £54: patron, T. Morse, Esq: impropriator, Rev. T. K. W. Harries, Esq.

C & C: 1 service, partially in English and Welsh, performed by the incumbent.

I & C: resident.

[Note: Beulah Baptist Chapel, 592. 4. 18(36), should be included here.]

12   St. Dogwells Parish.
Area: 3,347 acres. *Popn.* 228 males, 273 females: total 501.

(23)   SAINT DOGWELL'S PARISH CHURCH.
Endowed: land purchased by Queen Anne's Bounty Money £4. 10s; tithe by commutation £45; glebe £34.
Space: free 50; other 70.
Present: morn. 35.
Average (12 *months*): morn. 50.
Remarks: Divine Service is always performed at eleven in the morning at St. Dogwells.

Peter David Richardson.   Vicar.

Lewis: discharged vicarage, rated at £4. 16. 0½; net income £71 with a glebe-house: patrons and impropirators, Dean and Chapter of St. David's.

C & C: 1 service, partially in English and Welsh, performed by the incumbent.

I & C: resident.

13   Ambleston Parish.
Area: 3,956 acres. *Popn.* 279 males, 319 females: total 598.

(24)   AMBLESTON PARISH CHURCH.
Endowed: land £40; tithe £122; glebe £10.
Space: free 200.
Present: morn. 40.

Jno. Pugh.   Vicar.

Lewis: discharged vicarage, rated £3. 19. 4½; endowed with £600 royal bounty, and £200 parliamentary grant; net income £183: in the gift of the Crown: impropriator, Lloyd Phillips, Esq.

C & C: 1 service in Welsh, performed by the incumbent.

I & C: no return.

(24)   AMBLESTON PARISH CHURCH.
Space: free 40.
Usual number of attendants: 80-100.
General congregation: 80-100; scholars 50.

Infomant: Sam. E. Lloyd.

[Endorsed: duplicate of 24]
[Informant's form]

(25) WOODSTOCK. CALVINISTIC METHODISTS.
Erected 1754.
Space: free 11; other 28.
Present: morn. 230; aft. 52.

> Thomas Harries. Deacon.
> Henry's Moat.

14 Spittal Parish.
Area: 2,674 acres. *Popn.* 209 males, 221 females: total 430.

(26) SPITTAL PARISH CHURCH.
Endowed: Bounty lands £80; glebe £21. 10s. 10d; permanent endowment
£6. 13. 4d.
Space: free 145; other 15.
Present: morn. 63.
Average: aft. 80, some times more.
Remarks: £21. 10. 10—Annual Interest on Queen Anne's Bounty and
Parliamentary Grants £6. 13. 4. Stipend from the Rector the Dean of St.
David's.

> Thomas Jenkins. Incumbent.
> Haverfordwest.

Lewis: perpetual curacy, endowed with £800 royal bounty, and £200 parliamentary
grant; net income £79: patrons and appropriators, Precentor and Chapter of St.
David's: appropriated tithes commuted for £152, with a glebe of 32 acres valued at
£20 per annum.
C & C: 1 service in English.
I & C: not resident.
ICBS: grant of £20 in 1834.

(27) WESLEYAN CHAPEL, SPITTAL GREEN. WESLEYAN METHODIST.
Erected 1826.
Space: free 86; other 37; standing 50.
Present: morn. 102; aft. 64 scholars.
Average: general congregation 120; scholars 60.

> George Llewellin. Trustee.
> Spittal.

(28) SALEM, SPITTLE. BAPTIST.
Erected 1827.
Space: all free about 40 feet by 30.
Present: aft. 96.

> Essex Lewis. Elder.
> Treffgarn Bridge, Spittle.

(29)   Zion's Hill, Spittal.   Independent.
Erected 1823.
Space: free 200; other 100 (all free).
Present: aft. 96 + 25 scholars.

Daniel Davies.   Minister.
Ambleston.

15   East Walton Parish.
Area: 1,893 acres. *Popn.* 124 males, 155 females: total 279.

(30)   Walton East Parish Church.
Endowed: land £36; permanent endowment £27.
Space: When rebuilt free 100; other 130.
Present: morn. 50; aft. 50.
Average: morn. 50; aft. 50.

James Thomas.   Incumbent.

Lewis: perpetual curacy, endowed with £600 royal bounty, and £200 parliamentary grant; net income £60; patron and impropriator, Lloyd Philipps, Esq: tithes commuted for £170.

C & C: 1 service in English.

I & C: no return.

ICBS: grant of £80 in 1849.

16   Henrys Moat Parish.
Area: 3,166 acres. *Popn.* 155 males, 168 femaes: total 323.

(31)   Henry's Moat, dedicated to St. Bernard, Parish Church.
Space: free 13.
Present: even. 12.
Average (12 *months*): morn. 16.
Remarks: The Church is endowed by Land, Tithe, and a small Glebe—but being not the Rector I am unable to state the amount of its annual Endowment. The Services are morning and evening on alternate Sundays.

Lewis Davies.   Curate.

Lewis: discharged rectory, rated at £5. 6. 8; endowed with £200 private benefaction, and £200 bounty: net income £185: patron, W. H. Scourfield, Esq.: tithes commuted for £145; glebe of about 5 acres, valued at £5 per annum.

C & C: 1 service in Welsh, performed by the curate.

I & C: not resident: curate, who resides at Temple Druid, 3 miles distant, has stipend of £70.

(32) HOREB, HENDRYSMOAT. BAPTIST.
Erected 1835.
Space: free 29, 40 by 20; standing 4 yards.
Present: morn. 200; even. 70.

William John
Ebenezer Eynon } Deacons.

(33) SILO CHAPEL, NERY'S MOAT. INDEPENDENT.
Erected 1842; Day School kept.
Space: 15 x 6 (90); 10 x 6 (60).
Present: morn. 75; aft. 47 scholars; even. 90.
Average: morn. 100; aft. 60 scholars; even. 120.

David Owen. Minister.

17 Castle Bythe, or Castle Bigh, Parish.
Area: 2,537 acres. *Popn.* 134 males, 132 females: total 266.

(34) CASTLE BYTHE PARISH CHURCH.
[This return is missing.]
Lewis: discharged rectory, rated at £6; in the patronage of the Crown.
C & C: 1 service in Welsh performed by the incumbent.
I & C: no return.

18 Puncheston Parish.
Area: 1,725 acres. *Popn.* 121 males, 124 females: total 245.

(35) PUNCHESTON PARISH CHURCH.
Endowed: land £30; tithe £70; fees £1.
Space: free 90; other 13.
Present: morn. 54.

William Davies. Curate.

Lewis: discharged rectory, rated at £5. 6. 8; net income £101, with a glebe-house:
patron, Rev. James Williams James.
C & C: 1 service in Welsh performed by the incumbent.
I & C: no return.
(36 & 36A)

(36) BEULAH, PARISH OF LITTLE NEWCASTLE. BAPTIST.
Erected 1808.
Space: free 20; other 30.
Present: aft. 300; even. 400.
Average: general congregation 400; scholars 40.

(36A) SMYRNA, PUNCHESTON PARISH. BAPTIST.
Erected 1824.
Average: general congregation 250; scholars 50.

D. W. Morris. Minister.

[This return contains 2 places of worship, numbered as above. (36) is wrongly numbered, and should be included under 592. 4. 11.]

(37) BETHEL. WELSH CALVINISTIC METHODIST.
Erected 827.
Space: free 100; standing 200.
Present: morn. 27 scholars; aft. 79; even. 39.
Average (12 *months*): general congregation 80; scholars 50.
Remarks: Some from the adjoining parishes.

Henry Evans. Deacon.

(38) SMYRNA. BAPTIST.
Erected 1827.
Space: free 250; standing 100.
Present: morn. 300; aft. 39 scholars.
Average (12 *months*): morn. general congregation 250; scholars 50.
Remark: Attendants from joining Parishes.

Ebenezer Williams. Deacon.
Llysdref, Puncheston.

[Cf. 592. 4. 18(36a).]

19   Morvil Parish.
Area: 2,551 acres. *Popn.* 73 males, 66 females: total 134.

(39) MORVIL PARISH CHURCH.
Endowed: land £60; tithe £68; permanent endowment £3. 0. 4d.
Space: free 200.
Average (12 *months*): morn. 15; aft. 15.
Remark: The Parish has been much neglected and the Church is not yet in proper repair.

Llewelyn Lloyd Thomas. Rector.
Newport Rectory, Haverfordwest.

Lewis: discharged rectory, rated at £2; endowed with £400 bounty; net income £81: patron, R. B. P. Phillips, Bart.; tithes commuted for £68.

C & C: 1 service in Welsh, performed by the incumbent.

I & C: not resident.

20 Pontfaen Parish.

Area: 695 acres. *Popn.* 19 males, 22 females: total 41.

(40) PONTFAEN PARISH CHURCH.
Endowed: land £70.
Space: free 120.
Average (12 *months*): morn. 9; even. 9.
Remark: The Church has been some time in a dilapidated state.

Lewis Davies.   Perpetual Curate.
Temple Druid, Nr. Narberth.

Lewis: perpetual curacy, rated at £3. 6. 8; endowed with £1,200 bounty, and £400 parliamentary grant: net income £72: patron and impropriator, Mr. Rees.

C & C: 1 service in English.

I & C: not resident.

[End of Fishguard Subdistrict, end of Haverfordwest District, and end of Pembrokeshire Registration County]

CARDIGANSHIRE

Area: 594,883 acres. *Popn.* 45,155 males, 52,459 females: total 96,614.

593   CARDIGAN (District)

Area: 85,481 acres. *Popn.* 8,812 males, 11,374 females: total 20,186

1 NEWPORT (Subdistrict)
Area: 37,639 acres. *Popn.* 2,589 males, 3,541 females: total 6,130.

1   Llanychlwydog Parish, co. Pembroke.
Area: 2,283 acres. *Popn.* 100 males, 109 females: total 209.

[(1) St. Mary's Newport Parish Church, 593. 1. 3(1), inserted here by mistake. For details, see below, p. 461.]

(2) THE RECTORY OF LLANYCHLWYDOG, WITH LLANELAWEN ANNEXED: PARISH CHURCH
Endowed: tithe £108.
Space: sufficient for the attendants, total for about 70.
Present: 'The service this day was performed at the Chapel of Llanllawen annexed, where the number was 26.'
Average: 'The Congregation at Llanychllwydog Church is uncertain and generally small.'
Remarks: Llanychllwydog church and the Chapel of Llanllawen annexed are served alternately in the afternoon. The number at Llanllawen on the 30th of March 1851 was 26. The average numbers at Llanychllwydog is not so large.

Watkin William Thomas.   Rector.
Dinas Rectory.

Lewis: sub Llanerchllwydog: discharged rectory, with that of Llanllawer [592. 4. 5(13)] annexed; rated at £8; net income £155: patron, Thomas Lloyd, ESQ.
C & C: sub Llanllawer with Llanychllwydog: 1 service in Welsh performed by the incumbent.
I & C: not resident.

(3) TREDAVID CHAPEL, LLANYCHLWYDOG.   CALVINISTIC METHODIST.
Erected before 1800.
Space: free 120; other 32; standing 50.
Present: aft. 35 + 25 scholars.
Average: morn. 40 + 35 scholars; aft. 40 + 35 scholars.
Remarks: As the school has only been open two or three months, the average is for that time.

Thomas George.   Manager.
Mywyd Melyw, Fishguard.

(4) JABEZ. BAPTIST.
Erected 1803; rebuilt 1842.
Space: free 'on the flour and galery for 240 persons'; other 'sittings for 174 persons': standing 'nine but the passages'.
Present: morn. 203; aft. 130 scholars; even. 136.
Average (12 *months*): morn. 260; aft. 118 scholars.

David George. Minister.
Trewern, nr. Newport.

2. Dinas Parish, co. Pembroke.

Area: 2,328 acres. *Popn.* 331 males, 525 females: total 856.

(5) DINAS PARISH CHURCH.
Endowed: tithe £140; glebe £30.
Space: nave 36 ft. long by 14 broad: aisle 18 ft. long by 12 broad; chancel 18 ft. long by 12 broad. Total sittings 93.
Present: morn. 56.
Average: 'The foregoing number is supposed to be below the average'.
Remarks: There are 13 pews and about 16 benches. It is supposed that none of the seats have ever been legally appropriated, though they are taken possession of by particular parishioners who attend. Dinas Church is situated on an isthmus. The Chancel was washed away by an encroachment of the sea in November last and it has not been rebuilt. It is greatly desired in the Parish if there were funds for the purpose to transfer to a new site.

Watkin William Thomas, B.C. Rector.
Dinas Rectory.

Lewis: discharged rectory, rated at £8; patron, Thomas Lloyd, Esq.: rectorial tithes commuted for £140; glebe-house, with glebe of 40 acres, valued at £50 per annum.

C & C: 1 service in Welsh performed by the incumbent.

I & C: resident.

(6) TABOR, BAPTIST.
Erected 1792; rebuilt 1842.
Space: free 50; other 600; standing 100.
Present: morn. 50 scholars; aft. 390; even. 241.
Average (12 *months*): morn. from 400 to 450; aft. from 400 to 540; even. from 300 to 400.
Remarks: Sunday Scholars average during 12 months: morning from 70 to 125; evening from 100 to 150.

David Davies. Minister.
Dinas.

(7) Brynhenllan Chapel. Calvinistic Methodist.
Erected before 1800.
Space: free 236; other 184; standing 50.
Present: morn. 145; aft. 79 scholars; even. 110.
Average (6 *months*): morn. 170 + 80 scholars; aft. 170 + 80 scholars; even. 170.

> David Evans. Deacon.
> Parc gwin bach.

(8) Gideon. Independents.
Erected 1830.
Space: free 108; other 216; standing 108.
Present: morn. school; aft. 128; even. 100.
Average: general congregation 134; scholars 70.

> John Davies. Minister.
> Newport.

3 Newport Parish, co. Pembroke.
Area: 4,711 acres. *Popn.* 605 males, 1,111 females: total 1,716.

(1) Newport, St. Mary's Parish Church.
Endowed: tithe £258; glebe £30; permanent endowment £17. 8s.
Space: free 218; other 444.
Present: morn. 400 + 100 scholars; aft. 400 + 100 scholars.
Average: morn. 400 + 100 scholars; aft. 400 + 100 scholars.

> Llewelyn Lloyd Thomas. Rector.

Lewis: discharged rectory, rated at £16; endowed with £400 parliamentary grant; net income £216 with glebe-house; patron, Thomas Lloyd of Bronwydd, Esq.

C & C: 1 service partially in English and Welsh, performed by the incumbent.

I & C: resident.

[This return, numbered 593. 1. 3(1), is wrongly numbered and bound: it is here placed in its proper order.]

(9) Bethlehem. Particular Baptist.
Erected before 1770.
Space: Galary free; other 50.
Usual number of attendants: morn. general congregation 300; aft. 140 scholars. even. general congregation 320.

> David Owen. Informant.
> Market Street

[Informant's form.]

(10)　TABERNACLE.　WELSH CALVINISTIC METHODIST.
Erected 1815, rebuilt 1837.
Space: free about 150; other about 220; standing about 80.
Present: morn. 120; aft. 65 scholars; even. 130.
Average (12 *months*): morn. 130; aft. 68 scholars; even. 140.
Remarks: The Welsh Calvinistic Methodists have no stated ministers, their system being Presbyterian, they are supplied regularly by their own County Ministers in rotation, and also at times from the neighbouring counties of Cardigan and Carmarthen.

John Harries.　Secretary.

(11)　EBENEZER.　INDEPENDENTS OR CONGREGATIONALISTS.
Erected before 1800; rebuilt in 1844.
Space: free 100; Pews to let than can contain 500.
Present: morn. 361; aft. 157 scholars; even. 270.
Remarks: The attendance at Ebenezer on March the 30th 1851 was about a 100 or 150 less than usual on account of illness and other causes.

Samuel Thomas.
Independent Minister.
Ebeneyzer.

(12)　BETHLEHEM.　BAPTIST.
Erected before 1800.
Space: free 8 and the galary; other 55.
Present: morn. 270; aft. 144 scholars; even. 261.
Average: morn. 300; aft. 140 scholars; even. 310.
Remarks: There is upwards of 350 members belonging to this Chapel. Great part of them is off on sea and other places. Having no stated minister at present, but are supplied by the ministers of the neighbroad in rotation.

David Owen.　Secretary.
Saddler etc., Newport.

[This return refers to the same chapel as 593. 1. 3(9).]

4　Nevern Parish, co. Pembroke.
Area: 14,637 acres. *Popn.* 773 males, 869 females: total 1,642.

(13)　KILGWYN.　[Endorsed: Nevern Parish Church.]
Consecrated: It is nor known. Marriages were about to be performed here years ago, but not now.
Endowed: Kilgwyn Church has never been endowed. Service in the Church performed gratuitously and voluntarily.
Sittings: see Nevern return.
Present: no service performed at Kilgwyn Church this day.
Average: aft. 70.

Remarks: See an account of Kilgwyn Church in Nevern Church Return. The service in Kilgwyn Church is performed every other Sunday at ½ past 2 o'clock in the afternoon. There is no schoolroom at Kilgwyn, but ground has lately been given for building one and a house for the master. Funds are greatly wanted.

John Jones, M.A.
Vicar of Nevern.

Lewis: chapelry in the parish of Nevern.

C & C: see Nevern.

(14) NEVERN PARISH CHURCH.

Nevern Church, dedicated to St. Brynach, a Welsh Saint, of the 6th century, and a contemporary of St. David. The architecture was Norman originally. In 1809 a few of the Gothic were replaced by modern (or parlour) windows. In 1819 the entire of the remaining windows were replaced in like manner, the roof ceiled, etc. In the south wall is the following notice: "The Body of the Church rebuilt A.D. 1819. The Rev. Dd. Griffiths Vicar, J. E. Evans, Esq., E. W. Jones, Esq., W. Symonds, Gent., Mr. Vaughan, Church-wardens".

Endowed: See the accompanying paper.

Space: In the Body of the Church, allowing 18 inches to each sitting

44 pews containing sittings, in all	241
the clerk's seat	1
12 moveable forms	48
6 fixed forms	24
4 benches	21
In the gallery 4 fixed forms	28
	363

Present: morn. 173 + 63 scholars.
Average: morn. 206 + 63 scholars.

Nevern Village consists of only six small Cottages, Parsonage and the Church. N.B. Within the circuit of one quarter of a mile from the Church are Eleven cottages, one Mill and one Farm. The remaining Cottages and Farm house are distant from the Church from about one mile and upwards, as far, at least, as six miles. The parish is mountainous and the Population scattered, and their living at a great distance from the Church is the reason why there is only morning service on Sundays (every Sunday at ten o'clock in the morning), Christmas Day, Good Friday, etc. The Congregations in the Church are larger or smaller according to the state of the weather. In dry weather especially on Sacrament Sunday the congregation amounts to 300 on an average. The number of communicants is upwards of 100 monthly.

John Jones, M.A.   Vicar.

[Endorsed: see accomp. sheet.]
The area of the parish contains, by the Tithe Commissioners' Map 14,522

acres. The commutation of Tithes for Rent charge, as per the Tithe Commissioners' map stands thus, viz.

To the Lay Impropriator (Mr. Atwood) is assigned   £579. 7. 6. per an.
To the Vicar of the Parish   £193. 2. 6. per an.

The Glebe, in the possession of the Vicar, consists of 46*a* 32*r* 28*p*.
The Glebe in the Vicar's own hands.
NB.   The fields are no. according to the Rent Charge Map

	a.	r.	p.
Nos. 583 Parsonage (a poor and uncomfortable house) with a field in front of it		3.	20.
582 Field pasture	0.	3.	8.
585 Field pasture	1.	3.	0.
541 Field pasture	4.	2.	6.
	7.	3.	34.

The remainder of the Glebe, upon which there is one house and one cottage, is rented at £39 per ann.

NB.   The Lay Impropriator, who does not reside in the Parish, contributes nothing towards the spiritual wants of the Parishioners, save and except a few Bottles of Wine at Easter, which he, as well as the Vicar, in conformity to an old custom, gives for the Table of the Lord's Supper.

The Parish of Nevern is divided into Four Quarters, or Districts, called Morfa Quarter, Crugiau Quarter, Trewern Quarter and Kilgwyn Quarter. In each of which Quarters there was formerly a church or chapel, belonging to private Families, but recognizing Nevern as being the mother or Parish Church. None of these Chapels now remain, save and except Kilgwyn, which has never been endowed, and over which the Bishop of the Diocese has not, it is said, any jurisdiction, as over the mother or Nevern Church. The Registrar of the Diocese can find no account of Kilgwyn Church among the Papers in his Registry, and the Churchwardens of Nevern Parish maintain that they have no right to contribute from the Church Rates towards keeping Kilgwyn Church in repairs. There is at present no private Family, or Mansion, claiming possession of the Church. It would be a great blessing to Kilgwyn Quarter if the Church was endowed and a Clergyman appointed to it. The shell of the building is in good repairs, it having been lately repaired by public subscriptions; but the inside is destitute of Pews, Forms, etc. a few Benches only and a wretched Pulpit and a Reading Desk are its present furniture.

John Jones, M.A.
Vicar of Nevern. 21st April 1851.

[On an attached sheet.]

There ought to be a District Church in each of the Four Quarters into which the Parish is divided. The Parish is so extensive that the distant inhabitants cannot attend their Parish Church. They would be living the lives of heathens had not the Dissenters built Chapels in different parts of the Parish, of which there are *six* Chapels. Those who attend New Nevern Church in the morning attend Chapel in their different localities in the evening.

(15) MORVA ROOM. INDEPENDENTS OR CONGREGATIONALISTS. Rented 1843.
Space: free 100.
Present: no service—general congregation aft. 45 scholars.

> Samuel Thomas.
> Independent Minister.

(16) GETHSEMANE. WELSH CALVINISTIC METHODIST.
Erected 1844.
Space: free 120; other 120; standing 60.
Present: morn. 48 scholars; aft. 110; even. 82.
Average (12 *months*): morn. 60 scholars; aft. 110; even. 80.
Remarks: The Welsh Calvinistic Methodists are on thE Presbyterian sistem, and have no Stated Ministers but supply their places of worship in rotation. Mr. S. Lewis of Hall supplied on the 30th March 1851.

> Thomas Jones. Manager.
> Trefach, nr. Newport.

(17) PENUEL. BAPTIST.
Erected 1824.
Space: free 24.
Present: morn. 161; aft. 41 scholars; even. 63.
Average: general. congregation 150; scholars 50.

> John Gwynne. Deacon.
> Grasyforwyn, Cardigan.

(18) GLANRHYD. CALVINISTIC METHODIST.
Erected about 1807.
Space: free 72; other 66.
Present: morn. 85; aft. 45 scholars; even. 75.
Average (12 *months*): morn. 110; aft. 52 scholars; even. 110.
Remarks: Service Time and Sunday School once every Sunday in our Chapel. Service once a week and Prayer Meeting once every week.

> Evan Morgan. Elder.
> Waensegur, St. Dogmells.

(19) BRYNBERIAN. INDEPENDANT.
Erected 1693: last erected 1843.
Space: free 222; other 216; standing about 200.
Present: morn. 64 scholars; aft. 264.

> Evan Lewis. Minister.

(20) CAERSALEM. BAPTIST.
Erected 1841.
Space: free 172; other 178; standing, none but the passages.
Present: morn. 130 scholars; aft. 234; even. 201.
Average (6 *months*): general congregation 240; scholars 140.
Remarks: The public worship and the School are alternately in the Morning and Evening.

> David George. Minister.
> Trewern.

5 Bayvil Parish, co. Pembroke.

Area: 1,344 acres. *Popn.* 52 males, 72 females: total 124.

(21) BAYVILL PARISH CHURCH, CONSOLIDATED WITH THE PARISH CHURCH OF MOYLGROVE.
Endowed: land £173; tithe £14.
Space: free 72; other 42.
Present: aft. 40.
Average (12 *months*): aft. 50.
Remarks: The above annual amount of Land rent is the whole amount of Land rent belonging to the two consolidated parish churches of Bayvill and Moylgrove.

> David Evan Morgan. Minister.

Lewis: discharged vicarage, consolidated with that of Moylgrove [593. 2. 5(9)], rated at £5; endowed with £800 royal bounty: net income £224: impropriators, the landowners.
C & C: 1 service in Welsh performed by the incumbent.
I & C: resident.

(22) COLLEGRE GREEN. INDEPENDENT.
Erected 1791.
Space: free 120; other 115; standing about 110.
Present: morn. 132; aft. 92 scholars.

> Evan Lewis. Minister.
> Brynberian, Eglwyswrw.

6 Meline Parish, co. Pembroke.

Area: 4,523 acres. *Popn.* 220 males, 254 females: total 474.

(23) MELINE PARISH CHURCH.
Endowed: land £10; tithe £140; glebe 6 acres.
Space: free 84; other 30.
Present: morn. 30; aft. 50.

Remarks: The Sunday School has been discontinued in consequence of my not being able to attend in person since last summer. I serve another parish besides.

David Davies.   Rector.

Lewis: sub Meliney, or Melineu: discharged rectory, rated at £10; patrons, alternately Thomas Lloyd, Esq., and the freeholders: tithes commuted for £160: glebe of 6 acres worth £10 12*s.* per annum.

C & C: 1 service in Welsh performed by the incumbent.

I & C: legally not resident.

(24)   PANTGYNON CHAPEL.   INDEPENDENT.
Erected before 1840.
Space: other 110; standing 90.
Present: aft. 87 scholars; even. 113.

Evan Lewis.   Minister.
Brynberian, Eglwyswrw.

7   Eglwyswrw Parish, co. Pembroke.
Area: 3,664 acres. *Popn.* 254 males, 305 females: total 559.

(25)   EGLWYSWRW PARISH CHURCH.
Patron the Prince of Wales.
Re-erected 1827, 1828 and 1829.
Total cost £346. 10. 2½.
Endowed: land £16;   tithe £80;   glebe £20;   permanent endowment £6. 15.; fees—'a mere trifle'. Total £122. 15.
Space: free 20; other (pews) 90.
Present: morn. 103; aft. 120.
Average (12 *months*): morn. 100; aft. 120.
Remarks: There is no Sunday School at present owing to the infirmities and extreme age of the Vicar, but it is his intention to revive it again when his health is in any degree restored to catechise as many of the children of our Day School as are taught the Church Catechism in the Summer Months.

David Prothero.   Vicar.

Lewis: discharged vicarage, rated at £3. 13. 4.; endowed with £200 royal bounty and £200 parliamentary grant; net income £105, with glebe-house: patron, the Crown; impropriators John Davies and George Griffiths, Esqrs: impropriated tithes commuted for £170, with glebe of 30*a.* 1*r.* 14*p.* valued at £21. 10: vicarial tithes commuted for £80, with a glebe of 25*a.* 0*r.* 27*p.* valued at £15. 10.

C & C: 1 service in Welsh performed by the incumbent.

I & C: resident.

(26) ELIM. BAPTIST.
Erected 1839.
Space: free 48; other 138.
Present: even. 180.

John Morris. Minister.
Eglwyswrw.

8 Whitechurch Parish, co. Pembroke.
Area: 2,481 acres. *Popn.* 152 males, 197 females: total 349.

(27) WHITECHURCH [Parish Church]
Space: free 100; other 30.
Attendants: morn. 30; aft. 45; even. no service.

Thos. Hughes. Informant.

Lewis: discharged rectory, rated at £6; endowed with £200 royal bounty: net income £113: patron Thomas Lloyd, Esq., tithes commuted for £140.
C & C: 1 service in Welsh performed by the incumbent.
I & C: no return.

(28) PENYGROES, EGLWYSWEN OR WHITECHURCH. INDEPENDENT.
Erected before 1800.
Space: free 336; standing 120.
Present: morn. 214.
Remarks: The Sunday Scholars are included in the Congregation as they are not seated apart. A Sunday School is held in the Chapel every Sunday afternoon, the account of which is not inserted here.

John Picton. Deacon.
Maesgwynne, Eglwyswrw.

(29) BETHABARA. BAPTIST.
Erected 1826.
Space: with the exception of one seat all the gallery is free; other 26.
Present: morn. 204; aft. 90 scholars.

John Morris. Minister.

9 Llanfair-Nant-Gwyn Parish, co. Pembroke.
Area: 1,668 acres. *Popn.* 102 males, 99 females: total 201.

(30) LLANFAIR NANT GWYN PARISH CHURCH.
Endowed: Land £70: tithe £4.
Sittings: free 80; other 20.
Present: morn. 40.
Average (12 *months*): morn. 30; aft. 45.

William James. Incumbent.

Lewis: perpetual curacy; endowed with £800 royal bounty; net income £80; patron and impropriator Thomas Bowen, Esq: tithes commuted for £105.
C & C: 1 service partially in English and Welsh, performed by the incumbent.
I & C: not resident.

(31) EBENEZER. BAPTIST.
Erected about 1776; rebuilt 1820.
Space: "with the exception of one seat, all the Gallery is free"; other "about 34 sittings on the ground floor".
Present: morn. 63 scholars besides teachers; aft. 249.

David Rees.   Deacon.
Treclyn Isaf.

[End of Newport Subdistrict]

2 CARDIGAN (Subdistrict)
Area: 17,982 acres. *Popn.* 4,258 males, 5,465 females: total 9,723.

1 Llantood Parish, co. Pembroke.
Area: 1,792 acres. *Popn.* 142 males, 161 females: total 303.

(1) LLANTOOD PARISH CHURCH.
Rebuilt about 1821.
Space: free 64; other 14.
Attendants: aft. 35. No Sunday School.

William Thomas.   Informant.

[Informant's form.]

Lewis: sub Llantyd: vicarage not in charge, annexed with that of Monington [593. 2. 4(8)], to the vicarage of St. Dogmael's; endowed with £200 royal bounty: tithes commuted for £157, of which £125 belong to the impropriator and £32 to the vicar, the latter subject to rates averaging £1. 10.
C & C: sub St. Dogmell's; 1 service per fortnight, in Welsh, performed by the incumbent.
I & C: no return.

[For Monington see 593. 2. 4(8) recorded as missing. There is no reference to the missing return for St. Dogmell's which should come under 593. 2. 6.]

2 Bridell Parish, co. Pembroke.
Area: 2,179 acres. *Popn.* 158 males, 177 females: total 335.

[(2)]   BRIDELL PARISH CHURCH.
Space: free 88; other 12.
Present: morn. 30; No Sunday School.

William Thomas.   Informant.

[Informant's form.]

Lewis: discharged rectory, rated at £9: patrons, the freeholders of the parish: net income £150; rectorial tithes commuted for £180; no glebe. Day and Sunday School discontinued for want of support

C & C: 1 service partially in English and Welsh, performed by the incumbent.

I & C: not resident.

(3) PENYBRYN. BABTIST.
Erected: 1818.
Space: free 156; other 138.
Present: morn. 275; aft. 90 scholars; even. 130.

Maurice Evans.   Baptist Minister.

3   Kilgerran Parish, co. Pembroke.

Area: 2,672 acres. *Popn.* 603 males, 663 females: total 1,266.

(4) KILGERRAN PARISH CHURCH.
Endowed: tithe £143; glebe £21; fees £1.
Space: free 180; other 40.
Present: morn. 150 + 80 scholars; even. 103.
Average (12 *months*): morn. 150 + 80 scholars; even. 110.

D. Evans.   Rector.

Lewis: discharged rectory, rated at £9: patron, the Crown: tithes commuted for £190; glebe of 9 acres valued at £9. 10.: body of the church lately taken down and rebuilt with the aid of a grant of £100 from the Church Building Commissioners, and £60 from Abel Anthony Gower, Esq: a few free sittings added by the rector.

C & C: 2 services in English.

I & C: resident.

ICBS: grant of £100 in 1836, and 2nd grant of £100 in 1851.

(5) PENOD [OR PENUEL?] BABTIST.
Erected 1820.
Space: free 156; other 156.
Present: aft. 104 scholars; even. 289.

Maurice Evans.   Babtist Minister.

(6) TABERNACLE. CALVINISTIC METHODIST.
Erected 1763: re-erected 1822.
Space: free 288; other 168.

Present: morn. 132 + 85 scholars; aft. 192; even. 310.
Average (12 *months*): morn. 106 + 85 scholars; 112; even. 180.

Ebenr. Bowen. Steward.

(7) "TY RHOS" CHAPEL. INDEPENDENT.
Erected 1810.
Space: free 150; other 125.
Present: morn. 120 + 25 scholars; even. 100 + 20 scholars.
Averge: morn. 180 + 30 scholars; even. 100 + 20 scholars.
Remarks: There are numerous meetings in the week and Sunday Teachers meetings.
The meetings are held morning and afternoon alternately.
The attendance this Sunday in every month is decidedly smaller than any other on an average. There are no Evening Services every Sunday.

David Thomas. Deacon.
Fynnonau Gleision, Nr. Boncath.

[This return is endorsed '8 Monnington Church missing'.]

4 Monington Parish, co. Pembroke.
Area: 1,010 acres. *Popn.* 58 males, 69 females: total 127.

(8) MONINGTON PARISH CHURCH missing.
Lewis: vicarage not in charge united to that of St. Dogmael's: tithes commuted for £80, of which £45 belong to the impropriator, and £35 to the vicar.
C & C: 1 service a fortnight in Welsh, performed by the incumbent.
I & C: no return.

5 Moylgrove Parish, co. Pembroke.
Area: 2,442 acres. *Popn.* 207 males, 246 females: total 453.

(9) MOYLGROVE PARISH CHURCH, CONSOLIDATED WITH THE PARISH CHURCH OF BAYVILL.
Endowed: land £173; tithe £60; glebe £2.
Space: free 120; other 60.
Present: morn. 50.
Average (12 *months*): morn. 80; aft. 90.
Remarks: The above annual amount of Land rent is the whole amount of Land rent belonging to the two consolidated Parish Churches of Bayvill and Moylgrove.

David Evan Morgan. Vicar.

Lewis: perpetual curacy, annexed to the vicarage of Bayvill [593. 1. 5(21)], endowed with £600 royal bounty.
C & C: 1 service in Welsh performed by the incumbent.
I & C: resident.

(10) BETHEL, MOILGROVE.   INDEPENDENTS.
Erected before 1800.
Space: free 12; other 366.
Present: morn. 118 scholars; aft. 288; even. 314.
Average (12 *months*): general congregation 400; Sunday scholars 100.
Remarks: The Service is Morning and Afternoon alternately. The number
of sittings on the floor only are inserted. Most of the Gallery is provided
with free sittings.

> Llewhelyn Rees and D. M. Evans.
> Ministers.

6   St. Dogmell's Parish, co. Pembroke.

Area: 6,220 acres. *Popn.* 1,123 males, 1,566 females: total 2,689.
[There is no return for St. Dogmell's Parish Church.]

Lewis: discharged vicarage with those of Llantyd [593. 2. 1(1)] and Monington
[593. 2. 4(8)] annexed; rated at £4 13s. 4d.;. endowed with £200 private benefaction and £600 royal bounty; net income £143: patron, the Crown; impropriator,
W. Deedes, Esq: impropriate tithes commuted for £408 11s., and the vicarial for
£70.

(11) BLAEN Y WAUN, ST. DOGMAELS.   BAPTIST.
Erected 1745.
Space: free 50.
Present: aft. 567.

> John Phillips Williams.   Minister.

(12) BETHSAIDA.   BAPTIST.
Erected 1813.
Space: free 240; other 156.
Present: morn. 281 scholars; even. 690.

> John Phillips Williams.   Minister.

(13) CAPEL DEGWELL, ST. DOGMELLS.   INDEPENDENTS.
Erected 1820.
Space: all free.
Present: aft. 320 + 80 scholars.

> Daniel Davies.   Minister.

(14) CHAPEL SION.   CALVINISTIC METHODISTS.
Erected 1838.
Present: morn. 49 scholars; aft. 100; even. 90.

> Thomas Davies.   Elder.
> Farmer. Penywern.

(15) [illegible] CHAPEL.   INDEPENDENTS.
Erected 1835.
Space: free 84.
Present: aft. 90.
Remarks: It is used as a place of worship and a Day School.
This Schedule not arrived in due time could not be filled up before to day,
although all preparations thereto were made March 30.

> David M. Evans.   Minister.

(16) GEREZIM.   BAPTIST.
Erected 1848.
Space: free 66; other 132.
Present: morn. 164; even. 152.

> John Phillips Williams.   Minister.

7   Cardigan Borough.   St. Mary Parish.
Area: 2,517 acres. *Popn.* 1,246 males, 1,735 females: total 2,689.
Military in barracks 60.

(17) ADDITIONAL SCHOOL ROOM, CARDIGAN, ST. MARY PARISH.
Licensed for public worship by the Bishop of St. David's, March 1850.
It was licensed for an additionl curate in the Parish by an Annual Grant
from the Curates Aid Society.
Space: free 250.
Present: morn. 100; even. 200 + 50 scholars.
Average (12 *months*): morn. 100; even. 120 + 50 scholars.
Remarks: An additional church is very much wanted in this parish in order
that Divine Service be conveniently performed both in *Welsh* and in *English*
at the same time, and with a proper Endowment for the support of the
same.

> Griffith Thomas.
> Vicar of St. Mary's, Cardigan.

(18) ST. MARY'S PARISH CHURCH.
Endowed: land £100, tithe £10; other endowments £27. 3.; fees £5.
Space: free 316; other 285.
Present: morn. 208 + 201 scholars; even. 132.
Average (12 *months*): morn. 274 + 200 scholars; even. 161 + 50 scholars.
Remarks: There is no Vicarage House nor any Glebe. An additional church
with proper Endowment is very much wanted in this Parish for the perfor-
mance of Divine Service in Welsh and English at the same time.

> Griffith Thomas.   Vicar.

Lewis: discharged vicarage, rated at £9. 15. 10; endowed with £200 private benefaction, and £400 royal bounty; net income £153, with a glebe-house: patron, the Crown; impropriator, P. J. Miles, Esq: impropriate tithes commuted for £300. Gallery erected at the sole expense of Pryse Pryse, Esq., in 1821.

C & C: 3 services, of which 2 in English entirely, the other in Welsh, performed by the incumbent.

I & C: incumbent resident; curate, who has stipend of £30, resides in the parish.

(19)   HOPE CHAPEL.   INDEPENDENT.
Erected 1837.
Space: free 50; other 150.
Present: morn. 71 + 35 scholars; aft. 67 scholars; even. 85.

Richard Hancock.   Pastor.

(20)   EBENEZER.   WESLEYAN METHODISTS.
Erected 1827.
Space: free 72; other 124; standing 90.
Present: even. 85 + 31 scholars.
Average (7 months): even. 100.

David Evans.   Minister.

(21)   ST. MARY'S CHAPEL.   INDEPENDENT.
Erected before 1800.
Space: free 236; other 144.
Present: morn. 300; aft. 126 scholars; even. 390.

David Davies.   Independent Minister.

(22)   BETHANY.   PARTICULAR BAPTIST.
Erected 1775.
Space: free 500; other 400.
Present: morn. 560; aft. 353 scholars; even. 781.
Average (12 months): morn. 560; aft. 250 scholars; even. 800.
Remarks: The Chapel measures in the clear 61 feet long by 47 feet wide.

Evan Thomas.   Minister.

(23)   TABERNACLE.   CALVINISTIC METHODISTS.
Erected before 1800.
Space: free 84; other 318.
Present: morn. 272; even. 401.

Thomas Edwards.   Elder.
Bridge Street, Cardigan.

8   Llangoedmore Parish.
Area: 4,946 acres. *Popn.* 425 males, 565 females: total 990.

(24) LLANGOEDMORE PARISH CHURCH.
Endowed: No land. Tithe gross value £440.
Space: free 112; other 78.
Present: morn. 55 + 37 scholars; aft. 56 scholars; even. 50.
Average (12 *months*): morn. 110 + 70 scholars; aft. 110 scholars; even. 70.
Remarks: The congregation at Llangoedmore Church was very small yesterday, in consequence of some of our communicants being sick, and others from home.

Thomas Evans. Curate.

Lewis: rectory, rated at £12. 8. 6½; patrons, St. David's College, Lampeter; tithes commuted for £440. Church entirely rebuilt in 1830.
C & C: 2 services, evening service in Welsh, performed by the incumbent.
I & C: incumbent not resident; curate, who resides at Cardigan, 1¾ miles distant, has stipend of £135.
ICBS: grant of £35 in 1829.

(25) BLAENWENEN. BAPTIST.
Erected 1838.
Space: free 198; other, none.
Present: morn. 60.

David Griffith. Deacon.
Blaenwaenwen.
Farmer.

(26) PENYPARK. PARTICULAR BAPTIST.
Erected 1769; rebuilt 1838.
Space: free 340; other 96; standing 90.
Present: morn. 93 scholars; aft. 322; even. 197.
Average: morn. 320 (once a month) + 90 scholars (alternative morn. and aft.); aft. 300 + 90 scholars; even. 190.

Thomas Davies. Deacon..
Cwmarch.

9 Verwick Parish.
Area: 3,062 acres. *Popn.* 177 males, 201 females: total 378.

(27) VERWIC PARISH CHURCH.
Endowed: tithe Gross £80; other endowments £16. 10.
Space: pews 12 x 4 = 48.
Present: morn. 26.
Average (12 *months*): morn. under 20.

Thomas Rees. Minister.

Lewis: discharged vicarage; rated at £10. 13. 4; endowed with £200 royal bounty; net income £69: patron, the Crown: impropriators, Arthur Jones and J. P. Miles, Esqrs: tithes commuted for £240, of which the impropriators receive two-thirds and the vicar one-third.
C & C: 1 service in Welsh performed by the incumbent.
I & C: not resident.

(28) SILOAM, VERWIG. BAPTIST.
Erected 1796.
Space: galary free; other 31.
Present: morn. 84; even. 103.
Average (12 *months*): morn. 140; aft. 90 scholars; even. 120.

> Josiah Williams. Deacon.
> Bryn Pedair, Verwig.

(29) BLAENCEFN, VERWICK. CALVINISTIC METHODIST.
Erected: 1808. Not a separate building: not used exclusively as a place of worship.
Space: free 130; other 70; standing 40.
Present: morn 102; aft. Sunday School; even. 90.
Average: general congregation, morn. 100; even. 100.

> Evan Davies.
> Heol Ias.

10 Mount Parish
Area: 1,142 acres. *Popn.* 49 males, 82 females: total 141.

(30) HOLY CROSS PARISH CHURCH.
Endowed: land £47. 10; tithe £4; other endowments £13.
Space: pews 9 x 4 = 36.
Present: aft. 15.
Average: aft. under 20.

> Thomas Rees. Minister.

Lewis: perpetual curacy; endowed with £1,000 royal bounty: net income £55: patron, David Lewis, Esq.; impropriators T. Lloyd and C. Longcroft, Esqrs..
C & C: 1 service in Welsh performed by the incumbent.
I & C: not resident.

[End of Cardigan Subdistrict]

3 LLANDYGWIDD (Subdistrict)
Area: 19,860 acres. *Popn.* 1,965 males, 2,368 females: total 4,333.

1 Aberporth Parish.
Area: 2,200 acres. *Popn.* 218 males, 296 females: total 514.

(1) ABERPORTH PARISH CHURCH.
Endowed: tithe £104; other permanent endowment £33. 13; fees 15*s*.
Space: all sittings free. The Church can contain but few more than 115.
Present: morn. 30 + 85 scholars.

> Griffith Evans. Rector.

Lewis: discharged rectory; rated at £5. 14. 9; endowed with £200 royal bounty, and £800 parliamentary grant: patron, Bp. of St. David's: rectorial tithes commuted for £104. 13. 4, and the impropriate tithes for £57.6.8.

C & C: 1 service in Welsh performed by the incumbent.

I & C: not resident.

ABERPORTH PARISH CHURCH.
Space: free 114; other 66.
Present: morn. 30 + 85 scholars.
Average (3 months): morn. 31 + 76 scholars; aft. 31 + 76 scholars.
Remarks: Divine Service once a month in the evening.

Thomas Rees. Churchwarden.

(1)   [Endorsed Duplicate.]

(2)   BLAENANNERCH.   CALVINISTIC METHODIST.
Erected 1794.
Space: free 42; other 294.
Present: morn. 190 scholars; aft. 332; even. 288.
Average (5 months): general congregation 171; Sunday Scholars 206.

Griffith Davies. Preacher.
Cwmcoed.

(3)   ABERPORTH.   WELSH CALVINISTIC METHODIST.
Erected 1833.
Space: free 72; other 162.
Present: aft. 231; even. 227.

David Davies. Clerk. Helyg
Ben Shadrack, Minister.

2   Blaenporth Parish

Area: 3,548 acres. *Popn.* 330 males, 389 females: total 719.

(4)   BLAENPORTH PARISH CHURCH.
Endowed: land £80, tithe £8; other endowments £29.
Space: free 24; other 108.
Present: lorn. 70.
Average: morn. 75.

Isaac Hughes. Incumbent.

Lewis: perpetual curacy, formerly a prebend in the College of St. David's at Llandewy-Brevi, and rated as such at £6; endowed with £800 royal bounty, and £800 parliamentary grant; in the alternate patronage of Earl of Lisburne and J. V. Lloyd, Esq., who are the impropriators of the parish and pay £8 per annum to the curate: net income £97, with a glebe-house: impropriate tithes commuted for £260.

C & C: 1 service in Welsh performed by the incumbent.

I & C: resident.

ICBS: grant of £30 in 1829.

(5) BRYNMAIR. INDEPENDENTS.
Erected 1833.
Space: all free.*
Present: morn. 64; aft. 141; even. 125.
Remarks: The chapel is 36 feet by 32 within with a gallery able to contain 150.
The congregation has also built a house for the Minister and a neat school-room.

> David Jones. Deacon.
> Felin, Blaenporth.

[*Endorsed: See Letter.]

(6) GLANDWR. INDEPENDENT.
Erected 1831.
Space: free 140; other 7.
Present: morn. Sunday School 90; aft. 92; even.: members Society 70.
Remarks: The chapel is 30 ft. long by 12 broad and free from debt.

> William Jones. Minister.
> Glynarthin, nr. Newcastle Emlyn.

[Endorsed: see letter.]

3   Tremain Parish
Area: 1,658 acres. *Popn.* 130 males, 146 females: total 276.

(7) TREMAIN PARISH CHURCH.
Rebuilt in 1846, 47, 48 by subscription and a grant from the Incorporated Building Society.
Endowed: land £49; tithe £8. 14. 6; glebe £6. 10. 0; other permanent endowments £10; fees 10s.
Space: free 121.
Present: aft. 30.
Remarks: The Congregation on the above day was much under the usual average of attendants, several being absent by reason of illness.

> Griffith Evans. Incumbent.

Lewis: perpetual curacy; endowed with £200 royal bounty, and £291. 4. 10. parliamentary grant; net income £72: patron and impropriator, Philip John Miles, Esq: tithes commuted for £124: small farm in the parish of Llansawel is attached to the benefice.

C & C: 1 service in Welsh, performed by the incumbent.

I & C: not resident.

ICBS: grant of £60 in 1846.

4 Llechryd Parochial Chapelry
Area: 943 acres. *Popn.* 204 males, 269 females: total 473.

(8) LLECHRYD PARISH CHURCH.
Space: free 120; other 20.
Usual number of attendants: from 30 to 40.
Remarks: The service performed morning and evening alternately, only one
on a Sunday, and the average congregation is from 30 to 40.

> Theophilus Davies.   Churchwarden.
> Informant.

From enquries I have made in the Parish I believe the above statement
correct. *Signed:* George Devonald.
[Informant's form.]

Lewis: reputed to have been a parochial chapelry to Llangoedmore [593. 2. 8(24)],
but now a parish of itself: perpetual curacy: endowed with £1,200 royal bounty;
net income £131: Joint patrons and impropriators, T. Lloyd, Esq., Mrs. Lloyd,
and C. R. Longcroft, Esq: tithes commuted for £36. 6. subject to rates averaging
£1. 6. per annum. Church recently much improved through exertions of the
incumbent.

C & C: 1 service in Welsh, performed by the incumbent.

I & C: not resident.

(9) LOWER CHAPEL.   INDEPENDENTS.
Erected 1700.
Space: all free except 16 pews.
Average (12 *months*): general congregation 310; scholars 170.
Remarks: NB. It is the Congregation in general that make up the Sunday
Scholars as in most places in Wales.

> Daniel Davies.   Minister.

(10) CAPEL LLWYN ADDA.   CALVINSTIC METHODIST.
Erected 1791, rebuilt 1829.
Space: free 30; other 234; standing 432 feet.
Present: morn. 245; aft. 140 scholars; even. 276.
Average: morn. 270; aft. 165 scholars. even. 280.
Remarks: The Sunday School is carried on upwards than 40 years with
great deficiency for School supplys.

> John Jones.   Steward.
> Tailor, Llechryd.

5 Llandygwidd Parish.
Area: 5,595 acres. *Popn.* 480 males, 583 females: total 1,063.

(11) LLANDYGWYDD PARISH CHURCH.
Endowed: land £108. 10; other sources £23. 3. 6.
Space: free 84; other 124.
Present: morn. 63 + 56 scholars; aft. 30 + 56 scholars.
Remarks: Gross value of Living with residence £134. 13. 6. The Tithe commuted at £450.0.0. is in the hands of Lay Impropriators, £8 per annum only being paid as a Salary to the Perpetual Curate.

> David Joshua Evans, M.A.
> Perpetual Curate.

Lewis: prebend in the collegiate church at Brecon; valued at £10. 12. 8½; in the gift of Bp. St. David's. Living a perpetual curacy, endowed with £200 private benefaction, £400 royal bounty, and £400 parliamentary grant: net income £107: patron, the Prebendary, whose appropriated tithes are commuted for £450.

C & C: 2 services, English in the morning, Welsh in the afternoon, performed by the incumbent.

I & C: resident.

(12) BETHESDA. INDEPENDENT.
Erected 1839.
Space: free 250; other 90.
Present: morn. 277.

> Lewis Lloyd.   Deacon.
> Penalltybie.

6 Manordivy Parish, co. Pembroke.
Area: 3,506 acres. *Popn.* 438 males, 518 females: total 956.

(13) MANORDIVY PARISH CHURCH.
Endowed: tithes, glebe only, both may be placed at about £175.
Space: free 66; other 72.
Present: morn. 123; aft. 54.
Average (12 *months*): morn. 150; aft. 50.
Remarks: a greater fallacy can barely be entertained than for anyone to suppose that they will receive accurate information upon these subjects from the several returns made under these enquiries.

> W. Lloyd. Rector.

Lewis: rectory, rated at £9; patron, the Crown: tithes commuted for £345, of which £25 is payable to the rector who also has a glebe of £40 acres valued at £50 per annum, and £80 to the impropriator.

C & C: 2 services, English in the morn; Welsh in aft., performed by the incumbent.

I & C: resident.

(14) CILFOWYR. BAPTIST.
Erected 1716.
Space: free 9; other 31; besides there are three score of free sittings and the gallery.
Present: morn. 475; aft. 66 scholars.

Rees Price. Baptist Minister.

(15) NEW CHAPEL. CALVINISTIC METHODISTS.
Erected 1763.
Space: free 80; other 84.
Present: morn. 65 scholars; aft. 125; even. 60.
Average: general congregation 200; scholars 114.

Stephen Hughes.   One of the members.
Whitegate

(16) RAMOTH. BAPTIST.
Erected 1827.
Space: other 25; Two free was in the gallery.
Present: aft. 80 scholars; even. 153.

Rees Price. Baptist Minister.
Cilyfowyr.

7 Llanfihangel-Penbedw Parish, co. Pembroke.
Area: 2,410 acres. *Popn.* 165 males, 167 females: total 332.

(17) LLANFIHANGEL PENBEDW PARISH CHURCH.
Endowed: tithe £135; glebe £110 net value.
Space: free 40; other 20.
Present: aft. 26.
Average (12 months): nearly the same.
Remarks: Service performed Morning and Evening alternately. A considerable increase of Congregation during the Summer Months.

George Devonald.   Rector.

Lewis: discharged rectory; rated at £6: patron, the Crown: tithes commuted for £135, subject to rates averaging £12. 6. 4. per annum.

C & C: 1 service in Welsh performed by the incumbent.

I & C: no return.

[*End of Llandygwydd Subdistrict and End of Cardigan District*]

Area: 113,346 acres. *Popn.* 9,385 males, 10,788 females: total 20,173.

1 KENARTH (Subdistrict)
Area: 47,459 acres. *Popn.* 4,088 males, 4,598 females: total 8,868.

1 Chapel Colman Parish, co. Pembroke.
Area: 770 acres. *Popn.* 68 males, 69 females: total 137.

(1) CHAPEL COLMAN PARISH CHURCH.
Endowed: land £44; tithe £4; other £26.
Space: free 80, other 20.
Present: aft. 45 scholars.
Average (12 *months*): morn. 30, aft. 36.

William James.   Incumbent.

Lewis: sub Capel-Colman: perpetual curacy, endowed with £800 royal bounty; net income £72: patron and impropriator, Miss Jones of Cilwendêg.
C & C: 1 service, partially in English and Welsh, performed by the incumbent.
I & C: not resident.
ICS: grant of £100 in 1834.

2 Penrith Parish, co. Pembroke. Consisting of Penrith, or Penrhydd, and Castellan Chapelry.
Area of Penrith: 2,182 acres. *Popn.* 127 males, 123 females: total 250.
Area of Castellan Chapelry: 899 acres. *Popn.* 94 males, 77 females: total 171.
Area of whole parish: 3,081 acres. *Popn.* 221 males, 200 females: total 421.

(2) PENRITH PARISH CHURCH.
Space: free 130, other 10.
Present: morn. 12.
Average (12 *months*): morn. 30; aft. 50.
Remarks: The services are alternate morning and evening.

Hugh Howell.   Rector.

[Endorsed: See letter.]

Lewis: sub Penrieth: discharged rectory, rated at £4; endowed with £400 royal bounty; patron, the Crown; net income £100: tithes commuted for £107, of which

£71 payable to the rector, and £36 to the impropriator of Castellan. Castellan Chapel now in ruins; incumbent receives one guinea per annum from the impropriator, Sir R. B. P. Phillips, of Picton Castle.

C & C: 1 service in Welsh performed by the incumbent.

I & C: not resident.

(3) BLAENFFOS, CASTELLAN. BAPTIST.
Consecrated before 1800.
Space: free 42; other 198; standing 300.
Present: aft. 335 + 148 scholars; even. 256.
Average: general congregation 335; scholars 148.

> James David Thomas.
> Baptist Minister.
> Blaenffos.

3 Llanfyrnach Parish, co. Pembroke.
Area: 6,238 acres. *Popn.* 439 males, 494 females: total 933.

(4) LLANFERNACH PARISH CHURCH.
Space: free 200; other 20.
Present: morn. 25.
Average (12 *months*): morn. 50; aft. 200.
Remarks: The Services are alternate morning and afternoon.
[Endorsed: See letter.]

Lewis: discharged rectory, rated at £10: patron, the Crown: glebehouse: tithes commuted for £251, of which £245 are payable to the rector, and £6 to the impropriator.

C & C: 1 service in Welsh, performed by the incumbent.

I & C: not resident.

(5) HERMON CHAPEL. BAPTIST.
Erected: 1808.
Space: free 270.
Present: morn. 180; aft. 120 scholars; even. 151.

> Walter Davies. Baptist Minister.

(6) GLANDWR. INDEPENDENTS.
Erected before 1800.
Space: free 396.
Present: morn. 331; aft. 114 scholars.
Average (12 *months*): morn. 340; aft. 110 scholars.
> John Davies. Minister.

[Endorsed: See letter.]

(7) Tymawr. Independent.
Erected about 1820.
Not a separate building, not used exclusively as a place of worship.
Space: all free.
Present: aft. 50.
Remarks: Tymawr is a dwelling house licensed for religious exercises. There is preaching in it every other Sunday. Sabbath School for the present suspended. It has a weekly expository meeting in it during the winter months and a monthly prayer meeting around the year.

> John Davies. Minister.
> Glandŵr.

(8) Antioch. Independent.
Erected 1846.
Space: free 108.
Present: aft. 156; even. 46.
Remarks: It is used also as a day school. The bulk of those who attend the Sunday School are members of the Congregation, but not seated apart.

> Simon Evans. Minister.
> Eglwyswrw.

4 Kilrhedin Parish, cos. Pembroke and Carmarthen.
Area of pt. in co. Pembroke: 2,183 acres. *Popn.* 124 males, 133 females: total 256. *Area* of pt. in co. Carmarthen: 5,673 acres. *Popn.* 374 males, 432 females: total 806.
Area of whole parish: 7,856 acres. *Popn.* 498 mlaes, 565 females: total 1,063.

(9) Kilrhedin Parish Church.
Endowed: land £12; tithe £367. [? £177]
Space: free 250, other 30.
Present: morn. 160.
Average: 'The estimated number of attendants would be from 70 to 150.'
Remarks: The Church is situated in one corner of the Parish and is in a very dilapidated state, and offering very little advantage or convenience for public worship.

> William Harries. Curate.

Lewis: rectory, rated at £8. 12. 8½: patron, the Crown; net income £192.

C & C: 1 service in Welsh performed by the incumbent.

I & C: no return.

(10) CAPEL EVAN, KILRHEDYN. CONGREGATIONALISTS OR INDEPENDENTS.
Erected 1723; re-erected 1795 and enlarged again 1844.
Space: free 150; other 332; standing 550.
Present: morn. (at 9) 326; aft. 136 scholars; even. (prayer meeting) 102.
Average (12 *months*): morn. 450; aft. school; even. prayer meeting 123.
Remarks: The chapel is calculated to hold nearly 1,200 persons. Prayer
meetings are generally held here in the evening at which the attendance is
generally less. Several prayer meetings being held in the neighbourhood at
dwelling houses account for the small attendance here on the evenings here

Thomas Davies. Deacon.

(11) PANT-TEG. UNITARIAN FREE BAPTISTS.
Erected 1764: repaired 1843.
Space: free 75, standing 420.
Present: morn. and aft. 'no service today'; even. 'prayer meeting'.
Average: morn. and aft. 45. No scholars.
Remarks: Service at 10 one Sunday and at 2 the other Sunday alternately
one Sunday in the month no service except a prayer meeting in the evening
at 6. No Sunday School.

James Morris. Deacon.
Penrheol, Nr. Capel Evan.

(12) REHOBOTH, CILRHEDYN. BAPTIST.
Erected 1807.
Space: sittings free.
Present: morn. 103 + 60 scholars; aft. 49; even. 105.
Average: morn. 103 + 55 scholars; even. 150 + 65 scholars.
Remarks: Stephen Davies attending.

David Jones. Baptist Minister.

5 Clydey Parish, co. Pembroke.
Area: 8,120 acres. *Popn.* 559 males, 641 females: total 1,200.

(13) CLYDEY PARISH CHURCH.
Space: free 22.
Present: morn. 12.
Remarks: No Sunday scholars. No ecclesiastical division or township in
the parish.

John Williams. Curate.

Lewis: prebend in the cathedral church of St. David's rated at £12; in the gift of
the bishop. The living, a discharged vicarage, rated at £6: endowed with £600
parliamentary grant: patron, the bishop; net income £44. The impropriate tithes,
vested in the Ecclesiastical Commissioners, commuted for £250, subject to rates
averaging £24. 1. 8.; and £12 payable to—Bloodworth, Esq subject to rates of

£1. 10. 0: the vicarial tithes commuted for £125 subject to rates averaging £12. 0. 10 per annum.

C & C: 1 service in Welsh performed by the incumbent and curate.

I & C: incumbent not resident: curate, who has stipend of £60, resides at Llwynledw, 2½ miles distant.

(14) SOAR CHAPEL. BAPTIST.
Erected 1830.
Space: sittings free.
Present: 150 + 60 scholars; even. 120.
Average: general congregation 150.
Remarks: W. Lewis attending.

David Jones.   Minister.
Berllan, Clydey.

(15) LLWYNHWRDD. INDEPENDENTS.
Erected 1806.
Space: free 476.
Present: morn. 350; aft. 185 scholars; even. 165.
Average: general congregation 450; scholars 180.

Samuel Thomas.   Elder.
Treowen.

(16) BWLCHYGROES. CALVINISTIC METHODIST.
Erected 1747.
Space: free 108, other 228, standing 200.
Present: morn. 400; aft. 300 + 100 scholars; even. 200.

Edward R. Reynolds.   Steward.
Bank Farm.

6 Kenarth Parish, co. Carmarthen, including the town of Newcastle
Area: 6,429 acres. *Popn.* 934 males, 1,046 females: total 1,980.

(17) TRINITY CHURCH, NEWCASTLE EMLYN.
Having a consolidated District assigned to it, under 6th sect. of 59th Geo. 3. cap. 134.
Licensed: Sept. 1842.
Built instead of another Chapel previously existing, which was then taken down.
Erected by the Inhabitants of the place and others.
Church Building Society gave £250; Subscriptions, etc. £1,150. Total cost £1,400.

Endowed: land £63. 17; other £85. 3; fees about £1. 15; pew rents about £22, which are appropriated for repairs and necessary expenses.
Space: free 390; other 110.
Present: morn. 132 + 60 scholars; aft. 85 + 40 scholars; even. 66 + 12 scholars.
Average: morn. 142 + 60 scholars; aft. 95 + 40 scholars; even. 82 + 18 scholars.

John Price Jones.   Incumbent

Lewis: perpetual curacy; endowed with £800 royal bounty, and £200 parliamentary grant: net income £71: patron, vicar of Kenarth.
C & C: 3 services, English 11 a.m., Welsh 3 p.m., partially English and Welsh at 6 p.m., performed by the incumbent.
I & C: no return.
ICBS: grant of £250 in 1840.

(18)   KENARTH PARISH CHURCH.
Endowed: land £6; tithe £130; other £1,500 at 3¼ per. cent.; fees £1. 10. 0.
Space: free sittings, including gallery, 105; other 32.
Present: morn. 60 + 45 scholars; even. 55 + 40 scholars.
Average: morn. 57 + 45 scholars; even. 55 + 45 scholars.

Augustus Brigstocke.   Vicar.

Lewis: discharged vicarage, rated at £4. 6. 8; endowed with £400 royal bounty, and £800 parliamentary grant; net income £185: patron, Bp. of St. David's: impropriator, Rev. A. Brigstocke: great tithes commuted for £266. 13. 4. and vicarial tithes for £133. 6. 8.
C & C: 2 services in Welsh performed by the incumbent.
I & C: resident.

(19)   THREE (sic) SOMON [?Salmons]. Room. LATER DAY SAINTS.
Erected 1850: part of a dwelling house, not used exclusively [as a place of worship].
Present: morn. 16; even. 60.
Average: morn. 16; even. 60.
Remarks: all free.

Thomas Jones.   elder.

(20)   BETHEL.   WELSH CALVINISTIC METHODISTS.
Erected 1821.
Space: free 150; other 230; standing 150'
Present: morn. 209; aft. 149 scholars; even. 251.
Average (12 *months*): morn. 240; aft. 178 scholars; even. 260.

John Jones.   Minister.

(21) TABERNACLE. WESLEYAN.
Erected 1833.
Space: 11 free sittings.
Present: morn. 5.

> Thomas Williams.
> Member of Society.
> Adpar.

(22) EBENEZER CHAPEL. INDEPENDENTS.
Erected 1807.
Space: free 114; other 258.
Present: morn. 320; even. 250.
Remarks: The free sittings in the gallery settles placed round the wall, and in three rows round the chapel about $2\frac{1}{2}$ feet apart.

> Theophilus James.   Deacon.
> Saddler.

(23) GRAIG CHAPEL, NEWCASTLE EMLYN. BAPTIST.
Erected 1776; rebuilt 1821.
Space: all free sittings.
Present: morn. 128 scholars; aft. 330; even. 250.

> Timothy Thomas.   Baptist Minister.

[Endorsed: see letter]

(24) PONTGARREG. WELSH CALVINISTIC METHODISTS.
Erected 1818; rebuilt 1844.
Space: free 80; other 110; standing 100.
Present: morn. 71 scholars; aft. 150; even. 130.
Average (12 *months*): morn. 145; aft. 160; even. 140; 'Sunday Scholars included'.

> Jonathan Thomas.   Secretary.
> Pontgarreg

(25) BRYN SION. INDEPENDENTS.
Erected 1831.
Space: free 420; other 90; standing 'no such room'.
Present: aft. 257; even. 103.

> Abednego Jenkyn.   Minister.

7 Penboyr Parish, co. Carmarthen.
Area: 6,876 acres. *Popn.* 586 males, 685 females: total 1,271.

(26)   PENBOYR PARISH CHURCH.
Consecrated 1 Jan. 1800.
Built about the year 1809 at the sole expense of the Rev. Archdeacon
Beynon, the Rector.
Endowed: tithe £320; glebe £100; fees £2.
Space: free 168; other 12.
Present: morn. 100.
Average (12 months): morn. from 60 to 100.

Thomas Evans.   Curate.

Lewis: rectory, with Trinity Chapel [594. 1.7(27)] annexed; rated at £9. 9. 4½; net
income £325, with glebe-house: patron, Earl Cawdor: tithes commuted for £310,
and glebe of 162*a.* 1*r.* 25*p*, valued at £105 per annum. The old church was taken
down and rebuilt in 1809 at the sole expense of the incumbent, Rev. Thomas
Beynon, Archdeacon of Cardigan.

C & C: *sub* Penboyr with Trinity Chapel: 1 service each in the church and the
chapel, in Welsh, performed by the curate.

I & C: not resident: curate, who resides in the glebe-house, has stipend of £150·

(27)   TRINITY CHAPEL.   A CHAPEL OF EASE UNDER PENBOYR.
Licensed 1 Jan. 1800. 'Doubtful whether ever consecrated'.
Space: free 72.
Present: morn. no service; 45 scholars; aft. 40.
Average: morn. no service 40-45 scholars; aft. 30-40.
Remarks: There is no Endowment belonging to the Chapel. Sittings in the
Chapel of Ease for about 50 persons.

Thomas Evans.   Clerk.

(28)   SOAR.   DISSENTERS OR INDEPENDENTS.
Erected 1835.
Space: other 170.
Present: morn. 70 scholars; aft. 210.
Average (12 months): morn. 100 scholars; aft. 250.

Evan Beynon.   Elder Deacon.
Penrhiw Trial, Penboyr.

(29)   PANTYBWLCH.   WELSH CALVINISTIC METHODIST.
Erected 1834.
Space: free 84; other none; standing 200.
Present: morn. 21 scholars; aft. 52.
Average (12 months): morn. 31 scholars; aft. 62.
Remarks: Building used 'occasionally for a Day School'.

John Jones.   Minister.

8   Llangeler Parish, co. Carmarthen.

Consisting of Upper Llangeler: *popn.* 294 males, 326 females: total 620; and Lower Llangeler: *popn.* 489 males, 572 females: total 1,061. *Area of whole parish*: 7,999 acres. *Popn.* 783 males, 898 females: total 1,681.

(30)   LLANGELER PARISH CHURCH.

Endowed: tithes £120; glebe £40; other £6.

This is the gross amount and not the net amount.

Space: free 250; other 100; total 350, 'or in the Welsh fashion of packing in 400'.

Present: morn. 200 + 800 scholars; aft. 300 + 90 scholars.

Average (12 *months*): morn. 300 + 60 scholars; even. 400 + 60 scholars.

Remarks: In the columns 'How endowed', the Great Tithe of the parish go to the College at Lampeter, as it is a sinecure Rectory, which amount to £240 per annum. Divine service is held for three Sundays in the month in the morning and evening, but once a month in the morning and afternoon.

John Griffiths.   Vicar.

Lewis: rectory and vicarage: sinecure rectory rated at £12. 18. 9; net value £176; appropriated to St. David's College, Lampeter; discharged vicarage, rated at £6. 13. 4; endowed with £200 royal bounty: net value £136 with glebe-house; patron, Bp. of St. David's. Tithes divided into two portions, the Grange and the Gwlâd; of the Gwlâd portion, St. David's College receives two-thirds and the vicar one third: of the Grange portion, one third belongs to the Llŷs Newydd family, two thirds of the remainder going to St. David's College, and one third to the vicar. Tithes commuted for £430, of which £244 are payable to the sinecure rector, subject to rates averaging £35. 16. 10, with a glebe of ½ acre valued at 10s per annum; £122, subject to rates averaging £17. 18. 5. per annum, to the vicar who has a glebe of 44 acres valued at £40; and £64, less £9. 9. 11. annual rates, to the impropriator.

C & C: 2 services in Welsh performed by the incumbent.

I & C: resident.

ICBS: grant of £70 in 1829.

(31)   PENRHIW.   PRESBYTERIAN.

Erected 1771.

Space: free 164; other 36.

Present: aft. 43.

Average: general congregation 80.

John Thomas.   Minister at Llandyssil
and supply at above place of worship.

(32)   DREFACH.   CALVINSTIC BAPTIST.

Erected 1809, rebuilt 1840.

Space: free 172; other 150.

Present: morn. 267; even. 279.

Average (12 *months*): morn. 290; aft. 200; even. 310.
Remarks: Internal Dimensions of the Chapel: Floor 36 feet by 26: Gallery 18 feet by 13. *Total* 54 feet by 39.

John Lewis. Deacon and Clerk.
Llwynbedw, Penboyr.

(33) SARON. INDEPENDANT.
Erected before 1800.
Space: free 138; other 180.
Present: morn. 279; even. 233.
Average (12 *months*): morn. 330; aft. 80; even. 110.
Remarks: More than half of the Sunday School Scholars are adults and but very few under 12 years of age. The school is kept but once a day either morning or afternoon and not immediately preceeding Divine Service, which service is not held that part of the day the School is held.
The Clear Space inside of the Building is 40 feet by 24 feet. The free sittings are Benches, the most part of which are on the Gallery and 18 of which are 10 feet long on an average, the other five benches are 6 feet long on an average, the other 30 sittings will contain 6 persons to sit upon an average.

David George. Deacon and Clerk.
Parkyotia, Llangelei.

(34) CLOS Y GRAIG. CALVINISTIC METHODIST.
Erected 1754.
Present: morn. 88.
Average (12 *months*): morn. 200.
Remarks: The public worship is continually at Ten in the morning on one Sunday and other Sunday at 2 and 6 evening and Sunday School besides.

David Jones.
Daniel Rees. Deacon.

[End of Kenarth sub-district]

2 PENBRYN (Subdistrict)
Area: 25,165 acres. *Popn.* 2,418 males, 2,942 females: total 5,360.

1 Llanfair-Tref-Helygen Parish
Area: 648 acres. *Popn.* 43 males, 54 females: total 97.
[There is no entry for the Parish Church.]
Lewis: rectory not in charge annexed to that of Llandyfriog [594. 2. 2(2)]: church in ruins.

(1) Bryngwenith. Independent.
Erected 'since 1800'.
Space: chapel inside 36 ft. by 24 ft.: 'all free yet'.
Present: morn. 'society'; aft. 'school'; even. 'sermon'.
Average: morn. 85; aft. 83; even. 115.
Remarks: The expense of the building was paid by the congregation by free contributions.

William Jones.   Minister.
Glynarthen.

2   Llandyfriog Parish.
Area: 2,867 acres. *Popn.* 434 males, 525 females: total 959.

(2)   Llandyfriog Parish Church.
Endowed: land £30; tithe £84; glebe £10.
Space: free 150; other 18.
Present: morn. 110.
Average: morn. 200.

Isaac Hughes.   Vicar.

Lewis: prebend in the Cathedral Church of St. David's: rated at £18, annexed to the archdeaconry of Cardigan: the living a discharged vicarage, with rectory of Llanvair Trêlygon [594.2.1(-)] annexed, rated at £8; endowed with £600 royal bounty; net income £147 with a glebe-house; patron, Bp. St. David's: tithes commuted for £250, of which £166. 13. 4. are payable to the impropriator, who has a glebe of 13 acres valued at £52 per annum, and £83. 6. 8. to the vicar, who has a glebe of 26 acres valued at £15 per annum.
C & C: 1 service in Welsh performed by the incumbent.
I & C: resident.
ICBS: grant of £60 in 1843.

3   Brongwyn Parish.
Area: 1,620 acres. *Popn.* 177 males, 190 females: total 367.

(3)   'It is belongs to the Parish of Penbryn'.
Endowed: tithe £139.
Space: free 20.
Present: aft. 9.
Remarks: The minister refuse to full up this paper.

John Jones.   Churchwarden.

Lewis: perpetual curacy, annexed, with that of Bettws-Evan [594. 2. 5(9)], to the vicarage of Pembryn [594. 2. 6(11)].
C & C: vide Pembryn.
I & C: ditto.
ICBS: grant of £35 made in 1829.

(4) TREWEN. INDEPENDENT.
Erected about 1736.
Space: free 400 except the galery.
Present: morn. 142 scholars; aft. 446; even. 69.
Average: general congregation between 400 and 500; scholars 130.

> Owen Davies. Deacon.
> Llwynbedw.

4 Troedyraur Parish.
Area: 4,660 acres. *Popn.* 466 males, 554 females: total 1,020.

(5) TROEDYRAUR PARISH CHURCH.
Endowed: tithe £307.
Present: no service.
Average: general congregation about 100.
Remarks: The church has been taken down for the sake of rebuilding it
since last May. The new church is not yet finished, so I can not say how
many sittings it will contain.

> H. L. Davies. Curate.

Lewis: discharged rectory, rated at £13; patron, the Crown: tithes commuted for
£305, subject to rates averaging £5 per annum; glebe of 12 acres valued at £12.
C & C: 2 services partially in English and Welsh.
I & C: not resident: curate, who resides in the glebe-house, has stipend of £130.
ICBS: grant of £40 made in 1850.

(6) TWRGWYN CHAPEL. CALVINISTIC METHODISTS.
Erected before 1800.
Space: free 150; other 260; standing 100.
Present: morn. 235; aft. 143 scholars; even. prayers 200.
Average: general congregation 300; scholars 60.
Remarks: Most part of the congregation attend the Sunday School as
Scripture readers. That accounts for the number being only sixty, other-
wise they would be counted twice.

> Samuel Morris. Deacon.
> Rhydlewis.

(7) HAWEN. INDEPENDENTS.
Builded in 1747 and rebuilded in 1790, Ditto in 1811 and Ditto in 1838.
Space: all free (including gallery) for about 400.
Present: morn. 200 scholars; aft. sermon 361; even. prayer 198.
Remarks: The demensions of the Chapel is 40 feet by 30 feet clear inside,
with gallery. The whole expences of building was paid for by free contributions. The collections towards Missions, Colleges, poor etc., are large
annually. There is a large burial ground belonging to the chapel, and all
free property.

> William Jones. Minister.

(8)   SALEM CHAPEL, NEAR BRONGEST VILLAGE.   CALVINISTIC METHODISTS.
Erected 1811.
Space: free 116; other 104; standing 286.
Present: morn. 72 scholars; aft. 177; even. 147.

> John Thomas.   Deacon.
> Crynant.

5   Bettws-Evan Parish.
Area: 2,640 acres. *Popn.* 184 males, 220 females: total 404.

(9)   BETTWS EVAN PARISH CHURCH.
Space: 140 sittings.
Usual attendants: morn. 40; aft. 50; even. 80.
No Sunday School.

> John Morgan.   Registrar.
> Informant.

[Informant's form.]

Lewis: perpetual curacy, annexed with that of Brongwyn [594. 2. 3.(3)] to the vicarage of Pembryn [594. 2. 6(11)]: impropriate tithes commuted for £82. 10, and the vicarial tithes for £77. 10, both subject to rates averaging £10 per annum. Incorporated Society gave grant of £25 towards additional sittings.

C & C: vide sub Penbryn [594. 2. 6(11)].

I & C: ditto.

ICBS: grant of £25 made in 1829.

(10) BRYNGWYN.   INDEPENDENT.
Erected 1838.
Space: see letter.
Present: morn. 50 scholars; even. 156.
Average: morn. 73 scholars; even. 150.

> Davies Davies.   Superintendent.
> Llain, Cwmsylltyn.

[Endorsed: see letter.]

6   Penbryn or Pembryn Parish.
Area: 8,347 acres. *Popn.* 748 males, 911 females: total 1,659.

(11) LLANFIHANGEL PENYBRYN, COMMONLY CALLED PENBRYN PARISH CHURCH.
Endowed: tithes commuted at £320.
Space: free about 150; other about 50.
Present: morn. 44; even. 30.
Average: morn. 60; even.: once a month 200.

> J. Hughes.   Vicar.

Lewis: vicarage, with the perpetual curacies of Bettws Evan [594. 2. 5(9)] and

Brongwyn [594. 2.3(3)] annexed: rated at £15; patron, Bp. St. David's; impropriator, Major W. Rice: tithes commuted for £700, of which £320 is payable to the vicar, £355 to the impropriator, both subject to rates averaging £46. 10. per annum. £25 are payable to the treasurer of St. David's cathedral.

C & C: 1 service in the church and 1 in the chapels, in Welsh, performed by the incumbent and curate.

I & C: resident; curate has stipend of £40.

(12) GLYNARTHEN CHAPEL. INDEPENDENTS.
Erected before 1800; rebuilded 1841.
Space: 120 pews rented; all others free; a space to accommodate 500 persons in standing and sitting. All free.
Present: morn. sermon 473; aft. school; even. Society.
Average: morn. 473; aft. 224; even. 161.
Remarks: The dimension of the Chapel is 57 feet length and 37 feet width clear inside, with a large Gallary. The expences in re-building was £700 and all was paid by free contributions. The Collections towards Missions, Bible Society, Colleges, poor etc. annually are large. There is a British School House builded by the Congregation on their own property and supported by themselves and free for the poor's children.

William Jones. Minister.

(13) TANYGROES CHAPEL. CALVINISTIC METHODIST.
Erected 1850.
Space: 'unfinished with them all free at present'.
Present: morn. 129 scholars; aft. 234; even. 264.
Remarks: The seats in Tanygroes Chapel is not finished but after been finished they will be rented. The free space in the center will be furnished with benches. The number of school and of persons attending Divine Service Service on Sunday, March 30 1851 is the average number of attendants since Divine Service and Sunday School commenced in March 1850.

Thomas Evans. Secretary.
Esgerathen, Penbryn.

(14) PENMORFA. CALVINISTIC METHODIST.
Erected 1796 rebuilt 1846.
Space: free 150; other 252; standing '23 feet by 18 feet or 414 feet superficial with Benches, free'.
Present: morn. 387+25 scholars; aft. 241 scholars; even. 302+30 scholars.
Average (12 months): morn. 400 + 31 scholars; aft. 311 scholars; even. 300 + 30 scholars.
Remarks: The chapel are 43 by 34 feet clear and 22 feet high with gallary both sides and back 10½ feet wide and 18½ feet in the Angles.
The expence of building was £650 and paid by free contribution by the

Assembly belong to the Chapel in two years and quite finish on the day of opening. The Collection towards Mission and Bible Societies are about £40 annually in this Chapel, besides the Expence of Home Ministry.

Timothy Timothy.   Secretary.
Rhydser.

(15)   BRYN MORIAH.   INDEPENDENTS.
Erected 1848.
Space: All free.
Present: morn. 'no service'; aft. 'school'; even. 'sermon'.
Average: aft. 113; even. 160.
Remarks: The Dimension of the chapel is 26 ft. in length by 21 ft. clear inside. The expences of building was £60, and paid be free contribution. The Collection towards Missions etc. are very good annually in this Chapel.

William Jones.   Minister.
Glynarthen.

[Endorsed: See Letter.]

7   Llangranog Parish.
Area: 4,383 acres. *Popn.* 366 males, 488 females: total 854.

(16)   LLANGRANOG PARISH CHURCH.
Space: 200.
Present: morn. 64 + 36 scholars; even. 70 + 20 scholars.
Average: morn. 70 + 40 scholars; aft. 140 + 40 scholars; even. 200 + 36 scholars.
Remarks: The afternoon service takes place only on alternate Sundays.

Josiah Rees.   Vicar.

Lewis: vicarage, not in charge, annexed to that of Llandysilio-Gogo [596. 1. 3(8)]; endowed with £600 parliamentary grant: tithes commuted for £240, of which £130 payable to the treasurer of St. David's cathedral, and £110 to the vicar, subject to rates averaging £20. 10. per annum; glebe of 60 acres valued at £42. Vicarage recently built under Gilbert's Act.
C & C: *vide sub* Llandysilio-Gogo [596. 1. 3(8)].
I & C: ditto.

(17)   GWNDWN CHAPEL.   BAPTIST.
Erected 1830.
Space: free 66; other 42.
Present: morn. 15 scholars; aft. 50.
Average: general congregation 60; scholars 23.

D. Williams.   Baptist Minister.

[Endorsed: See Letter.]

(18) WORVILLE BROOK CHAPEL.   CALVINSTIC METHODIST.
Erected 1849.
Space: free (see Remarks).
Present: morn. 135; aft. 108 scholars; even. 149.
Remarks: free 7 pews on the ground floor together with all the gallery; other 34 pews = 204 sittings.

> Owen Evans.   Deacon.
> Penar.

(19) CHAPEL-WIG.   INDEPENDENTS.
Erected 1813.
Space: free 216; other 312.
Present: morn. 151 scholars; aft. 319.
Average (12 *months*): morn. 180 scholars; aft. 400; even. 200.

> Thomas Rees.   Minister.

(20) PANTYCREIGIAU CHAPEL.   INDEPENDENTS.
Erected 1847.
Space: free 108; other 92; standing 108.
Present: morn. 147; aft. 83 scholars; even. 64.
Average (6 *months*): general congregation 140; scholars 70.

> Robert Thomas.   Minister.

[End of Penbryn Subdistrict]

3 LLANDYSSIL (Subdistrict)
Area: 40,722 acres. *Popn.* 2,879 males, 3,248 females: total 6,127.

1 Llangunllo Parish.
Area: 3,650 acres. *Popn.* 255 males, 308 females: total 563.

(1) BWLLYGROES.   CONGREGATIONALISTS.
Erected 1833.
Space: free 90; other 144; standing 50.
Present: morn. 126; aft. 75 scholars.
Average (12 *months*): general congregation 200; scholars 96.
Remarks: We are generally called Independents, but with more propriety we are called Congregationalists. 3 Sabbaths in every month School in the morning, preaching in the afternoon and sometimes in the evening, the other Sabbath preaching in the morning school in the evening or afternoon. The members in communion are 107. As many of the Sunday Scholars are members the Congregation is generally from 170 to 200.

> Samuel Griffiths.   Minister.
> Horeb, Nr. Llandyssul.

(2)   LLANGUNLLO PARISH CHURCH.
Space: free 200; other 40; standing 100.
Present: morn. 60 + 40 scholars.
Average (12 *months*): morn. 100 + 45 scholars.

J. H. Davies.   Rector.

[This return is on a Form B.]

Lewis: discharged rectory; rated at £6. 13. 4; in the patronage of the freeholders and leaseholders of the parish; tithes commuted for £175; glebe of 120 acres valued at £80 per annum, with a glebe-house.

C & C: 1 service, partially in English and Welsh.

I & C: no return.

2   Henllan Parish.
Area: 387 acres. *Popn.* 55 males, 62 females: total 117.

(3)   HENLLAN PARISH CHURCH.
Endowd: tithe £20. 10; glebe £7.
Space: free 96.
Present: morn. 45; aft. 81 scholars.
Remarks: Children and adults from the adjoining Parishes attend the Sunday School.

John Sinnett.   Rector.

Lewis: rectory, not in charge, annexed to that of Bangor [594. 3. 4(6)]; tithes commuted for £25. 8; with glebe of 4 acres valued at £ 7 per annum.
C & C: vide sub Bangor [594. 3. 4(6)].

I & C: ditto.

ICBS: grant of £30 in 1850.

(4)   CAPPEL DRINDOD.   INDEPENDENT AND METHODIST.
Erected before 1800.
Space: free 300; other 'a pew for Bronwydd family'; standing 300.
Present: aft. 300.
Average (12 *months*): general congregation 300; scholars 71 elders (sic.)
Remarks: This chapel was built and endowed by the late Colonel and Mrs. Lloyd of Bronwydd who invested the sum of £1,500 in the 3 *p.c.* Consols for its maintainance. The appointment of Ministers (of which there are *four*, three *Methodist* and *one Independent*) is in the hands of Thomas Davies Lloyd Esq. of Bronwydd, grandson of the above Colonel Lloyd, who is a member of the Church of England. The Ministers receive £1. 1s. 0d. every Sunday.

Thomas Davies Lloyd, J.P., D.L.
Patron.

3   Llanfair-Orllwyn Parish.
Area: 1,744 acres. *Popn.* 197 males, 236 females: total 433.

(5)   LLANFAIR ORLLWYN PARISH CHURCH.
Endowed: land £26; tithe £100; glebe £18.
Space: free 200.
Present: morn. 150; aft. 70 scholars.
Average: morn. 180; aft. 80 scholars.

Thomas Lloyd.   Rector.

Lewis: discharged rectory; rated at £4. 13. 4; endowed with £600 royal bounty; net income £155: patron, Bp. St. David's: tithes commuted for £120, subject to rates averaging £12; glebe of 25 acres valued at £18 per annum.

C & C: 1 service in Welsh performed by the incumbent.

I & C: not resident.

ICBS: grant of £20 in 1842.

6   Bangor Parish
Area: 1,392 acres. *Popn.* 93 males, 105 females: total 198.

(6)   BANGOR PARISH CHURCH.
Endowed: land £22. 10; tithe £72. 13; glebe £50.
Space: free 75; other 10.
Present: morn. 45 scholars; aft. 160.
Remarks: There are not near enough sittings in the Church for the Congregation.

John Sennett.   Rector.

Lewis: discharged rectory with that of Henllan [594. 3. 2(3)] annexed; rated at £5. 6. 8; endowed with £200 royal bounty; net income £163; patron, Bp. of St. David's: rectorial tithes commuted for £87; glebe of 52 acres valued at £45 per annum.

C & C: (with Henllan): 1 service in each church, in Welsh, performed by the incumbent and curate.

I & C: no return.

7   Llandyssil Parish, consisting of Llandyssil-is-Kerdin and Llandyssil-uwch-Kerdin.
Popn. of Llandyssil-is-Kerdin, 724 males, 817 females: total 1,541; of Llandyssil-uwch-Kerdin, 667 males, 722 females: total 1,389. *Area* of the whole parish: 17,556 acres. *Popn.* 1,391 males, 1539 females: total 2,930.

(7)   LLANDYSSUL PARISH CHURCH.
Endowed: land £25. 4; tithe (called stipend) £25; permanent endowment
£101. 1. 8; fees surplice etc. about £2. 10.
Space: free 400; other 70.
Present: morn. 250 + 50 scholars.
Average: general congregation morn. from 300 to 400; aft. from 300 to 400.
Remarks: The Parish being near 7 miles long and between 5 and 6 broad,
a Cottage lecture is delivered every other Sunday in the evening in a distant
part of the Parish. The lecture yesterday was delivered at a place distant
about three miles from the Parish Church.

Evan Morgan.   Vicar.

Lewis: rectory and vicarage united: sinecure rectory rated at £14, and the vicarage
at £7. 10; patron, Bp. St. Asaph: tithes commuted for £500; glebe of 16 acres,
with house, valued at £35 per annum.
C & C: no return.
I & C: resident.

(8)   JOHN THOMAS'S SCHOOLROOM.   UNITARIAN.
Erected since 1800: 'used for a Day School'.
Space: 100 all free.
Present: morn. 20; aft. and even. 'no service'.

John Thomas.   Minister.

(9)   EBENEZER.   PARTICULAR BAPTISTS.
Erected 1833.
Space: 20 by 32 in clear for Divine Service.
Present: morn. 37 scholars; aft. 300; even. 50.
Average: morn. 63 scholars; aft. 250; even. 260.

John Jones.   Baptist Minister.

(10)   PENUEL.   WESLEYAN METHODIST.
Erected 1808.
Space: free 150; other 150.
Present: morn. 200 + 50 scholars; even. 60.

David Evans.   Minister.

(11)   TABERNACLE.   CALV. METH.
Erected 1832.
Space: free 204; standing 324 'near'.
Present: morn. 35 + 40 scholars; even. 50.
Average: morn. 45 + 40 scholars; even. 50.

Morris James.   Deacon.
Currier.

(12) WAUNIFOR CHAPEL. CALVINISTIC METHODISTS.
Erected 1760.
Space: free 21.
Present: morn. 22.
Remarks: This old Chapel is in neediness of repair or rebuilt and the average of attendants is from 30 to 40. First built by Thomas Bowen, Esq., Waunifor, on his Estate and his Expence.

> Evan Edwards. Elder.
> Dolwilym.

(13) BETHEL. WESLEYAN METHODISTS.
Erected 1833.
Space: free 250.
Present: morn. 180 + 20 scholars.

> David Evans. Minister.

(14) LLWYNRHYDOWEN. PRESBYTERIAN.
Erected 1733; rebuilt 1791; rebuilt 1834.
Space: free 42; other 'none'.
Present: morn. about 500.
Average: general congregation from 400 to 600.

> John Davies. Minister.
> Adpar.

(15) PANTYDEFAID. UNITARIANS.
Erected 1803; rebuilt 1840.
Space: free 210; standing from 20 to 30.
Present: aft. 150.
Remarks: The attendance at the Morning Service every alternate Sunday is more numerous than at the afternoon Service. The average number may be 250.

> Thomas Thomas. Minister.
> Pantydefaid.

(16) CARMEL. INDEPENDENTS.
Erected 1819; rebuilt 1832.
Space: free 96; other 168.
Present: morn. 40 scholars; aft. 98.
Average (12 months): general congregation 180; scholars 50.
Remarks: 2 Sabbaths in every month preaching in the morning, school for reading and religious instruction in the afternoon. 2 other Sabbaths, school in the morning, preaching in the afternoon.
The members in full communion 138, the Sunday Scholars 50, but as many Sunday Scholars are members the general congregation in all are from 175 to 180.

> Samuel Griffiths. Minister.
> Horeb.

(17) HOREB. CONGREGATIONAL.
Erected 1784; rebuilt 1826.
Space: free 480.
Present: morn. 252; aft. 85 scholars.
Average (12 *months*): general congregation 290, scholars 145.
Remarks: We are generally called Independents but with more propriety we are called Congregationalists. 3 Sabbaths in every month preaching in the morning Sunday School in the afternoon. The other Sabbath, school in the morning preaching in the afternoon.
The numbers in Communion are 334. There is an infant school in a separate building belonging to the Congregation, contains on the books 42 Sunday Scholars 21 per return of Mr. Evan Thomas Superintendent.

Samuel Griffiths. Minister.

6   Llanfihangel-ar-arth Parish, co. Carmarthen.

Area: 15,993 acres. *Popn.* 888 males, 998 females: total 1,886.
(18) LLANFIHANGEL-AR-ARTH PARISH CHURCH.
Endowed: land £27; tithe £78; glebe £50; other £9. 16. 10; fees about £2.
Space: free 222.
Present: morn. 150; aft. 42 scholars.
Average (3 *months*): morn. 200; aft. 35 scholars.
Remarks: Rates and Taxes etc. are not deducted from the above Statement of the value of the said Living.

John Edwards. Vicar.

Lewis: discharged vicarage, rated at £6. 6. 8; endowed with £200 royal bounty; patrons and impropriators, W. Lewes, Esq., and J. E. Lloyd, Esq.: tithes commuted for £508, of which £430 are payable to the impropriators, and £78 to the vicar; glebe of 85 acres valued at £60 per annum.

C & C: sub Llanfihangel Yeroth: no return.

I & C: not resident: curate, who resides at Llandysil, 2 miles distant, has stipend of £50.

(19) PENYBONT, LLANFIHANGEL YEROTH. BAPTIST.
Erected before 1800.
Space: free 174; standing 200 people.
Present: morn. 19 scholars; aft. 61.
Average (12 *months*): morn. 140 + 38 scholars; aft. 70; even. 55.

David Evans. Steward.
Pelican, Llandyssil.

(20) HEBRON. PARTICULAR BAPTIST.
Erected 1830.
Space: 'about 28 by 22 in clear'.
Present: morn. 70.

John Jones. Baptist Minister.

(21)   PENCADER CHAPEL.   INDEPENDENTS.
Erected 'about 1650'.
Space: free 462; standing 30.
Present: morn. 305.
Remarks: The Congregation is divided into different sections which on Sunday Evenings meet in different Dwelling Houses for prayer and where sermons are occasionally delivered.

John Owen.   Minister.

(22)   NEW INN.   CALV. METHODIST.
Erected 1797, rebuilt 1832.
Space: free 'for about 100'; other '25 seats will hold 7'; standing 'our chapel can hold more than 300 persons and very often does'.
Present: morn. Sunday School; aft. sermon 167; even. sermon 63.
Average: general congregation '200 about': scholars '128-33'.
Remarks: We did not take the male and female numbers separate in this case as it would take too much of our time. This paper is as correct as possible, and if any more Information is required on application shall be given.

Thomas Rhys Saunders.   Deacon.
Perthyberllan, New Inn.

(23)   TROEDYRHIW CHAPEL.   INDEPENDENTS.
Erected 1833.
Used also as a Day School.
Space: free 110; other 110; standing 80.
Present: morn. 137.
Average: morn. 200.
Remarks: The Congregation is divided into different sections and meet in different Dwelling Houses for Prayer on Saturday Evenings.

John Owen.   Minister.

[*End of Llandyssil Subdistrict, and end of Newcastle-in-Emlyn District*]

595   LAMPETER (District)

Area: 75,710 acres.   *Popn.* 4,705 males, 5,169 females: total 9,874.

1 LLANYBYTHER (Subdistrict)
Area: 25,667 acres. *Popn.* 1,234 males, 1,396 females: total 2,630.

1   Llanllwny Parish, co. Carmarthen.
Area: 6,624. *Popn.* 388 males, 437 females: total 825.
Erected 1810.
Space: free 150; other 280.
Present: morn. 380 + 120 scholars.

David Davies.   Deacon.

(2)   LLANLLWNI PARISH CHURCH.
Endowed: land £32; annuity in lieu of tithes from the Rector the Bishop of Lincoln £16; other £62; fees about £2.
Space: free 130; other 34.
Present: morn. 32 scholars; aft. 67.
Average: morn. and aft. alternately 110.
Remarks: The Congregation in the mornings is generally much larger than in the afternoon. Hence the difference between the average and that actually in attendance on the 30th. There is another Church and Parish belonging to the Living, distant between 7 and 8 miles *unendowed*—Llanfihangel Rhosycorn.

Richard Davies.   Vicar.

Lewis: discharged vicarage, with Llanvihangel-Rhôsycorn [595. 1. 2(3)] annexed; rated at £5, endowed with £600 parliamentary grant; net income £103, with glebe-house: patron, Bishop St. David's: tithes commuted for £233 payable to the Bishop of Lincoln; glebe of 86 acres valued at £55.

C & C: 1 service in Welsh performed by the incumbent.

I & C: resident; curate has stipend of £40.

2   Llanfihangel-Rhos-y-Corn Parish, co. Carmarthen.
Area: 9,012 acres. *Popn.* 326 males, 355 females: total 681.

(3)   LLANFIHANGEL RHOS-Y-CORN PARISH CHURCH.
Space: now in building and not finished.
Present: morn. 20.

Average: morn. 60.
Remarks: Dependent on Llanllwyn Church.   No separate endowment.

David Jones.   Curate.

Lewis: vide Llanllwni [595. 1. 1(2)].

C & C: sub Llanllwni: 1 service in chapel in Welsh performed by the curate.

I & C: vide Llanllwni.

(4)   GWERNOGE CHAPPEL.   INDEPENDENTS.
Erected before 1800.
Space: free 288; standing 200.
Present: morn. 180; even. 65.
Average: morn. 250; even. 60.
Remarks: Divine Service performed every Sunday in the Morning;
occasionally performed also in the afternoon on Sundays, also frequently on
weekdays. Sunday School kept generally on every Sunday Evenings, teach-
ing Religious Instructions and reading the Scripture in Welsh.

Daniel Evans.   Occasional Preacher.

(5)   TYMAWR, LLANFIHANGEL RHOSYCORN.   LATTER DAY SAINTS.
Part of a dwelling house.
Usual attendance: morn. 30.

James Evans.   Informant.

[Informant's form.]

(6)   CWMWRDY.   UNITARIANS.
Erected 1835.
Space: All free.
Usual attendance: morn. 29.

James Evans.   Informant.

[Informant's form, endorsed 'See Letter'.]

3   Llanybyther Parish, co. Carmarthen.
Area: 10,031 acres. *Popn.* 520 males, 603 females: total 1,124.

(7)   ST. PETER'S LLANBYTHER PARISH CHURCH.
Endowed: Land £70; tithe £70; glebe £9; other £12; fees £1.
Space: free 203.
Present: aft. 80 + 24 scholars.
Average: morn. 90 + 24 scholars.

Remarks: Service is performed in this Church morning and afternoon on alternate Sundays.

Hugh Felix.   Vicar.

Lewis: discharged vicarage, endowed with £600 royal bounty and £400 parliamentary grant; patron, the Crown: net income £117, with a glebe-house; impropriators, C. Longcroft and T. Lloyd, Esqs: tithes commuted for £230, of which £160 payable to the impropriators and £70 to the vicar; glebe of 7½ acres valued at £10. Church recently thoroughly repaired.

C & C: no return.

I & C: no eturn.

ICBS: grant of £50 in 1830.

(8)   ABERGORLECH CHAPEL.   A PERPETUAL CURACY.
Endowed: land £60.
Space: free 100.
Present: even. 15.
Average: from 20 to 30.

David Jones.   Perpetual curate.

Lewis: sub Llanybyther: perpetual curacy, endowed with £1,000 royal bounty: net income £60: in the gift of the vicar of Llanybyther.

C & C: 1 service in Welsh performed by the incumbent.

I & C: not resident.

ICBS: grant of £50 in 1834.

(9)   RHYDYBONT.   INDEPENDENT.
Space: free 547.
Present: morn. 320 + 70 scholars.

David Lewis.   Deacon.

(10)   ABERDUAR.   BAPTIST.
Erected before 1800.
Space: free 415.
Present: morn. 300 + 20 scholars.

John Williams.   Minister.

(11)   RHYDCYMERE.   CALVINISTIC METHS.
Erected: 1847.
Space: free 125; other 125.
Present: morn. 130 + 50 scholars,* morn. 117; even. 39.

John Williams.   Deacon.

[*Endorsed: Probably the average attendance.]

(12)   Abergorlech New Chapel.   Independents Denomination.
The first meeting house was blt in the years 1740 and the second in the year
1781 and this in the yr 1828.
Space: See letter.
Present: morn. 214; aft. 75 scholars; even. 91.
Average: general congregation 200; scholars 150.
Remarks: There are three other Schools besides the one held in the Chapel
whose attendants average together about eighty, but the Congregation had not
been supplied with a schedule for the making of a return of the Sunday
Schools.

Stephen Griffiths.   Deacon.

[Endorsed: See Letter. The remarks are in another hand, and refer to the
Education Census Schedule, form C, for which see Census of Great Britain
1851, *Education* (1854), p. cvi.]

[End of Llanybyther Subdistrict]

2 PENCARREG (Subdistrict)
Area: 22,231 acres. *Popn.* 1,304 males, 1,402 females: total 2,706.

1   Pencarreg Parish, co. Carmarthen.
Area: 10,392 acres. *Popn.* 552 males, 571 females: total 1,123.

(1)   Pencarreg Parish Church.
Endowed: land £8; tithe £110; other £40. 7s. 6d.; fees £1.
Space: free 150.
Present: morn. 40; aft. 55 scholars.
Average: general congregation 40 to 50.
Remarks: the above term [average] is yearly and the school recently opened.

Thomas Jones.   Vicar.

Lewis: discharged vicarage, rated at £4; endowed with £200 royal bounty and £1,200
parliamentary grant: patron, Pryse Pryse, Esq.: impropriators, Edmund H. Stacey,
Esq., and Rev. B. Williams; tithes commuted for £330, of which £110 belong to
the vicar, the remainder to the impropriators.

C & C: 1 service in Welsh perfofmed by the incumbent.

I & C: resident.

ICBS: grant of £20 in 1834.

(2) CAERSALEM. BAPTIST.
Erected 1840.
Space: free 160.
Present: aft. 50 + 10 scholars.
Average (12 *months*): aft. 120 + 15 scholars.

John Williams. Minister.
Aberduar.

(3) PARK Y RHOS. INDEPENDENTS.
Used first as a chapel in 1841. It was previously a dwelling house.
Space: free none; other 150; standing 50.
Present: morn. 95.
Average (12 *months*): general congregation 120; scholars 25.

William Davies, Ph.D. Minister.

(4) ESGERDAWE. INDEPENDENT.
Erected 1844.
Space: free 100; other 150; standing 50.
Present: morn. 171 + 53 scholars.
Average (12 *months*): morn. 180 + 50 scholars.

Rees Jones. Minister.

2-3 Llanycrwys Parish, co. Carmarthen, consisting of [2] the Hamlet of Fforest and [3] the Hamlet of Mynachty.
Area: 3,379 acres. *Popn.* 244 males, 251 females: total 495.

2 Fforest Hamlet.
Popn. 131 males, 146 females: total 277.

(5) LANYCRWYS PARISH CHURCH.
Endowed: land £59; tithe £8; other £6. 10s.
Space: all free.
Present: morn. 15.
Average (12 *months*): morn. 20.

D. Price Lewis. Perpetual Curate.

Lewis: perpetual curacy; endowed with £600 royal bounty and £200 parliamentary grant; net income £60: patron and impropriator, John Johnes, Esq: tithes commuted for £90, subject to rates averaging £4. 1. 10d. per annum.

C & C: 1 service in Welsh performed by the incumbent.

I & C: not resident.

3 Mynachty Hamlet.
Popn. 113 males, 115 females: total 218.

(6) FFALDYBRENIN. INDEPENDENT.
Erected 1833.
Space: free 150; other 160; standing 60.
Present: aft. 176.
Average (12 months): general congregation 200; Scholars 100.

Rees Jones. Minister.

4 Cellan Parish.
Area: 3,645. *Popn.* 237 males, 263 females: total 500.

(7) CELLAN PARISH CHURCH.
Endowed: land £15; tithes £120; glebe £12; fees 10s.
Space: free 120; other 20.
Present: aft. from 60 to 70.
Average (12 months): 50 to 75.
Remarks: The Church was partly rebuilt about Eight years ago, the Parishioners etc Charity. P.S. The Service in church is performed Morning and Afternoon, alternately in the evening. No service used in the Evening. [Signed:] T.D.

Timothy Davies. Churchwarden.

Lewis: discharged rectory, rated at £5. 7. 8½.; endowed with £200 royal bounty; net income £83, with a glebe-house: patron, Bp. St. David's.

C & C: 1 service in Welsh performed by the incumbent.

I & C: not resident.

(8) CAERONNEN. UNITARIAN.
Erected 1846.
Space: 'See letter'.
Present: morn. general congregation 100.
Remarks: The service is held alternately having but one service on the Sabbath day.

John Jones. Deacon.

[Endorsed: See letter.]

(9) CAPEL YR ERW. INDEPENDENTS.
Erected 1811.
Space: free 200; standing 200.
Present: morn. 95 + 68 scholars.
Average (12 months): general congregation 100.

Rees Jones. Minister.

5 Llanfair Clydogau Parish.
Area: 4,815 acres. *Popn.* 271 males, 317 females: total 588.

(10) LLANFAIRCLYDOGE PARISH CHURCH.
Endowed: land £95; tithe £4; fees £1.
Space: free 120.
Present: morn. 63.
Remarks: service morning and evening alternately.

Morgan Williams.   Incumbent.

Lewis: perpetual curacy, endowed wih £800 royal bounty: net income £63: patrons
and impropriators, Lord Carrington and Capt. George Laurence Vaughan: tithes
commuted for £180.
C & C: 1 service in Welsh performed by the incumbent.
I & C: resident.

(11) CAPEL MAIR, LLANFAIR CLYDOGE.   INDEPENDENTS.
Erected 1825.
Space: free 42; other 228.
Present: aft. 135 + 45 scholars.
Average: general congregation 140; scholars 55.

David Stephens.
Independent Minister.

[End of Pencarreg Subdistrict]

3 LAMPETER (Subdistrict)
Area: 14,612 acres. *Popn.* 1,264 males, 1,370 females: total 2,634.

1 Bettws Bleddrws Parish.
Area: 2,216 acres. *Popn.* 119 males, 116 females: total 235.

(1) BETTWS BLEDRWS PARISH CHURCH.
Endowed: land £8; tithe £120; glebe £12; other £6. 10s.
Space: free 130; other 20.
Present: morn. 80 + 50 scholars.
Average: morn. from 60 to 100; aft. do.

Charles Lloyd.   Rector.

[Endorsed: See letter]

Lewis: discharged rectory, rated at £4. 7. 8½; endowed with £400 royal bounty;
net income £143, with glebe-house; patron, Bp. St. David's: tithes commuted for
£120; glebe of 10 acres, valued at £15. Church altered and repaired in 1831.

C & C: 1 service in Welsh performed by the incumbent.

I & C: resident.

[According to *Lewis*, the parish contained places of worship belonging to the Baptists and Calvinistic Methodists; these do not appear in the Census.]

2   Llangyby Parish.

Area: 1,809 acres. *Popn.* 118 males, 150 females: total 268.

(2)   LLANGYBI PARISH CHURCH.

Endowed: land £88; tithe £2.

Present: even. 58.

Remarks: Seats not completed since rebuilt. Service morning and evening alternately.

Morgan Williams.   Incumbent.

Lewis: perpetual curacy, rated at £1. 6. 8., and endowed with £800 royal bounty: net income £60: patrons, Lord Carrington and Capt. G. L. Vaughan, alternately; impropriators, the same: tithes commuted for £90, subject to rates averaging £14. 9. 6. p.a.

C & C: 1 service in Welsh performed by the incumbent.

I & C: not resident.

(3)   CAPEL FFYNNON.   CALVINISTIC METHS.

Erected first in 1795 in the Parish of Bettws Bledrws, rebuilt in the Parish of Llangybi 1838.

Space: free 18; other 84.

Present: even. 58 + 20 scholars.

Average (12 *months*): even. 70 + 30 scholars.

John Jones.   Manager.

(4)   CILGWYN CHAPEL.   ARMINIAN PRESBYTERIANS.

Established in 1654 and removed and rebuilded in 1840 in the same parish.

Space: free 42; other 156; standing space 15 ft. by 8½.

Present: aft. 75 + 12 scholars.

Average (12 *months*): general congregation 100 + 30 scholars.

Remarks: N.B. This place of Public Religious Worship was first erected on a part of a Farm called Cilgwyn in the parish of Llangybi (as it was engraved on a stone on the front of the Building) in the year 1654. And now on a more convenient site on a part of a Farm called Penybanc in the same Parish and commonly called Cilgwyn Chapel.

Evan Lewis.   Minister.

[According to *Lewis*, there was also a place of worship for the Independents.]

3   Trefilan Parish.
Area: 2,201 acres. *Popn.* 151 males, 157 females: total 308.

(5)   TREFILAN PARISH CHURCH.
Space: free 87; other 78.
Present: morn. 90 + 25 scholars.
Average: morn. 80 + 20 scholars.

David Griffiths.   Incumbent.

[Endorsed: See letter.]
Lewis: discharged rectory; rated at £5; endowed with £400 royal bounty; net income £118: patron, Bp. St. David's: tithes commuted for £110, of which £5 payable to an impropriator and £105 to the rector; glebe of 3 acres, valued at £9. 9s. p.a. Church taken down in 1806 and rebuilt.
C & C: 1 service in Welsh performed by the incumbent.
I & C: resident.
ICBS: grant of £50 in 1834.

4   Silian Parish.
Area: 2,182 acres. *Popn.* 154 males, 181 females: total 335.

(6)   SILIAN.   A CHAPEL ANNEXED TO LLANWNNEN.
Endowed: tithe £30; glebe £35; Q.A.B. £11.
Space: free 100.
Present: aft. 80.
Average (12 *months*)*:* morn. 75.
Remarks: The morning and afternoon services alternate, being in the morning one Sunday and in the afternoon the other Sunday.

David Williams.   Vicar.

Lewis: consolidated with the vicarage of Llanwnnen [595. 4. 2(7)].
ICBS: grant of £40 in 1839.

(7)   BETHEL.   BAPTIST.
Erected about the year 1833.
Space: free 185; standing 100.
Present: morn. 150; even. 160.
Average: 35 (? scholars).

Timothy Davies.   Deacon.

5-6   Lampeter-Pont-Stephen Parish, consisting of the [5] town of Lampeter and [6] the Hamlet of Tref-y-coed.
Area of the whole: 6,204 acres. *Popn.* 722 males, 766 females: total 1,488.

5   Lampeter Borough.
Popn. 682 males, 711 females: total 1,393.

(8) St. Peters, or in Welsh Llanbedr, corrupted into Lampeter.
Endowed: tithe £175; glebe £100.
Space: free 300.
Present: morn. 250 + 10 scholars; even. 200 + 10 scholars.
Average (12 months): morn. 200 + 10 scholars; even. 180 + 10 scholars.

Llewelyn Llewellin. Vicar.

Lewis: discharged vicarage; rated at £6. 13. 4.; net income £240; patron, Bp. St. David's; appropriator, Precentor of St. David's: tithes commuted for £229. Church entirely rebuilt recently.

C & C: 2 services in Welsh performed by the incumbent and curate.

I & C: legally not resident: curate has stipend of £100.

(9) Tabernacle. Calv. Meth.
Erected 'one hundred and six' 1806 (sic).
Space: free 90; other 288; standing 120.
Present: morn. 220 + 95 scholars; even. 200.
Average: general congregation 300; scholars 130.

Enoch Stephen. Deacon.

(10) Soar. Independents.
Erected 1842.
Space: free 180; other 36; standing 150.
Present: morn. 53 scholars; aft. 350; even. 150.
Average (12 months): general congregation 300.
Remarks: By the sittings I understand the seats and benches which are of different lengths.

David Davies. Independent Minister.

(11) Wesleyan Chapel.
Erected 1810.
Space: free 120; other 150; standing 100.
Present: morn. 53; aft. 39 scholars; even. 150.
Average (12 months): morn. 160; aft. 60 scholars; even. 250.
Remarks: The term sitting is here used in the same sense as Pew.

Edmunds. Class Leader.

(12) Ebenezer. Independent.
Erected 1772.
Space: free 24; other 192; standing 40.
Present: morn. 137.
Average: general congregation 140; scholars 60.

David Stephens. Independent Minister.

(13) PENYBONT. WESLEYAN METHODISTS.
Present: aft. 35.
Average (8 months): general congregation 40.

> William Davies.   Leader.

[End of Lampeter Subdistrict]

4 LLANWENOG (Subdistrict)
Area: 13,200 acres. *Popn.* 903 males, 1,001 females: total 1,904.

1 Llanwenog Parish.
Area: 10,720 acres. *Popn.* 749 males, 826 females: total 1,575.

(1) LLANWENOG PARISH CHURCH.
Endowed: tithe £147; other £19; fees £2.
Space: free 300.
Present: morn. 150.
Average: morn. 160.

> Hugh Felix.   Vicar.

Lewis: formerly a prebend in the collegiate church of Llanddewi-Brevi [598. 2. 4.
(return missing)], rated at £17. 12. 11: discharged vicarage; endowed with £600
parliamentary grant; net income £138: patron, Bp. St. David's: impropriators,
the High Mead estate and the Crosswood estate.
C & C: no return.
I & C: no return.

(2) CRUG. BABTISTS.
Erected 1711.
Space: free 150.
Average: general congregation 100; scholars 26.
Remarks: Sunday School morning and evening every other afternoon every
other Sunday.

> Thomas Griffiths.   Manager.

(3) TREFACH SCHOOL ROOM. INDEPENDENTS A BRANCH OF BRYNTEG.
Used as a place of worship 1847, formerly used as a Shop Room, at present
only a place of worship and Sunday School.
Space: free 120; standing about 120.
Present: even. including scholars, 76.
Average (some months): evening including scholars about 88.
Remarks: Divine Service at this Place yet is only at 6 Every Evening.
Sunday School is kept every morning and afternoon alternately.

> Thomas Thomas.   Deacon.

(4) ALLTYPLACA. UNITARIAN.
Erected 1837.

Space: free 240.
Present: aft. 84.
Average (6 *months*): general congregation 160.

David Evans.   Minister.

(5) Capelsion.   Baptist.
Erected 1820.
Space: free 100.
Present: aft. 110.

Evan Jenkins.   Deacon.

[Endorsed: See letter.]

(6) Brynteg.   Independents.
Erected 1838.
Space: free about 230; gallery about 160.
Present: morn: 'Sunday School'; aft. 138; even. 'only occasionally'.
Average (*Summer months*): about 300.
Remarks: On some Sundays and Special Meetings the attendants in number much exceed the two specified insertions.

Thomas Thomas.   Deacon.
Trefail.

2   Llanwnen Parish.
Area: 2,480 acres. *Popn.* 154 males, 175 females: total 329.

(7) Llanwennen Parish Church.
Endowed: tithe £50.
Space: free 100.
Present: morn. 34.
Average (12 *months*) : morn. 25.
Remarks: the morning and afternoon services alternate.

David Williams.   Vicar.

Lewis: discharged vicarage with that of Silian [595. 3. 4(6)] consolidated: rated at £3. 4. 9½.; endowed with £400 royal bounty and £400 parliamentary grant; net income £102: patron, Bp. St. David's: impropriator, Rev. D. H. T. G. Williams.
C & C: 1 service each in the church and chapel, performed by the incumbent.
I & C: resident.

(8) Capel y Groes.   Unitarian.
Erected 1802.
Space: all free, about 500.
Present: morn. 250 + 50 scholars.
Average (12 *months*): morn. 350 + 50 scholars.
Remarks: Service is usually held in the morning and afternoon alternately every other Sunday.

Rees Davies.   Minister.

[*End of Llanwenog Subdistrict and end of Lampeter District*]

Area: 65,704 acres. *Popn.* 5,991 males, 7,233 females: total 13,224.

1 LLANDISILIO (Subdistrict)
Area: 33,730 acres. *Popn.* 2,903 males; 3,512 females: total 6,415.

1 Dihewid Parish.
Area: 3,215 acres. *Popn.* 219 males, 270 females: total 489.

(1)   DIHEWYD PARISH CHURCH.
Licensed 1824.
Endowed: land £83; tithe £192. 15*s.*; glebe £18; fees 13*s.*
Space: free 125; other 15.
Present: aft. 40.
Remarks: Dihewyd Church was rebuilt in the year 1827 in lieu of an old one, at the expense of the tithe owners and parishioners, amounting to £170. 7*s.* 6*d.*

> Thomas Davies.   Curate.

Lewis: prebend in the collegiate church of Brecknock, rated at £6. 13. 4.; patron, the Bp.: the living a perpetual curacy, consolidated with that of Llanychaeron [596. 2. 4(11)]; endowed with £800 royal bounty; net income £83; patrons and impropriators, Earl of Lisburne and Major Lewis.

C & C: 1 service in Welsh performed by the curate.

I & C: not resident: curate, who has stipend of £50, resides in the parish.

(2)   TROEDYRHIW.   INDEPENDENT.
Erected 1808.
Space: free 200; standing 60.
Present: morn. 193; aft. 55 scholars.
Average (6 *months*): morn. 150; aft. 40.
Remarks: two Sabbaths in the month preaching in the morning instructing youth in religious knowledge and reading in the evening. The two other Sabbaths school in the morning and preaching in the evening.

> Rees Evans.   Deacon.

2 Llanarth Parish.
Area: 15,044 acres. *Popn.* 1,068 males, 1,269 females: total 2,377.

(3) LLANARTH PARISH CHURCH.
Endowed: tithe ⅓, £123; fees £1.
Space: free 570; other 198.
Present: morn. 205 + 50 scholars.
Average (12 *months*): 300 + 60 scholars.

David Evans. Vicar.

Lewis: vicarage, with the perpetual curacy of Llanina [596. 1. 5(19)] annexed: rated at £4. 18. 1½; patron, the Bp: tithes commuted for £460, of which £303. 8. 4. are payable to the Bp. £151. 14. 2. to the vicar, and £4. 17. 6. to an impropriator.

C & C: with Llanina; 2 services in Welsh performed by the incumbent.

I & C: resident.

(4) CAPEL VICAR. WESLEYAN METHODISTS.
Erected 1810.
Space: free 72; other 150; standing 100.
Present: morn. 42 scholars; aft. 119.
Average: general congregation 200; scholars 50.

John Rees. Local Preacher.

(5) PENYCAE CHAPEL. INDEPENDENTS.
Erected 1825.
Space: free 96 on the gallery; other 150.
Present: morn. 223; aft. 150 scholars.
Average: cannot answer the question.
Remarks: Our Congregation on the appointed day was as is seen 223. The Sunday School 150 which generally speaking is made up from among those that attend divine service. Could not return an average only by guess because we do not keep a weekly account of the Sunday School and other things. Therefore sent none at all.

Evan Williams. Minister.

(6) MYDROILIN. INDEPENDENTS.
Erected 1835.
Space: free 30; other 162; standing 100.
Present: morn. 141; aft. 59 scholars.
Average (12 *months*): general congregation 160; scholars 70.

David Davies. Teacher.

3 Llandisilio-Gogo Parish.
Area: 10,224 acres. *Popn.* 649 males, 746 females: total 1,395.

(7) CAPEL CYNON.
Erected in lieu of an old and previously existing one by the parishioners of Llandisiliogogo.
Endowed: land £7;
Present: aft. 45.
Average: aft. 45.

David Griffiths. Perpetual curate.
Tresilian Rectory.

Lewis: sub Llandysilio-Gogo: decayed chapel, rebuilt by the parishioners in 1820; subsequently endowed by Major Parry of Gernos with £200, and £2,000 parliamentary grant: perpetual curacy, net income £75; patron, the vicar of the parish of Llandysilio-Gogo.

C C: 1 service in Welsh performed by the curate.

I & C: not resident: the curate, who has a stipend of £45, resides at Llangunllo [594. 3. 1(2)], 3 miles distant.

(8) LLANDISSILIO GOGO PARISH CHURCH.
Endowed: tithe £30: glebe, none; land, none; permanent outgoings deducted net annual income £20.
Space: 250.
Present: morn. 100 + 32 scholars; aft. 55 + 34 scholars.
Average: morn. 95 + 30 scholars; aft. 84 + 30 scholars; even: 71 + 27 scholars.

Edward James. Curate.

Lewis: discharged vicarage with that of Llangrannog [594. 2. 7(16)] annexed: rated £3. 18. 1½; net income £166, with a glebe-house: tithes commuted for £350, of which £320 payable to the Treasurer of the Cathedral, and £30 to the vicar.

C & C: (with Llangrannog): 3 services in 2 Sundays, in Welsh except at Llanrannog where services are partially in English, performed by the curate.

I & C: resident: curate has stipend of £90.

(9) PISGAH. INDEPENDANT.
Erected 1821.
Space: 48 feet by 21 feet.
Present: aft. 207.
Average: general congregation 307; scholars 235.

Robert Thomas. Minister.

(10) BWLCHYFADFA CHAPEL. PRESBYTERIAN.
Erected 'about forty years ago'.
Space: free 192.
Present: aft. about 200.
Average: general congregation morn. 120; aft. 200.

John Davies. Minister.

(11) LLWYNDAFYDD. PARTICULAR BAPTIST.
Erected 1779.
Space: free 48; other 198; standing 89.
Present: morn. 135; aft. 49 scholars; even. 77.
Average (12 *months*): general congregation morn. 135; scholars 50.

Thomas Griffiths. Baptist Minister.

(12) PENSARN CHAPEL. CALV. METH.
Erected 1794.
Space: free 72; other 300; standing 70.
Present: morn. 91 scholars; aft. 211.

Evan Evans. Secretary.

(13) FANNWEN CHAPEL [or Tonwen?], LLANARTH PARISH. CALV. METH.
Erected about 1779.
Space: free 12; other 228; standing 11 yards by 3.
Present: aft. 160; even. average 102.
Average: general congregation 153; scholars 100.
Remarks: We usually have two sermons one Sunday and one and a prayer
meeting every other Sunday considering that we are joined to the Chapel
called Ffos y ffin. [596. 2. 5(15).]

William Lewis. Elder.
[Note: this return is misplaced.]

4 Llanllwchaiarn Parish.
Area: 3,249 acres. *Popn.* 751 males, 987 females: total 1,738.

(14) LLANLLWCHAIARN PARISH CHURCH.
Endowed: tithe £256; glebe £15; fees £3.
Space: free 200.
Average (3 *months*): morn. 130 + 30 scholars; aft. 60 + 10 scholars.

David Evans. Rector.

Lewis: discharged rectory, rated at £6. 7. 8½; net income £180, with a glebe-house;
patron, the Bp.
C & C: 2 services, Welsh in the morn. English in the aft., performed by the
incumbent.
I & C: resident.

(15) PENRHIWGALED. INDEPENDENTS OR CONGREGATIONALISTS.
Erected before 1800.
Space: free 80; other 400; standing 80.
Present: morn. 210 + 81 scholars; aft. 112 scholars; even. no service.
Average: morn. 350 + 90 scholars; aft. 120 scholars.

Thomas Richard. Deacon.

(16)   BETHEL, NEW QUAY.   PARTICULAR BAPTIST.
Erected 1849.
Space: free 54; other 60; standing 60.
Present: aft. 120; even. 110.

Thomas Griffiths.   Baptist Minister.

(17)   MAESYGROES, NEW QUAY.   WELSH INDEPENDENTS OR CONGREGATIONALISTS.
Erected 1828.
Space: free 60; other 234; standing 'None but the alleys and free seats'.
Present: morn. 300 scholars; aft. 500 + 200 scholars; even. 370 + 230 scholars.
Remarks: At 6 o'clock we have many meetings held occasionally for Divine Worship at different places in the neighbourhood.

Thomas Rees.   Minister.

(18)   TABERNACLE, NEW QUAY.   WELSH CALVINISTIC METHODIST.
Erected 1807, rebuilt 1837.
Space: free 180; other 540; standing 100 or upward.
Present: morn. 280 + 120 scholars; aft. 'a school is always kept at 2 o'clock'; even. 300 + 118 scholars.
Average: 420 to 450 incl. Sunday scholars.
Remarks: other meetings are held occasionally during the week.

Evan Jones.   Minister.

5 Llanina Parish.
Area: 1,998 acres. *Popn.* 216 males, 240 females: total 456.

(19)   LLANINA PARISH CHURCH.
Endowed: tithe ⅓—£23.
Space: free 112; other 39.
Present: morn. 35 + 9 scholars.
Average: morn. 56 + 18 scholars.

David Evans.   Vicar.

Lewis: perpetual curacy, annexed to the vicarage of Llanarth [596. 1. 2(3)]: tithes commuted for £115, of which £61. 13. 4 are payable to the Bp., £30. 16. 8 to the vicar of Llanarth, and £22. 10. to the vicar of Llanllwchaiarn [596. 1. 4(14)].

C & C: vide Llanarth.

I & C: ditto.

[End of Llandisilio Subdistrict]

2 LLANSANTFFRAID (Subdistrict)
Area: 31,974 acres. *Popn.* 3,088 males, 3,721 females: total 6,809.

1 Llanfihangel—Ystrad Parish.
Area: 7,467 acres. *Popn.* 568 males, 615 females: total 1,183.

(1) Capel Beynon, Llanfihangel Ystrad.
Licensed about July 1847; cost defrayed by subscription only, about £880.
Endowed: no endowment or pay for any service.
Space: all free, benches 24, with 1 pew, 6.
Present: There was no duty today. Duty every other Sunday.
Average: morn. 45; no scholars.
Remarks: 4 miles from Lampeter. New Chapel built for the accommodation
of a part of the parish.

David Griffiths.   Minister.
Rector of Trefilan.

(2) Llanfihangel Ystrad Parish Church.
Space: total sittings 250.
Present: morn. 60 + 24 scholars.
Average: morn. 60 + 24 scholars.

David Griffiths.   Vicar.

[Endorsed: see letter.]

Lewis: discharged vicarage, rated at £4. 18. 1½; endowed with £678. 18. 6. parliamentary grant and £200 royal bounty; net income £126; patron, the Bp.: tithes
commuted for £410, of which £282 are impropriated, £128 payable to the vicar.

C & C: Sub Ystrad: 1 service each Sunday in the church, one on alternate Sundays
in the chapel, in Welsh performed by the incumbent.

I & C: not resident.

(3) Ty'n y gwndwn.   Independents.
Erected before 1800.
Space: free 100; other 200; standing 100.
Present: aft. 250 + 100 scholars.

William Davies.   Deacon.

(4) Crybyn Chapel.   Unitarian.
Erected 1790.
Space: all free; standing about 500.
Present: even. 100.
Average (12 *months*): morn. and even. alternate Sundays 250.
Remarks: A Sunday School is sometimes kept, a singing one at present,
about 30 scholars. The service is held morn—even alternately.

John Jeremy. Occasional Minister.

(5) RHYDYGWIN. UNITARIAN.
Erected 1848.
Space: All free sittings sufficiently large to accommodate from 300 to 400 persons.
Present: aft. 100 + 30 scholars.
Average: general congregation 200 + 30 scholars.
Remarks: This Chapel was erected in lieu of a previously existing Building in the neighbourhood which was built in the year 1812.

Rees Davies.   Minister.

2   Cilcennin Parish.

Area: 3,405 acres. *Popn.* 294 males, 346 females: total 640.

(6) CARNE. WESLEYAN.
Space: free 12; other 9.
Present: even. 54 + 40 scholars.
Average: general congregation 54 + 40 scholars.

David M. Evans.
Assistant Overseer.

(7) CILCENNIN. INDEPENDENT.
Erected 1775.
Space: free none; other 41.
Present: morn. 400; aft. 150 scholars.

Thomas Jones.   Independent Minister.

(8) KILCENNIN PARISH CHURCH.
Endowed: land £5; tithe £50; glebe 2.
Other permanent endowment: Attached to Llanbadarn. Endowed Queen Anne's Bounty £40 per annum.
Space: free 120.
Present: morn. 100 + 20 scholars.
Average: 20 scholars.
Remarks: This is a Parish Church consolidated with Llanbadarn Trefeglwys.

James James.   Vicar.

Lewis: vicarial, consolidated with Llanbadarn Trefeglwys [596. 2. 7(22)]: impropriate tithes commuted for £106. 13. 4., and the vicarial for £53. 6. 8., with a glebe of 4 acres, valued at £4. Church rebuilt in 1835, cost defrayed by public contribution.

C & C: 1 service in Welsh performed by the incumbent.

I & C: resident.

3 Cilie-Aeron, or Kilie-Ayron Parish.
Area: 1,914 acres. *Popn.* 129 males, 173 females: total 302.

(9) CILIAU AYRON: ST. MICHAEL'S PARISH CHURCH.
Endowed: land £20; tithe £115.
Space: free 50; other 150.
Present: morn. 130.
Average: morn. 150.
Remarks: number of communicants 46.

William Hughes, M.A.   Rector.

Lewis: discharged rectory, rated at £5; endowed with £400 royal bounty: patron, the Bp.: tithes commuted for £115, subject to rates averaging £14. 4. 3½ p.a.

C & C: 1 service in Welsh performed by the incumbent.

I & C: resident.

(10) CILIAU CHAPEL.   UNITARIAN.
Erected about 1750.
Space: free 156; standing 100.
Present: morn. 70 + 15 scholars.
Average (12 *months*): morn. 80 + 20 scholars.

John Evans.   Deacon.
Bont.

4 Llanerch-ayron Parish.
Area: 1,606 acres. *Popn.* 117 males, 142 females: total 259.

(11) LLANERCHAERON PARISH CHURCH.
Endowed: land £73; tithes £160.
Space: total 140.
Present: morn. 15.
Remarks: This Church of Llanerchaeron was re-erected in the year 1797 at the expense of the Lewis family and parishioners.

Thomas Davies.   Curate.

Lewis: sub Llanychaeron: perpetual curacy, endowed with £600 royal bounty and £1,200 parliamentary grant; net income £73: alternate patrons, and the impropriators, Earl of Lisburne and Major Lewis: impropriate tithes commuted for £120.

C & C: 1 service, partially in English and Welsh, performed by the curate.

I & C: not resident: curate, who has stipend of £50, resides at Dihewid, 2 miles distant.

5 Henfynyw Parish.
Area: 2,261 acres. *Popn.* 394 males, 496 females: total 890.

(12)   TRINITY CHURCH CHAPEL OF EASE.
Built by subscription: total cost £700.
Licensed in 1838 as an additional Church to Henfynyw and Llanddewi Aberarth churches.
Endowed: £800 at interest; pew rents £15.
Sittings: free 60; other 200.
Present: morn. 45 + 65 scholars; aft 20 + 50 scholars.
Average: morn. 70 + 60 scholars; aft. 25 + 40 scholars.

Evan Jones.   Officiating Minister.

(13)   TABERNACLE.   CALVINISTIC METHODISTS.
Erected 1833.
Space: free 60; other 248; standing, 'none but alleys'.
Present: morn. 235; even. 294.
Average (12 *months*): morn. 220; even. 270.
Remarks: Most of our Congregation attend Sunday School. Many that are on the Sunday School's books are mariners being seldom at home and not included in the average.

Benjamin Evans.   Sec.
Timber Merchant.

(14)   HENFYNYW PARISH CHURCH.
Endowed: land £60.
Space: free 60; other 20.
Present: morn. 45 + 12 scholars.
Average: morn. 55 + 14 scholars.
Remarks: The Church was originally endowed with £800 Royal Bounty and £1,000 Parliamentary Grant some of which about the value of £60 per annum has been invested in land.   That is all I know about the income as I am authorised by the incumbent to collect that sum as part payment of my salary.

E. T. Evans.   Curate.

Lewis: perpetual curacy; endowed with £800 royal bounty £1,000 parliamentary grant; patron and appropriator, Precentor and Chapter St. David's Cathedral; incumbent has stipend of £8; net income £109.

C & C: 1 service in Welsh performed by the curate.

I & C: no return.

(15)   FFOS Y FFIN.   CALVC. METHS.
Erected before 1800.
Space: free 66; other 240; other 200 (sic).
Present: morn. 309; aft. 150 scholars; even. 160.
Average: morn. 252 + 100 scholars; aft. 190 + 150 scholars; even. 80.

David Hughes.   Deacon.

(16) NEUADDLWYD HENFENYW.   INDEPENDENTS.
Erected before 1800.
Space: free 72; other 390; standing 70.
Present: morn. 367 + 165 scholars.
Average: morn. 500 + 165 scholars; even. 600 + 200 scholars.
Remarks: No service but once but occasionally from 500 to 600 occasionally
165 on Sunday.

David Davies.   Deacon.

(17) HENFENYW, ABERAERON.
WESLEYAN METHODISTS.
A dwelling house.
Present: even. 35 + 10 scholars.

David Evans.   Wesleyan Minister.

6 Llanddewi-Aberarth Parish.
Area: 3,595 acres. *Popn.* 560 males, 724 females: total 1,284.

(18) LLANDDEWI ABERARTH PARISH CHURCH.
Endowed: land £91; tithe £6; other £21 7s. 2d.
Space: free 100; other 300.
Present: aft. 160.
Average: aft. 200.
Remarks: The Number of communicants average from 90 to 100. It is
impossible to state correctly the average number of attendants. I believe
the number stated is rather under than above the average.

Wm. Hughes, M.A.
Perpetual Curate.

Lewis: sub Llandewy-Aberarth: prepend in the cathedral church, rated at £10, in
the patronage of the bishop: perpetual curacy, endowed with £800 royal bounty and
£400 parliamentary grant: patron and appropriator, the Prebendary; tithes
commuted for £255; net income £100.

Note: Lewis also mentions a family chapel, dedicated to St. Alban, erected in 1809
by Rev. Alban Thomas Jones Gwynne, who endowed it with land worth £20 per
annum: perpetual curacy, endowed additionally with £200 royal bounty and £800
parliamentary grant: patron, proprietor of Ty-Gwyn estate.

C & C: 1 service in Welsh performed by the incumbent.

I & C: not resident.

(19) PENIEL.   INDEPENDENTS.
Erected 1833.
Space: free 60; other 318; standing 70.
Present: morn. 255; aft. 195 scholars; even. 270.
Average (12 months): morn. 280; aft. 220 scholars; even. 300.

William Evans.   Minister.

(20) TANYBRYN. CALVINISTIC METHODIST
Erected 1830.
Space: free.
Present: none.
Average: morn. 100 + 30 scholars.

John Phillips. Secretary.

[Endorsed: See Letter.]

(21) BETHEL, ABERARTH. CALVINISTIC METHODIST
Erected before 1800; rebuilt 1803.
Space: free 108; other 288; standing 10 sq. ft.
Present: morn. 174 scholars; aft. 268; even. 248.
Average (12 *months*): morn. 180 scholars: general congregation. 270.

Thomas Evans. Minister.

7 Llanbadarn-Tref-Eglwys Parish.
Area: 6,283 acres. *Popn.* 402 males, 533 females: total 965.

(22) LLANBADARN TREFEGLWYS PARISH CHURCH.
Tithe £150.
Space: free 30.
Present: morn. 200 + 124 scholars.
Average: morn. 124 scholars.

James Jones. Vicar.

Lewis: discharged vicarage, with that of Kilkennin [596. 2. 2(8)] annexed, rated at £6; endowed with £1,200 parliamentary grant; net income £70: patron and impropriator, the Bishop: tithes commuted for £245, of which £175 payable to the impropriator and £70 to the vicar.
C & C: 1 service in Welsh, performed by the incumbent.
I & C: resident.

(23) PENNANT MEETING HOUSE. CALVINISTIC METHODIST
Erected 1760.
Space: free 24; other 288; standing 25 square yards.
Present: morn. 217; even. 142.
Average: morn. 250 + 173 scholars; even. 160.

Thomas Lewis. Minister.

(24) BETHANIA. CALVINISTIC METHODIST
Erected 1809.
Space: free 78; other 216; standing 100.
Present: morn. 120 scholars; aft. 204.
Average: morn. 192 scholars; aft. 264.

Edward Evans. Deacon.

(25) PONTSAESON. CALVINISTIC METHODIST.
Erected 1824.
Space: free 57; other 104.
Present: morn. 105; even. 102.

David Jones. Deacon.

[Endorsed: See Letter.]

8 Llansantffraid Parish.
Area: 5,443 acres. *Popn.* 594 males, 692 females: total 1,286.

(26) LLANSANTFREAD PARISH CHURCH.
Endowed: tithe £92; glebe £6; other endowments £14.
Space: free 100; other 368.
Present: morn. 168 + 135 scholars; aft. 317 + 148 scholars.
Average (12 months): morn. 216 + 172 scholars; aft. 347 + 179 scholars

William Herbert. Minister.

Lewis: discharged vicarage, rated at £6. 13s. 4d; endowed with £400 parliamentary grant; net income £91: patron, the bishop: impropriators, Vicars Choral.

C & C: 2 services in Welsh performed by the incumbent.

I & C: resident.

(27) LLANNON. CALVINISTIC METHODIST.
Erected 1762.
Space: free 8; other 496.
Present: morn. 200 scholars; aft. 315; even. 409.
Average: general congregation 350; scholars 255.

Daniel Evans. Secretary.

(28) NEBO. INDEPENDENT.
Erected 1809; rebuilt 1833.
Space: free; other 150; standing 100.
Present: morn. 170; aft. 125 scholars; even. 120 (see below).
Average: church members, 96.
Remarks: Chiefly a place of worship, but it has been occasionally employed as a Day School. The Sunday School is always held therein. The Chapel will hold about 400 persons. Evening: Either a sermon or a prayer meeting at which on an average, 120 persons attend.
In this part, grown up persons and regular members of the churches as well as very young children regularly attend Sunday Schools.

Thomas Jones. Independent Minister.

[End of Llansantffraid Subdistrict and end of Aberayron District]

597   ABERYSTWYTH (District)

Area: 132,592 acres. *Popn.* 11,359 males, 12,394 females: total 23,753.

1 LLANRHYSTYD (Subdistrict)
Area: 22,403 acres. *Popn.* 1,615 males, 1,794 females: total 3,409.

1-2   Llanrhystyd Parish, consisting of [1] Haminiog Township and [2] Mefenydd Township.
Area: 8,770 acres. *Popn.* 712 males, 804 females: total 1,516.

Haminiog Township.
Popn. 412 mlaes, 451 females: total 863.

(1)   LLANRHYSTYD PARISH CHURCH.
[This return is missing.]
Lewis: discharged vicarage; rated at £6. 13. 4.: patron, the Bishop: tithes commuted for £620, of which £450 payable to the impropriators, Precentor and Chapter of St. David's, and £170 to the vicar.

C & C: 1 service in Welsh performed by the incumbent.

I & C: resident (Rev. John Lewis).

ICBS: grant of £160 in 1852.

(2)   CARMEL.   WELSH CALVINISTIC METHODIST.
Erected 1824.
Space: free 414; other 102; standing 20 feet by 10.
Present: morn. 277; even. 355.
Average (12 *months*): general congregation 350; scholars 331.
Remarks: 30 Pews in the Gallery.

> Joel [?] Rowlands.   Superintendent.
> Tanyrallt, Aberystwyth.

(3)   RHIWBWYS.   CALVINISTIC METHODIST.
Erected 1781: repaired 1820; rebuilt 1832.
Space: free 150; other 246; standing 150.
Present: morn. 360; aft. Sunday School; even. 288.
Average: morn. 450-500; even. 350-400.
Remarks: The attendance on the 30th was not so great as usual. Great many families being invalids. The chapel will accomodate from 500 to 550

comfortably. There are two other places in connection with this chapel at a distance of less than two miles each where sermons are delivered in one (Penrhiw) in the afternoon of every Sunday except in one in every six weeks when the minister officiates at Brynwyre. They are both School houses built for keeping Sunday School in. Another branch Sunday School in another direction is kept in a dwelling house called Hafod. Average attendance at Penrhiw about 200 Brynwyre about 100.

David Jacob Davies.   Deacon.
Pentremawr, Llanrhystyd.

(4)   PENRHIW TRAWSNANT.   CALVINISTIC METHODIST.
Erected 1834.
Space: free 100;   other 12;   standing 150.
Present: aft. 100 + 120 scholars.
Average (12 *months*): aft. 100 + 120 scholars.
Remarks: This place of worship belongs to Rhiwbwys. Sermon every Sunday afternoon and occasionally during the week. The Sunday School is held in the morning generally.

Thomas Evans.   Chief Manager.
Talwrn, Llanrhystyd.

2   Mefenydd Township.
Popn. 300 males, 353 females: total 653.

(5)   BRYNWYRE.   CALVINISTIC METHODIST.
Erected 1849.
Space: free 88;   standing 50.
Present: aft. 51 scholars.
Average: general congregation 'none but occasionally': aft. scholars 60.
Remarks: This house (Brynwyre) was entirely for Sunday School except public worship occasionally.

Edward Jones.
Sunday School Teacher.

(6)   SALEM.   BAPTIST.
Erected 1823.
Space: free 80;   other 87;   standing 50.
Present: morn. 28 + 15 scholars;   aft. 48 + 20 scholars;   even. Sunday School.
Average (12 *months*): morn. 40 + 20 scholars;   aft. 80 + 22 scholars, even. School.

John Dd. Jones.   Deacon.
Grocer, Llanrhystyd.

3 Llanddeiniol Parish.
Area: 2,077. *Popn.* 127 males, 124 females: total 251.

(7) Llanddeiniol Parish Church.
Consecrated about 16 years ago, in lieu of the old parish church;
Built principally at the expense of the Revd. Thomas Richards, a landed
proprietor of the parish.
Total cost probably £700.
Endowed: land £66; other sources £17.
Space: All free, ample accomodation.
Present: morn. 100.
Average (12 *months*): from 80 to 90.

John   Lewis.   Curate.

Lewis: Perpetual curacy; endowed with £1,000 royal bounty: net income £66:
patrons and impropriators, Earl of Lisburne and R. Price, Esq., alternatively;
tithes commuted for £123. 8. 4.
C & C: 1 service in Welsh performed by the curate.
I & C: no return.
ICBS: grant of £80 in 1834.

(8) Elim.   Calvinistic Methodist.
Erected 1832.
Space: free 32; other 181; standing 167.
Present: morn. 122 scholars; aft. 169; even. 102.
Remarks: The average number of attendants answers to the number of
March 30, 1831.

Evan Evans.   Deacon.
Spite, Llanddeiniol.

4 Llangrwyddon, or Llanygwyryfon Parish.
Area: 3,846 acres. *Popn.* 270 males, 325 females: total 595.

(9) Llangwyryfon Parish Church.
[Return missing.]
Lewis: Perpetual curacy; endowed with £800 royal bounty and £1,200 parlia-
mentary grant; net income £176: patron and impropriator J. P. B. Chichester, Esq.
C & C: 1 service in Welsh performed by the incumbent.
I & C: not resident (Rev. John Morgan).

(10) Tabor, Llangwiryfon.   Calvinistic Methodist.
Erected after 1800.
Space: free 60; other 200; standing 'it will accomodate 200 persons'.
Present: morn. 245; aft. 144 scholars; even. 183.
Average: general congregation 150; scholars 150.

Remarks: We have no particulars remarks to add except that great many of
the this congregation do occassionally attend Church. They are properly
Dissenters and many of them members of the forementioned chapel. But
church being near and its services commencing when that of the chapel is
finished they occassionally attend. The class of hearers would be in the
chapel were the two services held same time.

John James. Deacon.
Penycwm, Llangwiryfon.

(11) SARON, LLANGWYRYFON. INDEPENDENTS.
Erected 1843.
Space: free 48; other 24.
Present: aft. 60; even. 35.
Average: general congregation 60; scholars 30.
Remarks: In the morning at Saron's chapel, by 10 o'clock we have Sunday
School to be held always, and by 2 and 6 sermon is to be delivered. Today
in the morning in our Sunday School the scholars are 30 in number. The
congregation by 2 was 60 and 6, 35 in number.

Thomas Jones.
Independent Minister.

(12) BETHEL, LLANGWIRYFON. CALVINISTIC METHODIST.
Erected 1808.
Space: free 156; other 96; standing accomedation for 450 persons.
Present: morn. 100; aft. 208; even. 181.

David Jones. Deacon.
To be left at D. Jones, National Bank,
Aberystwyth.

**5-6 Llanilar Parish, consisting of [5] Lower Llanilar Township, and
[6] Upper Llanilar Tonwship.**
Area: 6,403 acres. *Popn.* 445 males, 479 females: total 924.

5 Lower Llanilar Township.
Popn. 225 males, 233 females: total 458.

(13) LLANILAR PARISH CHURCH.
[This return is missing.]

Lewis: discharged vicarage, rated at £6. 13. 4; net income £95, with glebe-house:
patron, the bishop: impropriator J. P. B. Chichester, Esq.
C & C: 1 service in Welsh performed by the incumbent, and additionally 1 service
in English on first Sunday of the month.

I & C: resident (Rev. Peter Felix).

[*Lewis* states that the parish contained 1 Calvinistic Methodist chapel.]

7 Rhostie Parish.
Area: 1,307 acres. *Popn.* 61 males, 62 females: total 123.

(14) RHOSTIE PARISH CHURCH.
[This return is missing.]

Lewis: sub Rhôsdiau: discharged rectory, rated at £1. 6. 8; endowed with £200 royal bounty; net income £101: patron, the bishop: tithes commuted for £63, subject to rates averaging £5; glebe of 40 acres valued at £21. 10. 0. per annum. Church rebuilt in 1818.

C & C: 1 service in Welsh performed by the incumbent and curate.

I & C: not resident: curate, who has stipend of £40, resides at Lledrod, 2½ miles distant.

[*End of Llanrhystyd Subdistrict*]

2 ABERYSTWYTH (Subdistrict)
Area: 15,440 acres. *Popn.* 3,862 males, 4,580 females: total 8,442.

1 Llanychaiarn Parish.
Area: 4,181 acres. *Popn.* 260 males, 278 females: total 538.

(1) LLANGORWEN CHURCH, LLANBADARN FAWR PARISH.
Erected: 'ten years ago'.
Space: free 400.
Present: morn. 150 scholars; even. 200.
[no signature]
[Informant's form]

C & C: 2 services in Welsh performed by the incumbent and curate.

I & C: resident (Rev. Lewis Gilbertston): curate has stipend of £70.

[Note: this should be included under 597. 2. 8.]

(2) LLANYCHAIARN CHURCH, LLANBADARN FAWR PARISH.
Erected 'about 200 hundred years'.
Space: free 200.
Present: morn. about 50; aft. about 100.
[no signature]
[Informant's form]

Lewis: perpetual curacy, endowed with £600 royal bounty; net income £97: patron and impropriator J. P. B. Chichester, Esq.

C & C: 1 service in Welsh performed by the incumbent.

I & C: resident (Rev. John Morgan).

(3) BLAENPLWY CHAPEL, LLANYCHAIARN.   CALFINISTIC METHODIST.
Erected 1819
Space: free 132; other 116; standing 120.
Present: morn. 172; aft. 201 scholars; even. 224.
Remarks: Average of atendans for the preceeding twelve months answers to
the attendance on March 30, 1851.

> William Rowlands.
> Cwrt-y-cwm, Llanychaiarn.

**2-9   Part of Llanbadarn-Fawr Parish, consisting of [2] the Chapelry
and Borough of Aberystwyth, and the townships of [3] Uchayndre, [4]
Issayndre, [5] Upper Vainor, [6] Lower Vainor, [7] Broncastellau, [8]
Clarach, and [9] Lower Llanbadarn-y-Croyddin.**
Area: 11,259 acres. *Popn.* 3,602 males, 4,304 females: total 7,904.

2   Aberystwyth Borough: Chapelry.
Area: 734 acres. *Popn.* 2,284 males, 2,905 females: total 5,189.

(4) ST. MICHAEL'S CHAPEL, ABERYSTWYTH.
Rebuilt and enlarged 1833 by the inhabitants.
Total cost: £4,335.
Defrayed by Parliamentary grant £1,000, private subscription £3,335.
Endowed: land £33; other endowments £18; pew rents £134; fees £8;
other sources £13.
Space: free 529; other 591.
Present: morn. (English) 600 + 60 scholars; aft. (Welsh) 320; even.
(English) 450.
Average (12 *months*): morn. (English) 700 + 60 scholars; aft. (Welsh)
320; even. (English) 600.
Remarks: The English and Welsh congregations are quite distinct.

> J. Hughes. Vicar of Llanbadarn Fawr.

Lewis: sub. Aberystwyth: perpetual curacy; endowed with £600 royal bounty, and
£400 parliamentary grant; net income £139: patron, Vicar of Llanbadarn Fawr.
The chapel built by subscription in 1797; another church recently (1833) built by
subscription aided by £1,000 grant from parliamentary commissioners and £400
from Society for Enlargement of Churches.

C & C: sub Aberystwyth: 4 services, 2 in Welsh and 2 in English performed by
the incumbent and curate.

I & C: sub Aberystwyth: incumbent (John Hughes) resident: curate (David
Joseph Jones) has stipend of £90.

ICBS: grant of £400 in 1829.

(5)   A LICENSED SCHOOL HOUSE, CHAPELRY OF ABERYSTWYTH.
Licensed by the Bishop for divine service.
Remarks: It is neither church nor chapel, therefore no person is consecrated
caused to be Licensed Because the Welsh part of the population had no
place to assemble for divine worship on Sunday evenings. It was erected
above 50 or 60 years of age—by public subscription for a sermon or school.
Not endowed at all.
Space: about 400 all free.
Present: even. 400.
Average (12 *months*): even. 400.

					J. Hughes. Incumbent of Aberystwyth

(6) and (7)
These returns are in respect of chapels in the parish of Aberystwyth, co.
Monmouth, and are to be found between 578. 5 and 578. 6.

(8)   SOAR, LEWIS TERRACE, ABERYSTWYTH.   WESLEYAN METHODIST
ASSOCIATION.
Erected 1839.
Space: free 84; other 174; standing 400.
Present: morn. 52; aft. 72; even. 98.
Average: morn. 52; aft. 72; even. 98.

					William Roberts. Minister.
					Chapel House, Lewis Terrace.

(9)   TABERNACLE, MILL STREET.   WELSH CALVINISTIC METHODIST.
Erected 1785.
Space: free 400; other 840; standing 'no free space except the aisles'.
Present: morn. 680; even. 1,022.
Remarks: The Bulk of our Congregation attend the Sunday School; there-
fore could not accurately make the distinction required under the 8th head.

					Edward Jones. Minister.

(10)   WESLEYAN ENGLISH CHAPEL, LEWIS TERRACE.
Erected 1846.
Space: free 166; standing 90.
Present: morn. 15 + 7 scholars; even. 16 + 6 scholars.
Remarks: In Summer the 'general congregation' is larger—arising from the
influx of Visitors.

					Geo. Williams. Leader (by Authority of
					the Minister).
					Custom House.

(11)   BETHEL CHAPEL, BAKER STREET.   BAPTIST.
Erected 1798; rebuilt 1833.
Space: free 150; other 500.

Present: morn. 205; aft. 244 scholars; even. 388.
Average (12 *months*)*:* morn. 200; aft. 260-300 scholars; even. 400-450.
Remarks: Many of the congregation are seafaring men and cannot attend every Sunday. When they are at home the congregation may be about 500.

> Edward Williams. Minister.
> 2 Portland Street.

(12) GOSEN. CALFINISTICK METHODIST.
Erected before 1800; rebuilt 1824.
Space: free none; other 240; standing 150.
Present: morn. 250 + 291 scholars; aft. 390 + 291 scholars; even. 390 + 291 scholars.
Average: the same.

> Isaac Rowlands. Elder.
> Abermaide.

(13) MORIAH. BAPTIST.
Erected 1828.
Space: free 30; other 102; standing 72 feet.
Present: morn. 50; aft. 46 scholars; even. 59.

> Lewis Lewis. Deacon.
> Tanyfron.

(14) SALEM. INDEPENDENT.
Erected 1826.
Space: [endorsed: See letter].
Present: morn. 96 scholars; aft. 190; even. 180.
Average: morn. 131 scholars; aft. 220; even. 180.

> R. W. Roberts. Minister.
> Clarach.

(15)
This return is in respect of Zion Chapel, Ebbw Vale in the parish of Aberystruth, co. Monmouth, for which see above 578. 5, p.60.

(16) QUEEN STREET CHAPEL. WESLEYAN METHODIST.
Erected before 1810; rebuilt 1842.
Space: free 180; other 504; standing 500.
Present: morn. 281; aft. 260 scholars; even. 464.
Average (12 *months*)*:* morn. 300; aft. 310 scholars; even. 550.
Remarks: All the services in this Chapel are performed in the Welsh Language.

> David Lloyd. Leader.
> Great Dark Gate Street.

(17) SION CHAPEL, TOWN OF ABERYSTWYTH. INDEPENDENTS.
Erected 1823.
Space: free 150; other 320.
Present: morn. 152; even. 238.

John Saunders. Minister.

(18) SOAR, LLANBADARN FAWR VILLAGE. THE INDEPENDENTS.
Erected 1803.
Space: free 70; other 214.
Present: morn. Sunday School; even. 160.
Average (12 *months*): aft. 200; even. 160.
Remarks: Great many persons were absent of reason of the small pox and other complaints; and others of reason of poverty wanting clothes fit to attend. The Sunday Scholars use to attend very well.

Benjamin Rees. Minister.
Llanbadarnfawr.

5   Upper Vainor Township in the parish of Llanbadarn-Fawr.
Area: 1,459 acres. *Popn.* 225 males, 220 females: total 445.

(19) DEWI CHAPEL, TOWNSHIP OF VAINOR UPPER. CALVINISTIC METHODIST
Erected about 1810.
Space: free 90; other 210; standing 200.
Present: morn. school 1,42; aft. sermon 332. even. prayer meeting 210.
Average: general congregation 152.
Remarks: The Sunday School is usual to be from 152 to 169.

John Davies. Deacon.
Cefn y Vainor.

6   Lower Vainor Township in the parish of Llanbadarn Fawr.
Area: 1,148 acres. *Popn.* 104 males, 113 females: total 217.

(20) CWMYNSCOCH, DISTRICT OF VAINOR. INDEPENDENTS.
Space: free 150.
Present: morn. 70 + 52 scholars; even. 60.
Average (12 *months*): general congregation 60; scholars 48.

Benjamin Rees. Minister.
Llanbadarnfawr.

8   Clarach Township, in the parish of Llanbadarn Fawr.
Area: 1,702 acres. *Popn.* 121 males, 119 females: total 240.

(21) CLARACH. [ANGLICAN]
['schoolroom?' (in another Land)].

It is neyther consecrated or licensed prayer meetings only being held in it every Sunday evening.

Erected by the late Hugh Jones, Esq. and other gentlemen from London.

Sittings: free 140?

Present: aft. 67; even. 136.

There is no service kept in the morning, the congregation attending Llanbadarn parish Church.

> William Herbert.   Schoolmaster.
> Clarach.

[Note: Llangorwen church [597. 2. 1(1)] should be included here.]
Note also that the following return is included under 605. 2. 8 (Llanbadarn FawrParish, Nantmel Subdistrict, Rhayadr District, county of Radnor).

HEPHZEBAH (?).   INDEPENDENT.

Erected 1837.

Space: other 35.

Present: morn. 82; aft. 60 scholars; even. 80.

Average (12 *months*): morn. 70 scholars, aft. 165; even. 150.

> R. W. Roberts.   Minister.
> Clarach, Aberystwyth.

4 Issayndre Township, parish of Llanbadarn Fawr.

Area: 730 acres (with (3) Uchayndre): *Popn.* 163 males, 215 females: total 378.

(22) SARON CHAPEL. WELSH CALVINISTIC METHODIST.

Erected 1842.

Space: free 200; other 144.

Present: morn. 110 scholars; aft. 140; even. 102.

> John Davies.   Superintendent.
> Cefnllau.

9 Lower Llanbadarn-y-Croyddin Township, in the parish of Llanbadarn Fawr.

Area: 4,981 acres. *Popn.* 425 males, 414 females: total 839.

(23) BEULAH, DYFFRYN POETH. INDEPENDENT.

Erected 1842.

Space: free 40; other 80.

Present: morn. 50 + 48 scholars; aft. 38; even. 69.

Average (12 *months*): general congregation 50; scholars 48.

Remarks: Several persons absent by reason of illness.

> Benjamin Rees.   Minister.
> Llanbadarnfawr.

[End of Aberystwyth Subdistrict]

3 GENEUR-GLYNN (Subdistrict)
Area: 32,290 acres. *Popn.* 2,182 males, 2,320 females: total 4,502.

1 Elerch Township, part of Llanbadarn Fawr Parish.
Area: 4,173 acres. *Popn.* 112 males, 98 females: total 210.
[No returns]

2-6 Part of Llanfihangel-Geneur-Glynn Parish, consisting of the townships of [2] Henllys, [3] Cynnill-Mawr, [4] Ceulan-y-Maes-Mawr, [5] Cyfoeth-y-Brenin, and [6] Tir-y-Mynach.

2 Henllys Township.
Area: 5.144 acres. *Popn.* 240 males, 219 females: total 459.

(1) Llanfihangel Geneu'r glyn Parish Church.
Endowed: tithe £224.
Space: free 100; other 400.
Average attendance: morn. 420; aft. 276 scholars; even. 150.
Remarks: There are two schoolrooms in the Parish which have been licensed by the Bishop for the purpose of performing Divine Service therein and this is done once in each every Sunday at 4 and 6 o'clock p.m. Estimate number attending at each is 100.

John Jones. Vicar.

Lewis: discharged vicarage, rated at £12; net income £221, with a glebe-house: patron, the Bishop; impropriator, T. P. Chichester, Esq. Part of township of Cyfoeth-y-Brenin pays the great tithes to the vicar, who receives ¼ of the small tithes of the parish.
C & C: 2 services in Welsh performed by the incumbent.
I & C: with Llanfihangel Edwin's Chapelry [606. 1. 1.( )]; resident; curate has stipend of £60.

(2) Eglwysfach.
A Chapel of Ease built about two hundred years ago, rebuilt and enlarged 1834.
Erected by grant of £150 from the Incorporated Society for Building Churches, by private subscription £250, by Parochial Rate £100; Total cost £500.
Endowed: land £80.
Space: free 110; other 310.
Present: aft. 120 + 40 scholars.
Average (12 *months*): aft. 130 + 40 scholars.

John Davies. Curate.

[This return lacks the parish numeration: it is numbered 597. 3. (2). It is misplaced, and should be numbered under Machynlleth, i.e. 606. 1. 1( ), township of Scybor-y-Coed, parish of Llanfihangel-Geneur-Glynn, District and Subdistrict of Machynlleth.]

Lewis: Eglwys-Vâch, or Llanvihangel-Capel-Edwin: perpetual curacy, endowed with £800 royal bounty; patron, Mrs. Jane Davies: net income, £80: impropriator, T. P. Chichester, Esq.

C & C: 1 service in Welsh performed by the curate.

I & C: See *sub* Llanfihangel Geneu'r Glyn [597. 3. 2(1)].

ICBS: grant of £150 in 1831.

(3) PENYGARN. CALVINISTIC METHODIST.
Erected '20 years'.
Space: free 450.
Average number of attendants: morn. 400; aft. 200 scholars; even. 420.

> William James. Informant.
> Rhydypene.

[Informant's form.]

(4) LLANCYNFELYN PARISH CHURCH.
Endowed: parliamentary grant £80.
Space: free 100; other 19.
Present: morn. 80; even. 60.
Average (12 months): morn. 120 + 20 scholars; even. 80 + 15 scholars.

> John Davies. Perpetual curate.

[Endorsed: See Letter.]

Lewis: perpetual curacy; net income £83; patron and impropriator, J. P. B. Chichester, Esq.

C & C: 2 services in Welsh performed by the incumbent.

I & C: resident.

ICBS: grant of £20 in 1834.

[Note: this return is misplaced, and should be under 597. 3. 7. For details of population and remainder of parish returns see below p.41.]

(5) MORFA'R BORTH CHAPEL OF EASE UNDER LLANFIHANGEL GENEU'R GLYN CHURCH.
Erected 'about 15 years'.
Space: free 400.
Usual number of attendants: morn. none, no Sunday School, aft. 250, even. none.

> John James. Informant.

[Informant's form.]

(6) RHYDMEIRIONYDD. [ANGLICAN]
Erected '15 years'.
Usual number of attendants: aft. 45 scholars. even. 70.

> John James. Informant.

[Informant's form.]

3 Cynnill-Mawr Township.

Area: 3,748 acres. *Popn.* 306 males, 309 females: total 615.

(7) DOLYBONT SCHOOL HOUSE USED AS AN OCCASIONAL PLACE OF WORSHIP.
CALVINISTIC METHODIST.
Erected May 1848.
Used for a Day School and Sunday School.
Space: 7 forms or benches across building: standing 21 feet by 6 feet.
Present: morn. 'S. School'; even. 110.
Average: even. 120 or 130.
Remarks: The building is 21 feet long by 21 feet broad and 12 feet in height,
furnished with 7 forms across the building containing room for 15 persons to
sit on each form. The space for standing room is furnished with 3 small
forms. Sunday Scholars included.

> Jenkin Jenkins. Superintendant of
> Sunday School.

(8) PENYGARN. CALVINISTIC METHODIST.
Erected 'before 1800'.
Space: free 75; other 366; standing 100.
Present: morn. 329; aft. 262 scholars; even. 397.

> Thomas James. Deacon.
> Tynyrhos, Nr. Rhydypene.

[This is a duplicate return for 597. 3. 1(3) above.]

4 Ceulan-y-Maes-Mawr Township

Area: 7,439 acres. *Popn.* 358 males, 349 females: total 707.

(9) BETHEL, TALYBONT. INDEPENDENTS.
Erected 1805.
Space: free 154; other 470; standing 218.
Present: morn. 396; aft. 325 scholars; even. 447.

> Owen Thomas. Independent Minister.
> Talybont.

(10) TABERNACLE, TALYBONT. BAPTISTS.
Erected 1812.
Space: free 84; other 228; standing 150.
Present: morn. 125 scholars; aft. 173; even. 157.

> John Evans. Baptist Minister.
> Talybont.

(11) SILOH, PANTYGEIFR. BAPTIST.
Erected 1845.
Present: morn. 38 scholars; even. 66.
Average (12 months): morn. general congregation 120; scholars 56.

Evan Roberts.

5 Cyfoeth-y-Brenin Township.
Area: 2,514 acres. *Popn.* 530 males, 672 females: total 1,202.

(12) BORTH. CALVINISTIC METHODIST.
Erected 1831.
Space: other 111.
Present: morn. 298 scholars; aft. 354; even. 295.
Average: morn. 454 + 335 scholars; aft. 433; even. 397.

Lumley Edwards. Steward.
Glanlery, Borth.

(13) SHILO. WESLEYAN METHODISTS.
Erected 1832, rebuilt and enlarged 1842.
Space: free 64; other 225; standing 120.
Present: morn. 94 scholars; aft. 161; even. 149.
Average (12 months): morn. 164 scholars; aft. 308; even. 320.
Remarks: All the services here are performed in the Welsh language.

John Lloyd. Leader.
(Rev. J. Lloyd, Wesleyan Minister.)

6 Tyr-y-Mynach Township.
Area: 2,716 acres. *Popn.* 162 males, 188 females: total 350.

(14) BONTGOCH. WESLEYAN METHODISTS.
Erected 1836.
Space: free 48; other 66; standing 80.
Present: morn. 79; aft. 64 scholars; even. 62.
Average (12 months): morn. 85; aft. 55 scholars; even. 90.
Remarks: All the services are performed in the Welsh language.

William Rees. Secretary.
Mill, Bontgoch.

7 Llancynfelin Parish.
Area: 6,556 acres. *Popn.* 474 males, 485 females: total 959.
[For the return of the Parish Church see 597. 3. 2(4).]

(15) SOAR. WESLEYAN METHODISTS.
Erected: 1806; rebuilt 1845.
Space: free 44; other 206; standing 80.
Present: morn. 114; aft. 184 scholars; even. 213.
Average: morn. 150 + 130 scholars; aft. 250 + 200 scholars; even. 270.

> Thomas Jones. Class Leader.
> Post Office, Taliesin.

(16) REHABOTH. CALVINISTIC METHODIST.
Erected 1833.
Space: free 48; other 264; standing 60.
Present: morn. 159 scholars; aft. 228; even. 178.
Average (12 *months*): morn. 150 scholars; aft. 250; even. 260.

> Thomas Davies. Elder.
> Taliesin.

[End of Geneur-Glynn Subdistrict]

4 RHEIDOL (Subdistrict)
Area: 62,459 acres. *Popn.* 3,700 males, 3,700 females: total 7,400.

1-5   Part of Llanbadarn-Fawr Parish, consisting of the townships of [1] Upper Llanbadarn-y-Croyddin, [2] Cwmrheidol, [3] Melindwr, [4] Parcel Canol, and [5] Trefeirig.
Area: 37,318 acres. *Popn.* 2,396 males, 2,266 females: total 4,662.

1   Upper Llanbadarn-y-Croyddin Township.
Area: 9,342 acres. *Popn.* 458 males, 483 females: total 941.

(1) LLANBADARN FAWR VICARAGE.
Endowed: land £105; glebe, 4 acres and a house and garden.
Other endowments: £20 from Lay impropriator; fees about £20.
Space: free 886; other 14.
Present: morn. 415 + 35 scholars; aft. 60 + 40 scholars.
Average (12 *months*): morn. 500 + 35 scholars. aft. 60 + 40 scholars.

> J. Hughes. Vicar.

Lewis: discharged vicarage, rated at £20: endowed with £450 private benefaction; net income £135, with a glebe-house: patron, the bishop; impropriator, J. P. Brice Chichester, Esq.
C & C: 2 services in Welsh performed by the incumbent and curate.
I & C: resident: curate (Morgan Evans) has stipend of £90.

(2) SALEM. DECENTERS.
Erected 'near the year 1840'.
Usual number of attendants: morn. 300 + 40 scholars; aft. 260.
Remarks: Small School Upper Salem is included in Salem School.

[no signature.]

[Informant's form.]

(3) HOREB, PENRHYNCOCH. BAPTIST.
Erected before 1800.
Space: free 30; other 210.
Present: morn. 240; aft. 174 scholars; even. 235.

William Jones. Deacon.
Tynllechwedd, Penrhyncoch.

(4) ABERFFRWD CHAPEL. CALVINISTIC METHODIST.
Erected 1835.
Space: free 78; other 180.
Present: morn. 199; aft. 216 scholars; even. 220.
Average (12 *months*): morn. 200; aft. 200 scholars; even. 210.
Remarks: I Division 8 [Present] the number of Sunday School Teachers,
being 30, is not included.

Evan Evans. Minister.
Abernant, Cwmrheidol.

2 Cwmrheidol Township.
Area: 7,824 acres. *Popn.* 541 males, 525 females: total 1,066.

(5) YSTUMTIEN. WESLEYAN METHODIST.
Erected 1821: enlarged 1839.
Space: free 150; other 156; standing 150.
Present: morn. 217; aft. 210 scholars; even. 163.
Remarks: All the services here are performing in the Welsh Language.

John Jones. Leader.
Joiner, Ystymtien.

(6) PONTERWYD. CALVINISTIC METHODIST.
Erected before 1800.
Space: free 85; other 30; standing 52.
Present: morn. 185 scholars; aft. 218; even. 182.
Average (12 *months*): morn. 270; aft. 300 scholars; even. 250.

John Stephens. Deacon.
Grocer, Ponterwyd.

3   Melindwr Township.
Area: 6,677 acres. *Popn.* 596 males, 555 females: total 1,151.

(7)   BANGOR CHAPEL OF EASE.
Consecrated 1839.
Erected by the late Richard Jones, Aberystwyth.
Cost: by subscription £700.
Space: free 200; other 200.
Present: morn. 80 + 70 scholars.

John Thomas Morgan.   Warden.
Tynllidiart.

(8)   SION.   CALVINISTIC METHODIST.
Erected 1826.
Space: free 60; other 162.
Present: morn. 184 scholars; aft. 211; even. 100.
Average (12 *months*)*:* morn. 184 scholars; aft. 200; even. 200.

John Davies.   Elder.
Bryn [. . . .]

(9)   JEZREEL, GOGINAN.   BAPTIST.
Erected 1842.
Space: free 72; other 228.
Present: morn. 79 scholars; aft. 190; even. 187.

David Jenkins.   Baptist Minister.

(10)   PENLLWYN.   CALVINISTIC METHODIST.
Erected 1790.
Space: uncompleted inside, building inside 54 ft. by 42 ft.
Present: morn. 271; aft. 249 scholars; even. 354.
Average (12 *months*)*:* morn. 320; afr. 266 scholars; even. 340.
Remark: This chapel is now bring rebuild the third time. It is yet only completed the outside.

Thomas Edwards.   Minister.
Trering.

(11)   DYFFRYN CHAPEL.   CALVINISTIC METHODIST.
Erected 1842.
Space: free 96 feet of sitting room; other 30 seats of 7 feet long; standing 232 squ. feet.
Present: morn. 209; aft. 225 scholars; even. 197.
Average (6 *months*)*:* morn. 220 scholars; aft. 230; even. 230.

John Edwards.   Deacon.
Blaendyffryn, Goginan.

5 Trefeirig Township.
Area: 9,150 acres. *Popn.* 478 males, 409 females: total 887.

(12) CWMSYMLOG. BAPTIST.
Erected 1843.
Space: free 54; other 84.
Present: morn. 89; aft. 75 scholars; even. 93.

David Jenkins.   Baptist Minister.

6 Llanafan Parish.
Area: 2,588 acres. *Popn.* 198 males, 221 females: total 419.

(13) LLANAVAN PARISH CHURCH.
Space: free 150; other 72.
Usual number of attendants: morn. 70 + 50 scholars; even. 60.

[No signature.]

[Informant's form.]

Lewis: perpetual curacy; net income £97: patron and impropriator, J. P. B. Chichester, Esq. Rebuilding of church completed in 1840 at expense of the parish, liberally assisted by the Church Building Commissioners and local benefactors.

C & C: sub Llanavanytrawscoed: 3 services in 2 Sundays, 1 a fortnight in English and 2 a fortnight in Welsh performed by the curate.

I & C: no return.

ICBS: grant of £100 in 1839.

(14) CHAPEL AVAN. CALVINISTIC METHODIST.
Erected about 1808.
Present: morn. 180; aft. 188 scholars; even. 188.
Average: morn. 184; aft. 188 + 180 scholars; even. 188.
Remark: Attending Divine service on March 30 1851 in the Morning 150, in the Evening 130.

John Davies }
John Hughes } Elders.

7-8 Llanfihangel-y-Croyddin Parish, consisting of [7] Lower Llanfihangel-y-Croyddin Township and [8] Upper Llanfihangel-y-Croyddin, or Eglwys Newydd Chapelry.
Area of the whole parish: 22,553 acres. *Popn.* 1,106 males, 1,213 females: total 2,319.

7 Lower Llanfihangel-y-Croyddin Township.
Area: 6,592 acres. *Popn.* 446 males, 485 females: total 931.

(15)   LLANFIHANGEL Y CROYDDIN PARISH CHURCH.
Erected 'about the year 651'.
Space: free 288; other 78.
Usual number of attendants: morn. 250 + 35 scholars; aft. school; even. 120.

[No signature.]

[Informant's form.]
Lewis: discharged vicarage, rated at £8: endowed with £200 royal bounty; net income £126: patron, the bishop; impropriator, T. P. Chichester, Esq.
C & C: 2 services in Welsh performed by the incumbent.
I & C: *sub* Llanvihangel y Croythin, alias Gelindrod: resident.

(16)   CYNON.   CALVINISTIC METHODIST.
Erected 1821.
Space: free 72; other 276.
Usual number of attendants: morn. 400 + 60 scholars; aft. 600; even. 300.

John Jenkins.   Informant.
Llwyn y brain, Nr. Llanfihangel-y-Croyddin.

[Informant's form.]

(17)   CARMEL.   WESLEYAN METHODISTS.
Erected 1843.
Space: free 60; other 100.
Present: morn. 59; aft. 76; even. 106.

John Hopkins.   Preacher.
Cnwch Coch, Llanfihangel Upper.

8   Upper Llanfihangel-y-Croyddin, or Eglwys Newydd Chapelry.
Area: 15,961 acres. *Popn.* 660 males, 728 females: total 1,388.

(18)   YSPYTTY CENVIN.
'Erected 1400 as far as known'.
Space: free 114; other 60.
Usual number of attendants: aft. 65.

[no signature.]

[Informant's form.]
Lewis: sub Llanbadarn Fawr: chapel of ease; perpetual curacy.
C & C: 1 service in Welsh performed by the incumbent.
I & C: resident.
ICBS: grant of £60 in 1835.

[Note: there is no return for Eglwys Newydd in this parish.]
Lewis: perpetual curacy, endowed with £1,000 royal bounty and £1,200 parliamentary grant; net income £97, derived partly from tithes and partly from a rate

estimated according to an old survey. Church built by Mr. Johnes of Hafod; rebuilt in 1841: patron, Duke of Newcastle.

C & C: 2 services, Welsh in the morn., English in the aft., performed by the incumbent.

I & C: resident.

(19) CWMYSTWYTH. CALVINISTIC METHODIST.
Erected 1835.
Space: free 120; other 252; standing—free space or floor may accomodate 120.
Present: morn. 170 scholars; aft. 306; even. 205.
Average: general congregation 400; scholars 307.

> John Thomas. Member of the Society.
> Gwarallt, Cwmystwyth.

(20) TRISAINT CHAPEL. CALVINISTIC METHODIST.
Erected 1820: rebuilt 1850.
Present: morn. 217; aft. 93 scholars; even. 174.
Average (12 *months*): morn. 300; aft. 110 scholars.
Remarks: The sittings is not let yet they are 40 in number.

> William Mason. Deacon.
> Nantgwyn.
> Nr. Devil's Bridge.

(21) FRONGOCH. WESLEYAN METHODISTS.
Space: free 40; other none; standing 20.
Present: morn. 30 + 16 scholars; aft. 33; even. 32.
Average (12 *months*): morn. 30 + 16 scholars; aft. 30; even. 30.

> J. Collins.

(22) SALEM. WESLEYAN METHODIST.
Erected 1812.
Space: free 35; other 175; standing 50.
Present: morn. 67 scholars; aft. 121; even. 52.
Average: morn. 80 scholars; aft. 150; even. 120.

> John Davies.

[End of Rheidol Subdistrict and Aberystwyth District]

Area: 122,050 acres. *Popn.* 4,903 males, 5,501 females: total 10,404.

1 GWNNWS (Subdistrict)
Area: 33,140 acres. *Popn.* 1,524 males, 1,623 females: total 3,147.

1-2 Llanfihangel Lledrod Parish, consisting of the townships of [1] Lower Lledrod and [2] Upper Lledrod.
Area: 8,692 acres. *Popn.* 535 males, 583 females: total 1,118.

1 Lower Lledrod Township.
Popn. 277 males, 307 females: total 584.

(1) RHYDLWYD. CALVINISTIC METHODIST.
Erected 1833.
Space: other 342; standing 24 ft. by 15.
Present: morn. 262; aft. 306 scholars; even. 241.
Average: morn. 330; aft. 350 scholars; even. 300 scholars (sic).

John Rees. Minister.
Tregaron.

(2) BRONNANT. CALVINISTIC METHODIST.
Erected 1836.
Space: free 78; other 210; standing 250.
Present: morn. 103 scholars; aft. 185; even. 117.
Remark: Present in the Sunday School including teachers 126.

David Daniel. Deacon.
Bwadrain, Lledrod.

2 Upper Lledrod Township.
Popn. 258 males, 276 females: total 534.

(3) BETHEL SWYDDFYNNON. BABTIST.
Erected 1823.
Present: morn. 50; aft. 50 scholars; even. 90.
Average: morn. 50; aft. 50; even. 90.

Robert Roberts. Babtist Minister.
Penlan.

(4)   SWYDDFYNNON.   CALVINISTIC METHODIST.
Erected 1837 'in lieu of one erected about 50 years before'.
Space: other 300.
Present: morn. 137 scholars; aft. 150; even. 50.
Average: morn. 137 scholars; aft. 250; even. 70.
Remark: The reason of so little on March 30th were there was an Imersion
by the Baptist on the same hour and many of the young went to see the
same.

> David Meredith.   Elder or Deacon.
> Ffosybleiddiaid.

**3-4   Gwnnws Parish, consisting of the townships of [3] Lower
Gwnnws, and [4] Upper Gwnnws.**
Area: 17,959 acres. *Popn.* 585 males, 588 females: total 1,173.

3   Lower Gwnnws Township.
Popn. 263 males, 268 females: total 531.

(5)   GWNNWS PARISH CHURCH.
Space: free 595.
Present: morn. about 200.
Average: morn. about 300.
Remarks: The 30th of March was very rainy and boisterous.

> William Hughes.   Minister.
> Tregaron.

Lewis: sub Llanwnws: perpetual curacy; endowed with £800 royal bounty and
£1,400 parliamentary grant; net income £106; patron T. P. B. Chichester, Esq.
Church built in 1829.
C & C: 1 service in Welsh performed by the curate.
I & C: not resident.
ICBS: grant of £150 in 1851.

4   Upper Gwnnws Township.
Popn. 322 males, 320 females: total 642.

(6)   CARMEL.   BAPTIST.
Erected 1836.
Space: free 54; other 216; standing 404 feet.
Present: morn. 110; aft. 450; even. 250.
Average (12 months): morn. 110; aft. 300; even. 250.

> David Jenkins.   Deacon.
> Pontrhydfendigaid.

(7)   PENUEL, PONTRHYDFENDIGAID.   WELSH CALVINISTIC METHODIST.
Erected before 1800.
Space: free 78; other 252; standing 27 feet by 15.
Present: morn. 409 scholars; aft. 206; even. 203.
Average (12 *months*): morn. 350; aft. 455 scholars; even. 400.

> James Morgan.   Deacon.
> Pontrhydfendigaid.

5   Yspytty-Ystwyth Parish.

Area: 5,544 acres. *Popn.* 343 males, 375 females: total 718.

(8)   YSPYTTY YSTWYTH PARISH CHURCH.
Endowed: land £80; fees £1.
Space: free 250.
Present: morn. 100 + 40 scholars.
Average (12 *months*): morn. 150 + 35 scholars.

> J. W. Morris.   Perpetual Curate.
> Ystradmeuric.

Lewis: perpetual curacy with that of Yspytty-Ystrad-Meuric [598. 1. 6(10)] annexed: endowed with £800 royal bounty; net income £86: patron, earl of Lisburne.
C & C: no return.
I & C: no return.

(9)   YSYTTY YSTWYTH CHAPEL, YSBYTTY [Ystwyth: deleted] ESTRAD MEURIG.   CALVINISTIC METHODIST.
Erected: the first chapel 1818, the second 1845.
Space: other 240; standing 86.
Present: morn. 152; aft. 186 scholars; even. 167.
Average: morn. 216 scholars; aft. 231; even. 192.

> David Morgan.   Minister.

[Note: this return should be under 598. 1. 6.]

6   Yspytty-Ystrad-Meiric Parochial Chapelry.

Area: 945 acres. *Popn.* 61 males, 77 females: total 138.

(10)   YSTRADMEURIC CHAPEL OF EASE.   ANGLICAN.
Present: morn. 100 + 40 scholars.
Average: even. 60.

> J. W. Morris.   Incumbent.

Lewis: served by the incumbent of Yspytty-Ystwyth or his curate: no separate endowment: impropriate tithes commuted for £37. 7s. subject to rates averaging £3.
C & C: *sub.* Spytty Ystwith, no return.
I & C: no return.

> [*End of Gwnnws Subdistrict*]

2 LLANGEITHIO (Subdistrict)
Area: 21,622 acres. *Popn.* 1,555 males, 1,738 females: total 3,293.

1 Llanbadarn-Odwyn Parish.
Area: 4,425 acres. *Popn.* 235 males, 257 females: total 492.

(1) PENUWCH CHAPEL. CALVINISTIC METHODIST.
Erected 1817; rebuilt 1837.
Space: other 184; standing 100.
Present: morn. 150 scholars; aft. 173; even. 135.
Average (12 *months*): much the same.

> Daniel Davies. Deacon.

(2) LLWYNPIOD. CALVINISTIC METHODIST.
Erected before 1760.
Space: free 30; other 40; standing 40.
Present: morn. 52 scholars; aft. 80; evn. 55.
Average (12 *months*): general congregation from 70 to 90; scholars 70 to 52 (sic).

> David Evans.
> Deacon.
> Drewernfain.

[Note: there is no return for the Parish Church: for details of the living.
Lewis: perpetual curacy, annexed to that of Llandewy-Brevi[; endowed with £600 royal bounty; impropriators, Earl of Lisburne and H. Price, Esq., formerly a prebend in the collegiate church of Llandewy-Brevi.]

(3) [Return: numbered 598. 2. 6. (2 crossed out and 6 inserted).]

BLAENPENAL. CHURCH OF AN ANCIENT CHAPELRY.
Endowed: land £114; fees 10*s.*
Space: free 80.
Present: aft. 60.
Average: aft. 30.

> Evan Evans. Perpetual Curate.
> Treflan Rectory.

Lewis: Chapelry in the parish of Llandewy-Brevi: living a perpetual curacy; endowed with £800 royal bounty and £200 parliamentary grant; net income £84, with a glebe-house: impropriators, Earl of Lisburne and H. Price, Esq., who are also patrons alternately.
C & C: 1 service in Welsh performed by the curate.
I & C: vacant.

(4)   [Return numbered 598. 2. 7 (2 crossed out and 7 inserted) (4).]

BETTWS LEIKI, an ancient chapel of an ancient separate chapelry in the parish of Llanddewibrefy.
Endowed: land £50.
Space: free 92; other 22.
Present: morn. 129 + 42 scholars.
Average (12 *months*): 'about the same'.
Remarks: Many of the hearers are obliged to stand in the aisle having not an adequate number of sitting.

> Thomas Edwardes. Perpetual Curate.
> Lampeter.

Lewis: perpetual curacy; endowed with £1,000 royal bounty; net income £50: patron, the perpetual curate of Llandewy-Brevi: erected in 1805.

C &vC: 1 service in Welsh performed by the incumbent.

I & C: not resident.

[This, and the previous return, are out of order: for parish details, see below 598. 2. 6 and 7.]

2   Llangeithio Parish.

Area: 2,150 acres. *Popn.* 219 males, 223 females: total 442.

(5)   LLANGEITHO PARISH CHURCH.
Endowed: land £11; tithe £115; glebe £21.
Space: free 94; other 55.
Present: morn. 42 scholars; aft. 175; even. none.
Average (12 *months*): 'About the same'.
Remarks: Many of the hearers are obliged to stand, not having an adequate number of sittings, There is a small gallery without a *single sitting* where the school children generally are.

> Thomas Edwardes.   Rector.

Lewis: discharged rectory; rated at £6; endowed with £200 royal bounty; gross income £154 with a glebe-house; patron, the bishop: tithes commuted for £115, subject to rates averaging £28. 7s. per annum; glebe valued at £20: church rebuilt in 1819.

C & C: 1 service in Welsh performed by the incumbent.

I & C: resident.

3   Nantcwnlle Parish.

Area: 4,603 acres. *Popn.* 368 males, 415 females: total 783.

(6)   NANTCWNLLE PARISH CHURCH.
Endowed: land £40; tithes £58; glebe £5; permanent endowment £20; fees £1.

Space: free 120.
Present: morn. 100.
Average (12 *months*): 'about the same'.

Evan Evans.   Vicar.

Lewis: prebend in the collegiate church of Brecknock, valued at £7. 6. 8: the living a discharged vicarage, rated at £3. 13. 4; endowed with £600 royal bounty, and £600 parliamentary grant; patron, the bishop: tithes commuted for £175, of which £116. 13. 4. are payable to the prebendary, and £58. 6. 8. to the vicar, both subject to rates averaging £13.

C & C: 1 service in Welsh performed by the incumbent.

I & C: not resident.

(7)   BWLCHLLAN OR PENUEL CHAPEL.   CALVINISTIC METHODIST.
Erected 1836.
Space: free 49; other 111; standing 200 persons.
Present: morn. 196; aft. 150 scholars; even. 140.
Average (12 *months*):   general congregation from 180 to 200 scholars from 140 to 160.

Rees Williams.   Deacon.
Bryngalem.

4-6   Part of the Parish of Llanddewi-brefi, consisting of [4] Garthely Chapelry, [5] Gwynfil Township, and [6] Blaenpenal Chapelry.

Area: 8,102 acres. *Popn.* 572 males, 645 females: total 1,217.

[*Note:* there is no return for the parish church of Llanddewi-brefi.]

Lewis: perpetual curacy, with that of Llanbadarn—Odwyn [598. 2. 1(1)] annexed: endowed with £800 royal bounty: impropriators and alternate patrons Earl of Lisburne and R. Price, Esq., net income £146.

C & C: 1 service in Welsh performed by the incumbent.

I & C: incumbent not resident: curate, who resides at Llangeitho 4 miles distant, has stipend of £100.

ICBS: grant of £100 in 1846.]

4   Garthely Chapelry

Area: 2,475 acres. *Popn.* 156 males, 181 females: total 337.

(8)   GARTHELI: an ancient chapel in the parish of Llanddewi Brefi, but wholly separate from the Mother Church.
Endowed: land £70.
Space: free 36; other 20.
Present: morn. 60.
Average (12 *months*): 'about the same'.

Remarks: There are people standing in the aisle which is capable of containing about 40 more than there are sittings.

Rees Williams.   Chapel Warden.

Lewis: perpetual curacy; endowed with £1,000 royal bounty; net income £60: patron, perpetual curate of Llandewy-Brevi.
C & C: 1 service in Welsh performed by the curate.
I & C: vacant.

(9)   ABERMIRIG CHAPEL.   CALVINISTIC METHODIST.
Erected: first chapel before 1800; re-erected 1816.
Space: free 250; other 270; standing 250.
Present: morn. 189 scholars; aft. 450; even. 150.
Average (12 *months*): morn. 171 scholars; aft. 420 to 460; even. 150.

Thomas Jones.   Deacon.
Trefynon, Gartheli.

5   Gwynfil Township.
Area: 1,522 acres. *Popn.* 177 males, 198 females: total 375.

(10)   CHAPEL GWYNFIL ALIAS CHAPEL LLANGEITHO.   CALVINISTIC METHODIST.
Erected 1760, rebuilt 1813.
Space: free 96; other 332; standing 120.
Present: morn. 490; aft. 164 scholars; even. 270.
Average (12 *months*): morn. from 450 to 500; aft. from 155 to 165 scholars; even. from 260 to 275.
Remarks: The late Revd. Daniel Rowlands was turned out of the Established Church of Llangeitho in 1763 and his congregation built for him the chapel and joined under his Ministry and was called Calvinisic Methodist and the chapel was called Chapel Llangeitho on account that Rowlands was called Rowlands Llangeitho, though the Chapel are in Township of Gwynfil Parish of Llanddewi Brefi.

David Jones.   Deacon.
Tyndolanbach.

6   Blaenpenal Chapelry.
Area: 4,105 acres. *Popn.* 239 males, 266 females: total 505.
[For the church of the chapelry see 598. 2. 1(3) above.]

(11)   BLAENPENAL METHODIST CHAPEL.   CALVINISTIC METHODIST.
Erected before 1800.
Space: free 300; standing 160 persons.

Present: morn. 200; aft. 150 scholars; even. 140.
Average (12 *months*): 'much the same'.

> Daniel Pugh. Superintendant of the
> School.
> Blaenpant, nr. Blaenpenal

7   Bettws-Leiki Parochial Chapelry.
Area: 2,342. *Popn.* 161 males; 198 females: total 359.
[For the church of the chapelry see 598. 2. 1(4) above.]

[End of Llangeitho Subdistrict]

3 TREGARON (Subdistrict)
Area: 67,288 acres. *Popn.* 1,824 males, 2,140 females: total 3,964.

1-7   Part of the Parish of Llanddewi-brefi, consisting of the Townships of [1] Llanio, [2] Gogoyan, [3] Garth and Ystrad, [4] Prisk and Carfan,

[5] Gorwydd, [6] Dothie-Camddwr, and [7] Dothie Piscottwr.
Area: 28,150 acres. *Popn.* 636 males, 735 females: total 1,371.

1   Llanio Township.
Area: 1,228 acres. *Popn.* 58 males, 66 females: total 124.
[No returns]

2   Gogoyan Township.
Area: 707 acres. *Popn.* 52 males, 52 females: total 104.
[No returns]

3   Garth and Ystrad Township.
Area: 853 acres. *Popn.* 32 males, 33 females: total 65.
[No returns]

4   Prisk and Carfan Township.
Area: 3,522 acres. *Popn.* 78 males, 75 females: total 153.
[No returns]

5   Gorwydd Township.
Area: 6,604 acres. *Popn.* 296 males, 379 females: total 675.

(1)   BETHESDA CHAPEL.   CALVINISTIC METHODIST.
Erected 1826.
Space: free 90; other 420; standing 312 feet.
Present: morn. 346; even. 206.
Average: morn. 346 + 210 scholars; even. 206.

Rees Jones.   Deacon.
Pistyllgwyn, Llanddewi brefi P.O.

6   Dothie-Camddwr Township.

Area: 7,467 acres. *Popn.* 72 males, 71 females: total 143.

(2)   SOAR.   CALVINISTIC METHODIST.
Erected 1828.
Space: free 30; other 126.
Present: morn. about 50.
Average: morn. about 100.

Nathaniel Williams.   Deacon.
Bronhelen, Caron uwch clawdd.

7   Dothie-Piscottwr Township.

Area: 7,769. *Popn.* 48 males, 59 females: total 107.

8-14   Caron-ys-Clawdd Parish, consisting of the Townships of [8] Argoed and Ystrad, [9] Tref-Lynn, [10] Blaen-caron, [11] Croes and Berwyn, [12] Tre-Cefel, [13] Blaen-Aeron, and [14] Caron-Uwch-Clawdd, or Strata Florida.

Area: 39,138 acres. *Popn.* 1,188 males, 1,405 females: total 2,593.

8   Argoed and Ystrad Township.

Popn. 372 males, 467 females: total 839.

(3)   STRATA FLORIDA CHAPEL OF EASE.
Endowed: land £80.
Space: free 300.
Present: aft. 50.
Average (12 *months*): aft. 80.

J. W. Morris.   Curate.
Ystrad meuric.

Lewis: perpetual curacy; endowed with £800 royal bounty and £400 parliamentary grant; net income £80: patron, Col Powell; impropriate tithes commuted for £287, and the vicarial for £120. 7s, with a glebe of 24 acres, valued at £36: chapel erected in 1815.

C & C: no return.

I & C: not resident; curate who has a stipend of £30 less than the whole emoluments, resides at Bronmeirie, 3 miles distant.

(4) CARON OR TREGARON PARISH CHURCH.
Endowed: tithe £143; glebe £20; parliamentary grant £9. 14*s*; fees £2.
Present: morn. 255; aft. 144 scholars; even. 200 + 160 scholars.
Average: morn. 260; aft. 180 scholars; even. 100.

John Hughes. Vicar of Caron.

Lewis: discharged vicarage, rated at £8; net income £156, with glebe-house: patron, the bishop: the prebend valued at £13. 6. 8.

C & C: 3 services in 2 Sundays in Welsh performed by the incumbent.

I & C: resident.

9 Tref-Lynn Township.
Popn. 70 males, 99 females: total 169.
[No returns]

10 Blaen-Caron Township.
Popn. 46 males, 54 females: total 100.

(5) BERTH. CALVINISTIC METHODIST.
Erected 1840.
Space: free 50; other 120; standing 100.
Present: morn. 103; aft. 113 scholars; even. 94.
Average (12 *months*): morn. 140; aft. 135 scholars; even. 100.

Benjamin Benjamin. Elder.
Llwyngwin.

(6) WESLEYAN CHAPEL. WESLEYAN METHODIST.
Erected 1840.
Space: free 60.
Present: morn. 30; even. 55.

[no signature.]

11 Croes and Berwyn Township.
Popn. 104 males, 122 females: total 226.
[No returns]

12 Tre-cefel Township.
Popn. 72 males, 68 females: total 140.

(7)   Bwlchgwynt Chapel.   Calvinistic Methodist.
Erected 1775.
Space: free 90; other 486; standing 29½ feet by 15½ feet.
Present: morn. 125 scholars; aft. 420; even. 352.
Average (12 *months*): morn. 198 scholars; aft. 700; even. 300.
Remarks: (used exclusively as a place of worship) 'except a day school kept
for a short time till a school house be erected'.

John Rees.   Minister.

13   Blaen-Aeron Township.
Popn. 119 males, 140 females: total 259.
[No returns]

14   Caron-Uwch-Clawdd or Strata Florida Township.
Popn. 405 males, 455 females: total 860.
[No returns]

[*End of Tregaron Subdistrict, end of Tregaron District, and end of
Cardigan Registration County*]

BRECKNOCKSHIRE

Area: 443,133 acres. *Popn.* 29,993 males, 29,185 females: total 59,178.

599 BUILTH (District)

Area: 102,953 acres. *Popn.* 4,152 males, 4,193 females: total 8,345.

1 ABERGWESSIN (Subdistrict)
Area: 46,144 acres. *Popn.* 1,419 males, 1,471 females: total: 2,890.

1 Llanddewi-Abergwessin Parish.
Area: 10,511 acres. *Popn.* 49 males, 54 females: total 103.

(1) LLANDDEWI-ABERGWESIN PARISH CHURCH.
Space: free 109.
Usual number of attendants: morn. 9.
Minister: Revd. Edward Jones.
Informant: Morgan Jones.

[Informant's form.]
Lewis: vide sub. Llangammarch [599. 1. 3(6)].

(2) MORIAH CHAPEL, LLANDDEWI-ABERGWYSIN. INDEPENDENT.
Erected 1828.
Day School held.
Space: free 100; other 18.
Present: aft. 33 + 18 scholars; even. 8 + 14 scholars.
Average: morn. 35 + 25 scholars; even. 8 + 14 scholars.

Rees Jenkins. Deacon.
Penybont,
Llanwrtyd Wells.

(3) LLANFIHANGEL BRYNPABUAN PARISH CHURCH.
[This return is misplaced: see below, between 599. 1. 11(51) and (16).]

2 Llanfihangel-Abergwessin Parish.
Area: 6,836 acres. *Popn.* 163 males, 155 females: total 318.

(4) LLANFIHANGEL ABERGWESIN PARISH CHURCH.
Space: free 102.
Usual number of attendants: aft. 5-6.
Minister: Revd. Edward Jones.
Remarks: Afternoon service only.
Informant: Morgan Jones.

[Informant's form.]

Lewis: perpetual curacy, annexed to the vicarage of Llanavan-vawr: [599.1. 10(15)]. tithes commuted for £180, of which £120 payable to Precentor and Chapter of St. David's, subject to rates averaging £8. 16. 8, and £60 to the incumbent subject to rates averaging £4. 8. 4.

C & C: *vide sub.* Llanafanfawr

I & C: no return.

(5)   PANTYCELYN CHAPEL.   PARTICULAR BAPTISTS.
Erected 1774.
Space: free 30; standing 100.
Present: morn. 101 + 9 scholars; aft. school; even. 42.

> Ezekiel Jones.   Baptist Minister.
> Pantycelyn, Nr. Builth.

[3-4]   Llangammarch Parish, consisting of the Hamlets of [3] Treflis and [4] Penbuallt.

Area of the whole parish: 11,748 acres. *Popn.* 491 males, 547 females: total 1,038.

3   Treflis Hamlet.

Area: 6,325 acres. *Popn.* 247 males, 249 females: total 496.

(6)   LLANGAMMARCH PARISH CHURCH.
Present: morn. 20.

> William Jenkins.   Vicar.

Lewis: prebend in the collegiate church at Brecon, rated at £27, and belonging to the Bishop of St. David's as Treasurer of the college; great tithes appropriated to the office. The living, a discharged vicarage with the perpetual curacies of Llanwrtyd [587. 7. 2(2)] and Llanddewi-Abergwessin [599. 1. 1(1)] annexed: rated at £8. 14. 5: patron, the Bishop; net income £209.

C & C: 1 service each in the parish church and chapels of Llanddewi Abergwesin and Llanwrtyd, in English in Llanddewi Abergwesin, Welsh in Llangammarch and Llanwrtyd, performed by the incumbent.

I & C: resident: curate has stipend of £40.

[3-4]   (7)   GOSEN AR GORWYDD.   CALVINISTIC METHODIST.
Erected 1778.
Space: free 70; standing 60.
Present: aft. 194; even. 100.
Average: 300.
Remarks: Several members of the Congregation are from the adjoining Parish Coled Torabbot and other parts of the neighbourhood.

> Rees Price.   Deacon.
> Builth.

4 Penbuallt Hamlet.
Area: 5,423 acres. *Popn.* 244 males, 298 females: total 542.

(8) NAZARETH. CALVINISTIC METHODIST.
Erected 1818.
Space: free 250; other 32.
Present: morn. 140; even. 180.
Remarks: Several members of the congregation are attending from the adjoining Hamlets.

> John Bevan. Deacon.
> Aberonell.

[5-6] Llanlleonvel Parish, consisting of [5] Llanlleonvel, and [6] Gwarafog Hamlet.
Area of the whole parish: 2,900 acres. *Popn.* 122 males, 113 females: total 235.

5 Llanlleonvel.
Area: 2,834 acres. *Popn.* 93 males, 89 females: total 182.

(9) LLANLLEONFEL PARISH CHURCH.
Endowed: land £30; permanent endowment £20.
Present: aft. 13.
Remarks: The Church, being in a solitary place, is better attended in summer than winter.

> Henry Morgan. Perpetual Curate.

Lewis: perpetual curacy, endowed with £800 royal bounty; net income £60; patron and impropriator, Prebendary of Llanwrthwl in the collegiate church of Brecon: no parsonage-house nor glebe.
C & C: 1 service in Welsh performed by the incumbent.
I & C: not resident.
ERCR: accom. 80.

(10) SALEM, LLANLLEONFIL. BAPTIST.
Erected 1845.
Space: free 156; other 60.
Present: morn. 62; aft. 51; even. 76.
Average: morn. 62; aft. 51; even. 76.

> Rees Jenkins. Deacon.

(11) BEULAH, LLANLLEONFIL. INDEPENDENTS.
Erected 1821; re-erected 1841.
Space: free 199; standing 68.
Present: morn. 125; aft. 83 scholars; even. 112.

Remarks: This chapel was erected first as a schoolroom by publick subscriptions in 1821. It was then 27 feet by 16 feet and 12 feet high. But in 1841 re-erected by publick subscription and is now 28 feet by 22 feet and 16 high with a galery and sittings for 80 persons on it and is free from any debt.

> Benjamin Wooding. Ordered by the Minister to take the Census.
> Shopkeeper. Beulah.

6   Gwarafog Hamlet.
Area: 66 acres. *Popn.* 29 males, 24 females: total 53.
[No returns]

7   Llanafan-fechan, or Llan-fechan Parish.
Area: 2,783 acres. *Popn.* 96 males, 77 females: total 173.

(12)   LLANAFANFECHAN, OR LLANFECHAN PARISH CHURCH.
Space: free 106.
Usual number of attendants: aft. 4.
Minister: Revd. Daniel Evans.

> Informant: Rees James.
> Llanfechan.

[Informant's form]

Lewis: perpetual curacy, annexed to the vicarage of Llanavan-Vawr [599. 1. 10(15)]: tithes commuted for £115, of which Precentor and Chapter of St. David's receive two-thirds and the Vicar one-third.
C & C: and *I & C: vide sub* Llanafan Fawr.

(13)   OLEWYDD.   INDEPENDENT.
Erected 1847.
Space: all free.
Present: morn. 41 scholars; even. 60.
Average: general congregation 150; scholars 50.

> David Williams.
> Independent Minister.
> at Troedrhiwdalar.

[8-9-10]   Part of Llanafan-fawr Parish, consisting [8] First Division, [9] Second Division, and [10] Third Division.
Area of this part of the parish: 7,971 acres. *Popn.* 364 males, 383 females: total 747.
(For the remainder of this parish, see below, 599. 3. 4.)

8   Llanafan-fawr, First Division.
Popn. 124 males, 142 females: total 266.
[No returns]

9   Llanafan-fawr, Second Division.
Popn. 113 males, 122 females: total 235.

(14)   TROEDRHIWDALAR.   INDEPENDENT.
Erected 1704.
Space: all free.
Present: morn. 101 scholars; aft. 360.
Remarks: I have three congregations under my charge, that meets at
Troedrhiwdolar—Beulah—and the Oliwydd, and our usual mode of carrying
on the service in both Chapels is as follows: A Sunday School, and a Sermon,
and a Prayer Meeting in each of them every Sunday. And as the neighbour-
hood is Rural and Mountainous, the attendance is not the same every
Sunday. But at an average the attendance is about four hundred at Troedrhiwdolar—and at Beulah about two hundred and at the Oliwydd about
hundred and fifty.

David Williams.
Independent Minister.

10   Llanafan fawr, Third Division.
Popn. 127 males, 119 females: total 246.

(15)   LLANAFANFAWR PARISH CHURCH.
Endowed: tithe £113; glebe £15.
Space: free 200.
Present: morn. 35.
Average: morn. 50.

David Evans.   Vicar.

Lewis: vicarage, with the perpetual curacies of Llanafanfechan [599. 1. 7(12)]
Llanfihangel-Abergwesin [599. 1. 2(4)], and Llanfihangel Bryn-Pabuan [599. 1. 11(3)
annexed; rated at £9. 8. 9; net income £273: patron, the Bishop; tithes (including
township of Llysdinam [599. 3. 4]) commuted for £470, subject to rates averaging
£6; two-thirds payable to Precentor and Chapter of St. David's, and one-third to the
vicar: glebe of 20 acres, valued at £20, and glebe-house.

C & C: 1 service each in the parish church and the Chapels of Llanafan-fechan,
Llanfihangel Abergwesin, and Llanfihangel Brynpabuan, all in Welsh, performed by
the incumbent and curate.

I & C: no return.

11   Llanfihangel Hamlet, part of Llanfihangel-Bryn-Pabuan Parish.
Area of the Hamlet: 3,395 acres. *Popn.* 134 males, 142 females: total 276.
(For the remainder of the parish see 599. 3. 5.)

(3) LLANFIHANGEL BRYNPABUAN PARISH CHURCH.
Space: free 112.
Usual number of attendants: morn. 6.
Minister: Revd. Daniel Evans.

Informant: David Gwillim.

[Informant's form.]

[This return is misnumbered.]

Lewis: perpetual curacy, annexed to the vicarage of Llanafan-fawr: tithes of the parish (including the hamlet of Rhosverrig [599. 3. 5.]), commuted for £203, of which two-thirds are payable to the Precentor and Chapter of St. David's, and one-third to the incumbent.

C & C: and *I & C: vide sub* Llanafan-fawr [599. 1. 10(15)].

(16) PISGAH. PARTICULAR BAPTIST.
Erected 1848.
Space: free 5 seats + 131 benches; standing 88.
Present: morn. 121 + 31 scholars.
Average (12 *months*): aft. 275 + 31 scholars.
Remarks: The service in the chapel every other Sunday—morning and evening. There is 5 seats and 13 long benches for siting.

Revd. David Jarman.   Minister.

[End of Abergwessin Subdistrict]

2 COLWYN (Subdistrict)
Area: 25,020 acres. *Po2n.* 1,017 males, 978 females: total 1,995.

[1-2] Disserth Parish, co. Radnor, consisting of [1] Disserth and [2] the Hamlet of Trecoed.
Area of the whole parish: 6,650 acres. *Popn.* 280 males, 284 females: total 564.

1 Disserth Parish.
Popn. 156 males, 167 females: total 323.

(1) DISSERTH PARISH CHURCH.
Endowed: tithe £289.
Space: free 6; other 33.
Present: morn. 79 + 32 scholars.
Average (3 *months*): aft. 250 + 45 scholars.

Remarks: The number of attendants in rural districts depends upon the state of the weather.

Jno. Thomas.   Rector.

Lewis: rectory, with perpetual curacy of Bettws-Disserth [599. 2. 4(4)] annexed; rated at £16: patron, the Bishop: tithes commuted for £299. 19. 11, subject to rates averaging £43. 13. 8¼, with glebe of ¾ acre, valued at £1. 1. 0.

C & C: 1 service each in English in the Church and Chapel.

I & C: resident.

2   Trecoed Hamlet.

Popn. 124 males, 117 females: total 241.

[No returns]

3   Llandrindod Parish, co. Radnor.

Area: 2,689 acres. *Popn.* 110 males, 107 females: total 217.

(2)   Llandrindod Parish Church.

Endowed: land £49; tithe £10.

Present: morn. 14.

Average (12 *months*): morn. 20.

Tho. Thonsby.   Minister.

Lewis: prebend in collegiate church of Brecon, rated at £5. 8. 9; in the gift of the Bishop: the living a perpetual curacy, endowed with £600 royal bounty and £200 parliamentary grant; net income £48; patron, the Bishop: tithes commuted for £100, payable to the Prebendary, who has also a glebe of ½ acre valued £1. 2. 0.

C & C: 1 service in English.

I & C: no return.

ERCR: accom. 225.

4   Bettws-Disserth Parochial Chapelry.

Area: 1,885 acres. *Popn.* 76 males, 64 females: total 140.

(4)   Bettws Parochial Chapelry.

Endowed: tithe £70.

Space: free 3; other 14.

Present: aft. 18.

Average (3 *months*): aft. 62.

Remarks: The number of attendants in rural districts depends upon the state of the weather.

Tho. Thomas.   Rector.

[This return is wrongly numbered.]

Lewis: perpetual curacy, consolidated with the rectory of Disserth [599. 2. 1(1); rectorial tithes commuted for £74 subject to rates averaging £8. 11. 0.

C & C: and *I & C:* *vide sub* Disserth.

5 Llansantfraed-in-Elvel Parish, co. Radnor.
Area: 4,000 acres. *Popn.* 165 males, 158 females: total 323.

(5) LLANSAINTFRAED PARISH CHURCH.
Endowed: tithe £198.
Space: free 30; other 28.
Present: aft. 165.
Average (3 *months*): morn. 40; aft. 50.

Hugh Vaughan. Vicar.

Lewis: prebend in the collegiate church of Brecon, rated at £5. 14. 9½; patron, the Bishop; vicarial tithes commuted for £198 subject to rates averaging £16.

C & C: 1 service in English.

I & C: resident.

(6) THE HUNDRED HOUSE CHAPEL. WELSH CALVINISTIC METHODIST.
Erected 1830.
Space: free 120; standing 80.
Present: even. 132.
Average (12 *month*): morn. 25; even. 100.

John James. Minister.

6 Cregrina Parish, co. Radnor.
Area: 1,595 acres. *Popn.* 56 males, 53 females: total 109.

(3) CREGRINA PARISH CHURCH.
Endowed: tithe £126 (gross): fees 10s.
Space: free 50; other 50.
Present: aft. 53 + 15 scholars.
Average (12 *months*): morn. aft. (alternately) 50 + 10 scholars.

Tho. Thomas. Rector.

[This return is wrongly numbered.]

Lewis: sub Caregrina: discharged rectory, with the perpetual curacy of Llanbadarn-y-Garreg [599. 2. 8(7)] annexed: rated at £9. 6. 8; net income £120: patron the Bishop: tithes commuted for £126, subject to rates averaging £15.

C & C: with Llanbadarn-y-Garreg: 1 service in English.

I & C: resident.

7 Rhulen Parochial Chapelry, co. Radnor.
Area: 756 acres. *Popn.* 56 males, 58 females: total 114.

(8)   RHULAN PAROCHIAL CHAPELRY (UNDER GLASCOMBE).
Endowed: tithe £33; free 5*s.*
Space: free 5; other 117.
Present: morn. 10.
Average (9 months): morn. 12.

David Vaughan.   Curate.

Lewis: chapelry consolidated with the living of Glascomb [603. 2. 1(1)]; valued at £4. 13. 4: tithes commuted for £82. 10., of which £49.10. payable to the Bishop as appropriator, subject to rates of £7. 14., and £33 to the vicar, subject to rates of £2. 4.
C & C: sub Glascombe with Colva and Ruben: 1 service in the chapel in English.
I & C: resident.

(9)   LLANTIDER.   PRIMITIVE METHODIST.
Erected before 1800.
Not a separate building.
Present: no service.
Average (6 months): aft. 20.
Remarks: The above place of worship is only used occasionally for publick worship, been a Dwelling House.

William Lloyd.   Class Leader.

8   Llanbadarn-y-Garreg Parochial Chapelry, co. Radnor.

Area: 900 acres. *Popn.* 30 males, 28 females: total 58.

(7)   LLANBADARN-Y-GARREG CHURCH OF ANCIENT CHAPELRY.
Endowed: tithe £60; fees 5*s.*
Space: free 60; other 20.
Present: morn. 27.
Average (12 months): morn. 30.
Remarks: It is difficult to make a correct estimate of the number of persons attending at Church in these mountainous districts as they vary from 7 or 20 to 100 and upwards.

Thomas Williams.   Churchwarden.

[This return is misnumbered.]
Lewis: annexed to the living of Caregrina [599. 2. 6(3)].
C & C: 1 service in English.
I & C: resident.

(10)   SALEM, LLANBADARNYGARREG.   INDEPENDENT.
Erected 1826.
Space: free 8; standing 60.
Present: aft. 29 + 12 scholars.
Average (6 months): general congregation 30; scholars 12.

David Williams.   Minister.
Aberedw.

9   Aberedw Parish, co. Radnor.
Area: 4,300 acres. *Popn.* 171 males, 159 females: total 330.

(11)   Aberedw Parish Church.
Endowed: tithes £245; glebe rated at £1.10.; fees 10s.
Space: free 10; other 96.
Present: aft. 37.
Average (12 months): morn. 25 + 6 scholars; aft. 50 + 8 scholars.
Remarks: There is no Sunday School in the winter months.

W. Rupell.   Rector.

Lewis: rectory, with that of Llanvaredd [599. 2. 10(3)] annexed; rated at £12. 13. 4; net income £355; patron, the Bishop.
C & C: 1 service in English.
I & C: resident.

(12)   Independents.
Licensed 1830.
Part of a dwelling house, not used exclusively as a place of worship.
Space: standing 60.
Present: morn. 12 scholars; even. 60.

David Williams. Independent Miniser.
Aberedw.

10   Llanvareth Parish, co. Radnor.
Area: 2,245 acres. *Popn.* 73 males, 67 females: total 140.

(13)   Llanfaredd Parish Church.
Endowed: tithe £250; fees 10s.
Space: 60.
Present: morn. 11.
Average: morn. 12; aft. 16.

W. Rupell.   Rector.

Lewis: annexed to the living of Aberedw.
C & C: sub. Aberedw: 1 service in English.
I & C: resdent.

[End of Colwyn Subdistrict]

3 BUILTH (Subdistrict)
Area: 31,789 acres. *Popn.* 1,716 males, 1,744 females: total 3,460

1   Llanelwedd Parish, co. Radnor.
Area: 2,020 acres. *Popn.* 91 males, 112 females: total 203.

(1)   LLANELWEDD PARISH CHURCH.
Endowed: land £60; tithe £6.
Space: free 70; other 4.
Present: morn. 49.
Average: morn. 50.

Hugh Vaughan.   Curate.

Lewis: prebend in the collegiate church of Brecon, rated at £6. 10., in the gift of the
Bishop. The living a perpetual curacy, endowed with £800 royal bounty: patron,
T. Thomas, Esq., lessee of the tithes under the prebendary; net income £70.

C & C: 1 service in English.

I & C: no return.

(2)   FFORDDLAS.   INDEPENDENT OR CONGREGATIONALIST.
Erected 1834.
A farm House.
Average attendants (12 *months*): even. 30 + 15 scholars.
Remarks: Service held on a weekday once in the month.

Septimus Davies.   Superintendant.

[Signed with a mark.]   Fforddlas, Nr. Builth.

2   Builth, other Llanfair-in-Buallt Parish.
Area: 712 acres. *Popn.* 555 males, 603 females: total 1,158.

(7)   LLANVAIR IN BUALLT PARISH CHURCH.
Endowed: Q.A's Bounty in land £375; parliamentary grant £23; fees £5;
salary for the lay rector £6.
Space: free 103; other 270.
Present: morn. 102 + 71 scholars; even. 130 + 50 scholars.
Average: morn. 200 + 80 scholars; even. 230 + 70 scholars.

Richd. H. Harrison.   Incumbent.

Lewis: sub Builth: perpetual curacy, with that of Llanddewi'r Cwm [599. 3. 8(13)]
annexed; endowed with £200 private benefaction, £400 royal bounty, and £600
parliamentary grant; net income £106: patrons and impropriators, alternately R.
Bell Price, Esq., and V. Pocock, Esq, tithes commuted for £90, subject to rates
averaging £1: 28 acres of bounty land, bought in 1739; no glebe-house.

C & C: 2 services in English.

I & C: no return.

(4)   ALPHA CHAPEL.   WELSH CALVINISTIC METHODIST.
Erected before 1800.
Space: free 103; other 297; standing 100.
Present: morn. 113; aft. 70 scholars; even. 221.
Average (3 *months*): morn. 130; aft. 90 scholars; even. 220.

David Charles Davies, M.A.   Minister.

(5) HOREB. INDEPENDENT.
Erected 1805.
Space: free 150; other 212; standing 364.
Present: morn. 110 + 21 scholars; even. 185 + 37 scholars.
Average (12 *months*): morn. 190 + 30 scholars; even. 250 + 40 scholars.

John Jones. Deacon.
New Hall, Builth.

(6) EBENEZER CHAPEL, BANK. BAPTIST.
Erected about 1794 [rebuilt 1842].
Space: free 6; other 244.
Present: morn. 30 + 20 scholars; even. 69 + 20 scholars.
Average (3 *months*): morn. 100 + 15 scholars; aft. 100 + 15 scholars; even.
100 + 15 scholars.
Remarks: This chapel was enlarged and rebuilt in 1842.

William Thomas. Deacon.

3 Llanganten Parish.
Area: 2,258 acres. *Popn.* 86 males, 95 females: total 181.

(7) LLANGANTEN PARISH CHURCH.
Endowed: land £95.
Space: free 96.
Present: 55.

Evan Joel Evans. Minister.

Lewis: perpetual curacy, endowed with £1,000 royal bounty: net income, £64;
patron and appropriator, Prebendary of Llandarog in the collegiate church of
Brecon: 4 acres of glebe, no glebe-house.

C & C: 1 service in English.

I & C: incumbent not resident: curate, who resides about ¼ mile distant, has stipend
of £80 for this and Llangynnog [599. 3. 10(15)].

(8) BETHESDA. INDEPENDENT.
Erected 1833.
Space: free, standing 150.
Present: even. 33 + 10 scholars.

Theophilus Jones. Foreman of the
Chapel.
Cefnbedd.

4 Llysdinam Hamlet, part of the parish of Llanafan-fawr [599. 1. 8.].
Area: 2,476 acres. *Popn.* 119 males, 119 females: total 238.
[No returns]

5   Rhosferig Hamlet, part of the parish of Llanfihangel-Bryn-Pabuan
[599. 1. 11].
Area: 1,320 acres. *Popn.* 51 males, 47 females: total 98.
[No returns].

6   Llanynys Parish.
Area: 2,250 acres. *Popn.* 78 males, 94 females: total 172.
(9)   LLANYNYS PARISH CHURCH.
Endowed: tithe £103; glebe £4.
Space: free 50; other 18.
Average attendants (9 *months*): morn. 10; aft. 15.
Remarks: There happened to be no congregation on March 30. The average
number varies from 6 to 30, according as the service is in the morning or
evening.

Wm. Williams.   Curate.

Lewis: discharged rectory, rated at £7. 0. 7½; patron, the Bishop: tithes commuted
for £103, with glebe of 3 acres valued at £7.
C & C: 1 service in Welsh performed by the incumbent.
I & C: resident.

(10)   LIBANUS CHAPEL.   WELSH CALVINISTIC METHODIST.
Erected about 1845.
Space: free 60; standing 100.
Present: aft. 70; even. 27 scholars.
Average (3 *months*): aft. 60; even. 38 scholars.
Remarks: A day school is also kept in the chapel.

David Charles Davies, M.A.   Minister.

7   Maes-Mynis Parish.
Area: 4,012 acres. *Popn.* 120 males, 114 females: total 234.

(11)   MAESMYNIS PARISH CHURCH.
Endowed: tithe £150; glebe £6.
Space: free 60; other 12.
Present: aft. 10.
Average: morn. 10; aft. 25.
Remarks: It is difficult to fix the average number of attendants there are
sometimes only ten and sometimes more than 50, according as the service
is in the morning or in the afternoon.

Wm. Williams.   Curate.

Lewis: discharged rectory, rated at £7. 1. 3; net income £128: patron, the Bishop:
glebe of 6 acres, with glebe-house erected by present incumbent.
C & C: 1 service in Welsh performed by the curate.
I & C: incumbent not resident: curate, who resides at Llanynys, 1½ miles distant,
has stipend of £50.

(12) SALEM, MAESYNIS. INDEPENDENT OR CONGREGATIONALIST.
Erected 1826.
Space: free 60; other 60; standing 30.
Present: aft. 80 + 15 scholars; even. 43.
Average (12 *months*): general congregation 70; scholars 20.

> D. Phillip Davies. Minister.

8 Llan-ddewi'r-Cwm Parish.
Area: 3,101 acres. *Popn.* 118 males, 105 females: total 223.

(13) LLANDDEWI'R CWM PARISH CHURCH.
Endowed: land £48; parliamentary grant £6; fees 15*s*; other sources paid
by Lay Rector £4.
Space: free 30; other 76.
Present: aft. 12 + 12 scholars.
Average: aft. 35 + 20 scholars.

> Richard H. Harrison.   Incumbent.

Lewis: perpetual curacy, endowed with £800 royal bounty; net income £64:
tithes commuted for £131; patrons and impropriators, Mrs. Sarah Price and
V. Pocock, Esq.
C & C: 1 service in English.
I & C: no return.
ICBS: grant of £20 in 1846.

9 Alltmawr Parish.
Area: 499 acres. *Popn.* 23 males, 20 females: total 43.

(14) ALLTMAWR PAROCHIAL CHAPEL.
Chapel formerly attached to the Mother Church, Llanafan Fawr in the same
district but now separate.
Endowed: land £60.
Present: morn. 12.
Average: morn. 20.
Remarks: the Population of the above parish does not amount to 20.

> J. W. Evans. Perpetual Curate.

Lewis: perpetual curacy, annexed to the vicarage of Llanavan-Fawr [599. 1. 10(15)];
endowed with £800 royal bounty, and £200 parliamentary grant; net income £48:
tithes commuted for £48, of which £25. 6. 8. payable to the chantor and chapter of
St. David's, and £12. 13. 4. to the vicar.
C & C: 1 service in English.
I & C: not resident.
ERCR: accom. 45.

10 Llangynog Parish.
Area: 1,429 acres. *Popn.* 27 males, 29 females: total 56.

(15) LLANGYNNOG PARISH CHURCH.
Endowed: land £40.
Space: free 60.
Present: morn. 7.
Average (2 months): morn. 10; aft. 15.

Evan Joel Evans. Minister.

Lewis: perpetual curacy: endowed with £800 royal bounty; net income £69: patron and appropriator, Prebendary of Llanddarog.

C & C: 1 service in Welsh performed by the curate.

I & C: incumbent not resident: curate, who resides at Rhosferig, 6 miles distant, has stipend of £80 for this and Llanganten [599. 1. 3(7)].

11 Gwen-ddwr Parish (excepting the Hamlet of Trawscoed [600. 5. 5].)
Area: 7,381 acres. *Popn.* 233 males, 207 females: total 440.

(16) GWENDDWR PARISH CHURCH.
Endowed: land £90.
Space: free 40; other 200.
Present: morn. 60.
Average: morn. 60; aft. 70.

William Williams. Minister.

Lewis; perpetual curacy, endowed with £800 royal bounty, and £700 parliamentary grant; net income £123: patron, John P. Pontywall, Esq: impropriate tithes commuted for £249. 10. 0.

C & C: 1 service in Welsh, performed by the incumbent; 1 English service a month.

I & C: resident.

(17) BAILIHALOG. INDEPENDENT.
Erected before 1750.
Space: free 4; standing 250.
Average number of attendants: aft. 60 + 12 scholars; even. 150 + 60 scholars.
Remarks: The lower columns in Division eight [i.e. estimated number of persons attending] stand for the upper section of the same division because of the mistake in the upper figures. [i.e. the average numbers are to be read as actual numbers present.]

Thomas Rees Davies. Minister.
Erwood.

12　Crickadarn Parish.
Area: 4331 acres; *Popn.* 215 males; 199 females; total 414.

(18)　Crickadarn Parish Church.
Endowed: tithe £200.
Space: free 50; other 80.
Present: morn. 50 + 14 scholars; aft. 60 + 14 scholars.
Average: aft. 84.

Charles Vaughan.　Vicar.

Lewis: endowed discharged vicarage, consolidated with that of Llandevalley [600. 5. 6(8)]: net income, £686, with a glebe-house: patron, George P. Watkins, Esq.

C & C: vide Llandefalley.

I & C: no return.

(19)　Epstiba.　Baptist.
Erected 1827.
Space: free 30; other 14; standing 100.
Present: morn. 60; even. 80.

Thomas Weeks.　Deacon.
Lynyorath, Crickadarn.

(20)　Hebron, Crigeadarn.　Independents.
Erected 1812.
Space: free 20; other 4; standing 50.
Present: morn. 60; aft. 30 scholars; even. 150.
Remarks: We are very short of Books in our School to carry the business on at present etc.

Wm. Morgan.　Secretary.
Abergwenddwr.

[End of Builth Subdistrict and end of Builth District]

600 BRECKNOCK (District)

Area: 196,793 acres. *Popn.* 8984 males, 9190 females:
total 18,174.

1 MERTHYR-CYNOG (Subdistrict)
Area: 34,651 acres. *Popn.* 858 males, 795 females: total: 1,653.

[1-4] Merthyr-Cynog Parish, consisting of the Hamlets of [1] Lower Dyffrin Honddu, [2] Upper Dyffrin, [3] Yscir-Vawr, and [4] Yscir-Fechan.
Area of the whole parish: 21,278 acres. *Popn.* 419 males, 406 females:
total 825.

1 Lower Dyffrin Honddu Hamlet.
Popn. 110 males, 91 females: total 201.

(1) Dyffryn Honddu Upper Chapel.
Endowed: land £69.
Space: about 80.
Present: morn. 45 + 19 scholars.
Remarks: All the sittings are Free.

Thos. Jones. Perpetual Curate.

Lewis: perpetual curacy; endowed with £1,000 royal bounty; net income £66:
patron, Vicar of Merthyr Cynog [600. 1. 4(5)].
C & C: 1 service in Welsh performed by the incumbent.
I & C: resident.

(2) Bethania. Independent.
Erected 1841.
Space: all free.
Present: morn. 38 scholars; aft. 78; even. 62.
Average: general congregation 120; scholars 30.

Morgan Morgans. Minister.

2 Upper Dyffrin Honddu.
Popn. 88 males, 95 females: total 183.

(3) EBENEZER. INDEPENDENT.
Erected 1805.
Space: other 10 seats; standing 22 ft. by 11 ft.
Present: morn. 61; aft. 37; even. 67.

> Thomas Jones. Secretary.
> Penwain, Nr. Upper Chapel.

3 Yscir-Vawr Hamlet.
Popn. 92 males, 99 females: total 191.

(4) TYDY. WELSH CALVINISTIC METHODIS.
Erected about 1792.
Space: free 1; other 18; standing 16 Bench 94 feet.
Present: morn. 47 scholars; aft. 95.

> Thomas Lloyd. Deacon.
> Trevers, Merthyr Cynog.

4 Yscir-Vechan Ḥamlet.
Popn. 129 males, 121 females: total 250.

(5) MERTHYR CYNOG PARISH CHURCH.
Endowed: land £71; permanent endowment £13. 6. 8.
Space: free 132.
Present: morn. 50.
Remarks: The sittings are all Free except a few Pews.

> Thomas Jones. Vicar.

Lewis: discharged vicarage, rated at at £7. 10. 5; endowed with £400 royal bounty, and £800 parliamentary grant; net income £90: impropriators, Marquess Camden and John Lloyd Vaughan Watkins, Esq.: impropriate tithes commuted for £410: patron, J. L. V. Watkins, Esq.

C & C: 1 service in Welsh performed by the incumbent.

I & C: resident.

(6) BRYN Y BONT, BONT VANE. CALVINISTIC METHODISTS.
Erected 1840.
Space: free 6 benches 10 feet long; other 20.
Present: morn. 50 + 12 scholars; aft. school; even. 61 + 23 scholars.

> Thomas Williams. Deacon.
> Bryn-y-bont, Bont Vane.

5 Garthbrengy Parish.
Area: 2,001 acres. *Popn.* 105 males, 84 females: total 189.

(7) GARTHBRENGY PARISH CHURCH.
Endowed: land £40; permanent endowment £20; fees 5s.
Space: free 85; other 80.
Present: morn. 25.
Average: morn. 30.
Remarks: The Sunday School is kept in the afternoon when there is no service in the Church.

David Price. Perpetual Curate.

Lewis: prebend in the collegiate church at Brecon, rated at £3. 6. 8: the living a perpetual curacy, endowed with £400 royal bounty, and £200 parliamentary grant; net income £71: patron, the Bishop: appropriator, Prebendary, whose tithes commuted for £200. 16. 6.
C & C: 1 service in Welsh performed by the incumbent.
I & C: not resident.
ICBS: grant of £100 in 1834.

6 Llanfihangel-fechan Chapelry, part of the parish of Llandefaelog-fach [600. 3. 6].
Area: 2,211 acres. *Popn.* 97 males, 84 females: total 181.

(8) LLANFIHANGELFECHAN PAROCHIAL CHAPELRY.
Endowed: land £67. 10.; fees 5s.
Space: free 32; other 52.
Present: aft. 40.
Average: aft. 40.

David Price. Perpetual Curate.

Lewis: perpetual curacy, endowed with £1,000 royal bounty: patron, Rector of Llandevaelog-Vach [600. 3. 6(7)]; net income £65.
C & C: 1 service in Welsh performed by the incumbent.
I & C: resident.

(9) SION. CALVINISTIC METHODIST.
Erected 1804.
Not used exclusively as a place of worship.
Space: 16 feet by 40 ft.
Present: morn. 43 scholars; even. 74.
Average: general congregation 80; scholars 50.

Thomas Havard (Shoemaker), Howell
Davies, David Morgan, Thomas
Steward, Watkin Powell. Deacons.

7　Llanfihangel-nant-brane Parish.

Area: 9,161 acres. *Popn.* 237 males, 221 females: total 458.

(10)　Llanfihangel Nant Brane Parish Church.
Space: free 150; other 50.
Usual number of attendants: morn. 20-40; aft. 30-60. No Sunday Scholars.

Thomas Powell (Enumerator).
Tyaryberllan.

[Informant's form]

Lewis: perpetual curacy, endowed with £800 royal bounty; net income £66: patrons and impropriator, Coheirs of W. Jeffrey, Esq.: impropriate tithes commuted for £227.

C & C: 1 service in Welsh performed by the incumbent.

I & C: not resident.

(11)　Soar.　Baptists.
Erected 1827.
Space: free 6; other 15; standing 60.
Present: morn. 100 + 50 scholars; even. 100 + 50 scholars.
Average (12 *months*): general congregation 120; scholars 50.
Remarks: Divine Service is held continually morning and evening.

Thomas Williams.　Baptist Minister.

(12)　Bethel.　Calvinistic Methodist.
Erected 1810.
Space: free 52; other 66.
Present: morn. 55 scholars; aft. 119; even. 89.
Average: general congregation 118; scholars 68.

Samuel Pugh.　Member.
Cooper.

(13)　Sardis [Upper part of the parish]　Old Baptist.
Erected 1822.
Not used exclusively as a place of worship.
Space: free 10; standing 50.
Present: morn. 27.
Average: morn. 40; even. 50; no school.

John Jones.　Minister.
Blandyrin

[End of Merthyr-Cynog Subdistrict]

2 DEVYNNOCK (Subdistrict)

Area: 65,053 acres. *Pon.* 2,147 males, 2,293 females: total 4,440.
[Note: some of the returns which follow have been wrongly bound and
numbered. As now presented they are grouped according to their parish of
origin.]

1   Llandilovane Parish.

Area: 10,491 acres. *Popn.* 252 males, 273 females: total 525.

(1)   Llandilovane Church.
Space: free 50; other 150.
Usual number of attendants: morn. 30; aft. 30.

Informant: Daniel Thomas. Registrar.

[Informant's form, wrongly numbered 600. 2. 3(3).]
Lewis: perpetual curacy, endowed with £600 royal bounty and £1,000 parliamentary
grant; net income £83: tithes commuted for £173, subject to rates averaging
£5. 8. 3: patrons and impropriators, Co-heirs of Walter Jeffreys, Esq.
C & C: sub Llandilorfaen: 1 service in Welsh performed by the incumbent.
I & C: sub Llandilo'r Vane: not resident.

(2)   Calvinistick Methodists, Llandilovane.
No seperate building: 'From House to House'.
Present: aft. 42; even. 39 scholars.
Average: morn. 80; aft. 45 scholars.

Isaac Davies.
Blaine Meeting house.
Bronant, Llandilovane.

[Wrongly numbered 600. 2. 1(5).]

[2-4]   Llywell Parish, consisting of the Hamlets of [2] Traian-Glas, [3] Traian-Mawr with Trecastle Ward, and [4] Ysclydach.

Area of the whole parish: 22,295 acres. *Popn.* 765 males, 862 females: total
1,627.

2   Traian Glas Hamlet.

Popn. 309 males, 339 females: total 648.

(3)   Llywell Parish Church.
Endowed: tithe £209.
Space: free 80; other 348.
Present: morn. 300 + 36 scholars; even. 200 + 90 scholars.

David Parry. Minister.

[Wrongly numbered 600. 2. 1(2).]

Lewis: vicarage, rated at £9. 10. 5; net income £152: patron, the Bishop: appropriators, Precentor and Chapter of St. David's.
C & C: 1 service in Welsh performed by the incumbent.
I & C: resident.

(4) [No return. Church of England according to the preliminary list.]

(5) TYNEWYDD.   CALVINISTICK METHODIST.
Erected 1765.
Space: other 68; standing 300.
Present: aft. 235.
Average (12 *months*): general congregation 300.
Remarks: Owing to illness.

> Jenkin Thos. Wilkins.   Deacon.
> Bryntwarch, near Trecastle.

[Original numbered 600. 2. 2.(6).]

(6) ZOAR.   INDEPENDENT.
Erected 1850.
Present: morn. 140 + 70 scholars.

> David Evan.   Minister.
> Ynysfawr, Trecastle.

[Original numbered 600. 2. 2(7).]

(7) SOAR CHAPEL.   CALVINISTIC METHODISTS.
Erected 1823.
Space: other 22; standing 150.
Present: morn. 80; aft. 58 scholars; even. 90.
Average (12 *months*): morn. 90; even. 100.

> Thomas Jenkins.   Deacon.
> Llwyncyntefin.

[Original numbered 600. 2. 2.(8).]

(8) SARON.   INDEPENDENT.
Erected 1822.
Building also serves as a Day School.
Space: free 96; other 60.
Present: morn. 120; aft. school; even. 90.
Remarks: This Region being very Hilly on borders of Carmarthenshire, open fields great trouble to mind the cattle and the little calves and hay. There-fore we are obliged to keep Sunday Schools from house to house in order to give Religious instruction to every rational being, before this and the

erection of the little capel there was here only paganism, ignorance, sabbath breaking and all wickedness committed.

David Evans.　Minister.

[Endorsed: See Letter.]

[The remarks are in a different hand from the signature. Original numbered 600. 2.(2-5) (10).]

(9)　Bailidw Chapel.　Welsh Calvinistic Methodist.

Erected before 1800.

Space: free 14 benches; other 5.

Present: morn. 85; aft. 50 scholars; even. 60.

Average (12 *months*): morn. 50 scholars; aft. 100 + 55 scholars.

John Lewis.　Deacon.
Fynnon.

[Original numbered 600. 2. (2-5) (10).]

3　Train-Mawr Hamlet with Trecastle Ward.

Popn. 297 males, 355 females: total 652.

(10)　Horeb.　Baptists.

Erected 1820.

School kept sometimes.

Space: free 100; other 150. Free space: in the aisles.

Present: morn. 42; aft. school; even. 80.

Average (12 *months*): general congregation 60:90; scholars 30.

Thomas Prichard.　Deacon.
Vardre

[Original numbered 600. 2. 3(11).]

4　Ysclydach Hamlet.

Popn. 159 males, 168 females: total 327.

(11)　＊Rhydybryw Chapel of Ease.

Endowed: land £185.

Space: free 12; other 192.

Present: aft. 200.

David Parry. Curate.

[Original numbered 600. 2. 4(1).]

Lewis: sub Llywel: perpetual curacy, in the gift of the Vicar of Llywel: net income £186.

5   Trallong Parish.
Area: 3,384 acres. *Popn.* 159 males, 160 females: total 319.

(12)   TRALLONG PARISH CHURCH.
Endowed: land £50; tithe £10; permanent endowment £6. 10.; fees 10*s.*
Present: aft. 82 + 21 scholars.

William Williams.   Churchwarden.

Lewis: prebend in the collegiate church at Brecon, rated at £7. 0. 7; in the gift of
the Bishop. The living, a perpetual curacy, endowed with £600 royal bounty; net
income £59; patron and impropriator, the Prebendary.

C & C: sub Trallwng: 1 service in Welsh performed by the incumbent.

I & C: not resident.

ERCR: accom. 250.

(13)   SALEM.   CALVINISTIC METHODISTS.
Erected 1831.
Space: free 9; other 14; standing 45-55 Persons.
Present: morn. 60; aft. 32 scholars; even. 100.

Owen Jones.   Deacon.
Cwmsevin, Trallong.

[6-10]   Devynnock Parish, consisting of the Hamlets of [6] Glyntawe, [7] Cray, [8] Glynn, [9] Maescar, and [10] Senny.
Area of the whole parish: 28,883 acres. *Popn.* 971 males, 998 females:
total 1,969.

6   Glyntawe Hamlet.
Popn. 55 males, 52 females: total 107.

(14)   CALLWEN DISTRICT CHAPEL, GLYNTAWE.
Endowed: land £22; glebe £10; permanent endowment £67; fees £1.
Space: free 22; other 58.
Present: morn. 42.
Average (12 *months*): morn. 50.

Evan Jenkins.   Incumbent.

Lewis: sub Capel-Callwen: perpetual curacy, endowed with £800 royal bounty and
£200 parliamentary grant; net income £56: patron, vicar of Devynock: tithes
commuted for £42, of which one third (£14) is payable to Vicar of Devynock, two-
thirds to Bishop of Gloucester and Bristol, and one-third to an impropriator.

C & C: 1 service in Welsh performed by the incumbent.

I & C: not resident.

ICBS: grant of £25 in 1840.

7 Cray Hamlet.
Popn. 232 males, 278 females: total 510.

(15) LLANULID PERPETUAL CURACY.
Endowed: land £12; permanent endowment £60.
Space: free 20; other 40.
Present: aft. 10.
Remarks: As to when the chapel was consecrated I have no means of ascertaining.

J. Morgan Downes. Perpetual Curate.

Lewis: sub Cray: perpetual curacy, endowed with £1,600 royal bounty: patron, the vicar of Devynnock: tithes commuted for £267. 6. 3, of which the patron receives one-third, the remaining two thirds being divided between Bishop of Gloucester and Bristol and the impropriator.
C & C: sub Llanulid: 1 service in Welsh performed by the incumbent.
I & C: resident.

(16) DEVYNNOCK PARISH CHURCH.
Endowed: land £8; tithe (gross) £306; glebe £5; total £319.
Space: free 100; other 499.
Present: morn. 200 + 80 scholars; even. 300 + 126 scholars.
Average: morn. 200 + 80 scholars; even. 300 + 126 scholars.

Timothy Davies.   Vicar.

Lewis: vicarage, with perpetual curacy of Ystrad-velltey annexed [584. 3. 6(9)], rated at £14. 14. 2½; net income £284, with 2 acres glebe and glebe-house; patron, Bishop Gloucester and Bristol who is impropriator of one-third of the great and small tithes, one-third belonging to Penry Williams, Esq., and the remaining one-third payable to the vicar: vicar is patron of the three perpetual curacies of Llanilid [600. 2. 7(15)], Llan Illtyd [600. 2. 8(23)], and Callwen [600. 2. 6(14)].
C & C: 2 services in Welsh in the church performed by the vicar.
I & C: resident: curate has stipend of £50.

[2. 6-10] (17) BRYCHGOED, DEVYNOCK.   INDEPENDENT.
Erected 1744.
Space: free 100; other 300; standing 50.
Present: morn. 100 + 20 scholars; even. 20 + 15 scholars.
Average: morn. 120 + 30 scholars; even. 40 + 20 scholars.
Remarks: There is no service held in one Chapel in the afternoon but there is constantly a Sunday School kept every afternoon.

John Stephens. Independent Minister.

[2. 6-10] (18) PARTICULAR BAPTIST, DEVINOCK.
A rented room.
Present: aft. 40; even. 25.

Revd. J. Jones.
Llanvihangelnant Bran.

[2. 6-10] (19) Sardis, Devynock. Independent.
Erected 1840.
Space: free 110; other 75.
Present: aft. 40 + 20 scholars; even. 10 + 17 scholars.
Average: aft. 50 + 30 scholars; even. 20 + 15 scholars.

> John Stephens. Minister.
> Brychgoed.

[2. 6-10] (20) Lower Chapel, Devynnock. Wesleyan Methodists.
Erected 1810.
Space: free 12; other 14; standing 100.
Present: morn. 39; aft. 17 scholars; even. 48.
Average: morn. 44; aft. 25 scholars; even. 50.

> Morgan Jones. Chapel Steward.
> Draper. Sennybridge.

[2. 6-10] (21) Trinity Chapel, Devynnock. Welsh Calvinistic Methodist.
Erected 1793.
Space: free 107; other 193.
Present: morn. 66 scholars; aft. 134; even. 112.
Average (12 *months*): morn. 76 scholars; aft. 143; even. 124.

> Edward Williams. Secretary.
> Maescur, Devynog.

[7] (22) Horeb, Cray. Calvinistic Methodist.
Erected 1808.
Day School held.
Space: free 13; other 22; standing 3 spaces free.
Present: morn. 110 + 52 scholars; even. 137 + 74 scholars.
Average (6 *months*): morn. 120 + 54 scholars; even. 130 + 76 Scholars.

> Thos. Thomas. Steward.
> Llwynmeusydd, Senny Bridge.

8 Glynn Hamlet.
Popn. 141 males, 135 females: total 276.

(23) Llanilltyd Chapelry, Glynn.
Endowed: land £49; permanent endowment £9. 10.; other sources £22.
Space: 72 sittings.
Present: aft. 34.
Average: aft. 30-40.
Remarks: The above named chapel is very inconveniently situated being

very near on the very top of Illtyd Mountain. The attendance varies very much owing to the weather, sometimes there are very few in chapel, sometimes all the sittings are occupied.

Jno. D. Morgan. Perpetual curate.

Lewis: vide sub. Devynnock.

C & C: 1 service in Welsh performed by the incumbent.

I & C: resident.

(24) LIBANUS. INDEPENDENT.
Erected 1823.
Space: free 75; other 70.
Present: morn. 50 + 15 scholars; even. 78 + 29 scholars.

John Stephens. Minister.

9 Maescar Hamlet.
Popn. 388 males, 394 females: total 782.
[No returns]

10 Senny Hamlet.
Popn. 155 males, 139 females: total 294.
[No returns]

[End of Devynnock Subdistrict]

3 BRECKNOCK (Subdistrict)
Area: 43,018 acres. *Popn.* 3,704 males, 3,811 females: total 7,515.

[1-3] Llanspyddid Parish, consisting of the Hamlets of [1] Llanspyddid, [2] Modrydd, and [3] Pen-Pont.
Area of the whole parish: 8,435 acres. *Popn.* 196 males, 208 females: total 404.

1 Llanspyddid Hamlet.
Area: 1,691 acres. *Popn.* 78 males, 86 females: total 164.

(1) LLANSPYDDID PARISH CHURCH.
Endowed: tithe £117; fees under 10s.
Space: other 100.
Present: morn. 55 + 14 scholars.
Average (12 *months*): morn. 60 + 14 to 18 scholars.

Remarks: The Vicar has only one Third of the Tithe the other two remaining parts belong to the Lay Rector, Marquis Camden & likewise the glebe the whole together may be valued at £12 per annum at the present time.

J. Morgan Downes.   Vicar.

Lewis: discharged vicarage, rated at £5. 17. 8½.: tithes (of the whole parish) commuted for £417: tithes of the Hamlet valued at £200: patron and impropriator, Marquess Camden: with the exception of £55 payable to archdeacon of Brecon, two-thirds of tithe payable to the impropriator, and remainder to the vicar; glebe of 4 acres valued at £6, and a glebe-house.
C & C: 1 service, alternately English and Welsh, performed by the incumbent.
I & C: not resident.
ERCR: accom. 200.

2   Modrydd Hamlet.

Area: 4,774. *Popn.* 61 males, 58 females: total 119.

(2)   Pont Estyll, Llanspythid.   Baptist.
Erected before 1800.
Space: free 150; other 160; standing 50.
Present: morn. 35 + 22 scholars; even. 70.
Remarks: As the above Chapel is situated in a country place, and many of the members and Hearers have a far way to come, the number of Hearers and Sunday Scholars is much less in Winter than in Summer. The number of Sunday Scholars is known is about 40; hearers in summer from 80 to 100 in the morning, from 160 to 200 in the evening.

Thomas Roberts.   Baptist Minister.

3   Pen-Pont Hamlet.

Area: 1,970 acres. *Popn.* 57 males, 64 females: total 121.

(3)   Bettws Penpont District Chapelry.
Endowed: permanent endowment £90.
Space: free 2 benches; other 14 pews.
Present: morn. 35; aft. 20.
Average (12 *months*): morn. 40; aft. 20.

Philip Howell Morgan.
Perpetual Curate.

Lewis: perpetual curacy, endowed with £1,000 royal bounty; net income £80: in the patronage of the resident parishioners: tithes commuted for £110, of which £55 payable to the archdeacon of Brecon, £36. 13. 4 to the impropriator, and £18. 6. 8. to the vicar of Llanspyddid.
C & C: 2 services in English.
I & C: not resident.
ERCR: accom. 60.

4 Aberyscir Parish.
Area: 1,918 acres. *Popn.* 64 males, 57 females: total 121.

(4) ABERYSCIR PARISH CHURCH.
Endowed: tithe £150.
Space: free open benches 18; other pews 5.
Present: morn. 25.
Average (12 *months*): morn. 30.
Remarks: Very small Agricultural Parish containing about ten farms.

D. Jones.   Rector.

Lewis: rectory; tithes communated for £150; rated as a vicarage at £3. 6. 3.:
patron, present incumbent.

C & C: 1 service in Welsh performed by the incumbent.

I & C: resident.

ERCR: accom. 'sufficient'.

(5) SILOAM.   INDEPENDENT.
Erected 1838.
Space: free 12; other 13; standing 20.
Present: morn. 12 scholars; aft. 15; even. 50.

William Davies.   Minister.
Gwarocllin, Merthyr Cynog.

5 Battle Parish.
Area: 1,544 acres. *Popn.* 76 males, 75 femles: total 151.

(6) BATTLE PARISH CHURCH.
Endowed: land £72; tithe £5. 5. 0.; fees £1.
Space: free 50; other 35.
Present: morn. 60 + 35 scholars; even. 45 + 30 scholars.
Average: morn. 55 + 30 scholars; even. 35 + 32 scholars.
Remarks: The Services are alternate, better attended in the morning than
evening.

Walter Williams.   Minister.

Lewis: perpetual curacy, endowed with £600 royal bounty and £200 parliamentary
grant; net income £73: patrons and impropriators, trustees of late John Browne,
Esq.: no glebe nor parsonage.

C & C: 1 service, alternate English and Welsh, performed by the incumbent.

I & C: not resident.

6 Llandefailog-fach parish—part of.
Area: 2,000 acres. *Popn.* 89 males, 115 females: total 204.

(7) LLANDEFEILOG FACH PARISH CHURCH.
Endowed: tithe £276. 11. 0; glebe £30; fees £1.
Space: free 55.
Present: morn. 39 + 20 scholars; aft. 22 + 10 scholars.
Average: morn. 30-45 + 20 scholars; aft. 15-20 + 10-15 scholars.

Thomas Vaughan, M.A., Rector.

Lewis: rectory, rated at £13; net income £258: patron, the Crown: church rebuilt 1831, of stone given by the rector, by subscription £200 and grant of £60 from the Incorporated Society.
C & C: 2 services, English in morn., Welsh in even., performed by incumbent and curate.
I & C: resident: curate has stipend of £60.
ICBS: grant of £60 in 1831.

(8) PWLLGLOYW.   WESLEYAN METHODIST.
Erected 1815.
Space: free 30; other 74.
Present: aft. 40; even. 50.
Average (12 months): aft. 50; even. 56.

Morgan Williams.   Steward.
Pan-y-llwyfen, Pwllgloyw.

(9) ELIM.   BAPTIST.
Erected 1844.
Space: free 56; other 44; standing 150.
Present: morn. 20; aft. 18 + 18 scholars; even. 101.
Average (12 months): general congregation 200; scholars 20.

Samuel Morgan.   Wrighter.
Sarne, Llandefailog Vach.

7 Llanthew Parish.
Area: 2,695 acres. *Popn.* 157 males, 143 females: total 300.

(10) LLANDDEW PARISH CHURCH.
Endowed: land £84; permanent endowment £14. 10s.
Space: free 12, other 92*.
Present: aft. 60.
Average (12 months): aft. 35-40.
Remarks: *Enough for all the *men, women* and *children* of the Parish.

Morgan Jones, B.A.   Incumbent.

Lewis: perpetual curacy, endowed with £1,000 royal bounty; net income £89; patron and impropriator, Archdeacon of Brecknock; tithes commuted for £300; glebe of 8 acres valued at £20.

C & C: 1 service in Welsh performed by the incumbent.
I & C: not resident.
ICBS: grant of £30 in 1836.

[8-9] Borough of Brecknock: St. John the Evangelist Parish, consisting of [8] Upper Division with Venny-Vach Hamlet, and [9] Lower Division or St. Mary Chapelry.
Area of whole parish: 3,637 acres. *Popn.* 2,237 males, 2,319 females: total 4,556.

8 Upper Division with Venny-Vach Hamlet.
Area: 2,932 acres. *Popn.* 1,005 males, 1,062 females: total 2,067.

(11) Priory or St. John's Parish Church.
Space: free 240; other 600.
Usual number of attendants: morn. 250 + 120 scholars; aft. 400 + 120 scholars.

Informant: J. D. Williams.

[Informant's form]
Lewis: discharged vicarage, with the perpetual curacy of St. Mary's [600. 3. 9(16)] annexed; rated at £6. 13. 4; endowed with £200 royal bounty and £200 private benefaction; patron, Archdeacon of Brecknock: impropriate tithes commuted for £192, and the vicarial for £172.
C & C: 2 services in English.
I & C: no return.
ICBS: grant of £120 in 1837.

(12) Tabernacle, Struet. Wesleyan Methodist.
Erected 1824.
Space: free 80; other 182.
Present: morn. 15; aft. 55 + 5 scholars; even. 73 + 7 scholars.
Average (12 *months*): aft. 75; even. 140.

John Hargest. Chapel Steward.
Dinas Row.

(13) Struet. Welsh Calvinistic Methodist.
Erected before 1800; re-erected 1820.
Space: free 170; other 280. 'No "free space" except the Aisles to the different sittings.'
Present: morn. 200; aft. 149 scholars; even. 231.
Average (12 *months*): morn. 210; aft. 130 scholars; even. 240.

Rees Williams. Assistant Secretary of the Connexion.
Orchard Street.

(14) KENSINGTON. ROMAN CATHOLIC.
Formerly a farm house, in occupation as a place of worship only 9 months.
Space: free 150; standing 60.
Present: morn. 191; aft. 36 + 15 scholars.
Average (9 *months*): morn. 200; aft 50 + 25 scholars.
Remarks: The place of worship herein described is only a temporary accomodation untill our new church St Michael situate in Wheat St. shall be opened affording ample space for 250 persons the sittings mostly free. The school is held only on afternoons before Vespers.

       Joseph Jones. Catholic Priest.
       Usk Terrace.

(15) KENSINGTON CHAPEL. BAPTIST.
Erected 1824.
Space: free 60; other 180.
Present: morn. 160; even. 140.

       James W. Evans. Minister.

9 Lower Division, or St. Mary Chapelry.
Area: 705 acres. *Popn.* 961 males, 1,257 females: total 2,218.

(16) ST. MARY'S CHAPEL OF EASE IN THE TOWN OF BRECON.
Endowed: land £143; tithe £90; fees £10.
Space: free 290; other 515; children 120.
Present: morn. 560 + 197 scholars; even. 480 + 120 scholars.
Remarks: Two Sunday Schools attend our Church in the morning.

       James Denning. Curate.

Lewis: sub Brecknock: impropriate tithes commuted for £40; and the dues of the perpetual curate for £60.
C & C: 2 services in English.
I & C: resident: curate has stipend of £90.

(17) WESLEYAN CHAPEL, LION STREET.
Erected 1834.
Space: free 84; other 274.
Present: morn. 180 + 20 scholars; even. 300.

       Paul Orchard, Jnr. Wesleyan Minister.
       Lion Street.

(18) PLOUGH CHAPEL, LION STREET. INDEPENDENTS.
Erected before 1800.
Space: free 900.
Present: morn. 550; even. 800.

       Caleb Gwion. Minister.
       Ship Street.

(19) GLAMORGAN STREET CHAPEL. INDEPENDENTS.
Erected 1835.
Space: free 242; other 192.
Present: morn. 130; even. 150.

> D. Henry Griffiths. Minister.
> Cottage Garden.

(20) WESTGATE WELSH BAPTIST CHAPEL. PARTICULAR BAPTIST.
Erected 1806; rebuilt 1833.
Space: free 260; other 278.
Present: morn. 264 + 40 scholars; aft. school; even. 328 + 50 scholars.
Average (12 *months*): morn. 250 + 50 scholars; even. 400 + 100 scholars.

> John Evans. Minister.
> High Street.

10 Christ's College, Ex. Parochial.
Popn. 55 males, 46 females: total 101.
[No returns]

11 Castle Inn, Ex. Parochial.
Popn. 8 males, 14 females: total 22.
[No returns]

[12-13] St. David Parish, consisting of [12] Lower Division or Llanfaes, and [13] Upper Division.
Area of the whole parish: 2,789 acres. *Popn.* 698 males, 721 females: total 1,419.

12 Lower Division of St. David Parish, or Llanvaes.
Popn. 622 males, 659 femles: total 1,281.

(21) ST. DAVID'S IN LLANFAES PARISH CHURCH.
Space: other 170.
Present: morn. 60 + 92 scholars; even. 51 + 81 scholars.

> R. Price. Vicar.

Lewis: discharged vicarage, rated at £5. 15. 7½.; endowed with £400 private benefactions, and £400 royal bounty; net income £160: patron, the archdeacon.

C & C: *sub* St. David's, Llanvaes: 2 services, three times a fortnight in English, once in Welsh, performed by the incumbent and curate.

I & C: incumbent not resident: curate has stipend of £10.

13   Upper Division of St. David Parish.
Popn. 76 males, 62 females: total 138.
[No returns]

[14-15]   Cantreff Parish, consisting of [14] Cantreff and [15] Nantddu Chapelry.
Area of the whole parish: 20,000 acres. *Popn.* 124 males, 113 females: total 237.

14   Cantreff Parish.
Popn. 60 males, 58 females: total 118.

(22)   CANTREFF PARISH CHURCH.
Space: other 64.
Average: morn. 16 + 14 scholars; even. 16 + 14 scholars.

Thos. M. Powell.   Rector.

Lewis: rectory, rated £9. 10. 7½; patron, Rev. Thomas Powell: tithes commuted for £230, subject to rates averaging £20; glebe of 38 acres, and glebe-house.

C & C: 1 service, in Welsh on alternate Sundays, performed by the incumbent.

I & C: resident.

15   Nantddu Chapelry.
Popn. 64 males, 55 females: total 119.

23)   NANTDDU CHAPEL.
Endowed: land £77. 10. 0.; permanent endowment £2. 10. 0.
Space: other 10.
Present: aft. 30.

John Rogers.   Minister.

Lewis: perpetual curacy, endowed with £1,000 royal bounty; net income £60: patron, rector of Cantrev [600. 3. 14(22)]; impropriator, Rev. W. Williams, the incumbent.

C & C: 1 service in Welsh performed by the curate.

I & C: incumbent not resident; curate has stipend of £57.
ERCR: accom. 55.

[End of Brecknock Subdistrict]

4 PENKELLY (Subdistrict)
Area: 25,749 acres. *Popn.* 754 males, 787 females: total 1,541.

1 Llanvrynach (Upper and Lower) Parish.
Area: 7,127 acres. *Popn.* 181 males, 177 females: total 358.

(1) LLANVRYNACH PARISH CHURCH.
Endowed: tithe £300; glebe 2 acres.
Space: free 110; other 93.
Present: morn. 73 + 30 scholars; even. 42.
Average (12 *months*): morn. (English service) 130 + 44 scholars; even.
(Welsh) 46.

William Meredith. Curate.

Lewis: rectory, rated at £4. 10. 7½.; tithes commuted for £300, subject to rates averaging £23. 16. 3.; glebe of 3 acres valued at £5, and glebe-house: patrons, family of Tynte.

C & C: 2 services, English and Welsh on alternate Sundays, performed by the curate.

I & C: incumbent not-resident: curate, who resides in the glebe-house, has stipend of £100.

(2) WESLEYAN.
[This return is missing.]

(3) MISPA CHAPPEL. BAPTISM.
Erected about 1835.
Space: free 61; other 90.
Present: morn. 58; even. 169.
Average (12 *months*): morn. 67; even. 180.

Thomas Smith. Deacon.
William Williams. Minister.

[2-3] Llanvigan Parish, consisting of [2] Glynn Collwn, or Upper Division, and [3] Penkelly, or Lower Division.
Area of the whole parish: 12,642 acres. *Popn.* 313 males, 321 females: total 634.

2 Glynn Collwn, or Upper Division.
Popn. 131 males, 144 females: total 275.
[No returns]

3 Penkelly, or Lower Division.
Popn. 182 males, 177 females: total 359.

(4)   LLANFIGAN PARISH CHURCH.
Endowed: tithe £450; glebe 27 acres.
Space: free 48; other 180.
Present: aft. 90.
Average (12 *months*): morn. 94.

Charles Williams.   Rector.

Lewis: rectory, rated at £20. 10. 0.; patron, C. K. Kemeys Tynte, Esq.: tithes commuted for £560, of which £110 payable to an impropriator, and £450 to the rector: glebe of 26 acres valued at £45, and glebe-house.

C & C: 2 services alternately English and Welsh performed by the incumbent.

I & C: resident.

(5)   PENTWYN.   CALVINISTIC METHODIST.
Erected before 1800.
Used also for Day School.
Space: free 50.
Present: morn. 16 scholars; aft. 32; even. 44.
Average (6 *months*): morn. 16 scholars; aft. 50.

John Watkins.   Deacon.

(6)   BENCIAH.   INDEPENDENTS.
Erected 1836.
Space: free 64.
Present: morn. 73 + 75 scholars; aft. 72; even. 130.
Average (12 *months*): morn. 70 + 72 scholars; aft. 60; even. 140.

Henry Powell.   Deacon.
Talybont.
Llanthetty.

(7)   GLYN COLLWYN CHAPEL OF EASE.
Endowed: land £80.
Space: free 50.
Present: aft. 40.

David Jones.   Officiating Minister.

Lewis: perpetual curacy, endowed with £1,000 royal bounty: net income £80; patron, rector of Llanvigan [600. 4. 3(4)].

C & C: 1 service in Welsh performed by the incumbent.

I & C: resident.

[This return should come under 600. 4. 2.]

(8)   TY NEWYDD AR ABER.   INDEPENDENTS.
Erected 1762.
Space: free 35; 36 feet length, 27 in breadth.

Present: morn. 88 + 59 scholars; even. 145.
Average (12 *months*): general. congregation 160; scholars 60.

David Jones.   Minister.

[This return should come under 600. 4. 2.]

[4-5]   Llanthetty Parish, consisting of the Hamlets of [4] Dyffrin, and [5] Vro.

Area of the whole parish: 5,980 acres. *Popn.* 260 males, 289 females: total 549.

4   Dyffrin Hamlet.

Popn. 90 males, 93 females: total 183.

(9)   LLANTHETTY PARISH CHURCH.
Endowed: tithe £340; glebe £35; fees £1.
Space: free 37; other 130.
Present: morn. 40. 'The service being entirely Welsh, the English part of the congregation were all absent.'
Average (12 *months*): From 50 to 60. Except when very wet.
Remarks: I was instituted in this living August 1846. There was then no school of any kind in the Parish. I have since built a spacious schoolroom at my own expence without any aid pecuniary or otherwise from any Individual or Society—on Sunday sennight I delivered a lecture at 6 p.m. I delivered a lecture in Welsh and about 100 persons attended—the Church is about 2 miles distant from the bulk of the Parishioners—peculiarly inconvenient. From Easter to Michaelmas there are two full duties in the Church—Welsh and English alternately Morning and evening. The school has just been commenced—it is open to all. It is intended to be a self-paying system after the Dean of Hereford's Plan.

John Jones.   Minister.

Lewis: rectory, with the perpetual curacy of Tâf-Vechan [600. 4. 5(12)] annexed, rated at £7. 10. 7½.; patron, J. P. Gwynne Holford, Esq.: tithes commuted for £395, of which £55 payable to the impropriator, and £340 to the vicar: glebe of 17 acres valued at £45. 15. 6, and a glebe-house.

C & C: 2 services in summer, one in winter, alternately English and Welsh, performed by the incumbent.

I & C: resident.

5   Nantddu Chapelry.

Popn. 170 males, 196 females: total 366.

(10)   YARD, TALYBONT YARD, LLANTHETTY.   BAPTISTS.
Erected 1813.
Space: standing 150.
Present: aft. 42.
Average: aft. 55.
Remarks: This is a Branch of Llangynidor Baptist Church and Service is only held here in the evening of each Sunday.   There is no School held here.

> Lewis Evans.   Baptist Minister.
> Llangynidr.

(11)   BETHANIA, TALYBONT.   CALVINISTIC METHODIST.
Erected 1834.
Space: free 15;   other 12;   standing 240 including gallery.
Present: morn. 42;   aft. 28 scholars;   even. 43.
Average (12 *months*): morn. 50;   aft. 28 scholars;   even. 55.
Remarks: This Chapel is used only for Public Worship and Sunday Schools the sermon is delivered by Circulating Ministers.

> Ebenezer Thomas.   Secretary of the Society.
> Watertender, Talybont.

(12)   TAFFECHAN CHAPEL OF EASE.
Endowed: land £80.
Space: free 72.
Present: morn. 40.

> David Jones.   Officiating Minister.

Lewis: sub Llanthetty: perpetual curacy endowed with £800 royal bounty and £200 parliamentary grant.

C & C: 1 service in Welsh performed by the incumbent.

I & C: not resident.

[End of Penkelly Subdistrict]

5 LLANGORSE (Subdistrict)
Area: 28,322 acres.   *Popn.* 1,521 males, 1,504 females: total 3,025.

1 Llansantffraed Parish.
Area: 2,247 acres.   *Popn.* 109 males, 122 females: total 231.

(1)   LLANSAINTFFREAD PARISH CHURCH.
Endowed: tithe £267;   glebe £27;   fees £1. 10. 0.*
Space: There is room in the Church for more than double the number of the inhabitants of the parish.

Present: morn. 24 + 8 scholars.
Average (3 *months*): morn. 35 + 10 scholars.
Remarks: This is a thinly populated parish. The greater part of the people live a *long distance from* the church. During the summer months there are two Church services morning and afternoon.
*It should here be noted that the amount of Income stated is the *gross*— there are of course many *deductions*.
During the summer months the number of attendants at Church is much greater than 45.

Thomas Watkins.   Rector.

(Additional remarks)
A return will doubtless be made by the minister of the Independent Chapel situated on one of the extremities of this Parish. The congregation ass[embled] there is obtained not from their part but from this and three or four other [adjoin]ing and neighbouring parishes.

Thomas Watkins.

Lewis: rectory, rated at £6. 4. 7; net income £271, with glebe house: patron, Earl of Ashburnham: portion of the tithes, anciently appropriated to the free chapel of Pencelly [600. 4. 3(7)] now held by the lords of the manors of Buckland and Scethrog.

C & C: 2 services in summer, 1 in winter, alternately English and Welsh performed by the incumbent.

I & C: resident.

ERCR: accom. 130.

(2) TABERNACLE. INDEPENDENT.
Erected 1841.
Space: free 16; other 14; standing 30.
Present: morn. 82 + 52 scholars; aft. 52 scholars; even. 117.
Average (12 *months*): morn. 78; aft. 47 scholars; even. 115.
Remarks: Before this Chapel was erected, Divine worship was held in a small village named Skethiog about half a mile from the present Chapel —Since the year 1814—the present Minister ordained in this small chapel in 1836—with 15 members and since maintained by voluntary subscriptions. Now in number about 72.

Evan Pritchard.   Minister.

2 Llanhamlach Parish.
Area: 1,867 acres. *Popn.* 174 males, 172 females: total 346.

(3) LLANHAMLACH PARISH CHURCH.
Endowed: tithes commuted in 1838.
Space: free 30; other 79.
Average: morn. 50; even. 30.

Remarks: There was a Sunday School by private subscription but it dropt off in consequence of the Minister's illness.

> Thomas M. Powell.   Rector.

Lewis: rectory, rated at £6. 1. 8.; patron, Rev. Thomas Powell: tithes commuted for £255, subject to rates averaging £26. 8. 2½; glebe of 40 acres valued at £40: church rebuilt 1802 by parochial rate.

C & C: 1 service in Welsh and English on alternate Sundays performed by the incumbent.

I & C: not resident.

(4)   BETHEL CHAPEL.   WESLEYAN METHODISTS.
Erected 1848.
Space: free 65.
Present: morn. 27 + 10 scholars; even. 37.
Average: general congregation 30; scholars 10.

> William Griffiths.   Steward.
> Canal Lockkeeper.

(5)   LLECHFAEN CHAPEL.   WELSH CALVINISTIC METHODISTS.
Erected 1837.
Space: free 100; other 20; standing 60.
Present: morn. 41 + 38 scholars; even. 48 + 40 scholars.
Average: aft. 40 + 50 scholars.

> John Rice.   Superintendent.
> Lechfaen.

3   Llanywern Parish.
Area: 1,430 acres. *Popn.* 73 males, 75 females: total 178.
[Llanywern Parish Church: see 600. 5. 8(14) below.]

4   Talachddu Parish.
Area: 1,818 acres. *Popn.* 96 males, 91 females: total 187.

(6)   TALACHDDU, ST. MARY'S PARISH CHURCH.
Endowed: tithe £135; glebe £30; fees £1.
Space: free 27; other 41.
Present: morn. 33 + 20 scholars.
Remarks: I have returned the gross amount of tithe and rent of glebe land without deductions for poor rates etc.

> Charles Griffiths.   Rector.

Lewis: discharged rectory, rated at £4. 12. 1; patron, Mrs. Anne Griffith: net income £143; glebe of 47 acres, with a glebe-house.

C & C: 1 service in English.

I & C: legally not resident.

(7) MAESYBERLLAN. BAPTISTS.
Erected 1746, rebuilt 1835.
Space: free benches 14; other pews 51.
Present: morn. 140 + 17 scholars.
Average: morn. 200 + 25 scholars.

                              Enoch Price.   Minister.

5 Trawsgoed Hamlet: part of Gwen-ddwr Parish [599. 3. 11.].
Area: 881 acres. *Popn.* 33 males, 30 females: total 63.
[No returns]

6 Llandefalley Parish.
Area: 8,509 acres. *Popn.* 359 males, 345 females: total 704.

(8) LLANDEFALLEY PARISH CHURCH.
Endowed: tithe £460; glebe £20.
Space: free 60; other 37.
Present: morn. 20.
Average: morn. 70; aft. 70.

                              Chas. Vaughan.   Rector.

Lewis: discharged vicarage, consolidated with that of Crickadarn [599. 3. 12(18)]; rated at £5: privately endowed with rectorial tithes of Llandefalley, Crickadarn, and part of Bronllys [602. 1. 6(11)], subject to payment of certain charities and £25 to curate of Crickadarn.

C & C: 2 services, English on morn. of alternate Sundays, Welsh on even. of alternate Sundays, performed by the incumbent.

I & C: sub Crickadarn with Llandevally: no return.

(9) BRECHFA, LLANVALLAN. INDEPENDENTS.
Erected 1803.
Space: free 12 seats; free gallery and down stairs free; standing 12 by 18.
Present: morn. 60; aft. 100; even. 100.
Average: morn. 60 incl. 24 scholars; aft. 100; even. 100.

                              Thomas Havard. Minister.
                              Talgarth.

(10) Wernos.   Calvinistic Methodists.
Farm House.
Present: morn. 35; aft. 40 scholars; even. 45.

> Thomas Jones. Deacon.
> Wernos.

7 Llanvillo Parish.

Area: 3,305 acres. *Popn.* 149 males, 158 females: total 307.

(11) Llanvillo Parish Church.
Endowed: tithe £322; glebe £15; fees £1.
Space: free 12; other 150.
Present: morn. 52 + 40 scholars; even. 30.
Average (12 *months*): morn. 60-70 + 50 scholars; even. 50.
Remarks: I have given you the gross amount of Tithe, the net amt. would
be about £220. Tithes *unlike other property* is rated without any reference to
personal labour and outlay, a *rate in fact upon real and personal property*. As
I hold it myself and have these last years been out of pocket by it. It is
situate in the midst of several hundred acres of Land now in the hands of
the Proprietor unable to let it and not likely to do so under the present aspect
of affairs and if he makes tithes, taxes and wages, he will be a clever fellow.
And he knows the reason why.

> William Bowcott. Rector.

Lewis: rectory, with that of Llandevailog-Tre'r-Graig [600. 5. 8(12)] annexed;
rated at £6. 14. 9½; net income £324, with glebe-house: patron, Earl of Ashburnham.

C & C: 3 services in 2 Sundays, in Welsh performed by the incumbent.

I & C: no return.

8 Llandefailog-Tre-Graig Parish.

Area: 540 acres. *Popn.* 22 males, 16 females: total 38.

(12) Llandefailog Tregraig Chapel of Ease.
Erected 1750 or 1760.
Not endowed.
Licensed to accomodate Gregory Parry's family then resident at Llane-
faelog House.
Space: other 25.
Average: aft. 8.

> William Bowcott. Minister.

Lewis: rectory, annexed to that of Llanvillo: church erected by Rev. Gregory
Parry, M.A., at his sole expense, in 1710.

C & C: sub Llavillo: 1 service in Welsh performed by the incumbent.

I & C: no return.
[Note: this return is numbered 600. 5. 7(12).]

(13)   CATHEDINE PARISH CHURCH.
[This return is misplaced: see under 600. 5. 12, below.]

(14)   LLANYWERN PARISH CHURCH.
Average (12 *months*): morn. 25 or 30.

Morgan Jones, B.A.   Vicar.

Lewis: perpetual curacy, endowed with £800 royal bounty; net income £81; patron the Bishop: parishioners, who once held the advowsons, contribute £4. 10. 0. towards stipend of incumbent.

C & C: 1 service in Welsh, performed by the curate.

I & C: incumbent not resident: curate, who resides at Llanspyddid, 4 miles distant, has stipend of £40.

ERCR: accom. 'sufficient'.

[This return is misplaced: it should be under 600. 5. 3.]

9   Llanfihangel-Tal-y-llyn Parish.
Area: 1,233 acres. *Popn.* 80 males, 83 females: total 163.

(15)   LLANFIHANGEL TAL-Y-LLYN PARISH CHURCH.
Endowed: tithe £172; glebe £25; permanent endowment £1. 1. 0.
Present: morn. 40.
Average (12 *months*): morn. 55.
Remarks: The Church is large enough to contain the whole population of the Parish. There is a day school attended by about [blank] scholars.

Hugh Bold, M.A.   Rector.

Lewis: discharged rectory, rated at £4. 12. 3½.; patron, Rev. Hugh Bold; tithes commuted for £170; glebe of 18 acres valued at £18, with an indifferent glebe-house.

C & C: 1 service in Welsh performed by the incumbent.

I & C: not resident.

ERCR: accom. 'sufficient'.

(16)   SION CHAPEL.   CALVINISTIC METHODIST.
Erected 1835.
Space: free sitting, 18 let.
Present: morn. 50; aft. 61 scholars; even. 115.

John Hargest.   Steward.

10   Llangorse Parish.
Area: 2,806 acres. *Popn.* 211 males, 190 females: total 401.

(17)   LLANGORSE PARISH CHURCH.
Usual number of attendants: morn. 20.

Informant: John Williams. Registrar.
[Informant's form.]

Lewis: vicarage, rated at £5. 10. 0.; net income £170, with glebe-house: tithes held on lease by Dean and Chapter of Windsor, the patrons.

C & C: 1 service in Welsh performed by the curate.

I & C: incumbent not resident: curate, who resides in the glebe-house, has stipend of £70.

ERCR: accom. 300.

(18)   LANGORS UPPER CHAPEL.   CALVINISTICK METHODIST.
Day School held.
Erected before 1800.
Space: free 35.
Present: morn. school; aft. 140; even. 101.
Remarks: The Sunday School is held in the morning.

Samuel Pugh.   Deacon.

(19)   BAPTIST CHAPEL.
Erected before 1820.
Space: free 200.
Present: morn. 104; aft. 42 scholars; even. 98.
Average (12 *months*): morn. 108; aft. 39 scholars; even. 120.

William Roberts.   Minister.

11   Llangasty-Tal-y-llyn Parish.
Area: 2,119 acres. *Popn.* 113 males, 120 females: total 233.

(20)   LLANGASTY TAL-Y-LLYN PARISH CHURCH.
Endowed: Rent charge £262; glebe 6 acres.
Space: free 105; other 145.
Present: morn. 19-23 + 12 children: aft. 63 + 25 children.
Average: morn. 30-40 + 30 children: aft. 40-50 + 30 children. even. 40.
Remarks: The Sunday Services alternate thus: morning Prayer English at ½ past 9 morning full service Welsh at 11.
afternoon public service Eng. at 3.
following Sunday: —
morning full service English at 11
afternoon full service Welsh at 3
evening Prayer English at 6
Daily service.
morning Prayer at 9

evening   Prayer at 9
             Wednesday ⎫
             Friday   ⎬ 7
                        ⎭

The above Parish Church was partially rebuilt and thoroughly repaired and restored in the year 1849 by private contribution.

Arthur Augustus Lewis. Curate.

Lewis: discharged rectory, rated at £4. 18. 9: patron, Rev. Richard Davies: tithes commuted for £260, with glebe of 6 acres.

C & C: 2 services in summer, 1 in winter, alternately English and Welsh, performed by the curate.

I & C: no return.

12   Cathedine Parish.
Area: 1,567 acres. *Popn.* 102 males, 102 females: total 204.

[(13)]   Cathedine Parish Church.
Endowed: tithe £160; glebe £4; fees 10s-15s.
Space: free 15; other 45.
Present: morn. 15.
Average (12 *months*): morn. 35; aft. 35.
Remarks: The attendance on the 30th March was less in number than has occurred during the two past years—which I attribute to the morning being stormy and wet and several sick in the Parish who usually attend.

Wm. Davies. Minister.

Lewis: discharged rectory, rated at £5. 2. 11; patron, Rev. Richard Davies: tithes commuted for £159. 10. 0; glebe of 1 acre valued at £3.

C & C: *sub* Kathedine: 1 service in English.

I & C: not resident.

[End of Llangorse Subdistrict and end of Brecknock District]

601 CRICKHOWELL (District)

Area: 53,692 acres. *Popn.* 11,410 males, 10,287 females: total 21,697.

1 CWMDU (Subdistrict)
Area: 10,068 acres. *Popn.* 560 males, 506 females: total 1,066.

[1-4] Llanfihangel Cwmdu Parish, consisting of the Parcels of [1] Blayney, [2] Cenol, [3] Cilwych, and [4] Tretower.
Area of the whole parish: 10,068 acres. *Popn.* 560 males, 506 females: total 1,066.

1 Blayney Parcel.
Popn. 80 males, 67 females: total 147.

(1) PENUEL. CWMRHOES. INDEPENDENT.
Erected 1805.
Space: free; standing 40.
Present: morn. 67 scholars; aft. 300; even. 100.
Average: morn. 300 + 67 scholars: aft. 300.

> William Hopkins.   Minister.
> Peutrebach.

(2) ZOAR TRETOWER.   PROTESTANT DISSENTERS.
Erected 1844.
Space: all free; standing 50.
Present: morn. 200 + 54 scholars; aft. do.; even. do.
Average: morn. 209 + 61 scholars.

> William Hopkins.   Minister.

[This return is numbered 601. 1. 4(2) and should be included after (5) below.]

2 Cenol Parcel.
Popn. 148 males, 135 females: total 283.

(3)   St. Michael Parish Church, Cwmdu.
Endowed: tithe £231; glebe £18 (gross).
Space: free 450; other 1,000.
Present: morn. 60.
Remarks: During the 12 Calendar Months next preceding March 30, 1851.
The estimated average attendance at Church is 80 persons. The parents
being chiefly Dissenters object to their children attending Church. There
is an afternoon service at the chapel of Ease.

John Hughes.   Minister.

Lewis: sub Llanvihangel-Cwm-Dû: sinecure rectory and vicarage: rectory rated at
£19. 15. 2½, net value £396; patron, Duke of Beaufort: vicarage rated at £9. 13. 1½;
net value £191; patron, the rector; vicarage endowed with one-third of the great
and small tithes, with the exception of certain appropriated tithes in Tretower [4],
Cenol [2] and Kilwych [3]. The church taken down in 1830 and rebuilt at a cost of
£1,600, of which about £225 raised by subscription.

C & C: no entry.

I & C: vacant.

ERCR: accom. 700.

[This return is numbered 601. 1. 2(3).]

3   Cilwych Parcel.
Popn. 170 males, 175 females: total 345.

(4)   Bwlch Chapel.   Calvinistic Methodist.
Erected 1818.
Space: all free.
Present: morn. 160 + 71 scholars; even. 180.
Average: morn. 160 + 89 scholars; even. 180.
Remarks: The Sunday School is held in the afternoon.

William Walters.   Deacon.
Bwlch.

4   Tretower Parcel.
Popn. 162 males, 129 females: total 291.

(5)   Tretower an ancient Chapel.
Space: other 300.
Present: aft. 50.
Average: aft. 50 to 60.

Jenkin Davies.   Perpetual curate.

Lewis: chapel of ease to the parochial church; perpetual curacy, endowed with £800
royal bounty; net income £64; patron, Morgan Morgans, Esq.: impropriator,
Mr. Jones.

C & C: 1 service in English, save once a month in Welsh, performed by the curate.

I & C: no return.

[*End of Cwmdû Subdistrict*]

2 LLANGUNIDER (Subdistrict)

Area: 13,908 acres. *Popn.* 1,756 males, 1,490 females: total 3,246.

[1-2] Llangunider Parish, consisting of the Parcels of [1] Blainey with Duffryn and [2] Vro.

Area and population of the whole parish as for the Subdistrict.

1   Blainey with Duffryn Parcel.

Popn. 1,466 males, 1,202 females: total 2,668.

(1) LLANGYNIDR PARISH CHURCH.

[For this return see under 601. 2. 2, below.]

(2) SARDIS, TREVIL. BAPTISTS.

Erected 1848.

Space: free 90; other 10.

Present: morn. 22; aft. 25 scholars; even. 40.

> Thomas Evans.   Deacon.
> Trevil Quarries.

(3) WELCH WESLEYAN METHODIST, LLANGYNIDR.

[For this return see under 601. 2. 2, below.]

(4) CARMEL CHAPEL, BEAUFORT IRONWORKS.   INDEPENDENTS.

Erected 1818; rebuilt 1829.

Space: free 500; other 250; standing 100.

Present: morn. 507; even. 616.

Remarks: The Sunday Scholars included in the general congregation.

> Thomas Rees.   Minister.
> Beaufort.

(5) SOAR.   INDEPENDENT.

Erected 1841.

Space: free 120.

Present: aft. 42 + 18 scholars; even. 42 + 18 scholars.

Average: aft. 38 + 17 scholars; even. 40 + 20 scholars.

> Sam Phillips.   Independent Minister.

(6) SARDIS COEDYRYNYS.   PARTICULAR BAPTIST.

Erected before 1800.

Space: free 400; standing 40.

Present: morn. 200 + 25 scholars; even. 300 + 30 scholars.

Average (12 *months*): morn. 150 + 30 scholars; even. 300 + 40 scholars.

> Lewis Evans.   Baptist Minister.
> Bishop's Cottage.

(7) HOREB, TREFIL. INDEPENDENT.
Erected 1839.
Space: all free: standing—Dimensions 2 ft by 15 ft within walls. No galleries.
Present: morn. 30.
Average: morn. 35; aft. 50; even. 40.
Remarks: We had no Service at the above place yesterday only in the morning. The Sunday School is kept in a Room rented for the purpose at Twrnyfin and not at the above place of worship. They have also occasional preaching at the place where the school is held. The number of attendance the thirty of April was 32.

> William Williams.   Minister.
> Adulam, Tredegar.

(8) SOAR. INDEPENDENTS.
Erected 1841.
Space: free gallery; other 40; standing 40.
Present: morn. 207; aft. 149 scholars; even. 219.

> John Thomas.   Minister.
> Rhymney.

(9) WESLEYAN METHODISTS, LLANGYNIDER.
Erected 1847.
Space: free 90; standing 40.
Present: aft. 33 + 25 scholars; even. 60 + 31 scholars.
Average (12 *months*): aft. 50 + 30 scholars; even. 50 + 30 scholars.

> Lewis Evans.   Weslean Preacher.
> Tafarnau Bach, Rhymney.

(10) SILOAM. BAPTIST.
Erected 1842.
Space: all free.
Present: morn. 106; aft. 30 scholars; even. 112.
Average: general congregation 25.

> John Jones.   Baptist Minister.
> Tavarnau Bach, Llangynidr.

2 Vro Parcel.
Popn. 290 males, 299 females: total 578.

[(1)] LLANGYNIDR PARISH CHURCH.
Endowed: tithe £424; glebe £60-£70; dues £5.
Space: free 65; other 140.
Present: aft. 43 + 82 scholars.

Average (12 *months*): 30 + 60 scholars; aft. 40 to 60 + 40 scholars; even. 20 to 30.

Remarks: The[re] was only one Service on Sunday March 30th. The greatest portion of the population of this parish lies from 7 to 9 miles from the parish church, which is built at one extremity of the parish—the population alluded to has been formed by the iron works—between which population and the parish church a large and extensive tract of mountain and wild uninhabited country. There are generally 2 services each Sunday—Morning and Afternoon or Morning and Evening.

W. Davies. Minister.

Lewis: rectory, rated at £13. 14. 7; net income £418: patron, Duke of Beaufort.

C & C: 2 services in Summer, 1 in winter, alternately English and Welsh performed by the incumbent.

I & C: resident.

[(3)] WELCH WESLEYAN METHODIST.
Erected 1808.
Space: free 56; other 52; standing 20.
Present: morn. 20 scholars; aft. 45; even. 36.
Average (3 *months*): morn. 66 + 20 scholars; aft. 90; even. 60.

William Rowlands.   One of the
Ministers.

(11) CARMEL. PARTICULAR BAPTIST.
Erected 1833.
Space: free 370; other 138.
Present: morn. 330; aft. 355 scholars; even. 581.
Average (12 *months*): morn. 360; aft. 280 scholars; even. 550.

Robert Ellis. Minister.
Sirhowy Ironworks.

(12) EBENEZER. INDEPENDENT.
Erected 1836.
Space: free gallery; other 400.
Present: morn. 372; aft. 335 scholars; even. 544.
Average (12 *months*): morn. 372; aft. 355 scholars; even. 544.

Noah Stephens. Minister.
Sirhowy.

(13) TABERNACLE. PARTICULAR BAPTIST (WELSH)
Erected 1833.
Space: free 100; other 100; standing 40.

Present: morn. 41; even. 61.
Average (12 *months*)*:* morn. 60; even. 100.

> David Williams. Deacon.
> Miner.
> Near the Rising Sun Duke's town.

(14) SARDIS. INDEPENDENT.
Erected 1838.
Space: free 240; standing 30; gallery contains 120 sittings.
Present: morn. 50 + 15 scholars; even. 77 + 20 scholars.
Average (12 *months*)*:* morn. 50 + 13 scholars; even. 70 + 18 scholars.
Remarks: The Independent cause commenced in this neighbourhood before the year 1830 but the present Chapel was built in the year 1838.

> The Revd. Sam Phillips.
> Independent Minister.
> Llangynidr.

[End of Llangynidr Subdistrict]

3 LLANGATTOCK (Subdistrict)
Area: 9,597 acres. *Popn.* 2,907 males, 2,508 females: total 5,415.

[1-2] Llangattock Parish, consisting of the Parcels of [1] Penallt, and

[2] Prisk and Killey.
Area and population as for the Subdistrict.

1 Penallt Parcel.
Popn. 329 males, 318 females: total 647.

(1) LLANGATTOCK PARISH CHURCH.
Endowed: tithe £527; glebe £70; fees £5.
Space: free 60; other 440.
Present: morn. 250 + 20 scholars; even. 150 + 20 scholars.
Average: morn. 270 + 30 scholars; even. 340 + 30 scholars.

> Geo. Howell. Rector.

Lewis: rectory, with perpetual curacies of Llanelly [601. 4. 1(2(2))] and Llangeney [601. 5. 2(11)]; rated at £31. 13. 9; net income £1,123, with a glebe-house: patron, Duke of Beaufort.

C & C: sub Llangattock with Llanelly and Llangenny: 2 services, in Welsh alternately morn. and even., performed by the curate.

I & C: sub Llangattock with Llanelly and Llangenny: incumbent (Lord W. G. H. Somerset) not resident: 2 curates, one of whom resides in the glebe-house and the other in the parish, have joint stipend of £220.

(2)   EBENEZER CHAPEL.   PRIMITIVE METHODIST.
Erected 1824, re-erected 1836.
Space: free 100; other 213.
Present: morn. 134 + 83 scholars; aft. 107 scholars; even. 200.
Average (12 *months*): morn. 5,200 + 4,160 scholars; aft. 5,200 scholars;
even. 11,440.

> William Rowe.   Minister.
> Beaufort, Brynmawr.

(3)   BETHESDA.   INDEPENDENTS.
Erected 1835.
Space: free 209; other 148; standing 25.
Present: morn. 128; aft. 67 scholars; even. 125.
Remarks: The actual numbers attending D.S. on March 30th 1851. Many
persons and members owing to their residing at a distance from the chapel
are unable to attend in the morning and evening.

> Evan Watkins.   Independent Minister.
> Llangattock.

(4)   UNION WORKHOUSE CHAPEL.
Erected 3 years.
Day School held.
Space: free 70.
Present: morn. 40 + 20 scholars.
Average (12 *months*): morn. 40 + 20 scholars.
Remarks: The Service is conducted by a Clergyman and therefore it is a
Church.

> John Evans.   Chaplain.
> to the Crickhowell Union.

(5)   BETHESDA INDEPENDENT CHAPEL.   CONGREGATIONALISTS.
Erected 1835.
Space: 32 (pews)
Usual number of attendants: morn. 250; aft. 120 scholars; even. 320.

> Informant, Thomas Evans.
> Penallt Isha.

[Informant's form.]
[This duplicates 601. 3. 1(3).]

2 Prisk and Killey Parcel.
Popn. 2,578 males, 2,190 : total 4,768.

(6)   SCHOOLROOM, BEAUFORT.   ENGLISH WESLEYAN METHODIST.
Erected 1845.
Space: free 160; standing 40.

Present: morn. 50 + 60 scholars; aft. school; even. 170 + 25 scholars.
Remarks: A new chapel capable of holding 400 will be immediately erected
in this place for the English Wesleyans.

William B. Longfellow.   Trustee.
Victoria Place, Beaufort.

(7) JAMES LEWIS CLUB ROOM, BEAUFORT.   ENGLISH INDEPENDENTS.
Religious worship held since January 1850.
Not a seperate building and not used exclusively as a place of worship.
Space: free 100.
Present: aft. 20 + 48 scholars; even. 35.

Thomas Rees.   Minister.
Beaufort.

[End of Llangattock Subdistrict]

4 LLANELLY (Subdistrict)
Area: 5,183 acres. *Popn.* 5,064 males, 4,580 females: total: 9,644.

1 Llanelly Parochial Chapelry.
Area and population as for the Subdistrict.

(1) LICENSED LECTURE ROOM (near the forge).
Erected by the Clydach Iron Company.
Licensed 1842 by the Bishop of St. David's.
Space: free 150.
Present: even. 120.
Average: even. 150.
Remarks: Licensed in consequence of the parish Church being inconveniently
situated in regard to population.

Arthur Griffiths.   Curate.

(2) LLANELLY PARISH CHURCH.
Endowed: tithe £423; fees, dues £50.
Space: free 70; other 230.
Present: morn. 122 + 35 scholars; aft. 45.
Average: morn. 150 + 40 scholars; aft. 50.

Arthur Griffiths.   Curate.

Lewis: perpetual curacy, united with that of Llangeney [601. 5. 2(11)] to the rectory
of Llangattock [601. 3. 1(1)]: tithes commuted for £423.
C & C: 2 services, alternately English and Welsh, performed by the curate.
I & C: vide sub Llangattock.

(3) WESLEYAN METHODIST, GILWERN.
Erected 1848.
Space: free 100.
Present: aft. 26; even. 40.
Average (12 *months*): aft. 26; even. 40.

> Thomas Rogerson.
> Wesleyan Methodist Minister.
> Abergavenny.

(4) PRIMITIVE METHODIST.
Erected 1838.
Space: free 80; other 100.
Present: morn. 40 + 20 scholars; aft. 30 scholars; even. 68.
Average (12 *months*): morn. 40 + 40 scholars; even. 75.

> Joseph Langford.   Steward.
> Gilwern. Clydach Iron Works.

(5) *Present:* morn. 46; aft. 56 scholars; even. 64.
Remarks: Return attached to 'Beersheba' in District No. 4.
[See 601. 4. 1.(7).]

(6) CARMEL, DAREN-FELEN. METHODIST.
Erected 1842.
Space: free 191; other 33; standing 20.
Present: morn. 130 scholars; aft. 152; even. 125.
Average (12 *months*): general congregation 152; scholars 130.

> Thomas Davies.   Secretary.
> Miner.
> Daren-felen, Clydach Iron Works.

(7) BEERSHEBA, DAREN-FELEN. BAPTIST.
Erected 1836.
Space: free 190; other 108; standing 30.
Present: morn. 270 + 170 scholars; even. 313.
Average (12 *months*): general congregation 300; scholars 170.
Remarks: The undermentioned is a branch of Beersheba church—a Rented appartment. It's seize—10 feet at 11. Attendants March the 30 1851: morning 46; afternoon 56 Sunday scholars; evening 4: Total 166.
[The whole of this entry under remarks has been deleted and the information transferred to 601. 4. 1(5) as it constituted a separate building.]
[Added in another hand] Sunday School return gives only 144 children.

> James Jones.   Deacon.
> Darenfelen, Clydach Ironworks.

(8) SION, BRYNMAWR. BAPTIST.
Erected 1846.
Space: free 260; other 220.
Present: morn. 210 + 40 scholars: aft. 166 scholars; even. 310.
Average: morn. 220; even. 360.

> Enoch Williams. Minister.
> King Street, Brynmawr.

(9) ENGLISH WESLEYAN CHAPEL, BRYNMAWR.
Erected 1850.
Space: free 282; other 172; standing 150 to 200.
Present: morn. 220; aft. 150 scholars; even. 400.

> John Swain, jnr. Steward, trustee, etc.
> Brynmawr.

(10) TABOR, BRYNMAWR. BAPTIST.
Erected 1835.
Space: free 310; other 260; standing 40.
Present: morn. 257 + 60 scholars; aft. 213 scholars; even. 330.
Average (12 *months*): morn. 300 + 70 scholars; aft. 220 scholars; even. 400.
Remarks: The reason that the attendance on March 30th was below the average of the last 12 months is that the revival of religion which followed the Cholera (1848) in this country was extraordinary in all *Chapels* and *Churches*. It should be also noticed that about 150 or nearly so may be added to the 330 to be considered as those who attend our Chapel. For the number of communicants is 281, but they never can attend always at the same time. Some must stop at home in each family with all denominations the same.

> James Davies. Minister.
> Waunesgyrn, Nantyglo.

(11) TOWN HALL, LLANELLY. WELSH WESLEYAN METHODISTS.
Space: free 172; standing 200.
Present: morn. 70; aft. 57 scholars; even. 59.
Average (3 *months*): morn. 50; aft. 60 scholars; even. 60.

> William Rowlands. One of the
> Ministers.

(12) PRIMITIVE METHODIST, BRYNMAWR.
Erected about 1841.
Space: free 185; other 267.
Present: morn. 118 + 40 scholars; aft. 64 scholars; even. 221.

Average (12 *months*): morn. 6,136 + 1,300 scholars; aft. 1,300 scholars; even. 10,600.

Remarks: The average number as stated below is the average number that attend on one Sabbath, and which number is multiplied by the 52 Sabbaths which are in the year.

John Hall Adams.   Minister.
Beaufort Hill, Brynmawr.

(13)   Libanus Chapel.   Welsh Calvinistic Methodist.
Erected 1841.
Space: free 267; other 221.
Present: morn. 180; aft. 116 scholars; even. 230.

David Edwards.   Preacher.
Brynmawr.

(14)   Calvary, Brynmawr.   English Particular Baptist Chapel.
Erected 1836.
Space: free 200; other 131; standing 20.
Present: morn. 134; even. 165.

Thomas Powell.   Deacon.
Stocktaker, Nantyglo Ironworks.

(15)   Green Street Chapel, Brynmawr.   Independent.
Erected 1850.
Space: free 200; other 200.
Present: morn. 124; even. 225.
Average: general congregation 200; scholars 138.

John Thomas.   Preacher.
Care of Rev. W. Jenkins,
Brynmawr.

(16)   Bethania.   Independents.
Erected 1845.
Space: free 210; other 70.
Present: morn. 127 + 50 scholars; even. 155 + 40 scholars.

David Cadwalader.   Secretary.
Llanelly.

(17)   Horeb.   Welsh Wesleyan Methodist.
Erected 1821.
Space: free 87; other 72; standing 36.
Present: morn. 83; aft. 70 scholars; even. 90.
Average (9 *months*): morn. 90; aft. 55 scholars; even. 95.

William Rowlands.   One of the
Ministers.

(18) SILOAM. INDEPENDENTS.
Erected 1829.
Space: free 264; other 168.
Present: morn. 321 + 19 scholars; even. 363 + 38 scholars.
Average: morn. 330 + 25 scholars; even. 360 + 40 scholars.
Remarks: Two schoolrooms have been lately built by this congregation, which have been respectively returned as Siloam Gilwern Schoolroom and Siloam Darenfelen Schoolroom.

> John Davies. Minister.
> Llanelly.

(19) INDEPENDENT.
Hired room, not used exclusively as a place of worship.
Space: 150.
Present: aft. 25 + 5 scholars; even. 30 + 7 scholars.
Average: aft. 27 + 6 scholars; even. 32 + 9 scholars.
Remarks: This little interest was established in 1850.

> Revd. John Davies. Minister.
> Llanelly.

(20) ENGLISH WESLEYAN METHODIST.
Erected 1829.
Space: free 720; other 80.
Present: morn. 110 + 30 scholars; even. 130 + 30 scholars.
Average: morn. 100; aft. 70 scholars; even. 110.

> William Ellis. Steward.
> Clydach Ironworks.

(21) EBENEZER. WELSH CALVINISTIC METHODISTS.
Erected 1828.
Space: free 45; other 33; standing 20.
Present: morn. 109; aft. 91 scholars; even. 111.
Average (12 *months*): morn. 110; aft. 90 scholars; even. 120.

> Revd. D. Miles. Minister.
> Clydach Iron Works.

(22) BETHLEHEM. PARTICULAR BAPTIST.
Erected 1830.
Space: 4 + 3 galleries; other 35.
Present: morn. 260; even. 510 [deleted].
Average (12 *months*): morn. 300; aft. 200; even. 500 [deleted].
Remarks: Are thankful for the liberty we enjoy. Wish all to pay the

expences of their own Religion. Are making constant and earnest prayers for our beloved Sovereign the Queen.

> Dan Davies.   Minister.

The statement as the evening attendance I do not think correct, the place would not hold five hundred persons.

> John Thomas.   Registrar.

(23) REHOBOTH, BRYNMAWR.   INDEPENDENT.
Erected 1829.
Space: free 888; other 312.
Present: morn. 810 + 230 scholars; even. 1,014 + 475 scholars.
Average (12 *months*): morn. 840 + 250 scholars; even. 1,050 + 450 scholars.

> William Jenkins.   Independent
> Minister.

Remarks: This place is stated to hold 1,500 upon a calculation of one foot to each individual. I do not think it will hold more than one thousand.

> John Thomas.   Registrar.

(24) CWMBACH CHAPEL.   BAPTISTS.
Erected 1847.
Space: free 693; other 173 (free).
Present: aft. 50 scholars; even. 100.
Average: aft. 50 scholars; even. 110.
Remarks: By 693 in column the 7th we mean so many square feet available for public worship and by 173 so many sittings which are all free.

> James Spencer.   Baptists Minister.

[The county is given as Carmarthen.]

(601. 4. 6.) BRYNMAWR TOWN.   CHURCH OF ENGLAND.
Divine service is performed every Sunday—morning and evening in English, afternoon in Welsh, Thursday evening in English.
Was opened by License of the Bishop of St. David's in January 1850. Average attendance about three hundred. Were not counted on the 30th March 1851. I have personally applied to the Revd. J. W. Morgan for the return which he declined to give and said he had lost or mis-laid the printed form left with him.
The room is also used as a schoolroom.

> John Thomas.   Registrar of Llanelly.
> 21 April 1851.

[Informant's form]

[*End of Llanelly Subdistrict*]

5 CRICKHOWELL (Subdistrict)
Area: 14,936 acres. *Popn.* 1,123 males, 1,203 females: total 2,326.

1 Crickhowell Parish.
Area: 1,941 acres. *Popn.* 662 males, 741 females: total 1,403.

(1) St. Edmund's Parish Church, Crickhowell.
Endowed: land £45; tithe £50. 10s.; glebe £25; permanent endowment £25; fees £10.
Space: free 81; other 600.
Present: morn. 256 + 75 scholars; aft. 200 + 50 scholars.
Average: morn. 350 + 60 scholars; aft. 200 + 50 scholars.

John Evans. Minister.

Lewis: discharged vicarage, rated £3. 17. 8½; endowed with £200 private benefaction and £200 royal bounty: patron, the rector, Lord W. G. H. Somerset: the rectory a sinecure, rated at £5. 9. 9½; patron, Duke of Beaufort, the lay impropriator: rectorial tithes commuted for £100. 13. with glebe of 2 acres valued at £4. 10.; vicarial tithes commuted for £50. 6. 6, with glebe etc., valued at £5.
C & C: 2 services in English.
I & C: resident.
ICBS: grant of £70 in 1828.

(2) Bethabara. Particular Baptists.
Erected 1840.
Space: free 300; other 100.
Present: morn. 120; aft. 35 scholars; even. 248.
Average (12 *months*): morn. 130; aft. 45 scholars; even. 270.

James Williams. Deacon.
Carpenter.
Oak field cotage.

(3) Three Salmon's Long Room. Independents.
Present: morn. 40 + 15 scholars; even. 70 + 20 scholars.

John Price. Steward.
Carpenter.
Llangatock.

(4) English Wesleyan Chapel.
Erected since 1800.
A separate room.
Space: free 50; other 120.
Present: morn. 30 + 10 scholars; even. 100 + 20 scholars.
Average (12 *months*): general congregation 110; scholars 10.
Remarks: There is a new chapel in Building in Bailey Street, Crickhowell which will be opened for Divine Service in May next.

Henry Williams. Class Leader.
No. 4 Lanbedr Rd.

(5)   Danycastle Chapel.   Welsh Calvinistic Methodist.
Erected 1807.
Space: free 100; other 300; standing 100.
Present: morn. 150; aft. 100 scholars; even. 230.
Average: morn. 200; aft. 100 scholars; even. 300.
Remarks: A great proportion of the Sunday Scholars form our Congregation.

> Thomas Morris.   Deacon.

(6)   Welsh Wesleyan Methodists Chapel.
Erected 1810.
Space: free 100; standing 80.
Present: aft. 50 + 6 scholars; even. 60 + 10 scholars.
Average (12 *months*): general congregation 80; scholars 10.

> Thomas Williams.
> Steward and Class Leader.
> High Street.

(7)   Primitive Methodist Chapel.
Erected 1849.
Space: free 68.
Present: aft. 20 + 8 scholars; even. 40 + 10 scholars.
Average (6 *months*): even. 40.

> Thomas Parry.   Class Leader.
> Castle Street.

(8)   Zion Chapel, Beaufort Hill.   Wesleyan Methodist.
Erected 1849.
Used for a Day School.
Space: free 205; other 53.
Present: morn. 80 + 104 scholars; aft. Sunday School; even. 160 + 40 scholars.

> John Rees.   Leader and Trustee.
> Care Sheppard Surgeon
> Beaufort Iron Works

(9)   Bethel, Beaufort.   Welsh Wesleyan.
Erected 1850.
Space: free 84; other 60; standing 12.
Preset: morn. School; aft. 45; even. 35.

> Edward Price.   Trustee.
> at Mr. Wm Thomas, Beaufort.

(10) BETHESDA, WAUNGOCH CHAPEL. WELSH CALVINISTIC METHODISTS.
Erected 1818.
Space: free 309; other 188.
Present: morn. 165; aft. 120 scholars; even. 321.
Average (12 *months*): morn. 195; aft. 13 + 130 scholars; even. 351.

> John Lewis. Deacon.
> Collier.
> Beaufort.

2 Llangenny Parochial Chapelry.
Area: 2,783 acres. *Popn.* 223 males, 232 females: total 455.

(11) LLANGENNEY PARISH CHURCH. VILLAGE OF LANGROINEY.
Endowed: land, tithe, glebe £335.
Space: free 80; other 220.
Present: morn. 140; aft. 170.
Average (12 *months*): morn. 127 + 50 scholars; aft. 124 + 51 scholars.
Remarks: The Finales are written in Red ink Total 177-175.

> Wm. Parry. Churchwarden.

Lewis: perpetual curacy, united with that of Llanelly [601. 4. 1(2)], to the rectory
of Llangattock [601. 3. 1(1)]: tithes commuted for £320; glebe of about 8½ acres
valued at £14.
C & C: 1 service in English.
I & C: vide sub Llangattock.

(12) LLANGENNEY CHAPEL. WELSH CALVINISTIC METHODIST.
Erected about 1820.
Space: free 150; standing 50.
Average: aft. 30.
Remarks: service once a month.

> Thomas Morris. Deacon.

3 Llanbedr Parish.
Area: 3,831 acres. *Popn.* 146 males, 140 females: total 286.

(13) LLANBEDER PARISH CHURCH.
Endowed: tithe £215; glebe £30; fees £2.
Space: free 75; other 220.
Present: morn. 70.
Average (6 *months*): morn. 62.
Remarks: The Services being alternately in Welsh and English the
congregation is divided—the Church much too large for the population.

> Edward Lewis: Rector.

Lewis: rectory, with Patrishow [601. 5. 4(14)] annexed: rated at £16. 17. 6: patron, Duke of Beaufort: tithes commuted for £212. 13. 4; glebe of 34½ acres valued at £40.

C & C: 2 services in summer, 1 in winter, alternately English and Welsh.

I & C: resident.

4   Patrishow Parochial Chapelry.
Area: 1,481 acres. *Popn.* 38 males, 38 females: total 76.

(14)   PATRISHOW CHAPEL.
Endowed: tithe £55; dues £7.
Space: free 60; other 18.
Present: aft. 26.
Average (6 *months*): morn. 29; aft. 35.
Remarks: The whole of this Chapel is now opened into free services and affords abundant room for the inhabitants. There are no Sunday Scholars as they attend the school at Llanbeder.

Edward Lewis.   Rector.

Lewis: consolidated with the rectory of Llanbedr [601. 5. 3(13)]: rectorial tithes commuted for £57. 10.

C & C: vide. sub. Llanbedr: 1 service.

I & C: ditto.

[5-6]   Part of Talgarth Parish consisting of the Hamlets of [5] Grwyne-fawr and [6] Grwyne-fechan.
Area of both hamlets: 4,900 acres. *popn.* 54 males, 52 females: total 106.

5   Grwyne-fawr Hamlet.
Popn. 7 males, 7 females: total 14.
[No returns]

6   Grwyne-fechan Hamlet
Popn. 47 males, 45 females: total 92.

(15)   GROYNEY VYCHAN CHAPEL.   CALVINISTIC METHODIST.
Erected before 1800.
Space: all free.
Present: morn. 29 scholars; aft. 54; even. 25.
Average (12 *months*): general congregation 57; scholars 60.

William Powell.   Deacon.
Groyneyvydran.

[*End of Crickhowell Subdistrict and end of Crickhowell District*]

Area: 89,695 acres. *Popn.* 5,447 males, 5,501 females: total 10,962.

1 TALGARTH (Subdistrict)
Area: 28,155 acres. *Popn.* 1,280 males, 1,269 females: total 2,549.

1-4   Part of Talgarth Parish, consisting of the hamlets of [1] Talgarth Borough, [2] Forest, [3] Pwll-y-wrach, and [4] Trefecca.
Area of this part of the Parish: 12,000 acres; *popn.* 607 males, 615 females: total 1,222.

1   Talgarth Borough Hamlet.
Popn. 336 males, 341 females: total 677.

(1)   TALGARTH PARISH CHURCH.
Endowed: tithe £285; glebe £20; fees £5.
Space: free 50; other 400.
Present: morn. 57 + 30 scholars; even. 40.
Average: morn. 70 + 40 scholars; even. 50.

James Morgan.   Vicar.

Lewis: vicarage not in charge: net income £250: patrons, Deans and Canons af Windsor: tithes commuted for £895 and appropriated as follows: by the Bishop of Gloucester and Bristol £40, by the deans and canons £590, with a glebe of 22 acres valued at £22, to the vicar £285 subject to rates averaging £2, with a glebe of 22 acres valued at £22.

C & C: 2 services, partially in Welsh in the evening performed by the incumbent and curate.

I & C: not resident.

(2)   BETHANIA.   INDEPENDENT.
Erected 1811.
Space: free 198; other 120; standing 40.
Present: morn. 119; aft. 119 scholars; even. 267.
Remarks: There are two other Sunday Schools belonging to Bethania Chapel, the number of scholars are to be seen in the Sunday School Census.

David Jones.   Deacon.
Post Office.

(3) BETHLEHEM.   CALVINISTIC METHODISTS.
Erected 1821.
Space: free 70; other 200; standing 50.
Present: morn. school; aft. 182; even. 152.
Average: 180.
Remarks: The Sunday Scholars are included in the General Congregation.

David Davies.   Deacon.

(4) TABERNACLE.   PARTICULAR BAPTISTS.
Erected 1838.
Space: free 55; other 64; standing 80.
Present: aft. 70; even. 40.
Average (12 *months*): aft. 80; even. 50.

Wm. Price.   Steward.
Penrheol.

(5) WESLEYAN CHAPEL.   WESLEYAN METHODISTS.
Erected 1849.
Space: free 20; other 50; standing 30.
Present: morn. 7; aft. 21; even. 12.
Average (6 *months*): morn. 7; aft. 25; even. 14.

David Price.   Steward.
Grocer.

(6) TREDWSTAN.   INDEPENDENT.
Erected 1672 [deleted]; before 1800.
Space: free 480; standing 50.
Present: morn. 60; aft. 100; even. 100.
Average (12 *months*): morn. 60; aft. 100; even. 100.

Thomas Havard.   Minister.

(7) TREVECCA CHAPEL.   WELSH CALVINISTIC METHODIST.
Erected 1748 [deleted]; before 1800.
Space: free 76; standing 60.
Present: morn. 49 scholars; even. 56.
Average (6 *months*): morn. 49 scholars; even. 66.
Remarks: The congregation attends at Talgarth in the Afternoon.

David Charles.   Minister.
Trevecca College.

[9] (8) PENRHEOL CHAPEL.   BAPTISTS.
Erected before 1800.
Space: free 300.
Present: even. 173.

William Richards.   Minister.
Hay
[This return is wrongly numbered: it should follow 602. 1. 9(16).]

(9) MORIAH. TREVECCA. CALVINISTIC METHODIST.
Erected 1835.
Space: free 90; other 5; standing 20.
Present: morn. 67; even. 98.
Average: morn. 70 ; even. 100.
Remarks: Sunday scholars are included in the general congregation.

> John Williams. Deacon.
> Carpenter.
> Penygenffordd.

5 Llanelieu Parish.
Area: 5,537 acres. *Popn.* 61 males; 50 females: total 111.

(10) LLANELIEU PARISH CHURCH.
In private patronage.
Endowed: tithe £100; glebe £20.
Space: free 50; other 100.
Present: morn. 16.
Average (12 months): aft. 40.

> John J. Jones   Rector.

Lewis: discharged rectory, endowed with £200 royal bounty: patron, Earl of
Ashburnham: tithes commuted for £100, subject to rates averaging £3; glebe of
28 acres and glebe-house.

C & C: 1 service in English.

I & C: vacant.

6 Broynllis Parish.
Area: 2,109 acres. *Popn.* 167 males, 163 females: total 330.

(11) BROYNLLYS PARISH CHURCH.
Endowed: tithe £192; glebe £12.
Space: other 286.
Present: aft. 105 + 15 scholars.
Average (12 months): alternate morn./aft. 150 + 25 to 30 scholars.

> John J. Jones.   Curate.

Lewis: discharged vicarage, rated at £4. 16. 0½: patron, Walter Wilkins de Winton,
Esq.; impropriator, rector of Llandevalley [006.5. 6(8)]; rectorial tithes commuted
for £118, and the vicarial for £192, the latter subject to rates averaging £20; glebe
of 6 acres valued at £6.

C & C: sub Brynllys: 2 services on alternate Sundays, in English morn. and
even., in Welsh even. performed by the curate.

I & C: incumbent not resident (Walter de Winton): curate, who resides in the
parish, has stipend of £100.

(12) UNION CHAPEL. CALVINISTIC METHODISTS, WESLEYAN METHODISTS, AND BAPTISTS.
Set apart in 1848.
Space: free 50.
Remarks: There has been no Divine Service held in Union Chapel on the Sabbath since it was set apart. Only a Sunday School on Sunday morning and a sermon on one evening in the week at which time about 20 generally attend.

> William Morgan. Superintendant of Sunday School.
> Broynllis

(13) CALVINISTIC METHODIST, BRONLLYS.
Not a separate building and not used exclusisely as a place of worship.
Space: standing 40.
Present: even. 38.
Average: even. 42.

> Simon Roberts. Minister.
> Trevecca College.

7 Llyswen Parish.
Area: 2,067 acres. *Popn.* 117 males, 108 females: total 225.

(14) LLYSWEN PARISH CHURCH.
Endowed: tithe £105; glebe £35; fees £1.
Space: free 40; other 50.
Present: morn. 49; aft. 57.
Average (12 *months*): morn. 50; aft. 55.

> William Morgan Williams. Rector.

Lewis: discharged rectory, rated at £3. 14. 7: patron, Mrs. Macnamara: tithes commuted for £96. 4., with glebe valued at £88.
C & C: 1 service in English.
I & C: resident.

(15) PHILADELPHIA. CALVINISTIC METHODIST.
Erected 1838.
Space: free 20 feet by 15; standing 32.
Present: aft. 40.
Average (12 *months*): general congregation 40; scholars 30.

> David Griffiths.
> Draper and Grocer.

8 Aberllunvey Parish.
Area: 626 acres. *Popn.* 50 males, 52 females: total 102.
[No entries.]
[*Lewis:* benefice ceased about middle of eighteenth century.]

[9-10] Part of Glasbury Parish consisting of the hamlets of [9] Tregoyd and Velindre and [10] Pipton.
Area of the above: 5,816 acres. *Popn.* 278 males, 281 females: total 559.

9 Tregoyd and Velindre Hamlet.
Popn. 206 males, 214 females: total 420.

(16) FELINDRE FARM HOUSE. CALVINISTIC METHODISTS.
Part of a dwelling house.
Space: free 20; standing 40.
Present: aft. 32.
Average (6 *months*): aft. 35.
Remarks: Supplied by Trevecca College Students gratis.

> Tho. Rob. Davies. Elder.
> Velindre.

[See also (8) above, Penrheol Chapel (misplaced).]

[End of Talgarth Subdistrict]

2 CLYRO (Subdistrict)
Area: 31,753 acres. *Popn.* 1,850 males, 1,778 females: total 3,628.

1 Part of Glasbury Parish: partly in co. Radnor.
Area: 3,400 acres. *Popn.* (in co. Brecon) 125 males, 116 females: total 241: (in co. Radnor) 274 males, 301 females: total 575: total population 399 males, 417 females: total 816.

(1) GLASBURY PARISH CHURCH.
Consecrated 1848 on being rebuilt on the site of the old church.
Space: free 362; other 328.
Present: morn. 120 + 63 scholars; aft. 60 + 29 scholars.
Remarks: The *Parish* of Glasbury is partly in Radnorshire, and partly in Brecknockshire—The Boundary of the counties is (in these parts) disputed. The Church stands on this disputed land. But it is now *believed* that this land is now held to be part of Brecknockshire.

> Revd. Sam. Alford. Minister.

[Note: that part of the parish situated on the Breconshire side of the River Wye was transferred from Radnorshire to Breconshire by 7 & 8 Vict. cap. 61.]

Lewis: vicarage, rated at £10: patron and appropriator, Bp. Gloucester and Bristol: rectorial tithes commuted for £400, subject to rates averaging £43. 9. 2:

and the vicarial for £470, subject to rates averaging £50. 18. 4: the old church, due to dilapidation, taken down in 1836, and the present church opened in May 1838.

C & C: 2 services in English.

I & C: incumbent not resident: curate, who resides in the glebe-house, has stipend of £150.

ICBS: grant of £200 in 1838.

(2) CWMBACH CHAPEL. WESLEYAN.
Erected 1818.
Space: free 100; other 44.
Present: even. 100.
Average: 100.

George Jones.   Chapel Steward.

(3) MAESIONEN. INDEPENDENT.
Erected 1691.
Space: free 25 + 5: standing 18 feet by 15.
Present: morn. 50; aft. 80 ; even. 80.
Average: 50.

Thomas Harvard.   Minister.

2 Boughrood Parish, co. Radnor.

Area: 1,633 acres. *Popn.* 152 males, 162 females: total 314.

(4) BOUGHROOD PARISH CHURCH.
Endowed: tithe £259; glebe £15; fees £2.
Space: free 40; other 75.
Present: morn. 86; aft. 33.
Remarks: The Sunday School discontinued at present to be reorganized on the opening of a new day School lately erected. I have perferred confining myself to a statement of the actual number of persons attending divine service on the day named—for that is a matter of fact, while an average must be matter for conjecture. At the same time I feel it necessary to add that the attendance in the afternoon was below the average.

Henry de Winton.   Minister.

Lewis: with Llanbedr-Painscastle [602. 2. 5(9)] a prebend in the collegiate church of Brecon, valued at 13s. 4d: discharged vicarage, endowed with the rectorial tithes; rated at £12. 6. 8: patron, the Bp.: tithes commuted for £259 subject to rates averaging £23. 10, and glebe of 10 acres valued at £13.

C & C: 2 services in English.

I & C: incumbent not resident: curate has stipend of £80.

(5) Llanirhimp, Ebenezer Chapel. Primitive Methodist.
Erected 1829.
Space: free 150.
Present: morn. 30; aft. 107; even. 64.

> Edward Powell. Occasional Minister.
> Boughrood Court.

3 Llanstephen Parish, co. Radnor.
Area: 2,407 acres. *Popn.* 143 males, 112 females: total 255.

(6) Llanstephan Parish Church.
Endowed: land £60; tithe £10.
Space: 250.
Present: aft. 70.
Average (12 *months*): morn. 35; aft. 40.
Remarks: Duty, morning and afternoon, alternately.

> William Morgan Williams, M.A.
> Officiating Minister.

Lewis: perpetual curacy, endowed with £400 royal bounty and £200 parliamentary grant; net income £67: patron and appropriator, Prebendary in the Collegiate Church of Brecon: tithes commuted for £180, with glebe of 2 acres valued at £2.

C & C: 1 service in English.

I & C: not resident.

4 Llandilo-Graban Parish, co. Radnor.
Area: 3,059 acres. *Popn.* 131 males, 129 females: total 260.

(7) Llandilo-Graban Parish Church.
Endowed: land £80.
Space: other 150.
Present: aft. 27.
Average (12 *months*): morn. 15; aft. 25.

> John Lloyd. Perpetual Curate.

Lewis: sub Llandeilo-Graban: prebend in the Collegiate Church of Brecon, valued at £9. 13. 4: the living, a perpetual curacy, endowed with £800 royal bounty: net income £72: patron, prebendary of Llandeilo-Graban: appropriated tithes, payable to the prebendary, commuted for £250 subject to rates averaging £28. 11. 11, with glebe of 9 acres valued at £9.

C & C: 1 service in English.

I & C: not resident.

(8) MORIAH. BAPTISTS.
Erected 1834.
Space: free 300; standing 300.
Present: morn. 150; even. 150.

Ed. Owen. Appointed Minister.
Painscastle.

5 Llanbedr-Painscastle Parish, co. Radnor.
Area: 3,877 acres. *Popn.* 176 males, 146 females: total 322.

(9) LLANBEDR PAINSCASTLE PARISH CHURCH.
Endowed: land £68.
Space: other 83.
Present: morn. 4.
Average: morn. 14; aft. 24.

John Lloyd. Officiating Minister.

Lewis: with Boughrood [602. 2. 2(4)] a prebend in the collegiate Church of Brecon, valued at 13*s.* 4*d*: the living a perpetual curacy, endowed with £600 royal bounty; patron, the prebendary: net income £68.

C & C: 1 service in English.

I & C: incumbent not resident: curate, who resides at Hay, 5 miles distant, has stipend of £40.

(10) ADDULLAM CHAPEL. BAPTIST.
Erected 1848.
Space: free 150.
Present: morn. 110 + 37 scholars; aft. 110.
Average: morn. 110 + 37 scholars.

Edward Owens. Minister.

(11) PAINSCASTLE CHAPEL. PRIMITIVE METHODIST.
Erected 1828.
Space: free 120.
Present: aft. 15.
Average (12 *months*): morn. 25.

Thomas Jones. Local Preacher.
Pencwm.

6 Llandewyfach Parish, co. Radnor.
Area: 2,297 acres. *Popn.* 60 males, 69 females: total 129.

(12)   LLANDDEWIFACH PARISH CHURCH.
Endowed: tithe £128.
Space: sufficient.
Present: morn. 23.
Average: aft. 25.

John Williams.   Minister.

Lewis: perpetual curacy, annexed to the vicarage of Llowes [602. 2. 10(18)]; patron and appropriator, archdeacon of Brecknock.

C & C: 1 service in English.

I & C: resident.

ERCR: accom. 'sufficient'.

7   Bryngwyn Parish, co. Radnor.
Area: 4,536 acres. *Popn.* 146 males, 144 females: total 290.

(13)   BRYNGWYN PARISH CHURCH.
Endowed: tithe £300; glebe 8 acres; fees £2 or £3; Easter offerings 4s. 6d.
Space: free 30.
Present: aft. 35.
Average: morn. 30; aft. 40.
Remarks: There is no school in this Parish.

Rees Lloyd.   Curate.

Lewis: rectory, rated at £11. 6. 8; net income £294; patron, the Bp.

C & C: 1 service in English.

I & C: incumbent not resident: curate, who resides at Hay, 5 miles distant, has stipend of £40.

(14)   HERMON.   INDEPENDENT OR CONGREGATIONALIST.
Erected 1849.
Space: free 180.
Present: morn. 37; aft. 30 scholars; even. 66.
Average (12 *months*): morn. 60 + 34 scholars; aft. 180 + 45 scholars; even. 120.

John Griffiths.   Preacher.
Portway, Bryngwyn.

[8-9]   Clyro Parish, co. Radnor, consisting of [8] the parish and [9] Bettws-Clyro Chapelry.
Area of the whole: 7,225 acres. *Popn.* 471 males, 412 females: total 883.

8 Clyro Parish.
Popn. 357 males, 301 females: total 658.

(15) Clyro Parish Church.
Endowed: land £279. 10s; fees £5.
Space: free 109; other 110.
Present: morn. 76 + 50 scholars. No service aft. or even.
Remarks: There is an unendowed Chapel of Ease called Bettws Chapel in
the parish in which the Incumbent officiates in the afternoon.

R. Lister Venables.   Vicar.

Lewis: prebend in the collegiate church of Brecknock, rated at £7. 6. 8, and in the
patronage of the Bishop. The living a discharged vicarage with the perpetual
vicarage of Bettws-Clyro [602. 2. 8(16)] annexed; rated at £6; net income £330,
with a glebe-house: patron, the Bp.: impropriate tithes, payable to the prebendary,
commuted for £675, subject to rates averaging £45; vicarage has glebe of 4 acres,
valued at £6.
C & C: 1 service each in the church and chapel in English.
I & C: resident.

(16) Bettws Clyro Chapel.
No endowment of any kind whatsoever.
Space: free 90.
Present: afr. 37. No service morn. and even.
Remarks: This is a very ancient Chapel. There is no burial ground and no
separate district allotted to it. Service is performed every Sunday in the
afternoon by the Incumbent of the Parish.

R. Lister Venables.   Vicar of Clyro.

Lewis: tithes included in the commutation of the parish.
C & C and *I & C:* see (15) above.

(17) Bronith Chapel.   P. Methodist.
Erected 1844.
Space: free 100; other 12.
Present: aft. 50.

James Allen.   Steward.
Wheelwright.

10 Llowes Parish, co. Radnor.
Area: 3,319 acres. *Popn.* 172 males, 187 females: total 359.

(18) Llowes Parish Church.
Endowed: tithe £170.
Space: free 30; other 150.

Present: aft. 43 + 19 scholars.
Average: aft. 70 + 30 scholars.

John Williams.   Minister.

Lewis: discharged vicarage, with the perpetual vicarage of Llanddewi-fach [602. 2. 6(12)] annexed; rated at £8. 10*s*; net income £132; patron and appropriator, archdeacon of Brecknock.

C & C: 1 service in English.
I & C: vide 602. 2. 6(12).
ICBS: grant of £75 in 1851.

(19)   New Zion Primitive Methodists.
Erected 1846.
Space: free 40; other 35.
Present: aft. 40; even. 50.

Tho. Williams.   Steward.

[End of Clyro Subdistrict]

3 HAY (Subdistrict)
Area: 29,787 acres. *Popn.* 2,317 males, 2,468 females: total 4,785.

[1-2]   Llanigon Parish consisting of [1] the parish and [2] Glynfach Hamlet.
Area of the whole: 9,256 acres. *Popn.* 251 males, 267 females: total 918.

1   Llanigon Parish.
Popn. 216 males, 236 females: total 452.
[Note: there is no return for Llanigon Parish Church. Details are as follows:]

Lewis: discharged vicarage, rated at £7. 12. 8½; in patronage of the crown: net income £202: endowed with half the tithes, the rest of which belong to Visc. Hereford and J. Spencer, Esq.

C & C: 2 services in English.

I & C: incumbent (Walter de Winton) not resident: curate, who resides at Hay, 1½ miles distant, has stipend of £70.

ERCR: accom. 'sufficient'.

(1)   Llandthomas.   Wesleyan.
Not a chapel.
Space: free 60.
Present: aft. 30.

Paul Richard.   Wesleyan Minister.
Lion Street, Brecon.

2   Glynfach Hamlet.
Popn. 35 males, 31 females: total 66.

(2)   CAPELYFRYN CHURCH OF AN ANCIENT CHAPELRY.
Endowed: land £50; permanent endowment £13.
Space: free 60.
Present: morn. 18 to 20.
Average: morn. 30.
Remarks: The Endowment is put down from recollection as accurately as I can.

George Griffiths.   Officiating Minister.

Lewis: sub Llanigon: no details of the living are given, however.
C & C: 1 service in English.
I & C: incumbent (George Griffith) not resident: curate, who resides at Cwmyoy (co. Hereford), 6 miles distant, has stipend of £30.

(3)   CAPELYFEEN.   BAPTIST.
Erected 1737.
Space: free 84.
Present: aft. 59.
Average (12 *months*): 80 to 90.

Morgan Lewis.   Minister.
Cwmyoy.

[3-4]   Hay Parish, consisting of [3] the parish and [4] Hay Town.
Area 2,602 acres. *Popn.* of the whole: 907 males, 1,045 females: total 1,952.
Area 2,602 acres. *Popn.* of Hay Parish: 342 males, 372 females: total 714.
Popn. of Hay Town: 565 males, 673 females: total 1,238.

3   Hay Parish.
Popn. 342 males, 372 females: total 714.

(4)   HAY PARISH CHURCH.
Endowed: land £45; tithe £124; glebe £13; permanent endowment £6. 6s; fees £6; Easter offerings £5.
Space: free 248; other 450.
Present: morn. 205 + 103 scholars; even. 316.
Average (3 *months*): morn. 230 + 115 scholars; even. 320.
Remarks: Sunday being a stormy day, the congregation fell somewhat below the average number.

W. L. Bevans.   Vicar.

Lewis: discharged vicarage, rated at £7. 0. 5; endowed with £200 private benefaction, and £400 royal bounty: patron, Mrs. McNamara: net income £140: impropriator, Thomas A. Williams, Esq.: church rebuilt 1833-4.

C & C: 2 services in English.

I & C: no return.

ICBS: grant of £350 in 1833.

[Note: this and the following returns should evidently be under [4] Hay Town, for which there are no entries.]

[(5) mis-numbered, being in respect of Clifford Parish Church, co. Hereford.]

(6) BRIDGE STREET, HAY. QUAKER.
Erected 1832.
Space: 40.
Present: morn. 3.
Remarks: The number of Individuals in this particular meeting is only 4. A family of 2 Individuals has recently left it. The building used as a meeting house is a separate one attached to a private dwelling house.

Benjamin Trusted.

[(7) mis-numbered, being in respect of Bredwordine parish church, co. Hereford.]

[(8) mis-numbered, being in respect of a Calvinistic Methodist chapel in Clifford, co. Hereford.]

(9) TABERNACLE CHAPEL, BACK LANE, HAY. CALVINISTIC METHDOSIT.
Erected 1829.
Space: free 50; other 250; standing 100.
Present: morn. 60 + 20 scholars; even. 80 + 10 scholars.
Average (12 *months*): general congregation 100; scholars 50.

John Hope.
Appointed by the Society.

(10) EBENEZER, HAY. INDEPENDENT.
Erected 1845.
Space: free 66; other 127.
Present: morn. 40 + 30 scholars; even. 60 + 10 scholars.
Average: morn. 40 + 30 scholars; even. 60 + 10 scholars.
Remarks: Preaching in dwelling houses. Cottage at Clyro Radnorshire 30

average attendance Farmhouse Bettws Do. 46 average attendance. Farmhouse Penrheol Clyro Parish Radnorshire 50 average attendance.

David Griffiths. Minister.

[Note: there are no entries for these Independent places under 602. 2. 8-9.]

(11) SALEM, HAY. BAPTIST.
Erected about 1814.
Day School held.
Space: free 100; other 110.
Present: morn. 64 + 80 scholars; aft. 80 scholars; even. 125.

John Henry Hall. Minister.
Oxford Road.

(12) EBENEZER, CASTLE ROAD, HAY. WESLEYAN.
Erected before 1800.
Space: free 260; other 140.
Present: morn. 60 + 30 scholars; even. 200.

Paul Orchard, Jun. Minister.
Lion Street.

[Note: the remaining 7 returns in this subdistrict relate to places of worship in co. Hereford.]

[*End of Hay Subdistrict, end of Hay District and end of Brecknockshire Registration County.*]

RADNORSHIRE

Area of the Registration County, excluding those parts situated in England: 232,186 acres. *Popn. of same:* 9,608 males, 9,052 females: total 18,660.

Area of the Registration District, excluding those parts situated in co. Hereford: 56,132 acres. *Popn. of same:* 2,638 miles, 2,510 females: total 5,148.

1 BRILLEY (Subdistrict)

Area of the parts wholly in Wales: 3,724 acres. *Popn.* 171 males, 137 females: total 308.

6   Michaelchurch-on-Arrow Parish.   Diocese of Hereford

Area 1,926 acres. *Popn.* 87 males, 67 females: total 155.

(13)   MICHAELCHURCH PARISH CHURCH.
Endowed: tithe £160.
Space: free 60; other 50.
Present: aft. 15.
Average: morn. 30; aft. 60.
Remarks: Full service alternately morning and afternoon.

Edward Watkins.   Churchwarden.

Lewis: perpetual curacy annexed to the vicarage of Kington [603. 3. 1(1)] co. Hereford (for which, see the entry from *Lewis* below).
603. 3. 1(1), Kington Parish Church.

(14)   PRIMITIVE METHODIST, MICHAEL CHURCH UPON HARROW.
Not a seperate building.
Present: aft. 24.
Average (12 *months*): aft. 30.
Remarks: This is a private Dwelling occupyed by a trades man and in which we meet for Divine Service sometimes every week and some times but once in a fortnight sometimes on the week Nights and atended to by diferent Local Preachers and Minesters of the Primitive Methodists Denomination.

William Went.   Local preacher and
Class Leader.   Carpenter.
Huntingdon, Nr. Kingston.

7   Newchurch Parish.   Diocese of St. Davids.

Area: 1,788 acres. *Popn.* 84 males, 69 females: total 153.

(15)   NEWCHURCH PARISH CHURCH.
Endowed: tithe £148; glebe £5.
Space: free 30; other 84.
Present: morn. 25.
Average (12 *months*): morn. 25; even. 36.

J. B. Richards.   Curate.

Lewis: discharged rectory, rated at £5. 6. 8; endowed with £200 private benefaction, and £200 royal bounty; net income £171: patron, the Bp.: benefice possessed of the small estate of Catriggin.

C & C: 1 service in English.

I & C: incumbent not resident; curate, who resides in the adjoining parish, distant 4 miles, has stipend of £52.

(16)   NEWCHURCH CHAPEL.   WELSH CALVINISTIC METHODIST.
Erected 1847.
Day School held.
Space: free 108; standing 60.
Present: morn. 47; aft. 18 scholars.
Average (12 *months*): morn. 35 + 10 scholars; aft. 14 scholars; even. 85.

John James.   Minister.

[*End of Brilley Subdistrict*]

2 RADNOR (Subdistrict)
Area, excluding the part in co. Hereford: 38,365. *Popn.* 1,901 males, 1,731 females: total 3,632.

[1-2]   Glascomb Parish, consisting of [1] Drewern Township and [2] Vaynor-Glare Township.
Area of the Parish: 6,984 acres. *Popn.* 280 males, 244 females: total 524.

1   Drewern Township.
Popn. 122 males, 109 females: total 231.

(1)   GLASCOMBE PARISH CHURCH.
Endowed: tithe £135.2s; fees 10s.
Space: free 10; other 110.
Present: even. 34.
Average (6 *months*): even. 45.

David Vaughan.   Curate.

Lewis: vicarage, with Colva and Rulen [603. 2. 3(3)] annexed; rated at £13. 6. 8.:

patron and appropriator of the rectorial tithes, the Bp.: rectorial tithes commuted for £206, subject to rates averaging £33, with glebe of 11½ acres: vicarial tithes commuted for £135, subject to rates averaging £11, with glebe of 1½ acres, and glebe-house.

C & C: 1 service in the church in English.

I & C: resident.

2 Vaynor-Glare Township.
Popn. 158 males, 135 females: total 293.

(2) WELSH CALVINISTIC METHODIST.
Not a separate building and not used exclusively as a place of worship.
Erected before 1800.
Space: free 30; other 40.
Present: aft. 41.
Average (12 *months*): aft. 30.
       John James. Minister.
       Newchurch.

[Note: Bethel, Baptist, return (15) below should be included here.]

3 Colva Parochial Chapelry.
Area: 2,293 acres. *Popn.* 96 males, 88 females: total 184.

(3) COLVA. A PAROCHIAL CHAPELRY (under Glascombe).
Endowed: tithe £62; fees 5*s.*
Space: free 40; other 120.
Present: aft. 24.
Average (6 *months*): aft. 30.
       David Vaughan. Curate.

Lewis: chapel of Glascomb: patron and appropriator, the Bp.: appropriate tithes commuted for £95, subject to rates averaging £15. 15*s*, and the vicarial tithes for £62, subject to rates averaging £6. 15*s.*

C & C: sub Glascomb: 1 service in the chapel in English.

I & C: resident.

4 Gladestry Parish.
Area: 3,798 acres. *Popn.* 187 males, 175 females: total 362.

(4) GLADISTRY PARISH CHURCH.
Endowed: tithe £355; fees £1.
Space: free 40; other 150.
Present: morn. 22 + 11 scholars.

Average (12 *months*): morn. about 40 + 20 scholars; aft. about 15.
Remarks: This was *Mid Lent* Sunday, when more were absent than usual, both of the general congregation and the Sunday Scholars; and of the latter the youngest are allowed to go home. The afternoon service is performed from Easter to Michs.

J. N. Welsh.   Curate.

Lewis: rectory, rated at £12. 19. 4½; patron, the Crown: net income £308.
C & C: 1 service in English.
I & C: incumbent not resident: curate, who resides at Kington, 3 miles distant, has stipend of £100.

(5) ZION CHAPEL. BAPTIST.
Erected 1842.
Day School held.
Space: free 80; other 86.
Present: morn. 35 + 18 scholars.
Remarks: We hold service every alternate Sunday evening the average number of attendants at that time is about one hundred and fifty.

Josephus Judson.   Baptist Minister.

(6) GLADESTRY CHAPEL. WESLEYAN.
Erected 1838.
Space: free 40; other 72.
Present: aft. 80; even. 40.
Average (12 *months*): aft. 80.
Remarks: Every other Sunday in Evening.

Wm. Ferries.   Steward.
Huntingdon Park.

[5-6]   Llanvihangel-Nantmellan Parish, consisting of [5] the Township of Trewern and Gwythla and [6] part of Llanvihangel-Nantwellan Township with part of Llandegley Parish.
Area of the whole: 8,250 acres. *Popn.* 231 males, 206 females: total 437.

5   Trewern and Gwythla Township.
Area: 2,423 acres. *Popn.* 58 males, 58 females: total 116.

(7) LLANFIHANGEL NANTMELAN PARISH CHURCH.
Re-erected recently on the site of the Ancient Parish Church.
Endowed: land £18; tithe £130; glebe £2.
Space: free 50; other 100.
Present: morn. 35.
Average (12 *months*): morn. 35 to 50.

Remarks: The Sunday School has been discontinued for some time back, and the weekly Charity School transferred to another parish. There is however a Charity School at Weithel, Old Radnor, to which Children are admissible from this Parish. The Church was rebuilt on the Ancient Site in the year 1847 and 8 with all the available materials of the Old Church—and consequently not deemed necessary to be reconsecrated—at the Cost of £450; of which £150 was by 'Parochial Rate', and the Residue by 'Private Subscription'.

It is situated near the lower Extremity of the Township of Llanfihangel in a thinly populated Locality, with a large Tract of Hill land lying between it and the upper Portion of the Township and a still larger between it and the Lower Division of the Parish, comprising the Township of Trewerne and Part of Harpton which circumstance satisfactorily accounts for the smallness of the Congregation, as the Inhabitants usually attend the adjoining Churches of Llandegley, Gladestry, New or Old Radnor, all being much more convenient. At the extreme Western Boundary of the Parish abt. 3 Miles from the Church, near Llandegley, a Dissenting Chapel has been erected, on Land given by the Inhabitants of Llandegley for the accomodation of the Inhabitants of that Parish and to which some of my Parishioners resident near the St. occasionally resort. But beg to observe that all my Parishioners are Church-going People, excepting one Farmer and his Household, resident on the border of Glascombe.

Wm. Prosser Williams.   Vicar.

Lewis: discharged vicarage, rated at £4. 13. 4; endowed with £600 royal bounty: net income, £142, incl. produce of 14 acres of bounty land and 40 acres in Merthyr Cynog, co. Brecon [600. 1. 1-4]; impropriators of two-thirds tithes, Mrs. Crummer and Rt. Hon. T. F. Lewis; remainder belongs to the vicar.

C & C: 1 service in English.

I & C: resident.

6   Llanvihangel-Nantmellan Township.

Area: 5,727 acres. *Popn.* of that part of the township in the parish, 143 males, 116 females: total 259; *popn.* of that part of the township in the parish of Llandegley, 30 males, 32 females: total 62; *popn.* of the whole township 173 males, 148 females: total 321.

(8)   CORN HILL CHAPEL.   CALVINISTIC METHODISTS.
Erected 1843.
Space: free 70; other 40.
Present: morn. 60.
Average (12 months): morn. 35 scholars; aft. 80.

Ebenezer Williams.
Calvinistic Methodist Minister.
Mission House, Penybont.

7 Swydd, Graig, and Tynlan Township in Llandegley Parish.
Area: 3,729 acres. *Popn.* 169 males, 170 females: total 339.

(9) LLANDEGLEY PARISH CHURCH.
Endowed: tithe £115; glebe £19; permanent endowment £6. 10*s*. fees £1; Easter Offerings £1.
Space: free 20; other 96.
Present: aft. 27.
Average (12 *months*)*:* aft. 40.

John Jones. Vicar.

Lewis: prebend in the collegiate church at Brecknock, rated at £5, in the patronage of the Bp: the living, a discharged vicarage, rated at £3. 5. 5.; endowed with £200 royal bounty; net income, £120, with a glebe-house:patron, the Bp.: tithes commuted for £230, equally divided between Christ's College, Brecon, and the vicar, the whole subject to rates averaging £30: appropriators have glebe of 20 acres valued at £27, and the vicar 20 acres valued at £22.

C & C: 1 service in English.

I & C: resident.

[Note: 603. 2. 8(12) below, is misnumbered and should be included in the above parish.]

8 New Radnor Parish. Diocese Hereford.
Area: 3,342 acres. *Popn.* 249 males, 232 females: total 481.

(10) NEW RADNOR PARISH CHURCH.
Rebuilt July 1845.
Endowed: tithe £291. 18*s*.; glebe 19 acres (14 of which being waste); fees £2.
Space: free 153; other 150.
Present: morn. 82 + 35 scholars; aft. 56 + 23 scholars.
Average (3 *months*)*:* morn. 90 + 30 scholars; aft. 65 + 18 scholars.
Remarks: There wd be a longer attendance of children at church both morning and afternoon if there was on General good School, which is sorley weenting in this parish.

William Neaton. Rector.

Lewis: rectory, rated at £13. 10. 10; patron, the Crown: net income £304, with glebe of 3 acres in the parish and 12 of hilly ground allocated under an enclosure act.

ICBS: grant of £100 in 1842.

(11) ZION CHAPEL. CALVINISTIC METHODIST.
Erected 1832.
Space: free 100; other 80.

Present: morn. 37; aft. 33 scholars; even. 110.
Average (12 *months*): morn. 35; even. 120.

> Moses Williams. Assistant Minister to
> the Rev. Ebenezer.
> Mission House, Penybont.

(12) THE PALES. MEETING HOUSE OF THE SOCIETY OF FRIENDS.
Erected: 1745; re-erected 1828.
Admeasurement in superficial feet: 18 feet square each room.
Present: morn. 16.

> Thomas Rogers.

[Note: this return should be under Llandegley Parish, 603. 2. 8. above.]

[9-14] Old Radnor Parish, consisting of the Townships of [9] Old Radnor and Burlingjobb, [10] Walton and Womaston [11] Evenjobb, Newcastle, Barland and Burfa, [12] Kinnerton, Salford, and Badland, [13] Ednol, and [14] pt. of Upper Harpton (the remainder of Harpton being in co. Hereford).
Area of the whole: 10,069 acres. *Popn.* 668 males, 595 females: total 1,263.

9 Old Radnor and Burlingjobb Township.
Popn. 175 males, 158 females: total 333.

(13) OLD RADNOR, ST. STEPHEN'S PARISH CHURCH. DIOCESE HEREFORD.
Endowed: land £3; permanent endowment £133; fees £3.
Space: free 20; other 200.
Present: morn. 70.
Average: morn. 90 to 100.
Remarks: The Chapel of Ease of Kinnerton not included in No. of congregation.

> H. N. Moonase. Vicar.

Lewis: vicarage, with the chapel of Kinnerton [603. 2. 9(14)] annexed, rated at £35. 1. 0½: endowed with £800 parliamentary grant; net income £171: tithes commuted for £1,330, subject to rates averaging £125; glebe of 3 acres valued at £5: patrons and appropriators of all the tithes, Dean and Chapter of Worcester.

(14) KINNERTON, CHAPEL OF EASE TO THE MOTHER CHURCH OF OLD RADNOR.
Space: free 50; other 250.
Present: morn. 30 + 33 scholars; aft. 46.
Remarks: The number attending Morn. and Afternoon service on the 30th of March are much below the average owing to bad weather. The average attendance being more than 200.

> George Armstrong Blakeley, M.A.
> Curate.

(15) BETHELL, DUWERN TOWNSHIP. BAPTIST.
Erected 1834.
Space: free 350; standing 50.
Present: morn. 80; even. 50.
Average (12 *months*): morn. 80 + 40 scholars; aft. 250 + 45 scholars; even. 260.
Remarks: The reason of the congregation been small on Sunday last was the visit of an Eminent Minister to A Neighbouring Chappel.

Richard Rogers. Minister.
Llangoverous, Glascomb.

[Note: this return is misplaced: it should be under 603. 2. 1, parish of Glascomb.]

(16) YARDIS CHAPEL. CALVINISTIC METHODISTS.
Erected 1840.
Space: free 100.
Present: aft. 50.
Average (12 *months*): aft. 50.
Remarks: No School. The Chapel is used on times for carrying on a Day School.

Moses Williams. Assistant Minister.
Mission House, Penybont.

(17) GORE. INDEPENDENTS.
Erected before 1800.
Space: free 110; other 40; standing 40.
Present: aft. 92.
Average (12 *months*): morn. 140.

William Jones. Minister.

(18) STRINDS. PRIMITIVE METHODISTS.
Not a Chapel.
Present: aft. 25; even. 50.
Average: aft. 30; even. 50.

Jarvis Pike. Minister.
Evenjobb.

(19) WESLEYAN.
Erected before 1800.
Space: free 50; standing 50.
Present: morn. 26.
Average (12 *months*): 40.

Joseph Lewis. Steward.
Evenjobb.

10   Walton and Womaston Township.

Popn. 110 males, 97 females: total 207.

[Note: return for the Quaker Meeting House, (22) should be included here.]

11   Evenjobb, Newcastle, Barland, and Burfa Township.

Popn. 187 males, 178 females: total 365.

(20)   BETHEL CHAPEL.   BAPTIST.
Erected 1849.
Space: free 70;   other 75.
Present: morn. 34 scholars; aft. 100.
Remarks: We hold service every alternate Sabbath Morning;   the average number of attendants at that time is about fifty.

> Josephus Judson.   Baptist Minister.
> Gladesbry.

12   Kinnerton, Salford, and Badland Township.

Popn. 121 males, 99 females: total 220.

(21)   KEIT BROOK.   PRIMITIVE METHODISTS.
Erected 1820.
Not a separate building, and not used exclusively as a place of worship.
Space: free 33;   standing 33.
Present: even. 33.
Average (3 *months*): general congregation 26.

> John Russbutch.   Local Preacher.
> [alias] Rus bach,
> Bridge Street, Kington.

(22)   QUAKER, WALTON, OLD RADNOR.
Admeasurement in superficial feet: 100 feet square.
Space: 20.
Present: morn. 7; aft. 7.
Remarks: This house belongs to an estate called Wallow Court and was no built or intended for a place of Worship.

> William Peter Edwards.

[Note: this return should be under 603. 2. 10 above.]

13   Ednol Township.

Popn. 19 males, 16 females: total 35.
[No returns]

14 Part of Upper Harpton Township.
Popn. 77 males, 68 females: total 145.
[No returns]

[*End of Radnor Subdistrict*]

3 KINGTON (Subdistrict)
Entirely within co. Hereford.

4 PRESTEIGNE (Subdistrict)
Area (excluding those parts in England): 14,043 acres. *Popn.* of the same: 1,129 males; 1,149 females: total 2,278.

1 Knill Parish, co. Hereford.

[2-4] Presteigne Parish, consisting of [2] High Street and St. David Street Ward, [3] Broad Street and Hereford Street Ward, and [4] Discoed, or Discoyd Township.
Area: 3,697 acres. *Popn.* 742 males, 826 females: total 1,568.

2 High Street and St. David Street Ward, Presteigne.
Popn. 315 males, 350 females: total 665.

(1)   St. David Street Chapel.   Wesleyan Methodist.
Erected about 1810.
Space: free 60; other 150; standing 20.
Present: morn. 8; aft. 9; even. 27.

James Davies.   Steward.
Broad Street.

[(2) Return mis-numbered, and relates to a place of worship in Combe Township in that portion of Presteigne Parish in co. Hereford.]

3 Broad Street and Hereford Street Ward, Presteigne.
Popn. 371 males, 417 females: total 788.

(3)   Presteigne Parish Church.
Endowed: tithe £1,300.
Space: free 735.
Present: morn. 400 + 54 scholars; even. 200.

Charles Indor.   Curate.

Lewis: rectory with Chapel of Discoed [603. 4. 4(6)] annexed; rated at £20: net income £795, with a glebe-house.
C & C:
I & C:

(4)   CHAPEL.   PRIMITIVE METHODISTS.
Erected 1833.
Space: free 140; other 160.
Present: morn. 42 scholars; aft. 58 + 46 scholars; even. 110.

> Joseph Hutchings.   Minister.
> Broad Street.

(5)   HEREFORD STREET CHAPEL.   BAPTISTS.
Erected 1845.
Space: free 143; other 123.
Present: morn. 40 + 10 scholars; even. 70 + 10 scholars.
Average (12 *months*): morn. 50 + 8 scholars; even. 100 + 6 scholars.
Remarks: Many of the Scholars of the Baptist Sabbath School are required
to attend divine service at Presteign Church, on account of their being
pupils of the Free Grammar School.

> T. W. Jones.   Deacon.
> Radnorshire Bank.

4   Discoed, or Discoyd Township.
Popn. 56 males, 59 females: total 115.

(6)   DISCOYD CHAPEL OF EASE OF PRESTEIGNE.
Space: free 150.
Present: aft. 20.

> Charles Indor.   Curate.

[See 603. 4. 3(3) above.]

(7)   COTTAGE MEETING HOUSE.   PRIMITIVE METHODIST.
Dwelling house.
Space: standing 35.
Present: morn. 11.
Average: morn. 20.

> James Hutchings.   Superintendent.
> Broad Street.

(8)   BRIDGE END COTTAGE.   PRIMITIVE METHODISTS.
Not used exclusively as a place of worship.
Space: free 40; standing 40.
Present: even. 30.
Average (12 *months*): morn. 30.

> James Hutchings.   Superintendant.
> Broad Street.

(9)   GRUNNERY.   PRIMITIVE METHODIST.
A Farm House, not used exclusively as a place of worship.
Erected 1844.
Present: even. 25.

George Middleton.   Local Preacher.
Gunnery.

[5–9, Township of Presteigne Parish in co. Hereford.]
10   Part of Litton and Cascob Township (formerly in co. Hereford).
Area: 1,208 acres. *Popn.* 29 males, 22 females: total 51.
[No returns]

11   Cascob Parish, including remainder of [10].
Area: 2,548 acres. *Popn.* 83 males, 72 females: total 155.

(12)   CASCOB PARISH CHURCH.
Endowed: land £8; tithe £130; glebe £20; fees 13*s.* 4*d.*
Space: free 36; other 100.
Present: aft. 50.
Average: morn. 40; aft. 50.
Remarks: Divine Service is performed in the Church but once every
Sunday morning and afternoon alternately. The Church is served in
conjunction with the Church of the Parish of Heyhop [604. 1. 11(15)].

W. Rees.   Rector.

Lewis: discharged rectory, rated at £7. 0. 7½; endowed with £200 royal bounty:
patron, the Bp: tithes commuted for £140, subject to rates averaging £8. 8.: glebe
of 14 acres valued at £20, with a glebe-house.
C & C: 1 service in English.
I & C: incumbent resident: curate has stipend of £60 for this and Heyhop.

12   Pilleth Parish
Area: 1,897 acres. *Popn.* 45 males, 47 females: total 92.
[For the parish church see (17) below.]

13   Whitton Parish.
Area: 1,549 acres. *Popn.* 71 males, 47 females: total 118.

(13)   WHITTON PARISH CHURCH.
Space: free 24; other 55.*
Present: morn. 40 + 25 scholars.
Average: morn. 50 to 60.

Remarks: [Col. VI] Sufficient for population. March 30 was cold and wet, and in Country Parishes the attendance not so large.

J. N. Price.   Curate.

[Endorsed: See Letter.]
Lewis: discharged rectory, rated at £4. 7. 11: net income £126, with a glebe-house: patron, the Bp.
C & C: 1 service in English.
[Return (18) below should be included here.]

[(14) is the return for Kinsham Parish Church, co. Hereford.]

14   Norton Parish.
Area: 3,144 acres. *Popn.* 159 males, 135 females: total 294.

(15)   NORTON PARISH CHURCH.   DIOCESE OF HEREFORD.
Endowed: tithe £147. 10s.
Space: free 90; other 118.
Present: morn. 80 + 20 scholars.
Average: morn. 120 to 150 + 30 to 40 scholars.

John Jenkins.   Minister.

Lewis: discharged vicarage, rated at £5; endowed with £200 royal bounty; patron, the Crown: net income £147: living endowed with a part of the rectorial tithes.

(16)   CASCOB PARISH CHURCH.
Space: free 30; other 16.
Usual number of attendants: 20.

Informant: Jeremiah Griffiths.

[Informant's form]

[Note: this probably duplicates 603. 4. 11(12) above.]

(17)   PILLETH PARISH CHURCH.
Endowed: land £5; tithe £20; permanent endowment £35; fees 5s.
Space: free 20; other 80.
Present: morn. 18.
Average (12 months): morn. 20; aft. 30.
Remarks: With respect to the Day School and Sunday School—see the return from the parish of Whitton—The Children of the parish attend school there, which school is jointly endowed for the instruction of the children of both parishes.

D. Davies.   Vicar.

Lewis: perpetual curacy, annexed to Llangunllo [604. 2. 2(1)] endowed with £200 royal bounty; net income £59: patron, the Bp.; impropriator, prebendary of Llangunllo in the Collegiate Church at Brecknock.

C & C: 1 service in English.

I & C: incumbent not resident.

[Note: the remarks probably refer to the Education Census.]

[This is misnumbered and should be under 603. 2. 12 above.]

(18) ROSSAMERCH, WHITTON. WESLEAN.
Dwelling house.
Present: even. 27.

William Duggan.
Agriculturer Labourer, occupier of house.

[This return is misnumbered and should be included under 603. 4. 13 above.]

(19) PREACHING ROOM. PRIMITIVE METHODIST.
Not used exclusively as a place of worship.
Erected 1849.
Space: all free.
Present: morn. 15; aft. 11; even. 12.

Joseph Hutchings. Minister.
Broad Street, Presteyne.

[The three remaining parishes in the subdistrict, total population 549, in co. Hereford.]

[End of Presteigne Subdistrict and end of Presteigne District]

Area of the Registration District, excluding those parts situated in cos. Hereford and Salop: 70,522 acres. *Popn. of same:* 3,398 males, 3,135 females: total 6,533.

1   KNIGHTON (Subdistrict)
Area (incl. the whole of Llanfihangel Beguildy Parish): 20,286 acres. *Popn.* 1,199 males, 1,170 females: total 2,369

10   Knighton Parish.   Diocese of St. David's.
Area: 2,461 acres. *Popn.* 770 males, 796 females: total 1,566.

(13)   KNIGHTON PARISH CHURCH.
Endowed: land £145; glebe £30; permanent endowment £72; fees £4. 10s.
Space: free 50; other 700.
Present: morn. 300; even. 200.
Average: morn. 400 + 150 scholars; even. 300 + 40 scholars.
Remarks: In consequence of the change of Master and Sunday school was not open'd on the 30th March.

James   Perpetual Curate.

Lewis: perpetual curacy, endowed with £600 royal bounty, and £600 parliamentary grant; net income £155: patron and impropriator, Warden of the Hospital of Clun: great tithes commuted for £290, subject to rates averaging £29.9.8½; with glebe of 9 acres valued at £30.
C & C:
I & C:

(14)   CHAPEL WESLEYANS.   WESLEYANS.
Erected about 1805.
Space: free 20; other 75; standing 40.
Present: morn. 12 scholars; aft. 80; even. 30

Edward Oldbury.   Society Steward.

11   Heyhop Parish, including part of the Township of Heyhop.
[For the remainder of the Township, see Llanbister Parish, see 604. 2. 9.]
Area: 1,180 acres. *Popn.* 95 males, 74 females: total 169.

(15) Heyhop Parish Church.
Endowed: tithe £10. 2*s*; glebe £2. 1*s*; permanent endowment £6. 10*s*; fees £1.
Space: free 42; other 88.
Present: morn. 35 + 40 scholars.
Average: morn. 45 + 35 scholars; aft. 60 + 30 scholars.
Remarks: There is only one service on a Sunday which is held alternately in the morning and afternoon. The Church is in bad repairs. The County adjoining stands in need of a new ecclesiastical division for the sake of efficiency.

Abraham Thomas. Assistant Curate.

Lewis: discharged rectory; rated at £5. 6. 8; endowed with £200 royal bounty; glebe of 18½ acres: net income £118: patron, the Bp.
C & C: 1 service in English.
I & C: incumbent not resident; curate has stipend of £60 for this and Cascob [603. 4. 11(12)].

14 Part of Llanfihangel Beguildy Parish.
Area, including the part in 604. 2. 1, 16,645 acres. *Popn.,* of 604. 1. 14 only, 334 males, 300 females: total 634.
[For the remainder see 604. 2. 1.]

(21) Beguildy Parish Church.
Endowed: tithe £190; land £28; fees £3. 10*s*.
Space: free 140; other 40.
Present: morn. 48.
Average (12 *months*): morn. 85.
Remarks: This Parish is about fifteen miles in length, it's average breadth for ten miles is about 2½ miles, ½ of which only is enclosed. The Church is situated near the Centre. The Inhabitants of the Lower Division have the opportunity of attending the Churches of adjoining Parishes, at a convenient distance. But parts of the upper division are from four to six miles distant from any church.

Rich. Hamer. Vicar.

Lewis: discharged vicarage rated at £7. 15. 7½; net income £164: patron, the Bp; impropriators, Dean and Chapter of St. David's.
C & C: 1 serivce in English.
I & C: resident.

(22) Velindre Chappel. Wesleyan Methodist.
Erected 1827.
Space: free 100; other 44.
Present: morn. 30; even. 100.
Average (12 *months*): general congregation 100.

John Griffiths. Steward.
Killowent, Beguidy.

[*End of Knighton Subdistrict*]

2 LLANBISTER (Subdistrict)
Area, excluding that part of Llanfihangel Beguildy already included in 604. 1. 14: 47,848 acres. *Popn.* 2,199 males, 1,965 females: total 4,164.

1   Part of Llanfihangel Beguildy Parish.
Popn. 215 males, 188 females: total 403.
[For the remainder see 604. 1. 14.]

(23)   BROOK HOUSE.   PRIMITIVE METHODIST.
Erected before 1800.
Not a separate building.
Space: all free.
Present: morn. 14; aft. 70; even. 20.

> Joseph Hutchings.   Minister.
> Broad Street, Presteigne.

[2-4]   Llangynllo, or Llangunllo Parish, consisting of the Townships of [2] Lower Llangynllo, [3] Upper Llangynllo, and [4] part of Heyhop.
Area: 5,627 acres. *Popn.* 251 males, 238 females: total 489.

2   Lower Llangynllo Township.
Popn. 99 males, 84 females: total 183.

(1)   LLANGUNLLO PARISH CHURCH.
Endowed: tithe £92; glebe £3; fees £1; easter offerings £1.
Space: free 40; other 210.
Present: morn. 41 scholars; aft. 81 + 41 scholars.
Average (12 months): morn. 80 + 45 scholars; aft. 100 + 45 scholars.
Remarks: There is but one Service in this Church on the Sunday. The Duty is performed alternately morning and afternoon. In order that the Church might become more efficient in this parish there ought to be two services on each Sunday, but owing to the smallness of the living (the Vicar receiving only ¼ of the rent charge paid in lieu of tithe) the endowment as above stated is insufficient for the maintainance of the clergyman and his family—consequently he is obliged to take the duty of another Parish.

> D. Davies.   Vicar.

Lewis: with Pilleth [603. 4. 12(17)] a prebend in the Collegiate Church at Brecknock, valued at £13, in the gift of the Bp: the living a discharged rectory, with the perpetual curacy of Pilleth annexed: rated at £5. 1. 0½; endowed with £200 royal bounty: net income £98, with a glebe-house; patron, the Bp. ¾ of the tithes appropriated to the prebend, the remainder to the vicar: tithes commuted for £400, the vacarial ¼ subject to rates of £6. 13. 6: glebe of 4 acres, valued at £5.

C & C: 1 service in English.

I & C: resident.

(2)   TEMPLE CHAPEL GRAVEL.   PARTICULAR BAPTIST.
Erected 1844.
Space: free 150.
Present: morn. 39; even. 43.
Average (12 *months*): general congregation 80.

> William Davies.   Deacon.
> Halegood.

3   Upper Llangynllo Township.
Popn. 115 males, 117 females: total 232.
[No returns]

4   Part of Heyhop Township.
Popn. 37 females, 7 males: total 74.
[No returns]

5   Blethvaugh, or Bleddfa Parish.
Area: 2,740 acres. *Popn.* 119 males, 115 females: total 234.
(3)   Not a separate building.
[No other details given: the Registrar's preliminary list gives 'None'.]

> Edward Thomas.   Enumeratee.

(4)   BLEDDFA PARISH CHURCH.
Endowed: tithe £220; glebe £12; rates reduce it below £200 per an.
Space: free 48; other 474.
Present: morn. 36 scholars; aft. 40 + 38 scholars.
Average (12 *months*): morn. 50 scholars; aft. 60 + 42 scholars.
Remarks: March 30. *This day* weather was *cold* and wet which makes a considerable difference in the numbers in country parishes—where many live at a distance.

> John Price.   Rector.

Lewis: rectory, rated at £10. 12. 1; patron, the Bp: tithes commuted for £220, subject to rates averaging £20; glebe of 8 acres valued at £10.

C & C: 1 service in English.

I & C: legally not resident.

6   Llanfihangel-Rhydithon Parish, consisting of part of Llanfihangel-Rhydithon Township.
Area: 3,204 acres. *Popn.* 190 males, 163 females: total 353.
[(5) misnumbered: see 604. 2. 9 below.]

(6) Llanvihangel rhydithon Parish Church (Penybont).
Rebuilt 1838.
Endowed: land £140; tithe £10; fees £2.
Space: free 101; other 200.
Present: morn. 60.

D. Lewis. Curate.

Lewis: perpetual curacy, annexed to that of Llandewi-Ystradenny [604. 2. 6-8];
endowed with £800 royal bounty and £200 parlimentary grant: appropriator,
Prebendary of Llanbister [604. 2. 9(5)]: tithes commuted for £196: church rebuilt
in 1838 on site of the northern portion of the old one taken down because of dilapidation.

C & C: *sub* Llanddewi-Ystradenny with Llanfihangel Rhydithon: 2 services in
English.

I & C: resident.

ICBS: grant of £60 in 1837.

**[6-8] Llandewy-Ystradenny Parish, consisting of [6] part of Llanfi-
hangel-Rhydithon Township [7] Mystyrrhoesllowdy Township, and
[8] Church Township.**
Area of the whole parish: 8,075 acres. *Popn.* 362 males, 324 females: total
692.
[There are no returns for this parish.]

Lewis: perpetual curacy, with that of Llanvihangel-Rhyd-Ithon [604. 2. 6(6)]
annexed: endowed with £600 royal bounty and £200 parliamentary grant; net
income £112: patron, Chancellor of the Collegiate Church at Brecknock; appropriator, Prebendary of Llanbister: tithes commuted for £365, subject to rates
averaging £42. 15. 7: church extensively altered 'lately'.

C & C: and *I & C:* vide 604. 2. 6(6).

ERCR: accom. (with Llanfinangel Rhydithon) 800.

9 Llanbister Parish.
Area: 14,837 acres. *Popn.* 575 males, 509 females: total 1,084.

(5) Llanbister Parish Church.
Endowed: tithe £160.
Space: free 128; other 222.
Present: morn. 36 + 32 scholars.
Average (12 *months*): gen. cong. 50 to 100 and upwards: scholars 40-60.
Remarks: Baptisms 145; Marriages 53; burials 128. The above numbers
are true copies of the Registers of Baptisms, Marriages and burials extracted

the 31st day of March 1851 and contain all the insertions for the last ten years.

Evan Powell.   Vicar.

[Endorsed: See Letter.]

Lewis: discharged vicarage; rated at £6. 11. 5½; endowed with part of the great tithes; net income £148; patron, the Bp; appropriator, Chancellor of Brecknock.

C & C: 1 service in English.

I & C: resident.

(7)   Cwmllechwedd Chapel.   Primitive Methodists.
Erected 1831.
Space: all free 24 ft. by 36 ft.
Present: aft. 25.
Average (12 *months*): aft. 45.

James Meredith.   Steward.

10   Llananno Parish.
Area: 4,400 acres. *Popn.* 201 males, 173 females: total 374.

(8)   Llananno Parish Church.
Endowed: land £47; tithe £10.
Space: free 13; other 90.
Present: aft. 63.
Remarks: Sunday School kept in Church during summer and autumn. Scholars 35.

John Rees Lewis.   Perpetual Curate.

Lewis: perpetual curacy, with that of Llanbadarn-Vynydd annexed [604. 2. 11(10)]: endowed with £600 royal bounty and £400 parliamentary grant: net income £95: patron and impropriator, Chancellor of Brecknock.

C & C: 1 service in English.

I & C: not resident.

ICBS: grant of £18 in 1834.

(9)   Maesyrhalen.   Baptist.
Erected about 1805.
Space: free 120.
Present: morn. 80.
Average (12 *months*): general congregation 4,160 (sic).

John George.   Deacon.
Thomas Havard.   Minister.
Hendy, Llanbister.

11   Llanbadarn-Fynydd Parish.

Area: 8,965 acres. *Popn.* 280 males, 255 females: total 535.

(10)   LLANBADARN-FYNYDD PARISH CHURCH.
Endowed: land £35; tithe £10; permanent endowment £6. 10*s*; fees £1.
Space: free 26; other 100.
Present: aft. 85.
Remarks: A Sunday school is kept in the church during summer and autumn, there being no schoolhouse in the Parish.   Scholars 47.

John Rees Lewis. Perpetual Curate.

Lewis: perpetual curacy, annexed to that of Llananno [604. 2. 10(8)].

C & C: and *I & C:* as for Llananno.

ICBS: grant of £30 in 1841.

[End of Llanbister Subdistrict and end of Knighton District]

605 RHAYADER (District)

Area: 105,532 acres. *Popn.* 3,480 males, 3,316 females:
total 6,796

1 RHAYADER (Subdistrict)
Area: 74,004 acres. *Popn.* 1,862 males, 1,827 females: total 3,689.

[1-2] Abbey-cwm-hir Parish, consisting of the Townships of [1] Cefnpawl and [2] Golon.
Area: 10,965 acres. *Popn.* 287 males, 281 females: total 568.

1 Cefnpawl Township.
Popn. 83 males, 83 females: total 166.

(1) Bwlchsarnau, Abbycwmhar. Baptist.
Erected 1829.
Space: free 150; standing 150.
Present: aft. 200.

        Stephen Pugh.   )
        Edward Brunt   )Ministers.

(2) Abbeycwmhir Parish Church.
Erected by Sir [Hans] Fowler.
Endowed: land £52; permanent endowment of £400 from the Bounty Office; dues £5.
Space: free 40; other 70.
Present: aft. 75 + 20 scholars.
Average: aft. 80 + 20 scholars.

        James John Evans. Perpetual Curate.

Lewis: perpetual curacy, endowed with £800 royal bounty; net income £61; parton, - Wilson Esq: impropriator, Chancellor of Brecknock.

C & C: 1 service in English.

I & C: not resident.

2 Golon Township
Popn. 204 males; 198 females; total 402.
[No returns]

[3-5]   St. Harmon Parish, consisting of the Townships of [3] Cenarth, [4] Clase, and [5] Rhiwrhiad.
Area: 12,000 acres. *Popn.* 464 males, 394 females: total 858.

3   Cenarth Township.
Popn. 248 males, 199 females: total 447.
[(3) is wrongly numbered: see under 605. 1. 4, below.]

(4)   SYCHNANT.   CALVINISTIC METHODIST.   ·
Erected about 1825.
Private or Domestic Chappel.
Space: free 24; other 84; standing 40 square yards.
Present: morn. school; aft. 70; even. 30.
Average (12 *months*): aft. 60-90; even. 40-50.
Remarks: Another meeting about two miles distant on the same hour which caused the evening meeting to be less numbers kept by members of Sychnant Chappel.

John Jones.   Deacon.
Pantydwr.

4   Clase Township.
Popn. 131 males, 133 females: total 264.

(3)   NANTGWYN.   BAPTISTS.
Erected 1792.
Space: free 192.
Present: morn. 49; aft. 39 scholars; even. 98.
Average (12 *months*): morn. 100; aft. 40; even. 200.
Remarks: As the congregation happened to be less than usual we have inserted the average for twelve months.

David Davies.   Minister.

[Endorsed: See Letter.]

(5)   ST. HARMON PARISH CHURCH.
Endowed: land £0. 2. 6; tithe £152. 10; permanent endowment £31. 9. 10.
Space: free 128; other 308.
Present: aft. 205 + 32 scholars.
Average (12 *months*): morn. 205 + 35 scholars; aft. 205 + 35 scholars.

J. B. Evans, Vicar.

Lewis: prebend in the collegiate church of Brecknock, rated at £3. 17. 3½; patron, the Bp: the living a discharged vicarage, rated at £5. 15. 2½; endowed with £800 parliamentary grant; net income £161: patron, the Bp: appropriate tithes, payable to the prebendary, commuted for £152. 10., and the vicarial for £152. 10, both subject to rates averaging £33. 6; vicar has glebe of ½ acre, valued at 5*s*: church rebuilt in 1823.

C & C: 1 service, partially in English and Welsh, performed by the incumbent.

I & C: resident.

(6)　St. Harmon Wesleyan Chapel.　Wesleyan Methodists.
Erected 1807.
Space: free 8; other 14; standing 200.
Present: morn. 10; aft. 27; even. 27.
Average (12 *months*): morn. 10; aft. 27; even. 27.
Remarks: No Sunday School at present.

> John Jones.　Wesleyan Minister.
> Llanidloes.

5　Rhiwrhiad Township.
Popn. 85 males, 62 females: total 147.
[No returns]

6　Rhayader Parish, incl. the Borough of Rhayadr.
Area: 188 acres. *Popn.* 384 males, 445 females: total 829.
[Returns (7) and (8) are misnumbered: see below under 605. 1. 8. and 605. 1. 7. respectively: and (9) is missing.]
[No returns]

Lewis: perpetual curacy; endowed with half the tithe; patron, the vicar of Nantmêl. Church repaired and gallery added in 1829.

C & C: 2 services in English.

I & C: incumbent resident.

ICBS: grant of £300 in 1839.

(10)　Tabernacle.　Independents.
Erected 1721; rebuilt 1836.
Space: free 250; other 340; standing 60.
Present: morn. 260 + 30 scholars; even. 550 + 70 scholars.
Average: morn. 200 + 20 scholars; even. 600 + 60 scholars.

> William Pugh.　Deacon.
> Glanllyn.

(11) MOUNT ZION. WESLEYAN METHODISTS.
Erected 1836.
Space: other 146; standing 100.
Present: even. 60 + 30 scholars.
Average (12 months): 90 + 30 scholars.

John Jones. Minister.
Llanidloes.

(12) MAES CHAPEL. CALVINISTIC METHODISTS.
Erected before 1815.
Space: free 125; other 100; standing 150.
Present: morn. 78; aft. 82 scholars; even. 148.
Average (12 months): morn. 80; aft. 94 scholars; even. 170.

Evan Morgan. Deacon.

(13) NORTH STREET CHAPEL. BAPTIST.
Erected 1839.
Space: free 100; other 50; standing 50.
Present: morn. 31 scholars; aft. 113; even. 41.

Evan Powell. Deacon.

[7-8] Cwmtoyddwr Parish, consisting of the Townships of [7] Dyffryn-Gwy and [8] Dyffryn-Elan.
Area of the Parish: 32,000 acres. *Popn.* 416 males, 419 females: total 835.

7 Dyffryn-Gwy Township.
Popn. 243 males, 248 females: total 491.

(8) LLAN ST. FREAD.
Erected 1782.
Space: free 100; other 180.
Usual number of attendants: morn. 80.

Informant: David Evans.

[Informant's form.]

Lewis: discharged vicarage, endowed with £200 royal bounty, and £400 parliamentary grant: net income £95; patron, the Bp.; tithes commuted for £311; of which Bp. and vicar receive £124. 3. 4. each, and the impropriator £72. 13. 4.

C & C: 1 service, alternately English and Welsh.

I & C: not resident.

8 Dyffryn-Elan Parish.
Popn. 173 males, 171 females: total 344.

(7)   NANTGWILLT CHAPEL OF ENGLAND.
Erected 1785.
Space: free 30; other 40.
  Usual number of attendants: aft. 65 + 30 scholars.

> Informant: Thos. Meredith.
> Parish Clerk.

[Informant's form.]

Lewis: sub Cwmtoyddwr *and* Dyfryn-Ellan: Nant-Wyllt, chapel of ease, erected 1772, four miles from the mother-church of Llansantfraid-Cwm-Toyddwr.

C & C: sub Cwmtoyddwr: 1 service in the chapel, alternately English and Welsh.

(14)   BETHANY, ELAN VALE.   PARTICULAR BAPTIST.
Erected 1845.
Space: free 36; other 78.*
Present: morn. 60; even. 160.
Remarks: I have nothing to add only to certify you that I cannot mention the average number of attendants here during any number of past months here because as our vicinity is mountainous the inhabitants dispersing, and the weather changable, so if the weather be fair we would have a very good congregation, but if the weather be wintry the attendants are very few.

> Richard Davies.   Minister.

[Endorsed: *See Letter.]

(15)   PENTRECEITHON.   CALVINISTIC METHODISTS.
Erected before 1815.
Not a separate building.
Space: all free.
Present: morn. 26 scholars; aft. 66.
Average: morn. 30 scholars; aft. 75.

> Edward Davies.   Superintendant.

[9-10] Llanwrthwl Parish, co. Brecon, consisting of [9] Upper Division and [10] Lower Division.
Area: 18,851 acres. *Popn.* 311 males, 288 females: total 599.

9 Upper Division of Llanwrthwl Parish.
Popn. 159 males, 159 females: total 318.
[No returns]

10   Lower Division.
Popn. 152 males, 129 females: total 281.

(16)   PENUEL.   INDEPENDENT.
Erected 1832.
Space: free 249; standing 98.
Present: aft. 78 + 17 scholars; even. 89 + 21 scholars.
Average (12 *months*): aft. 90 + 18 scholars; even. 100 + 25 scholars.
Remarks: The inclemency of the season rendered congregation below the general estimate this Sabbath.

Thomas Evans.   Minister.

(17)   LLANWRTHWL PARISH CHURCH.
Endowed: land £9; tithe £91. 14*s*; fees £1. 10*s*.
Space: other 200.
Average (12 *months*): morn. 60; aft. 70.
Remarks: On the 30 of March there was no service. I was summoned away on a sudden to attend the funeral of my father in a distant part of the country. Mrs. Bevans schoolmaster who for three years rendered service to the parish has been lately withdrawn, as a result of my experience the people of this parish are eager for education, but the poverty of the people is an obstacle unless the government aid us little can be done.

Charles R. Rees.   Minister.

Lewis: prebend in the collegiate church of Brecknock, rated at £9. 12. 1; patron, the Bp.:the living a discharged vicarage, endowed with £200 royal bounty: net income, £85.

C & C: 1 service, partially in English and Welsh, performed by the incumbent.

I & C: not resident.

[End of Rhayader Subdistrict]

2 NANTMEL (Subdistrict)
Area: 31,528 acres. *Popn.* 1,618 males, 1,489 females: total 3,107.

[1-4]   Nantmel Parish, consisting of the Townships of [1] Gwastedin, [2] Maesgwyn, [3] Coedlasson, and [4] Vainor.
Area: 16,387 acres. *Popn.* 749 males, 666 females: total 1,415.

1   Gwastadin Township.
Popn. 246 males, 232 females: total 478.

(1) MAESYCELYN. BAPTIST.
Dwelling house.
Present: aft. 61.
Average (12 *months*): 75.
Remarks: There has been a Sunday School kept in this place for the seven
last years but closed for the last Nine Months, its general numbers was from
35 to 40 scholars and will be reopened in a short time. Books and Teachers
all gratis.

> Lewis Jones.   Deacon.
> Holmes, Rhayadr.

2 Maesgwyn Township.

Popn. 212 males, 182 females: total 394.
[No returns.]

3 Coedlasson Township.

Popn. 137 males, 121 females: total 258.

(2) GOOSETREE CHAPEL. WESLEYANS.
Erected 1842.
Space: free 60.
Present: even. 27.

> Richard Wilding.
> Wesleyan Local Preacher.
> Bridgend, Nr. Penybont.

4 Vainor Township.

Popn. 154 males, 131 females: total 285.

(3) NANTMEL PARISH CHURCH.
Endowed: tithe £410; glebe £23; fees £5.
Space: free 39; other 350.
Present: morn. 39 [No] Sunday School owing to the weather.
Average: morn. 80 + 20 scholars.
Remarks: [C]ongregations are much affected by the state of the weather in
this church many of the congregation having to walk or ride 4 or 5 miles and
in some cases more [illegible] very many of the Inhabitants attend other
Parish Churches being more convenient to them.

> James John Evans.   Curate.

Lewis: vicarage, with Llanyre annexed [605. 2. 6(8)]; rated at £11. 17. 6; net
income £350; glebe-house with 15 acres: patron, the Bp; impropriators,
Precentor and Chapter of St. David's.

C & C: 1 service in English in the church and chapel.

I & C: incumbent not resident: curate has stipend of £50.

(4) DOLEU CHAPEL. BAPTIST.
Erected before 1800.
Space: free 232.
Present: morn. 106; aft. 34 scholars; even. 88.
Remarks: Owing to unfavourable weather the number of attendants at the evening service is below the average. On fine weather the average number of attendants at the Evening Service is about 150.

David Davies. Minister.

(5) CARMEL. INDEPENDENT.
Erected about 1829.
Space: free 151; standing 50.
Present: morn. 66 + 4 scholars; even. 35 + 13 scholars.
Average (12 *months*): general congregation 80; scholars 11.
Remarks: There are two services held on every Sabbath, one always in the evening and the other every alternate Sabbath in the morning and afternoon the attendance in the afternoon is much larger than in the morning or evening, consequently the average for the twelve months is as near as can be ascertained stated in section 8.

Thomas Evans. Minister.

5 Llanfihangel-Helygen Parish.
Area: 1,459 acres. *Popn.* 51 males, 49 females: total 100.

(6) LLANFIHANGEL-HELYGON PARISH CHURCH.
Endowed: land £62. 10*s*; tithe £44. 15*s*; glebe £1. 10*s*.
Space: free 20; other 50.
Present: aft. 27.

Charles Davies Rees. Curate.

Lewis: perpetual curacy, endowed with £800 royal bounty, and with half the tithes of the parish: patron, vicar of Nantmel [605. 2. 4(3)].
C & C: 1 service in English.
I & C: vacant.

(7) FRON AND DEUAETH. WESLEYAN METHODIST.
Not a separate building.
Present: morn. 30.
Average: morn. 40.
Remarks: Only on Sunday morning we have preaching in Fron and Deuaeth, and the preaching is carried on in rotation; so that the two places are only equivalent to one. There is no Sunday School connected with these places.

John Jones. Wesleyan Preacher.
Llanidloes.

6 Llanyre Parish.
Area: 5,901 acres. *Popn.* 397 males, 376 females: total 773.

(8)   LLANYRE CHAPEL.
Endowed: tithes £152; fees 15*s.*
Space: free 40; other 56.
Present: aft. 50.

> Thomas Lloyd.   Chapel Warden.
> Dolwoner.

[Endorsed: See Letter.]
Lewis: vicarage, not in charge, annexed to the vicarage of Nantmel [605. 2. 4(3)].

C & C: *sub* Nantmel with Llanyre: 1 service in English.

I & C: *vide sub* 605. 2. 4(3).

(9)   PENTRE NEWYDD OR NEW BRIDGE.   PARTICULAR BAPTIST.
Erected 1760; rebuilt 1828.
Space: free 500.*
Present: morn. 115 + 67 scholars; even. 125.
Average (12 *months*): general congregation 300; scholars 67.

> William Probert.   Assistant Minister.
> Newbridge & Llanyre.

(10)   NEWBRIDGE CHAPEL.   WESLEYAN METHODISTS.
Erected 1811.
Space: free 6; other 60; standing 30.
Present: aft. 34.
Average (12 *months*): general congregation 60; scholars 20.

> John Jones.   Minister.
> Llanidloes.

7 Cefnllys Parish.
Area: 4,135 acres. *Popn.* 200 males, 186 females: total 386.

(11)   CEFNLLYS OR KEVENLUSE PARISH CHURCH.
Endowed: tithe £204; glebe £42.
Average attendants (12 *months*): aft. 20.
Remarks: Many of the parishioners go to other churches nearer to their residence.

> Tho. Thoresby.
> Minister.

Lewis: *sub* Kevenlleece (Cefn-llŷs): rectory, rated at £8. 19. 4½; patron, the Bp: tithes commuted for £196, with a glebe of 40 acres valued at £40.

C & C: 1 service in English.
I & C: no return.
ERCR: accom. 400.

(12)   CAE BACH.   INDEPENDENTS.
Present building erected 1804 on site of another.
Space: free 200; standing 50.
Presnt: morn. 37; aft. 52; even. occasionally 60.
Remarks: Being the above place of worship is the nearest to Llandrindod
Wells (Dissenter), the average during the summer months may be morning
70 to 80, even. 100-180.

> David Price.   Independent Minister.
> Llandrindod.

8   Llanbadarn-fawr Parish.

Area: 3,646 acres. *Popn.* 221 males, 212 females: total 433.

(13)   LLANBADARN FAWR PARISH CHURCH.
Endowed: tithe £261. 6*s*; glebe £38. 18*s*.
Space: free 540; other 280.
Present: morn. 50.
Average (12 *months*): morn. 100; aft. 200.

> William E. Jones.   Curate.

Lewis: discharged rectory, rated at £7. 12. 6; patron, the Bp: tithes commuted for
for £756, subject to rates averaging £22. 10; glebe of 37 acres valued at £40.

(14)   PENYBONT CHAPEL.   CALVINISTIC METHODISTS.
Erected 1822.
Space: free 140; other 64 (98 square yards).
Present: even. 137.
Average (12 *months*): morn. 90 scholars; even. 170.

> Ebenezer Williams.
> Calvs Methodist Minister.
> Mission House, Penybont.

(15)   ROCK.   BAPTIST.
Erected before 1800.
Space: free 200.
Present: morn. 80; aft. 100.
Average (12 *months*): morn. 20 scholars; even. 90.

> John Jones.   Baptist Minister.
> Penybont.
> Rock.

(16) LLANBADARN FAWR, CO. CARDIGAN.
HEPHZEBAH. INDEPENDENT.
Space: other 35.
Present: morn. 82; aft. 60 scholars; even. 80.
Average (12 *months*): morn. 70; aft. 165; even. 150.

R. W. Roberts. Minister.
Clarach, Aberystwyth.

[Note: the above return has been misnumbered and wrongly bound: it should be under 597. 2. 8.]

[*End of Nantmêl Subdistrict, end of Rhayader District and end of Radnorshire Registration County.*]

APPENDIX A

Blank schedules of inquiry, Forms A and B.
[Reproduced from the Report, pp. clxxii-clxxv].

Form A.

CENSUS OF GREAT BRITAIN, 1851.
(13 & 14 Victoriæ, Cap. 53.)

A **Return** of the several Particulars to be inquired into respecting the under-mentioned Church or Chapel in England, belonging to the United Church of England and Ireland.

A similar Return (*mutatis mutandis*) will be obtained with respect to Churches belonging to the Established Church in Scotland, and the Episcopal Church there, and also from Roman Catholic Priests, and from the Ministers of every other Religious Denomination throughout Great Britain, with respect to their Places of Worship.]

I.	**NAME AND DESCRIPTION OF CHURCH OR CHAPEL.**

		Parish, Ecclesiastical Division or District, Township, or Place.	Superintendent Registrar's District.	County and Diocese.
II.	**WHERE SITUATED.**			

	WHEN CONSECRATED OR LICENSED.	**UNDER WHAT CIRCUMSTANCES CONSECRATED OR LICENSED.**
III.		

IV. — IN THE CASE OF A CHURCH OR CHAPEL CONSECRATED OR LICENSED SINCE THE 1st JANUARY 1800 ; STATE

HOW OR BY WHOM ERECTED.	COST, HOW DEFRAYED.
	By Parliamentary Grant - - - Parochial Rate - - - Private Benefaction or Subscription, or from other Sources - Total Cost - - £

V.	VI.
HOW ENDOWED.	**SPACE AVAILABLE FOR PUBLIC WORSHIP.**

	£		£	
Land - - -		Pew Rents - - -		Free Sittings - - -
Tithe - - -		Fees - - - -		
Glebe - - -		Dues - - - -		Other Sittings - - -
Other Permanent Endowment - - -		Easter Offerings - - Other Sources - -		Total Sittings -

VII.

ESTIMATED NUMBER OF PERSONS ATTENDING DIVINE SERVICE ON SUNDAY, MARCH 30, 1851.		Morning.	Afternoon.	Evening.	AVERAGE NUMBER OF ATTENDANTS during Months next preceding March 30, 1851. (See Instruction VII.)		Morning.	Afternoon.	Evening.
General Congregation - - Sunday Scholars -					General Congregation - - Sunday Scholars -				
Total -					Total -				

VIII.	**REMARKS.**	

I certify the foregoing to be a true and correct Return to the best of my belief.

Witness my hand this _______________ day of_____________________ 1851.

IX. (*Signature*) ____

(*Official Character*)____ *of the above-named.*

(*Address by Post*) ____

CENSUS OF GREAT BRITAIN, 1851.

INSTRUCTIONS FOR FILLING UP THE SCHEDULE ON THE ADJOINING PAGE.

(Prepared under the direction of one of Her Majesty's Principal Secretaries of State.)

I.—*Name and Description of Church or Chapel.*—In the column thus headed insert—1st. The Name given to the Church on its Consecration, or the Name by which it is commonly known, if only licensed for Public Worship by the Bishop of the Diocese :—2ndly. Its Description,—(that is to say) Whether it be an ancient Parish Church, or the Church of an ancient Chapelry, the Church of a distinct and separate Parish, District Parish, District Chapelry or Consolidated District, or of a new Parish under the provisions of 6 & 7 Vict. c. 37. (Sir R. Peel's Act,) or of a District under the provisions of 1 & 2 W. 4. c. 38. (the Private Patronage Act), or a Chapel of Ease, or a Church or Chapel built under the authority of a local or private Act of Parliament; and if such information can be given, state the year, reign, and chapter of such Act.

II.—*Where situated.*—Describe accurately in the proper columns,—
The Parish, Ecclesiastical Division or District, Township, or Place, in which the Church is situated; and if it be in a Town, the Name of the Street or other locality.
The Superintendent Registrar's District or Poor Law Union.
The County and Diocese.

III.—*When consecrated or licensed.*—State in this Column whether the Church was consecrated, or only licensed by the Bishop of the Diocese. This will be sufficiently done by writing the word "Consecrated," or "Licensed," as the case may require. And if the Consecration or License was *before the 1st January* 1800, write after "Consecrated" or "Licensed" as follows,—"Before 1800." But if it took place *on or after the 1st January* 1800, insert, as nearly as can be, the *precise date* of such Consecration or License.

Under what circumstances Consecrated or Licensed.—If the Consecration or License was *before* the 1st January 1800, this column *may be left blank;* but, if it was on or after that date, state under this heading whether the Church, if consecrated, was consecrated as an additional Church, or in lieu of an old or previously existing one.

IV.—*How or by whom erected.*—If the Church was consecrated *before* the year 1800, the column thus headed, and also the column headed "Cost, how defrayed," *are to be left blank.* If the Church was consecrated or licensed *since* the 1st January 1800, and as an additional Church, *but not else,*—insert under this heading the words "By Parliamentary Grant,"—"By Parochial Rate,"—"By Private Benefaction or Subscription," —or the Name of the individual at whose expense the Church was built, or such other words as will briefly express the facts of the case.

Cost.—And, in the same circumstances, *but not else,*—state in the column headed "Cost, how defrayed," as nearly as may be known, the total cost of the Building. And if it was erected partly by Parliamentary Grant and partly by Private Subscription, or from other sources, state also the respective proportions contributed.

V.—*How endowed.*—Insert under this heading in what manner it is endowed,—whether by land, tithe, glebe, or other permanent endowment ; by pew rents, fees, dues, Easter-offerings, or now otherwise, and the aggregate annual amount of such endowment.

VII.—*Estimated Number of Attendants on March* 30, 1851.—
If—as is sometimes the case in Wales and elsewhere—two or more Congregations successively assemble in the Building during the same part of the day,—and also in all cases where two or more distinct services are performed in the morning, afternoon, or evening, either by the same Minister, or by different Ministers,—denote the fact by drawing a line immediately *under* the gross number of attendants during that part of the day, thus | 750 | —in order to show that it expresses the aggregate of persons attending at *all* such distinct services. Make a × under each portion of the day—if there be any— during which *no* service is performed.

Average Number.—
If from any cause the figures in the first three columns of Division VII. should not truly represent the numbers *usually* in attendance, the person making the Return is at liberty to add in the fourth, fifth, and sixth columns of the same Division, the estimated *average* number of attendants on Sunday during the 12 calendar months next preceding March 30, 1851, or during such portion of that period as the Building has been open for Public Worship, stating in the heading over the numbers so inserted the exact number of months for which the additional Return is made.

And if, in consequence of repairs, or from any other temporary cause, the Building should not be open for Public Worship on March 30, 1851, write across the first three columns the words "No Service," and insert in the remaining columns the average number who are supposed to have attended at each Sunday during twelve months next preceding the Sunday on which Divine Service was last performed.

VIII.—*Remarks.*—Any observations in explanation of the Return may be inserted in this column ; or—if the space provided for the purpose be insufficient—they may be written on a separate paper and appended to the Return.

IX.—*Signature, &c.*—The Return is to be made and signed by the Minister, or by a Church or Chapel Warden, or other recognized and competent officer; and the person signing will have the goodness to state in what capacity he signs, by writing immediately below his name the word "Minister," "Churchwarden," &c., as the case may be. He will also add his *Address by the Post,* in order that, if necessary, he may be communicated with direct from the Census Office in London, on the subject of the Return.

Approved,

GEORGE GRAHAM,
Registrar General.

Whitehall,
28th Jan. 1851. } G. GREY.

N.B.—The Return must not relate to more than ONE *Church or Chapel. Clergymen having the charge of two or more Churches will be furnished with a separate Form for each. And any Minister, Warden, or other person requiring an additional supply of Forms, may obtain them, free of postage or other charge, on application by letter (the postage of which may be left unpaid), addressed to "Horace Mann, Esq., Census Office, Craig's Court, London."*

Form B.

CENSUS OF GREAT BRITAIN, 1851.

(13 & 14 Victoriæ, Cap. 53.)

A RETURN of the several Particulars to be inquired into respecting the under-mentioned Place of Public Religious Worship.

[N.B.—A similar Return will be obtained from the Clergy of the Church of England, and also from the Ministers of every other Religious Denomination throughout Great Britain.]

The Particulars to be inserted in Divisions I. to VI. inclusive, and in IX., may be written either along or across the Columns, as may be more convenient.

I.	II.			III.	IV.	V.	VI.	VII.		VIII.				IX.
Name or Title of Place of Worship.	Where situate; specifying the			Religious Denomination.	When erected.	Whether a separate and entire Building.	Whether used exclusively as a Place of Worship (except for a Sunday School).	Space available for Public Worship.		Estimated Number of Persons attending Divine Service on Sunday March 30, 1851.				REMARKS.
	Parish or Place.	District.	County.					Number of Sittings already provided.			Morning.	Afternoon.	Evening.	
								Free Sittings.	Other Sittings.					
	(1)	(2)	(3)					(4)	(5)	General Congregation } Sunday Scholars } TOTAL -				
								Free Space or *Standing Room* for		Average Number of Attendants during Months. (See Instruction VIII.)				
										General Congregation } Sunday Scholars } TOTAL -				

I certify the foregoing to be a true and correct Return to the best of my belief.   Witness my hand this ____________________ day of ________________ 1851.

X. (*Signature*) ____

(*Official Character*) ______________________________________ of the above-named Place of Worship.

(*Address by Post*) ________________________________

CENSUS OF GREAT BRITAIN, 1851.

INSTRUCTIONS FOR FILLING UP THE SCHEDULE ON THE ADJOINING PAGE.

(Prepared under the direction of one of Her Majesty's Principal Secretaries of State.)

I.—*Name or Title of Place of Worship.*—In the column thus headed insert the distinguishing Name, Title, or other Appellation by which the Place of Worship is commonly known. But if by reason of its being only a *part* of some Dwelling House or other Building, or from any other cause it have *no* distinguishing Name write in this column the word "None."

II.—*Where situate.*—Describe accurately,
   (1.) The Parish, Township, or Place in which the Building is situated; and if it be in a Town, the Name of the Street or other locality.
   (2.) The Superintendent Registrar's District or Poor Law Union.
   (3.) The County.

III.—*Religious Denomination.*—Insert here the name of the Religious Denomination or Society now occupying the Building.

IV.—*When erected.*—If the Building was erected *before* the year 1800—or, if it has been erected since 1800 on the site or in lieu of one which existed before that year,—in either of those cases write "Before 1800." If it was erected *in* the year 1800, or has been erected *since* and *not* on the site or in lieu of a previously existing Building, insert, as nearly as can be ascertained, the precise year in which it was built, thus—"*In the year* 1800," or—"*About the year* 1801," according to the fact of the case.

V.—*Whether a separate and entire Building*—as contra-distinguished from a mere *Room* or *Part of a Building.*—Insert in this column "Yes" or "No," as the case may be.
   Bear in mind that, for the purposes of this Return, a building must not be deemed the less a "separate" Building by reason of its adjoining, or having an internal communication with, a Dwelling House or other Building, as frequently happens in the case of Roman Catholic Chapels and those of some other Religious Denominations; the term "separate" being employed simply to denote a Building which is *separated or set apart* for religious uses.
   In this Division (V.) should also be included *Private or Domestic* Chapels, if commonly used as places of *Public* Religious Worship, but not else.

VI.—*Whether exclusively a Place of Worship* (except as it may be also used as a Sunday School).—Write also in this column "Yes" or "No," according to the fact.

VII.—*Space available for Public Worship.*—
   (4.) The term "Free Sittings" is used to denote sittings which are not appropriated for the use of particular individuals, and to which, therefore, *any* person is entitled to have free access.
   (5.) "Other Sittings" are those which are either let, or have become private property, or which for any other reason do not answer strictly the description of *free* sittings.
   "Free Space or Standing Room."—If, as is the case in some *Roman Catholic* Churches and Chapels there is, besides or instead of *free sittings*, an open space allotted as *standing room*, for the accommodation of the poor, state immediately below this heading the number of persons that such space will accommodate.

VIII.—*Number of Attendants.*—
   If—as is sometimes the case in Wales and elsewhere—two or more Congregations successively assemble in the Building during the same part of the day, and also in all cases where two or more distinct services are performed in the morning, afternoon, or evening, either by the same Minister or by different Ministers, denote the fact by drawing a line immediately *under* the gross number of attendants during that part of the day, thus [750]—in order to show that it expresses the aggregate of persons attending at *all* such distinct services. Make a × under each portion of the day—if there be any—during which *no* service is held.

   Average Number.—
   If from any cause the figures in the *upper* section of Division VIII. should not truly represent the numbers *usually* in attendance, the person making the Return is at liberty to add in the *lower* columns of the same Division, the estimated *average* number of attendants on Sunday during the 12 calendar months next preceding March 30, 1851, or during such portion of that period as the Building has been open for Public Worship, stating in the heading over the numbers so inserted the exact number of months for which the additional Return is made.
   And if, in consequence of repairs, or from any other temporary cause, the Building should not be open for Public Worship on March 30, 1851, write across the *upper* columns the words "No Service," and insert in the *lower* columns the average number who are supposed to have attended on Sundays during twelve months next preceding the Sunday on which Divine Service was last performed.

IX.—*Remarks.*—Any observations which it may be deemed requisite to make in explanation of the Return may be written along this column; or—if the space provided for the purpose should be insufficient—may be written on a separate paper and appended to the Return.

X.—*Signature, &c.*—The Return is to be made and signed by the Minister, or by some person acting under his authority; if there be no Minister, by an Elder, Deacon, Manager, Steward, or other recognized and competent officer: and the person signing will have the goodness to state in what capacity he signs, by writing immediately below his name the word "Minister," "Elder," "Deacon," "Manager," "Steward," &c., as the case may be. He will also add his *Address by the Post*, in order that, if necessary, he may be communicated with direct from the Census Office, in London, on the subject of the Return.

Approved.   GEORGE GRAHAM,
Whitehall,   } G. GREY.   *Registrar-General.*
28th Jan. 1851. }

N.B.—The Return must relate to only ONE *Place of Worship. Ministers having the charge of two or more such Places will be furnished with a separate Form for each. And any person requiring an additional supply of Forms, may obtain them free of postage or other charge, on application by letter (the postage of which may be left unpaid) addressed to "Horace Mann, Esq., Census Office, Craig's Court, London."*

APPENDIX B

Places of Worship, Sittings, and Attendants, in
Registration Districts, or Poor Law Unions.

[Reprinted from the Report, pp. 120-126]

DIVISION XI.—WELSH COUNTIES.*   [MONMOUTH.

RELIGIOUS DENOMINATION	Number of Places of Worship	Number of Sittings.			Number of Attendants at Public Worship on Sunday, March 30, 1851, [including Sunday Scholars].			Number of Places of Worship	Number of Sittings.			Number of Attendants at Public Worship on Sunday March 30, 1851, [including Sunday Scholars].		
		Free.	Appropriated.	Total.	Morning.	Afternoon.	Evening.		Free.	Appropriated.	Total.	Morning.	Afternoon.	Evening.
	576. CHEPSTOW. Population, 19,057.							**577. MONMOUTH.** Population, 27,379.						
TOTAL -	70	5409	4537	11,054	4268	2598	2762	103	10,419	7343	18,532	7776	5047	4987
PROTESTANT CHURCHES:														
Church of England -	37	2456	3513	7077	2993	1718	996	47	4681	5366	10,817	4446	3629	1592
Independents - -	4	434	216	650	82	80	107	3	379	598	977	461	..	400
Baptists - -	7	490	250	740	461	109	440	16	1766	740	2506	1477	268	1389
Moravians - -	1	200	..	200	120	..	160	..	..	..	..	..	..	..
Wesleyan Methodists -	11	1141	416	1557	345	270	491	14	1743	253	1996	505	521	614
Primitive Methodists -	1	100	..	100	60	100	140	14	1052	129	1181	487	521	737
Bible Christians - -	6	300	70	370	57	252	348	4	228	5	233	38	62	90
Wesleyan Reformers -	..	..	..	..	..	..	..	2	330	72	402	85	..	165
Calvinistic Methodists	1	100	..	100	..	69	..	..	..	..	..	..	..	..
OTHER CHRISTIAN CHS.:														
Roman Catholics - -	1	28	72	100	100	..	80	3	240	180	420	277	46	..
Cath. and Apos. Church	1	160	..	160	50	..	..	..	..	..	..	..	..	..

RELIGIOUS DENOMINATION	Number of Places of Worship	Number of Sittings.			Number of Attendants.			Number of Places of Worship	Number of Sittings.			Number of Attendants.		
		Free.	Appropriated.	Total.	Morning.	Afternoon.	Evening.		Free.	Appropriated.	Total.	Morning.	Afternoon.	Evening.
	578. ABERGAVENNY. Population, 59,229.							**579. PONTYPOOL.** Population, 27,993.						
TOTAL -	124	22,961	17,177	41,436	18,546	4962	23,927	82	12,833	6588	20,608	11,230	1774	10,977
PROTESTANT CHURCHES:														
Church of England -	34	4482	3592	9172	3670	1751	2410	28	3054	2028	6269	2837	750	2185
Independents - -	13	3074	2616	5690	3722	111	4476	12	1575	654	2229	1268	93	1273
Baptists - - -	30	8285	4465	12,750	5701	322	8479	16	4328	1593	5921	3011	156	3555
Wesleyan Methodists -	16	2928	2826	5754	2337	903	3712	15	2541	1713	4254	2757	296	2890
Primitive Methodists -	11	1419	730	2149	541	575	1258	4	445	395	840	422	219	690
Bible Christians - -	..	..	..	..	..	..	..	1	100	..	100	21	..	40
Calvinistic Methodists	13	2203	2708	5111	2073	739	3274	3	482	153	635	434	50	286
Undefined - -	1	200	..	200	..	235	123	1	68	52	120	70	..	58
OTHER CHRISTIAN CHS.:														
Roman Catholics -	2	270	240	510	353	131	..	2	240	..	240	410	210	..
Latter Day Saints -	4	100	..	100	149	195	195	..	..	..	..	..	..	..

*Division XI. consisting of *Monmouthshire* and *Wales*—commences with District 576 (CHEPSTOW) and terminates with District 623 (ANGLESEY).

576. CHEPSTOW.—The returns omit to state the number of *sittings* in one place of worship belonging to the ESTABLISHED CHURCH, attended by a maximum number of 45 persons at a service; in three places belonging to the PARTICULAR BAPTISTS, attended by a maximum of 151 persons at a service; and in two belonging to the BIBLE CHRISTIANS, attended by a maximum of 59 persons at a service.—*Neither sittings nor attendants* are given in the case of one place of worship belonging to the ESTABLISHED CHURCH.

577. MONMOUTH.—The returns omit to state the number of *sittings* in four places of worship belonging to the ESTABLISHED CHURCH, attended by a maximum of 604 persons at a service; in one place belonging to the BAPTISTS, attended by a maximum of 11 at a service; in two belonging to the WESLEYAN METHODISTS, attended by a maximum of 150 at a service; in one belonging to the PRIMITIVE METHODISTS, attended by a maximum of 35 at a service; and in one belonging to the BIBLE CHRISTIANS, attended by a maximum of 12 at a service.—The number of *attendants* is not given for three places of worship belonging to the ESTABLISHED CHURCH, containing 261 sittings.

578. ABERGAVENNY.—The returns omit to state the number of *sittings* in one place of worship belonging to the ESTABLISHED CHURCH, attended by a maximum of 10 persons at a service; in one place belonging to the INDEPENDENTS, attended by a maximum of 214 at a service; in one belonging to the BAPTISTS, attended by a maximum of 61 at a service; in one belonging to the WESLEYAN METHODISTS, attended by a maximum of 132 at a service; in one belonging to the PRIMITIVE METHODISTS, attended by a maximum of 45 at a service; and in two belonging to the LATTER DAY SAINTS, attended by a maximum of 135 at a service.—The number of *attendants* is not given for three places of worship belonging to the ESTABLISHED CHURCH, containing 1200 sittings.—*Neither sittings nor attendants* are given for one place of worship belonging to the BAPTISTS, one place belonging to the PRIMITIVE METHODISTS, and one belonging to the LATTER DAY SAINTS.

579. PONTYPOOL.—The returns omit to state the number of *sittings* in three places of worship belonging to the ESTABLISHED CHURCH, attended by a maximum of 78 persons at a service; in one place belonging to the INDEPENDENTS, attended by a maximum of 70 at a service; in one belonging to the WESLEYAN METHODISTS, attended by a maximum of 50 at a service; and in one belonging to the ROMAN CATHOLICS, attended by a maximum of 160 at a service.—The number of *attendants* is not given for one place belonging to the INDEPENDENTS, containing 300 sittings.

GLAMORGAN.]   DIVISION XI.—WELSH COUNTIES.

580. NEWPORT. / 581. CARDIFF.

RELIGIOUS DENOMINATION.	Number of Places of Worship.	Number of Sittings. Free.	Appropriated.	Total.	Attendants, March 30, 1851. Morning.	Afternoon.	Evening.	Number of Places of Worship.	Number of Sittings. Free.	Appropriated.	Total.	Attendants, March 30, 1851. Morning.	Afternoon.	Evening.
	580. NEWPORT. Population, 43,472.							581. CARDIFF. Population, 46,491.						
TOTAL	111	13,014	9415	24,636	12,697	1674	13,622	140	18,038	9996	29,944	13,369	4918	14,413
PROTESTANT CHURCHES:														
Church of England	36	2228	1455	5860	2080	622	891	50	4289	2989	9188	3359	1777	439
Independents	20	2739	1850	4589	2451	77	3275	19	3684	1354	5038	2274	..	2813
Baptists	20	4139	2321	6460	3683	..	4785	24	4187	1997	6184	3090	158	4750
Society of Friends	..	..	..	..	..	..	..	1	200	..	200	5	3	..
Wesleyan Methodists	15	1349	1696	3045	1697	272	1970	18	1495	1106	2601	969	803	2024
Primitive Methodists	2	200	100	300	181	..	157	..	..	..	..	..	..	..
Bible Christians	2	62	252	314	71	38	84	..	..	..	..	..	..	..
Wesleyan Reformers	3	425	250	675	349	..	500	..	..	..	..	..	..	..
Calvinistic Methodists	8	842	491	1333	706	145	681	25	3361	2370	5731	2422	1747	3977
Undefined	2	460	..	460	19	20	19	1	60	..	60	..	80	60
OTHER CHRISTIAN CHS.:														
Roman Catholics	1	300	1000	1300	1300	200	700	1	762	180	942	1200	150	100
Latter Day Saints	2	300	..	300	160	300	560	1	..	..	..	50	200	250

582. MERTHYR TYDFIL. / 583. BRIDGEND.

RELIGIOUS DENOMINATION.	Number of Places of Worship.	Number of Sittings. Free.	Appropriated.	Total.	Attendants, March 30, 1851. Morning.	Afternoon.	Evening.	Number of Places of Worship.	Number of Sittings. Free.	Appropriated.	Total.	Attendants, March 30, 1851. Morning.	Afternoon.	Evening.
	582. MERTHYR TYDFIL. Population, 76,804.							583. BRIDGEND. Population, 23,422.						
TOTAL	122	21,021	18,976	41,763	25,920	5739	30,974	98	9909	6944	18,478	7053	2333	9390
PROTESTANT CHURCHES:														
Church of England	17	2017	1111	4894	1726	192	1837	40	1433	1807	4865	1677	956	662
Independents	26	3809	5642	9451	8746	862	9347	17	2764	1892	4656	2093	256	2850
Baptists	30	6981	5947	12,928	10,600	769	11,782	14	1672	806	2478	1159	272	2361
Unitarians	2	261	200	461	263	..	204	1	40	..	40	..	9	..
Wesleyan Methodists	16	1788	2173	3961	1020	234	1914	11	1176	644	1820	314	342	850
Primitive Methodists	4	320	382	702	180	128	412	..	..	..	..	..	..	..
Wesleyan Reformers	2	120	..	120	40	..	115	..	..	..	..	..	..	..
Calvinistic Methodists	15	3390	3451	6841	2260	2193	4095	15	2824	1795	4619	1810	498	2667
Undefined	1	265	40	305	226	..	462	..	..	..	..	..	..	..
OTHER CHRISTIAN CHS.:														
Roman Catholics	1	300	..	300	600	150	..	..	..	..	..	..	..	..
Latter Day Saints	7	1760	..	1760	825	1190	783	..	..	..	..	..	..	..
Jews	1	10	30	40	34	21	23	..	..	..	..	..	..	..

580. NEWPORT.—The returns omit to state the number of *sittings* in one place of worship belonging to the ESTABLISHED CHURCH, attended by a maximum of 200 persons at a service; in one place belonging to the INDEPENDENTS, attended by a maximum of 200 at a service; in three belonging to the BAPTISTS, attended by a maximum of 352 at a service; in six belonging to the WESLEYAN METHODISTS, attended by a maximum of 219; in one belonging to the CALVINISTIC METHODISTS, attended by a maximum of 60; in one belonging to the WESLEYAN REFORMERS, attended by a maximum of 41; and in one belonging to the LATTER DAY SAINTS, attended by a maximum of 400.—The number of *attendants* is not given in the case of one place of worship belonging to the ESTABLISHED CHURCH, containing 13 sittings.—*Neither sittings nor attendants* are given in the case of one place of worship belonging to the ESTABLISHED CHURCH.

581. CARDIFF.—The returns omit to state the number of *sittings* in five places of worship belonging to the ESTABLISHED CHURCH, attended by a maximum number of 105 persons at a service; in one place belonging to the INDEPENDENTS, attended by a maximum of 109 persons at a service; in two belonging to the BAPTISTS, attended by a maximum of 124 at a service; in seven belonging to the WESLEYAN METHODISTS, attended by a maximum of 457 at a service; in two belonging to the CALVINISTIC METHODISTS, attended by a maximum of 441 at a service; and in one belonging to the LATTER DAY SAINTS, attended by a maximum of 250 at a service.

582. MERTHYR TYDFIL.—The returns omit to state the number of *sittings* in four places of worship belonging to the INDEPENDENTS, attended by a maximum of 855 persons at a service; in one place belonging to the BAPTISTS, attended by a maximum of 200 at a service; in one belonging to the WESLEYAN REFORMERS, attended by a maximum of 35 at a service; in one belonging to the CALVINISTIC METHODISTS, attended by a maximum of 95; and in three belonging to the LATTER DAY SAINTS, attended by a maximum of 379 persons at a service.—The number of *attendants* is not given for one place of worship belonging to the CHURCH OF ENGLAND, containing 176 sittings; and two places belonging to the BAPTISTS, containing 252 sittings.—*Neither sittings nor attendants* are given in the case of one place of worship belonging to the WESLEYAN METHODISTS.

583. BRIDGEND.—The returns omit to state the number of *sittings* in two places of worship belonging to the ESTABLISHED CHURCH, attended by a maximum of 73 persons at a service; in one place belonging to the INDEPENDENTS, attended by a maximum of 75 at a service; in four belonging to the BAPTISTS, attended by a maximum of 558; and in one belonging to the WESLEYAN METHODISTS, attended by a maximum of 40.—*Neither sittings nor attendants* are given for four places of worship belonging to the ESTABLISHED CHURCH, and one place belonging to the INDEPENDENTS.

C.

DIVISION XI.—WELSH COUNTIES.   [GLAMORGAN.

RELIGIOUS DENOMINATION.	Number of Places of Worship.	Number of Sittings.			Number of Attendants at Public Worship on Sunday March 30, 1851, [including Sunday Scholars].			Number of Places of Worship.	Number of Sittings.			Number of Attendants at Public Worship on Sunday March 30, 1851, [including Sunday Scholars].		
		Free.	Appropriated.	Total.	Morning.	Afternoon.	Evening.		Free.	Appropriated.	Total.	Morning.	Afternoon.	Evening.
	584. NEATH. Population, 46,471.							585. SWANSEA. Population, 46,907.						
TOTAL -	100	13,512	12,064	28,285	14,290	4757	16,476	109	14,846	15,726	33,618	14,039	3778	15,859
PROTESTANT CHURCHES:														
Church of England -	25	2313	1503	6109	2202	1092	1545	27	2416	4305	9367	3022	2052	1488
Independents - -	27	5827	4048	10,291	6607	2001	7223	25	3730	5212	8942	5797	220	6115
Baptists - -	17	2377	1872	4249	2002	74	2691	15	2494	2142	4636	1743	270	2849
Society of Friends -	1	154	..	154	40	16	..	1	240	..	240	22	13	..
Unitarians - -	2	15	120	135	93	..	125	2	500	..	900	221	..	121
Wesleyan Methodists -	6	406	849	1255	356	..	548	14	1166	1099	2265	657	162	1530
Primitive Methodists -	1	60	..	60	105	..	35	4	460	160	620	200	50	540
Bible Christians -	1	40	100	140	..	..	120	..	..	..	..	..	..	..
Calvinistic Methodists -	17	2320	3572	5892	2853	1560	4125	13	2684	2154	4838	1417	711	2116
L'Huntingdon'sConnex.	..	..	..	..	..	..	..	1	50	600	650	450	..	600
Undefined - -	..	..	..	..	..	..	..	4	876	..	876	160	230	100
OTHER CHRISTIAN CHS.:														
Roman Catholics -	..	..	..	..	..	..	..	1	200	12	212	300	..	200
Latter Day Saints -	3	..	..	..	32	14	64	1	..	..	..	50	70	200
Jews - - -	..	..	..	..	..	..	..	1	30	42	72	..	..	..
	586. LLANELLY. Population, 23,507.							587. LLANDOVERY. Population, 15,055.						
TOTAL -	51	7118	5186	14,760	8316	4032	9737	52	4919	8094	14,099	6956	1970	4947
PROTESTANT CHURCHES:														
Church of England -	11	1251	313	4020	1313	2251	706	15	818	2369	4069	1396	629	967
Independents - -	13	1977	2392	4369	2659	519	3150	15	2232	2250	4686	3212	203	2293
Baptists - - -	14	2637	435	3072	3380	214	3421	8	668	927	1595	781	334	294
Wesleyan Methodists -	5	414	591	1005	219	191	477	2	70	205	275	81	32	123
Calvinistic Methodists	7	679	1455	2134	665	707	1777	12	1131	2343	3474	1486	772	1270
OTHER CHRISTIAN CHS.:														
Latter Day Saints -	1	160	..	160	80	150	206	..	..	..	..	..	..	..

584. NEATH.—The returns omit to state the number of *sittings* in one place of worship belonging to the INDEPENDENTS' attended by a maximum number of 146 persons at a service; in one place belonging to the UNITARIANS, attended by a maximum of 13 persons at a service; in one belonging to the BAPTISTS, attended by a maximum of 76 persons at a service; and in two belonging to the LATTER DAY SAINTS, attended by a maximum of 64 persons at a service.—*Neither sittings nor attendants* are given for one place of worship belonging to the LATTER DAY SAINTS.

585. SWANSEA.—The returns omit to state the number of *sittings* in one place of worship belonging to the ESTABLISHED CHURCH, attended by a maximum of 70 persons at a service; in five places belonging to the INDEPENDENTS, attended by a maximum of 822 persons at a service; in two belonging to the WESLEYAN METHODISTS, attended by a maximum number of 202 persons at a service; in one belonging to the CALVINISTIC METHODISTS, attended by a maximum of 117 at a service; and in one belonging to the LATTER DAY SAINTS, attended by a maximum of 200 at a service.—The number of *attendants* is not given for one place of worship belonging to the ESTABLISHED CHURCH, containing 400 sittings; and one place belonging to the JEWS, containing 72 sittings.—*Neither sittings nor attendants* are given in the case of one place of worship belonging to the ESTABLISHED CHURCH.

586. LLANELLY.—The returns omit to state the number of *sittings* in two places of worship belonging to the INDEPENDENTS, attended by a maximum number of 350 persons at a service; and in five places belonging to the BAPTISTS, attended by a maximum of 1115 persons at a service. The number of *attendants* is not given for two places of worship belonging to the ESTABLISHED CHURCH, containing 659 sittings; and one place belonging to the CALVINISTIC METHODISTS, containing 20 sittings.

587. LLANDOVERY.—The returns omit to state the number of *sittings* in one place of worship belonging to the CALVINISTIC METHODISTS, attended by a maximum number of 130 persons at a service.

CARMARTHEN, PEMBROKE.] DIVISION XI.—WELSH COUNTIES.

RELIGIOUS DENOMINATION.	Number of Places of Worship.	Number of Sittings.			Number of Attendants at Public Worship on Sunday March 30, 1851, [including Sunday Scholars].			Number of Places of Worship.	Number of Sittings.			Number of Attendants at Public Worship on Sunday March 30, 1851, [including Sunday Scholars].		
		Free.	Appro-priated.	Total.	Morn-ing.	After-noon.	Even-ing.		Free.	Appro-priated.	Total.	Morn-ing.	After-noon.	Even-ing.
	588. LLANDILOFAWR. *Population, 17,968.*							**589. CARMARTHEN.** *Population, 38,142.*						
TOTAL -	72	6994	6227	14,520	6626	2933	6633	123	11,060	12,822	27,597	15,597	6653	12,223
PROTESTANT CHURCHES:														
Church of England -	18	2335	1754	5388	2027	809	954	35	2259	2870	8844	3949	1614	1794
Independents - -	22	2378	996	3374	2334	191	2369	32	3454	3935	7389	5879	2604	3646
Baptists - - -	11	548	1059	1607	1354	240	1403	17	1662	1849	3511	2703	751	2535
Unitarians - -	1	100	..	100	50	..	..	2	106	210	316	170	..	180
Wesleyan Methodists -	6	273	715	988	365	90	475	6	637	852	1489	386	95	602
Calvinistic Methodists	13	1260	1703	2963	496	1585	1394	29	2722	3106	5828	2365	1540	3355
OTHER CHRISTIAN CHS.:														
Roman Catholics -	..	..	..	..	..	..	..	1	120	..	120	99	..	46
Latter Day Saints -	1	100	..	100	..	18	38	1	100	..	100	46	49	65

RELIGIOUS DENOMINATION.	Number of Places of Worship.	Number of Sittings.			Number of Attendants at Public Worship on Sunday March 30, 1851.			Number of Places of Worship.	Number of Sittings.			Number of Attendants at Public Worship on Sunday March 30, 1851.		
		Free.	Appro-priated.	Total.	Morn-ing.	After-noon.	Even-ing.		Free.	Appro-priated.	Total.	Morn-ing.	After-noon.	Even-ing.
	590. NARBERTH. *Population, 22,130.*							**591. PEMBROKE.** *Population, 22,960.*						
TOTAL -	90	9714	7368	18,897	7943	6022	3430	71	6824	9215	17,263	7781	2905	7159
PROTESTANT CHURCHES:														
Church of England -	41	2489	3108	7204	2499	1873	357	28	2273	4440	7807	3366	1296	1666
Independents - -	23	3719	2408	6335	3309	1706	1130	10	586	1210	1926	1242	175	1225
Baptists - -	13	2121	1329	3450	1689	1555	1045	11	1468	1573	3041	1301	498	1685
Unitarians - -	1	80	..	80	76	..	..	..	..	..	..	..	..	..
Wesleyan Methodists -	4	388	153	541	108	370	254	8	1276	1175	2451	1164	255	1554
Primitive Methodists -	2	240	80	320	70	30	250	3	227	78	305	..	230	130
Calvinistic Methodists	6	677	290	967	192	488	394	7	614	739	1353	538	361	851
Undefined - - -	..	..	..	..	..	..	..	3	250	..	250	60	60	48
OTHER CHRISTIAN CHS.:														
Roman Catholics -	..	..	..	..	..	..	..	1	130	..	130	110	30	..

588. LLANDILOFAWR.—The returns omit to state the number of *sittings* in two places of worship belonging to the ESTA-BLISHED CHURCH, attended by a maximum number of 55 persons at a service; in one place belonging to the INDEPENDENTS, attended by a maximum of 280 at a service; and in two places belonging to the BAPTISTS, attended by a maximum of 297 at a service.—*Neither sittings nor attendants* are given for one place of worship belonging to the ESTABLISHED CHURCH; and one place belonging to the INDEPENDENTS.

589. CARMARTHEN.—The returns omit to state the number of *sittings* in three places of worship belonging to the ESTA-BLISHED CHURCH, attended by a maximum number of 260 persons at a service; in eleven places belonging to the INDE-PENDENTS, attended by a maximum of 1825 at a service; in three places belonging to the BAPTISTS, attended by a maximum of 1215 at a service; and in three places belonging to the CALVINISTIC METHODISTS, attended by a maximum of 504 at a service.—*Neither sittings nor attendants* are given for two places of worship belonging to the ESTABLISHED CHURCH.

590. NARBERTH.—The returns omit to state the number of *sittings* in one place of worship belonging to the INDE-PENDENTS, attended by a maximum number of 50 persons at a service; and one place of worship belonging to the BAPTISTS, attended by a maximum of 250 persons at a service.—The number of *attendants* is not given in the case of one place of worship belonging to the ESTABLISHED CHURCH, containing 14 sittings.

591. PEMBROKE.—The returns omit to state the number of *sittings* in two places of worship belonging to the ESTABLISHED CHURCH, attended by a maximum number of 270 persons at a service; in two places belonging to the INDEPENDENTS, attended by a maximum of 286 persons at a service; in one place belonging to the BAPTISTS, attended by a maximum of 65 at a service; and in one place belonging to an UNDEFINED DENOMINATION, attended by a maximum of 60 at a service.—The number of *attendants* is not given in the case of one place of worship belonging to the ESTABLISHED CHURCH, containing 1028 sittings.

DIVISION XI.—WELSH COUNTIES.   [CARDIGANSHIRE.

RELIGIOUS DENOMINATION.	Number of Places of Worship.	Number of Sittings.			Number of Attendants at Public Worship on Sunday March 30, 1851, [including Sunday Scholars].			Number of Places of Worship.	Number of Sittings.			Number of Attendants at Public Worship on Sunday March 30, 1851, [including Sunday Scholars].		
		Free.	Appropriated.	Total.	Morning.	Afternoon.	Evening.		Free.	Appropriated.	Total.	Morning.	Afternoon.	Evening.
	592. HAVERFORDWEST. Population, 39,382.							593. CARDIGAN. Population, 20,186.						
TOTAL -	156	16,053	12,778	30,844	14,026	6017	11,044	78	8349	8396	18,918	7718	5413	7808
PROTESTANT CHURCHES:														
Church of England -	67	4283	4160	10,356	3124	1687	1233	27	1539	1311	4373	2474	1027	485
Independents - -	26	3676	2386	6062	4056	763	2787	17	2188	2063	4901	1599	1359	1317
Baptists - - -	26	3839	2695	6634	4067	1737	3444	20	3146	2946	6092	2459	1762	3701
Society of Friends -	1	60	..	60	5	..	..	..	..	..	..	..	..	..
Wesleyan Methodists -	17	2241	1676	3917	1233	364	1892	1	72	124	196	..	..	116
Primitive Methodists -	1	100	..	100	..	30	60	..	..	..	..	..	..	..
Calvinistic Methodists	14	1540	1841	3381	1302	1406	1276	13	1404	1952	3356	1186	1265	2189
Brethren - - -	1	200	..	200	90	..	173	..	..	..	..	..	..	..
Undefined - -	1	..	..	..	89	..	89	..	..	..	..	..	..	..
OTHER CHRISTIAN CHS.:														
Roman Catholics -	1	84	..	84	40	..	30	..	..	..	..	..	..	..
Latter Day Saints -	1	30	20	50	20	30	60	..	..	..	..	..	..	..

	Number of Places of Worship.	Number of Sittings.			Attendants Morning.	Afternoon.	Evening.	Number of Places of Worship.	Number of Sittings.			Attendants Morning.	Afternoon.	Evening.
	594. NEWCASTLE IN EMLYN. Population, 20,173.							595. LAMPETER. Population, 9,874.						
TOTAL -	77	8727	4635	16,364	8998	6357	5339	44	4885	2312	8874	4417	1588	1212
PROTESTANT CHURCHES:														
Church of England -	22	888	152	4042	2025	819	383	15	217	98	1992	852	325	268
Independents - -	23	4362	2044	6406	3331	2529	1691	13	2286	1411	3697	1975	887	317
Baptists - - -	10	1074	390	1464	890	1273	1359	5	1010	..	1010	596	170	160
Unitarians - -	5	649	336	985	517	193	..	5	1019	156	1175	429	171	..
Wesleyan Methodists -	3	411	150	561	455	..	60	2	120	150	270	53	35	150
Calvinistic Methodists	13	1343	1563	2906	1764	1543	1786	3	233	497	730	482	..	317
OTHER CHRISTIAN CHS.:														
Latter Day Saints -	1	..	..	..	16	..	60	1	..	..	..	30	..	..

592. HAVERFORDWEST.—The returns omit to state the number of *sittings* in one place of worship belonging to the ESTABLISHED CHURCH, attended by a maximum number of 26 persons at a service; in two places belonging to the INDEPENDENTS, attended by a maximum of 314 at a service; in three belonging to the BAPTISTS, attended by a maximum of 620 at a service; in one belonging to the CALVINISTIC METHODISTS, attended by a maximum of 140 at a service; and in one belonging to a DENOMINATION UNDEFINED, attended by a maximum of 89 at a service. · The number of *attendants* is not given for three places belonging to the ESTABLISHED CHURCH, containing 272 sittings.—*Neither sittings nor attendants* are given for two places belonging to the ESTABLISHED CHURCH.

593. CARDIGAN,—The returns omit to state the number of *sittings* in one place of worship belonging to the INDEPENDENTS, attended by a maximum of 350 persons at a service; in one place belonging to the BAPTISTS, attended by a maximum of 567 at a service; and in one place belonging to the CALVINISTIC METHODISTS, attended by a maximum of 100 at a service.—The number of *attendants* is not given for two places of worship belonging to the INDEPENDENTS, containing 750 sittings; and one place belonging to the BAPTISTS, containing 350 sittings.—*Neither sittings nor attendants* are given in the case of two places of worship belonging to the ESTABLISHED CHURCH.

594. NEWCASTLE IN EMLYN.—The returns omit to state the number of *sittings* in one place of worship belonging to the ESTABLISHED CHURCH, attended by a maximum number of 100 persons at a service; in four places belonging to the INDEPENDENTS, attended by a maximum of 972 persons at a service; in four places belonging to the BAPTISTS, attended by a maximum of 625 at a service; in one place belonging to the UNITARIANS, attended by a maximum of 17 at a service; in one place belonging to the CALVINISTIC METHODISTS, attended by a maximum of 264 at a service; and in one place belonging to the LATTER DAY SAINTS, attended by a maximum of 60 at a service.

595. LAMPETER.—The returns omit to state the number of *sittings* in three places of worship belonging to the ESTABLISHED CHURCH, attended by a maximum number of 93 persons at a service; in one place belonging to the WESLEYAN METHODISTS, attended by a maximum of 35 at a service; and in one place belonging to the LATTER DAY SAINTS, attended by a maximum of 30 at a service.

CARDIGAN, BRECKNOCK.]   DIVISION XI.—WELSH COUNTIES.

596. ABERAYRON. *Population, 13,224.*   597. ABERYSTWITH. *Population, 23,753.*

RELIGIOUS DENOMINATION.	Number of Places of Worship.	Number of Sittings.			Number of Attendants at Public Worship on Sunday March 30, 1851, [including Sunday Scholars].			Number of Places of Worship.	Number of Sittings.			Number of Attendants at Public Worship on Sunday March 30, 1851, [including Sunday Scholars].		
		Free.	Appropriated.	Total.	Morning.	Afternoon.	Evening.		Free.	Appropriated.	Total.	Morning.	Afternoon.	Evening.
TOTAL	47	2724	6450	11,353	5984	3878	3591	75	7906	10,311	20,258	9806	6713	12,302
PROTESTANT CHURCHES:														
Church of England	16	334	1024	3537	1780	894	..	20	2429	1481	5951	2260	1062	1511
Independents	11	858	2310	3168	2605	557	808	7	660	1336	1996	768	523	1213
Baptists	2	102	258	360	135	120	187	9	656	1439	2095	677	431	1255
Unitarians	4	698	..	698	85	330	100	..	..	..	..	..	..	..
Wesleyan Methodists	3	84	246	330	..	119	139	10	937	1582	2519	967	601	1443
Primitive Methodists	..	..	..	..	..	..	..	1	100	112	212	..	97	114
Wesleyan Association	..	..	..	..	..	..	..	1	84	174	258	52	72	98
Calvinistic Methodists	11	648	2612	3260	1379	1858	2357	27	3040	4187	7227	5082	3927	6668

598. TREGARON. *Population, 10,404.*   599. BUILTH. *Population, 8,345.*

RELIGIOUS DENOMINATION.	Places of Worship.	Free.	Appropriated.	Total.	Morning.	Afternoon.	Evening.	Places of Worship.	Free.	Appropriated.	Total.	Morning.	Afternoon.	Evening.
TOTAL	28	1385	3724	6568	3325	2399	3075	49	2976	2332	6263	1701	1348	2025
PROTESTANT CHURCHES:														
Church of England	10	130	75	1664	1126	285	360	26	872	1343	3050	618	505	180
Independents	..	..	..	..	..	..	..	12	759	342	1101	336	559	967
Baptists	2	54	216	270	160	450	340	5	512	318	830	494	..	245
Wesleyan Methodists	1	60	..	60	30	..	55	..	..	..	..	..	..	..
Primitive Methodists	..	..	..	..	..	..	..	1	..	..	..	..	20	..
Calvinistic Methodists	15	1141	3433	4574	2009	1664	2320	5	833	329	1282	253	264	633

600. BRECKNOCK. *Population, 18,174.*   601. CRICKHOWELL. *Population, 2,1697.*

RELIGIOUS DENOMINATION.	Places of Worship.	Free.	Appropriated.	Total.	Morning.	Afternoon.	Evening.	Places of Worship.	Free.	Appropriated.	Total.	Morning.	Afternoon.	Evening.
TOTAL	91	6700	7670	15,315	7098	2761	6711	65	9652	7978	18,430	9495	1537	10,833
PROTESTANT CHURCHES:														
Church of England	41	1807	3538	6290	3056	1370	1655	11	1011	2878	4339	1138	717	290
Independents	14	2209	903	3112	1693	325	1880	16	2673	1788	4581	3433	458	4557
Baptists	12	1337	992	2329	1029	118	1211	12	2961	1246	4417	2245	..	2590
Wesleyan Methodists	5	271	544	815	274	100	478	13	1649	642	2291	1109	230	1496
Primitive Methodists	..	..	..	..	..	..	..	5	433	580	1013	481	28	603
Calvinistic Methodists	18	926	1693	2619	855	797	1487	7	925	844	1769	835	84	1097
Undefined	..	..	..	..	..	..	..	1	..	..	..	254	20	200
OTHER CHRISTIAN CHS.:														
Roman Catholics	1	150	..	150	191	51	..	..	..	..	..	..	..	..

596. ABERAYRON.—The returns omit to state the number of *sittings* in one place of worship belonging to the ESTABLISHED CHURCH, attended by a maximum number of 200 persons at a service; in one place belonging to the INDEPENDENTS, attended by a maximum of 400 persons at a service; in one place belonging to the UNITARIANS, attended by a maximum of 100 at a service; and in one place belonging to the WESLEYAN METHODISTS, attended by a maximum of 35 at a service. The number of *attendants* is not given for one place of worship belonging to the ESTABLISHED CHURCH, containing 80 sittings; and one place belonging to the BAPTISTS, containing 114 sittings.

597. ABERYSTWITH.—The returns omit to state the number of *sittings* in one place of worship belonging to the CHURCH OF ENGLAND, attended by a maximum number of 100 persons at a service; and in six places belonging to the CALVINISTIC METHODISTS, attended by a maximum of 1378 persons at a service. The number of *attendants* is not given for one place belonging to the ESTABLISHED CHURCH, containing 500 sittings; and one place belonging to the CALVINISTIC METHODISTS, containing 88 sittings.—*Neither sittings nor attendants* are given in the case of four places belonging to the ESTABLISHED CHURCH.

598. TREGARON.—The returns omit to state the number of *sittings* in two places of worship belonging to the ESTABLISHED CHURCH, attended by a maximum number of 355 persons at a service; and in one place belonging to the BAPTISTS, attended by a maximum of 90 persons at a service.

599. BUILTH,—The returns omit to state the number of *sittings* in four places of worship belonging to the ESTABLISHED CHURCH, attended by a maximum number of 59 persons at a service; in five places belonging to the INDEPENDENTS, attended by a maximum of 483 persons at a service; and in one place belonging to the PRIMITIVE METHODISTS, attended by a maximum of 20 persons at a service.

600. BRECKNOCK.—The returns omit to state the number of *sittings* in five places of worship belonging to the ESTABLISHED CHURCH, attended by a maximum number of 214 persons at a service; in two places belonging to the INDEPENDENTS, attended by a maximum of 218 persons at a service; in two places belonging to the BAPTISTS, attended by a maximum of 82 persons at a service; and in three places belonging to the CALVINISTIC METHODISTS, attended by a maximum of 161 persons at a service.

601. CRICKHOWELL.—The returns omit to state the number of *sittings* in three places belonging to the INDEPENDENTS, attended by a maximum number of 400 persons at a service; in one place belonging to the PRIMITIVE METHODISTS, attended by a maximum of 64 persons at a service; in one place belonging to the CALVINISTIC METHODISTS, attended by a maximum of 180 at a service; and in one place belonging to a DENOMINATION UNDEFINED, attended by a maximum of 254 at a service.

DIVISION XI.—WELSH COUNTIES. [Radnor, Montgomery.

602. HAY. Population, 10,962. — 603. PRESTEIGNE. Population, 15,149.

RELIGIOUS DENOMINATION.	Number of Places of Worship.	Number of Sittings.			Number of Attendants at Public Worship on Sunday March 30, 1851, [including Sunday Scholars].			Number of Places of Worship.	Number of Sittings.			Number of Attendants at Public Worship on Sunday March 30, 1851, [including Sunday Scholars].		
		Free.	Appropriated.	Total.	Morning.	Afternoon.	Evening.		Free.	Appropriated.	Total.	Morning.	Afternoon.	Evening.
Total -	54	4590	3219	8758	2426	1783	2287	73	4738	5828	11,896	3517	1460	2447
Protestant Churches:														
Church of England -	21	1172	2042	4163	1422	734	356	33	1638	3926	6894	2416	455	875
Independents - -	4	948	150	1098	266	180	513	4	546	96	642	59	223	106
Baptists - -	7	989	174	1163	391	239	488	5	943	414	1357	413	215	430
Society of Friends -	1	40	..	40	3	..	..	2	20	..	20	23	7	..
Wesleyan Methodists -	5	500	234	734	97	91	312	8	468	622	1090	268	138	301
Primitive Methodists -	5	410	37	447	30	227	114	14	545	500	1045	129	263	525
Calvinistic Methodists-	9	481	582	1063	217	294	504	7	578	270	848	209	159	210
Undefined - -	1	50	..	50	..	..	..	..	..	..	..	..	..	..
Other Christian Chs.:														
Latter Day Saints -	1	..	..	..	..	18	..	..	..	..	..	..	..	..

604. KNIGHTON. Population, 9,480. — 605. RHAYADER. Population, 6,796.

RELIGIOUS DENOMINATION.	Places	Free.	Appropriated.	Total.	Morning.	Afternoon.	Evening.	Places	Free.	Appropriated.	Total.	Morning.	Afternoon.	Evening.
Total -	33	1402	2871	4583	1462	984	978	33	3632	2491	6323	1455	1552	1909
Protestant Churches:														
Church of England -	15	722	2692	3724	1129	405	421	11	1017	1369	2586	379	714	80
Independents - -	2	70	..	70	..	37	..	5	850	540	1390	479	147	918
Baptists - -	4	270	..	270	194	..	43	8	1410	128	1538	479	494	452
Wesleyan Methodists -	3	220	149	369	75	160	230	5	66	206	272	40	61	144
Primitive Methodists -	9	120	30	150	64	382	284	..	..	..	..	..	..	..
Calvinistic Methodists-	.	..	..	..	..	..	..	4	289	248	537	78	136	315

602. Hay.—The returns omit to state the number of *sittings* in two places of worship belonging to the Established Church, attended by a maximum of 77 persons at a service; in one place belonging to the Primitive Methodists, attended by a maximum of 15 at a service; in two belonging to the Calvinistic Methodists, attended by a maximum of 78; and in one belonging to the Latter Day Saints, attended by a maximum of 18. The number of *attendants* is not given for one place of worship belonging to the Baptists, containing 300 sittings; and one place belonging to a Denomination Undefined, containing 50 sittings. - *Neither sittings nor attendants* are given for one place of worship belonging to the Baptists.

603. Presteigne.—The returns omit to state the number of *sittings* in one place of worship belonging to the Established Church, attended by a maximum of 14 persons at a service; in one place belonging to the Society of Friends, attended by a maximum of 16 at a service; in two places belonging to the Wesleyan Methodists, attended by a maximum of 109; and in seven places belonging to the Primitive Methodists, attended by a maximum of 217.

604. Knighton.—The returns omit to state the number of *sittings* in one place of worship belonging to the Baptists, attended by a maximum of 75 persons at a service; and in seven places belonging to the Primitive Methodists, attended by a maximum of 411 at a service. - *Neither sittings nor attendants* are given in the case of one place of worship belonging to the Baptists.

605. Rhayader.—The returns omit to state the number of *sittings* in one place of worship belonging to the Established Church, attended by a maximum of 20 persons at a service; in one place belonging to the Baptists, attended by a maximum of 61 at a service; in two places belonging to the Wesleyan Methodists, attended by a maximum of 57; and in one place belonging to the Calvinistic Methodists, attended by a maximum of 66.

INDEX OF PLACE NAMES

BRE	Brecknockshire	MON	Monmouthshire
CRD	Cardiganshire	PEM	Pembrokeshire
CRM	Carmarthenshire	RAD	Radnorshire
GLA	Glamorgan		

(Note: the index follows the spellings of the Calendar. Corrected forms and spellings are given in brackets.)